LOCOMOTIVE NAMES

Inside Swindon Works. Castle class no. 4000 *North Star* undergoing a heavy repair in 1953, with the replica broad gauge locomotive *North Star* on its pedestal in the background.

An Illustrated Dictionary

JIM PIKE

SUTTON PUBLISHING

First published in the United Kingdom in 2000 by
Sutton Publishing Limited · Phoenix Mill
Thrupp · Stroud · Gloucestershire · GL5 2BU

British Library Cataloguing in Publication Data
A catalogue record for this book is available from the British Library.

ISBN 0-7509-2284-2

To my wife Patricia, who suggested the need for this book, and then put up with my efforts to compile it. For her unwavering support, my grateful thanks.

Typeset in 11/14pt Bembo
Typesetting and origination by
Sutton Publishing Limited.
Printed in Great Britain by
Bookcraft, Midsomer Norton, Somerset.

CONTENTS

'Tell Sir Herbert I have no objection [to giving the locomotives names], but I warn you it won't make any difference to the working of the engine!'

R.E.L. Maunsell, Chief Mechanical Engineer, Southern Railway

INTRODUCTION

The aim of this work is to help those who, while not necessarily railway enthusiasts as such, may nevertheless find themselves employed or otherwise involved in the railway preservation industry. One can use the word 'industry', since many museums, steam centres and preserved railways employ staff. Such employees may well find themselves on the receiving end of queries from their visitors. Finding the answer is one thing; knowing what the enquirer is talking about is another! Questions such as 'How many locomotives have there been with the name *Coronation*?' or 'I have a nameplate from an engine called *Rooke*; can you tell me anything about it?' or even 'When was *Flying Scotsman* built?' can all be answered from the following pages.

For those of us who 'worship at the shrine of the steam locomotive', in Loughnan Pendred's phrase, there has always been something special about engines bearing names. Everyone has heard of Stephenson's *Rocket*. Naming locomotives is a tradition dating back to the earliest days when the steam locomotive was regarded as a replacement for the horse for hauling coal. Horses have names so names were bestowed on their successors, and the tradition happily survives on modern diesel and electric power.

Some names have been very appropriate indeed. *Thunderer* and *Volcano* gave our ancestors a good idea of what to expect, though *Racer* might have been something of a hostage to fortune. Other names have been less happy. It seemed a good idea to name engines after racehorses, and *Diamond Jubilee* has a pleasant ring to it. But what of *Bachelor's Button*? Naming locomotives after the company's directors also seemed promising, and *Viscount Churchill* has a dignified sound. *The Rt. Hon. Viscount Cross, G.C.B., G.C.S.I.* was perhaps a little over the top, while *Strang Steel* sounds more like a product than a person!

The first practicable Great Western engine was named *North Star*, and succeeding engines were named after stars. The idea of a theme is attractive in that an engine's class or type can readily be identified. One class was named after country houses, or Halls. The class was then multiplied to over three hundred, and with names like *Willey Hall*, *Westminster Hall*, *Guild Hall* and *Albert Hall* one felt that the bottom of the barrel was being well and truly scraped.

Classical names had a great attraction in Victorian times, though less so latterly. The Great Western occasionally misspelt names. Sometimes names were applied without really understanding them: the Southern's King Arthur class included *King Uther* and *Pendragon*, *Elaine* and *Maid of Astolat*. But Uther Pendragon was one person, and Elaine *was* the Maid of Astolat!

There were a number of railways, including some large and important ones, which made a policy of not naming any engines. From Archibald Sturrock's time until the Grouping in 1923, the Great Northern had only three named engines and the Midland only two. The North Eastern had none from Edward Fletcher's time, and the Great Eastern had just three. At the other extreme, the London, Chatham & Dover and the London, Brighton & South Coast went through a period of naming almost everything – Chatham engines, in William Martley's time, had had names and no numbers – followed, in both cases, by a reaction. There is a slight correlation between anonymous engines and Quaker locomotive superintendents, but not enough to permit generalization. In addition, there were railways like the London & North Western which reserved names for express passenger engines, while others, like the London & South Western, reserved names for only the smallest dock shunters. In recent years British Railways have had a policy of reviving the best steam era names, a policy of naming engines after anything that will generate a bit of (preferably free) publicity, such as provincial newspapers, and a policy of encouraging depots to give homely names to their charges. *Cookie*, for instance, was the depot cat.

It is interesting to see which names were the most popular. *Vulcan* attracted twenty-seven locomotives, and there were twenty-eight *Victorias*. But the clear winner, with thirty-five entries, was *Hercules*! So, take your pick. There are names of every kind, from the sublime to the ridiculous.

How to Use this Book

As stated in the Introduction, this book is aimed at the non-enthusiast who may find himself or herself involved in the railway preservation or museum business. The intention is not to give a detailed history of every named locomotive; such a work would comfortably fill a library shelf or two. Rather, it is to provide a starting point. Given the locomotive's name, herein may be found its number (if any), class or wheel arrangement, date of introduction and owning railway. Where necessary, footnotes have been used for amplification. For further details, the user is referred to the sources listed at the end.

Some names have proved to be very popular, with several locomotives so endowed. These are listed in chronological order; it is hoped that this may afford some guide to the user.

Terms of Reference

Industrial Locomotives. As a basic principle, industrial locomotives are omitted because in many cases the information is simply no longer available. Many civil engineering contractors changed their locomotives' names as they moved from contract to contract, and there were also renamings owing to changes of owner. Nevertheless, the Industrial Locomotive Society has done a great deal of work in this direction and the interested reader should refer to their publications. But the question 'what is an industrial locomotive?' needs to be addressed. Quite clearly, a small tank engine shunting wagons in a coalmine is 'an industrial', but what of the same tank engine hauling passengers on a preserved railway? Therefore all locomotives operating on the preserved lines of this country, or preserved in museums, are included regardless of their origins. I hope there are not too many anomalies.

War Department Locomotives. These are included as far as the information is available. But, again, the question needs to be asked, 'what is a WD locomotive?' Quite clearly, locomotives of the Longmoor Military Railway are WDs, but what of those of the Admiralty and Air Force? What, also, of Woolwich Arsenal? For the sake of completeness, I have included them as far as possible. If I have omitted any, I would be grateful to learn of them.

Also Included. I have included locomotives from the Isle of Wight, the Isle of Man and the Channel Islands. I have, however, omitted all Irish locomotives: full details of these can be found in J.W.P. Rowledge's *Irish Steam Loco Register*, published by Irish Traction Group, 1993.

Background Knowledge

Since this book is aimed at the non-enthusiast, I have assumed no prior knowledge of railways. The following notes may help the reader.

2–2–2, 4–4–0, 0–4–0T, etc.

This is a handy way of classifying locomotives by the arrangement of their wheels. It was invented by an American engineer named F.A. Whyte, and is generally known as the Whyte notation. For example, a locomotive with four small wheels at the front, six large driving wheels and two small wheels at the back is called a 4–6–2, while a locomotive with four driving wheels and no carrying wheels at either end is an 0–4–0.

The tender, where there is one, is not counted, but tank engines (carrying their own fuel and water without a separate tender) have the suffix T. Thus, if our 0–4–0 were a tank engine, it would be an 0–4–0T. And so on.

Atlantic, Pacific, etc.

Before the Whyte notation was devised, steam locomotive wheel arrangements were given names. Most of them originated in America, and some (but by no means all) spread to Britain. For reasons that need not concern us here, 4–4–2 locomotives were termed Atlantics and 4–6–2s were dubbed Pacifics. These are the two names most frequently encountered. Some of the other names were patently silly. For example, a 4–6–0 was called a 'Ten-Wheeler'. Mr H.A. Ivatt of the Great Northern Railway was once chided in the railway press for referring to his new 4–4–2 as a ten-wheeler. A ten-wheeler was a 4–6–0, someone wrote, and therefore Mr Ivatt's new locomotive was not a Ten-Wheeler in spite of having ten wheels! Ivatt's riposte was sturdy and to the point.

To avoid confusion, these names have not been used in the following pages. But, since some of them may be encountered by the user of this book, the following list is offered in a spirit of helpfulness:

Atlantic	4–4–2	Berkshire	2–8–4★
Mogul	2–6–0	Mastodon	4–8–0†
Prairie	2–6–2	Mountain	4–8–2★
Ten-Wheeler	4–6–0#	Northern	4–8–4★
Pacific	4–6–2	Decapod	0–10–0
Baltic (or Hudson)	4–6–4	Decapod	2–10–0
Consolidation	2–8–0	Santa Fe	2–10–2★
Mikado	2–8–2		

Name seldom used in Britain.   ★ Locomotive type not used in Britain.   † Only used for tank engines in Britain.

Bo-Bo, Co-Co, etc.

The Whyte notation does not fit diesel and electric locomotives very well, especially when, as is often the case, they are mounted on bogies. So a different notation, based on a German system, is used. Here the axles are counted, not the wheels. Powered axles are counted by letters (A=1, B=2, C=3, etc.) and unpowered axles are counted by numbers (1, 2, 3, etc.) The letter B on its own would therefore denote a two-axled (four-wheeled) locomotive, with the wheels coupled by rods. If the axles were independently motored, then the suffix o is added and our B locomotive would become a Bo. A locomotive mounted on two two-axle bogies, all motored independently, would thus be a Bo-Bo. Three-axle bogies, and we have a Co-Co. Just occasionally it is necessary to add an extra carrying axle at the outer ends, making a 1-Co-Co-1 (like the British Railways 40 class), or even to add the extra carrying axle between two powered axles, making an A-1-A - A-1-A (like the Brown Boveri gas turbine locomotive for the Western Region of British Railways). However, having said all that, smaller shunting locomotives which have two or three axles coupled by rods are more usually referred to as 0–4–0 or 0–6–0 diesel locomotives!

Gauge

The reader will realize that the distance between the inside edges of the rails must be constant, and that locomotives and rolling stock must be made to fit. The standard gauge for track is 4ft 8½in.[1] The main

[1] 4ft 8½in seems a very odd measurement: where does it come from? The answer is, nobody really knows! The early waggonways in Northumberland seem to have 'grown up' with this dimension, and George Stephenson made his earliest locomotives to fit. Beyond that, much scholarly ink has been expended, involving chariot ruts from Ancient Rome and sledge ruts from Ancient Babylon; the interested reader is referred to various erudite articles that have appeared from time to time in the *Railway Magazine*. I have my own theory, namely that a horse-drawn waggon containing a fair load of coal for one horse worked out at roughly 4ft 6in wide, 4ft 6in long, and 4ft 6in high, and the colliery waggonways were built to take such waggons. But this, it must be stressed, is just a theory, without a shred of evidence!

exception to this was the Great Western Railway, which began with a gauge of 7ft 0¼in and only converted the last of it to standard gauge in 1892. In addition, there have been narrower gauges, some of which are still in operation. All locomotives in this list are to standard gauge unless shown otherwise.

Classification

In the early days of locomotive development, hardly any two engines were alike. This situation has returned on many modern 'preserved' lines. It also persisted on smaller railways, and also for the occasional 'odd' engines which the larger railways acquired from time to time. These engines are shown by their wheel arrangement.

Once a locomotive design had been tried and found satisfactory, there was every incentive to build more to the same design. Thus arose the concept of 'classes', some of which were very large indeed. Where appropriate, each locomotive's class is shown.

Nameplates

Since nameplates fetch high prices these days, it is perhaps worth mentioning that not every named locomotive carried a nameplate. Many names were painted on, and simply reapplied every time the locomotive was repainted. Principal exponents were the Scottish companies and the London, Brighton & South Coast Railway.

Nicknames and Unofficial Names

These are given in inverted commas. On the question of nicknames, some are of better provenance than others. There was once a Southern Region locomotive with 'Superheater Sid' daubed on the tender! But when a nickname has entered railway literature, or I have otherwise become aware of it, I have included it.

Preserved Engines

These are shown in **bold type**.

In most cases, no attempt has been made to give the location of preserved locomotives. This is because they sometimes move from one location to another. It is strongly recommended that one should always telephone to ensure that a particular locomotive is at a given location before undertaking a special journey to see it.

Since locomotive maintenance is an ongoing activity, it does not automatically follow that, because a locomotive is shown as preserved, it is possible to view it. A locomotive may well be stripped down, its boiler perhaps sent away to one contractor for re-tubing, its wheels to another for re-profiling. Again, enquiries should always be made before embarking on a journey to see a specific locomotive.

Names bestowed since preservation are shown in brackets.

Date of Introduction

This is usually the date of construction. When a locomotive was placed in store on completion, for whatever reason, the date given is the date the locomotive entered traffic. Where possible, the month is given as well as the year.

Changes of Names

The names listed here were not always carried for the locomotives' entire lives. The reasons for this are many and varied. For example, the Highland and North British Railways were fond of naming locomotives after the towns or villages where they worked, and a locomotive transferred to another part of the company's system was often renamed. Locomotives named after directors were apt to be renamed if the gentlemen concerned severed their connection with the railway, or were knighted or raised to the peerage. There are instances of locomotives losing their names on being taken over by another railway, and/or on being rebuilt. In the case of the Great Western Railway 9000 'Dukedog' class, those locomotives which were named after directors of the railway saw their names transferred to larger and more imposing designs simply because the 9000 class comprised comparatively small 4–4–0s, and the gentlemen concerned, it is said, considered themselves affronted!

Names but No Numbers

Not every engine carried a number. As already mentioned, in the early days engines were known only by name on several railways, and this persisted on the GWR broad gauge for the 'Rover' class right down to 1892 and the abolition of the broad gauge. Also, departmental locomotives, for example those dedicated to the engineering departments, were often unnumbered. Those industrial engines which have survived often did not carry a number: sometimes names alone were preferred, but, of course, there was little point in numbering a locomotive if it was its owner's only one!

Alphabetical Order

In this list, names are placed in alphabetical order. Names are treated as if they were one word. That is to say, *His Majesty* would come before *Hispaniola*. Names that start with numbers, such as *257 Squadron*, are listed under the word Squadron, and then in numerical order. *St.*, *St* and *Saint* are all treated as if they were Saint (in full).

In the Class Notes, the class names are in alphabetical order on the same basis, regardless of railway. Thus, 'Castle class, Great Western Railway' comes before 'Castle class, Highland Railway'. Classes known by letter/number designations, such as N15 and N15x, come in alphabetical/numerical order. Thus 'B1 class, London & North Eastern Railway' comes before 'B4 class, Southern Railway'. Classes known by numbers only, such as '3021 class, Great Western Railway', '3029 class, Great Western Railway', and '3031 class, Great Western Railway' are given in numerical order.

Information Given

After each name comes the engine's number. This is usually the first one carried or the one by which the engine is best known. *Mallard*, for example, has carried the numbers 4498, 22, and 60022. In this instance, it makes more sense to refer to *Mallard* as 4498, which is also the number it carries in preservation.

After nationalization in 1948 ex-Great Western Railway engines kept their numbers unchanged, ex-Southern Railway engines had 30000 added, ex-London Midland & Scottish Railway engines had 40000 added, and ex-London & North Eastern Railway engines had 60000 added. Exceptions were diesel locomotives, which were numbered from 10000 upwards, and electric locomotives, numbered from 20000 upwards. The British Railways standard classes began at 70000.

The engine's class is given next. This can be either a name, a number, a letter, or a combination of these. The London & North Eastern Railway used a letter/number system whereby the letter denoted the wheel arrangement and the number denoted the individual locomotive type. The Southern used the works' order number, inherited from its three constituents, with the result that there was some duplication. The Great Western used the running number of the first member of the class, e.g. 9000, if there was no class name. The class number was often shown with XX replacing the last two zeros, for example 90XX. The London Midland & Scottish Railway followed the Midland Railway's policy of classifying locomotives by power, with 0 for the smallest shunting locomotives, and 7 or 8 for the most powerful. These figures were tailored to train weights, so that, it was hoped, any class 4 locomotive, for example, could do any other class 4 locomotive's work. This system was refined by using the suffixes F for freight, MT for mixed traffic or P for passenger. British Railways continued the system, culminating in class 8P for the one-off no. 71000 *Duke of Gloucester*, and the very successful 9F class 2–10–0 freight locomotives.

In many cases locomotives were 'one-offs', and no classification as such can be given. In these cases the wheel arrangement is shown, in order to give some idea of the size and type of the locomotive.

The date of introduction is given next. There are several variables here: the date of construction, the date of purchase, the date to traffic . . . In most cases differences will be only a day or two, but if it is important to the researcher then he or she is directed to specialist histories, most notably those published by the Railway Correspondence and Travel Society. The only case where it can be a matter of moment is when a locomotive is completed in the works on 31 December and entered traffic on 1 January – which year is appropriate? In the one or two cases found, the matter is amplified by a footnote and the reader may take his or her pick!

I have not assumed that the reader is necessarily familiar with railway companies' initials, and have spelt out in full the names of owning railways. Where locomotives were named after being taken over from another railway, the previous owner is shown where known.

Errors and omissions are my sole responsibility, and it would be deemed a favour if any spotted are drawn to my attention; one never knows, a second edition may emerge one day! If the work is helpful to someone, I shall be well content.

AJP
Leeds, 1999

ABBREVIATIONS

The problem with abbreviations is that one risks insulting one's reader's intelligence, or alternatively omitting items that puzzle! Steering a course between Scylla and Charybdis, the following is offered:

bg	Broad Gauge (7ft 0¼in)	Fs	Fireless locomotive[3]
CT	Crane Tank (a tank locomotive with a crane mounted on it)	G	Beyer-Garratt locomotive[4]
D	Diesel (transmission unspecified)	PE	Petrol-Electric (where a petrol engine drives a generator which powers electric motors that turn the wheels)
DE	Diesel electric locomotive (where a diesel engine drives a generator which powers electric motors that turn the wheels)	PT	Pannier Tank engine
		Rly	Railway
DH	Diesel hydraulic locomotive (transmission from a diesel engine to the wheels through a fluid coupling)	ST	Saddle Tank engine
		T	Tank engine (with *side* tanks)
DM	Diesel mechanical locomotive (transmission from a diesel engine to the wheels through a gearbox)	TG	Geared tank locomotive (for example, a Sentinel vertical-boiler geared locomotive)
DMU	Diesel Multiple Unit (a diesel-powered passenger train without a separate locomotive)	TT	Tank-tender engine (a tank engine which also has a tender – a very rare type)
		VB	Vertical Boiler locomotive
ed	Engineering Department[1]	w	Wheeled (for example, 4w = 4-wheeled, 6w = 6-wheeled, etc.)
F	Fairlie locomotive[2]	WT	Well Tank engine (where the water is stored in a tank mounted between the frames)

---

[1] In the early days it was the custom on some railways, notably the London & South Western, for the Engineering Department to maintain its own fleet of locomotives for ballasting work, etc.

[2] The Fairlie locomotive was invented by Robert Fairlie. It consists of two boilers mounted back-to-back and sharing a common firebox. Thus there is a chimney at each end. The whole assembly is mounted on two bogies, each with cylinders and coupling rods. It looks like two engines joined together back-to-back. The idea was to produce a very powerful locomotive which nevertheless could traverse very sharp curves. Standard gauge examples were not very successful in the UK, but on the 2ft gauge Ffestiniog Railway they were very successful and remain in operation to this day. British manufacturers built many for export, notably to Russia and Mexico. Several series of big Fairlies worked for years on the Mexican Railways.

[3] Here the conventional boiler and firebox are replaced by a steam 'receiver', a circular tank which resembles a boiler in shape, but the chimney is absent. Designed for industrial work, the receiver is charged with high temperature water by the works boiler or other convenient source, and the locomotive can then operate for about four or five hours before recharging becomes necessary. As the steam is used, the drop in pressure causes the water to provide more steam, until the pressure becomes too low for further work to be done. The used steam is exhausted to the atmosphere in the usual way. The absence of fire makes these locomotives particularly suitable for use where the risk of fire or explosion is particularly high, for instance in plants producing explosives, paper, petroleum and, for reasons of cleanliness, food factories.

[4] The Beyer-Garratt locomotive was invented by a Tasmanian called Herbert Garratt. It consisted of a large boiler slung between two engine units, each with its own cylinders and wheels. The front unit carried water and the rear unit carried coal and water. Thus the engine could traverse sharp curves while developing considerable power. Thirty-three such locomotives worked on the London Midland & Scottish Railway, and one on the London & North Eastern Railway. None of the main line locomotives had names, and so are not recorded in this work. One or two were built for industrial use, and one, *William Francis*, is preserved at Bressingham. Beyer Peacock & Co. Ltd of Manchester took up the idea, hence the Beyer prefix to the name, and built many for service abroad. Some examples built for South Africa were among the most powerful steam locomotives in the world.

Name	Number	Class	Date	Railway
Abberley Hall	4981	Hall	12/1930	Great Western Rly
Abbot	–	Abbot	6/1855	Great Western Rly (bg)
Abbotsbury Castle	4083	Castle	5/1925	Great Western Rly
Abbotsford	479	Abbotsford	7/1877	North British Rly
Abbotsford	879	H	8/1906	North British Rly
Abbotsford	60141	A1	12/1948	British Railways (Eastern Region)
Abdul Medjid	–	Victoria	10/1856	Great Western Rly (bg)

Great Western Railway Castle class 4–6–0 no. 4083 *Abbotsbury Castle*, at Old Oak Common, 11 October 1930. (*Photo: LCGB Ken Nunn Collection*)

Name	Number	Class	Date	Railway
Aberaman	–	0–6–0	9/1846	Taff Vale Rly
Aberaman	17	0–6–0	1859	Taff Vale Rly
Abercorn	208	B2	9/1897	London, Brighton & South Coast Rly
Abercrombie	1525	Newton	11/1866	London & North Western Rly
Abercrombie	1525	rPrecedent	5/1891	London & North Western Rly
Aberdare	–	0–4–2	4/1845	Taff Vale Rly
Aberdare	7	0–6–0	1863	Taff Vale Rly
Aberdare Valley	8	0–6–0ST	12/1880	Alexandra (Newport & South Wales) Docks & Co.
Aberddawan	37801	37/7	12/1960	British Railways [1]
Aberdeen	73	Peel	10/1852	Stockton & Darlington Rly
Aberdeen	332	bCrewe	3/1854	London & North Western Rly
Aberdeen	236	233	1860	North British Rly [2]
Aberdeen	486	Abbotsford	1878	North British Rly [3]
Aberdeen Commonwealth	21C7	MN	6/1942	Southern Rly
Aberdeen Corporation Gas Works	**3**	**0–4–0ST**	**1926**	**Scottish Industrial Railway Centre**
Aberdeenshire	249	D49/1	2/1928	London & North Eastern Rly
Aberdonian	868	H	1906	North British Rly
Aberdonian	9903	C11	8/1911	London & North Eastern Rly [4]
Aberdonian	60158	A1	11/1949	British Railways (Eastern Region)
Aberfeldy	17	Jones Tank	12/1879	Highland Rly [5]
Aberfoyle	98	72	1881	North British Rly [6]
Abergavenny	325	F	1/1877	London, Brighton & South Coast Rly

Name	Number	Class	Date	Railway
Abergavenny	325	J1	12/1910	London, Brighton & South Coast Rly
Abergavenny Castle	5013	Castle	6/1932	Great Western Rly
Abergwawr	24	0–6–0	1851	Taff Vale Rly
Aberporth Grange	6860	Grange	2/1939	Great Western Rly
Aberthaw	37801	37/7	12/1960	British Railways [7]
Aberystwyth	4	0–6–0	7/1868	Manchester & Milford Rly [8]
Aberystwyth	3712	Bulldog	6/1906	Great Western Rly
Aberystwyth Castle	4084	Castle	5/1925	Great Western Rly
Abney Hall	6900	Hall	6/1940	Great Western Rly
Aboukir	5681	Jubilee	1935	London Midland & Scottish Rly
Aboyeur	60148	A1	5/1949	British Railways (Eastern Region)
ABP Port of Hull	56039	56	1978	British Railways
Abraham Darby	86247	86/2	1965	British Railways
Accra EDL	40034	40	9/1959	British Railways [9]
Acheron	–	Priam	1/1842	Great Western Rly (bg)
Acheron	64	Alecto	12/1846	London & South Western Rly
Acheron	–	Hawthorn	2/1866	Great Western Rly (bg)
Acheron	64	Volcano	12/1866	London & South Western Rly
Achilles	–	2–2–0	12/1831	Warrington & Newton Rly
Achilles	–	Priam	6/1841	Great Western Rly (bg)
Achilles	43	0–4–2	7/1843	London, Brighton & South Coast Rly [10]
Achilles	65	Alecto	3/1847	London & South Western Rly
Achilles	32	Goliath	2/1849	East Lancashire Rly
Achilles	1005	L/Bloomer	1851	London & North Western Rly
Achilles	303	bCrewe	2/1853	London & North Western Rly
Achilles	16	A	8/1864	Metropolitan Rly
Achilles	65	Lion	1/1870	London & South Western Rly
Achilles	2165	0–6–0ST	12/1873	Great Western Rly (bg) [11]
Achilles	511	Dreadnought	1885	London & North Western Rly
Achilles	–	0–4–0ST	1885	Woolwich Arsenal [12]
Achilles	3031	3031	3/1894	Great Western Rly
Achilles	310	2Precursor	12/1904	London & North Western Rly
Achilles	5697	Jubilee	1936	London Midland & Scottish Rly
Achilles	50045	50	1968	British Railways
Acis	113	Acis	9/1861	London, Chatham & Dover Rly
Acklam	183	Windsor	3/1866	Stockton & Darlington Rly
Acmon	113	0–6–0	4/1853	Manchester, Sheffield & Lincolnshire Rly
Acorn	**–**	**0–4–0DM**	**1948**	**Penrhyn Castle Industrial Museum**
Actaeon	–	Priam	12/1841	Great Western Rly (bg)
Actaeon	66	Alecto	12/1847	London & South Western Rly
Actaeon	79	2–4–0	6/1849	Manchester, Sheffield & Lincolnshire Rly [13]
Actaeon	66	Volcano	1/1867	London & South Western Rly
Active	48	0–4–2	1844	Stockton & Darlington Rly [14]
Active	–	0–4–0ST	1882	Alexandra (Newport & South Wales) Docks & Co. [15]
Active	D600	Warship	1/1958	British Railways
Acton	356A	0–4–0T	?	London & North Western Rly [16]
Acton Burnell Hall	6991	M/Hall	11/1948	British Railways (Western Region)
Acton Hall	4982	Hall	1/1931	Great Western Rly
Ada	2146	0–6–0ST	1862	Great Western Rly (bg) [17]
Ad-a-Cab	**25**	**4wDM**	**1938**	**Leighton Buzzard Rly [18]**

---

[1] Named *Aberthaw* on the other side.

[2] Built for Edinburgh & Glasgow Railway.

[3] Later renamed *Eskbank*.

[4] Originally North British Railway no. 903 *Cock o' the North*. Renamed *Aberdonian* in May 1934 to free the original name for Sir Nigel Gresley's P2 class 2–8–2 no. 2001.

[5] Previously named *Breadalbane*. Renamed *Aberfeldy* in 1886, it was nameless by 1915.

[6] This engine was in service before the Aberfoyle line was opened; it may originally have carried another name.

[7] Named *Aberddawan* on the other side.

[8] Became Great Western Railway no. 1339.

[9] Previously no. D234 *Accra*.

[10] Built for London & Brighton and South Eastern Railways Joint Stock, and went to the London & Brighton (later the London, Brighton & South Coast Railway) on the dissolution of the joint stock.

[11] Formerly the South Devon Railway. After conversion to standard gauge and removal of its name, it became South Wales Mineral Railway no. 7.

[12] 18in gauge.

[13] May have been built originally as a 2–2–2.

[14] May have been obtained second-hand, in which case 1844 would be the date of purchase.

[15] Date of purchase. Previous history unknown.

[16] Acquired with the Shropshire Union Railway & Canal Co. Date of construction unknown.

[17] Originally South Devon Railway.

[18] 2ft gauge.

Name	Number	Class	Date	Railway
Adam	1	0–4–0ST	1916	**Cambrian Railways Society**
Adam Smith	60057	60	9/1991	British Railways
Adam Woodcock	428	Scott	8/1915	North British Rly
Addax	1024	B1	4/1947	London & North Eastern Rly
Adderley Hall	4901	Hall	12/1928	Great Western Rly
Addingston	109	19	1880	North British Rly
Addington	22	D1	8/1875	London, Brighton & South Coast Rly
Addison	–	0–4–2	12/1860	Preston & Longridge Rly
Adelaide	20	Director	4/1832	Stockton & Darlington Rly
Adelaide	22	0–6–0	4/1840	Newcastle & Carlisle Rly [19]
Adelaide	824	Samson	1/1866	London & North Western Rly
Adelaide	824	Whitworth	6/1893	London & North Western Rly
Adelaide	3394	Atbara	6/1901	Great Western Rly
Aden	3395	Atbara	7/1901	Great Western Rly
Aden	5633	Jubilee	1934	London Midland & Scottish Rly
Adjutant	159	bCrewe	8/1856	London & North Western Rly [20]
Adjutant	675	2Precursor	4/1906	London & North Western Rly
Admiral	172	bCrewe	10/1847	London & North Western Rly
Admiral	772	2Precursor	4/1906	London & North Western Rly
Admiral Jellicoe	2408	Prince/W	12/1915	London & North Western Rly
Adonis	55	2–4–0	6/1848	Manchester, Sheffield & Lincolnshire Rly
Adrian	127	Adrian	8/1866	London, Chatham & Dover Rly
Adriatic	150	E1	11/1880	London, Brighton & South Coast Rly

North Eastern Railway 2–2–4T no. 66 *Aerolite*, at Newcastle Central on 27 April 1920. (*Photo: LCGB Ken Nunn Collection*)

Name	Number	Class	Date	Railway
Adriatic	1309	Teutonic	6/1890	London & North Western Rly
Adriatic	322	2Experiment	12/1908	London & North Western Rly
Aelfred	–	0–6–0T	10/1898	Lambourn Valley Rly [21]
Aeolus	–	Wolf	11/1837	Great Western Rly (bg)
Aeolus	26	2–2–2	1838	Grand Junction Rly
Aeolus	5	2–2–2	1/1842	Manchester, Sheffield & Lincolnshire Rly
Aeolus	15	Aurora	3/1847	East Lancashire Rly
Aeolus	67	Alecto	10/1847	London & South Western Rly
Aeolus	26	aCrewe	11/1847	London & North Western Rly
Aeolus	849	L/Bloomer	1851	London & North Western Rly
Aeolus	71	Aeolus	9/1860	London, Chatham & Dover Rly
Aeolus	67	Gem	3/1863	London & South Western Rly
Aerolite	66	2–2–4T	1869	**North Eastern Rly [22]**
Aetna	104	0–6–0	4/1852	Manchester, Sheffield & Lincolnshire Rly
Africa	55	Europa	10/1873	London, Chatham & Dover Rly
Agamemnon	56	Rossendale	1/1853	East Lancashire Rly
Agamemnon	3032	3031	7/1894	Great Western Rly
Agamemnon	1923	Jubilee	3/1900	London & North Western Rly
Agamemnon	5693	Jubilee	1936	London Midland & Scottish Rly
Agecroft No. 2	–	0–4–0ST	1948	**Southport Railway Centre**
Agecroft No. 3	–	0–4–0ST	1951	**Museum of Science and Industry in Manchester**
Agenoria	–	0–4–0	1829	**Shutt End Rly [23]**
Agincourt	1931	Jubilee	9/1900	London & North Western Rly
Agincourt	50013	50	1968	British Railways
AGW1 Pet	2	4wP	1939	**Hampshire Narrow Gauge Railway Society [24]**
A. Harold Bibby	1250	B1	10/1947	London & North Eastern Rly [25]
A.H. Mills	3704	Bulldog	5/1906	Great Western Rly [26]
A.H. Peppercorn	525	A2	12/1947	London & North Eastern Rly
Ahwaz	5028	J94	10/1943	Longmoor Military Rly
Ahwaz	203	J94	5/1953	Longmoor Military Rly
Ailsa Craig	60044	60	9/1991	British Railways
Airborne	511	A2/3	7/1946	London & North Eastern Rly
Airdrie	284	165	1875	North British Rly [27]
Airdrie	60	72	1882	North British Rly
Aire	17	2–2–2	11/1840	Manchester & Leeds Rly
Airedale	–	0–6–0ST	1923	**Yorkshire Dales Rly**
Airey	1678	Newton	4/1868	London & North Western Rly
Airey	1678	rPrecedent	4/1892	London & North Western Rly
Airey Neave	86411	86/6	1965	British Railways
Airtour Suisse	73212	73/2	10/1965	British Railways
Aisne	631	C	3/1890	North British Rly
Ajax	29	2–2–0	1832	Liverpool & Manchester Rly
Ajax	–	0–4–2	1838	Leicester & Swannington Rly
Ajax	–	Fury	12/1838	Great Western Rly (bg)
Ajax	41	1Hercules	11/1841	London & South Western Rly
Ajax	24	2–2–2	3/1846	Manchester, Sheffield & Lincolnshire Rly
Ajax	17	Pegasus	4/1847	East Lancashire Rly
Ajax	21	0–6–0	1855	South Staffordshire Rly
Ajax	41	2Hercules	3/1855	London & South Western Rly
Ajax	144	0–6–0	8/1860	London, Chatham & Dover Rly
Ajax	2149	0–6–0ST	9/1860	Great Western Rly (bg) [28]
Ajax	408	4	8/1864	Manchester, Sheffield & Lincolnshire Rly [29]
Ajax	41	2Vesuvius	12/1874	London & South Western Rly
Ajax	509	Dreadnought	1885	London & North Western Rly
Ajax	–	0–4–0T	1895	Woolwich Arsenal [30]
Ajax	639	2Precursor	10/1904	London & North Western Rly
Ajax	38	0–6–0T	1918	**Isle of Wight Steam Rly**
Ajax	6139	Royal Scot	10/1927	London Midland & Scottish Rly [31]
Ajax	5689	Jubilee	1936	London Midland & Scottish Rly
(Ajax)	–	0–4–0ST	1941	**Chatham Dockyard [32]**
Ajax	50046	50	1968	British Railways
(A.J. Hill)	9621	N7	1924	**London & North Eastern Rly**
Alan-a-dale	1355	0–6–0T	1876	Great Western Rly [33]

[19] Became North Eastern Railway no. 470, either 0–6–0 or 0–4–2.

[20] Formerly Grand Junction Railway. Later London & North Western Railway no. 18 *Cerberus*, then renumbered and renamed no. 159 *Adjutant*.

[21] Became Cambrian Railways no. 35 in June 1904.

[22] Built as 2–2–2WT, it was rebuilt as 4–2–2T in 11/1892, and as 2–2–4T in April 1902.

[23] The name comes from classical Greek. Homer uses the word in the *Iliad* to describe Hector. It means haughty, and also strong – all the manly virtues.

[24] 2ft gauge.

[25] Nameplates fitted in December 1947.

[26] Renamed *Sir Edward Elgar* in August 1932.

[27] Later renamed *Grahamston*.

[28] Built for the South Devon Railway.

[29] Originally built for Logan & Hemingway, contractors, as their no. 5 *Ajax*. Purchased in June 1876 by the MS&LR, it may have lost its name on purchase.

[30] 18in gauge.

[31] Renamed *The Welch Regiment* in May 1936.

[32] Built for Chatham Dockyard; now at Chatham Dockyard Historic Trust.

[33] Built for the Severn & Wye & Severn Bridge Railway.

Name	Number	Class	Date	Railway
Alan	**3**	**4wDM**	**1956**	**Gartell Light Rly** [34]
Alan	**–**	**0–4–0DM**	**1957**	**Severn Valley Rly**
Alan Bloom	**–**	**0–4–0DM**	**1992**	**Bressingham Steam Museum** [35]
Alan George	**–**	**0–4–0ST**	**1894**	**Teifi Valley Rly**
Alan Meaden	**5**	**4wDM**	**1965**	**Corris Rly** [36]
Alaric	29	2–2–2	1838	Grand Junction Rly
Alaric	29	aCrewe	11/1846	London & North Western Rly
Alaric	71	Alecto	12/1847	London & South Western Rly
Alaric	990	L/Bloomer	1851	London & North Western Rly
Alaric	71	Falcon	9/1863	London & South Western Rly
Alaric	282	2Precursor	4/1906	London & North Western Rly
Alarm	70	Priam	2/1852	Stockton & Darlington Rly
Alaska	315	1Experiment	1884	London & North Western Rly
Alaska	117	2Precursor	10/1905	London & North Western Rly
Albany	349	G	5/1882	London, Brighton & South Coast Rly
Albany	3456	Bulldog	1/1904	Great Western Rly
Albatross	162	bCrewe	5/1856	London & North Western Rly [37]
Albatross	1169	1Precursor	1879	London & North Western Rly
Albatross	3033	3031	7/1894	Great Western Rly
Albatross	510	2Precursor	6/1904	London & North Western Rly
Albemarle	1961	Alfred	7/1903	London & North Western Rly
Albert	–	0–6–0	1839	Llanelly Rly
Albert	–	2–2–2	1840	Lancaster & Preston Junction Rly
Albert	18	Fairbairn	9/1841	London & South Western Rly
Albert	116	2–2–2	11/1845	Great Western Rly [38]
Albert	29	0–4–2	1847	Newcastle & Carlisle Rly [39]
Albert	18	Tartar	7/1852	London & South Western Rly
Albert	84	Peel	7/1854	Stockton & Darlington Rly
Albert	898	0–4–2	1857	Great Western Rly [40]
Albert	18	2Vesuvius	7/1871	London & South Western Rly
Albert	647	C	2/1891	North British Rly
Albert	–	B-B DM	1934	Woolwich Arsenal [41]
Albert Brassey	3414	Bulldog	12/1902	Great Western Rly
Albert Edward	–	0–4–0ST	12/1873	Woolwich Arsenal [42]
Albert Edward	–	0–4–0ST	1/1882	Swansea Harbour Trust
Albert Edward	3062	3031	5/1897	Great Western Rly
Albert Fields	**–**	**0–6–0DM**	**1958**	**Midland Railway Centre**
Albert Hall	**4983**	**Hall**	**1/1931**	**Great Western Rly**
Alberta	5562	Jubilee	1934	London Midland & Scottish Rly
Albion	76	aCrewe	9/1845	Grand Junction Rly
Albion	5	0–4–2	1848	South Yorkshire Rly
Albion	129	Saxon	9/1855	London & South Western Rly
Albion	30	Small Pass	3/1863	Cambrian Railways
Albion	1215	Newton	4/1872	London & North Western Rly
Albion	95	L/Scotchmen	2/1873	London, Chatham & Dover Rly
Albion	312	Lyons	9/1883	London, Brighton & South Coast Rly
Albion	1215	rPrecedent	4/1893	London & North Western Rly
Albion	2971	Saint	12/1903	Great Western Rly [43]
Albion	610	Prince/W	12/1915	London & North Western Rly
Albion	D803	Warship	3/1959	British Railways
Albion	47509	47/4	1966	British Railways
Albrighton Hall	4984	Hall	1/1931	Great Western Rly
Alcazar	60136	A1	11/1948	British Railways (Eastern Region)
Alchemist	210	bCrewe	7/1848	London & North Western Rly
Alchemyst	210	DX	1859	London & North Western Rly
Alchymist	645	Dreadnought	1888	London & North Western Rly
Alchymist	365	2Precursor	4/1905	London & North Western Rly
Aldam	–	2–2–2	1847	Huddersfield & Manchester Railway & Canal
Aldaniti	86428	86/6	7/1966	British Railways

Name	Number	Class	Date	Railway
Aldborough Hall	6931	Hall	12/1941	Great Western Rly [44]
Aldeburgh Festival	47596	47/4	1965	British Railways
Aldenham Hall	4902	Hall	12/1928	Great Western Rly
Alderman	185	aCrewe	2/1848	London & North Western Rly
(Alderman A.E. Draper)	**5305**	**5**	**1937**	**London Midland & Scottish Rly**
Alderney	107	E1	10/1876	London, Brighton & South Coast Rly
Alderney	85	B4	10/1891	London & South Western Rly
Aldersey Hall	6930	Hall	11/1941	Great Western Rly [45]
Aldgate	283	D1	10/1879	London, Brighton & South Coast Rly
Ald Hague	**–**	**4wPM**	**1954**	**Moseley Railway Museum**
Aldingbourne	456	E3	4/1895	London, Brighton & South Coast Rly
Aldourie	2	Raigmore	10/1855	Highland Rly
Aldourie	69	Duke	8/1874	Highland Rly [46]
Aldrington	161	E1	11/1891	London, Brighton & South Coast Rly
Aldwark	09008	09	1959	British Railways
(Aldwych)	**111**	**0–6–0ST**	**1882**	**Air Ministry** [47]
Alecto	9	2–2–2	1837	Grand Junction Rly
Alecto	20	2–2–2	12/1845	Manchester, Sheffield & Lincolnshire Rly
Alecto	9	aCrewe	11/1846	London & North Western Rly
Alecto	63	Alecto	12/1846	London & South Western Rly
Alecto	63	Volcano	12/1866	London & South Western Rly
Alecto	2003	Newton	4/1871	London & North Western Rly
Alecto	2003	rPrecedent	6/1891	London & North Western Rly
Alecto	–	2–4–0	1904	Woolwich Arsenal [48]
Alecto	1516	2Precursor	8/1907	London & North Western Rly
Alencon	129	E1	10/1878	London, Brighton & South Coast Rly
Alert	22	Tory	1/1848	Stockton & Darlington Rly
Alert	33	Dawn	10/1862	London, Chatham & Dover Rly

Great Western Railway Saint class 4–6–0 no. 2971 *Albion*, at Swindon. (*Photo: RAS Marketing*)

Name	Number	Class	Date	Railway
Alexander	77	Peel	2/1854	Stockton & Darlington Rly
Alexander	–	Victoria	11/1856	Great Western Rly (bg)
Alexander	2232	cSentinel	1929	London & North Eastern Rly
Alexander Fleming	60014	60	1/1993	British Railways
Alexander Graham Bell	60061	60	9/1991	British Railways
Alexander Hubbard	3299	Badminton	6/1898	Great Western Rly [49]
Alexander Reith Gray	1242	B1	10/1947	London & North Eastern Rly
Alexandra	1	0–6–0	3/1863	Brecon & Merthyr Rly

[34] 2ft gauge.
[35] 15in gauge.
[36] Corris Railway Museum, Corris. 2ft 3in gauge.
[37] Built for the Grand Junction Railway.
[38] Built for the Chester & Birkenhead Railway.
[39] Became North Eastern Railway no. 477. Rebuilt as 2–4–0 (date unknown).

[40] Built for the Llanelly Railway.
[41] 18in gauge.
[42] 18in gauge.
[43] Altered to 4–4–2 in 1904, and back to 4–6–0 in 1907. Renamed *The Pirate* in March 1907; reverted to *Albion* in July 1907.
[44] Named in September 1947.
[45] Named in May 1946.

[46] Previously named *The Lord Provost* and *Sir James*.
[47] Now at the Leeds City Museum of Science & Industry.
[48] Paraffin/mechanical. 18in gauge.
[49] Originally named *Hubbard*. Renamed in August 1903.

Name	Number	Class	Date	Railway
Alexandra	–	0–6–0	1865	Llanelly Rly [50]
Alexandra	4	S/Goods	6/1872	Cambrian Railways
Alexandra	–	0–4–0ST	?	Alexandra (Newport & South Wales) Docks & Co. [51]
Alexandra	185	O2	6/1890	London & South Western Rly [52]
Alexandra	3061	3031	5/1897	Great Western Rly [53]
Alexandra	**12**	**0–4–0ST**	**1902**	**Lakeside & Haverthwaite Rly**
Alexandra	237	233	1860	North British Rly
Alexandria	11	0–6–0ST	1/1871	Alexandra (Newport & South Wales) Docks & Co.
Alf	**9**	**0–4–0DM**	**1950**	**Talyllyn Rly [54]**
(Alfie)	D2246	04	1956	**British Railways [55]**
Alfred	897	0–4–2	9/1839	Great Western Rly [56]

British Railways Deltic class Co-Co diesel locomotive no. 9009 *Alycidon*, at Finsbury Park in November 1969. (*Photo: RAS Marketing*)

Name	Number	Class	Date	Railway
Alfred	–	**0–4–0ST**	**1953**	**Bodmin & Wenford Rly**
Alfred Baldwin	3415	Bulldog	1/1903	Great Western Rly [57]
Alfred Fletcher	1327	Claughton	5/1913	London & North Western Rly
Alfred Paget	1429	Problem	1865	London & North Western Rly
Alfred Paget	**11**	**0–4–0ST**	**1882**	**Chasewater Light Rly**
Alfred Paget	412	2Precursor	6/1904	London & North Western Rly
Alfred the Great	1941	Alfred	5/1901	London & North Western Rly
Alfred the Great	70009	Britannia	5/1951	British Railways
Alfriston	346	G	4/1882	London, Brighton & South Coast Rly
Algiers	891	Bo-Bo	1941	War Department [58]
Alice	896	0–4–2	7/1839	Great Western Rly [59]
Alice	194	Peel	10/1866	Stockton & Darlington Rly
Alice	–	**0–4–0ST**	**1902**	**Leighton Buzzard Rly [60]**
Alice	–	0–6–2T	4/1912	Longmoor Military Rly [61]

Name	Number	Class	Date	Railway
Alison	20903	20	8/1961	Hunslet-Barclay Ltd
Alison	**5**	**4wDH**	**1983**	**Gartell Light Rly [62]**
Alistair	**4**	**4wDM**	**1950**	**Gartell Light Rly [63]**
Allan-Bane	2692	D11/2	11/1924	London & North Eastern Rly
Allen	32	0–6–0	10/1848	Newcastle & Carlisle Rly [64]
Allenby	611	C	8/1892	North British Rly
Allen Sarle	188	Gladstone	5/1889	London, Brighton & South Coast Rly
Allersley Hall	4985	Hall	1/1931	Great Western Rly [65]
Allerton	281	bCrewe	2/1852	London & North Western Rly
Allerton T&RS Depot Quality Approved	90127	90/1	4/1989	British Railways
Allesley Hall	4985	Hall	1/1931	Great Western Rly [66]
Alliance	104	4–4–2	6/1905	Great Western Rly [67]
Alligator	–	Caesar	7/1848	Great Western Rly (bg)
(Allington Castle)	**12228**	**0–4–0DH**	**1968**	**Chatham Dockyard**
Allt	30	0–6–0ST	1874	Brecon & Merthyr Rly
Alma	1816	2–4–0	?	London & North Western Rly [68]
Alma	24	2–4–0	1853	St Helens Canal & Rly [69]
Alma	351	bCrewe	10/1854	London & North Western Rly
Alma	–	Iron Duke	11/1854	Great Western Rly (bg)
Alma	36	0–6–0	1855	Taff Vale Rly
Alma	2185	Precedent	4/1875	London & North Western Rly
Alma	–	Rover	11/1880	Great Western Rly (bg)
Alma	2185	rPrecedent	1/1896	London & North Western Rly
Almon B. Strowger	20131	20/0	2/1966	British Railways
Alnwick Castle	2822	B17/1	1/1931	London & North Eastern Rly
Alpha	–	0–4–0	7/1835	London & South Western Rly
Alpha	–	**0–6–2T**	**1932**	**Sittingbourne & Kemsley Light Rly [70]**
Alrewas	13	0–6–0	1/1851	South Staffordshire Rly
Alston	33	0–6–0	6/1850	Newcastle & Carlisle Rly [71]
Altyre	8	Seafield	8/1858	Highland Rly [72]
Aluminium 100	37410	37/4	1965	British Railways
Alverstone	W29	O2	8/1891	Southern Rly [73]
Alycidon	**55009**	**Deltic**	**7/1961**	**British Railways**
Amadis	60149	A1	5/1949	British Railways (Eastern Region)
Amanda	**1**	**4wDH**	**1966**	**Gartell Light Rly [74]**
Amazon	–	Iron Duke	3/1851	Great Western Rly (bg)
Amazon	861	Precedent	5/1877	London & North Western Rly
Amazon	–	Rover	9/1878	Great Western Rly (bg)
Amazon	3001	3001	1/1892	Great Western Rly [75]
Amazon	861	rPrecedent	9/1901	London & North Western Rly
Amazon	D1675	47	1965	British Railways
Ambassador	216	aCrewe	7/1848	London & North Western Rly
Ambassador	216	DX	1859	London & North Western Rly
Ambassador	647	Dreadnought	1888	London & North Western Rly
Ambassador	333	2Precursor	12/1904	London & North Western Rly
Amberley	372	D3	12/1892	London, Brighton & South Coast Rly

50 Became Great Western Railway no. 907.
51 Became Great Western Railway no. 1341 after 1923. Built probably *c*. 1884.
52 Specially named *Alexandra* for the opening of the Brookwood–Bisley branch on 12 July 1890, and the first shoot of the National Rifle Association at the Bisley Ranges, an event attended by HRH the Princess of Wales, afterwards Queen Alexandra. No. 185 hauled the special train and, as well as the name, received a representation of the Prince of Wales's feathers and a monogram of the company's initials. It became nameless again in November 1896, the date of the next repaint. It was the only member of its class to bear a name until Southern Railway days, when engines transferred to the Isle of Wight were named after places on the island.
53 Name removed in November 1910; renamed *George A. Wills* in October 1911.

54 Former National Coal Board underground mining locomotive. 2ft 3in gauge.
55 Later named *Bluebell*.
56 Built for the Llanelly Railway. *Prince Alfred* until 1862.
57 Originally named *Baldwin* until April 1903.
58 Ex-WD no. 1233. Built by Whitcomb in the USA under the US Government's Lend-Lease Programme.
59 Built for the Llanelly Railway.
60 2ft gauge.
61 Great Northern Railway no. 1590. Stayed at Longmoor for a year, during which time it was experimentally armour-plated. The name was carried only at Longmoor. Returned to GNR in 1922.
62 2ft gauge.
63 2ft gauge.
64 Became North Eastern Railway no. 480.

65 Later renamed *Allesley Hall*.
66 Originally named *Allersley Hall*.
67 Name not fitted until 1907.
68 Came from the Whitland & Cardigan Railway. Date of construction unknown. May have been built for the Liverpool & Manchester Railway.
69 Believed to be ex-Liverpool & Manchester Railway *Ostrich*, *Partridge* or *Redwing*.
70 2ft 6in gauge.
71 Became North Eastern Railway no. 481. Rebuilt as 2–4–0 in 1869.
72 Later renamed *Beauly*.
73 Formerly London & South Western Railway (and Southern Railway) no. 202. Renamed *Alverstone* by the Southern Railway on transfer to Isle of Wight, April 1926.
74 2ft gauge.
75 Rebuilt to 4–2–2 in October 1894.

Name	Number	Class	Date	Railway
Ambersham	589	E5	3/1904	London, Brighton & South Coast Rly
America	56	Europa	10/1873	London, Chatham & Dover Rly
America	365	1Experiment	1884	London & North Western Rly
America	1509	2Precursor	8/1905	London & North Western Rly
Amethyst	69	Ruby	10/1861	London, Chatham & Dover Rly
Amethyst	45700	Jubilee	1936	British Railways [76]
Amlwch Freighter	47330	47/3	1965	British Railways
Amman	900	2-4-0	9/1865	Great Western Rly [77]
Amos	–	4wPE	1927	Ashover Rly [78]
Amphion	–	Caesar	11/1852	Great Western Rly (bg)
Amphion	342	aCrewe	8/1854	London & North Western Rly
Amphion	988	2Precursor	4/1906	London & North Western Rly
Amyas	3272	Duke	8/1896	Great Western Rly
An Comunn Gaidhealach	37418	37/4	1965	British Railways
Ancona	134	E1	12/1878	London, Brighton & South Coast Rly
Andania CLS	**40013**	**40**	**1959**	**British Railways [79]**
Anderton	289	2-4-0	5/1861	Lancashire & Yorkshire Rly
Andes	106	0-6-0	6/1852	Manchester, Sheffield & Lincolnshire Rly
Andre Chapelon	86103	86/1	1966	British Railways
Andrew	**2**	**4wDH**	**?**	**Gartell Light Rly [80]**
Andrew Bain	48	F	10/1920	Great North of Scotland Rly
Andrew Carnegie	47517	47/4	1907	British Railways
Andrew K. McCosh	4494	A4	8/1937	London & North Eastern Rly [81]
Andromeda	1388	Prince/W	10/1911	London & North Western Rly
Andy	**–**	**0-4-0DM**	**1923**	**Midland Railway Centre**
Anemone	4111	Flower	6/1908	Great Western Rly
Anerley	9	D1	4/1874	London, Brighton & South Coast Rly
An Gearasdan	37073	37/0	1962	British Railways
Angerstein	11	0-4-2	1850	South Staffordshire Rly
Anglesea	–	0-6-0WT	6/1862	Anglesey Rly [82]
Anglesey	260	bCrewe	5/1850	London & North Western Rly
Anglia	226	DFG	5/1866	London & South Western Rly
Anglia	2295	Prince/W	4/1916	London & North Western Rly
Angmering	371	D3	12/1892	London, Brighton & South Coast Rly
Anker	–	2-2-2	11/1839	Birmingham & Derby Junction Rly
Ann	**–**	**4wVB**	**1927**	**Yorkshire Dales Rly**
(Annabel)	**08398**	**08**	**1958**	**British Railways**
Annan	91	Scotchmen	11/1866	London, Chatham & Dover Rly
Annie	–	0-4-0ST(?)	1873	Alexandra (Newport & South Wales) Docks & Co.
Annie	**–**	**0-4-0ST**	**1904**	**Lavender Line**
Annie	**–**	**0-4-0ST**	**1908**	**Yorkshire Dales Rly**
Annie	**–**	**0-4-2T**	**1998**	**Groudle Glen Rly [83]**
Annington	505	E4	10/1900	London, Brighton & South Coast Rly
Anson	319	bCrewe	5/1854	London & North Western Rly
Anson	1932	Jubilee	9/1900	London & North Western Rly
Anson	5672	Jubilee	1935	London Midland & Scottish Rly
Anson	50022	50	1968	British Railways
Anstruther	101	19	1881	North British Rly

Name	Number	Class	Date	Railway
Ant	300	bCrewe	1/1853	London & North Western Rly
Antaeus	68	bCrewe	5/1852	London & North Western Rly
Antaeus	561	2Precursor	4/1906	London & North Western Rly
An Teallach	60091	60	2/1992	British Railways
Antelope	9	2-2-2	1840	York & North Midland Rly
Antelope	46	2-2-0	8/1840	Stockton & Darlington Rly [84]
Antelope	–	Wolf	8/1841	Great Western Rly (bg)
Antelope	23	Fairbairn	4/1842	London & South Western Rly [85]
Antelope	5	2-2-2	8/1848	Liverpool, Crosby & Southport Rly [86]
Antelope	317	bCrewe	9/1853	London & North Western Rly
Antelope	27	2-4-0	1855	Newport, Abergavenny & Hereford Rly
Antelope	7	0-6-0	1857	Brecon & Merthyr Rly
Antelope	38	0-6-0	1/1857	Taff Vale Rly [87]
Antelope	66	Giraffe	7/1857	East Lancashire Rly
Antelope	2114	4-4-0ST	7/1859	Great Western Rly (bg) [88]
Antelope	23	Lion	11/1871	London & South Western Rly
Antelope	2183	Precedent	3/1875	London & North Western Rly
Antelope	2183	rPrecedent	5/1895	London & North Western Rly
Anteus	68	0-4-2	3/1841	Grand Junction Rly
Anti-Aircraft Command	21C149	BB	12/1946	Southern Rly
Antiquary	–	Abbot	6/1855	Great Western Rly (bg)
Anthony Ashley Cooper	60033	60	2/1991	British Railways
Anthony Manor	7801	Manor	1/1938	Great Western Rly
Antonia CLS	**40014**	**40**	**6/1959**	**British Railways [89]**
(Antwerp)	**75130**	**J94**	**8/1944**	**War Department**
Anubis	–	0-4-2T	1885	Woolwich Arsenal [90]
Anzac	126	Prince/W	3/1916	London & North Western Rly
Anzac	70046	Britannia	6/1954	British Railways
Apapa EDL	40035	40	10/1959	British Railways [91]
Apis	–	0-4-2T	1885	Woolwich Arsenal [92]
Apollo	–	Wolf	1/1838	Great Western Rly (bg)
Apollo	4	2-2-2	12/1841	Manchester, Sheffield & Lincolnshire Rly
Apollo	75	aCrewe	9/1845	Grand Junction Rly
Apollo	1388	0-6-0	1846	Great Western Rly [93]
Apollo	68	Alecto	11/1846	London & South Western Rly
Apollo	851	L/Bloomer	1851	London & North Western Rly
Apollo	43	0-6-0	1857	Taff Vale Rly
Apollo	68	Falcon	12/1863	London & South Western Rly
Apollo	1120	1Experiment	1884	London & North Western Rly
Apollo	1115	2Precursor	4/1905	London & North Western Rly
Apollo	70015	Britannia	6/1951	British Railways
Appleby	132	Peel	8/1858	Stockton & Darlington Rly
Appleby Frodingham	47222	47/0	1965	British Railways
Appledore	34100	rWC	12/1949	British Railways (Southern Region)
Appollo	5	A	1864	Metropolitan Rly
Aquarius	–	Leo	6/1842	Great Western Rly (bg)

[76] Originally named *Britannia*. Renamed by British Railways to commemorate HMS *Amethyst*'s exploits in the Yangtse River in China, and also to free the name *Britannia* for British Railways no. 70000.

[77] Built for the Llanelly Railway.

[78] 1ft 11½in gauge.

[79] Formerly D213 *Andania*.

[80] 2ft gauge.

[81] Originally named *Osprey*; renamed in October 1942.

[82] Became *Miers* on the Neath & Brecon Railway. Later became no. 42 on the Waterford & Limerick Railway in Ireland, and was converted to the 5ft 3in gauge.

[83] 2ft gauge.

[84] Bury type. Formerly no. 14 *Antelope* of the Midland Counties Railway.

[85] Rebuilt from *Sam Slick* (unnumbered), which was not a satisfactory design. The whole class was sent to Fairbairns for reconstruction, returning in April 1842 as no. 23 *Antelope*. Sam Slick, by the way, was a character in a series of comic stories written by Judge J.C. Halliburton of Nova Scotia, popular in England during the 1830s.

[86] Originally named either *Southport* or *Waterloo*. It is uncertain whether *Southport* was renamed *Antelope* and *Waterloo* became *Gazelle* by October 1850, or vice versa.

[87] This engine, and Brecon & Merthyr no. 7 listed immediately above, were by the same builder (Slaughter, Gruning & Co.), with almost identical dimensions (wheels 4ft 6in or 4ft 6½in; cylinders 16in × 24in) and both were of long-boiler type. It is very tempting to assume that they were the same engine, but no. 38 was supplied to the Taff Vale by the makers new in January 1857 and was broken up in January 1878, while no. 7 was purchased by the Brecon & Merthyr from an unknown source at an unknown date, and its disposal is likewise shrouded in mystery.

[88] Built for the South Devon Railway.

[89] Previously no. D214 *Antonia*.

[90] 18in gauge.

[91] Previously no. D235 *Apapa*.

[92] 18in gauge.

[93] Built for the West Cornwall Railway in 1846 or 1847.

Name	Number	Class	Date	Railway
Aquitania CLS	40015	40	6/1959	British Railways [94]
Arab	37	Vivid	9/1839	London & South Western Rly
Arab	–	Priam	5/1841	Great Western Rly (bg)
Arab	37	2Hercules	4/1853	London & South Western Rly
Arab	346	bCrewe	9/1854	London & North Western Rly
Arab	1152	1Precursor	1874	London & North Western Rly
Arab	37	2Vesuvius	2/1874	London & South Western Rly
Arab	2576	2Precursor	12/1905	London & North Western Rly
Arabic	2092	Prince/W	4/1916	London & North Western Rly
Arborfield Hall	6992	M/Hall	11/1948	British Railways (Western Region)
Arbroath	96	165	1878	North British Rly
Arbury Hall	5986	Hall	11/1939	Great Western Rly
Archibald Sturrock	60118	A1	11/1948	British Railways (Eastern Region)
Archilles [sic]	27	2-2-2	11/1846	Manchester, Sheffield & Lincolnshire Rly
Archimedes	6	2-2-2	5/1839	London & Croydon Rly
Archimedes	25	2-4-0	3/1846	Manchester, Sheffield & Lincolnshire Rly
Archimedes	103	aCrewe	5/1847	London & North Western Rly
Archimedes	989	L/Bloomer	1851	London & North Western Rly
Archimedes	6	0-6-0	3/1858	Manchester, Sheffield & Lincolnshire Rly
Archimedes	1395	Dreadnought	1886	London & North Western Rly
Archimedes	648	2Precursor	10/1904	London & North Western Rly
Archimedes	26046	EM1	8/1952	British Railways
Arcidae	47224	47/0	1965	British Railways
Arcuil	60089	60	1/1992	British Railways
(Ardent)	**D2192**	**03**	**1962**	**British Railways**
Ardingly	236	D1	11/1881	London, Brighton & South Coast Rly
Ardingly	917	Schools	5/1933	Southern Rly
Ardross	4	Raigmore	9/1857	Highland Rly
Ardross	4	Duke	7/1876	Highland Rly [95]
Ardvuela	66	Duke	7/1874	Highland Rly [96]
Arenig Fawr	60017	60	10/1990	British Railways
Arethusa	849	Prince/W	3/1916	London & North Western Rly
Arethusa	5696	Jubilee	1936	London Midland & Scottish Rly
Argo	–	Fury	7/1846	Great Western Rly (bg)
Argo	2151	0-6-0ST	10/1863	Great Western Rly (bg) [97]
Argus	–	Priam	8/1842	Great Western Rly (bg)
Argus	21	2-2-2	12/1845	Manchester, Sheffield & Lincolnshire Rly
Argus	69	Alecto	4/1847	London & South Western Rly
Argus	69	Falcon	12/1863	London & South Western Rly
Argus	2056	Dreadnought	1885	London & North Western Rly
Argus	323	2Precursor	2/1905	London & North Western Rly
Argyll	–	0-6-2T	1906	Campbeltown & Machrihanish Rly [98]
Argyll and Sutherland Highlander	6107	Royal Scot	8/1927	London Midland & Scottish Rly
Argyll and Sutherland Highlander	55021	Deltic	5/1962	British Railways
Argyllshire	270	D49/1	1/1928	London & North Eastern Rly
Ariadne	67	2-2-2	9/1848	Manchester, Sheffield & Lincolnshire Rly [99]
Ariadne	–	Caesar	11/1852	Great Western Rly (bg)
Ariadne	166	Undine	12/1859	London & South Western Rly
Ariadne	1666	Newton	3/1868	London & North Western Rly
Ariadne	1666	rPrecedent	6/1891	London & North Western Rly
Ariadne	**27001**	**EM2**	**1954**	**British Railways**
Ariel	–	2-2-2	3/1838	Great Western Rly (bg)
Ariel	1	2-2-0	5/1839	Midland Counties Rly [100]
Ariel	10	2-2-2	1840	York & North Midland Rly
Ariel	70	Alecto	9/1847	London & South Western Rly
Ariel	20	bCrewe	4/1848	London & North Western Rly
Ariel	994	L/Bloomer	1851	London & North Western Rly
Ariel	70	Falcon	11/1864	London & South Western Rly
Ariel	29	Venus	10/1868	East Lancashire Rly
Ariel	70016	Britannia	6/1951	British Railways
Ariel's Girdle	28	2-2-0WT	1851	Eastern Union Rly [101]
Aries	–	Leo	6/1841	Great Western Rly (bg)
Aries	116	0-6-0	9/1853	Manchester, Sheffield & Lincolnshire Rly
Arkle	**13**	**4wDM**	**1937**	**Leighton Buzzard Rly [102]**
Ark Royal	D601	Warship	3/1958	British Railways
Ark Royal	**50035**	**50**	**1968**	**British Railways**
Arley Hall	6901	Hall	7/1940	Great Western Rly
Arlington	247	D1	12/1881	London, Brighton & South Coast Rly
Arlington Court	2931	Saint	10/1911	Great Western Rly
Arlington Grange	6800	Grange	8/1936	Great Western Rly
Armada	5679	Jubilee	1935	London Midland & Scottish Rly
Armington	570	E5	12/1902	London, Brighton & South Coast Rly
Armistice	**–**	**0-4-0ST**	**1919**	**Bredgar & Wormshill Rly [103]**
Armorel	3273	Duke	11/1896	Great Western Rly
Armorel	3273	Bulldog	2/1902	Great Western Rly
Armstrong	7	No.7	3/1894	Great Western Rly
Armstrong	212	B2	12/1897	London, Brighton & South Coast Rly
Armytage	667	627	7/1881	Lancashire & Yorkshire Rly [104]
Arnhem	1443	J94	4/1945	Longmoor Military Rly [105]
Arnold Kunzler	47219	47/0	1965	British Railways
Arquebus	–	0-4-0ST	3/1889	Woolwich Arsenal [106]
Arran	84	Scotchmen	5/1866	London, Chatham & Dover Rly
Arras	643	C	2/1891	North British Rly
Arrow	2	0-2-2	1830	Liverpool & Manchester Rly
Arrow	52	2-2-2	1837	Liverpool & Manchester Rly
Arrow	26	2-2-2	5/1837	Stockton & Darlington Rly [107]
Arrow	–	Priam	7/1841	Great Western Rly (bg)
Arrow	72	Alecto	11/1847	London & South Western Rly
Arrow	72	Falcon	12/1864	London & South Western Rly
Arrow	70017	Britannia	6/1951	British Railways
Arsenal	2848	B17/4	3/1936	London & North Eastern Rly
Arthog Hall	6993	M/Hall	11/1948	British Railways (Western Region)
Arthur	903	0-6-0	1858	Great Western Rly [108]
Arthur	**–**	**0-6-0ST**	**1901**	**Middleton Rly**
Arthur	**–**	**0-6-0ST**	**1953**	**Buckinghamshire Railway Centre**
Arthur Otway	190	Gladstone	12/1888	London, Brighton & South Coast Rly
(Arthur Vernon Dawson)	**08774**	**08**	**1960**	**British Railways**
Arthur Wright	**D4279**	**0-4-0DE**	**1952**	**Great Central Rly**
Arundel	236	2-2-2	4/1867	London, Brighton & South Coast Rly
Arundel	180	Gladstone	3/1890	London, Brighton & South Coast Rly
Asbestos	**4**	**0-4-0ST**	**1909**	**Chasewater Light Rly**
A.S.Harris	756	756	12/1907	Southern Rly [109]
Ashburne	225	D1	6/1885	London, Brighton & South Coast Rly
Ashburnham	284	D1	9/1879	London, Brighton & South Coast Rly
Ashburnham	1	0-6-0ST	1900	Burry Port & Gwendraeth Valley Rly [110]
ASHBURNHAM	08993	08/9	1959	British Railways
(Ashburton)	**1450**	**14XX**	**7/1935**	**Great Western Rly**
Ashchurch	26	4-2-0	1/1841	Birmingham & Gloucester Rly

---

[94] Previously no. D215 *Aquitania*.

[95] Later renamed *Auchtertyre*.

[96] Previously named *Ross-shire*.

[97] Built for the South Devon Railway.

[98] 2ft 3in gauge.

[99] Renamed *Chapman* in 1856.

[100] Renamed *Bee* in 1841.

[101] This locomotive was close-coupled to a four-wheeled saloon and operated as a steam railcar. It was shown at the Great Exhibition of 1851, but seems never to have entered service in its original form. The locomotive part, however, later worked on the Millwall Extension line.

[102] 1ft 11½in gauge.

[103] 2ft gauge. Bagnall works no. 2088.

[104] Some authorities give the date of construction as August 1881.

[105] Originally named *Constantine*.

[106] 18in gauge.

[107] Some sources show this locomotive as no. 27.

[108] Built for the Llanelly Railway.

[109] Built for the Plymouth, Devonport & South Western Junction Railway. An 0-6-0T with outside cylinders, it was the only one of its class.

[110] Became Great Western Railway no. 2192.

Name	Number	Class	Date	Railway	Name	Number	Class	Date	Railway
Ascupart	–	0–4–0ST	7/1872	Southampton Docks	*Atlas*	26	0–6–0	5/1846	Manchester, Sheffield & Lincolnshire Rly
Ashey	W28	O2	7/1890	Southern Rly [111]	*Atlas*	22	Samson	11/1847	East Lancashire Rly
Ashford	1872	0–6–0ST	1920	War Department	*Atlas*	140	bCrewe	3/1852	London & North Western Rly
Ashford	**33052**	**33/0**	**1961**	**British Railways**	*Atlas*	7	0–6–0	c.1853	Newcastle & Carlisle Rly [125]
Ashford 150	33114	33/1	1961	British Railways [112]	*Atlas*	28	0–6–0	7/1853	Taff Vale Rly
Ashfordby Mine	58046	58	10/1986	British Railways [113]	*Atlas*	–	?	?	Brampton Rly
Ashington	485	E4	5/1899	London, Brighton & South Coast Rly	*Atlas*	42	2Hercules	2/1854	London & South Western Rly
Ashley	**1**	**0–4–0ST**	**1942**	**South Devon Rly [114]**	*Atlas*	2152	0–6–0ST	10/1863	Great Western Rly (bg) [126]
Ashley Grange	6824	Grange	1/1937	Great Western Rly	*Atlas*	18	0–6–0ST	12/1865	Brecon & Merthyr Rly
Ashover	**–**	**4wDM**	**1948**	**Festiniog Rly [115]**	*Atlas*	2150	Samson	11/1874	London & North Western Rly
Ashtead	53	A1	12/1875	London, Brighton & South Coast Rly [116]	*Atlas*	42	2Vesuvius	1/1875	London & South Western Rly
Ashton Court	2932	Saint	10/1911	Great Western Rly	*Atlas*	2150	Whitworth	6/1893	London & North Western Rly
Ashurst	248	D1	12/1881	London, Brighton & South Coast Rly	*Atlas*	2417	Prince/W	2/1916	London & North Western Rly
Ashwicke Hall	5976	Hall	9/1938	Great Western Rly	*Atlas*	6134	Royal Scot	9/1927	London Midland & Scottish Rly [127]
Asia	54	Europa	9/1873	London, Chatham & Dover Rly	*Atlas*	5737	Jubilee	1936	London Midland & Scottish Rly
Askam Hall	**15**	**0–4–0ST**	**1935**	**Lakeside & Haverthwaite Rly**	*Atlas*	47016	47/0	1963	British Railways
Aske Hall	2827	B17/1	3/1931	London & North Eastern Rly	*ATLAS*	47626	47/4	1965	British Railways
Assagais	–	Wolf	9/1841	Great Western Rly (bg)	*Atropos*	–	2–4–0	1901	Woolwich Arsenal [128]
Assam	5583	Jubilee	1934	London Midland & Scottish Rly	*Auchtertyre*	31	Duke	7/1876	Highland Rly [129]
Astley Hall	4903	Hall	12/1928	Great Western Rly	*Auckland*	10	Tory	8/1839	Stockton & Darlington Rly
Aston	28	0–6–0	1858	South Staffordshire Rly	*Auckland*	3393	Atbara	6/1901	Great Western Rly
Aston Hall	4986	Hall	1/1931	Great Western Rly	*Audley End*	2806	B17/1	12/1928	London & North Eastern Rly
Atalanta	97	aCrewe	11/1846	London & North Western Rly	*Audus*	287	2–4–0	4/1861	Lancashire & Yorkshire Rly
Atalanta	96	2–4–0	2/1850	Manchester, Sheffield & Lincolnshire Rly	*Auld Reekie*	872	H	1906	North British Rly
Atalanta	18	2–2–2T	1853	Edinburgh & Glasgow Rly	*Auld Reekie*	H	2–4–2T	3/1909	War Department [130]
Atalanta	97	Problem	1860	London & North Western Rly	*Auld Reekie*	60160	A1	12/1949	British Railways (Eastern Region)
Atalanta	3002	3001	1/1892	Great Western Rly [117]	*Aultnaskiah*	9	Seafield	8/1858	Highland Rly [131]
Atalanta	61	2Experiment	11/1906	London & North Western Rly	*Aultnaskiah*	50	Glenbarry	7/1864	Highland Rly [132]
Atbara	3373	Atbara	4/1900	Great Western Rly [118]	*Ault Wharrie*	62	Duke	6/1874	Highland Rly [133]
Athelhampton Hall	6971	M/Hall	10/1947	Great Western Rly	*Aurania*	363	1Experiment	1884	London & North Western Rly
Athelney Castle	7009	Castle	5/1948	British Railways (Western Region)	*Aurania*	113	2Precursor	7/1905	London & North Western Rly
Atholl	33	Glenbarry	10/1863	Highland Rly [119]	**Aureol EDL**	**40012**	**40**	**1959**	**British Railways [134]**
Atholl	79	Clyde Bogie	6/1886	Highland Rly	*Auricula*	4101	Flower	5/1908	Great Western Rly
Atkinson	290	2–4–0	6/1861	Lancashire & Yorkshire Rly	*Aurora*	10	Venus	9/1838	London & South Western Rly
Atlanta	167	Undine	12/1859	London & South Western Rly	*Aurora*	–	Wolf	12/1840	Great Western Rly (bg)
Atlanta	3002	3001	1/1892	Great Western Rly [120]	*Aurora*	14	Aurora	2/1847	East Lancashire Rly
Atlantic	7	4–2–0	11/1839	Birmingham & Gloucester Rly	*Aurora*	80	2–4–0	7/1849	Manchester, Sheffield & Lincolnshire Rly
Atlantic	–	0–6–2T	1906	Campbeltown & Machrihanish Rly [121]	*Aurora*	2099	4–4–0ST	1/1852	Great Western Rly (bg) [135]
Atlantic College	47749	47/7		British Railways	*Aurora*	10	Chaplin	7/1856	London & South Western Rly
(Atlantic Conveyor)	**D306**	**40/1**	**1960**	**British Railways**	*Aurora*	10	Lion	1/1871	London & South Western Rly
Atlas	23	0–4–0	1831	Liverpool & Manchester Rly	*Aurora*	1962	2–4–0	7/1903	London & North Western Rly
Atlas	–	0–6–0	2/1834	Leicester & Swannington Rly	*Aurora*	27002	EM2	1954	British Railways
Atlas	7	0–6–0	1836	Newcastle & Carlisle Rly [122]	**Austins No. 1**	**–**	**0–4–0DM**	**1961**	**Keighley & Worth Valley Rly**
Atlas	–	Wolf	6/1838	Great Western Rly (bg)	*Australia*	91	Peel	3/1855	Stockton & Darlington Rly
Atlas	42	1Hercules	11/1841	London & South Western Rly	*Australia*	1947	Alfred	6/1901	London & North Western Rly [136]
Atlas	81	2–4–0?	1842	Liverpool & Manchester Rly [123]	*Australia*	48	B4	7/1901	London, Brighton & South Coast Rly
Atlas	23	2–2–2	3/1846	Joint Board of Management [124]	*Australia*	3455	Bulldog	1/1904	Great Western Rly

[111] Formerly London & South Western Railway (and Southern Railway) no. 186. Named *Ashey* on transfer to Isle of Wight by the Southern Railway in March 1926.

[112] Later renamed *Sultan*.

[113] Later named *Thoresby Colliery*.

[114] The modern, preserved, South Devon Railway.

[115] Originally on Ashover Light Railway. 1ft 11½in gauge.

[116] Rebuilt to class A1x in January 1912. Sold by Southern Railway (their no. 2653) in April 1937 to the Weston, Clevedon & Portishead Railway. Became their no. 4, losing its name, and in 1940 became Great Western Railway no. 6.

[117] Rebuilt to 4–2–2 in June 1894.

[118] Temporarily renamed *Maine* for City Imperial Volunteers' Special Train on 29 October 1900, and *Royal Sovereign* for Queen Victoria's funeral train on 2 February 1901.

[119] Converted from 2–2–2 to 2–4–0 in March 1883, renamed *Birnam* in August 1886.

[120] Rebuilt to 4–2–2 in June 1894.

[121] 2ft 3in gauge.

[122] Sold 1853. Its replacement carried the same name and number.

[123] Became London & North Western Railway no. 140 in 1846.

[124] Birmingham & Gloucester and Bristol & Gloucester Railways, formed on 14 January 1845. Standard gauge. The locomotives passed to the Midland Railway on 3 August 1846, and were renumbered into Midland stock wef February 1847.

[125] Replacement of earlier engine with same name and number. Became North Eastern Railway no. 456.

[126] Built for the South Devon Railway.

[127] Renamed *The Cheshire Regiment* in May 1936.

[128] Paraffin/mechanical. 18in gauge.

[129] Previously no. 4 *Ardross*. Renumbered in 1899 and renamed in 1901.

[130] Formerly LNER F4 class no. 7071.

[131] Later renamed *Golspie*.

[132] Later renamed *Badenoch*. Altered from 2–2–2 to 2–4–0 in April 1878.

[133] Previously named *Perthshire*, *Stemster* (1889), and *Huntingtower* (1899). Renamed *Ault Wharrie* in 1903.

[134] Formerly D212 *Aureol*. ELD stands for Elder Dempster Lines.

[135] Built for the South Devon Railway.

[136] Renamed *Zillah* from June 1911.

Name	Number	Class	Date	Railway	Name	Number	Class	Date	Railway
Australia	1218	George V	6/1911	London & North Western Rly	*Avon*	110	Rocklia	11/1848	London & South Western Rly
Australia	5563	Jubilee	1935	London Midland & Scottish Rly	*Avon*	–	Caesar	6/1857	Great Western Rly (bg)
Austria	153	E1	3/1881	London, Brighton & South Coast Rly	*Avon*	110	Lion	1/1869	London & South Western Rly
Autocrat	321	bCrewe	5/1854	London & North Western Rly	*Avon*	2189	Precedent	4/1875	London & North Western Rly
Autocrat	321	aCrewe	3/1858	London & North Western Rly [137]	*Avon*	69	River	1/1896	Great Western Rly [140]
Autocrat	2064	Dreadnought	1885	London & North Western Rly	*Avon*	2189	rPrecedent	7/1897	London & North Western Rly
Autocrat	306	2Experiment	6/1905	London & North Western Rly	*Avondale Castle*	7010	Castle	6/1948	British Railways (Western Region)
Autumn	191	Panther	4/1866	Stockton & Darlington Rly	*Avonside*	–	Hawthorn	12/1865	Great Western Rly (bg) [141]
Avalanche	–	Banking	2/1846	Great Western Rly (bg)	*Avonside*	4114	0–6–0ST	1916	War Department
Avalanche	3003	3001	2/1892	Great Western Rly [138]	*Avora*	15	A	8/1864	Metropolitan Rly
Avalon	3332	Bulldog	11/1899	Great Western Rly	**(Awdas)**	**870**	**0–6–0DH**	**1966**	**War Department**
Aveley	81	79	1909	London, Tilbury & Southend Rly	*Axe Edge*	60085	60	12/1991	British Railways
Avenger	D804	Warship	4/1959	British Railways	*Axial*	47228	47/0	1965	British Railways
Aviemore	22	S/Goods	9/1863	Highland Rly	*Axminster*	21C118	rWC	12/1945	Southern Rly
Aviemore	39	M/Goods	5/1864	Highland Rly	*Aylburton Grange*	6801	Grange	8/1936	Great Western Rly
Aviemore Centre	47546	47/4	1964	British Railways	*Aylesbury College*	51899	DMU	?	British Railways
Aviemore Centre	47976	47/4	7/1964	British Railways [139]	**Aylwyn**	**7**	**0–4–2T**	**1923**	**Snowdon Mountain Rly** [142]
Avignon	128	E1	10/1878	London, Brighton & South Coast Rly	*Ayrshire Yeomanry*	5156	5	1935	London Midland & Scottish Rly
Avocet	**89001**	**89**	**10/1986**	**British Railways**	*Ayton*	99	Pierremont	7/1855	Stockton & Darlington Rly
Avon	14	0–6–0	7/1846	Taff Vale Rly	*Azalia*	–	Metro	4/1864	Great Western Rly (bg)
Avon	198	bCrewe	2/1848	London & North Western Rly	**(Aznar Line)**	**31874**	**N**	**9/1925**	**Southern Rly** [143]

[137] Built as replacement for previous engine, which was sold to the Lancaster & Carlisle Railway.

[138] Rebuilt to 4–2–2 in May 1894.

[139] Originally named *Bolton Wanderer*.

[140] Rebuild of 2–2–2 no. 69 of 1855.

[141] Originally (and somewhat unimaginatively) named *Slaughter*, after a partner in Slaughter, Gruning & Co., Bristol, the firm which built the locomotive and which became the Avonside Engine Co. in late 1865. It was quickly renamed!

[142] Formerly *Eryri*. Rack and pinion, 800mm gauge.

[143] Withdrawn by British Railways in March 1964, and subsequently went to the Mid-Hants Railway. The name was carried from April 1977 to January 1979. In May 1957 the engine underwent a thorough reconstruction at Ashford Works, involving new front ends to the main frames, new cylinders with outside steam pipes, and British Railways class 4 blast pipe and chimney. In preservation, therefore, the engine carries its BR number.

B

Name	Number	Class	Date	Railway
Babylon	2637	2Experiment	6/1909	London & North Western Rly
Bacchante	1951	Alfred	1/1902	London & North Western Rly
Bacchus	–	Fury	12/1837	Great Western Rly (bg)
Bacchus	18	2–2–2	12/1845	Manchester, Sheffield & Lincolnshire Rly
Bacchus	7	Bacchus	5/1846	East Lancashire Rly
Bacchus	72	Aeolus	11/1860	London, Chatham & Dover Rly
Bacchus	2643	2Experiment	6/1909	London & North Western Rly
Bachelor's Button	60537	A2	6/1948	British Railways (Eastern Region)
Back Tor	60064	60	9/1991	British Railways
Bactria	2639	2Experiment	6/1909	London & North Western Rly
Badajos	1677	Newton	4/1868	London & North Western Rly
Badajos	1677	rPrecedent	1/1890	London & North Western Rly
Badenoch	50	Glenbarry	7/1864	Highland Rly [1]
Baden Powell	3374	Atbara	4/1900	Great Western Rly [2]
Baden-Powell	59	B4	8/1901	London, Brighton & South Coast Rly
Badminton	3292	Badminton	12/1897	Great Western Rly
Baggrave Hall	6994	M/Hall	12/1948	British Railways (Western Region)
Baglan Hall	4913	Hall	2/1929	Great Western Rly
Bagnall	–	0–4–0DH	1961	Foxfield Rly
(Bagnall)	873	0–6–0DH	1966	War Department
Bagshot	69	B4	9/1901	London, Brighton & South Coast Rly
Bahamas	5596	Jubilee	1935	London Midland & Scottish Rly
Bahram	60531	A2	3/1948	British Railways (Eastern Region) [3]
Bailie MacWheeble	2671	D11/2	7/1924	London & North Eastern Rly
Bailie Nicol Jarvie	245	Scott	10/1911	North British Rly
Balaklava	–	Iron Duke	12/1854	Great Western Rly (bg)
Balaklava	–	Rover	10/1871	Great Western Rly (bg)
Balcombe	223	D1	7/1885	London, Brighton & South Coast Rly
Baldwin	3415	Bulldog	1/1903	Great Western Rly [4]
Balfron	320	317	1860	North British Rly [5]
Balham	34	D1	6/1876	London, Brighton & South Coast Rly
Ballindalloch	3	2Raigmore	7/1877	Highland Rly
Ballindalloch Castle	141	Castle	1900	Highland Rly
Balloch	318	317	1859	North British Rly [6]
Ballymoss	55018	Deltic	11/1961	British Railways
Balmenach	2	0–4–0ST	1936	Strathspey Rly
Balmoral	178	Windsor	6/1865	Stockton & Darlington Rly
Balmoral	862	Precedent	5/1877	London & North Western Rly
Balmoral	862	rPrecedent	7/1897	London & North Western Rly
Balmoral	66	B4	8/1901	London, Brighton & South Coast Rly [7]
Balmoral	60140	A1	12/1948	British Railways (Eastern Region)
Balnain	56	Lochgorm	2/1869	Highland Rly [8]
Baltic	42	0–4–2	11/1842	Manchester & Leeds Rly
Baltic	350	bCrewe	9/1854	London & North Western Rly
Baltic	2151	Samson	11/1874	London & North Western Rly [9]
Baltic	2151	Whitworth	12/1895	London & North Western Rly
Baltic	2445	Claughton	7/1917	London & North Western Rly [10]
Baltimore	15	4–2–0	9/1840	Birmingham & Gloucester Rly
Bamburgh	–	0–6–0ST	1898	North Sunderland Rly
Bampton Grange	6802	Grange	9/1936	Great Western Rly
Banbury Castle	7011	Castle	6/1948	British Railways (Western Region)
Banffshire	309	D49/1	3/1928	London & North Eastern Rly
Bangor	5523	Patriot	3/1933	London Midland & Scottish Rly [11]
Bang Up	43303	Clayton	1928	London & North Eastern Rly
Banks	3	0–4–2ST	1878	West Lancashire Rly
Banks of Don	313	cSentinel	1931	London & North Eastern Rly
Banshee	50	Venus	4/1850	East Lancashire Rly
Banshee	–	Caesar	9/1854	Great Western Rly (bg)
Banshee	369	aCrewe	6/1855	London & North Western Rly
Banshee	369	DX	1859	London & North Western Rly
Banshee	16	0–4–0ST	4/1863	Whitehaven & Furness Junction Rly
Banshee	757	Samson	5/1863	London & North Western Rly
Banshee	757	Whitworth	1/1892	London & North Western Rly
Banshee	2628	2Experiment	3/1909	London & North Western Rly
Banstead	10	D1	4/1874	London, Brighton & South Coast Rly
Banstead	18	III	7/1892	Mersey Rly
Bantam Cock	3401	V4	2/1941	London & North Eastern Rly
"Bantam Hen"	3402	V4	3/1941	London & North Eastern Rly
Barbados	3466	Bulldog	3/1904	Great Western Rly
Barbados	5597	Jubilee	1935	London Midland & Scottish Rly
(Barbara)	107	J94	12/1943	War Department [12]
Barber	–	0–6–2ST	1908	Harrogate Gasworks [13]
(Barbouilleur)	–	0–4–0T	1950	Amberley Chalk Pits Museum [14]
Barbury Castle	5043	Castle	3/1936	Great Western Rly [15]
Barbury Castle	5095	Castle	6/1939	Great Western Rly
Barcelona	157	E Special	9/1884	London, Brighton & South Coast Rly
Barcombe	514	E4	3/1901	London, Brighton & South Coast Rly
Barcote Manor	7803	Manor	1/1938	Great Western Rly
Bardon Hill	56063	56	1979	British Railways
Barfleur	1933	Jubilee	9/1900	London & North Western Rly
Barfleur	5685	Jubilee	1936	London Midland & Scottish Rly
Barham	5653	Jubilee	1935	London Midland & Scottish Rly
Barham	50016	50	1968	British Railways
Bari	271	0–6–0DE	1944	Longmoor Military Rly [16]
Baring	75	Peel	8/1853	Stockton & Darlington Rly
Barking	7	Class 1	1880	London, Tilbury & Southend Rly
Barnard Castle	107	Peel	3/1856	Stockton & Darlington Rly
Barnes	301	2–4–0	12/1861	Lancashire & Yorkshire Rly
Barnes	669	627	9/1881	Lancashire & Yorkshire Rly
Barnham	259	D1	3/1882	London, Brighton & South Coast Rly [17]
Barningham Hall	6920	Hall	7/1941	Great Western Rly [18]
Barnsley	2869	B17/4	5/1937	London & North Eastern Rly
Barnsley	08492	08	1958	British Railways
Barnstaple	21C105	rWC	7/1945	Southern Rly
Barnum	–	2–2–2	7/1844	London & South Western Rly (bg) [19]
Barochan	911	908	1906	Caledonian Rly
Baroda	5587	Jubilee	1934	London Midland & Scottish Rly
Baronet	101	bCrewe	2/1847	London & North Western Rly
Baronet	997	L/Bloomer	1872	London & North Western Rly
Baron of Bradwardine	2672	D11/2	8/1924	London & North Eastern Rly
Barrington	3293	Badminton	4/1898	Great Western Rly
Barrington	–	0–4–0ST	1921	Colne Valley Rly
Barrow	172	Panther	12/1863	Stockton & Darlington Rly
Barrow Steel No 7	FR18	0–6–0ST	1863	Steamtown Carnforth
Barrow Steel No 17	FR25	0–4–0ST	1865	Steamtown Carnforth
Barry Castle	7012	Castle	6/1948	British Railways (Western Region)

---

[1] Previously named *Aultnaskiah*. Altered from 2–2–2 to 2–4–0 in April 1878.

[2] Temporarily renamed *Pretoria* for City Imperial Volunteers' Special Train on 29 October 1900, *Britannia* for Royal Trains on 7 and 10 March 1902, and *Kitchener* for a Special Train on 12 July 1902.

[3] Entered service as no. E531.

[4] Renamed *Alfred Baldwin* in April 1903.

[5] Ex-Edinburgh & Glasgow Railway, absorbed by the NBR in 1865.

[6] Ex-Edinburgh & Glasgow Railway, absorbed by the NBR in 1865.

[7] Renamed *Billinton* in July 1906.

[8] Renamed *Dornoch* in 1902.

[9] Transferred to Engineer's Department 1901–June 1923, and renamed *Engineer Walsall*.

[10] Named March 1923.

[11] Rebuilt with taper boiler in October 1948.

[12] Named *Foggia* on Longmoor Military Railway.

[13] 2ft gauge. Now preserved at Armley Mills Museum, Leeds.

[14] 2ft gauge. Built by Decauville, France.

[15] Renamed *Earl of Mount Edgcumbe* in September 1937 and preserved.

[16] Later numbered 70271, and then 876. LMS-type.

[17] Originally *Telford*. Renamed *Barnham* in April 1898.

[18] Named May 1946.

[19] Thought to be the locomotive built for the Bristol & Gloucester Railway as their no. 5 *Gloucester*. Broad gauge. In November 1855 it was sold to Thomas Brassey for working the North Devon Railway, and is thought to have become their *Barnum*.

Name	Number	Class	Date	Railway
Barrymore	2974	Saint	3/1905	Great Western Rly [20]
Barton	–	2-2-2	7/1839	Birmingham & Derby Junction Rly
Barton Hall	4905	Hall	12/1928	Great Western Rly
Basildon	70	69	1903	London, Tilbury & Southend Rly
Basilisk	22	2-2-2	1837	Grand Junction Rly
Basilisk	18	2-2-0	8/1840	Midland Counties Rly
Basilisk	22	aCrewe	4/1845	London & North Western Rly
Basilisk	852	L/Bloomer	1872	London & North Western Rly
Basilisk	–	0-4-0ST	1886	Woolwich Arsenal [21]
Basra	877	0-6-0DE	1944	Longmoor Military Rly
Basra	2220	0-4-0D	1945	Longmoor Military Rly [22]
Basra	272	0-6-0DE	3/1945	Longmoor Military Rly [23]
Bassethound	2495	George V	5/1911	London & North Western Rly
Bassetlaw	58034	58	1985	British Railways
Basutoland	5598	Jubilee	1935	London Midland & Scottish Rly
Bat	–	0-4-2	5/1842	Swansea Vale Rly [24]
Bat	135	aCrewe	9/1852	London & North Western Rly
Bat	135	DX	1859	London & North Western Rly
Bath	–	Swindon	1/1866	Great Western Rly (bg)
Bath Abbey	5083	Castle	6/1937	Great Western Rly [25]
Bathgate	238	233	1861	North British Rly [26]
Batley	10	0-4-0ST	7/1924	London Midland & Scottish Rly [27]
Battersea	3	D1	12/1873	London, Brighton & South Coast Rly
Battle of Britain 50th Anniversary	73109	73/1	1966	British Railways
Bauxite	**2**	**0-4-0ST**	**1874**	**National Railway Museum**
Baxter	**–**	**0-4-0T**	**1877**	**Bluebell Rly**
Bayardo	2578	A3	10/1924	London & North Eastern Rly
Baydon Manor	7804	Manor	2/1938	Great Western Rly
Baynards	268	D1	5/1880	London, Brighton & South Coast Rly
Bayonne	124	E1	8/1878	London, Brighton & South Coast Rly
BBC East Midlands Today	43076	43	12/1977	British Railways
B.B.C. Look East	86221	86/2	1965	British Railways
BBC Look North	43155	43	1/1981	British Railways
BBC Midlands Today	90001	90/0	4/1988	British Railways
BBC North West	90015	90/0	11/1988	British Railways
BBC Radio One FM	91025	91	11/1990	British Railways
BBC Wales Today	43149	43	6/1981	British Railways
Beachamwell Hall	6934	Hall	12/1941	Great Western Rly [28]
Beachy Head	469	E4	6/1898	London, Brighton & South Coast Rly
Beachy Head	2424	H2	9/1911	Southern Rly [29]
Beacon	19	0-6-0ST	12/1865	Brecon & Merthyr Rly
Beaconsfield	1122	Queen	4/1875	Great Western Rly
Beaconsfield	16	4-4-0	8/1878	Cambrian Railways
Beaconsfield	211	Richmond	3/1880	London, Brighton & South Coast Rly [30]
Beaconsfield	218	Gladstone	11/1885	London, Brighton & South Coast Rly
Beagle	361	George V	7/1911	London & North Western Rly
Bear	**–**	**0-4-0ST**	**1896**	**Sittingbourne & Kemsley Light Rly**
Bearley Grange	6831	Grange	8/1937	Great Western Rly
Beatrice	895	0-4-2	1860	Great Western Rly [31]
Beatrice	2190	Precedent	4/1875	London & North Western Rly [32]
Beatrice	1757	1738	1887	Midland Rly
Beatrice	**7**	**0-6-0ST**	**1945**	**Yorkshire Dales Rly**
Beattie	2331	Remembrance	4/1936	Southern Rly [33]
Beatty	5677	Jubilee	1935	London Midland & Scottish Rly
Beaufort	163	Cobham	11/1879	Great Western Rly
Beaufort	74	Duke	9/1885	Highland Rly
Beaufort	3035	3031	7/1894	Great Western Rly [34]
Beaufort	5078	Castle	5/1939	Great Western Rly [35]
Beaufort Castle	147	Castle	1902	Highland Rly
Beauly	8	Seafield	8/1858	Highland Rly [36]
Beauly	26	S/Goods	11/1863	Highland Rly
Beauly	47	Glenbarry	6/1864	Highland Rly [37]
(Beaumont)	13809	7F	7/1925	London Midland & Scottish Rly [38]
Bechuanaland	5599	Jubilee	1935	London Midland & Scottish Rly
Beckford Hall	5977	Hall	9/1938	Great Western Rly
Becton	**1**	**0-4-0ST**	**1892**	**Bressingham Museum**
Becton	**25**	**0-4-0ST**	**1896**	**Bressingham Museum**
Bedale	20028	20	1959	British Railways
Beddgelert	–	0-6-4ST	1878	North Wales Narrow Gauge Rly [39]
Beddgelert	**–**	**0-6-4ST**	**1979**	**Fairbourne & Barmouth Steam Rly [40]**
Beddington	21	D1	7/1875	London, Brighton & South Coast Rly
Bedfordshire	1412	2Experiment	11/1909	London & North Western Rly
Bedfordshire	335	D49/3	8/1928	London & North Eastern Rly [41]
Bedhampton	169	E3	12/1894	London, Brighton & South Coast Rly
Bedlington	2	Locomotion	1825	Stockton & Darlington Rly [42]
Bedlington	2	Majestic	1831	Stockton & Darlington Rly [43]
Bedwelly	–	0-6-0	?	Sirhowy Rly [44]
Bee	–	?	1832	Bolton & Leigh Rly [45]
Bee	1	2-2-0	5/1839	Midland Counties Rly [46]
Bee	–	0-4-0	10/1839	Swansea Vale Rly
Bee	11	Tory	9/1842	Stockton & Darlington Rly [47]
Bee	240	bCrewe	5/1849	London & North Western Rly [48]
Bee	240	DX	1859	London & North Western Rly
Bee	–	Metro	7/1862	Great Western Rly (bg)
Bee	642	Samson	7/1864	London & North Western Rly
Bee	–	0-4-0ST	1865	Bishops Castle Rly [49]
Bee	642	Whitworth	8/1890	London & North Western Rly
Bee	–	0-4-0ST	1901	Lancashire & Yorkshire Rly
Beeding	476	E4	10/1898	London, Brighton & South Coast Rly
Beehive	11	Enterprise	2/1838	Stockton & Darlington Rly [50]
Beelah	139	Peel	12/1858	Stockton & Darlington Rly
Beenham Grange	6808	Grange	9/1936	Great Western Rly
Beethoven	92003	92		British Railways
Begonia	4102	Flower	5/1908	Great Western Rly

[20] Later renamed *Lord Barrymore*.

[21] 18in gauge.

[22] Later named *Chittagong*.

[23] Formerly *Chittagong*. Later named *Eisenhower*.

[24] Formerly Liverpool & Manchester Railway no. 76 *Bat*, purchased January 1856. Renamed *Merlin* in 1861.

[25] Rebuilt from Star class no. 4063 *Bath Abbey*, built November 1922.

[26] Ex-Edinburgh & Glasgow Railway, absorbed by the NBR in 1865.

[27] 3ft gauge. Purchased 1945 for use at Batley Creosote Works.

[28] Named *March* 1948.

[29] Built for the London, Brighton & South Coast Railway. Name applied by the Southern Railway in September 1924.

[30] Renamed *Cavendish* in November 1885.

[31] Built for the Llanelly Railway.

[32] Originally named *Beatrice* for a short while, then *Lady Beatrice* until 1888, then *Princess Beatrice*.

[33] Rebuilt from London, Brighton & South Coast Railway L class 4-6-4T no. 331, built in December 1921.

[34] Originally named *Bellerophon*. Renamed in December 1895.

[35] Originally named *Lamphey Castle*. Renamed in January 1941.

[36] Previously named *Altyre*.

[37] Originally named *Bruce*, and then *Lovat*. Altered from 2-2-2 to 2-4-0 in July 1880.

[38] Name carried occasionally. Built as no. 89 for the Somerset & Dorset Joint Railway. Became LMS no. 9679, then 13809. Withdrawn in June 1964 as British Railways no. 53809.

[39] 1ft 11½in gauge.

[40] 12¼in gauge.

[41] As originally built with Lentz Oscillating Cam poppet valves. In November 1938 altered to piston valves and assimilated into class D49/1.

[42] Named *Hope*. If it carried the name *Bedlington* originally, it can only have been for a very short while.

[43] No. 12 *Majestic* entered service with this name and number. Renamed and renumbered 2 August 1831. First of the class.

[44] Dated between 1832 and 1853.

[45] There is some doubt as to whether it was originally named *Bee* and renamed *Bury*, or *vice versa*.

[46] Originally named *Ariel*. Renamed in 1841.

[47] May have originally been no. 30. Rebuilt from no. 11 *Bee*.

[48] Charged in current A/C as *Peel*.

[49] Obtained from the contractor who built the line.

[50] Rebuilt in 1842 and renamed *Bee*.

Name	Number	Class	Date	Railway
Behemoth	–	Caesar	3/1848	Great Western Rly (bg)
Behemoth	3034	3031	7/1894	Great Western Rly
Beighton	08436	08	1958	British Railways
Bela	89	bCrewe	8/1846	London & North Western Rly
Bela	621	S/Bloomer	1857	London & North Western Rly
Belfast	164	Saltburn	1862	Stockton & Darlington Rly
Belgian Marine	21C17	MN	4/1945	Southern Rly
Belgian Monarch	4022	Star	6/1909	Great Western Rly [51]
Belgic	372	2Experiment	6/1905	London & North Western Rly [52]
Belgravia	201	Belgravia	11/1872	London, Brighton & South Coast Rly
Belgravia	610	Richmond	9/1879	London, Brighton & South Coast Rly [53]
Belisarius	2640	2Experiment	6/1909	London & North Western Rly
Belladrum	12	Belladrum	5/1862	Highland Rly [54]
Belladrum	49	Glenbarry	7/1864	Highland Rly [55]
Bellerophon	–	Fury	7/1846	Great Western Rly (bg)
Bellerophon	38	0–4–2	5/1848	Manchester, Sheffield & Lincolnshire Rly
Bellerophon	296	bCrewe	11/1852	London & North Western Rly
Bellerophon	296	DX	1860	London & North Western Rly
Bellerophon	–	0–6–0WT	1874	Keighley & Worth Valley Rly [56]
Bellerophon	3035	3031	7/1894	Great Western Rly [57]
Bellerophon	80	2Precursor	4/1906	London & North Western Rly
Bellerophon	5694	Jubilee	1936	London Midland & Scottish Rly
Belle Vue	123	Peel	6/1857	Stockton & Darlington Rly
Bellgrove	295	165	5/1877	North British Rly [58]
Bellgrove	33	72	1881	North British Rly
Bellona	–	Priam	11/1841	Great Western Rly (bg)
Bellona	9	2–2–2	10/1844	Manchester, Sheffield & Lincolnshire Rly
Bellona	2641	2Experiment	6/1909	London & North Western Rly
Bellshill	259	165	11/1875	North British Rly [59]
Belmont	–	0–4–2ST	1873	Snailbeach District Rly [60]
Belmont	19	D1	7/1875	London, Brighton & South Coast Rly
Belmont Hall	6903	Hall	7/1940	Great Western Rly
Belted Will	79	aCrewe	2/1846	London & North Western Rly
Belted Will	24	2–2–2	1857	Lancaster & Carlisle Rly [61]
Belted Will	1220	Newton	4/1872	London & North Western Rly
Belted Will	1220	rPrecedent	1887	London & North Western Rly
Belvedere	–	0–4–0TG	1946	**Northamptonshire Ironstone Railway Trust**
Belvidere	10	0–6–0	c.1850	South Staffordshire Rly
Belvoir	–	0–6–0ST	1954	**East Anglian Railway Museum**
Belvoir Castle	2832	B17/2	5/1931	London & North Eastern Rly [62]
Belvoir Castle	1632	B2	7/1946	London & North Eastern Rly [63]
Bembridge	–	0–6–0ST	1875	Isle of Wight Rly [64]
Bembridge	W4	A1x	7/1880	**Southern Rly [65]**
Bembridge	338	G	11/1881	London, Brighton & South Coast Rly
Bembridge	W33	O2	8/1892	Southern Rly [66]
Ben a'Bhuird	47	Small Ben	1906	Highland Rly
Ben a'Chait	65	Large Ben	1908	Highland Rly
Ben a'Chaoruinn	62	Large Ben	1909	Highland Rly
Benachie	46	F	9/1921	Great North of Scotland Rly
Benachie	08882	08	1961	British Railways
Ben Alder	2	Small Ben	1898	Highland Rly
Ben Aliskey	13	Small Ben	1900	Highland Rly
Ben Alligan	17	Small Ben	1901	Highland Rly
Ben Armin	6	Small Ben	1899	Highland Rly
Ben Attow	7	Small Ben	1899	Highland Rly
Ben Avon	16	Small Ben	1901	Highland Rly
Ben Bhach Ard	41	Small Ben	1906	Highland Rly
Ben Bhreac'Mhor	60	Large Ben	1909	Highland Rly
Benbow	1952	Alfred	1/1902	London & North Western Rly
Benbow	D805	Warship	5/1959	British Railways
Benbow	50012	50	1968	British Railways
Ben Clebrig	8	Small Ben	1899	Highland Rly
Ben Cruachan	37404	37/4	1965	British Railways
Ben Dearg	14	Small Ben	1900	Highland Rly
Benfleet	13	Class 1	1881	London, Tilbury & Southend Rly
Benfleet	40	37	1897	London, Tilbury & Southend Rly
Bengal	5577	Jubilee	1934	London Midland & Scottish Rly
Ben Hope	12	Small Ben	1900	Highland Rly
Beningbrough Hall	6972	M/Hall	10/1947	Great Western Rly
Benjamin Disraeli	14	Bo-Bo	1921	Metropolitan Rly [67]
Benjamin Gimbert G.C.	47574	47/4	1964	British Railways
Ben Jonson	52	2–2–2WT	1859	Oxford, Worcester & Wolverhampton Rly
Ben Line	47457	47/4	1964	British Railways
Ben Loyal	15	Small Ben	1901	Highland Rly
Ben Lui	60031	60	9/1991	British Railways
Ben Macdui	60096	60	5/1992	British Railways
Ben Machdui	11	Small Ben	1899	Highland Rly
Ben Mheadhoin	63	Large Ben	1908	Highland Rly
Ben Mholach	64	Large Ben	1908	Highland Rly
Ben More	4	Small Ben	1899	Highland Rly
Ben More Assynt	60093	60	2/1992	British Railways [68]

Bellerophon, an 0–6–0WT of 1874 preserved by the Vintage Carriages Trust, pictured at Keighley with a train of vintage carriages in 1998. (*Photo: Author*)

[51] Originally named *King William* until June 1927. Renamed *The Belgian Monarch* in June or July 1927, and *Belgian Monarch* in October 1927. Nameplates removed in May 1940, and the words STAR CLASS were painted on the splashers.

[52] Originally named *Germanic*. Renamed *Belgic* during the First World War: the old name was defaced and the new nameplate mounted above it, so that nobody should miss the point!

[53] Formerly no. 52 *Cornwall*, until October 1901.

[54] Subsequently renamed *Breadalbane* in 1871 and *Strathpeffer* in 1885. Rebuilt as 2–2–2T in May 1871.

[55] Later renamed *Helmsdale*. Altered from 2–2–2 to 2–4–0, April 1879.

[56] Owned by the Vintage Carriages Trust; based at Ingrow, West Yorkshire.

[57] Renamed *Beaufort* in December 1895.

[58] Later renamed *Carnoustie*.

[59] Later renamed *Queensferry*.

[60] 2ft 4½in gauge.

[61] Later renamed *Ingleboro*.

[62] Rebuilt to B2, July 1946.

[63] Date when rebuilt from B17 no. 2832 *Belvoir Castle*, originally built May 1931. As no. 61632, was renamed *Royal Sovereign* in October 1958 following the withdrawal of no. 61671.

[64] Purchased by IWR (from unknown source) in 1882.

[65] Formerly London, Brighton & South Coast Railway no. 78 *Knowle*.

[66] Previously London & South Western Railway no. 218. Name applied by the Southern Railway on transfer to Isle of Wight, May 1936.

[67] Nominally a rebuild of an earlier, unnamed, locomotive; actually virtually a new machine.

[68] Later named *Jack Stirk*.

Name	Number	Class	Date	Railway
Ben More Assynt	60099	60	12/1992	British Railways
Ben na Caillich	61	Large Ben	1908	Highland Rly
Ben Nevis	60029	60	11/1990	British Railways
Ben Rinnes	9	Small Ben	1899	Highland Rly
Ben Slioch	10	Small Ben	1899	Highland Rly
Benthall Hall	6995	M/Hall	12/1948	British Railways (Western Region)
Ben Udlaman	38	Small Ben	1906	Highland Rly
Ben Vrackie	5	Small Ben	1899	Highland Rly
Ben Wyvis	3	Small Ben	1898	Highland Rly
Ben-y-Gloe	1	Small Ben	1898	Highland Rly
Bere Alston	34104	rWC	4/1950	British Railways (Southern Region)
Berengaria	2644	2Experiment	6/1909	London & North Western Rly
Berenice	2642	2Experiment	6/1909	London & North Western Rly
Beresford	200	Gladstone	1/1888	London, Brighton & South Coast Rly
Bergion	–	Fury	1/1847	Great Western Rly (bg)
Berkeley	262	2-2-2	7/1844	Midland Rly (bg) [69]
Berkeley	–	0–4–0T	1916	Woolwich Arsenal [70]
Berkeley Castle	4085	Castle	5/1925	Great Western Rly
Berkshire	2755	D49/1	3/1929	London & North Eastern Rly
Berlin	–	0–4–0WT	**1901**	**Leighton Buzzard Rly** [71]
Berlioz	92033	92		Société Nationale des Chemins de Fer Français
Bermondsey	7	D1	3/1874	London, Brighton & South Coast Rly
Bermuda	5600	Jubilee	1935	London Midland & Scottish Rly
Berne	90	E1	5/1883	London, Brighton & South Coast Rly
Berrington Hall	4912	Hall	2/1929	Great Western Rly
Berry Pomeroy Castle	5012	Castle	7/1927	Great Western Rly
Bertolt Brecht	92036	92		British Railways
Bervie	241	165	1/1876	North British Rly [72]
Berwick	467	E4	5/1898	London, Brighton & South Coast Rly
Berwickshire	277	D49/1	1/1928	London & North Eastern Rly
Beryl	–	4wPM	**1937**	**Swanage Rly**
Bescot	7	2-2-2	6/1849	South Staffordshire Rly
Bescot TMD	31105	31/1	1959	British Railways
Bescot Yard	47238	47/0	1966	British Railways
Bessborough	3295	Badminton	5/1898	Great Western Rly
Bessborough	45	B4	6/1902	London, Brighton & South Coast Rly [73]
Bessborough	326	J2	3/1912	London, Brighton & South Coast Rly
Bessemer	431	1Precursor	1/1879	London & North Western Rly
Bessemer	3022	3021	5/1891	Great Western Rly [74]
Bessemer	213	B3	12/1897	London, Brighton & South Coast Rly [75]
Betty	171	GWR2301	9/1897	War Department [76]
Betty	1769	0–4–0ST	1917	War Department
Betty	8411/04	0–4–0DH	**1965**	**Rutland Railway Museum**
"Betty Baldwin"	A763	L	8/1914	Southern Rly [77]
Beulah	81	A1	7/1880	London, Brighton & South Coast Rly [78]
Beult	26	0–4–0	12/1842	London & Brighton and South Eastern Railways Locomotive Pool
Bevendean	479	E4	12/1898	London, Brighton & South Coast Rly
Bevere	1746	Newton	11/1869	London & North Western Rly

Name	Number	Class	Date	Railway
Bevere	1746	rPrecedent	2/1890	London & North Western Rly
Bevere	192	Claughton	5/1921	London & North Western Rly
Beverston Castle	5044	Castle	3/1936	Great Western Rly [79]
Beverston Castle	5068	Castle	6/1938	Great Western Rly
Bexhill	397	D3	11/1896	London, Brighton & South Coast Rly
Bey	–	Metro	7/1862	Great Western Rly (bg)
Beyer	–	Hawthorn	12/1865	Great Western Rly (bg)
Bhopal	5594	Jubilee	1935	London Midland & Scottish Rly
Bibby	3416	Bulldog	2/1903	Great Western Rly [80]
Bibby Line	21C20	MN	6/1945	Southern Rly
Bibury Court	2933	Saint	11/1911	Great Western Rly
Bickersteth	194	Gladstone	7/1888	London, Brighton & South Coast Rly
Bickmarsh Hall	5967	**Hall**	**3/1937**	**Great Western Rly**
Bicton	2	**4wDM**	**1942**	**Bicton Woodland Rly** [81]
Bidder	10	2–4–0	9/1864	London & South Western Rly (ed) [82]
Bidean Nam Bian	60038	60	3/1991	British Railways
Bideford	21C119	WC	12/1945	Southern Rly
Big Ben	12	0–6–0	8/1855	Whitehaven & Furness Junction Rly
Bigga	–	**0–4–0DH**	**1947**	**South Yorkshire Rly**
Biggin Hill	21C157	BB	3/1947	Southern Rly
"Big Jim"	5820	S160	1945	Keighley & Worth Valley Rly [83]
Bihar and Orissa	5581	Jubilee	1934	London Midland & Scottish Rly
Billingham Enterprise	47363	47/3	1965	British Railways
Billingshurst	373	D3	12/1892	London, Brighton & South Coast Rly
Billinton	66	B4	8/1901	London, Brighton & South Coast Rly [84]
Billy	–	**0–4–0**	**?1816**	**Killingworth Colliery** [85]
Billy	–	0–4–0T	7/1875	London & North Western Rly [86]
Bilston	22	0–4–2	1858	South Staffordshire Rly
Binderton	408	E6	12/1904	London, Brighton & South Coast Rly
Binegar Hall	4904	Hall	12/1928	Great Western Rly
Bingley Hall	5921	Hall	5/1933	Great Western Rly
Birchenwood	4	**0–6–0ST**	**1944**	**North Norfolk Rly**
Birch Grove	473	**E4**	**6/1898**	**London, Brighton & South Coast Rly**
Birchwood Grange	6807	Grange	9/1936	Great Western Rly
Birdwood	662	C	11/1891	North British Rly
Birkbeck	63	Birkbeck	2/1849	Stockton & Darlington Rly
Birkenhead	8	2–2–2	4/1845	Chester & Birkenhead Rly [87]
Birkenhead	11	0–6–0	3/1849	Birkenhead, Lancashire & Cheshire Junction Rly [88]
Birkenhead	25	2–4–0	1/1853	Birkenhead, Lancashire & Cheshire Junction Rly [89]
Birkenhead	8	I	1/1886	Mersey Rly
Birkenhead	3443	Bulldog	9/1903	Great Western Rly
Birkenhead	7386	**0–4–0ST**	**1948**	**Southall Railway Centre**
Birmingham	–	2–2–2	7/1839	Birmingham & Derby Junction Rly
Birmingham	9	4–2–0	8/1840	Birmingham & Gloucester Rly
Birmingham	8	0–6–0	7/1849	South Staffordshire Rly
Birmingham	–	Swindon	1/1866	Great Western Rly (bg)
Birmingham	–	0–4–0T	1916	Woolwich Arsenal [90]
Birnam	20	S/Goods	8/1863	Highland Rly

---

[69] Built for the Bristol & Gloucester Railway as their no. 6. Broad gauge. In April 1856 it was sold to Thomas Brassey for working the North Devon Railway, and is thought to have become their *Exe*.

[70] 18in gauge.

[71] 1ft 11½in gauge.

[72] Previously named *Roslin* and *Penicuik*.

[73] Rebuilt to class B4x in April 1923. The name was then removed.

[74] Built as broad gauge convertible. Originally named *Rougement*; converted to 4–2–2 in July 1894 and renamed *Bessemer* in 1898.

[75] The only member of its class. Basically, it was a B2 with a slightly larger boiler. It was rebuilt to class B2x, November 1908.

[76] Originally GWR no. 2545.

[77] Built for the South Eastern & Chatham Railway. The name was neatly painted on the splasher by a volunteer driver during the General Strike of 1926.

[78] Sold in January 1918 to the Admiralty, and resold in July 1921 to the Shropshire & Montgomeryshire Railway, becoming their no. 7 *Hecate*.

[79] Renamed *Earl of Dunraven* in September 1937.

[80] Renamed *Frank Bibby* in April 1903.

[81] Formerly at Woolwich Arsenal, where it was unnamed. 18in gauge.

[82] Formerly no. 202. Transferred to Engineer's Dept in April 1872 and withdrawn in January 1889.

[83] Built for Transportation Corps, US Army, during the Second World War. Purchased for the Keighley & Worth Valley Railway from Poland.

[84] Originally named *Balmoral*. Renamed in July 1906.

[85] Built 1816–26. Preserved at the Stephenson Railway Museum & North Tyneside Steam Railway.

[86] 18in gauge for Crewe Works tramway.

[87] Later renamed *Monk*.

[88] Later named *Blazer* and passed to the Great Western Railway.

[89] Passed to the Great Western Railway as their no. 99.

[90] 18in gauge.

Name	Number	Class	Date	Railway
Birnam	33	Glenbarry	10/1863	Highland Rly [91]
Birtles Hall	6933	Hall	12/1941	Great Western Rly [92]
Bishop Eric Treacy	86240	86/2	1965	British Railways
Bishops Castle	–	2-4-0	1861	Bishops Castle Rly [93]
Bishop's Castle	5053	Castle	5/1936	Great Western Rly [94]
Bishop's Castle	5064	Castle	6/1937	Great Western Rly [95]
Bishopsgate	49	A1	12/1876	London, Brighton & South Coast Rly
Bishopstone	270	2-4-0T	3/1873	London, Brighton & South Coast Rly [96]
Bishopstone	170	E3	12/1894	London, Brighton & South Coast Rly
Bismarck	455	4	3/1879	Manchester, Sheffield & Lincolnshire Rly [97]
Bison	49	Bison	12/1845	London & South Western Rly
Bithon	–	Banking	10/1854	Great Western Rly (bg)
Bittern	142	bCrewe	3/1853	London & North Western Rly [98]
Bittern	**4464**	**A4**	**12/1937**	**London & North Eastern Rly [99]**
Bittern	47209	47/0	1965	British Railways
Blackbird	3731	Bulldog	5/1909	Great Western Rly
Blackbuck	1006	B1	3/1944	London & North Eastern Rly
Blackburn	7	2-4-0	4/1862	West Lancashire Rly [100]
Blackcap	47314	47/0	1965	British Railways
Blackcomb	–	2-2-0	1841	North Western Rly [101]
Black Diamond	3	Locomotion	4/1826	Stockton & Darlington Rly [102]
Black Diamond	1905	Jubilee	3/1899	London & North Western Rly
Black Douglas	87030	87/0	1974	British Railways
Black Duncan	500	Scott	11/1920	North British Rly
Blackheath	411	E6	5/1905	London, Brighton & South Coast Rly [103]
Blackhorse Road	40	37	1897	London, Tilbury & Southend Rly
Black Horse Road	13	Class 1	1881	London, Tilbury & Southend Rly
Black Knight	5100	J94	4/1944	War Department
Black Knight	5250	J94	1945	War Department
Black Knight	191	J94	1/1953	War Department [104]
Blacklock	73	Craven	3/1862	East Lancashire Rly
Blackmoor Vale	**21C123**	**WC**	**2/1946**	**Southern Rly**
Blackpool	–	2-4-0	?	Preston & Wyre Railway, Harbour & Dock Co.
Blackpool	–	2-6-0T	1909	Garstang & Knott End Rly [105]
Blackpool	2233	George V	7/1916	London & North Western Rly
Blackpool	5524	Patriot	3/1933	London Midland & Scottish Rly [106]
Blackpool Tower	37407	37/4	1965	British Railways
Black Prince	3004	3001	2/1892	Great Western Rly [107]
Black Prince	1902	Jubilee	6/1897	London & North Western Rly
Black Prince	**10**	**4-6-2**	**1931**	**Romney, Hythe & Dymchurch Rly [108]**
Black Prince	**11**	**4-6-2**	**1937**	**Romney, Hythe & Dymchurch Rly [109]**
Black Prince	70008	Britannia	4/1951	British Railways
(Black Prince)	92203	9F	12/1958	**British Railways**
Blackstone	577	E4	6/1903	London, Brighton & South Coast Rly
Blacktail	1038	B1	12/1947	London & North Eastern Rly
Blackwall	3	2-2-2WT	1848	London & Blackwall Rly
Blackwall	75	A1	12/1872	London, Brighton & South Coast Rly
Black Watch	1907	Jubilee	4/1899	London & North Western Rly
Black Watch	6102	Royal Scot	8/1927	London Midland & Scottish Rly
Blackwell Grange	6806	Grange	9/1936	Great Western Rly
Blackwell Hall	6996	M/Hall	1/1949	British Railways (Western Region)
Blairadam	485	165	1/1878	North British Rly [110]
Blair Atholl	51	Glenbarry	5/1864	Highland Rly [111]
Blair Athol	2557	A3	2/1925	London & North Eastern Rly
Blair Castle	144	Castle	1900	Highland Rly
Blake	5650	Jubilee	1935	London Midland & Scottish Rly
Blakemere Grange	6810	Grange	11/1936	Great Western Rly
Blakeney	3	0-6-0T	12/1880	Lynn & Fakenham Rly [112]
Blakesley Hall	4909	Hall	1/1929	Great Western Rly
Blanche	17	0-6-0ST	12/1861	Brecon & Merthyr Rly [113]
Blanche	–	**2-4-0TT**	**1893**	**Festiniog Rly [114]**
Blandford Forum	34107	WC	4/1950	British Railways (Southern Region) [115]
Blasius	3353	Bulldog	5/1900	Great Western Rly
Blatchington	165	E3	11/1894	London, Brighton & South Coast Rly
Blazer	108	0-6-0	3/1849	Great Western Rly [116]
Bleaklow Hill	60081	60	12/1991	British Railways
Blenheim	237	aCrewe	5/1849	London & North Western Rly
Blenheim	237	DX	c.1860	London & North Western Rly
Blenheim	3294	Badminton	5/1898	Great Western Rly
Blenheim	1934	Jubilee	9/1900	London & North Western Rly
Blenheim	2598	A3	4/1930	London & North Eastern Rly
Blenheim	5073	Castle	7/1938	Great Western Rly [117]
Blenkinsop	–	Hawthorn	12/1865	Great Western Rly (bg)
Blenkinsop	941	Newton	8/1873	London & North Western Rly
Blenkinsop	941	rPrecedent	10/1888	London & North Western Rly
Blenkinsopp	37	?	1853	Newcastle & Carlisle Rly [118]
Bletchingly	474	E4	8/1898	London, Brighton & South Coast Rly
Blickling	2807	B17/1	12/1928	London & North Eastern Rly [119]
Blickling	1607	B2	5/1947	London & North Eastern Rly [120]
Blink Bonny	2550	A3	10/1924	London & North Eastern Rly
Blinkin Bess	–	**4wDM**	**1950**	**Scottish Industrial Railway Centre**
Bloodhound	43	0-4-0	11/1840	Midland Counties Rly
Bloodhound	1532	George V	5/1911	London & North Western Rly
Bloxwich	25	0-6-0	1858	South Staffordshire Rly
Blucher	–	0-4-0	1814	Hetton Colliery [121]
Bluebell	42	Bluebell	6/1863	London, Chatham & Dover Rly
(Bluebell)	323	P	7/1910	**Southern Rly [122]**
(Bluebell)	D2246	04	1956	**British Railways [123]**

[91] Previously named *Atholl*. Altered from 2–2–2 to 2–4–0, March 1883; and renamed *Birnam*, August 1886.

[92] Named in December 1946.

[93] Purchased from the Somerset & Dorset Railway in 1865.

[94] Renamed *Earl Cairns* in August 1937.

[95] *Tretower Castle* until September 1937.

[96] Previously no. 53. Renumbered 270 and name applied, November 1875. Renamed *Fratton* in May 1878 and sent to Hayling Island branch. Renumbered 357 in April 1880 and 497 in April 1886, it was withdrawn in September 1890.

[97] 0–6–0ST built for Logan & Hemingway, contractors, who named it *Bismarck*. Purchased by MS&LR in May 1880.

[98] Formerly Liverpool & Manchester Railway no. 84.

[99] In recent preservation years *Bittern* has been restored as 2509 *Silver Link*.

[100] Originally London, Brighton & South Coast Railway no. 151. Sold to WLR in April 1883, who applied the name.

[101] Said to be formerly London & North Western Railway no. 179 *Nun*. But this locomotive was a 2–4–0, and built in November 1849.

[102] Rebuilt to 0–6–0 in 1830.

[103] Rebuilt to class E6x, November 1911.

[104] Preserved on the Kent & East Sussex Railway as *Holman F. Stephens*.

[105] Became London Midland & Scottish Railway no. 11680.

[106] Originally named *Sir Frederick Harrison*; renamed *Blackpool* in March 1936.

[107] Rebuilt to 4–2–2 in November 1894.

[108] 15in gauge. Later renamed *Doctor Syn*.

[109] 15in gauge. Built by Krupp for a German miniature railway; purchased by RHDR after the Second World War.

[110] May have originally been named *Yoker*.

[111] Originally named *Caithness*. Renamed *Blair Atholl* 1874, and altered from 2–2–2 to 2–4–0 in July 1875.

[112] Bought from the Cornwall Minerals Railway.

[113] Originally named *Pioneer*. Renamed by 1871.

[114] Formerly 0–4–0ST on the Penrhyn Railway. 1ft 11½in gauge.

[115] Originally *Blandford*, but soon renamed.

[116] Built for the Birkenhead, Lancashire & Cheshire Junction Railway, and originally named *Birkenhead*.

[117] *Cranbrook Castle* until January 1941.

[118] Became North Eastern Railway no. 485 in 1862, and rebuilt as 0–6–0 in 1871.

[119] Rebuilt to B2, May 1947.

[120] Date when rebuilt from B17 no. 2807 *Blickling*, originally built in December 1928.

[121] George Stephenson's first locomotive.

[122] Named *Bluebell*, and repainted blue, after sale to the Bluebell Railway.

[123] Originally named *(Alfie)*.

Name	Number	Class	Date	Railway
Bluebird	–	D/E Railcar	10/1933	London Midland & Scottish Rly [124]
Bluebottle	–	0–4–0Fs	1916	**Bressingham Museum**
Blue Circle	–	2–2–0TG	1926	**Bluebell Rly** [125]
Blue Circle Cement	47210	47/0	1965	British Railways
Blue Funnel	21C13	MN	2/1945	Southern Rly
Blue Peter	60532	A2	3/1948	**British Railways (Eastern Region)**
Blue Star	21C10	MN	8/1942	**Southern Rly**
Blundell	1	0–4–2	7/1848	Liverpool, Crosby & Southport Rly
Blundells	932	Schools	2/1935	Southern Rly
Blyth	3	2–4–0T	1879	Southwold Rly [126]
Blythe	–	2–2–2	11/1839	Birmingham & Derby Junction Rly
Blyth Power	56134	56	1984	British Railways
Boadicea	1148	1Precursor	10/1878	London & North Western Rly
Boadicea	1963	Alfred	7/1904	London & North Western Rly
Boadicea	70036	Britannia	12/1952	British Railways
Boarhound	1504	George V	4/1911	London & North Western Rly

British Railways (Eastern Region) A1 class 4–6–2 no. 60155 *Borderer*, at Haymarket on 16 August 1958. (*Photo: RAS Marketing*)

Name	Number	Class	Date	Railway
Boar of Badenoch	60092	60	1/1992	British Railways [127]
Boar of Badenoch	60100	60	12/1992	British Railways
Bob Ridley	15	0–4–0ST	1862	Whitehaven & Furness Junction Rly
Bobs	–	0–4–0ST	1900	Caldon Low Quarry [128]
Bodiam	3	A1x	12/1872	**Kent & East Sussex Rly** [129]
Bodicote Grange	6870	Grange	3/1939	Great Western Rly
Bodinnick Hall	5978	Hall	9/1938	Great Western Rly
Bodmin	–	0–4–0ST	1863	London & South Western Rly [130]
Bodmin	21C116	rWC	11/1945	**Southern Rly**
Bognor	76	0–4–2ST	5/1869	London, Brighton & South Coast Rly [131]
Bognor	508	E4	12/1900	London, Brighton & South Coast Rly
Bohemia	490	E4	6/1899	London, Brighton & South Coast Rly
Bois Roussel	60117	A1	10/1948	British Railways (Eastern Region)
Bologna	87	E1	3/1883	London, Brighton & South Coast Rly
Bolton	–	0–4–0	5/1838	Manchester & Bolton Rly
Bolton Wanderer	47976	47/4	7/1964	British Railways [132]
Bolton Wanderer	47831	47/4	9/1964	British Railways
Bombay	3470	Bulldog	4/1904	Great Western Rly

Name	Number	Class	Date	Railway
Bombay	5576	Jubilee	1934	London Midland & Scottish Rly
Bon Accord	2	0–4–0ST	1897	**Caledonian Rly (Brechin)**
Bon-Accord	870	H	7/1906	North British Rly
Bon Accord	60154	A1	9/1949	British Railways (Eastern Region)
Bonaventura	3354	Bulldog	6/1900	Great Western Rly
Bonaventure	1452	Prince/W	11/1911	London & North Western Rly
Bonchurch	297	D1	12/1877	London, Brighton & South Coast Rly
Bonchurch	–	2–4–0T	1883	Isle of Wight Rly [133]
Bonchurch	W32	O2	11/1892	Southern Rly [134]
Boness	165	165	11/1875	North British Rly [135]
Bongo	1005	B1	2/1944	London & North Eastern Rly
Bongrace	60128	A1	5/1949	British Railways (Eastern Region)
Boniface	2646	2Experiment	7/1907	London & North Western Rly
Bonnie Dundee	11	0–4–2T	1901	Ravenglass & Eskdale Rly [136]
Bonnie Dundee	869	H	7/1906	North British Rly [137]
Bonnie Dundee	60159	A1	11/1949	British Railways (Eastern Region)
Bonnie Prince Charlie	1	0–4–0ST	1949	**Didcot Railway Centre**
Bonnington	97	165	7/1878	North British Rly
Bonnybridge	418	418	1873	North British Rly
Bont y Bermo	37402	37/4	1965	British Railways
Bookham	80	A1	7/1880	London, Brighton & South Coast Rly
Book Law	2599	A3	7/1930	London & North Eastern Rly
Booth	308	bCrewe	4/1853	London & North Western Rly
Booth	308	Newton	9/1870	London & North Western Rly
Booth	308	rPrecedent	5/1890	London & North Western Rly
Bootle	–	0–4–0	4/1839	Manchester & Bolton Rly
Boots	2	0–4–0Fs	1935	**Midland Railway Centre**
Boots	–	0–4–0DE	1955	**Midland Railway Centre**
Bordeaux	99	E1	12/1874	London, Brighton & South Coast Rly
Borderer	881	H	8/1906	North British Rly
Borderer	60155	A1	9/1949	British Railways (Eastern Region)
Bordon	4	0–6–0ST	1906	Longmoor Military Rly
Boreas	270	0–4–0	1851	Monklands Rly [138]
Boris	1	0–4–0D	1952	**Chinnor & Princes Risborough Rly**
Borough	31	D1	5/1876	London, Brighton & South Coast Rly
Borough of Kettering	43044	43	3/1977	British Railways
Borough of Stevenage	43162	43	6/1981	British Railways
Borrowstounness	–	0–4–0T	1899	**Bo'ness & Kinneil Rly** [139]
Borth	24	0–6–0ST	1/1863	Cambrian Railways
Borwick Hall	6921	Hall	7/1941	Great Western Rly [140]
Boscastle	21C139	rWC	9/1946	**Southern Rly**
Boscawen	3254	Duke	7/1895	Great Western Rly
Boscawen	5642	Jubilee	1934	London Midland & Scottish Rly
Bostock Hall	5988	Hall	11/1939	Great Western Rly
Boston	14	4–2–0	8/1840	Birmingham & Gloucester Rly
Boswell	60138	A1	12/1948	British Railways (Eastern Region)
Bothwell	166	165	1875	North British Rly [141]
Bothwell	268	72	1/1883	North British Rly
Bounds Green	43057	43	7/1977	British Railways
Bourton Grange	6871	Grange	3/1939	Great Western Rly
Bouverie	12	II	12/1887	Mersey Rly
Bow	5	2–2–2WT	1848	London & Blackwall Rly
Bow Fell	60015	60	3/1993	British Railways
Bow Road	55	51	1900	London, Tilbury & Southend Rly [142]

---

[124] Built by English Electric of Preston, and remained their property. It was demonstrated on the LMS, but that company never purchased it.

[125] A traction engine on railway wheels, built by Aveling & Porter, Rochester, 1926.

[126] 3ft gauge.

[127] Later renamed *Reginald Munns*.

[128] 3ft gauge. Caldon Low Quarries were owned by the London & North Western Railway.

[129] Originally London, Brighton & South Coast Railway no. 70 *Poplar*. Sold to the Kent & East Sussex Railway in May 1901. Taken into British Railways stock on nationalization in 1948.

[130] Employed on the then isolated Bodmin & Wadebridge line.

[131] Unnamed until January 1872.

[132] Later named *Aviemore Centre*.

[133] Later Southern Railway no. W18. Scrapped in 1928.

[134] Originally London & South Western Railway no. 226. Name applied by Southern Railway on transfer to Isle of Wight, May 1928.

[135] May have originally been named *Coatbridge*.

[136] 15in gauge. Rebuilt from a 2ft gauge 0–4–0WT from Dundee Gas Works.

[137] Previously named *Dundonian*.

[138] Absorbed by the North British Railway in 1865. May have been *Boreas*, built for the Glasgow, Dumfries & Carlisle Railway.

[139] 3ft gauge.

[140] Named in January 1948.

[141] Later renamed *Newport*.

[142] Originally named *Wellington Road*.

Name	Number	Class	Date	Railway
Boxer	–	0–4–0ST	11/1873	Woolwich Arsenal [143]
Boxgrove	489	E4	6/1899	London, Brighton & South Coast Rly [144]
Boxhill	**82**	**A1**	**8/1880**	**London, Brighton & South Coast Rly**
Boyne	–	Caesar	8/1857	Great Western Rly (bg)
Braddyll	**–**	**0–6–0**	**?**	**South Hetton Rly [145]**
Bradfield	923	Schools	12/1933	Southern Rly [146]
Bradfield Hall	4906	Hall	1/1929	Great Western Rly

London, Brighton & South Coast Railway A1 class 0–6–0T no. 82 *Boxhill*, at Brighton in umber livery on 4 September 1902 and, surprisingly for those days, none too clean. (*Photo: LCGB Ken Nunn Collection*)

Name	Number	Class	Date	Railway
Bradford	9	0–4–2	9/1839	Manchester & Leeds Rly
Bradford	2867	B17/4	4/1937	London & North Eastern Rly
Bradford City	2868	B17/4	4/1937	London & North Eastern Rly
Brading	–	2–4–0T	1876	Isle of Wight Rly [147]
Brading	257	D1	3/1882	London, Brighton & South Coast Rly
Brading	W22	O2	6/1892	Southern Rly [148]
Bradley Manor	**7802**	**Manor**	**1/1938**	**Great Western Rly**
Bradshaw	5518	Patriot	2/1933	London Midland & Scottish Rly
Braeriach	60074	60	11/1991	British Railways
Brahan Castle	26	Castle	1913	Highland Rly
Brahms	92016	92		British Railways
Braich	**10**	**4wDM**	**1942**	**Llanberis Lake Rly [149]**
Bramber	246	D1	12/1881	London, Brighton & South Coast Rly
Brambletye	24	D1	11/1875	London, Brighton & South Coast Rly
Brambridge Hall	**4**	**4wP**	**1936**	**Hampshire Narrow Gauge Railway Society [150]**
Bramley	36	A1	6/1878	London, Brighton & South Coast Rly
Bramley No 4	1659	0–6–0ST	1930	War Department
Bramley No 6	1660	0–6–0ST	1930	War Department
Brancepeth Castle	2826	B17/1	3/1931	London & North Eastern Rly

Name	Number	Class	Date	Railway
Braunton	**21C146**	**rWC**	**11/1946**	**Southern Rly**
Brasenose	3333	Bulldog	11/1899	Great Western Rly
Breadalbane	12	Belladrum	5/1862	Highland Rly [151]
Breadalbane	17	JonesTank	12/1879	Highland Rly [152]
Breadalbane	789	Precedent	10/1880	London & North Western Rly
Breadalbane	75	Duke	10/1886	Highland Rly
Breadalbane	789	rPrecedent	7/1894	London & North Western Rly
Breadalbane	779	766	1898	Caledonian Rly
Breadalbane	169	Claughton	4/1921	London & North Western Rly
Breccles Hall	6936	Hall	7/1942	Great Western Rly [153]
(Brechin City)	**08046**	**08**	**1953**	**British Railways [154]**
Brecknock	2	0–6–0	3/1863	Brecon & Merthyr Rly
Brecon	2	2–4–0	?	Neath & Brecon Rly
Brecon Beacons	60040	60	2/1992	British Railways
Brecon Castle	5023	Castle	4/1934	Great Western Rly
Bredon	18	4–2–0	10/1840	Birmingham & Gloucester Rly
Brenchley	576	E5	4/1903	London, Brighton & South Coast Rly [155]
Brenner	155	E1	3/1881	London, Brighton & South Coast Rly
Brentor	34095	rWC	10/1949	British Railways (Southern Region)
Brest	89	E1	5/1883	London, Brighton & South Coast Rly
Bret Harte	964	Prince/W	2/1914	London & North Western Rly
Bretwalda	408	0–4–0ST	11/1878	London & South Western Rly [156]
Brewster	–	2–4–0T	1861	Colne Valley & Halstead Rly
(Brian Fisk)	**31874**	**N**	**9/1925**	**Southern Rly**
Briareus	67	0–4–2	1/1841	Grand Junction Rly
Briareus	67	bCrewe	5/1851	London & North Western Rly
Briareus	995	L/Bloomer	1872	London & North Western Rly
Bricklehampton Hall	6973	M/Hall	10/1947	Great Western Rly
Bride of Lammermoor	2987	Saint	8/1905	Great Western Rly [157]
Bridget	–	4–6–0T	1917	Ashover Rly [158]
Bridgwater Castle	5045	Castle	3/1936	Great Western Rly [159]
Bridgwater Castle	5096	Castle	6/1939	Great Western Rly
Brigand	–	Bogie	9/1849	Great Western Rly (bg)
Brigand	1	0–4–2	8/1861	London, Chatham & Dover Rly
Brigand	–	?	?	South Wales Mineral Rly [160]
Brigham Hill	6	0–6–0ST	1894	Cockermouth & Workington Rly
Brighton	130	2–2–2	1/1839	South Eastern Rly
Brighton	163	2–2–2	10/1863	London, Brighton & South Coast Rly [161]
Brighton	–	0–6–0	3/1866	Manchester, Sheffield & Lincolnshire Rly [162]
Brighton	–	0–4–2ST	?	London, Brighton & South Coast Rly(?) [163]
Brighton	**40**	**A1**	**3/1878**	**London, Brighton & South Coast Rly [164]**
Brighton	587	E5	12/1903	London, Brighton & South Coast Rly
Brighton	915	Schools	5/1933	Southern Rly
Brighton Evening Argus	73101	73/1	1965	British Railways
Bright Star	–	Wolf	4/1841	Great Western Rly (bg)

[143] Originally named *Victoria*, renamed *c.* 1901. 18in gauge.

[144] Rebuilt to class E4x, May 1909.

[145] Called the *Buddle* in one source. Built *c.* 1835–7 by Timothy Hackworth.

[146] Originally named *Uppingham*. Before entering service, it was renamed *Bradfield* following objections from the headmaster at Uppingham School. He considered that displaying the school's name on a locomotive constituted advertising, which he did not deem proper.

[147] Later Southern Railway no. W17. Scrapped in 1926.

[148] Formerly London & South Western Railway no. 215. Name applied by Southern Railway on transfer to Isle of Wight, June 1924.

[149] 1ft 11½in gauge.

[150] 2ft gauge.

[151] Previously named *Belladrum*. Renamed *Breadalbane* 1871. Later renamed *Strathpeffer* 1885. Nameless by 1890.

[152] Renamed *Aberfeldy* in 1886. Altered from 2–4–0T to 4–4–0T in July 1887.

[153] Named in February 1947.

[154] Also numbered D3059.

[155] Rebuilt to class E5x, July 1911.

[156] Built for the Southampton Docks Co., which the London & South Western Railway absorbed.

[157] Named *Robertson* in November 1905, and renamed *Bride of Lammermoor* in April 1907.

[158] Ex-War Department locomotive by Baldwins (USA) for service in France. 1ft 11½in gauge.

[159] Renamed *Earl of Dudley* in September 1937.

[160] May have been broad gauge.

[161] Modified by Stroudley and named *Brighton* in February 1873. Renamed *Sandown* in 1878.

[162] Built by London, Brighton & South Coast Railway, and named when sold to C. Braddock, contractor, November 1885. It became MS&LR property, but was never taken into their running stock and was never numbered. It was scrapped in July 1895.

[163] Of uncertain origin, this engine was used by Fred Furniss, contractor, to build the Hayling Island branch and then to work it. Said to have been obtained originally from the London, Brighton & South Coast Railway, but there is no trace in their records. Purchased by Boultons, *c.* 1871.

[164] Exhibited at the 1878 Paris Exhibition, where it was awarded a Gold Medal. Sold to the Isle of Wight Central Railway in January 1902, and named *Newport* by the Southern after 1923.

Great Western Railway 3001 class 4–2–2 no. 3005 *Britannia* at Westbourne Park shed on 26 April 1902. To the left can be glimpsed the combined name, number and works plate of no. 3341 *Mars*, a Bulldog class 4–4–0. These combined plates enjoyed a very short vogue on the GWR. (*Photo: LCGB Ken Nunn Collection*)

Name	Number	Class	Date	Railway
Brill	**14**	**0–4–0ST**	**1912**	**Northamptonshire Ironstone Railway Trust**
Brill	97	G	3/1916	Metropolitan Rly [165]
Brill No. 1	–	0–6–0ST	12/1894	Metropolitan Rly [166]
Brilliant	22	aSentinel	1927	London & North Eastern Rly
Brindisi	136	E1	1/1879	London, Brighton & South Coast Rly [167]
Brindley	–	Victoria	5/1864	Great Western Rly (bg)
Brindley	1489	Newton	5/1866	London & North Western Rly
Brindley	1489	rPrecedent	4/1893	London & North Western Rly
Brindley	1363	2Precursor	10/1905	London & North Western Rly [168]
Brisbane	3396	Atbara	7/1901	Great Western Rly
Bristol	260	2–2–2	4/1844	Midland Rly (bg) [169]

Name	Number	Class	Date	Railway
Bristol	36	0–6–0	6/1844	Birmingham & Gloucester Rly
Bristol	4	2–2–2	7/1844	Bristol & Gloucester Railway (bg) [170]
Bristol	16	0–6–0	10/1846	Taff Vale Rly
Bristol	–	Swindon	12/1865	Great Western Rly (bg)
Bristol	–	0–4–0T	1915	Woolwich Arsenal [171]
Bristol Barton Hill	47738	47/7		British Railways
Bristol Bath Road	47805	47/4	3/1966	British Railways
Bristol Bath Road Quality Assured	47816	47/4	1/1965	British Railways
Bristol Castle	7013	Castle	7/1948	British Railways (Western Region) [172]
Bristol Evening Post	43150	43	6/1981	British Railways
Britain	17	?	?	St Helens Canal & Rly

[165] Sold to LNER in November 1937, becoming their no. 6157 of class M2.

[166] Originally built for the Wotton Tramway, Bucks.

[167] In 1932 became Southern Railway no. W1 *Medina*, in the Isle of Wight.

[168] Originally named *Cornwall*, but when it was decided to keep the 8ft 6in single, now preserved, no. 1363 was renamed *Brindley*.

[169] Built for the Bristol & Gloucester Railway as their no. 4. In June 1855 it was sold to Thomas Brassey for working the North Devon Railway, where it is thought to have been renamed *Star*.

[170] In February 1847 this locomotive passed to the Midland Railway, who sold it to Thomas Brassey, the famous contractor. Brassey used it to work the North Devon Railway, which was broad gauge, and this locomotive is thought to have been renamed *Star*.

[171] 18in gauge.

[172] This engine exchanged identities with 4082 *Windsor Castle* in February 1952. The genuine *Windsor Castle* was under repair, and the exchange of identities (which was permanent) was so that an engine named *Windsor Castle* could haul HM King George VI's funeral train from Paddington to Windsor.

Name	Number	Class	Date	Railway
Britannia	–	0-6-0	1829	Sirhowy Rly
Britannia	122	1Vesuvius	5/1853	London & South Western Rly
Britannia	1748	Newton	11/1869	London & North Western Rly
Britannia	122	2Vesuvius	12/1869	London & South Western Rly
Britannia	–	?	1879	Alexandra (Newport & South Wales) Docks & Co.
Britannia	1748	rPrecedent	7/1889	London & North Western Rly
Britannia	3005	3001	2/1892	Great Western Rly [173]
Britannia	3374	Atbara	4/1900	Great Western Rly [174]
Britannia	2235	cSentinel	1929	London & North Eastern Rly
Britannia	5700	Jubilee	1936	London Midland & Scottish Rly [175]
Britannia	**70000**	**Britannia**	**1/1951**	**British Railways**
Britannia	87004	87/0	1973	British Railways
Britannia	**70000**	**4-6-2**	**1988**	**Conwy Valley Railway Museum [176]**
Britannic	323	1Experiment	1884	London & North Western Rly
Britannic	353	2Experiment	6/1905	London & North Western Rly
British Columbia	5559	Jubilee	1934	London Midland & Scottish Rly
British Empire	502	George V	6/1911	London & North Western Rly
British Guiana	5601	Jubilee	1935	London Midland & Scottish Rly
British Gypsum	**4**	**0-4-0ST**	**1953**	**Steamtown Carnforth**
British Honduras	5602	Jubilee	1935	London Midland & Scottish Rly
British India Line	**21C18**	**MN**	**5/1945**	**Southern Rly**
British International Freight Association	37194	37/0	1964	British Railways
British Legion	6170	Royal Scot	12/1929	London Midland & Scottish Rly [177]
British Monarch	4021	Star	6/1909	Great Western Rly [178]
British Petroleum	47223	47/0	1965	British Railways
British Queen	2236	cSentinel	1929	London & North Eastern Rly
British Red Cross 125th Birthday 1995	43195	43	7/1982	British Railways
British Steel Corby	37716	37/7	2/1963	British Railways
British Steel Hunterston	37156	37/0	1963	British Railways
British Steel Llanwern	37902	37/9	6/1963	British Railways
British Steel Llanwern	56054	56	1979	British Railways
British Steel Ravenscraig	37152	37/0	1963	British Railways
British Steel Shelton	37503	37/5	1961	British Railways
British Steel Skinningrove	37506	37/5	1961	British Railways
British Steel Teesside	37502	37/5	1962	British Railways
British Steel Workington	37505	37/5	1961	British Railways
British Transport Police	90012	90/0	11/1988	British Railways
Britomart	–	**0-4-0ST**	**1899**	**Pen-yr-Orsedd Quarries [179]**
Britomart	2645	2Experiment	7/1907	London & North Western Rly
Briton	12	Enterprise	6/1837	Stockton & Darlington Rly [180]
Briton	19	Fairbairn	10/1841	London & South Western Rly [181]
Briton	19	2Sussex	12/1852	London & South Western Rly
Briton	19	2Vesuvius	7/1871	London & South Western Rly
Brittany	104	E1	10/1876	London, Brighton & South Coast Rly
Brittany	97	B4	11/1893	London & South Western Rly
Brittany	–	Sentinel	1927	Jersey Eastern Rly [182]
Britten	92026	92		British Railways
Brixton	67	A1	8/1874	London, Brighton & South Coast Rly
Broadbridge	453	E3	4/1895	London, Brighton & South Coast Rly
Broadlands	73201	73/2	1/1967	British Railways
Broadwater	235	D1	10/1881	London, Brighton & South Coast Rly
Brocket Hall	5987	Hall	11/1939	Great Western Rly
Brockhurst	455	E3	4/1895	London, Brighton & South Coast Rly
Brockington Grange	6804	Grange	9/1936	Great Western Rly
Brocklebank Line	**35025**	**MN**	**11/1948**	**British Railways (Southern Region)**
Brockley	8	D1	3/1874	London, Brighton & South Coast Rly
Brockley Hall	4987	Hall	1/1931	Great Western Rly
Brockton Grange	6832	Grange	8/1937	Great Western Rly
Brodie	44	M/Goods	6/1864	Highland Rly
Brodie Castle	50	Castle	1917	Highland Rly
Bromley	4	Class 1	1880	London, Tilbury & Southend Rly
Brompton	15	D1	1/1875	London, Brighton & South Coast Rly
Bromsgrove	1	2-2-2	7/1839	Birmingham & Gloucester Rly
Broneirion	14	S/Goods	9/1875	Cambrian Railways
Bronllwyd	–	**0-6-0WT**	**1930**	**Bressingham Museum [183]**
Brontes	–	Fury	5/1847	Great Western Rly (bg)
Bronzino	60539	A2	8/1948	British Railways (Eastern Region)
Brook	–	2-2-2	1847	Huddersfield & Manchester Railway & Canal
Brookes No. 1	–	**0-6-0ST**	**1941**	**Middleton Rly**
Brookhouse	230	D1	10/1884	London, Brighton & South Coast Rly
Brookfield	–	**0-6-0PT**	**1940**	**Pontypool & Blaenavon Rly**
Brookside	124	Peel	10/1857	Stockton & Darlington Rly
Brookside	86632	86/6	4/1966	British Railways
Broome Hall	4908	Hall	1/1929	Great Western Rly
Broome Manor	7805	Manor	3/1938	Great Western Rly
Brough	120	Peel	12/1856	Stockton & Darlington Rly
Brougham	17	2-4-0	1857	Lancaster & Carlisle Rly
Brougham	160	Brougham	8/1860	Stockton & Darlington Rly
Brougham	393	Newton	8/1870	London & North Western Rly
Brougham	393	rPrecedent	4/1893	London & North Western Rly
Brougham	2011	2Precursor	8/1907	London & North Western Rly
Broughton Castle	5033	Castle	3/1935	Great Western Rly
Broughton Grange	6805	Grange	9/1936	Great Western Rly
Broughton Hall	4907	Hall	1/1929	Great Western Rly
Brown Jack	2508	A3	1/1935	London & North Eastern Rly
Browsholme Hall	6935	Hall	12/1941	Great Western Rly [184]
Bruce	6	Seafield	5/1858	Highland Rly [185]
Bruce	47	Glenbarry	6/1864	Highland Rly [186]
Bruce	60	Duke	6/1874	Highland Rly [187]
Bruce	72	Duke	7/1884	Highland Rly [188]
Bruce	76	Clyde Bogie	12/1886	Highland Rly
Brunel	2	2-4-0	4/1858	London & South Western Rly (ed)
Brunel	–	Victoria	5/1863	Great Western Rly (bg)
Brunel	2	2-4-0	9/1864	London & South Western Rly (ed) [189]
Brunel	14	No.7	5/1894	Great Western Rly
Brunel	207	B2	6/1897	London, Brighton & South Coast Rly [190]
Brunlees	13	II	1/1888	Mersey Rly
Brunswick	68	Priam	7/1850	Stockton & Darlington Rly
Brush Veteran	31146	31/1	1959	British Railways
Brussels	**118**	**J94**	**1945**	**Longmoor Military Rly [191]**
Brutus	–	Caesar	1/1854	Great Western Rly (bg)
Brutus	2150	0-6-0ST	10/1862	Great Western Rly (bg) [192]

[173] Rebuilt to 4-2-2 in November 1894.

[174] Originally named *Baden Powell*. Temporarily renamed *Pretoria* for City Imperial Volunteers' Special Train on 29 October 1900, *Britannia* for Royal Trains on 7 and 10 March 1902, and *Kitchener* for a Special Train on 12 July 1902.

[175] Later renamed *Amethyst* by British Railways.

[176] 15in gauge.

[177] Rebuilt from no. 6399 *Fury* in November 1935, and formed the prototype of the 'Converted Royal Scot' class.

[178] Originally named *King Edward*. Renamed *The British Monarch* in June or July 1927, and then *British Monarch* in October or November 1927.

[179] Privately owned; occasionally operates on the Festiniog Railway. 1ft 11½in gauge.

[180] May have originally been no. 31. Rebuilt in 1842 and renamed *Trader*.

[181] Rebuilt from *Deer* (no number) of June 1838.

[182] Sentinel-Cammell steam railcar.

[183] 1ft 11½in gauge.

[184] Named in January 1947.

[185] Renamed *Helmsdale*, c. 1874.

[186] Later renamed *Lovat*, and then *Beauly*. Altered from 2-2-2 to 2-4-0, July 1880.

[187] Later renamed *Sutherland*.

[188] Later renamed *Grange*.

[189] Replacement of previous engine. Formerly Somerset & Dorset Railway. Became LSWR no. 147 *Isis*, and was transferred to Engineer's Dept in March 1883.

[190] Rebuilt to class B2x, July 1909.

[191] Now preserved on the Keighley & Worth Valley Railway.

[192] Built for the South Devon Railway.

London & North Eastern Railway A3 class 4–6–2 no. 2508 *Brown Jack* near Potters Bar with the Up Edinburgh–King's Cross 'Flying Scotsman' on 8 March 1936. (Photo: *LCGB Ken Nunn Collection*)

Name	Number	Class	Date	Railway	Name	Number	Class	Date	Railway
Brutus	–	0–4–0ST	1912	Woolwich Arsenal [193]	*Buckingham*	382	Newton	1/1870	London & North Western Rly
Bryndu No. 3	–	0–4–2ST	1853	Port Talbot Rly [194]	*Buckingham*	–	0–4–0T	12/1876	Metropolitan Rly [197]
Bryngwyn Hall	6974	M/Hall	10/1947	Great Western Rly	*Buckingham*	382	rPrecedent	5/1890	London & North Western Rly
Bryn-Ivor Hall	6997	M/Hall	1/1949	British Railways (Western Region)	*Buckingham*	986	Claughton	8/1917	London & North Western Rly
BSC No 2	–	0–4–0ST	1927	**Rutland Railway Museum**	*Buckinghamshire*	336	D49/2	6/1929	London & North Eastern Rly [198]
Buachaille Etive Mor	60088	60	1/1992	British Railways	*Buckland*	264	Precedent	1/1882	London & North Western Rly
Buccaneer	37184	37/0	1963	British Railways	*Buckland*	264	rPrecedent	1/1896	London & North Western Rly
Buccleuch	905	I	8/1911	North British Rly	*Buckland*	503	E4	8/1900	London, Brighton & South Coast Rly
Bucephalus	253	bCrewe	11/1849	London & North Western Rly [195]	*Buckland*	2625	2Experiment	2/1909	London & North Western Rly
Bucephalus	780	S/Bloomer	1858	London & North Western Rly	*Bucklebury Grange*	6803	Grange	9/1936	Great Western Rly
Bucephalus	990	2Precursor	4/1906	London & North Western Rly	*Bude*	21C106	WC	7/1945	Southern Rly
Buck	–	2–2–0	7/1837	Manchester & Bolton Rly	*Budleigh Salterton*	21C114	rWC	11/1945	Southern Rly
Buckenhill Grange	6830	Grange	8/1937	Great Western Rly	**Budley**	–	4wDM	**1945**	**Bicton Woodland Rly [199]**
Buckhaven	161	165	4/1877	North British Rly [196]	*Buffalo*	67	0–4–2	1839	Liverpool & Manchester Rly [200]
Buckhurst	252	D1	1/1882	London, Brighton & South Coast Rly	*Buffalo*	42	0–4–0	11/1840	Midland Counties Rly

[193] 18in gauge.

[194] Built as no. 36 of the Oxford, Worcester & Wolverhampton Railway and became GWR no. 222 in 1863. It was sold to Bryndu Colliery in October 1873. It passed to the Cefn & Pyle Railway, which was purchased by the Port Talbot Railway on 1 January 1897. The Port Talbot offered it for sale in April 1897, and it passed out of their possession by the end of the year. Its subsequent history is unknown.

[195] Charged to current A/C as *Tantalus*.

[196] Originally named *Partick*.

[197] Ex-Wotton Tramway.

[198] Renamed *The Quorn* in May 1932.

[199] 18in gauge.

[200] Became London & North Western Railway no. 121 in 1846.

Name	Number	Class	Date	Railway	Name	Number	Class	Date	Railway
Buffalo	–	Leo	3/1841	Great Western Rly (bg)	*Burma*	5580	Jubilee	1934	London Midland & Scottish Rly
Buffalo	50	Bison	3/1846	London & South Western Rly	*Burmah*	993	L/Bloomer	1872	London & North Western Rly
Buffalo	121	DX	c.1850	London & North Western Rly	*Durmington Grange*	6829	Grange	3/1937	Great Western Rly
Buffalo	2160	0–6–0ST	6/1872	Great Western Rly (bg) [201]	*Burnham Thorpe*	2805	B17/1	12/1928	London & North Eastern Rly [210]
Buffalo	1134	1076	11/1874	Great Western Rly	*Burnley*	21	2–2–2	1/1841	Manchester & Leeds Rly
Buffalo	2181	Precedent	3/1875	London & North Western Rly	*Burnley*	17	III	6/1892	Mersey Rly
Buffalo	2630	2Experiment	3/1909	London & North Western Rly	*Burntisland*	480	157	6/1877	North British Rly [211]
Builth Castle	4086	Castle	6/1925	Great Western Rly	*Burntisland*	–	0–4–0ST	1889	Llanelly & Mynydd Mawr Rly
Bullidae	37431	37/4	1965	British Railways	*Burry Port*	6	0–6–0ST	8/1874	Burry Port & Gwendraeth Valley Rly
Bullidae	47194	47/0	1965	British Railways	*Burry Port*	3	0–6–0T	1901	Burry Port & Gwendraeth Valley Rly [212]
Bulkeley	–	Sir Watkin	12/1865	Great Western Rly (bg) [202]	**Burt**	**2**	**4wDM**	**1951**	**North Downs Steam Rly**
Bulkeley	–	Rover	7/1880	Great Western Rly (bg)	*Burton*	–	2–2–2	7/1839	Birmingham & Derby Junction Rly
Bulkeley	3072	3031	6/1898	Great Western Rly [203]	*Burton*	5	2–2–2	5/1849	South Staffordshire Rly
Bulldog	306	bCrewe	3/1853	London & North Western Rly	*Burton Hall*	6922	Hall	7/1941	Great Western Rly [213]
Bulldog	627	S/Bloomer	1854	London & North Western Rly	**Burton Agnes Hall**	**6998**	**M/Hall**	**1/1949**	**British Railways (Western Region)**
Bulldog	3312	Duke	10/1898	Great Western Rly	**Burtonwood Brewer**	**–**	**0–6–0ST**	**1932**	**Llangollen Rly**
Bulldog	3312	Bulldog	3/1906	Great Western Rly	*Burwarton*	–	0–6–0ST	1908	Cleobury Mortimer & Ditton Priors Light Rly [214]
Bull Dog	956	George V	4/1911	London & North Western Rly [204]	*Burwarton Hall*	6932	Hall	12/1941	Great Western Rly [215]
Bulldog	D602	Warship	11/1958	British Railways	*Burwick*	–	?	1856	North British Rly [216]
Buller	57	B4	8/1901	London, Brighton & South Coast Rly	*Bury*	–	0–4–0	1832	Bolton & Leigh Rly [217]
Bullfinch	152	bCrewe	7/1855	London & North Western Rly [205]	*Bury*	–	Hawthorn	7/1865	Great Western Rly (bg)
Bullfinch	3732	Bulldog	5/1909	Great Western Rly	*Bury*	08495	08	1958	British Railways
(Bulliver)	**1420**	**14XX**	**11/1933**	**Great Western Rly**	*Buryhill*	287	D1	6/1879	London, Brighton & South Coast Rly
Bulwark	50041	50	1968	British Railways	*Bury St Edmunds*	4	2–2–2	10/1846	Eastern Union Rly
Bulmers of Hereford	47207	47/0	1965	British Railways	*Bushbuck*	1017	B1	1/1947	London & North Eastern Rly
Bulwell Hall	4988	Hall	1/1931	Great Western Rly	*Busy Bee*	–	0–4–0ST	12/1872	Chatham Dockyard [218]
Bulwer Lytton	951	Prince/W	12/1913	London & North Western Rly	*Bute*	22	0–6–0	6/1851	Taff Vale Rly
Bunsen	1679	Newton	4/1868	London & North Western Rly	*Bute*	82	Scotchmen	4/1866	London, Chatham & Dover Rly
Bunsen	167	rPrecedent	1/1888	London & North Western Rly	*Butleigh Court*	2934	Saint	11/1911	Great Western Rly
Bunsen	1177	Claughton	1/1920	London & North Western Rly [206]	**Butler-Henderson**	**506**	**11F**	**12/1919**	**Great Central Rly**
Bunsen	5512	Patriot	9/1932	London Midland & Scottish Rly [207]	*Butlers Hall*	6902	Hall	7/1940	Great Western Rly
Bunting	47307	47/3	1964	British Railways	*Buttermere*	15	0–6–0ST	1873	Whitehaven, Cleator & Egremont Rly [219]
Bunty	**–**	**0–4–0DM**	**1950**	**Northampton & Lamport Rly**	*Buz*	134	0–6–0	7/1873	London, Chatham & Dover Rly
Burcot	16	III	5/1892	Mersey Rly	*Buzzard*	47102	47/0	1963	British Railways
Burdett Road	18	Class 1	1881	London, Tilbury & Southend Rly	**Byfield No. 2**	**–**	**0–6–0ST**	**1941**	**Gloucestershire Warwickshire Rly**
Burgess Hill	369	D3	10/1892	London, Brighton & South Coast Rly	*Byng*	628	C	1/1890	North British Rly
Burghclere Grange	6809	Grange	9/1936	Great Western Rly	*Byron*	1516	Newton	11/1866	London & North Western Rly
Burghead	58	JonesTank	12/1878	Highland Rly [208]	*Byron*	1516	rPrecedent	6/1891	London & North Western Rly
Burgoyne	–	0–4–0ST	4/1873	School of Military Engineering, Chatham [209]	*Byron*	70031	Britannia	11/1952	British Railways
Burgundy	110	E1	3/1877	London, Brighton & South Coast Rly	*Bywell*	38	0–6–0	12/1853	Newcastle & Carlisle Rly [220]
					Byzantium	2638	2Experiment	6/1909	London & North Western Rly

[201] Built for the South Devon Railway.

[202] Not put into stock until December 1866. This locomotive was sold to the South Devon Railway in August 1872, retaining its name and still unnumbered. In 1876 the Great Western absorbed the South Devon, and the SDR engines received numbers, *Bulkeley* becoming no. 2157. It ceased work in December 1890.

[203] Originally named *North Star*. Renamed *Bulkeley* in September 1906.

[204] Originally named *Dachshund*; renamed in December 1915.

[205] Formerly Liverpool & Manchester Railway no. 94.

[206] Name applied in March 1922.

[207] Rebuilt with taper boiler in July 1948.

[208] Converted from 2–4–0T to 4–4–0T, October 1885.

[209] 18in gauge.

[210] Renamed *Lincolnshire Regiment* in April 1938.

[211] Originally named *Roseneath*.

[212] Became Great Western Railway no. 2193.

[213] Named in December 1946.

[214] Became Great Western Railway no. 29. Rebuilt to 0–6–0 pannier tank, 1924.

[215] Named in March 1946.

[216] Ex-Port Carlisle Railway.

[217] There is some doubt as to whether it was originally named *Bee* and renamed *Bury*, or *vice versa*.

[218] 18in gauge.

[219] Became Furness Railway no. 111.

[220] Became North Eastern Railway no. 486 in 1862.

C

Name	Number	Class	Date	Railway
Cabot	39	0–6–0DH	1965	**Dean Forest Rly**
Cadboll	48	Glenbarry	6/1864	Highland Rly [1]
Cadboll	83	Clyde Bogie	10/1886	Highland Rly [2]
Cadbury No. 1	–	0–4–0T	1925	**Birmingham Railway Museum**
Cadbury Castle	7028	Castle	5/1950	British Railways (Western Region)
Cadeby 41A	08919	08	1962	British Railways
Cader Idris	34	S/Goods	12/1861	Cambrian Railways [3]
Cader Idris	41	Small Pass	3/1864	Cambrian Railways [4]
Cader Idris	6	2–4–2T	1896	Manchester & Milford Rly [5]
Cader Idris	60011	60	10/1991	British Railways
(Cadley Hill)	1	J94	6/1962	**Snibston Discovery Park**
Cadmus	68	2–2–2	10/1848	Manchester, Sheffield & Lincolnshire Rly
Cadmus	256	bCrewe	3/1850	London & North Western Rly
Cadmus	789	S/Bloomer	1854	London & North Western Rly
Caen	301	Lyons	3/1877	London, Brighton & South Coast Rly
Caen	90	B4	11/1892	London & South Western Rly
Caen	2214	0–4–0D	1945	War Department
Caerhays Castle	7014	Castle	7/1948	British Railways (Western Region)
Caerleon	4	0–6–0	4/1865	Brecon & Merthyr Rly
Caernarvon	5515	Patriot	9/1932	London Midland & Scottish Rly
Caerphilly	5	0–6–0	4/1865	Brecon & Merthyr Rly
Caerphilly	10	0–6–0ST	8/1866	Alexandra (Newport & South Wales) Docks & Rly [6]
Caerphilly Castle	4073	Castle	8/1923	**Great Western Rly**
Caerphilly Castle	37887	37/7	3/1963	British Railways [7]
Caerphilly Castle	47615	47/4	1966	British Railways [8]
Caersws	–	0–6–0ST	1877	Van Rly [9]
Caesar	3	2–2–2	1/1842	South Eastern Rly
Caesar	–	Caesar	8/1851	Great Western Rly (bg)
Caesar	1964	Alfred	1904	London & North Western Rly
Caesarea	–	0–4–2T	1872	Jersey Eastern Rly
(Cairngorm)	75061	J94	1943	**War Department [10]**
Cairn Gorm	60073	60	11/1991	British Railways
Cairn Toul	60072	60	10/1991	British Railways
Caithness	1885	ELBloomer	1861	London & North Western Rly
Caithness	51	Glenbarry	5/1864	Highland Rly [11]
Caithness	68	Duke	8/1874	Highland Rly [12]
Caithness	37261	37/0	1965	British Railways
Caithness-shire	68	Duke	8/1874	Highland Rly [13]
Calbourne	93	E1	11/1883	London, Brighton & South Coast Rly
Calbourne	W24	O2	12/1891	**Southern Rly [14]**
Calceolaria	4103	Flower	5/1908	Great Western Rly
Calcot Grange	6833	Grange	8/1937	Great Western Rly
Calcutta	3468	Bulldog	3/1904	Great Western Rly
Caldarvon	322	317	1861	North British Rly [15]
Calder	18	2–2–2	11/1840	Manchester & Leeds Rly
Caldercruix	322	317	1861	North British Rly [16]
Calder Hall Power Station	31130	31/1	1959	British Railways
Calder Hall Power Station	31276	31/1	1961	British Railways
Caldicot Castle	4074	Castle	12/1923	Great Western Rly
Caleb Balderstone	413	Scott	5/1914	North British Rly
Caledonia	15	0–6–0T	1885	**Isle of Man Rly [17]**
Caledonia	70	0–4–0WT	1931	**Hollycombe Steam Collection [18]**
Caledonian	28	0–4–0	1832	Liverpool & Manchester Rly
Caledonian	6141	Royal Scot	10/1927	London Midland & Scottish Rly [19]
Caledonian	86224	86/2	1965	British Railways
Calendula	4104	Flower	5/1908	Great Western Rly
Caliban	17	2–2–2	1837	Grand Junction Rly
Caliban	17	2–2–0	5/1840	Midland Counties Rly
Caliban	17	aCrewe	10/1844	London & North Western Rly
Caliban	–	Caesar	2/1848	Great Western Rly (bg)
Caliban	45	John Bull	1/1850	East Lancashire Rly
Caliban	99	2–2–2	7/1850	Manchester, Sheffield & Lincolnshire Rly
Caliban	602	S/Bloomer	1854	London & North Western Rly
Caliban	17	bCrewe	1/1857	London & North Western Rly
Caliban	805	Samson	9/1873	London & North Western Rly
Caliban	805	Whitworth	4/1893	London & North Western Rly
Caliban	2392	Prince/W	12/1915	London & North Western Rly
Caliban	1	0–4–0ST	1937	**Lakeside & Haverthwaite Rly**
Caliph	–	Caesar	5/1854	Great Western Rly (bg)
Call Boy	2795	A3	4/1930	London & North Eastern Rly
Callington	21C147	rWC	11/1946	Southern Rly
Calstock	34103	WC	2/1950	British Railways (Southern Region)
Calvados	–	0–4–2T	1872	Jersey Eastern Rly
Calvados	100	E1	3/1875	London, Brighton & South Coast Rly
Calveley Hall	6939	Hall	7/1942	Great Western Rly [20]
Calverton Colliery	22	0–6–0DM	1958	**Midland Railway Centre [21]**
Calypso	75	2–4–0	8/1849	Manchester, Sheffield & Lincolnshire Rly
Cam	–	2–4–0T	?	Colne Valley & Halstead Rly [22]
Camber	–	2–4–0T	1895	Rye & Camber Tramway [23]
Camberwell	30	D1	4/1876	London, Brighton & South Coast Rly
Camborne	–	2–4–0T	4/1852	West Cornwall Rly
Cambrai	–	0–6–0T	1888	**Irchester Narrow Gauge Railway Museum [24]**
Cambria	6	0–6–0	1863	Pembroke & Tenby Rly [25]
Cambria	27	S/Goods	2/1863	Cambrian Railways
Cambria	222	DFG	4/1866	London & South Western Rly
Cambria	98	L/Scotchmen	3/1873	London, Chatham & Dover Rly
Cambria	3296	Badminton	5/1898	Great Western Rly
Cambrian	–	0–6–0	1846	Taff Vale Rly
Cambrian	249	bCrewe	10/1849	London & North Western Rly
Cambrian	10	0–6–0	1861	Taff Vale Rly [26]

[1] Altered from 2–2–2 to 2–4–0 in January 1881, and renamed *Dingwall* in 1886.

[2] Renamed *Monkland* in 1900.

[3] Originally named *Talerddig*.

[4] Later renamed *Countess Vane*.

[5] Became Great Western Railway no. 1306.

[6] Originally London, Brighton & South Coast Railway no. 229.

[7] Also named (on the other side) *Castell Caerffili*.

[8] Also named (on the other side) *Castell Caerffili*.

[9] The Van Railway was taken over by the Cambrian Railways in 1896. *Caersws* became no. 22. But the Van Railway had another Manning, Wardle 0–6–0ST, un-named, which became Cambrian no. 25. No. 22 was withdrawn by the end of 1899,

and was replaced by a new no. 22 in 1901. Thereafter records and diagrams show no. 25 as built in 1877. It is thought that the best parts of both locomotives were used to make one serviceable engine 'No. 25' was sold to HM Office of Works, and by 1922 was at 'HM Filling Factory, Hereford'.

[10] Preserved on the Strathspey Railway.

[11] Renamed *Blair Atholl* in 1874, and altered from 2–2–2 to 2–4–0 in July 1875.

[12] Previously named *Caithness-shire*, and later renamed *Muirtown*.

[13] Later renamed *Caithness*, and then *Muirtown*.

[14] Previously London & South Western Railway no. 209. Named by Southern Railway on transfer to Isle of Wight, April 1925.

[15] Later renamed *Caldercruix*. Ex-Edinburgh & Glasgow Railway, absorbed by NBR in 1865.

[16] Originally named *Caldarvon*. Ex-Edinburgh & Glasgow Railway, absorbed by NBR in 1865.

[17] Built for Manx Northern Railway. 3ft gauge.

[18] 2ft gauge.

[19] Renamed *The North Staffordshire Regiment* in June 1936.

[20] Nameplates fitted August 1946.

[21] 2ft gauge.

[22] Hired in 1860 from Monro, the contractor who built the line.

[23] 3ft gauge.

[24] Built in France by Corpet Louvet. Metre gauge.

[25] Renamed *Tenby* when the original *Tenby*, no. 1, was withdrawn in 1886. In 1896 it became Great Western Railway no. 1364.

[26] Not to be confused with unnumbered engine of the same name shown above.

Name	Number	Class	Date	Railway
Cambrian	2194	Precedent	5/1875	London & North Western Rly
Cambrian	2194	rPrecedent	10/1896	London & North Western Rly
Cambrian	D806	Warship	6/1959	British Railways
Cambridge	–	2–2–0T	1850	Eastern Counties Rly [27]
Cambridge	08638	08	1958	British Railways
Cambridge	08714	08	1960	British Railways
Cambridgeshire	318	D49/3	5/1928	London & North Eastern Rly [28]
Cambridge Traction & Rolling Stock Depot	47462	47/4	1964	British Railways
Cambridge Traction & Rolling Stock Depot	47736	47/7		British Railways
Cambyses	–	Caesar	11/1854	Great Western Rly (bg)
Camden	62	51	1900	London, Tilbury & Southend Rly
Camden Town	62	51	1900	London, Tilbury & Southend Rly
Camel	–	4–wheel	1834	London & South Western Rly [29]
Camel	113	Peel	9/1856	Stockton & Darlington Rly
Camel	2162	0–6–0ST	8/1872	Great Western Rly (bg) [30]
Camel	3352	Bulldog	10/1899	Great Western Rly
Camelford	21C132	rWC	6/1946	Southern Rly
Camelia	–	Metro	12/1863	Great Western Rly (bg)
Camellia	4105	Flower	5/1908	Great Western Rly
Camelot	3355	Bulldog	6/1900	Great Western Rly
Camelot	742	King Arthur	6/1919	Southern Rly [31]
Camelot	**73082**	**5MT**	**6/1955**	**British Railways**

Name	Number	Class	Date	Railway
Camilla	94	Lion	6/1867	London & South Western Rly
Campania CLS	40016	40	6/1959	British Railways [33]
Campanula	4106	Flower	5/1908	Great Western Rly
Campbell Brick Works	**–**	**4wDM**	**1968**	**Midland Railway Centre [34]**
Camperdown	113	2–2–2	7/1844	South Eastern Rly
Camperdown	1948	Alfred	1902	London & North Western Rly
Camperdown	5680	Jubilee	1935	London Midland & Scottish Rly
Campion Hall	5941	Hall	2/1935	Great Western Rly
(Camulodonum)	**08772**	**08**	**1960**	**British Railways**
Canada	47	B4	6/1901	London, Brighton & South Coast Rly
Canada	882	George V	6/1911	London & North Western Rly
Canada	5553	Jubilee	1934	London Midland & Scottish Rly
Canadian Pacific	**21C5**	**MN**	**12/1941**	**Southern Rly**
Canary	C	0–4–2	1852	Oxford, Worcester & Wolverhampton Rly [35]
Cancer	–	Leo	10/1841	Great Western Rly (bg)
Candidate	170	bCrewe	10/1847	London & North Western Rly
Candidate	2149	1Precursor	8/1874	London & North Western Rly
Candidate	1301	2Precursor	10/1905	London & North Western Rly
Canisp	60077	60	11/1991	British Railways
Cannes	85	E1	3/1883	London, Brighton & South Coast Rly
Canning	110	aCrewe	6/1847	London & North Western Rly
Canning	504	Prince/W	3/1919	London & North Western Rly [36]
Cannock	24	0–6–0	1858	South Staffordshire Rly
Canopus	1913	Jubilee	1899	London & North Western Rly
Canopus	–	0–6–2ST	1901	Pentewan Rly [37]
Canute	9	2–2–2	4/1842	South Eastern Rly
Canute	135	Canute	5/1856	London & South Western Rly
Canute	–	0–4–0ST	7/1870	Southampton Dock Co.
Canvey Island	75	69	1908	London, Tilbury & Southend Rly
Capability Brown	60002	60	12/1992	British Railways
Capel Dowi Hall	6999	M/Hall	2/1949	British Railways (Western Region)
Capercailie	4901	A4	6/1938	London & North Eastern Rly [38]
Capesthorne Hall	6975	M/Hall	10/1947	Great Western Rly
Cape Town	3397	Atbara	8/1901	Great Western Rly
Capital Radio's Help a London Child	47710	47/7	1966	British Railways
Capricornus	–	Leo	4/1842	Great Western Rly (bg)
Captain Bill Smith RNR	**33109**	**33/1**	**1961**	**British Railways**
Captain Craigengelt	2681	D11/2	10/1924	London & North Eastern Rly
Captain Cuttle	2745	A3	9/1928	London & North Eastern Rly
Captain Fryatt	154	Claughton	3/1917	London & North Western Rly
Captain Peter Manisty RN	47788	47/7		British Railways
3rd Carabinier	6125	Royal Scot	8/1927	London Midland & Scottish Rly [39]
3rd Carabinier	**45135**	**Peak**	**1961**	**British Railways**
Caractacus	477	Precedent	11/1880	London & North Western Rly
Caractacus	477	rPrecedent	2/1896	London & North Western Rly
Caradoc	246	bCrewe	10/1849	London & North Western Rly
Caradoc	2192	Precedent	4/1875	London & North Western Rly
Caradoc	2192	rPrecedent	1/1894	London & North Western Rly
Caradoc	D807	Warship	6/1959	British Railways
Caradoc Grange	6873	Grange	4/1939	Great Western Rly

British Railways (ex-LNER) K4 class 2–6–0 no. 61995 *Cameron of Lochiel*. (Photo: RAS Marketing)

Name	Number	Class	Date	Railway
Cameron Highlander	6105	Royal Scot	8/1927	London Midland & Scottish Rly
Cameronian	6113	Royal Scot	9/1927	London Midland & Scottish Rly
Cameronian	2505	A3	10/1934	London & North Eastern Rly
Cameron of Lochiel	61995	K4	12/1938	London & North Eastern Rly
Camilla	38	2–2–2	1838	Grand Junction Rly
Camilla	5	2–2–2	12/1845	Joint Board of Management [32]
Camilla	38	aCrewe	9/1846	London & North Western Rly
Camilla	94	Fireball	5/1848	London & South Western Rly
Camilla	27	Venus	8/1848	East Lancashire Rly
Camilla	889	L/Bloomer	1851	London & North Western Rly

27   This locomotive was close-coupled to a four-wheeled saloon and operated as a steam railcar.

28   As originally built with Lentz Oscillating Cam poppet valves. In March 1938 altered to piston valves and assimilated into class D49/1.

29   Built by Neath Abbey Ironworks for the Bodmin & Wadebridge Railway. Beyond recording that this locomotive had four wheels, information on its wheel arrangement seems to be lacking. See also *Elephant*.

30   Built for the South Devon Railway.

31   Built for the London & South Western Railway to Robert Urie's design. Nameplates fitted by the Southern Railway in 1925.

32   Birmingham & Gloucester and Bristol & Gloucester Railways, formed on 14 January 1845. Standard gauge. The locomotives passed to the Midland Railway on 3 August 1846, and were renumbered into Midland stock with effect from February 1847.

33   Originally no. D216 *Campania*.

34   2ft gauge.

35   Date of purchase, second-hand, for the opening of the Worcester–Abbot's Wood Junction section, the first part of the Oxford, Worcester & Wolverhampton Railway (sometimes called the Old Worse & Worse, especially by its passengers and shareholders) on 5 October 1850.

36   Name applied in August 1922.

37   2ft 6in gauge.

38   Renamed *Charles H. Newton* in September 1942, and further renamed *Sir Charles Newton* in June 1943.

39   Originally named *Lancashire Witch*; renamed in June 1936.

Name	Number	Class	Date	Railway
Caradon	–	0–6–0ST	1862	Liskeard & Looe Rly
Caravan	6	4wDM	1938	**Leighton Buzzard Rly** [40]
Carbon	12	4wPM	1930	**Leighton Buzzard Rly** [41]
Carbrook	79	Carbrook	1889	Caledonian Rly
Cardean	903	903	1906	Caledonian Rly
Cardew	195	Gladstone	7/1888	London, Brighton & South Coast Rly
Cardiff	–	0–4–2	1841	Taff Vale Rly [42]
Cardiff	3444	Bulldog	9/1903	Great Western Rly

Caledonian Railway 4–6–0 no. 903 *Cardean* approaching Carlisle with a Glasgow–Euston express on 31 July 1912. (*Photo: LCGB Ken Nunn Collection*)

Name	Number	Class	Date	Railway
Cardiff	–	0–4–0T	1916	Woolwich Arsenal [43]
Cardiff Canton	56044	56	1978	British Railways [44]
Cardiff Castle	4075	Castle	1/1924	Great Western Rly
Cardigan	18	0–6–0ST	10/1862	Cambrian Railways
Cardigan Castle	4087	Castle	6/1925	Great Western Rly
Cardrona	323	317	1861	North British Rly [45]
Cardross	167	157	6/1877	North British Rly [46]
Carew Castle	5024	Castle	4/1934	Great Western Rly
Carew D. Gilbert	184	Gladstone	10/1889	London, Brighton & South Coast Rly [47]
Carinthia CLS	40017	40	7/1959	British Railways [48]
Carisbrooke	206	Belgravia	10/1875	London, Brighton & South Coast Rly
Carisbrooke	W3	A1X	7/1880	Southern Rly [49]
Carisbrooke	W36	O2	6/1891	British Railways (Southern Region) [50]
Carisbrooke	568	E5	12/1902	London, Brighton & South Coast Rly
Carlisle	12	0–4–0	6/1837	Newcastle & Carlisle Rly [51]
Carlisle	2	2–4–0	1846	Whitehaven & Furness Junction Rly [52]
Carlisle	12	0–6–0	c.1853	Newcastle & Carlisle Rly [53]
Carlisle	2	0–6–0ST	1855	Whitehaven, Cleator & Egremont Rly [54]
Carlisle	–	0–6–0	1868	Bishops Castle Rly [55]

Name	Number	Class	Date	Railway
Carlisle	476	Abbotsford	5/1877	North British Rly
Carlisle Currock	47588	47/4	1964	British Railways
Carlton	201	Eskdale	4/1867	Stockton & Darlington Rly
Carlton No 3	–	0–4–0DM	1941	**Rutland Railway Museum**
Carmania CLS	40018	40	7/1959	British Railways [56]
Carmarthen	2	2–4–0	6/1866	Manchester & Milford Rly
Carmarthen Castle	4076	Castle	2/1924	Great Western Rly
Carnarvon	–	0–4–0ST	1915	Woolwich Arsenal [57]
Carnarvon	984	George V	6/1916	London & North Western Rly
Carnarvon	47	0–6–0ST	1934	**Bulmer Railway Centre**
Carnarvonshire	1618	2Experiment	1/1910	London & North Western Rly
Carnation	4112	Flower	6/1908	Great Western Rly
Carn Brea	–	?	c.1838	West Cornwall Rly
Carn Brea Castle	7015	Castle	7/1948	British Railways (Western Region)
Carnedd Dafydd	60009	60	2/1993	British Railways
Carnedd Llewelyn	60034	60	12/1990	British Railways
Carnegie	3	0–4–4–0DM	1954	**Bicton Woodland Rly** [58]
Carnoustie	295	165	5/1877	North British Rly [59]
Caronia CLS	40019	40	7/1959	British Railways [60]
(Carr)	872	0–6–0DH	1966	**War Department**
Carroll	–	0–4–0DM	1946	**Middleton Rly**
Carronade	–	0–4–0ST	1884	Woolwich Arsenal [61]
Carshalton	20	D1	5/1875	London, Brighton & South Coast Rly
Carteret	–	0–4–2T	1898	Jersey Eastern Rly
Castell Caerfili	37887	37/7	3/1963	British Railways [62]
Castell Caerffili	47615	47/4	1966	British Railways [63]
Castell Conwy	–	4wDM	1958	**Festiniog Rly** [64]
Castell Deudraeth	35	S/Goods	12/1861	Cambrian Railways [65]
(Castell Dinas Bran)	76079	4MT	1955	**British Railways**
(Castell Dinas Bran)	25035	25	1963	**British Railways**
Castell Ogwr	56034	56	1977	British Railways [66]
Castle	–	0–4–2	1838	Bolton & Leigh Rly
Castlecary	217	211	5/1877	North British Rly [67]
Castle Donington Power Station	56091	56	1981	British Railways
Castle Hedingham	2814	B17/2	10/1939	London & North Eastern Rly [68]
Castle Hedingham	1614	B2	11/1946	London & North Eastern Rly [69]
(Castle Hedingham)	190	J94	1/1953	**Colne Valley Rly** [70]
Castleman	159	Clyde	1/1859	London & South Western Rly
Castor	–	Priam	8/1841	Great Western Rly (bg)
Castor	199	bCrewe	3/1848	London & North Western Rly
Castor	96	Fireball	5/1848	London & South Western Rly
Castor	94	2–4–0	·1/1850	Manchester, Sheffield & Lincolnshire Rly [71]
Castor	2121	4–4–0ST	6/1865	Great Western Rly (bg) [72]
Castor	746	Samson	1/1866	London & North Western Rly
Castor	96	Clyde	8/1868	London & South Western Rly
Castor	746	Whitworth	6/1894	London & North Western Rly
Castor	606	Prince/W	1/1916	London & North Western Rly

[40] 1ft 11½in gauge.

[41] 1ft 11½in gauge.

[42] Rebuilt to 0–6–0 in 1856, and numbered 37.

[43] 18in gauge.

[44] Later renamed *Cardiff Canton Quality Assured*.

[45] Ex-Edinburgh & Glasgow Railway, absorbed by the NBR in 1865.

[46] Later renamed *Dundee*.

[47] Renamed *Stroudley* in September 1906.

[48] Originally no. D217 *Carinthia*.

[49] Formerly London, Brighton & South Coast Railway no. 77 *Wonersh*. Rebuilt to class A1x in 1911. Transferred to Isle of Wight in 1927 as no. W3, later W13 *Carisbrooke*; returned to mainland in 1949 as no. 32677.

[50] Formerly London & South Western Railway no. 198. Named by British Railways (Southern) on transfer to Isle of Wight in April 1949.

[51] Sold 1853. Replacement carried same name and number.

[52] Sold in 1854 to the Stockton & Darlington Railway, becoming their no. 79 and keeping its name.

[53] Replacement of earlier locomotive with same name and number. This engine became NER no. 461 in 1862 and was rebuilt as 0–6–0ST in 1881.

[54] Became Furness Railway no. 99.

[55] Built by Kitsons of Leeds for Thomas Nelson of Carlisle, contractor, and sold to Bishops Castle Railway in 1895.

[56] Originally no. D218 *Carmania*.

[57] 18in gauge.

[58] Originally at Woolwich Arsenal. 18in gauge.

[59] Previously named *Bellgrove*.

[60] Originally no. D219 *Caronia*.

[61] 18in gauge.

[62] Also named (on the other side) *Caerphilly Castle*.

[63] Also named (on the other side) *Caerphilly Castle*.

[64] Also named *Conway Castle*. 1ft 11½in gauge.

[65] Originally named *Countess Vane*.

[66] Also named (on the other side) *Ogmore Castle*.

[67] Ex-Edinburgh & Glasgow Railway, absorbed by NBR in 1865.

[68] Rebuilt to class B2, November 1946.

[69] Date when rebuilt from class B17.

[70] Or *Hedingham Castle*.

[71] Date to stock. Built 1849 and delivered 31 December.

[72] Built for the South Devon Railway.

Name	Number	Class	Date	Railway
Catch-Me-Who-Can	–	0–4–0	1808	Richard Trevithick [73]
Catcliffe Demon	47186	47/0	1964	British Railways
Cathays C & W Works 1846–1993	37414	37/4	1965	British Railways
Catherington	506	E4	10/1900	London, Brighton & South Coast Rly
Cathryn	–	0–4–0ST	1955	**South Yorkshire Rly**
Cato	95	2–4–0	2/1850	Manchester, Sheffield & Lincolnshire Rly
Cato	–	Caesar	3/1853	Great Western Rly (bg)
Cato	362	bCrewe	4/1855	London & North Western Rly
Cato	2118	4–4–0ST	9/1863	Great Western Rly (bg) [74]
Caucasus	107	0–6–0	7/1852	Manchester, Sheffield & Lincolnshire Rly
Cavalier	1910	Jubilee	1899	London & North Western Rly
Cavendish	111	2–2–2	10/1864	London, Brighton & South Coast Rly [75]
Cavendish	211	Richmond	3/1880	London, Brighton & South Coast Rly [76]
Cawdor Castle	148	Castle	1900	Highland Rly
Caxton Hall	5922	Hall	5/1933	Great Western Rly
Caynham Court	2935	Saint	11/1911	Great Western Rly
Cecil Raikes	5	I	1/1896	**Mersey Rly**
Cecil Rhodes	44	B4	6/1902	London, Brighton & South Coast Rly

Name	Number	Class	Date	Railway
Centaur	12	2–2–2	11/1842	Grand Junction Rly
Centaur	95	Fireball	5/1848	London & South Western Rly
Centaur	74	2–4–0	8/1849	Manchester, Sheffield & Lincolnshire Rly
Centaur	51	John Bull	4/1850	East Lancashire Rly
Centaur	12	aCrewe	11/1853	London & North Western Rly
Centaur	95	Clyde	8/1868	London & South Western Rly
Centaur	651	Craven	6/1876	Lancashire & Yorkshire Rly [78]
Centaur	773	Samson	5/1879	London & North Western Rly [79]
Centaur	773	Whitworth	7/1895	London & North Western Rly
Centaur	D808	Warship	7/1959	British Railways
Centenary	2555	A3	1/1925	London & North Eastern Rly
Centipede	372	bCrewe	9/1855	London & North Western Rly
Central Provinces	5582	Jubilee	1934	London Midland & Scottish Rly
Centurion	1911	Jubilee	1899	London & North Western Rly
Centurion	50011	50	1968	British Railways
Cerberous	18	2–2–2	1837	Grand Junction Rly
Cerberus	16	2–2–0	5/1840	Midland Counties Rly
Cerberus	–	Priam	6/1841	Great Western Rly (bg)
Cerberus	18	aCrewe	2/1844	London & North Western Rly
Cerberus	19	2–2–2	12/1845	Manchester, Sheffield & Lincolnshire Rly
Cerberus	48	Pluto	3/1850	East Lancashire Rly
Cerberus	18	bCrewe	8/1856	London & North Western Rly [80]
Cerberus	15	Tiger	12/1861	London, Chatham & Dover Rly
Cerberus	10	A	7/1864	Metropolitan Rly
Cerberus	–	Hawthorn	2/1866	Great Western Rly (bg)
Cerberus	1174	1Precursor	10/1878	London & North Western Rly
Cerberus	1111	2Precursor	3/1905	London & North Western Rly
Ceres	1390	0–6–0	1847	Great Western Rly [81]
Ceres	81	2–4–0	8/1849	Manchester, Sheffield & Lincolnshire Rly
Ceres	–	Caesar	1/1854	Great Western Rly (bg)
Ceres	4A	2–4–0	?	East & West Junction Rly
Cerestar	90132	90/1		British Railways
Cernyw	–	4wDM	1940	**Bala Lake Rly** [82]
Cesar Franck	92032	92		EPS
Ceylon	5604	Jubilee	1935	London Midland & Scottish Rly
C.G. Mott	3417	Bulldog	2/1903	Great Western Rly [83]
Chaffinch	153	bCrewe	11/1853	London & North Western Rly [84]
Chaffinch	3733	Bulldog	5/1909	Great Western Rly
Chailey	351	D1	1/1886	London, Brighton & South Coast Rly
Chaka	–	0–4–2T	1940	**North Gloucestershire Rly** [85]
Chaka's Kraal No. 6	12	0–4–2T	1940	**South Tynedale Rly** [86]
Chale	W31	O2	4/1890	Southern Rly [87]
Challenger	888	George V	7/1911	London & North Western Rly
Chaloner	1	0–4–0VB	1877	**Leighton Buzzard Rly** [88]
Chalvington	458	E3	12/1895	London, Brighton & South Coast Rly
Chambery	144	E1	4/1879	London, Brighton & South Coast Rly
Chamois	1029	B1	6/1947	London & North Eastern Rly
Chamossaire	514	A2/3	9/1946	London & North Eastern Rly
Champion	226	bCrewe	11/1848	London & North Western Rly
Champion	–	Caesar	12/1862	Great Western Rly (bg)
Champion	46	Reindeer	7/1865	London, Chatham & Dover Rly
Champion	2147	1Precursor	8/1874	London & North Western Rly
Champion	515	2Precursor	12/1904	London & North Western Rly
Champion	D809	Warship	8/1959	British Railways

Mersey Railway 0–6–4T no. 5 *Cecil Raikes*, seen at Rock Ferry on 29 October 1901. Although the negative is scratched, this is one of the few photographs to show this locomotive actually in service. (*Photo: LCGB Nunn Collection*)

Name	Number	Class	Date	Railway
Cedric	18	0–6–0	1864	Whitehaven & Furness Junction Rly [77]
Cedric	847	1Precursor	10/1878	London & North Western Rly
Cedric	1104	2Precursor	2/1905	London & North Western Rly
(Cefn Coed)	–	J94	7/1956	**Cefn Coed Colliery Museum**
Cefntilla Court	2936	Saint	11/1911	Great Western Rly
Celerity	2238	cSentinel	1929	London & North Eastern Rly
Celt	141	Saxon	10/1857	London & South Western Rly
Celtic	1311	Teutonic	6/1890	London & North Western Rly
Celtic	754	2Precursor	7/1907	London & North Western Rly
Centaur	12	2–2–2	1837	Grand Junction Rly
Centaur	32	2–2–0	5/1841	Midland Counties Rly
Centaur	–	Priam	12/1841	Great Western Rly (bg)

---

[73] Operated for a few months on a circular track at what is now Torrington Square, near where Euston station now stands. The track was enclosed, and admission to the spectacle was one shilling. This included a ride for those who dared!

[74] Formerly the South Devon Railway.

[75] Originally no. 201, then 111 *Cavendish* (November 1872), no. 197 (March 1877), no. 487 (November 1877), renamed *Chichester* December 1887.

[76] *Beaconsfield* prior to November 1885.

[77] Became Furness Railway no. 43.

[78] Formerly the East Lancashire Railway.

[79] Transferred to Engineer's Department from 1895 to May 1923, and renamed *Engineer Watford*.

[80] Later renumbered 159 and renamed *Adjutant*.

[81] Built for the West Cornwall Railway.

[82] 1ft 11½in gauge.

[83] Renamed *Charles Grey Mott* in 1904.

[84] Formerly Liverpool & Manchester Railway no. 95.

[85] 2ft gauge.

[86] 2ft gauge. This and *Chaka* above are the same locomotive: Hunslet 2075 of 1940.

[87] Formerly LSWR no. 180. Name applied by the Southern Railway on transfer to Isle of Wight, May 1927.

[88] De Winton-type locomotive, 2ft gauge.

Name	Number	Class	Date	Railway
Champion Lodge	2843	B17/1	5/1935	London & North Eastern Rly
Chancellor	154	England	9/1862	Great Western Rly
Chancellor	3	0–6–0	1865	Wrexham, Mold & Connah's Quay Rly [89]
Chandos	325	aCrewe	1/1854	London & North Western Rly
Chandos	325	2–4–0	8/1856	London & North Western Rly [90]
Chandos	325	DX	c.1860	London & North Western Rly
Chandos	1187	Precedent	9/1878	London & North Western Rly
Chandos	1187	rPrecedent	7/1896	London & North Western Rly
Channel Packet	21C1	MN	6/1941	Southern Rly [91]
Chanter	–	?	c.1838	West Cornwall Rly [92]
Chaplin	9	Venus	7/1838	London & South Western Rly
Chaplin	9	Chaplin	7/1856	London & South Western Rly
Chaplin	–	0–4–0VB	11/1865	Southampton Dock Co. [93]
Chaplin	9	Lion	12/1870	London & South Western Rly
Chapman	67	2–2–2	9/1848	Manchester, Sheffield & Lincolnshire Rly [94]
Chard	21C133	WC	7/1946	Southern Rly
Charfield Hall	6904	Hall	7/1940	Great Western Rly
Charing Cross	64	51	1903	London, Tilbury & Southend Rly
Charles	–	0–4–0ST	1882	**Penrhyn Castle Industrial Railway Museum** [95]
Charles Babbage	60054	60	9/1991	British Railways
Charles C. Macrae	314	B2	6/1895	London, Brighton & South Coast Rly [96]
Charles C. Macrae	327	L	4/1914	London, Brighton & South Coast Rly [97]

London, Brighton & South Coast Railway L class 4–6–4T no. 327 *Charles C. Macrae*, at Victoria, 19 December 1918. (*Photo: LCGB Ken Nunn Collection*)

Name	Number	Class	Date	Railway
Charles Darwin	60068	60	10/1991	British Railways
Charles Dickens	955	Precedent	2/1882	London & North Western Rly
Charles Dickens	82	George V	1/1913	London & North Western Rly
Charles Dickens	70033	Britannia	12/1952	British Railways
Charles Dickens	92022	92		British Railways
Charles Francis Brush	60098	60	12/1992	British Railways

Name	Number	Class	Date	Railway
Charles Grey Mott	3417	Bulldog	2/1903	Great Western Rly [98]
Charles H. Dent	2338	Claughton	8/1916	London & North Western Rly
Charles H. Mason	1965	Alfred	1904	London & North Western Rly
Charles H. Newton	4901	A4	6/1938	London & North Eastern Rly [99]
Charles James Lever	2443	Prince/W	3/1914	London & North Western Rly
Charles J. Cropper	1567	Claughton	10/1914	London & North Western Rly
Charles J. Hambro	2978	Saint	4/1905	Great Western Rly [100]
Charles Jones	96	G	2/1916	Metropolitan Rly [101]
Charles Kingsley	2213	Prince/W	11/1913	London & North Western Rly
Charles Lamb	2152	Prince/W	2/1914	London & North Western Rly
Charles Mortimer	3302	Badminton	7/1898	Great Western Rly [102]
Charles N. Lawrence	2046	Claughton	6/1913	London & North Western Rly
Charles Rennie Macintosh	47561	47/4	1964	British Railways
CHARLES RENNIE MACKINTOSH	86226	86/2	1965	British Railways
Charles Saunders	16	No.7	6/1894	Great Western Rly
Charles Stuart-Wortley	437	11E	11/1913	Great Central Rly [103]
Charles Wesley	43118	43	3/1979	British Railways
Charles Wolfe	892	Prince/W	10/1913	London & North Western Rly
Charlotte	–	0–6–0	?	Sirhowy Rly [104]
Charlton	–	0–4–0T	1916	Woolwich Arsenal [105]
Charlwood	266	D1	5/1882	London, Brighton & South Coast Rly
Charon	–	Priam	5/1840	Great Western Rly (bg)
Charon	65	2–2–2	7/1840	Grand Junction Rly
Charon	12	2–2–2	3/1845	Manchester, Sheffield & Lincolnshire Rly
Charon	92	Fireball	1/1848	London & South Western Rly
Charon	65	aCrewe	10/1852	London & North Western Rly
Charon	64	Charon	7/1857	East Lancashire Rly
Charon	65	DX	c.1860	London & North Western Rly
Charon	735	Samson	5/1863	London & North Western Rly
Charon	92	Lion	5/1867	London & South Western Rly
Charon	735	Whitworth	1/1892	London & North Western Rly
Charwelton	14	0–6–0ST	1917	**Kent & East Sussex Rly**
Chatham	64	Sondes	2/1858	London, Chatham & Dover Rly
Chattenden	7	0–6–0DM	1949	**Welshpool & Llanfair Light Rly** [106]
Chaucer	92045	92		British Railways
Cheam	59	A1	10/1875	London, Brighton & South Coast Rly
Cheapside	35	0–4–2	5/1841	Manchester & Leeds Rly
Cheapside	47	A1	12/1876	London, Brighton & South Coast Rly
Cheesewring	1311	0–6–0ST	1864	Great Western Rly [107]
Chelsea	14	D1	12/1874	London, Brighton & South Coast Rly
Cheltenham	4	2–2–2	9/1839	Birmingham & Gloucester Rly
Cheltenham	8	2–2–2	7/1844	Bristol & Gloucester Rly (bg) [108]
Cheltenham	925	**Schools**	4/1934	**Southern Rly**
Chepstow Castle	3314	Duke	3/1899	Great Western Rly [109]
Chepstow Castle	4077	Castle	2/1924	Great Western Rly
Cherbourg	102	E1	3/1875	London, Brighton & South Coast Rly
Cherbourg	98	B4	11/1893	London & South Western Rly
Cherwell Hall	4989	Hall	2/1931	Great Western Rly
Chesford Grange	6812	Grange	11/1936	Great Western Rly
Cheshire	1418	2Experiment	11/1909	London & North Western Rly

[89] Date of acquisition by WM&CQR. Believed to be South Hetton Railway no. 11 *Tyne*, which became London & North Western Railway no. 1377.

[90] Formerly Birkenhead, Lancashire & Cheshire Junction Railway no. 38 *Dee*.

[91] Within a week of its introduction, Cockney enginemen had renamed the engine *Flannel Jacket*!

[92] Renamed *Coryndon* in 1851.

[93] Date purchased by Southampton Dock Co. from R. Brotherhood & Co. of Chippenham. Built by Alexander Chaplin of Glasgow and used in the construction of the Bristol & South Wales Union Railway.

[94] Originally *Ariadne*. Renamed *Chapman* in 1856.

[95] 1ft 11½in gauge.

[96] Rebuilt to class B2x, April 1911.

[97] Rebuilt to class N15x as no. 3327 *Trevithick* by Southern Railway, April 1935.

[98] Originally named *C.G. Mott*. Renamed in 1904.

[99] Originally named *Capercailie*. Renamed *Charles H. Newton* in September 1942, and further renamed *Sir Charles Newton* in June 1943.

[100] Originally named *Kirkland*. Renamed *Charles J. Hambro* in May 1935.

[101] Sold to the LNER in November 1937, becoming their no. 6156 (nameless) of class M2.

[102] Originally named *Mortimer*. Renamed in August 1904.

[103] Renamed *Prince George* in 1920.

[104] Built some time between 1832 and 1853.

[105] 18in gauge.

[106] 2ft 6in gauge.

[107] Originally the Liskeard & Looe Railway.

[108] In August 1856 this locomotive was sold to Thomas Brassey for working the North Devon Railway, a broad gauge concern which later passed to the London & South Western Railway. There it is thought to have become the NDR's *Tite*.

[109] Nameplate removed in May 1923 to avoid confusion with Castle class engine.

Name	Number	Class	Date	Railway	Name	Number	Class	Date	Railway
Cheshire	2753	D49/1	2/1929	London & North Eastern Rly	C.I.T. 75th Anniversary	86210	86/2	1965	British Railways
Chessington	495	E4	11/1899	London, Brighton & South Coast Rly	City Link	–	0–4–0ST	1949	Yorkshire Dales Rly
Chester	12	0–6–0	3/1849	Birkenhead, Lancashire & Cheshire Junction Rly [110]	City of Aberdeen	–	0–4–0ST	1887	Bo'ness & Kinneil Rly
Chester	342	0–4–2ST	10/1856	Great Western Rly [111]	City of Bath	3433	City	3/1903	Great Western Rly
Chester	–	Swindon	3/1866	Great Western Rly (bg)	City of Birmingham	3434	City	5/1903	Great Western Rly
Chester Castle	7016	Castle	8/1948	British Railways (Western Region)	City of Birmingham	6235	Duchess	7/1939	London Midland & Scottish Rly
Chevalier	–	0–4–0ST	1885	Campbeltown & Machrihanish Rly [112]	City of Birmingham	87009	87/0	1973	British Railways
Chevy Chase	43302	Clayton	1928	London & North Eastern Rly	City of Bradford	6236	Duchess	7/1939	London Midland & Scottish Rly
Chicheley Hall	6906	Hall	11/1940	Great Western Rly	City of Bradford	43085	43	3/1978	British Railways
Chichester	–	0–4–2ST	1847	West Sussex Light Rly [113]	City of Bristol	3435	City	5/1903	Great Western Rly
Chichester	172	Chichester	3/1864	London, Brighton & South Coast Rly	City of Bristol	6237	Duchess	8/1939	London Midland & Scottish Rly
Chichester	487	2–2–2	10/1864	London, Brighton & South Coast Rly [114]	City of Bristol	43126	43	5/1979	British Railways
Chichester	–	0–6–0ST	1871	West Sussex Light Rly [115]	City of Carlisle	2	Dreadnought	1886	London & North Western Rly
Chichester	386	D3	12/1893	London, Brighton & South Coast Rly	City of Carlisle	565	2Experiment	1/1906	London & North Western Rly
Chiddingfold	496	E4	12/1899	London, Brighton & South Coast Rly	City of Carlisle	6238	Duchess	9/1939	London Midland & Scottish Rly
Childrey Manor	7809	Manor	4/1938	Great Western Rly	City of Carlisle	86204	86/2	1965	British Railways
Chilgrove	410	E6	3/1905	London, Brighton & South Coast Rly	City of Chester	437	Dreadnought	1886	London & North Western Rly
Chillington	243	bCrewe	5/1849	London & North Western Rly	City of Chester	3436	City	5/1903	Great Western Rly
Chillington	2188	Precedent	4/1875	London & North Western Rly	City of Chester	893	2Experiment	1/1906	London & North Western Rly
Chillington	2188	rPrecedent	2/1895	London & North Western Rly	City of Chester	426	1	3/1913	Great Central Rly
Chillington	2626	2Experiment	2/1909	London & North Western Rly	City of Chester	6239	Duchess	9/1939	London Midland & Scottish Rly
Chilmark	–	4wDM	1939	Bala Lake Rly [116]	City of Chester	86208	86/2	1966	British Railways
Chiltington	558	E4	10/1901	London, Brighton & South Coast Rly	City of Chicago	366	1Experiment	1884	London & North Western Rly
Chilworth	504	E4	9/1900	London, Brighton & South Coast Rly	City of Coventry	6240	Duchess	3/1940	London Midland & Scottish Rly
Chimborazo	109	0–6–0	8/1852	Manchester, Sheffield & Lincolnshire Rly	City of Coventry	86209	86/2	1965	British Railways
Chimera	177	bCrewe	8/1848	London & North Western Rly	City of Discovery	43041	43	12/1976	British Railways
Chimera	177	DX	c.1860	London & North Western Rly	City of Dublin	640	Dreadnought	1888	London & North Western Rly
Chimera	733	Samson	5/1863	London & North Western Rly	City of Dublin	1074	2Experiment	1/1906	London & North Western Rly
Chimera	733	Whitworth	1/1890	London & North Western Rly	City of Durham	2403	2400	3/1924	London & North Eastern Rly
Chipstead	265	D1	5/1882	London, Brighton & South Coast Rly	City of Edinburgh	1353	Dreadnought	1886	London & North Western Rly
Chirk Castle	5025	Castle	4/1934	Great Western Rly	City of Edinburgh	1357	2Experiment	1/1906	London & North Western Rly
Chiru	1034	B1	10/1947	London & North Eastern Rly	City of Edinburgh	6241	Duchess	4/1940	London Midland & Scottish Rly
Chislet	9	0–6–0ST	1951	Buckinghamshire Railway Centre	City of Edinburgh	86210	86/2	1965	British Railways
Chittagong	2220	0–4–0D	1945	Longmoor Military Rly [117]	City of Edinburgh	43065	43	10/1977	British Railways
Chittagong	70272	0–6–0DE	3/1945	Longmoor Military Rly [118]	City of Exeter	3442	City	5/1903	Great Western Rly
"Chittaprat"	–	0–4–0	1825	Stockton & Darlington Rly [119]	City of Germiston	3052	15F	1944	South African Railways [121]
(Chloe)	18	0–4–0ST	1863	Furness Rly	City of Glasgow	1370	Dreadnought	1886	London & North Western Rly
Chough	3275	Duke	11/1896	Great Western Rly	City of Glasgow	1669	2Experiment	1/1906	London & North Western Rly
(Christine)	D4092	10	1962	British Railways	City of Glasgow	6242	Duchess	5/1940	London Midland & Scottish Rly
Christopher Wren	60003	60	1/1992	British Railways	City of Glasgow	87006	87/0	1973	British Railways
Christ's Hospital	913	Schools	12/1932	Southern Rly	City of Gloucester	3437	City	5/1903	Great Western Rly
Chronus	–	Caesar	9/1861	Great Western Rly (bg)	City of Hereford	3438	City	5/1903	Great Western Rly
Churchill	2984	Saint	7/1905	Great Western Rly [120]	City of Hereford	6255	Duchess	10/1946	London Midland & Scottish Rly
Churchtown	12	0–4–0T	1884	West Lancashire Rly	City of Hereford	09015	09	1961	British Railways
Cicero	–	Caesar	7/1853	Great Western Rly (bg)	City of Hereford	47575	47/4	1964	British Railways
Cicero	2797	A3	6/1930	London & North Eastern Rly	City of Kingston-upon-Hull	2401	2400	12/1922	North Eastern Rly [122]
(Cider Queen)	D2758	05	1955	British Railways	City of Kingston upon Hull	43116	43	3/1979	British Railways
Cilgwyn	–	4wDM	1936	Teifi Valley Rly	City of Lancaster	6243	Duchess	6/1940	London Midland & Scottish Rly
Cineraria	4107	Flower	6/1908	Great Western Rly	City of Lancaster	86205	86/2	1965	British Railways
Circe	165	Undine	12/1859	London & South Western Rly	City of Leeds	6244	Duchess	7/1940	London Midland & Scottish Rly [123]
Cir Mhor	60030	60	11/1990	British Railways					

---

[110] Later renamed *Gnome* and passed to the Great Western Railway.

[111] Built for the Commissioner of Chester General station, jointly owned by the Great Western, London & North Western, and Birkenhead Railways. Taken over by GWR in April 1865, numbered 342 and name removed. In February 1881 it was altered to 0–4–0ST, further rebuilt in August 1897 and finally withdrawn in August 1931.

[112] Later altered to 0–4–2ST. 2ft 3in gauge.

[113] Built as an 0–6–0ST. Said to have been in service with the Great Western, and then in industrial service.

[114] Originally no. 201, then 111 *Cavendish* (November 1872), no. 197 (March 1877), no. 487 (November 1877), renamed *Chichester* (December 1887).

[115] Obtained as a replacement for the first *Chichester*. It was originally built as an 0–4–0ST on the 3ft 6in gauge, and was purchased by the Plymouth, Devonport & South Western Junction Railway. They rebuilt it as a standard gauge 0–4–2ST and named it *Kelly*. They sold it to the West Sussex Railway in 1912.

[116] 1ft 11½in gauge.

[117] Originally named *Basra*.

[118] Later renamed *Basra* and then *Eisenhower*.

[119] Built by Robert Wilson and tried on S&DR; purchased and immediately dismantled. Boiler shell, and possibly wheels and other components, incorporated in no. 5 *Royal George*.

[120] Renamed *Viscount Churchill* in 1906, and then *Guy Mannering* in 1907.

[121] South African Railways 15F class 4–8–2, 3ft 6in gauge, preserved at East Somerset Railway.

[122] Name applied by the LNER.

[123] Renamed *King George VI* in April 1941.

Name	Number	Class	Date	Railway
City of Leeds	6248	Duchess	10/1943	London Midland & Scottish Rly
City of Leicester	6252	Duchess	6/1944	London Midland & Scottish Rly
City of Lichfield	641	Dreadnought	1888	London & North Western Rly
City of Lichfield	165	2Experiment	2/1906	London & North Western Rly
City of Lichfield	6250	Duchess	5/1944	London Midland & Scottish Rly
City of Lichfield	86207	86/2	1965	British Railways
City of Lincoln	424	1	1/1913	Great Central Rly
City of Lincoln	43061	43	8/1977	British Railways
City of Liverpool	410	Dreadnought	1886	London & North Western Rly
City of Liverpool	828	2Experiment	2/1906	London & North Western Rly
City of Liverpool	428	1	12/1913	Great Central Rly
City of Liverpool	6247	Duchess	9/1943	London Midland & Scottish Rly
City of Liverpool	87008	87/0	1973	British Railways
City of London	639	Dreadnought	1888	London & North Western Rly
City of London	3439	City	5/1903	Great Western Rly
City of London	978	2Experiment	2/1906	London & North Western Rly
City of London	427	1	3/1913	Great Central Rly
City of London	2870	B17/5	5/1937	London & North Eastern Rly [124]
City of London	6245	Duchess	6/1943	London Midland & Scottish Rly
City of London	87005	87/0	1973	British Railways
City of Manchester	173	Dreadnought	1886	London & North Western Rly
City of Manchester	1405	2Experiment	2/1906	London & North Western Rly
City of Manchester	425	1	2/1913	Great Central Rly
City of Manchester	6246	Duchess	8/1943	London Midland & Scottish Rly
City of Manchester	87007	87/0	1973	British Railways
City of Newcastle	2400	2400	12/1922	North Eastern Rly [125]
City of Newcastle-upon-Tyne	43113	43	2/1979	British Railways

North Eastern Railway 4–6–2 no. 2400, at York on 31 July 1926, in LNER livery and named *City of Newcastle*. (*Photo: LCGB Ken Nunn Collection*)

Name	Number	Class	Date	Railway
City of New York	637	Dreadnought	1888	London & North Western Rly
City of Norwich	3	2–2–2	5/1846	Eastern Union Rly
City of Nottingham	6251	Duchess	6/1944	London Midland & Scottish Rly
City of Oxford	47627	47/4	1965	British Railways
City of Paris	638	Dreadnought	1888	London & North Western Rly
City of Paris	1575	2Experiment	2/1906	London & North Western Rly
(City of Peterborough)	**73050**	**5MT**	**6/1954**	**British Railways**
City of Peterborough	43052	43	4/1977	British Railways
City of Plymouth	43188	43	4/1982	British Railways
City of Portsmouth	73130	73/1	1966	British Railways
City of Ripon	2404	2400	3/1924	London & North Eastern Rly
City of St. Albans	6253	Duchess	9/1946	London Midland & Scottish Rly
City of Salford	46257	Duchess	5/1948	British Railways

Name	Number	Class	Date	Railway
City of Sheffield	6249	Duchess	4/1944	London Midland & Scottish Rly
City of Stoke-on-Trent	6254	Duchess	9/1946	London Midland & Scottish Rly
City of Stoke-on-Trent	86206	86/2	1965	British Railways
City of Swansea	43019	43	7/1976	British Railways [126]
City of Truro	**3440**	**City**	**5/1903**	**Great Western Rly**
City of Truro	47625	47/4	1965	British Railways
City of Truro	43192	43	5/1982	British Railways
City of Wells	**34092**	**WC**	**9/1949**	**British Railways (Southern Region) [127]**
City of Westminster	43026	43	8/1976	British Railways
City of Winchester	3441	City	5/1903	Great Western Rly
City of Winchester	73129	73/1	1966	British Railways
City of Worcester	37114	37/0	1963	British Railways
City of York	2402	2400	3/1924	London & North Eastern Rly
City of York	43064	43	10/1977	British Railways
City University	86217	86/2	1965	British Railways

The preserved Great Western Railway 4–4–0 no. 3440 *City of Truro*, pictured at York in the 1970s with an excursion for Scarborough. (*Photo: Author*)

Name	Number	Class	Date	Railway
Civil Link	47333	47/3	1965	British Railways
Civil Service Rifleman	6163	Royal Scot	9/1930	London Midland & Scottish Rly
C.J. Bowen Cooke	2059	Claughton	5/1920	London & North Western Rly
Clachnacuddin	46	Glenbarry	6/1864	Highland Rly [128]
Clachnacuddin	71	Duke	12/1883	Highland Rly
Clackmannan	111	72	9/1880	North British Rly
Clan Buchanan	72000	Clan	12/1951	British Railways
Clan Cameron	57	Clan	1918	Highland Rly
Clan Cameron	72001	Clan	12/1951	British Railways
Clan Campbell	49	Clan	1918	Highland Rly
Clan Campbell	72002	Clan	1/1952	British Railways
Clan Chattan	54	Clan	1918	Highland Rly
Clan Fraser	51	Clan	1918	Highland Rly
Clan Fraser	72003	Clan	1/1952	British Railways
Clan Line	**35028**	**MN**	**12/1948**	**British Railways (Southern Region)**
Clan Macdonald	72004	Clan	2/1952	British Railways
Clan Macgregor	72005	Clan	2/1952	British Railways
Clan Mackenzie	56	Clan	1918	Highland Rly
Clan Mackenzie	72006	Clan	2/1952	British Railways
Clan Mackinnon	55	Clan	1918	Highland Rly
Clan Mackintosh	72007	Clan	2/1952	British Railways
Clan Macleod	72008	Clan	2/1952	British Railways
Clan Munro	52	Clan	1918	Highland Rly
Clanricarde	235	aCrewe	2/1849	London & North Western Rly
Clanricarde	1986	2Experiment	9/1906	London & North Western Rly
Clan Stewart	53	Clan	1918	Highland Rly
Clan Stewart	72009	Clan	3/1952	British Railways

---

[124] Originally *Manchester City*. Renamed *Tottenham Hotspur* (May 1937), and *City of London* and streamlined for working the 'East Anglian' express (September 1937).

[125] Name applied by the London & North Eastern Railway.

[126] Also named (on the other side) *Dinas Abertawe*.

[127] Originally named *Wells*.

[128] Altered from 2–2–2 to 2–4–0 in May 1880, and renamed *Kingussie* in 1883.

Name	Number	Class	Date	Railway		Name	Number	Class	Date	Railway
Clapham	68	A1	8/1874	London, Brighton & South Coast Rly		Clothes Show Live	86222	86/2	1965	British Railways
Clarence	–	0–4–2?	1832	Bolton & Leigh Rly		Clotho	–	2–4–0	1900	Woolwich Arsenal [144]
Claroncc	14	0–4–0	7/1840	Manchester & Leeds Rly		Clougha	–	2–2–0	6/1840	North Western Rly
Clarence	08602	08	1959	British Railways		Clovelly	21C137	rWC	8/1946	Southern Rly
(Clarence)	**08785**	**08**	**1960**	**British Railways**		Clumber	2820	B17/1	11/1930	London & North Eastern Rly
Clarendon	264	bCrewe	5/1850	London & North Western Rly [129]		**Clun Castle**	**7029**	**Castle**	**5/1950**	**British Railways (Western Region)**
Clarendon	69	Priam	11/1850	Stockton & Darlington Rly		Cluny	55	Glenbarry	10/1864	Highland Rly [145]
Clarendon	787	Newton	8/1873	London & North Western Rly		Cluny	32	Glenbarry	10/1868	Highland Rly [146]
Clarendon	787	rPrecedent	4/1893	London & North Western Rly		Cluny Castle	28	Castle	1913	Highland Rly
Clarkston	67	72	1/1883	North British Rly		Clwyd	–	0–4–2	1858	Vale of Clwyd Rly
Claud Hamilton	1900	D16	1900	Great Eastern Rly		**Clwyd**	**1**	**4wDM**	**1951**	**West Lancashire Light Rly [147]**
Claughton Hall	6905	Hall	7/1940	Great Western Rly		Clyde	26	0–4–2	1850	St Helens Canal & Rly
Clausentum	457	0–4–0ST	7/1890	London & South Western Rly [130]		Clyde	–	Caesar	8/1858	Great Western Rly (bg)
Claverhouse	415	Scott	6/1914	North British Rly		Clyde	157	Clyde	1/1859	London & South Western Rly
Clayton	396	D3	5/1896	London, Brighton & South Coast Rly [131]		Clyde	833	Problem	c.1860	London & North Western Rly
Cleator	8	0–6–0ST	1863	Whitehaven, Cleator & Egremont Rly [132]		Clyde	88	Scotchmen	8/1866	London, Chatham & Dover Rly
Cleckheaton	48	0–4–0	12/1845	Manchester & Leeds Rly		Clyde	1364	2Precursor	7/1907	London & North Western Rly
Cleeve Abbey	4071	Saint	2/1923	Great Western Rly [133]		Clydebank	313	165	1/1878	North British Rly [148]
Cleeve Abbey	5091	Castle	12/1938	Great Western Rly [134]		Clydebank	294	72	1882	North British Rly
Cleeve Grange	6850	Grange	10/1937	Great Western Rly		Clydebridge	37099	37/0	1962	British Railways
Cleobury	–	0–6–0ST	1908	Cleobury Mortimer & Ditton Priors Light Rly [135]		Clyde Iron	37137	37/0	1963	British Railways
Clevedon	2	2–2–2T	1857	Weston, Clevedon & Portishead Rly [136]		Clydesdale	37	cSentinel	1929	London & North Eastern Rly
Clevedon	1	2–4–0T	1879	Weston, Clevedon & Portishead Rly [137]		Clydesdale	37088	37/0	1963	British Railways
Clevedon	–	0–6–0T	?	Weston, Clevedon & Portishead Rly [138]		**Clydesmill**	**3**	**0–4–0ST**	**1928**	**Bo'ness & Kinneil Rly**
Clevedon Court	2937	Saint	12/1911	Great Western Rly		**Cnicht**	**36**	**4wDM**	**1941**	**Welsh Highland Rly [149]**
Cleveland	60	Cleveland	11/1848	Stockton & Darlington Rly		Coalbrookvale	–	0–6–0ST	1850	Monmouthshire Railway & Canal Co.
Cleveland	21	0–6–0	1861	Stockton & Darlington Rly [139]		Coal Merchants' Association of Scotland	37235	37/0	1964	British Railways
Cleveland	219	Gladstone	11/1885	London, Brighton & South Coast Rly		**(Coal Products)**	**168**	**J94**	**8/1943**	**War Department**
Cleveland	2133	cSentinel	1928	London & North Eastern Rly		**Coal Products No 6**	**–**	**0–6–0ST**	**1943**	**Rutland Railway Museum**
(Cleveland)	**07011**	**07**	**1962**	**British Railways**		Coatbridge	165	165	11/1875	North British Rly [150]
Cleveland Potash	20122	20	1962	British Railways		Coatbridge	240	165	1/1878	North British Rly [151]
Clifford Castle	5046	Castle	4/1936	Great Western Rly [140]		Coatbridge	74	72	5/1882	North British Rly [152]
Clifford Castle	5071	Castle	6/1938	Great Western Rly [141]		Cobham	162	Cobham	10/1879	Great Western Rly
Clifford Castle	5098	Castle	5/1946	Great Western Rly		Cobham Hall	4991	Hall	2/1931	Great Western Rly
Clifton	15	0–6–0	10/1846	Taff Vale Rly		Cobra RAILFREIGHT	47297	47/0	1966	British Railways
Clifton	168	Panther	12/1862	Stockton & Darlington Rly		Cockade	D810	Warship	9/1959	British Railways
Clifton	927	Schools	6/1934	Southern Rly		Cocker	2	–	1847	Cockermouth & Workington Rly
Clifton Hall	4990	Hall	2/1931	Great Western Rly		Cocker	9	0–4–2	1847	Maryport & Carlisle Rly [153]
Cliftonville	166	E3	11/1894	London, Brighton & South Coast Rly		Cockington Manor	7806	Manor	3/1938	Great Western Rly
Clinton	**4**	**0–4–0DM**	**1941**	**Bicton Woodland Rly [142]**		Cochrane	5656	Jubilee	1934	London Midland & Scottish Rly
Clio	53	2–2–2	1838	Grand Junction Rly		**Cochrane**	**–**	**0–4–0ST**	**1948**	**Tanfield Rly**
Clio	6	2–2–2	4/1842	Manchester, Sheffield & Lincolnshire Rly		Cock o' the North	903	I	8/1911	North British Rly [154]
Clio	53	bCrewe	10/1848	London & North Western Rly		Cock o'the North	2001	P2	5/1934	London & North Eastern Rly
Clio	3	Clio	1/1867	East Lancashire Rly		Cock o'the North	501	A2/2	9/1944	London & North Eastern Rly [155]
Clio	2230	Claughton	5/1917	London & North Western Rly		Cock o'the North	87022	87/0	1974	British Railways
Clive	723	Problem	c.1860	London & North Western Rly		Codrington	5676	Jubilee	1935	London Midland & Scottish Rly
Clive	1	2Precursor	6/1907	London & North Western Rly		Coedbach	37698	37/5	1964	British Railways
Clive of India	70040	Britannia	3/1953	British Railways		Coehorn	–	0–4–0ST	3/1878	Woolwich Arsenal [156]
Cloister	**3**	**0–4–0ST**	**1891**	**Hampshire Narrow Gauge Society [143]**		Coeur de Lion	–	Abbot	5/1855	Great Western Rly (bg)
						Coeur-de-Lion	70007	Britannia	4/1951	British Railways
						Coeur de Lion	87012	87/0	1974	British Railways
						"Coffee Pot"	126	0–4–0VB	9/1850	South Eastern Rly

[129] Charged to Current Account as *Tiger*.

[130] Ex-Southampton Docks Co., purchased by LSWR in December 1891.

[131] Rebuilt to class D3x, April 1909.

[132] Became Furness Railway no. 104.

[133] Rebuilt to Castle class, December 1938.

[134] Rebuilt from Star class no. 4071.

[135] Became GWR no. 28. Rebuilt to pannier tank in 1931.

[136] Formerly Furness Railway no. 12A.

[137] Formerly *General Don* of the Jersey Railway.

[138] Purchased 1897.

[139] Ex-West Hartlepool Harbour & Railway, absorbed by the North Eastern Railway in 1865.

[140] Renamed *Earl Cawdor* in August 1937.

[141] Renamed *Spitfire* in September 1940.

[142] 18in gauge.

[143] 2ft gauge.

[144] Paraffin/mechanical. 18in gauge.

[145] Renamed *Sutherland* in 1874, and altered from 2–2–2 to 2–4–0 in September 1874. Renamed *Invergordon* in 1884.

[146] Originally named *Sutherland*. Renamed *Cluny* in 1874, and altered from 2–2–2 to 2–4–0 in May 1884.

[147] 1ft 11½in gauge.

[148] Later renamed *Musselburgh*.

[149] 1ft 11½in gauge.

[150] Originally named *Boness*. There is some doubt as to whether the name *Coatbridge* was in fact ever carried.

[151] Later renamed *Polton*.

[152] Later renamed *Whiteinch* for a while.

[153] There is some doubt as to whether the engine ever actually carried this name. There is a possibility that this locomotive and the preceding entry are one and the same, but confirmation is not to hand.

[154] As LNER no. 9903, was renamed *Aberdonian* to make way for Gresley's P2 class locomotive no. 2001. The original *Aberdonian* had previously been scrapped.

[155] Rebuild of 2001 above.

[156] 18in gauge.

Name	Number	Class	Date	Railway
(Coffee Pot)	–	0–4–0VB	**1871**	**Beamish Museum** [157]
Cogan Hall	5952	Hall	**12/1935**	**Great Western Rly**
Coity Castle	5035	Castle	5/1935	Great Western Rly
Colchester	1	2–2–2	5/1846	Eastern Union Rly
Colchester	–	0–4–0T	1916	Woolwich Arsenal [158]
Coldstreamer	4844	V2	5/1939	London & North Eastern Rly
Coldstream Guardsman	6114	Royal Scot	9/1927	London Midland & Scottish Rly
Coldstream Guardsman	D64	Peak	4/1962	British Railways
Collingwood	31	0–6–0	9/1848	Newcastle & Carlisle Rly [159]
Collingwood	1935	Jubilee	1900	London & North Western Rly
Collingwood	5645	Jubilee	1934	London Midland & Scottish Rly
Collingwood	50005	50	1968	British Railways
Colne	148	Tweed	12/1858	London & South Western Rly
Colne	–	2–4–0T	?	Colne Valley & Halstead Rly [160]

London & North Eastern Railway P2 class 2–8–2 *Cock o' the North*, at King's Cross on 18 May 1935. (*Photo: LCGB Ken Nunn Collection*)

Name	Number	Class	Date	Railway
Colne	–	2–4–0T	1862	Colne Valley & Halstead Rly
Colne	148	2–4–0	9/1864	London & South Western Rly [161]
Colne	3	2–4–2T	1887	Colne Valley & Halstead Rly
Colombia	8	4–2–0	3/1839	Birmingham & Gloucester Rly [162]
Colombo	3398	Atbara	8/1901	Great Western Rly
Colombo	2501	A3	7/1934	London & North Eastern Rly
Colonel	188	aCrewe	12/1847	London & North Western Rly
Colonel Bill Cockburn CBE TD	90020	90/0	1/1989	British Railways
Colonel Edgcumbe	3375	Atbara	4/1900	Great Western Rly [163]
Colonel Gardiner	2675	D11/2	8/1924	London & North Eastern Rly
Colonel Lockwood	1429	Claughton	9/1914	London & North Western Rly
(Colonel Tomline)	D3489	10	**1957**	**British Railways**
Colorado	2748	A3	12/1928	London & North Eastern Rly
Colossus	66	0–4–2	1/1841	Grand Junction Rly
Colossus	66	bCrewe	10/1851	London & North Western Rly
Colossus	108	0–6–0	7/1852	Manchester, Sheffield & Lincolnshire Rly

Name	Number	Class	Date	Railway
Colossus	223	DFG	4/1866	London & South Western Rly
Colossus	1154	1Precursor	9/1874	London & North Western Rly
Colossus	1912	Jubilee	1899	London & North Western Rly
Colossus	–	4–6–2	**1915**	**Ravenglass & Eskdale Rly** [164]
Colossus	5702	Jubilee	1936	London Midland & Scottish Rly
Colossus	47564	47/4	1964	British Railways
Colossus	D1672	47/0	1965	British Railways
Colsterworth	1382	0–6–0DE	**1962**	**Rutland Railway Museum**
Colston Hall	5923	Hall	5/1933	Great Western Rly
Columbia	8	4–2–0	11/1839	Birmingham & Gloucester Rly [165]
Columbia	3472	Bulldog	4/1904	Great Western Rly
Columbine	49	2–2–2	1838	Grand Junction Rly
Columbine	49	aCrewe	7/1845	**London & North Western Rly** [166]
Columbine	850	L/Bloomer	1851	London & North Western Rly
Columbus	1530	Newton	11/1866	London & North Western Rly
Columbus	1530	rPrecedent	11/1888	London & North Western Rly
Columbus	1019	Claughton	5/1917	London & North Western Rly
Colville	81	Clyde Bogie	7/1886	Highland Rly
Colworth	406	E5	11/1904	London, Brighton & South Coast Rly
Colwyn	45	0–6–0ST	**1933**	**Northampton & Lamport Rly**
Colwyn Bay	226	George V	6/1916	London & North Western Rly
Colwyn Bay	5525	Patriot	3/1933	London Midland & Scottish Rly [167]
Combe Martin	21C143	WC	10/1946	Southern Rly
Combermere	379	bCrewe	11/1855	London & North Western Rly [168]
Combermere	563	Problem	c.1860	London & North Western Rly
Combermere	902	2Experiment	9/1907	London & North Western Rly
Comet	5	0–2–2	1830	Liverpool & Manchester Rly
Comet	–	0–4–0	5/1832	Leicester & Swannington Rly [169]
Comet	2	0–4–0	1835	Newcastle & Carlisle Rly
Comet	55	2–2–2	1837	Liverpool & Manchester Rly
Comet	36	Vivid	7/1839	London & South Western Rly
Comet	–	Wolf	10/1840	Great Western Rly (bg)
Comet	52	2–2–2	12/1840	Stockton & Darlington Rly
Comet	166	aCrewe	5/1847	London & North Western Rly
Comet	2096	4–4–0ST	10/1851	Great Western Rly (bg) [170]
Comet	36	2Sussex	6/1852	London & South Western Rly
Comet	45	0–6–0	1858	Taff Vale Rly
Comet	36	Standard	2/1872	London & South Western Rly
Comet	–	0–4–0ST	1883	Chatham Dockyard [171]
Comet	3315	Duke	3/1899	Great Western Rly
Comet	6129	Royal Scot	8/1927	London Midland & Scottish Rly [172]
Comet	2110	Clayton	1928	London & North Eastern Rly
Comet	5735	Jubilee	1936	London Midland & Scottish Rly
Commander B	–	0–4–0ST	**1899**	**Hollycombe Steam Collection**
Commerce	35	Commerce	1/1847	Stockton & Darlington Rly
Commerce	43301	cSentinel	1928	London & North Eastern Rly
Commercial Road	22	Class 1	1884	London, Tilbury & Southend Rly
Commercial Road	42	37	1897	London, Tilbury & Southend Rly
Commodore	4	2–2–2	6/1841	Chester & Birkenhead Rly
Commodore	175	bCrewe	11/1847	London & North Western Rly
Commodore	478	Precedent	11/1880	London & North Western Rly
Commodore	478	rPrecedent	8/1896	London & North Western Rly
Commonwealth	1966	Alfred	1904	London & North Western Rly
XIII Commonwealth Games Scotland 1986	43088	43	5/1978	British Railways

---

[157] Formerly at Dorking Greystone Co.'s works at Betchworth, Surrey. Built by Head Wrightson, 1871.

[158] 18in gauge.

[159] Became North Eastern Railway no. 479 in 1862. Rebuilt as 0–6–0ST in 1873.

[160] Hired in 1860 from Monro, the contractor who built the line.

[161] Formerly the Somerset & Dorset Railway. Transferred to Engineer's Department in April 1884, where it became no. 3 *Stephenson*.

[162] Later went to the Taff Vale Railway.

[163] Said to have been named *Conqueror* until May 1900. Named *Edgcumbe* until 1903.

[164] From Capt J.E.P. Howey's estate railway at Staughton Manor. Formerly named *John Anthony*. Chassis re-used to construct the first *River Mite*. 15in gauge.

[165] Later sold to the Aberdare Railway, and thence to the Taff Vale Railway. It was one of three purchased from the Birmingham & Gloucester Railway. The others were *W.S. Moorsom* and *Gloucester*.

[166] Later named *Engineer Bangor*. Preserved as no. 1868, without name.

[167] Originally named *E. Tootal Broadhurst*; renamed *Colwyn Bay* in late 1937 and rebuilt with taper boiler in August 1948.

[168] Later renumbered 149 and renamed *Petrel*.

[169] Later sold to the Birmingham & Gloucester Railway, becoming their no. 22 *Leicester*.

[170] Built for South Devon Railway.

[171] 18in gauge.

[172] Renamed *The Scottish Horse* in January 1936.

Name	Number	Class	Date	Railway
Commonwealth Institute	91017	91	7/1990	British Railways
Commonwealth of Australia	4491	A4	6/1937	London & North Eastern Rly
Como	308	Lyons	7/1883	London, Brighton & South Coast Rly
Competitor	33	0–4–2	4/1841	Manchester & Leeds Rly
Competitor	12	2–2–2WT	10/1851	North Western Rly
Compound	300	1Experiment	1882	London & North Western Rly
Compton Castle	5047	Castle	4/1936	Great Western Rly [173]
Compton Castle	5072	Castle	6/1938	Great Western Rly [174]
Compton Castle	5099	Castle	5/1946	Great Western Rly
Compton Manor	7807	Manor	3/1938	Great Western Rly
Comus	74	Aeolus	4/1861	London, Chatham & Dover Rly
Concrete Bob	37425	37/4	1965	British Railways [175]
Condor	158	bCrewe	3/1853	London & North Western Rly [176]
Condor	–	0–6–0ST	4/1866	Swansea Vale Rly
Condor	868	Precedent	6/1877	London & North Western Rly
Condor	868	rPrecedent	11/1896	London & North Western Rly
Condor	867	Prince/W	1/1916	London & North Western Rly
Condor	6145	Royal Scot	10/1927	London Midland & Scottish Rly [177]
Condover Hall	4915	Hall	2/1929	Great Western Rly
Condover Hall	47784	47/7		British Railways
Conductor	253	0–4–0DH	1978	Bicester Military Rly
Coney Hall	7920	M/Hall	9/1950	British Railways (Western Region)
Confederation of British Industry	47675	47/4	10/1965	British Railways
Conidae	37706	37/7	6/1961	British Railways
Connaught	335	G	10/1881	London, Brighton & South Coast Rly
Connaught	9	I	7/1886	Mersey Rly
Connaught	5742	Jubilee	1936	London Midland & Scottish Rly
Conon	27	S/Goods	11/1863	Highland Rly
Conqueror	132	Canute	3/1856	London & South Western Rly
Conqueror	3375	Atbara	4/1900	Great Western Rly [178]
Conqueror	1704	Prince/W	11/1911	London & North Western Rly
Conqueror	5701	Jubilee	1936	London Midland & Scottish Rly
Conqueror	50009	50	1968	British Railways
Conquest	D603	Warship	11/1958	British Railways
Conside	28	0–6–0	1845	Stockton & Darlington Rly [179]
Constance	817	Samson	1/1866	London & North Western Rly
Constance	817	Whitworth	4/1893	London & North Western Rly
Constantine	132	Adrian	10/1886	London, Chatham & Dover Rly
Constantine	71443	J94	4/1945	Longmoor Military Rly [180]
Contractor	175	0–6–0	10/1864	Stockton & Darlington Rly
Conway	207	bCrewe	5/1848	London & North Western Rly
Conway	1086	George V	7/1916	London & North Western Rly
Conway Castle	–	4wDM	**1958**	**Festiniog Rly** [181]
Conyngham Hall	6937	Hall	7/1942	Great Western Rly [182]
Cook	1529	Newton	11/1866	London & North Western Rly
Cook	1529	rPrecedent	9/1889	London & North Western Rly
Cook & Nuttal	1	0–4–0ST	**1947**	**Steamtown Carnforth**
Cookham Manor	7808	Manor	**3/1938**	**Great Western Rly**
Cookie	08616	08	1959	British Railways

Name	Number	Class	Date	Railway
Cooksbridge	384	D3	12/1893	London, Brighton & South Coast Rly
"Coppernob"	3	A2	**1846**	**Furness Rly**
Copthorne	574	E5	3/1903	London, Brighton & South Coast Rly
Coptic	1307	Teutonic	6/1890	London & North Western Rly
Coptic	723	2Precursor	2/1906	London & North Western Rly
Coquette	–	Caesar	10/1853	Great Western Rly (bg)
Coquette	28	Echo	4/1862	London, Chatham & Dover Rly
Coquette	1454	Prince/W	11/1911	London & North Western Rly
Corbiere	3	2–4–0T	7/1893	Jersey Rly [183]
Cordite	–	0–4–0WT	1893	Corringham Light Rly [184]
Corfe Castle	5034	Castle	5/1935	Great Western Rly
Cormorant	–	0–4–2T	1885	Woolwich Arsenal [185]
Cormorant	3734	Bulldog	5/1909	Great Western Rly
Cormorant	47338	47/3	1965	British Railways
Corndean Hall	6938	Hall	7/1942	Great Western Rly [186]
Cornishman	3274	Duke	11/1896	Great Western Rly
Cornubia	–	?	c.1838	West Cornwall Rly

Furness Railway 0–4–0 no. 3, *"Coppernob"*, seen at the Wembley Exhibition of 1927. *(Photo: LCGB Ken Nunn Collection)*

Name	Number	Class	Date	Railway
Cornubia	3255	Duke	7/1895	Great Western Rly
Cornwall	173	aCrewe	8/1847	London & North Western Rly
Cornwall	–	?	?	Cornwall Mineral Rly
Cornwall	3020	Problem	**c.1860**	**London & North Western Rly** [187]
Cornwall	210	Richmond	9/1879	London, Brighton & South Coast Rly [188]
Cornwall	74	B4	10/1901	London, Brighton & South Coast Rly
Cornwall	1363	2Precursor	10/1905	London & North Western Rly [189]
Cornwall	–	0–4–0ST	1915	Woolwich Arsenal [190]
Cornwallis	2242	cSentinel	1929	London & North Eastern Rly
Cornwallis	5666	Jubilee	1935	London Midland & Scottish Rly
Coronach	2747	A3	11/1928	London & North Eastern Rly
Coronation	13	Majestic	1831	Stockton & Darlington Rly
Coronation	1800	George V	6/1911	London & North Western Rly
Coronation	6220	Duchess	6/1937	London Midland & Scottish Rly [191]

[173] Renamed *Earl of Dartmouth* in August 1937.
[174] Renamed *Hurricane* in November 1940.
[175] Also named (on the other side) *Sir Robert McAlpine*.
[176] Formerly Grand Junction Railway.
[177] Later renamed *The Duke of Wellington's Regt. (West Riding)*.
[178] Said to have been named *Conqueror* until May 1900. Named *Edgcumbe* until 1903, and *Colonel Edgcumbe* thereafter.
[179] Purchased in May 1845 from West Hartlepool Iron Co.
[180] Later renamed *Arnhem*.
[181] Also named *Castell Conwy* in Welsh. 1ft 11½in gauge.
[182] Nameplates fitted October 1946.

[183] 3ft 6in gauge.
[184] Later renamed *Cordite Major*.
[185] 18in gauge.
[186] Nameplates fitted March 1946.
[187] Although latterly included with the Problem or Lady of the Lake class, *Cornwall* as originally built was a freak, with its boiler below the driving axle. Also, it is not clear whether it was originally a 2–2–2 or a 4–2–2. Although rebuilt as an orthodox 2–2–2, it retained its original framing, which made it unique.
[188] Renamed and renumbered 610 *Belgravia* in October 1901.
[189] Intended as a replacement for no. 3020 *Cornwall*; when it was decided to retain this engine, no. 1363 was renamed *Brindley*.

[190] 18in gauge.
[191] Ran as no. 6229 *Duchess of Hamilton* from 1939 to 1942. The genuine no. 6229 was temporarily renumbered 6220 and renamed *Coronation* for a visit to the World's Fair at New York in 1939. The locomotive was streamlined, and painted crimson with gold stripes, whereas the genuine *Coronation* was in blue with silver stripes. A new demonstration train in red and gold went with it to the USA, and the train made an extensive tour of North America. In 1942 the locomotive was brought back to the UK, and resumed its rightful name and number (as did the genuine *Coronation*). The coaches stayed in the USA until after the end of the war.

Name	Number	Class	Date	Railway
Coronation	3	0–4–0ST	1942	**Steamtown Carnforth**
Coronation	–	0–4–0DH	1953	**Foxfield Rly**
Corrall	–	4wDM	1946	**Bodmin & Wenford Rly**
Corringham	69	69	1903	London, Tilbury & Southend Rly
Corsair	–	Bogie	8/1849	Great Western Rly (bg)
Corsair	–	0–4–2	8/1861	London, Chatham & Dover Rly
Corsair	3037	3031	9/1894	Great Western Rly
Corsham Court	2938	Saint	12/1911	Great Western Rly
Corstrophine	212	211	3/1861	North British Rly [192]
Corunna	1667	Newton	3/1868	London & North Western Rly
Corunna	1667	rPrecedent	4/1893	London & North Western Rly
Coryndon	–	?	c.1838	West Cornwall Rly [193]
Coryndon	79	2–2–2	9/1844	South Eastern Rly
Cosham	258	D1	3/1882	London, Brighton & South Coast Rly
Cossack	6	1Sussex	7/1839	London & South Western Rly
Cossack	6	2Sussex	9/1852	London & South Western Rly
Cossack	347	bCrewe	9/1854	London & North Western Rly
Cossack	–	Caesar	11/1862	Great Western Rly (bg)
Cossack	6	2Vesuvius	1/1871	London & South Western Rly
Cossack	1145	1Precursor	9/1874	London & North Western Rly
Cossack	685	2Precursor	10/1904	London & North Western Rly
Cossack	D604	Warship	1/1959	British Railways
Cotherstone	102	Peel	9/1855	Stockton & Darlington Rly
Cotswold	3313	Duke	3/1899	Great Western Rly
Cottam Power Station	58040	58	3/1986	British Railways
Cottesloe	173	Gladstone	4/1891	London, Brighton & South Coast Rly
Coulsdon	34	2–2–2	9/1839	London & Brighton Rly
Coulsdon	356	D1	11/1886	London, Brighton & South Coast Rly
Councillor	112	bCrewe	9/1847	London & North Western Rly
Councillor	981	S/Bloomer	1854	London & North Western Rly
Countess	1518	Newton	11/1866	London & North Western Rly
Countess	1518	rPrecedent	5/1891	London & North Western Rly
Countess	2	0–6–0T	1903	**Welshpool & Llanfair Light Rly** [194]
Countess Vane	35	S/Goods	12/1861	Cambrian Railways [195]
Countess Vane	41	Small Pass	3/1864	Cambrian Railways [196]
Count Louis	–	4–4–2	1924	Fairbourne Miniature Rly [197]
County Carlow	3801	1County	10/1906	Great Western Rly
County Clare	3802	1County	10/1906	Great Western Rly
County Cork	3803	1County	10/1906	Great Western Rly
County Dublin	3804	1County	10/1906	Great Western Rly
County Kerry	3805	1County	10/1906	Great Western Rly
County Kildare	3806	1County	11/1906	Great Western Rly
County Kilkenny	3807	1County	11/1906	Great Western Rly
County Limerick	3808	1County	11/1906	Great Western Rly
County of Avon	47592	47/4	1964	British Railways
County of Bedford	3821	1County	12/1911	Great Western Rly
County of Berks	3831	1County	6/1904	Great Western Rly
County of Berks	1002	2County	9/1945	Great Western Rly [198]
County of Brecknock	1007	2County	12/1945	Great Western Rly [199]
County of Brecon	3822	1County	12/1911	Great Western Rly
County of Bucks	3811	1County	11/1906	Great Western Rly
County of Bucks	1001	2County	9/1945	Great Western Rly [200]
County of Cambridgeshire	47458	47/4	1964	British Railways

Name	Number	Class	Date	Railway
County of Cardigan	3812	1County	11/1906	Great Western Rly
County of Cardigan	1008	2County	12/1945	Great Western Rly [201]
County of Carmarthen	3813	1County	11/1906	Great Western Rly
County of Carmarthen	1009	2County	12/1945	Great Western Rly [202]
County of Carnarvon	3823	1County	12/1911	Great Western Rly
County of Carnarvon	1010	2County	1/1946	Great Western Rly [203]
County of Cheshire	87025	87/0	1974	British Railways
County of Chester	3814	1County	11/1906	Great Western Rly
County of Chester	1011	2County	1/1946	Great Western Rly [204]
County of Cleveland	43104	43	10/1978	British Railways
County of Clwyd	86248	86/2	1965	British Railways [205]
County of Cornwall	3824	1County	12/1911	Great Western Rly
County of Cornwall	1006	2County	11/1945	Great Western Rly [206]
County of Cornwall	43023	43	8/1976	British Railways
County of Denbigh	3825	1County	12/1911	Great Western Rly
County of Denbigh	1012	2County	2/1946	Great Western Rly [207]
County of Derbyshire	43084	43	2/1978	British Railways
County of Devon	3835	1County	8/1904	Great Western Rly
County of Devon	1005	2County	11/1945	Great Western Rly [208]
County of Dorset	3833	1County	8/1904	Great Western Rly
County of Dorset	1013	2County	2/1946	Great Western Rly [209]
County of Dyfed	37180	37/7	10/1963	British Railways [210]
County of East Sussex	73207	73/2	4/1966	British Railways
County of Essex	47580	47/4	1964	British Railways
County of Flint	3826	1County	1/1912	Great Western Rly
County of Glamorgan	3838	1County	10/1904	Great Western Rly
County of Glamorgan	1014	2County	2/1946	Great Western Rly [211]
County of Gloucester	3827	1County	1/1912	Great Western Rly
County of Gloucester	1015	2County	3/1946	Great Western Rly [212]
County of Gwynedd	47537	47/4	1965	British Railways [213]
County of Hants	3815	1County	11/1906	Great Western Rly
County of Hants	1016	2County	3/1946	Great Western Rly [214]
County of Hereford	3828	1County	1/1912	Great Western Rly
County of Hereford	1017	2County	3/1946	Great Western Rly [215]
County of Herefordshire	47583	47/4	1964	British Railways
County of Herefordshire	47711	47/7	1966	British Railways
County of Humberside	43053	43	5/1977	British Railways
County of Kent	47845	47/4	2/1965	British Railways
County of Lancashire	86613	86/6	11/1965	British Railways
County of Leicester	3816	1County	12/1906	Great Western Rly
County of Leicester	1018	2County	4/1946	Great Western Rly [216]
County of Leicestershire	43060	43	8/1977	British Railways
County of Merioneth	3829	1County	1/1912	Great Western Rly
County of Merioneth	1019	2County	4/1946	Great Western Rly
County of Merseyside	86249	86/2	1965	British Railways
County of Middlesex	3800	1County	5/1904	Great Western Rly
County of Middlesex	1000	2County	8/1945	Great Western Rly [217]
County of Mid Glamorgan	56053	56	1978	British Railways [218]

[192] Ex-Edinburgh & Glasgow Railway, absorbed by NBR in 1865.

[193] Named *Chanter* until 1851.

[194] 2ft 6in gauge. The Welshpool & Llanfair was worked by the Cambrian Railways and became part of the Great Western in 1923, *Countess* becoming their no. 823. Originally named *The Countess*, the GWR altered the name to *Countess*. The W&LLR Preservation Society, which now operates the line, has restored the original name. The lady commemorated was the Countess of Powis.

[195] Later renamed *Castell Deudraeth*.

[196] Originally named *Cader Idris*.

[197] 15in gauge Bassett-Lowke scale model, built for (and named after) Count Louis Zbrowski, a contemporary racing-car driver.

[198] Nameplates fitted in May 1947.

[199] Nameplates fitted in January 1948.

[200] Nameplates fitted in December 1947.

[201] Nameplates fitted in June 1947.

[202] Nameplates fitted in February 1948.

[203] Nameplates fitted in December 1947. Spelling altered to *Caernarvon*, November 1951.

[204] Nameplates fitted in November 1947.

[205] Also named (on the other side) *Sir Clwyd*.

[206] Nameplates fitted in April 1948.

[207] Nameplates fitted in July 1946.

[208] Nameplates fitted in July 1946.

[209] Nameplates fitted in January 1947.

[210] Also named, in Welsh, *Sir Dyfed*.

[211] Nameplates fitted in March 1948.

[212] Nameplates fitted in April 1947.

[213] Also named (on the other side) *Sir Gwynedd*.

[214] Nameplates fitted in September 1946.

[215] Nameplates fitted in March 1946.

[216] Nameplates fitted in April 1946.

[217] Nameplates fitted in March 1946.

[218] Also named (on the other side) *Sir Morgannwg Ganol*.

Name	Number	Class	Date	Railway
County of Monmouth	3817	1County	12/1906	Great Western Rly
County of Monmouth	1020	2County	12/1946	Great Western Rly
County of Montgomery	1021	2County	12/1946	Great Western Rly
County of Norfolk	47582	47/4	1964	British Railways
County of Northampton	1022	2County	12/1946	Great Western Rly
County of Nottingham	43077	43	12/1977	British Railways
County of Oxford	3830	1County	2/1912	Great Western Rly
County of Oxford	1023	2County	1/1947	Great Western Rly
County of Pembroke	3839	1County	10/1904	Great Western Rly
County of Pembroke	1024	2County	1/1947	Great Western Rly
County of Powis	37431	37/4	1965	British Railways [219]
County of Radnor	3818	1County	12/1906	Great Western Rly
County of Radnor	1025	2County	1/1947	Great Western Rly
County of Salop	3819	1County	12/1906	Great Western Rly
County of Salop	1026	2County	1/1947	Great Western Rly
County of Somerset	3834	1County	8/1904	Great Western Rly
County of Somerset	1004	2County	10/1945	Great Western Rly [220]
County of Somerset	47603	47/4	1965	British Railways
County of Somerset	43134	43	8/1979	British Railways
County of South Glamorgan	56032	56	1977	British Railways [221]
County of Stafford	3837	1County	10/1904	Great Western Rly
County of Stafford	1027	2County	3/1947	Great Western Rly
County of Suffolk	47584	47/4	1964	British Railways
County of Suffolk	47702	47/7	1966	British Railways
County of Surrey	73131	73/1	1966	British Railways
County of Warwick	3836	1County	10/1904	Great Western Rly
County of Warwick	1028	2County	3/1947	Great Western Rly
County of West Glamorgan	37899	37/7	7/1963	British Railways
County of Wilts	3832	1County	6/1904	Great Western Rly
County of Wilts	1003	2County	10/1945	Great Western Rly [222]
County of Worcester	3820	1County	12/1906	Great Western Rly
County of Worcester	1029	2County	4/1947	Great Western Rly
County School	**–**	**0–4–0DH**	**1963**	**County School**
County Wexford	3809	1County	11/1906	Great Western Rly
County Wicklow	3810	1County	11/1906	Great Western Rly
Couperin	92044	92		EPS
Courageous	5711	Jubilee	1936	London Midland & Scottish Rly
Courageous	50032	50	1968	British Railways
Courier	176	bCrewe	11/1847	London & North Western Rly [223]
Courier	–	Iron Duke	6/1848	Great Western Rly (bg)
Courier	866	Precedent	5/1877	London & North Western Rly
Courier	–	Rover	11/1878	Great Western Rly (bg)
Courier	3006	3001	3/1892	Great Western Rly [224]
Courier	866	rPrecedent	1/1896	London & North Western Rly
Courier	6147	Royal Scot	10/1927	London Midland & Scottish Rly [225]
Courier	2152	cSentinel	1928	London & North Eastern Rly
Coventry Colliery	58048	58		British Railways
Coventry No. 1	**–**	**0–6–0ST**	**1939**	**Buckinghamshire Railway Centre**
Covertcoat	**–**	**0–4–0ST**	**1898**	**Launceston Steam Rly [226]**
Cowes	W10	A1	7/1874	Southern Rly [227]
Cowes	4	2–4–0T	1876	Isle of Wight Central Rly [228]
Cowes	108	0–4–0ST	11/1877	London & South Western Rly
Cowes	W15	O2	12/1890	Southern Rly [229]
Cowfold	394	D3	4/1896	London, Brighton & South Coast Rly
Coxhoe	–	0–6–0	?	Clarence Rly
C.P.C.	**–**	**0–4–0ST**	**1929**	**Foxfield**
C.P. May	**–**	**4wPM**	**1944**	**Airfield Line**
Crabtree	**5**	**4wDM**	**1953**	**North Downs Steam Rly**
Craftsman	47501	47/4	1966	British Railways
Craigendoran	314	157	6/1877	North British Rly [230]
Craigendoran	494	Helensburgh	4/1879	North British Rly
Craigentinny	43100	43	8/1978	British Railways
Crampton	61	Sondes	3/1858	London, Chatham & Dover Rly
Crampton	1	0–6–0T	1866	East & West Junction Rly [231]
Cranbourne Grange	6811	Grange	11/1936	Great Western Rly
Cranbrook Castle	5048	Castle	4/1936	Great Western Rly [232]
Cranbrook Castle	5073	Castle	7/1938	Great Western Rly [233]
Cranbrook Castle	7030	Castle	6/1950	British Railways (Western Region)
Crane	137	bCrewe	5/1853	London & North Western Rly [234]
Cranford	**–**	**0–6–0ST**	**1924**	**Foxfield Rly**
Cranford No 2	**–**	**0–6–0ST**	**1942**	**Yorkshire Dales Rly**
Cranham	73	69	1903	London, Tilbury & Southend Rly
Cranleigh	275	D1	12/1879	London, Brighton & South Coast Rly
Cranleigh	936	Schools	6/1935	Southern Rly
Cranmore Hall	4914	Hall	2/1929	Great Western Rly
Cransley Hall	5989	Hall	12/1939	Great Western Rly
Craven	80	Craven	9/1863	East Lancashire Rly
Craven	–	0–4–0ST	1920	Nidd Valley Light Rly [235]
Crawley	269	D1	5/1880	London, Brighton & South Coast Rly
Crawley Grange	6872	Grange	3/1939	Great Western Rly
Cray	33	2–2–0	7/1843	South Eastern Rly
Crediton	21C148	rWC	11/1946	Southern Rly
Creedy	–	2–4–0	6/1855	London & South Western Rly (bg) [236]
Creepy	**29**	**4wDM**	**1963**	**Leighton Buzzard Rly [237]**
Creese	–	Wolf	1/1842	Great Western Rly (bg)
Creon	–	Caesar	3/1856	Great Western Rly (bg)
Crepello	55012	Deltic	9/1961	British Railways
Crescent	34	Fenton	8/1840	London & South Western Rly [238]
Crescent	133	Canute	4/1856	London & South Western Rly
Cressy	155	Nile	5/1859	London & South Western Rly
Cressy	1967	Alfred	1904	London & North Western Rly
Crewe	314	bCrewe	7/1853	London & North Western Rly
Crewe	–	0–4–0DM	1930	London Midland & Scottish Rly [239]
Crewe Basford Hall	90135	90/1	9/1989	British Railways
Crewe Diesel Depot	47489	47/4	1964	British Railways
Crewe Diesel Depot Quality Approved	47734	47/7		British Railways
Crewe International Electric Maintenance Depot	90126	90/1	3/1989	British Railways
Crewe Locomotive Works	56133	56	1984	British Railways
Crewkerne	21C140	rWC	9/1946	Southern Rly
Crib Goch	60095	60	3/1992	British Railways
Cricceith Castle	5026	Castle	4/1934	Great Western Rly
Cricket	96	0–4–0ST	9/1856	Great Western Rly [240]
Cricklewood	31102	31/1	1959	British Railways

[219] Also named (on the other side) *Sir Powis*.

[220] Nameplates fitted in August 1946.

[221] Also named (on the other side) *Sir De Morgannwg*.

[222] Nameplates fitted in August 1947.

[223] Crampton-type 4–2–0 locomotive.

[224] Rebuilt as 4–2–2 in 6/1894.

[225] Later renamed *The Northamptonshire Regiment*.

[226] 1ft 11½in gauge.

[227] Formerly London, Brighton & South Coast Railway no. 69 *Peckham*.

[228] Originally built for Ryde & Newport Railway. Later Southern Railway no. W4. Scrapped in 1925.

[229] Originally London & South Western Railway (and Southern Railway) no. 195. Name applied by Southern Railway when transferred to Isle of Wight in May 1936.

[230] Later renamed *Lochee*.

[231] Later renamed *Kineton*. Sold to the Shropshire & Montgomeryshire Railway and renamed *Morous*; later sold to the West Sussex Light Railway.

[232] Renamed *Earl of Devon* in August 1937.

[233] Renamed *Blenheim* in January 1941.

[234] Formerly Liverpool & Manchester Railway no. 78.

[235] Formerly named *Gadie*.

[236] Formerly North Devon Railway.

[237] 1ft 11½in gauge.

[238] Rebuilt as a 2–2–2WT, December 1851.

[239] 18in gauge, for Crewe Works tramway. This tiny Hudswell Clarke diesel-mechanical (works no. D563) was the first diesel locomotive to be owned by the LMS.

[240] Originally no. 39 of the Birkenhead, Lancashire & Cheshire Junction Railway.

Name	Number	Class	Date	Railway	Name	Number	Class	Date	Railway
Crimea	–	Iron Duke	5/1855	Great Western Rly (bg)	*Cudworth*	2330	Remembrance	9/1935	Southern Rly [250]
Crimea	–	Rover	9/1878	Great Western Rly (bg)	*Culford Hall*	2815	B17/2	10/1939	London & North Eastern Rly [251]
Crimpsall	08647	08	1959	British Railways	*Culford Hall*	1615	B2	4/1946	London & North Eastern Rly [252]
Criterion	2245	cSentinel	1929	London & North Eastern Rly	*Culverin*	–	0–4–0ST	1884	Woolwich Arsenal [253]
Crocus	39	Bluebell	4/1863	London, Chatham & Dover Rly	*Cumberland*	17	0–4–0	10/1838	Newcastle & Carlisle Rly
Croft	56110	56	1982	British Railways	*Cumberland*	1968	Alfred	1904	London & North Western Rly
Cromartie	67	Duke	8/1874	Highland Rly [241]	*Cumberland*	2759	D49/1	5/1929	London & North Eastern Rly
Cromwell	1531	Newton	11/1866	London & North Western Rly	*(Cumbria)*	**94**	**J94**	**1953**	**Lakeside & Haverthwaite Rly**
Cromwell	1531	rPrecedent	11/1890	London & North Western Rly	**Cumbria**	**11**	**0–4–0DM**	**1967**	**South Tynedale Rly**
Cromwell's Castle	7031	Castle	6/1950	British Railways (Western Region)	**Cunarder**	**47160**	**0–6–0T**	**1931**	**Swanage Rly**
Croome Court	2939	Saint	12/1911	Great Western Rly	*Cunard White Star*	21C4	MN	10/1941	Southern Rly
Crosby	–	0–4–0	1839	Manchester & Bolton Rly	*Cupid*	82	2–4–0	9/1849	Manchester, Sheffield & Lincolnshire Rly
Crosby Hall	4992	Hall	2/1931	Great Western Rly					
CROSSCOUNTRY VOYAGER	43013	43	5/1976	British Railways	*Cupid*	–	Caesar	10/1853	Great Western Rly (bg)
					Cupid	170	Undine	6/1860	London & South Western Rly
Crossens	11	0–4–0T	1884	West Lancashire Rly	*Curlew*	60122	A1	12/1948	British Railways (Eastern Region)
Cross Fell	80	2–2–2	1859	Lancaster & Carlisle Rly	*Curlew*	47313	47/3	1965	British Railways
Crossfell	140	Peel	2/1859	Stockton & Darlington Rly	*Cwmbargoed DP*	37898	37/7	11/1963	British Railways
Cross Fell	D5	Peak	10/1959	British Railways	*Cwmbran*	37430	37/4	1965	British Railways
Cross Fell	60084	60	1/1993	British Railways	*Cwm Mawr*	7	0–6–0ST	1881	Burry Port & Gwendraeth Valley Rly [254]
Crosswood Hall	4917	Hall	3/1929	Great Western Rly					
Crouch Hill	57	51	1900	London, Tilbury & Southend Rly	*Cwm Mawr*	5	0–6–0ST	1905	Burry Port & Gwendraeth Valley Rly [255]
Crow	145	bCrewe	10/1853	London & North Western Rly [242]	*Cyclops*	46	2–2–2	1836	Liverpool & Manchester Rly
Crow	2177	0–4–0ST	12/1874	Great Western Rly (bg) [243]	*Cyclops*	–	Priam	10/1840	Great Western Rly (bg)
Crowborough	84	A1	9/1880	London, Brighton & South Coast Rly [244]	*Cyclops*	13	2–2–2	4/1845	Manchester, Sheffield & Lincolnshire Rly
Crowborough	585	E5	12/1903	London, Brighton & South Coast Rly					
Crowhurst	224	D1	6/1885	London, Brighton & South Coast Rly	*Cyclops*	1389	0–6–0	1846	Great Western Rly [256]
Crown Point	86235	86/2	1965	British Railways	*Cyclops*	5	Roach	12/1846	East Lancashire Rly
Crowstone	82	79	1909	London, Tilbury & Southend Rly	*Cyclops*	93	Fireball	5/1848	London & South Western Rly
Croxteth	283	bCrewe	4/1852	London & North Western Rly	*Cyclops*	268	bCrewe	5/1851	London & North Western Rly
Croxteth	283	DX	c.1860	London & North Western Rly	*Cyclops*	30	0–6–0	1853	Taff Vale Rly
Croxteth	731	Samson	7/1864	London & North Western Rly	*Cyclops*	12	A	7/1864	Metropolitan Rly
Croxteth	731	Whitworth	11/1889	London & North Western Rly	*Cyclops*	20	0–6–0ST	2/1866	Brecon & Merthyr Rly
Croxteth	2511	Claughton	2/1920	London & North Western Rly [245]	*Cyclops*	93	Lion	5/1867	London & South Western Rly
Croxteth	5500	Patriot	11/1930	London Midland & Scottish Rly [246]	*Cyclops*	1102	1Experiment	1884	London & North Western Rly
Croxteth Hall	6923	Hall	7/1941	Great Western Rly [247]	*Cyclops*	17	0–6–4CT	4/1901	Great Western Rly
Croydon	2	2–2–2	8/1838	London & Croydon Rly	*Cyclops*	1545	2Precursor	4/1905	London & North Western Rly
Croydon	128	2–2–2	7/1871	London, Brighton & South Coast Rly	**Cyclops**	**112**	**0–4–0ST**	**1907**	**Tanfield Rly**
Croydon	181	Gladstone	3/1890	London, Brighton & South Coast Rly	*Cyclops*	5692	Jubilee	1936	London Midland & Scottish Rly
Croydon	21C156	rBB	2/1947	Southern Rly	*Cyclops*	47625	47/4	1965	British Railways
Croydon 1883–1983	73208	73/2	4/1966	British Railways	*Cyfarthfa*	24	0–6–0ST	8/1870	Brecon & Merthyr Rly
Cruckton Hall	5979	Hall	9/1938	Great Western Rly	*Cyfronydd*	40	S/Goods	6/1863	Cambrian Railways
Crumlin	–	0–6–0T	?	Swansea & Mumbles Rly	*Cygnet*	139	aCrewe	9/1852	London & North Western Rly [257]
Crumlin Hall	4916	Hall	2/1929	Great Western Rly	*Cygnet*	139	Problem	c.1860	London & North Western Rly
Crummock	10	0–6–0ST	1869	Whitehaven, Cleator & Egremont Rly [248]	*Cymbeline*	21	0–6–0ST	2/1866	Brecon & Merthyr Rly
Crusader	3036	3031	9/1894	Great Western Rly	*Cymmer*	–	0–6–0	1851	Taff Vale Rly
Crusader	1909	Jubilee	1899	London & North Western Rly	*Cymmer*	23	0–6–0	1863	Taff Vale Rly [258]
Crynant Grange	6861	Grange	2/1939	Great Western Rly	*Cynon*	26	2–4–0	12/1852	Taff Vale Rly
Crystal Palace	366	D3	7/1892	London, Brighton & South Coast Rly	*Cyprus*	–	Caesar	4/1854	Great Western Rly (bg)
Cuckfield	237	D1	11/1881	London, Brighton & South Coast Rly	*Cyprus*	2498	George V	7/1911	London & North Western Rly
Cuckmere	222	D1	7/1885	London, Brighton & South Coast Rly	*Cyprus*	5605	Jubilee	1935	London Midland & Scottish Rly
Cuckoo	161	bCrewe	3/1856	London & North Western Rly [249]	**Cyril**	**–**	**0–4–0DM**	**1987**	**Ravenglass & Eskdale Rly** [259]
Cuckoo	1168	Samson	7/1879	London & North Western Rly	*Czar*	328	bCrewe	3/1854	London & North Western Rly
Cuckoo	1168	Whitworth	6/1894	London & North Western Rly	*Czar*	–	Metro	8/1862	Great Western Rly (bg)
Cuddie Headrigg	417	Scott	7/1914	North British Rly	*Czar of Russia*	88	Prince/W	10/1915	London & North Western Rly

[241] Previously named *The Duke*. Renamed *Cromartie*, January 1977.

[242] Previously no. 87 of the Liverpool & Manchester Railway.

[243] Built for the South Devon Railway.

[244] Sold to Isle of Wight Central Railway in November 1903, becoming their no. 12, and nameless. Named *Ventnor* by the Southern Railway and numbered W12. Withdrawn in May 1936.

[245] Name only applied in July 1923.

[246] Date of rebuilding from Claughton class locomotive no. 5971. Renamed *Patriot* in February 1937.

[247] Nameplates fitted in August 1946.

[248] Became Furness Railway no. 106.

[249] Formerly the Grand Junction Rly.

[250] Rebuilt from London, Brighton & South Coast Railway L class 4–6–4T no. 330, built December 1921.

[251] Rebuilt to class B2, April 1946.

[252] Date rebuilt from class B17.

[253] 18in gauge.

[254] Later became no. 3 *Weston* on the Weston, Clevedon & Portishead Railway.

[255] No. 5 on the Burry Port & Gwendraeth Valley Railway. Became GWR no. 2195.

[256] Formerly the West Cornwall Railway.

[257] Formerly Liverpool & Manchester Railway no. 80.

[258] Not to be confused with previous, unnumbered engine.

[259] 15in gauge.

D

Name	Number	Class	Date	Railway
Dachshund	956	George V	4/1911	London & North Western Rly [1]
Daedalion	63	2–4–0	11/1848	Manchester, Sheffield & Lincolnshire Rly
Daedalus	98	aCrewe	1/1847	London & North Western Rly
Daedalus	896	L/Bloomer	1851	London & North Western Rly
Dagenham	19	Class 1	1884	London, Tilbury & Southend Rly
Dagenham Docks	78	69	1908	London, Tilbury & Southend Rly
Dagmar	1668	Newton	3/1868	London & North Western Rly
Dagmar	1668	rPrecedent	5/1891	London & North Western Rly
Dailuaine	1	0–4–0ST	1939	**Strathspey Rly**
Daisy	19	0–6–0ST	6/1886	Alexandra (Newport & South Wales) Docks & Rly [2]
Daisy	197	GWR2301	8/1897	War Department [3]
Daisy	228	0–6–0ST	1910	War Department
Dalcross	23	S/Goods	10/1863	Highland Rly [4]
Dalcross	45	M/Goods	6/1864	Highland Rly
Dalcross Castle	29	Castle	1913	Highland Rly
Dalemain	80	aCrewe	3/1846	Grand Junction Rly
Dalemain	854	L/Bloomer	1851	London & North Western Rly
Dalemain	22	2–2–2	1857	Lancaster & Carlisle Rly
Dalhousie	491	Abbotsford	1/1879	North British Rly
Dalkeith	274	165	1877	North British Rly
Dallington	347	G	4/1882	London, Brighton & South Coast Rly
Dalmuir	151	165	5/1877	North British Rly [5]
Dalraddy	65	Duke	7/1874	Highland Rly [6]
Dalton	1486	Newton	5/1866	London & North Western Rly
Dalton	1486	rPrecedent	3/1890	London & North Western Rly
Dalton	2516	Prince/W	11/1919	London & North Western Rly
Dalton Hall	4993	Hall	2/1931	Great Western Rly
Dalzell	37190	37/0	1964	British Railways
(Dame Vera Lynn)	73672	WD2–10–0	1943	**War Department**
Damon	–	Priam	3/1842	Great Western Rly (bg)
Damon	2101	4–4–0ST	2/1852	Great Western Rly (bg) [7]
Damon	115	0–6–0	8/1853	Manchester, Sheffield & Lincolnshire Rly
Damredub	17	4wDM	1936	**Leighton Buzzard Rly** [8]
Danby Lodge	–	0–6–0ST	1903	London Midland & Scottish Rly [9]
Dandie Dinmont	–	0–6–0T	?	Brampton Rly
Dandie Dinmont	896	Scott	7/1909	North British Rly
Dane	126	Saxon	5/1855	London & South Western Rly
(Danish Seaways)	740	S	1928	**Danish State Rly** [10]
Dante	513	A2/3	8/1946	London & North Eastern Rly
Dante	92029	92		British Railways
Danube	147	E1	10/1880	London, Brighton & South Coast Rly
Daphne	1433	Problem	c.1860	London & North Western Rly
Daphne	80	Rose	9/1863	London, Chatham & Dover Rly
Daphne	13	A	7/1864	Metropolitan Rly
Daphne	9	A1	9/1880	Shropshire & Montgomeryshire Rly [11]
Daphne	218	2Precursor	6/1907	London & North Western Rly
Dare	25	2–4–0	11/1852	Taff Vale Rly
Darfield No 1	–	0–6–0ST	1953	**Llangollen Rly**
Daring	D811	Warship	10/1959	British Railways

Name	Number	Class	Date	Railway
Darlington	19	Director	9/1832	Stockton & Darlington Rly
Darlington	38	0–4–2	10/1841	Manchester & Leeds Rly
Darlington	103	Peel	10/1855	Stockton & Darlington Rly
Darlington	2852	B17/4	4/1936	London & North Eastern Rly
Darlington	43110	43	1/1979	British Railways
Darnall	08857	08	1961	British Railways
Darnaway Castle	58	Castle	1917	Highland Rly
Dart	4	0–2–2	1830	Liverpool & Manchester Rly
Dart	48	2–2–2	1836	Liverpool & Manchester Rly
Dart	41	0–4–0	4/1840	Stockton & Darlington Rly
Dart	–	Priam	7/1841	Great Western Rly (bg)
Dart	–	2–2–2	8/1855	London & South Western Rly (bg) [12]
Dart	2119	4–4–0ST	12/1864	Great Western Rly (bg) [13]
Dart	70	River	10/1895	Great Western Rly [14]
Dart	–	(?)	?	Brecon & Merthyr Rly [15]
Dartington Hall	4918	Hall	3/1929	Great Western Rly
Dartmoor	3276	Duke	12/1896	Great Western Rly
Dartmoor	21C121	rWC	1/1946	Southern Rly
Dartmoor	08641	08	1959	British Railways
Dartmoor The Pony Express	43158	43	4/1981	British Railways
Dartmouth	3356	Bulldog	6/1900	Great Western Rly
Dartmouth Castle	4088	Castle	7/1925	Great Western Rly
Dauntless	5717	Jubilee	1936	London Midland & Scottish Rly
Dauntless	50048	50	1968	British Railways
Dava	43	M/Goods	6/1864	Highland Rly
Davenham Hall	6907	Hall	11/1940	Great Western Rly
David	13	0–4–0ST	1953	**Lakeside & Haverthwaite Rly**
David Lloyd George	37428	37/4	1965	British Railways
David Lloyd George	–	0–4–4–0F	1992	**Festiniog Rly** [16]
David MacIver	3421	Bulldog	2/1903	Great Western Rly [17]
David Payne	185	0–4–0DM	1950	**Darlington Railway Centre**
Davies	5	0–6–0	1867	Pembroke & Tenby Rly [18]
DAVIES THE OCEAN	47488	47/4	1964	British Railways
Daw Mill Colliery	58002	58	1983	British Railways
Dawn	32	Dawn	10/1862	London, Chatham & Dover Rly
Dean	100	Saint	2/1902	Great Western Rly [19]
Deanery	88	0–4–0	1845	Stockton & Darlington Rly [20]
Debussy	92043	92		Société National des Chemins de fer Français
Dee	14	0–6–0	3/1849	Birkenhead, Lancashire & Cheshire Junction Rly [21]
Dee	270	bCrewe	6/1851	London & North Western Rly
Dee	27	?	?	St Helens Canal & Rly
Dee	38	2–4–0	4/1856	Birkenhead, Lancashire & Cheshire Junction Rly [22]
Dee	9	0–4–0ST	1872	Wrexham, Mold & Connah's Quay Rly [23]
Dee	71	River	10/1895	Great Western Rly [24]
Deepdale	137	Peel	12/1858	Stockton & Darlington Rly
Deepdene	291	D1	5/1879	London, Brighton & South Coast Rly

[1] Renamed *Bulldog* in December 1915.
[2] Named *Daisy* when purchased in 1891 from a Mr Isaac Llewellyn; it is not known if the name continued to be carried.
[3] Formerly Great Western Railway no. 2540.
[4] Originally named *Murthly*.
[5] Later renamed *Guardbridge*.
[6] Originally named *Nairnshire*.
[7] Formerly the South Devon Railway.
[8] 2ft gauge.
[9] Built by Manning, Wardle for industrial use (their works no. 1595). Purchased by the London Midland & Scottish Railway in December 1933.
[10] Danish State Railways 2–6–4T. Preserved on Nene Valley Railway.
[11] Originally London, Brighton & South Coast Railway no. 83 *Earlswood*. Sold to the Admiralty in January 1918; resold to Shropshire & Montgomeryshire Railway in November 1923.
[12] Formerly the North Devon Railway.
[13] Formerly the South Devon Railway.
[14] Rebuild of 2–2–2 no. 70 of 1855.
[15] A tender engine acquired (source unknown) in about 1865 and disposed of (to an unknown destination) in about 1871.
[16] 1ft 11½in gauge.
[17] Originally named *Maciver* until April 1903.
[18] In 1896 became Great Western Railway no. 1363.
[19] Named *Dean* in June 1902, and *William Dean* in November 1902. Later no. 2900.
[20] Ex-Manchester & Leeds Railway, purchased in 1854.
[21] Later named *Gheber* and passed to London & North Western Railway.
[22] Later passed to London & North Western Railway as their no. 325 *Chandos*.
[23] Built for T. Butlin of Wellingborough. Acquired by WM&CQR 1881. Renumbered 402B by Great Central Railway after their absorption of WM&CQR.
[24] Rebuilt from 2–2–2 no. 71 of 1855.

Name	Number	Class	Date	Railway
Deer	–	Rennie	6/1838	London & South Western Rly [25]
Deerhound	1662	George V	5/1911	London & North Western Rly
De Falla	92030	92		British Railways
Defence	220	bSentinel	1932	London & North Eastern Rly
Defence	5722	Jubilee	1936	London Midland & Scottish Rly
Defford	19	4–2–0	11/1840	Birmingham & Gloucester Rly
Defiance	11	0–6–0	12/1844	Bristol & Gloucester Rly (bg) [26]
Defiance	1721	Prince/W	11/1911	London & North Western Rly
Defiance	2257	cSentinel	1929	London & North Eastern Rly
Defiance	5728	Jubilee	1936	London Midland & Scottish Rly
Defiance	**50049**	**50**	**1968**	**British Railways**
Defiant	–	?		Brassey [27]
Defiant	**5080**	**Castle**	**5/1939**	**Great Western Rly [28]**
Defiant	**22**	**0–4–0ST**	**1952**	**Yorkshire Dales Rly**
Deighton	**–**	**0–4–0DE**	**1959**	**Caerphilly Railway Society**
Delamere	228	bCrewe	11/1848	London & North Western Rly
Delamere	1940	ELBloomer	1861	London & North Western Rly
Delamere	2051	2Precursor	8/1907	London & North Western Rly
De la Warr	186	Gladstone	7/1889	London, Brighton & South Coast Rly
Delhi	1674	Newton	4/1868	London & North Western Rly
Delhi	1674	rPrecedent	11/1890	London & North Western Rly
Deltic	**–**	**Co-Co**	**10/1955**	**English Electric Co.**
Denbies	290	D1	6/1879	London, Brighton & South Coast Rly
Denbigh Castle	5049	Castle	4/1936	Great Western Rly [29]
Denbigh Castle	5074	Castle	7/1938	Great Western Rly [30]
Denbigh Castle	7001	Castle	5/1946	Great Western Rly [31]
Denbigh Castle	7032	Castle	6/1950	British Railways (Western Region)
Denbighshire	1621	2Experiment	1/1910	London & North Western Rly
(Denis)	**–**	**0–4–0VB**	**1958**	**Bo'ness & Kinneil Rly**
Denmark	39	A1	5/1878	London, Brighton & South Coast Rly
(Denmark)	**RE 002**	**railcar**	**1984**	**British Railways [32]**
Dennington	497	E4	5/1900	London, Brighton & South Coast Rly [33]
Dennis	1	0–4–2T	1888	Glyn Valley Tramway [34]
Dennis	1	0–6–0T	1910	Snailbeach District Rly [35]
Densworth	513	E4	3/1901	London, Brighton & South Coast Rly
Deptford	73	A1	10/1872	London, Brighton & South Coast Rly
Derby	–	2–2–2	7/1839	Birmingham & Derby Junction Rly
Derby	22	2–2–2	1/1841	Manchester & Leeds Rly
Derby	286	bCrewe	6/1852	London & North Western Rly
Derby	23	0–4–2	1858	South Staffordshire Rly
Derby	2	2–4–0T	1873	Isle of Man Rly [36]
Derby	–	0–6–0ST	1876	Port Talbot Rly [37]
Derby	–	0–4–0T	1916	Woolwich Arsenal [38]
Derby & Derbyshire Chamber of Commerce & Industry	47844	47/4	5/1964	British Railways
Derby County	2851	B17/4	3/1936	London & North Eastern Rly
Derby Etches Park	43072	43	12/1977	British Railways
Derby Evening Telegraph	47973	47/4		British Railways
Derbyshire	1420	2Experiment	11/1909	London & North Western Rly

Name	Number	Class	Date	Railway
Derbyshire	251	D49/1	11/1927	London & North Eastern Rly
Derek Crouch	**–**	**0–6–0ST**	**1924**	**Nene Valley Rly**
De Robeck	5678	Jubilee	1935	London Midland & Scottish Rly
Derwent	–	2–2–2	8/1839	Birmingham & Derby Junction Rly
Derwent	**25**	**Tory**	**11/1845**	**Stockton & Darlington Rly**
Derwent	?3	?	10/1846	Whitehaven & Furness Junction Rly
Derwent	–	0–4–2	10/1846	Cockermouth & Workington Rly
Derwent	1	0–4–0T	1854	Cockermouth & Workington Rly
Derwent	37012	37/0	1961	British Railways
Derwent Grange	6862	Grange	2/1939	Great Western Rly
Derwentwater	14	0–6–0ST	1873	Whitehaven, Cleator & Egremont Rly [39]
Desmond	**–**	**0–4–0ST**	**1906**	**Caerphilly Railway Society**
Despatch	D812	Warship	11/1959	British Railways [40]
Deva	74	aCrewe	10/1845	Grand Junction Rly
Devizes Castle	5050	Castle	5/1936	Great Western Rly [41]
Devizes Castle	5075	Castle	8/1938	Great Western Rly [42]

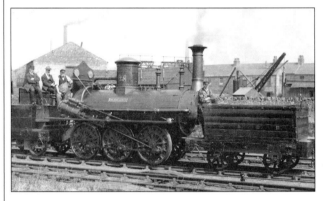

Stockton & Darlington Railway 0–6–0 no. 25 *Derwent*, seen at Darlington at the Railway Centenary of 1925. (*Photo: LCGB Ken Nunn Collection*)

Name	Number	Class	Date	Railway
Devizes Castle	7002	Castle	6/1946	Great Western Rly
Devon	–	0–6–0T	1874	Ravenglass & Eskdale Rly [43]
Devonia	3038	3031	9/1894	Great Western Rly
Devonport Royal Dockyard 1693–1993	43181	43	11/1981	British Railways
Devonshire	209	Richmond	8/1879	London, Brighton & South Coast Rly
Devonshire	70	B4	9/1901	London, Brighton & South Coast Rly [44]
De Winton	6	0–6–0	6/1862	Brecon & Merthyr Rly [45]
Dewi Sant	47790	47/7		British Railways [46]
Dewrance	–	Hawthorn	7/1865	Great Western Rly (bg)
Dewsbury	19	2–2–2	12/1840	Manchester & Leeds Rly

[25] An unsuccessful design. All five engines were sent to Fairbairns for rebuilding in February 1841. *Deer* returned as no. 19 *Briton*.

[26] Later taken over by the Midland Railway. In August 1857 this engine was sold to Thomas Brassey for working the North Devon Railway, a broad gauge line which later passed to the London & South Western Railway. On the NDR the engine lost its number but the name was unchanged.

[27] Thomas Brassey contracted to maintain the track of the London & South Western Railway from 4 November 1839 to December 1853. He provided his own locomotives, of which *Defiant* is one. Beyond their names, very little is known of them.

[28] *Ogmore Castle* until January 1941.

[29] Renamed *Earl of Plymouth* in August 1937.

[30] Renamed *Hampden* in January 1941.

[31] Renamed *Sir James Milne* in February 1948.

[32] Named on sale to ABB Transportation, Derby Carriage Works.

[33] Renamed *Donnington*, February 1905.

[34] 2ft 4½in gauge. Not the same as Snailbeach District Railway no. 1 below.

[35] 2ft 4½in gauge.

[36] 3ft gauge.

[37] Taken over by the Port Talbot Railway from the Cefn & Pyle Railway, which it purchased on 1 January 1897. The locomotive was sold in 1897 and became no. 5 at Swansea Harbour Trust, where it is said to have been briefly named *Harriet*. It was disposed of in 1911.

[38] 18in gauge.

[39] Became Furness Railway no. 110.

[40] Name never carried. Entered service as *Royal Naval Reserve 1859–1959*.

[41] Renamed *Earl of St. Germans* in August 1937.

[42] Renamed *Wellington* in October 1940.

[43] Officially 2ft 9in gauge; 3ft according to a tape measure, and according to recently excavated old sleepers!

[44] Originally *Holyrood*. Renamed in March 1907.

[45] At one time no. 16 of the Cambrian Railways. Thomas Savin, contractor, provided locomotives for both railways, and moved them around as traffic needs dictated. After his bankruptcy, there was some dispute as to which railway actually owned *De Winton*, and the Brecon & Merthyr was successful.

[46] Also named (on the other side) *Saint David*.

Name	Number	Class	Date	Railway
D H Lawrence	92015	92		British Railways
Diadem	1946	Alfred	6/1901	London & North Western Rly
Diadem	D813	Warship	12/1959	British Railways
Diamond	191	aCrewe	1/1848	London & North Western Rly
Diamond	–	0–4–0T	1850	Chester & Holyhead Rly
Diamond	67	Ruby	8/1861	London, Chatham & Dover Rly
Diamond Jubilee	2545	A3	8/1924	London & North Eastern Rly
Diamond Jubilee	47365	47/3	1965	British Railways
Diana	83	2–4–0	9/1849	Manchester, Sheffield & Lincolnshire Rly
Diana	–	Caesar	8/1853	Great Western Rly (bg)
Diana	377	bCrewe	11/1855	London & North Western Rly [47]
Diana	**1**	**J94**	**10/1943**	**Caledonian Rly (Brechin)**
Diana	**27003**	**EM2**	**1954**	**British Railways**
Diana	**–**	**4wDM**	**1957**	**Festiniog Rly [48]**
(Dianne)	**D2867**	**02**	**1961**	**British Railways**
Dibatag	1033	B1	8/1947	London & North Eastern Rly
Dickie	–	0–4–0T	5/1875	London & North Western Rly [49]
Dick Hardy	09012	09	1961	British Railways
Dickson	–	?	1857	Port Carlisle Rly
Dick Turpin	2579	A3	11/1924	London & North Eastern Rly
Dick Whittington	13	Bo-Bo	1921	Metropolitan Rly [50]
DICK WHITTINGTON	47712	47/7	1966	British Railways
Didcot Power Station	58014	58	1984	British Railways
Didlington Hall	6940	Hall	8/1942	Great Western Rly [51]
Dido	66	0–4–2	9/1848	Manchester, Sheffield & Lincolnshire Rly
Dido	–	Caesar	6/1851	Great Western Rly (bg)
Dido	2143	0–6–0ST	3/1860	Great Western Rly (bg) [52]
Dido	14	A	8/1864	Metropolitan Rly
Dido	8	A1x	6/1878	Shropshire & Montgomeryshire Rly [53]
Dieppe	200	2–2–2	8/1864	London, Brighton & South Coast Rly [54]
Dijon	137	E1	1/1879	London, Brighton & South Coast Rly
Diligence	4	Locomotion	5/1825	Stockton & Darlington Rly [55]
Diligence	2261	cSentinel	1929	London & North Eastern Rly
Dilston	39	0–6–0	1855	Newcastle & Carlisle Rly [56]
Dinan	746	B4	4/1908	London & South Western Rly
Dinard	747	B4	4/1908	London & South Western Rly
Dinas	–	0–4–2	1841	Taff Vale Rly
Dinas	4	0–6–0	1861	Taff Vale Rly [57]
Dinas Abertawe	43019	43	7/1976	British Railways [58]
Dingley Hall	5980	Hall	9/1938	Great Western Rly
Dingwall	7	Seafield	8/1858	Highland Rly [59]
Dingwall	19	S/Goods	8/1863	Highland Rly [60]
Dingwall	48	Glenbarry	6/1864	Highland Rly [61]
Dinmore Manor	**7820**	**Manor**	**11/1950**	**British Railways (Western Region)**
Dinton Hall	5924	Hall	5/1933	Great Western Rly
Diomed	10	Medusa	12/1846	East Lancashire Rly
Diomed	52	aCrewe	11/1849	London & North Western Rly
Diomed	52	DX	c.1859	London & North Western Rly
Diomed	821	Samson	5/1863	London & North Western Rly
Diomed	821	Whitworth	1/1892	London & North Western Rly
Diomede	52	2–2–2	1838	Grand Junction Rly
Diomede	115	Acis	12/1861	London, Chatham & Dover Rly
Diomedes	69	2–2–2	10/1848	Manchester, Sheffield & Lincolnshire Rly
Diomedes	26047	EM1	8/1952	British Railways
Director	16	Director	9/1832	Stockton & Darlington Rly
Director	289	bCrewe	8/1852	London & North Western Rly
Director	696	Newton	8/1873	London & North Western Rly
Director	696	rPrecedent	11/1888	London & North Western Rly
Dirk Hatteraick	359	Scott	12/1911	North British Rly
Dirleton	52	72	1/1883	North British Rly
Dispatch	6	Tory	1839	Stockton & Darlington Rly
Disraeli	–	0–6–0ST	1869	Mawddwy Rly
Disraeli	867	Precedent	6/1877	London & North Western Rly
Disraeli	867	rPrecedent	7/1894	London & North Western Rly
Disraeli	1325	Prince/W	8/1919	London & North Western Rly
Diss	–	?	?	Eastern Union Rly
Distillers MG	47214	47/0	1965	British Railways
Ditcheat Manor	**7821**	**Manor**	**11/1950**	**British Railways (Western Region)**
Ditchling	240	D1	11/1881	London, Brighton & South Coast Rly
Dixon	102	2–4–0	1857	North British Rly [62]
Djerid	–	Wolf	7/1841	Great Western Rly (bg)
Dochfour	84	Duke	12/1888	Highland Rly
Doctor Dalton	19	2–2–2	1837	Grand Junction Rly
Doctor Syn	**9**	**4–6–2**	**1931**	**Romney, Hythe & Dymchurch Rly [63]**
Doctor Syn	**10**	**4–6–2**	**1931**	**Romney, Hythe & Dymchurch Rly [64]**
Dodington Hall	7901	M/Hall	3/1949	British Railways (Western Region)
Dog Star	–	Priam	9/1839	Great Western Rly (bg)
Dog Star	4001	Star	2/1907	Great Western Rly
Dolbadarn	**3**	**0–4–0ST**	**1922**	**Llanberis Lake Rly [65]**
Dolgarrog	**9**	**4wDM**	**1962**	**Llanberis Lake Rly [66]**
Dolgoch	**2**	**0–4–0T**	**1865**	**Talyllyn Rly [67]**
Dolhywel Grange	6863	Grange	2/1939	Great Western Rly
Doll	**4**	**0–6–0T**	**1919**	**Leighton Buzzard Rly [68]**
Dollands Moor International	47053	47/0	1964	British Railways
Dolphin	**1**	**4wDM**	**1952**	**Groudle Glen Rly [69]**
Dominie Sampson	411	Scott	4/1914	North British Rly
Dominion	1969	Alfred	1904	London & North Western Rly
Dominion of Canada	3453	Bulldog	1/1904	Great Western Rly
Dominion of Canada	**4489**	**A4**	**5/1937**	**London & North Eastern Rly [70]**
Dominion of India	60011	A4	6/1937	British Railways [71]
Dominion of New Zealand	4492	A4	6/1937	London & North Eastern Rly
Dominion of Pakistan	**60020**	**A4**	**12/1937**	**British Railways [72]**
Don	298	bCrewe	11/1852	London & North Western Rly
Don 1	5519	0–4–0D	1940	War Department
Don 2	5520	0–4–0D	1940	War Department
Don 3	5521	0–4–0D	1940	War Department
Doncaster	2547	A3	8/1924	London & North Eastern Rly

[47] Later renumbered 10 and renamed *Dragon*.

[48] 1ft 11½in gauge.

[49] 18in gauge for Crewe Works tramway.

[50] Nominally a rebuild of an earlier, unnamed, locomotive; but using few (if any) of its parts.

[51] Nameplates fitted in August 1946.

[52] Built for the South Devon Railway.

[53] Formerly London, Brighton & South Coast Railway no. 38 *Millwall*. Sold to the Admiralty for use at Invergordon; resold to Shropshire & Montgomeryshire Railway in November 1923.

[54] Name applied in January 1871.

[55] Rebuilt to 0–6–0 in 1834.

[56] Became North Eastern Railway no. 487 in 1862.

[57] Later converted to 0–4–4T in 1876. Nameplates removed *c.* 1866.

[58] Also named (on the other side) *City of Swansea*.

[59] Originally *Fife*. Rebuilt from 2–4–0 to 4–4–0 and renamed in May 1875.

[60] Previously no. 18 *Inverness*; later renamed *Golspie*.

[61] Originally named *Cadboll*. Altered from 2–2–2 to 2–4–0 in January 1881, and renamed *Dingwall* in 1886.

[62] Built for Carlisle & Silloth Bay Railway. Absorbed by NBR in 1859.

[63] 15 inch gauge. Later renamed *Winston Churchill*.

[64] 15 inch gauge. Originally named *Black Prince*.

[65] 1ft 11½in gauge.

[66] 1ft 11½in gauge.

[67] 2ft 3in gauge. Ran as *Pretoria* during the Boer War period. Talyllyn locomotives only received numbers in Preservation Society days.

[68] 2ft gauge.

[69] 2ft gauge.

[70] Originally named *Woodcock*, renamed in June 1937. Preserved at Canadian Railroad Historical Museum.

[71] Built for London & North Eastern Railway. Originally named *Empire of India*; renamed *Dominion of India* by British Railways.

[72] Built for the London & North Eastern Railway. Originally named *Guillemot*; renamed *Dominion of Pakistan* by British Railways.

Dolbadarn, a 1ft 11½in gauge 0–4–0ST built in 1922 for the Padarn Quarries in North Wales, and seen here on the Llanberis Lake Railway. (*Photo: R.G. Pike*)

Name	Number	Class	Date	Railway
Doncaster	–	0–4–0DE	**1957**	**Nene Valley Rly**
Doncaster Enterprise	47522	47/4	1966	British Railways
Doncaster Rovers	2857	B17/4	5/1936	London & North Eastern Rly
Doncaster Works	58020	58	1984	British Railways
Donnington	497	E4	5/1900	London, Brighton & South Coast Rly [73]
Donnington Hall	4919	Hall	3/1929	Great Western Rly
Donnington Castle	4089	Castle	7/1925	Great Western Rly
Donovan	2546	A3	8/1924	London & North Eastern Rly
Dora	–	0–4–0ST	**1927**	**Rutland Railway Museum**
Dorchester	21C142	rWC	10/1946	Southern Rly
Dorchester Castle	4090	Castle	7/1925	Great Western Rly
Doreen	240	0–6–0ST	1931	War Department
Doric	1305	Teutonic	3/1890	London & North Western Rly
Doric	276	2Precursor	7/1907	London & North Western Rly
Dorking	235	2–2–2	11/1866	London, Brighton & South Coast Rly [74]

Name	Number	Class	Date	Railway
Dorking	229	D1	12/1884	London, Brighton & South Coast Rly
Dornden	273	D1	4/1880	London, Brighton & South Coast Rly
Dorney Court	2940	Saint	12/1911	Great Western Rly
Dornoch	56	Lochgorm	2/1869	Highland Rly [75]
Dornoch Firth	70054	Britannia	9/1954	British Railways
Dorothea	–	0–4–0ST	**1901**	**Launceston Steam Rly** [76]
Dorothy	–	0–4–0ST	1903	Powlesland & Mason [77]
(Dorothy)	D2337	04	**1961**	**British Railways**
Dorothy Garrod	60071	60	9/1991	British Railways
Dot	–	0–4–0ST	**1887**	**Lancashire & Yorkshire Rly** [78]
Dottin	3	2–2–0	1834	London & Greenwich Rly
Dottrel	8	Tiger	9/1861	London, Chatham & Dover Rly
Dougal	8	0–4–0T	**1946**	**Welshpool & Llanfair Light Rly** [79]
Douglas	9	2–4–0T	**1896**	**Isle of Man Rly** [80]
Douglas	4584	0–4–0ST	1900	War Department
(Douglas)	6	0–4–0T	**1918**	**Talyllyn Rly** [81]
Dounreay	37262	37/0	1965	British Railways
Dove	–	2–2–2	8/1839	Birmingham & Derby Junction Rly[82]
Dovedale	2370	George V	7/1916	London & North Western Rly
Dover	911	Schools	12/1932	Southern Rly
Dowlais	–	0–4–2	1841	Taff Vale Rly
Dowlais	47	0–6–0	1859	Taff Vale Rly
Downham Hall	6908	Hall	11/1940	Great Western Rly
Downside	912	Schools	12/1932	Southern Rly
Downton Hall	4994	Hall	2/1931	Great Western Rly
Dragon	10	2–2–2	1837	Grand Junction Rly
Dragon	26	2–2–0	6/1840	Midland Counties Rly
Dragon	10	aCrewe	2/1845	London & North Western Rly
Dragon	–	Iron Duke	8/1848	Great Western Rly (bg)
Dragon	10	bCrewe	11/1855	London & North Western Rly [83]
Dragon	176	Lion	1/1870	London & South Western Rly
Dragon	2164	0–6–0ST	9/1873	Great Western Rly (bg) [84]
Dragon	1155	1Precursor	9/1874	London & North Western Rly
Dragon	–	Rover	8/1880	Great Western Rly (bg)
Dragon	3007	3001	3/1892	Great Western Rly [85]
Dragon	60	2Precursor	10/1904	London & North Western Rly
Dragon	D814	Warship	1/1960	British Railways
Drake	1526	Newton	11/1866	London & North Western Rly
Drake	1526	rPrecedent	1/1890	London & North Western Rly
Drake	1559	George V*	11/1910	London & North Western Rly
Drake	5659	Jubilee	1934	London Midland & Scottish Rly
Drake	–	0–4–0ST	**1940**	**Rutland Railway Museum**
Drakelow Power Station	58007	58	1983	British Railways
Drax Power Station	56123	56	1983	British Railways
Draycott Manor	7810	Manor	12/1938	Great Western Rly
Drayton	198	2–2–2	7/1864	London, Brighton & South Coast Rly [86]
Drayton	391	D3	6/1894	London, Brighton & South Coast Rly
Dreadnought	10	0–6–0	7/1844	Bristol & Gloucester Rly (bg) [87]
Dreadnought	–	Fury	10/1846	Great Western Rly (bg)
Dreadnought	40	0–6–0	9/1856	Birkenhead, Lancashire & Cheshire Junction Rly [88]
Dreadnought	503	Dreadnought	1884	London & North Western Rly
Dreadnought	3039	3031	9/1894	Great Western Rly
Dreadnought	659	2Precursor	6/1904	London & North Western Rly
Dreadnought	5718	Jubilee	1936	London Midland & Scottish Rly
Dreadnought	–	0–4–0DM	**1939**	**Amerton Rly** [89]

[73] Originally *Dennington*. Renamed in February 1905.

[74] Name applied in February 1872 and renumbered 475 in May 1881. Sold to the West Lancashire Railway in January 1883, becoming their no. 5, retaining the name *Dorking*. No. 233 (later 487) *Horsham* was also sold to the WLR at the same time.

[75] Originally *Balnain* until 1902.

[76] 2ft gauge.

[77] Became Great Western Railway no. 942 when P&M were taken over in 1924, and the name was soon removed. The locomotive was further renumbered 1153 in November 1949. It was withdrawn by British Railways in October 1955.

[78] 18in gauge.

[79] 2ft 6in gauge.

[80] 3ft gauge.

[81] 2ft 3in gauge.

[82] Later went to the Cambrian Railways.

[83] Originally no. 377 *Diana*.

[84] Built for the South Devon Railway.

[85] Rebuilt to 4–2–2 in August 1894.

[86] Name applied in June 1872.

[87] Later passed to the Midland Railway, and in May 1856 was sold to Thomas Brassey for working the North Devon Railway, a broad gauge line which was later taken over by the London & South Western Railway. On the NDR this engine's name was unchanged.

[88] Became Great Western Railway no. 102.

[89] 2ft gauge.

Name	Number	Class	Date	Railway
Dreadnought	50001	50	1967	British Railways
Driver	34	Miner	3/1846	Stockton & Darlington Rly
Driver	–	0-4-0ST	1/1875	Wantage Tramway [90]
Driver John Axon G.C.	86261	86/2	1965	British Railways
Driver John Axon G.C.	86041	86/2	9/1965	British Railways
Driver John Elliot	37412	37/4	1965	British Railways
Driver Wallace Oakes G.C.	86048	86/2	10/1965	British Railways
Driver Wallace Oakes G.C.	86260	86/2	1966	British Railways
Droitwich	27	4-2-0	1/1841	Birmingham & Gloucester Rly
Dromedary	–	Leo	3/1841	Great Western Rly (bg)
Dromedary	168	aCrewe	8/1847	London & North Western Rly
Dromedary	2166	0-6-0ST	12/1873	Great Western Rly (bg) [91]
Druid	7	2-2-2	12/1844	Chester & Birkenhead Rly
Druid	272	bCrewe	8/1851	London & North Western Rly
Druid	–	Caesar	2/1852	Great Western Rly (bg)
Druid	1144	1Precursor	8/1874	London & North Western Rly
Druid	106	2Precursor	10/1904	London & North Western Rly
Druid	D815	Warship	1/1960	British Railways
Drysllwyn	–	0-6-0	10/1842	Llanelly Rly [92]

Name	Number	Class	Date	Railway
Duchess of Fife	43	B4	6/1902	London, Brighton & South Coast Rly [95]
Duchess of Gloucester	6225	Duchess	5/1938	London Midland & Scottish Rly
Duchess of Hamilton	**6229**	**Duchess**	**9/1938**	**London Midland & Scottish Rly [96]**
Duchess of Kent	6212	Princess	10/1935	London Midland & Scottish Rly
Duchess of Lancaster	71	2-2-2	1859	Lancaster & Carlisle Rly
Duchess of Lancaster	480	Precedent	11/1880	London & North Western Rly
Duchess of Lancaster	480	rPrecedent	2/1897	London & North Western Rly
Duchess of Montrose	6232	Duchess	7/1938	London Midland & Scottish Rly
Duchess of Norfolk	49	B4	7/1901	London, Brighton & South Coast Rly [97]
Duchess of Norfolk	6226	Duchess	5/1938	London Midland & Scottish Rly
Duchess of Rutland	6228	Duchess	6/1938	London Midland & Scottish Rly
Duchess of Sutherland	**6233**	**Duchess**	**7/1938**	**London Midland & Scottish Rly**

London & North Western Railway Dreadnought class 2-2-2-0 no. 503 *Dreadnought*, at Shrewsbury. (*Photo: RAS Marketing*)

London Midland & Scottish Railway 4-6-2 no. 6232 *Duchess of Montrose* passing Wembley with a Euston–Aberdeen express on 2 August 1938. (*Photo: LCGB Ken Nunn Collection*)

Name	Number	Class	Date	Railway
Drysllwyn Castle	**5051**	**Castle**	**5/1936**	**Great Western Rly [93]**
Drysllwyn Castle	5076	Castle	8/1938	Great Western Rly [94]
Drysllwyn Castle	7018	Castle	5/1949	British Railways (Western Region)
Dublin	180	Windsor	9/1865	Stockton & Darlington Rly
Duchess	–	2-2-2	1840	Lancaster & Preston Junction Rly
Duchess	1519	Newton	11/1866	London & North Western Rly
Duchess	1519	rPrecedent	6/1891	London & North Western Rly
Duchess of Abercorn	6234	Duchess	8/1938	London Midland & Scottish Rly
Duchess of Albany	674	627	9/1881	Lancashire & Yorkshire Rly
Duchess of Albany	3066	3031	12/1897	Great Western Rly
Duchess of Atholl	6231	Duchess	6/1938	London Midland & Scottish Rly
Duchess of Buccleuch	6230	Duchess	6/1938	London Midland & Scottish Rly
Duchess of Devonshire	6227	Duchess	6/1938	London Midland & Scottish Rly

Name	Number	Class	Date	Railway
Duchess of Teck	3067	3031	12/1897	Great Western Rly
Dudley	1	2-2-2	2/1849	South Staffordshire Rly
Dudley Castle	4091	Castle	7/1925	Great Western Rly
Dudley Castle	86245	86/2	1965	British Railways
Duffryn	20	0-6-0	5/1850	Taff Vale Rly
Dugald Dalgetty	414	Scott	6/1914	North British Rly
Dugdale	58	Rossendale	2/1854	East Lancashire Rly
Duiker	1015	B1	1/1947	London & North Eastern Rly
Duke	99	aCrewe	2/1847	London & North Western Rly
Duke	891	L/Bloomer	1851	London & North Western Rly
Duke	61	Duke	6/1874	Highland Rly [98]
Duke	7	0-4-0ST	1878	Wrexham, Mold & Connah's Quay Rly
Duke of Albany	257	Precedent	1/1882	London & North Western Rly
Duke of Cambridge	3068	3031	1/1898	Great Western Rly
Duke of Connaught	260	Precedent	1/1882	London & North Western Rly
Duke of Connaught	260	rPrecedent	1896	London & North Western Rly
Duke of Connaught	3065	3031	7/1897	Great Western Rly
Duke of Connaught	2427	Claughton	6/1917	London & North Western Rly
Duke of Cornwall	3252	Duke	5/1895	Great Western Rly
Duke of Edinburgh	3064	3031	6/1897	Great Western Rly

[90] Originally built for the Royal Arsenal, Woolwich, and said to have been named there *The Gunner*. Purchased by Wantage Tramway for £600 in 1919 and renamed *Driver*. It was not successful, being unable to maintain steam pressure (one old driver is quoted as saying 'She was only a good engine as long as she was standing still'). It was broken up at Wantage in 1920, after less than a year's service.

[91] Formerly South Devon Railway.

[92] Later named *Princess Royal*, and then *Royal*.

Became Great Western Railway no. 909.

[93] Renamed *Earl Bathurst* in August 1937. Since preserved.

[94] Renamed *Gladiator* in January 1941.

[95] Name removed by D.E. Marsh, 1905. Rebuilt to class B4x, June 1923.

[96] Temporarily renumbered 6220 and renamed *Coronation* for a visit to the World's Fair at New York in 1939. The locomotive was streamlined, and painted crimson with gold stripes, whereas the genuine *Coronation* was in blue with silver stripes. A new demonstration train went with it to the USA, and the train made an extensive tour of North America. In 1942 the locomotive was brought back to the UK, and resumed its rightful name and number (as did the genuine *Coronation*). The coaches stayed in the USA until after the end of the war.

[97] Originally named *Queensland*. Renamed in December 1904.

[98] Originally named *Sutherlandshire*. Renamed *Duke* in January 1877.

Name	Number	Class	Date	Railway
Duke of Edinburgh's Award	47716	47/7	1966	British Railways
Duke of Edinburgh's Award	47727	47/7		British Railways
Duke of Gloucester	71000	8P	5/1954	**British Railways** [99]
Duke of Lancaster	3	I	12/1885	Mersey Rly
Duke of Normandy	2	2–4–0T	9/1870	Jersey Rly
Duke of Rothesay	509	H	6/1921	North British Rly
Duke of Rothesay	508	A2/1	6/1944	London & North Eastern Rly
Duke of Sutherland	21	Claughton	6/1913	London & North Western Rly
Duke of Sutherland	5541	Patriot	8/1933	London Midland & Scottish Rly
Duke of York	1128	Queen	6/1875	Great Western Rly
Duke of York	3063	3031	6/1897	Great Western Rly
Dullatur	216	211	1856	North British Rly [100]
Dulwich	17	D1	4/1875	London, Brighton & South Coast Rly
Dulwich	907	Schools	7/1930	Southern Rly
Dumbarton	157	157	6/1877	North British Rly [101]
Dumbartonshire	281	D49/1	2/1928	London & North Eastern Rly [102]
Dumbiedykes	418	Scott	7/1914	North British Rly
Dumbleton Hall	4920	Hall	3/1929	**Great Western Rly**
Dumfries-shire	2757	D49/1	3/1929	London & North Eastern Rly
Dummer Grange	6834	Grange	8/1937	Great Western Rly
Dunalastair	721	721	1896	Caledonian Rly
Dunalastair 2nd	766	766	1897	Caledonian Rly
Dunbar	235	233	1865	North British Rly [103]
Duncan	5674	Jubilee	1935	London Midland & Scottish Rly

Name	Number	Class	Date	Railway
Duncannon	315	B2	7/1895	London, Brighton & South Coast Rly [104]
Duncraig	10	Seafield	9/1858	Highland Rly [105]
Duncraig Castle	149	Castle	1902	Highland Rly
Dundee	167	157	6/1877	North British Rly [106]
Dundonian	869	H	7/1906	North British Rly [107]
Dunedin	3399	Atbara	8/1901	Great Western Rly
Dunedin	874	H	8/1906	North British Rly
Dunedin	47704	47/7	1966	British Railways
Dunfermline	424	418	1873	North British Rly
Dunkeld	15	14	10/1862	Highland Rly [108]
Dunkery Beacon	60042	60	6/1991	British Railways
Dunley Manor	7811	Manor	12/1938	Great Western Rly
Dunlop No 7	–	0–4–0ST	1951	**Battlefield Steam Rly**
Dunphail	52	Glenbarry	9/1864	Highland Rly [109]
Dunraven	48	0–6–0	1859	Taff Vale Rly
Dunraven Castle	4092	Castle	8/1925	Great Western Rly
Dunrobin	–	2–4–0T	8/1870	Duke of Sutherland [110]
Dunrobin	396	Newton	9/1870	London & North Western Rly [111]
Dunrobin	2055	Dreadnought	1885	London & North Western Rly
Dunrobin	–	0–4–4T	7/1895	**Duke of Sutherland** [112]
Dunrobin	1573	2Precursor	4/1905	London & North Western Rly
Dunrobin Castle	142	Castle	1900	Highland Rly
Dunrobin Castle	37114	37/0	1963	British Railways
Dunster Castle	4093	Castle	5/1926	Great Western Rly
Dunton	76	69	1908	London, Tilbury & Southend Rly
Dunvant	913	0–6–0	1868	Great Western Rly [113]
Dunvegan Castle	30	Castle	1910	Highland Rly
Durban	3400	Atbara	8/1901	Great Western Rly
Durban	3400	City	4/1907	Great Western Rly
Durdans	113	E1	5/1877	London, Brighton & South Coast Rly [114]
Durford Hall	5990	Hall	12/1939	Great Western Rly
Durham	18	0–6–0	1839	Newcastle & Carlisle Rly
Durham	104	Peel	10/1855	Stockton & Darlington Rly
Durham Cathedral	91002	91	4/1988	British Railways
Durham School	4831	V2	5/1939	London & North Eastern Rly
Durn	82	Clyde Bogie	9/1886	Highland Rly [115]
Durn	74	Snaigow	1916	Highland Rly
Durrington	566	E4	6/1902	London, Brighton & South Coast Rly
Dutch Monarch	4024	Star	6/1909	Great Western Rly [116]
Dwarf	25	0–4–0ST	?	Brecon & Merthyr Rly [117]
Dwight D. Eisenhower	4496	A4	9/1937	**London & North Eastern Rly** [118]
Dwight D. Eisenhower	3278	S160	1944	**Gloucestershire Warwickshire Rly**
Dylan Thomas	–	0–4–0DH	1956	**Gwili Rly**
Dymock Grange	6864	Grange	2/1939	Great Western Rly
Dynevor Castle	4094	Castle	5/1926	Great Western Rly
Dyvatty	4	0–6–0ST	1891	Burry Port & Gwendraeth Valley Rly

Great Western Railway Hall class 4–6–0 no. 4920 *Dumbleton Hall*, at Oxley Shed on 4 May 1958. (*Photo: RAS Marketing*)

[99] The only 8P class Standard locomotive built by British Railways. Replaced no. 46202 *Princess Anne*, which was destroyed in the Harrow & Wealdstone accident. Something of a disappointment in service, *Duke of Gloucester* has been rebuilt for preservation (with an ashpan to the original design – an ashpan that did not accord with the workshop drawings as originally fitted) and has proved itself to be a very successful machine, far better than when in service with British Railways.

[100] Ex-Edinburgh & Glasgow Railway, absorbed by NBR in 1865.

[101] Later renamed *Markinch*.

[102] This is the name borne by the locomotive, which is incorrect. The name of the county is Dunbartonshire; Dumbarton is the county town. The mistake was never corrected.

[103] Ex-Edinburgh & Glasgow Railway, absorbed by NBR in 1865.

[104] Renamed *John Gay* in October 1906. Rebuilt to class B2x, March 1909.

[105] Originally named *Westhall*. Rebuilt from 2–4–0 to 4–4–0 and renamed *Duncraig* in June 1873.

[106] Formerly named *Cardross*.

[107] Later renamed *Bonnie Dundee*.

[108] Previously named *Sutherland*, then renamed *Dunkeld*, and then *Foulis*.

[109] Altered from 2–2–2 to 2–4–0, February 1876.

[110] Later taken into Highland Railway stock as no. 118 *Gordon Castle*.

[111] Renamed *Tennyson* in 1885.

[112] The second locomotive of this name to be owned by the Duke of Sutherland, this was a replacement for the first engine. Now preserved in Canada.

[113] Formerly the Llanelly Rly.

[114] Originally named *Granville*. Renamed in December 1883.

[115] Originally named *Fife*. Renamed *Durn* in 1900.

[116] Originally named *King James*. Renamed *The Dutch Monarch* in June or July 1927, and further renamed *Dutch Monarch* in October or November 1927.

[117] This engine was one of Thomas Savin's, and operated on the Brecon & Merthyr. It was never taken into their stock, and when Savin failed in February 1866 *Dwarf* was put up for sale. It was bought for £250 by I. W. Boulton, who renamed it *Dot*.

[118] Originally named *Golden Shuttle*, renamed in September 1945. Preserved at the National Railroad Museum, USA.

E

Name	Number	Class	Date	Railway
Eadbald	41	2–2–2	1/1844	South Eastern Rly
Eadweade	–	0–6–0T	6/1903	Lambourn Valley Rly [1]
Eagle	20	2–2–2	1837	Grand Junction Rly
Eagle	–	Wolf	11/1838	Great Western Rly (bg)
Eagle	–	1Sussex	12/1838	London & South Western Rly
Eagle	10	2–2–0	9/1839	Midland Counties Rly
Eagle	14	2–2–2	4/1840	London & Brighton Rly
Eagle	27	1Eagle	11/1843	London & South Western Rly
Eagle	20	aCrewe	3/1844	London & North Western Rly
Eagle	–	2–2–0WT	1849	Eastern Counties Rly
Eagle	108	Peel	6/1856	Stockton & Darlington Rly
Eagle	20	bCrewe	8/1856	London & North Western Rly
Eagle	2106	4–4–0ST	4/1859	Great Western Rly (bg) [2]
Eagle	–	0–6–0ST	3/1862	Swansea Vale Rly
Eagle	27	2Eagle	12/1862	London & South Western Rly
Eagle	2140	cSentinel	1928	London & North Eastern Rly
Eagle	**50043**	**50**	**1968**	**British Railways**
Eagle C.U.R.C.	08631	08	1959	British Railways
EAGLE C.U.R.C.	08711	08	1960	British Railways
Ealhswith	–	0–6–0T	11/1898	Lambourn Valley Rly [3]
Eamont	18	2–4–0	1857	Lancaster & Carlisle Rly
Eamont	394	Newton	1870	London & North Western Rly
Earl	100	bCrewe	2/1847	London & North Western Rly
Earl	626	S/Bloomer	1854	London & North Western Rly
Earl	**822**	**0–6–0T**	**9/1902**	**Great Western Rly [4]**
Earl Baldwin	5063	Castle	6/1937	Great Western Rly [5]
Earl Bathurst	**5051**	**Castle**	**5/1936**	**Great Western Rly [6]**
Earl Bathurst	3208	3200	2/1937	Great Western Rly
Earl Beatty	1164	9P	6/1920	Great Central Rly
Earl Cairns	5053	Castle	5/1936	Great Western Rly [7]
Earl Cairns	3210	3200	4/1937	Great Western Rly
Earl Cawdor	3297	Badminton	5/1898	Great Western Rly
Earl Cawdor	5046	Castle	4/1936	Great Western Rly [8]
Earl Cawdor	3203	3200	7/1936	Great Western Rly
Earles	08879	08	1960	British Railways
Earl Fitzwilliam	**–**	**0–6–0ST**	**1923**	**Elsecar at Barnsley**
Earl Grey	21	Director	1832	Stockton & Darlington Rly
Earl Haig	22	2–4–2T	1/1891	Longmoor Military Rly [9]
Earl Haig	1166	9P	8/1920	Great Central Rly
Earl Haig	70044	Britannia	6/1953	British Railways
Earlham Hall	2844	B17/1	5/1935	London & North Eastern Rly [10]
Earlham Hall	61644	B2	3/1949	British Railways (Eastern Region) [11]
Earl Kitchener of Khartoum	279	1A	12/1914	Great Central Rly
Earl Marischal	2002	P2	10/1934	London & North Eastern Rly
Earl Marischal	502	A2/2	6/1944	London & North Eastern Rly [12]
Earl Marischal	87029	87/0	1974	British Railways
Earl Mountbatten of Burma	33027	33/0	1961	British Railways
Earl Mountbatten of Burma	**33207**	**33/2**	**1961**	**British Railways [13]**
Earl of Airlie	–	0–2–4	9/1833	Dundee & Newtyle Rly [14]
Earl of Berkeley	5060	Castle	6/1937	Great Western Rly [15]
(Earl of Berkeley)	3217	3200	3/1938	Great Western Rly [16]
Earl of Birkenhead	5061	Castle	6/1937	Great Western Rly [17]
Earl of Chester	2	I	12/1885	Mersey Rly
Earl of Chester	3069	3031	1/1898	Great Western Rly
Earl of Clancarty	5058	Castle	5/1937	Great Western Rly [18]
Earl of Cork	3418	Bulldog	2/1903	Great Western Rly
Earl of Dartmouth	5047	Castle	4/1936	Great Western Rly [19]
Earl of Dartmouth	3204	3200	8/1936	Great Western Rly
Earl of Devon	3277	Duke	1/1897	Great Western Rly [20]
Earl of Devon	5048	Castle	4/1936	Great Western Rly [21]
Earl of Devon	3205	3200	9/1936	Great Western Rly
Earl of Ducie	5054	Castle	6/1936	Great Western Rly [22]
Earl of Ducie	3211	3200	3/1937	Great Western Rly
Earl of Dudley	5045	Castle	3/1936	Great Western Rly [23]
Earl of Dudley	3202	3200	6/1936	Great Western Rly
Earl of Dunraven	5044	Castle	3/1936	Great Western Rly [24]
Earl of Dunraven	3201	3200	4/1936	Great Western Rly [25]
Earl of Eldon	5055	Castle	6/1936	Great Western Rly [26]
Earl of Eldon	3212	3200	5/1937	Great Western Rly
Earl of Merioneth	**–**	**0–4–4–0F**	**1979**	**Festiniog Rly [27]**
Earl of Mount Edgcumbe	4	0–6–2T	12/1907	Plymouth, Devonport & South Western Junction Rly [28]
Earl of Mount Edgcumbe	**5043**	**Castle**	**3/1936**	**Great Western Rly [29]**
Earl of Mount Edgcumbe	3200	3200	5/1936	Great Western Rly
Earl of Plymouth	5049	Castle	4/1936	Great Western Rly [30]
Earl of Plymouth	3206	3200	11/1936	Great Western Rly
Earl of Powis	5056	Castle	6/1936	Great Western Rly [31]
Earl of Radnor	5052	Castle	5/1936	Great Western Rly [32]
Earl of Radnor	3209	3200	2/1937	Great Western Rly
Earl of St. Germans	5050	Castle	5/1936	Great Western Rly [33]
Earl of St Germans	3207	3200	12/1936	Great Western Rly

---

[1] Became Cambrian Railways no. 24 in June 1904, and Great Western Railway no. 819 in 1923.

[2] Formerly the South Devon Railway.

[3] Became Cambrian Railways no. 26 in June 1904, and Great Western Railway no. 820 in 1923.

[4] 2ft 6in gauge. Built as *The Earl* for the Welshpool & Llanfair Light Railway, which was operated by the Cambrian Railways from the opening. It was renamed *Earl* by the Great Western Railway after 1923; the original name has since been restored.

[5] *Thornbury Castle* until July 1937.

[6] *Dryslwyn Castle* until August 1937.

[7] *Bishop's Castle* until August 1937.

[8] *Clifford Castle* until August 1937.

[9] Formerly London & North Western Railway no. 658, London Midland & Scottish Railway no. 6613.

[10] Rebuilt to class B2, March 1949.

[11] Date rebuilt from class B17/1 to class B2.

[12] Rebuild of 2002 above.

[13] The name was transferred to 33207 (formerly D6592) on the withdrawal of 33027 (formerly D6545) in July 1991. Class 33/0 was the standard locomotive; class 33/1 were the nineteen push/pull fitted locomotives for working between Bournemouth and Weymouth with TC (Trailer Control) coach sets; and class 33/2 were the twelve locomotives built with specially slim bodies (2.64m as against 2.81m, or 8ft 8in as against 9ft 3in) for use on the Hastings line, with its narrow tunnels.

[14] 4ft 6in gauge.

[15] *Sarum Castle* until October 1937.

[16] Preserved on the Bluebell Railway.

[17] *Sudeley Castle* until October 1937.

[18] *Newport Castle* until September 1937.

[19] *Compton Castle* until August 1937.

[20] Name removed in May 1936 when 'Earl' names were allotted to the new 3200 or 'Dukedog' class 4–4–0s.

[21] *Cranbrook Castle* until August 1937.

[22] *Lamphey Castle* until September 1937.

[23] *Bridgwater Castle* until September 1937.

[24] *Beverston Castle* until September 1937.

[25] Originally named *St. Michael*. This name was removed in May 1936 and *Earl of Dunraven* affixed in June 1936.

[26] *Lydford Castle* until August 1937.

[27] 1ft 11½in gauge. Originally named *Livingston Thompson*, and then *Taliesin*. On being further renamed *Earl of Merioneth* (a title held by HRH the Duke of Edinburgh) it was also named (on the other side) *Iarll Meirionnydd*. Taliesin, incidentally, was a chief of the bards, and flourished around AD 570.

[28] Became Southern Railway no. 757 in 1923, and BR no. 30757 in 1948.

[29] *Barbury Castle* until September 1937.

[30] *Denbigh Castle* until August 1937.

[31] *Ogmore Castle* until September 1937.

[32] *Eastnor Castle* until July 1937.

[33] *Devizes Castle* until August 1937.

Name	Number	Class	Date	Railway
Earl of Shaftesbury	5062	Castle	6/1937	Great Western Rly [34]
Earl of Warwick	3070	3031	2/1898	Great Western Rly
Earl Roberts	23	2-4-2T	3/1891	Longmoor Military Rly [35]
Earl Roberts	2400	LBSC I2	4/1908	Longmoor Military Rly [36]
Earl Roberts of Kandahar	446	1A	11/1914	Great Central Rly
Earl St. Aldwyn	5059	Castle	5/1937	Great Western Rly [37]
Earl's Court	66	51	1903	London, Tilbury & Southend Rly
Earlstown	2359	Special Tank	12/1879	London & North Western Rly
Earlswood	83	A1	9/1880	London, Brighton & South Coast Rly [38]
Earl Waldegrave	5057	Castle	6/1936	Great Western Rly [39]
Easingwold	–	0-6-0ST	1891	Easingwold Rly
East Anglian	2859	B17/5	6/1936	London & North Eastern Rly [40]
East Asiatic Company	35024	MN	11/1948	British Railways (Southern Region)
Eastbourne	241	2-2-2	6/1867	London, Brighton & South Coast Rly
Eastbourne	183	Gladstone	12/1889	London, Brighton & South Coast Rly
Eastbourne	914	Schools	12/1932	Southern Rly
Eastbury Grange	6813	Grange	12/1936	Great Western Rly
Eastcote Hall	5925	Hall	5/1933	Great Western Rly
Eastergate	592	E5	4/1904	London, Brighton & South Coast Rly
Eastern Star	47733	47/7		British Railways
Eastfield	26001	26/0	1958	British Railways
East Ham	15	Class 1	1881	London, Tilbury & Southend Rly
Eastham Grange	6835	Grange	9/1937	Great Western Rly
East Hoathly	470	E4	6/1898	London, Brighton & South Coast Rly
East Horndon	22	Class 1	1884	London, Tilbury & Southend Rly
East Horndon	42	37	1897	London, Tilbury & Southend Rly
East Lancashire Railway	37418	37/4	1965	British Railways
Eastleigh	33008	33/0	1961	British Railways
Eastleigh Depot	58017	58	1984	British Railways
East Mount	128	Peel	8/1858	Stockton & Darlington Rly
Eastnor Castle	5052	Castle	5/1936	Great Western Rly [41]
Eastnor Castle	5077	Castle	8/1938	Great Western Rly [42]
Eastnor Castle	7004	Castle	6/1946	Great Western Rly
Easton Court	2941	Saint	5/1912	Great Western Rly
Easton Hall	4995	Hall	2/1931	Great Western Rly
Eaton Hall	4921	Hall	4/1929	Great Western Rly
Eaton Mascot Hall	7902	M/Hall	3/1949	British Railways (Western Region)
Ebor	226	aSentinel	1928	London & North Eastern Rly
Echo	27	Echo	3/1862	London, Chatham & Dover Rly
Eckington	25	4-2-0	1/1841	Birmingham & Gloucester Rly
Eclipse	40	0-4-2	1835	Liverpool & Manchester Rly
Eclipse	–	?	?	Birmingham & Gloucester Rly [43]
Eclipse	32	Fenton	8/1839	London & South Western Rly
Eclipse	–	Wolf	8/1840	Great Western Rly (bg)

Name	Number	Class	Date	Railway
Eclipse	202	bCrewe	4/1848	London & North Western Rly
Eclipse	32	2Hercules	4/1853	London & South Western Rly
Eclipse	–	2-2-2	8/1860	London, Chatham & Dover Rly [44]
Eclipse	32	2Vesuvius	7/1873	London & South Western Rly
Eclipse	636	Samson	9/1873	London & North Western Rly
Eclipse	636	Whitworth	4/1893	London & North Western Rly
Eclipse	3334	Bulldog	11/1899	Great Western Rly
Eclipse	404	George V	4/1913	London & North Western Rly
Eclipse	212	aSentinel	1928	London & North Eastern Rly
Eclipse	D816	Warship	2/1960	British Railways
Economist	301	1Experiment	1883	London & North Western Rly
E.C. Trench	2174	Claughton	8/1916	London & North Western Rly
E.C. Trench	5539	Patriot	7/1933	London Midland & Scottish Rly
Eddystone	3278	Duke	1/1897	Great Western Rly
Eddystone	**21C128**	**rWC**	**4/1946**	**Southern Rly**
Eden	9	0-4-0	1836	Newcastle & Carlisle Rly [45]
Eden	5	2-2-0	10/1842	London, Brighton & South Coast Rly [46]
Eden	87	bCrewe	8/1846	London & North Western Rly
Eden	7	0-6-0	1849	St Helens Canal & Rly
Eden	9	0-6-0	c.1857	Newcastle & Carlisle Rly [47]
Eden	7	2-4-0	1857	Lancaster & Carlisle Rly
Eden	135	The Duke	11/1858	Stockton & Darlington Rly
Eden	87	DX	c.1860	London & North Western Rly
Eden	724	Samson	2/1864	London & North Western Rly
Eden	724	Whitworth	3/1893	London & North Western Rly
Edenbridge	159	E1	7/1891	London, Brighton & South Coast Rly
Eden Hall	4996	Hall	3/1931	Great Western Rly
Edgcumbe	3375	Atbara	4/1900	Great Western Rly [48]
Edie Ochiltree	2677	D11/2	9/1924	London & North Eastern Rly
Edinburgh	179	Windsor	9/1865	Stockton & Darlington Rly
Edinburgh	906	0-6-0	9/1866	Great Western Rly [49]
Edinburgh	477	Abbotsford	6/1877	North British Rly
Edinburgh	336	G	10/1881	London, Brighton & South Coast Rly
Edinburgh	43101	43	10/1978	British Railways
Edinburgh International Festival				
Edinburgh Military Tattoo	43091	43	5/1978	British Railways
Edith	1427	Problem	c.1864	London & North Western Rly
Edith	2053	2Precursor	7/1907	London & North Western Rly
Edith Cavell	2275	Prince/W	11/1915	London & North Western Rly
Edmund Burke	7	Bo-Bo	1921	Metropolitan Rly [50]
Edmundsons	**–**	**0-4-0ST**	**1940**	**North Norfolk Rly**
Edstone Hall	7921	M/Hall	9/1950	British Railways (Western Region)
Edward Blount	189	Gladstone	3/1889	London, Brighton & South Coast Rly
Edward Fletcher	60142	A1	2/1949	British Railways (Eastern Region)
Edward Gibbon	2377	Prince/W	2/1914	London & North Western Rly
Edward Green	873	863	9/1885	Lancashire & Yorkshire Rly
Edward Holden	1	0-4-2	1877	West Lancashire Rly [51]
Edward Lloyd	**–**	**4wDM**	**1961**	**Sittingbourne & Kemsley Light Rly [52]**
Edward Paxman	43170	43	9/1981	British Railways
Edward Pease	114	Edward Pease	8/1856	Stockton & Darlington Rly

[34] *Tenby Castle* until November 1937.

[35] Formerly London & North Western Railway no. 608, and London Midland & Scottish Railway no. 6610.

[36] Formerly London, Brighton & South Coast Railway no. 13, and Southern Railway no. 2013. Withdrawn 1939 and sold to WD. Finally disposed of in 1952.

[37] *Powis Castle* until October 1937.

[38] Sold in January 1918 to the Admiralty, and resold in November 1923 to the Shropshire & Montgomeryshire Railway as their no. 9 *Daphne*.

[39] *Penrice Castle* until October 1937.

[40] Originally *Norwich City*. Renamed *East Anglian* and streamlined for working the 'East Anglian' express, September 1937.

[41] Renamed *Earl of Radnor* in July 1937.

[42] Renamed *Fairey Battle* in October 1940.

[43] An experimental tank engine designed by William Church. When on trial on the Lickey Incline of the Midland Railway, it exploded, killing its crew. On their tombstones in Bromsgrove churchyard the stonemason represented the first locomotive he saw; this has resulted in a legend that they were killed by a Norris-type 4-2-0 locomotive.

[44] Date of purchase. There is a suggestion that *Eclipse* and a sister engine *Meteor* were built to Government order for use in the Crimea, and were left uncompleted when that conflict ended. Both had seen previous service, for *Meteor* had received a new firebox, while *Eclipse*'s firebox had been patched.

[45] Withdrawn 1857. Replaced by a new engine with the same name and number.

[46] London & Brighton and South Eastern Joint Stock.

[47] Replacement for earlier locomotive with same name and number. This engine became NER no. 458 in 1862.

[48] Said to have been named *Conqueror* until May 1900. Renamed *Colonel Edgcumbe* in 1903.

[49] Formerly the Llanelly Railway.

[50] Officially a rebuild of an earlier, unnamed, locomotive, but incorporating few if any of its parts.

[51] Renamed *Southport* in 1880.

[52] 2ft 6in gauge.

Name	Number	Class	Date	Railway
(Edward Thomas)	4	0–4–2ST	1921	Talyllyn Rly [53]
Edward Thompson	500	A2/3	5/1946	London & North Eastern Rly
Edward Tootal	2177	Precedent	3/1875	London & North Western Rly
Edward Tootal	2177	rPrecedent	8/1895	London & North Western Rly
Edward Tootal	1193	George V	3/1913	London & North Western Rly
Edward VII	1	2–6–2T	1/1902	Vale of Rheidol Rly [54]
Edward VII	3413	Bulldog	12/1902	Great Western Rly
Edwin A. Beazley	431	11E	10/1913	Great Central Rly
Edwin Hulse	**2**	**0–6–0ST**	**1918**	**Avon Valley Rly**
Efficient	**–**	**0–4–0ST**	**1918**	**Southport Railway Centre**
Effie	–	0–4–0T	1874	Duffield Bank Rly [55]
Effingham	288	D1	7/1879	London, Brighton & South Coast Rly
Egbert	7	2–2–2	2/1842	South Eastern Rly
Egeria	1436	Problem	1865	London & North Western Rly
Egeria	1431	2Precursor	3/1905	London & North Western Rly
Eggborough Power Station	56030	56	1977	British Railways
Eggborough Power Station	56094	56	1981	British Railways
Eglington	287	bCrewe	7/1852	London & North Western Rly
Eglington	255	1Precursor	1/1879	London & North Western Rly
Eglington	124	Carbrook	1886	Caledonian Rly
Eglington	2061	2Precursor	4/1905	London & North Western Rly
Egmont	222	Egmont	5/1866	London, Brighton & South Coast Rly
Egmont	394	Newton	8/1870	London & North Western Rly
Egmont	359	D1	12/1886	London, Brighton & South Coast Rly
Egmont	394	rPrecedent	4/1893	London & North Western Rly
Egremont	7	0–6–0ST	1863	Whitehaven, Cleator & Egremont Rly [56]
Eigiau	**–**	**0–4–0WT**	**1912**	**Bressingham Museum [57]**
Eire	5572	Jubilee	1934	London Midland & Scottish Rly
Eisteddfod Genedlaethol	37429	37/4	1963	British Railways
E.J. Robertson Grant	–	0–6–0ST	8/1908	Llanelly & Mynydd Mawr Rly
Elaine	747	King Arthur	7/1922	Southern Rly [58]
Elaine	73110	5MT	10/1955	British Railways
(Elaine)	**73119**	**5MT**	**12/1955**	**British Railways [59]**
Eland	1001	B1	6/1943	London & North Eastern Rly
Elbe	41	0–4–2	10/1842	Manchester & Leeds Rly
Elder-Dempster Lines	35030	MN	4/1949	British Railways (Southern Region)
Elders Fyffes	21C16	MN	3/1945	Southern Rly
Eldon	32	Miner	2/1846	Stockton & Darlington Rly
Eleanor	1428	Problem	c.1864	London & North Western Rly
Eleanor	2181	2Precursor	7/1907	London & North Western Rly
Elector	189	aCrewe	1/1848	London & North Western Rly
Electra	–	Priam	3/1842	Great Western Rly (bg)
Electra	168	Undine	6/1860	London & South Western Rly
Electra	**27000**	**EM2**	**1953**	**British Railways**
Elephant	–	0–6–0	1815	Wallsend Colliery
Elephant	–	4–wheel	1836	Bodmin & Wadebridge Rly [60]
Elephant	65	0–4–2	1839	Liverpool & Manchester Rly [61]
Elephant	–	Leo	1/1841	Great Western Rly (bg)
Elephant	51	Bison	5/1846	London & South Western Rly
Elephant	113	bCrewe	6/1847	London & North Western Rly
Elephant	95	Peel	6/1855	Stockton & Darlington Rly
Elephant	8	0–6–0	1858	Brecon & Merthyr Rly
Elephant	2161	0–6–0ST	7/1872	Great Western Rly (bg) [62]
Elf	**5**	**0–6–0WT**	**1936**	**Leighton Buzzard Rly [63]**
Elfin	–	0–4–0ST	3/1898	Fishguard & Rosslare Railways & Harbours
Elgar	92009	92		British Railways
Elgin	834	Problem	c.1863	London & North Western Rly
Elidir	**1**	**0–4–0ST**	**1889**	**Llanberis Lake Rly [64]**
Eliseg	**–**	**0–4–0DM**	**1939**	**Llangollen Rly**
Elizabeth	**–**	**0–4–0ST**	**1928**	**Rutland Railway Museum**
Elizabeth	**–**	**0–4–0DM**	**1949**	**Alderney Rly**
Elizabeth Fry	60024	60	12/1990	British Railways
Elizabeth Garrett Anderson	86612	86/6		British Railways
Elk	24	1Sussex	5/1838	London & South Western Rly [65]
Elk	–	Priam	8/1846	Great Western Rly (bg)
Elk	23	Samson	1/1848	East Lancashire Rly
Elk	299	bCrewe	11/1852	London & North Western Rly
Elk	29	2–4–0	1855	Newport, Abergavenny & Hereford Rly
Elk	2107	4–4–0ST	4/1859	Great Western Rly (bg) [66]
Elk	45	Reindeer	7/1865	London, Chatham & Dover Rly
Elk	24	Lion	12/1871	London & South Western Rly
Elkhound	1706	George V	5/1911	London & North Western Rly
Ella	–	0–6–0T	1881	Ravenglass & Eskdale Rly [67]
Ellangowan	416	Scott	6/1914	North British Rly
Ellen Douglas	2688	D11/2	11/1924	London & North Eastern Rly
Eller	5	0–6–0	8/1864	Cockermouth & Workington Rly
Ellerman Lines	**35029**	**MN**	**2/1949**	**British Railways (Southern Region)**
Ellesmere	245	bCrewe	8/1849	London & North Western Rly
Ellesmere	245	DX	c.1860	London & North Western Rly
(Ellesmere)	**–**	**0–4–0WT**	**1861**	**Bo'ness & Kinneil Rly**
Ellesmere	634	Samson	5/1863	London & North Western Rly
Ellesmere	634	Whitworth	3/1893	London & North Western Rly
Ellington Colliery	56131	56	1984	British Railways
Elm Field	118	Woodlands	5/1857	Stockton & Darlington Rly
Elmley Castle	7003	Castle	6/1946	Great Western Rly
Elton	182	Windsor	12/1865	Stockton & Darlington Rly
Elton Hall	4997	Hall	3/1931	Great Western Rly
Elveden	2804	B17/1	12/1928	London & North Eastern Rly
Elwy	–	0–4–2	1858	Vale of Clwyd Rly
Ely	33	2–4–0	1853	Taff Vale Rly
Ely	08594	08	1959	British Railways
Ely Cathedral	47572	47/4	1964	British Railways
Emerald	195	aCrewe	2/1848	London & North Western Rly
Emerald	66	Ruby	8/1861	London, Chatham & Dover Rly
Emerald	626	1Precursor	1/1879	London & North Western Rly
Emerald	300	2Precursor	7/1905	London & North Western Rly
Emerald	2268	cSentinel	1929	London & North Eastern Rly
Emile Zola	92014	92		Société Nationale des Chemins de fer Français
Emily	10	0–6–0ST	5/1882	Wrexham, Mold & Connah's Quay Rly

[53] 2ft 3in gauge. Built for Corris Railway. May have carried the name *Tattoo* for a short while at first. 'Tattoo' was the maker's code-name for the design. This locomotive was successively Corris Railway no. 4, Great Western Railway no. 4, British Railways no. 4, and Talyllyn Railway no. 4! In more recent years, it has often carried the name *Peter Sam*, from the Revd W. Audrey's children's books.

[54] 1ft 11½in gauge. Became Great Western Railway no. 1212; scrapped in 1932.

[55] 15in gauge.

[56] Became Furness Railway no. 103.

[57] 2ft gauge.

[58] Built by the London & South Western Railway to Robert Urie's design. Nameplates fitted in 1925 by the Southern Railway.

[59] Restored as no. 73110.

[60] Built by Neath Abbey Ironworks for the Bodmin & Wadebridge Railway, which was opened on 4 July 1834 and purchased by the London & South Western Railway in 1846 – though it remained isolated from its parent until 1895 when the LSWR reached Wadebridge. The Great Western had previously made contact at Bodmin Road in 1888. Neath Ironworks supplied the first locomotive, named *Camel* after the local river. They named the next engine *Elephant*, thinking that *Camel* commemorated an animal!

[61] Became London & North Western Railway no. 113 in 1846, and rebuilt to 2–4–0 wheel arrangement.

[62] Formerly the South Devon Railway.

[63] 2ft gauge.

[64] 1ft 11½in gauge.

[65] Originally *Tiger*, by Charles Tayleur & Co. of May 1838. An unsuccessful design, it was rebuilt by Fairbairns in 1842.

[66] Formerly the South Devon Railway.

[67] 15in gauge Heywood type. Built for the Duffield Bank Railway, and later sold to the Ravenglass & Eskdale. Converted to petrol in 1927, and scrapped in 1930.

Name	Number	Class	Date	Railway
Emlyn	3041	3031	10/1894	Great Western Rly [68]
Emlyn	3071	3031	2/1898	Great Western Rly
Emlyn	82	0–6–0ST	1903	Weston, Clevedon & Portishead Rly [69]
Emperor	–	Iron Duke	9/1847	Great Western Rly (bg)
Emperor	217	aCrewe	7/1848	London & North Western Rly
Emperor	74	Peel	7/1853	Stockton & Darlington Rly
Emperor	2167	0–6–0ST	12/1873	Great Western Rly (bg) [70]
Emperor	–	Rover	9/1880	Great Western Rly (bg)
Emperor	374	1Experiment	1884	London & North Western Rly
Emperor	3008	3001	3/1892	Great Western Rly [71]
Emperor	55	B4	7/1901	London, Brighton & South Coast Rly [72]
Emperor	311	2Precursor	9/1905	London & North Western Rly
Empire of India	3467	Bulldog	3/1904	Great Western Rly
Empire of India	4490	A4	6/1937	London & North Eastern Rly [73]
Empress	363	aCrewe	4/1855	London & North Western Rly
Empress	372	1Experiment	1884	London & North Western Rly
Empress	–	0–4–0ST	1897	Aberford Rly
Empress	54	B4	5/1900	London, Brighton & South Coast Rly [74]
Empress	374	2Precursor	9/1905	London & North Western Rly
Empress of Britain CPS	40010	40	5/1959	British Railways [75]
Empress of Canada CPS	40032	40	9/1959	British Railways [76]
Empress of England CPS	40033	40	9/1959	British Railways [77]
Empress of India	3040	3031	9/1894	Great Western Rly
Emsworth	388	D3	5/1894	London, Brighton & South Coast Rly
Emu	–	0–6–0ST	8/1864	Swansea Vale Rly
Enborne Grange	6814	Grange	12/1936	Great Western Rly
Enchantress	1537	Prince/W	11/1911	London & North Western Rly
E. Nettlefold	228	George V	1/1911	London & North Western Rly
Enfield	–	S/Railcar	1849	Eastern Counties Rly
Enfield	–	0–4–0T	1916	Woolwich Arsenal [78]
Engineer	885	Samson	10/1874	London & North Western Rly [79]
Engineer	5099	Whitworth	6/1893	London Midland & Scottish Rly [80]
Engineer Bangor	**1868**	**aCrewe**	**7/1845**	**London & North Western Rly [81]**
Engineer Bangor	1166	Samson	6/1897	London & North Western Rly [82]
Engineer Crewe	209	Whitworth	8/1895	London & North Western Rly [83]
Engineer Lancaster	414	Samson	9/1873	London & North Western Rly [84]
Engineer Lancaster	5100	Whitworth	5/1894	London Midland & Scottish Rly [85]

Name	Number	Class	Date	Railway
Engineer Liverpool	742	Whitworth	3/1893	London & North Western Rly [86]
Engineer Manchester	2156	Whitworth	2/1895	London & North Western Rly [87]
Engineer Northampton	209	Samson	5/1879	London & North Western Rly [88]
Engineer Northampton	5086	Whitworth	11/1890	London Midland & Scottish Rly [89]
Engineer South Wales	155	1P	1876	London Midland & Scottish Rly [90]
Engineer South Wales	485	Whitworth	3/1893	London & North Western Rly [91]
Engineer South Wales	209	Whitworth	8/1895	London & North Western Rly [92]
Engineer Walsall	2151	Samson	11/1874	London & North Western Rly [93]
Engineer Walsall	5094	Whitworth	4/1893	London Midland & Scottish Rly [94]
Engineer Watford	773	Samson	5/1879	London & North Western Rly [95]
Engineer Watford	5101	Whitworth	5/1894	London Midland & Scottish Rly [96]
England	5	4–2–0	3/1839	Birmingham & Gloucester Rly
England	–	2–2–2T	9/1850	Liverpool, Crosby & Southport Rly
England	203	0–6–0	6/1867	Stockton & Darlington Rly
Enid	**2**	**0–4–2T**	**1895**	**Snowdon Mountain Rly [97]**
Enigma	50	Enigma	3/1869	London, Chatham & Dover Rly [98]
Ennerdale	1	0–6–0ST	1855	Whitehaven, Cleator & Egremont Rly [99]
Enterprise	25	Enterprise	6/1835	Stockton & Darlington Rly [100]
Enterprise	1	0–6–0T	1858	Cambrian Railways
Enterprise	**–**	**0–4–0ST**	**1884**	**Tanfield Rly**
Enterprise	4480	A3	8/1923	London & North Eastern Rly
Enterprise	**–**	**0–6–0DM**	**1953**	**South Yorkshire Rly [101]**
Enville Hall	4922	Hall	4/1929	Great Western Rly
Envoy	209	bCrewe	7/1848	London & North Western Rly
Envoy	209	cCrewe	4/1857	London & North Western Rly [102]
Envoy	865	Precedent	5/1877	London & North Western Rly
Envoy	865	rPrecedent	7/1894	London & North Western Rly
Epernay	132	E1	11/1878	London, Brighton & South Coast Rly
Epsom	40	2–4–0	11/1854	London, Brighton & South Coast Rly
Epsom	937	Schools	6/1935	Southern Rly
E.R. Calthrop	1	2–6–4T	1904	Leek & Manifold Light Rly [103]
Ercombert	33	2–2–2	2/1844	London & Brighton Rly [104]
Erebus	33	2–2–2	1838	Grand Junction Rly
Erebus	–	Priam	2/1842	Great Western Rly (bg)
Erebus	33	aCrewe	10/1846	London & North Western Rly
Erebus	46	0–6–0	10/1849	Manchester, Sheffield & Lincolnshire Rly
Erebus	33	Problem	c.1859	London & North Western Rly
Erebus	564	2Precursor	6/1907	London & North Western Rly
(Eric Treacy)	**5428**	**5**	**1937**	**London Midland & Scottish Rly**

[68] Renamed *The Queen* in 1897 and *James Mason* in June 1910.

[69] Date of hiring. Ran for part of its time on the WC&P as an 0–4–2T.

[70] Originally built for the South Devon Railway. After conversion to standard gauge and removal of its name, it became South Wales Mineral Railway no. 6.

[71] Rebuilt to 4–2–2 in October 1894.

[72] Name removed by D.E. Marsh, 1905. Rebuilt to class B4x, August 1922.

[73] As British Railways no. 60011, renamed *Dominion of India*.

[74] Name removed by D.E. Marsh, 1905. Renamed *Princess Royal* in August 1906.

[75] Originally no. D210 *Empress of Britain*.

[76] Originally no. D232 *Empress of Canada*.

[77] Originally no. D233 *Empress of England*.

[78] 18in gauge.

[79] Transferred to Engineer's Department 1897–May 1923. Formerly named *Vampire*.

[80] Built for the London & North Western Railway. Transferred to Engineer's Department May 1923–July 1932. Originally no. 792 *Theorem*.

[81] Originally Grand Junction Railway no. 49 *Columbine*; preserved as no. 1868, nameless.

[82] Transferred to Engineer's Department 1902–25. Formerly named *Wyre*.

[83] Transferred to Engineer's Department 1914–32. Formerly named *Petrel*. Became *Engineer South Wales* from January to August 1932.

[84] Transferred to Engineer's Department 1903–February 1924. Formerly named *Prospero*.

[85] Transferred to Engineer's Department February 1924–35. Formerly London & North Western Railway no. 737 *Roberts*.

[86] Transferred to Engineer's Department 1921–October 1932. Formerly named *Spitfire*.

[87] Transferred to Engineer's Department 1914–October 1927. Formerly named *Sphinx*.

[88] Transferred to Engineer's Department 1902–23. Formerly named *Petrel*. NB This is *not* the same locomotive as the Whitworth class engine of the same name and number which became *Engineer Crewe*!

[89] Transferred to Engineer's Department 1923–November 1927. Formerly London & North Western Railway no. 468 *Wildfire*.

[90] Ex-Midland Railway 2–4–0 no. 155, became no. 20155 on 24 March 1934, reverted to 155 immediately thereafter, became 20155 again in 1937, when the name was removed.

[91] Transferred to Engineer's Department 1921–January 1932. Formerly named *Euxine*.

[92] Transferred to Engineer's Department 1914–32 as *Engineer Crewe*. Formerly named *Petrel*. Became *Engineer South Wales* from January to August 1932.

[93] Transferred to Engineer's Department 1901–June 1923. Formerly named *Baltic*.

[94] Transferred to Engineer's Department June 1923–February 1928. Formerly London & North Western Railway no. 609 *The Earl of Chester*.

[95] Transferred to Engineer's Department 1895–May 1923. Formerly named *Centaur*.

[96] Transferred to Engineer's Department May 1923–April 1936. Formerly London & North Western Railway no. 793 *Martin*.

[97] 800mm gauge rack and pinion locomotive.

[98] Name removed by W. Kirtley when number applied.

[99] Became Furness Railway no. 98.

[100] Rebuilt in 1842 and became no. 8 *Leader*.

[101] The modern, preserved South Yorkshire Railway.

[102] Replacement of previous engine, which was sold to the Lancaster & Carlisle Railway.

[103] 2ft 6in gauge.

[104] London & Brighton and South Eastern Railways joint stock.

Name	Number	Class	Date	Railway
Eridge	271	D1	5/1880	London, Brighton & South Coast Rly
Erin	97	L/Scotchmen	2/1873	London, Chatham & Dover Rly
Erlestoke Manor	**7812**	**Manor**	**1/1939**	**Great Western Rly**
Ernest	905	0-6-0	4/1866	Great Western Rly [105]
Ernest Cunard	2998	Saint	3/1903	Great Western Rly [106]
Ernest Palmer	3420	Bulldog	2/1903	Great Western Rly [107]
Errol Lonsdale	**68011**	**0-6-0ST**	**1953**	**South Devon Rly** [108]
Eryri	**7**	**0-4-2T**	**1923**	**Snowdon Mountain Rly** [109]
Eryri	**8**	**0-4-2T**	**1923**	**Snowdon Mountain Rly** [110]
ESCAFELD	08691	08	1959	British Railways
Escomb	199	Roseberry	12/1866	Stockton & Darlington Rly
Escucha	**11**	**0-4-0ST**	**1883**	**Tanfield Rly** [111]
Escus	29	2-2-2	1/1843	South Eastern Rly
Eshton Hall	6942	Hall	4/1942	Great Western Rly [112]
Esk	–	Caesar	6/1857	Great Western Rly (bg)
Esk	94	Scotchmen	12/1866	London, Chatham & Dover Rly
Eskbank	486	Abbotsford	1878	North British Rly [113]
Eskdale	200	Eskdale	2/1867	Stockton & Darlington Rly
Eske	18	2-4-0	5/1853	South Staffordshire Rly
Esme	–	0-4-0WT	1917	Sand Hutton Rly [114]
Esperanza	–	0-6-0ST	1872	West Somerset Mineral Rly [115]
Essex	9 or 10	0-4-2	1846	Eastern Union Rly
Essex	–	0-4-0ST	1915	Woolwich Arsenal [116]
Esso	**–**	**Bo-Bo**	**1949**	**Steamtown, Carnforth**
Estaffete	–	Iron Duke	9/1850	Great Western Rly (bg)
Estevarney Grange	6836	Grange	9/1937	Great Western Rly
Etarre	751	King Arthur	11/1922	Southern Rly [117]
Etarre	73114	5MT	11/1955	British Railways
Ethelbert	6	2-2-2	2/1842	South Eastern Rly
Ethelred	754	Problem	c.1861	London & North Western Rly
Ethelred	2621	2Experiment	2/1909	London & North Western Rly
Etherley	18	Tory	2/1840	Stockton & Darlington Rly
Ethon	–	Caesar	3/1863	Great Western Rly (bg)
Etna	20	2-2-0	1831	Liverpool & Manchester Rly
Etna	51	2-2-2	1837	Liverpool & Manchester Rly
Etna	–	Leo	6/1841	Great Western Rly (bg)
Etna	118	1Vesuvius	12/1849	London & South Western Rly
Etna	343	2-4-0	1852	London & North Western Rly [118]
Etna	343	aCrewe	8/1854	London & North Western Rly
Etna	343	DX	c.1860	London & North Western Rly
Etna	2132	4-4-0ST	1864	Great Western Rly (bg) [119]
Etna	118	Volcano	8/1872	London & South Western Rly
Etna	481	1Precursor	1/1879	London & North Western Rly
Etna	2577	2Precursor	12/1905	London & North Western Rly
Eton	900	Schools	3/1930	Southern Rly
Etona	3335	Bulldog	11/1899	Great Western Rly
E. Tootal Broadhurst	856	Claughton	9/1914	London & North Western Rly
E. Tootal Broadhurst	5525	Patriot	3/1933	London Midland & Scottish Rly [120]
E. Tootal Broadhurst	5534	Patriot	4/1933	London Midland & Scottish Rly [121]
Eugenie	–	2-2-2	6/1855	[122]
Eugenie	142	Canute	1/1857	London & South Western Rly
Eunomia	1434	Problem	c.1865	London & North Western Rly
Eunomia	2622	2Experiment	2/1909	London & North Western Rly
Eupatoria	–	Iron Duke	5/1855	Great Western Rly (bg)
Eupatoria	–	Rover	10/1878	Great Western Rly (bg)
Eupatoria	3078	3031	2/1899	Great Western Rly [123]
Euphrates	2057	Dreadnought	1885	London & North Western Rly
Euphrates	622	2Precursor	12/1904	London & North Western Rly
Euripides	–	Bogie	2/1855	Great Western Rly (bg)
Europa	–	Caesar	3/1853	Great Western Rly (bg)
Europa	121	0-6-0	2/1854	London, Brighton & South Coast Rly [124]
Europa	53	Europa	9/1873	London, Chatham & Dover Rly
Europa	08661	08	1959	British Railways
European Community	86238	86/2	1965	British Railways
Euryalus	1971	Alfred	1904	London & North Western Rly
Eustace Forth	**7063**	**0-4-0ST**	**1942**	**Central Electricity Generating Board** [125]
Euston	340	aCrewe	7/1854	London & North Western Rly
Euston	3186	Special Tank	12/1875	London & North Western Rly
Euxine	354	bCrewe	11/1854	London & North Western Rly
Euxine	485	Samson	10/1874	London & North Western Rly
Euxine	485	Whitworth	3/1893	London & North Western Rly [126]
Evan Dhu	2673	D11/2	8/1924	London & North Eastern Rly
Evan Llewellyn	3419	Bulldog	2/1903	Great Western Rly
Evanton	32	14	9/1862	Highland Rly [127]
Evening Star	–	Priam	7/1839	Great Western Rly (bg)
Evening Star	4002	Star	3/1907	Great Western Rly
Evening Star	**92220**	**9F**	**3/1960**	**British Railways**
Evenley Hall	4923	Hall	4/1929	Great Western Rly
Evenwood	–	0-6-0	?	Clarence Rly
Everton	2863	B17/4	2/1937	London & North Eastern Rly
Evesham	33	2-2-0	6/1842	Birmingham & Gloucester Rly
Evesham Abbey	4065	Star	12/1922	Great Western Rly
Evesham Abbey	5085	Castle	7/1939	Great Western Rly [129]
Ewell	60	A1	11/1875	London, Brighton & South Coast Rly
Excalibur	72	Mails	11/1865	South Eastern Rly [130]
Excalibur	3256	Duke	8/1895	Great Western Rly
Excalibur	736	King Arthur	8/1918	Southern Rly [131]
Excalibur	73081	5MT	6/1955	British Railways
Excelsior	1	0-4-2	10/1856	Whitehaven & Furness Junction Rly

[105] Formerly Llanelly Railway.

[106] Named *Vanguard* in March 1907, and renamed *Ernest Cunard* in December 1907.

[107] Renamed *Sir Ernest Palmer* in February 1916.

[108] The modern, preserved South Devon Railway.

[109] Later renamed *Aylwyn*. 800mm gauge rack and pinion locomotive.

[110] 800mm gauge rack and pinion locomotive.

[111] 2ft gauge.

[112] Nameplates fitted April 1948.

[113] Originally named *Aberdeen*. Renamed in 1880, having been transferred to the Carlisle route after the fall of the first Tay Bridge.

[114] Previously no. 10 at Royal Army Service Corps Depot, Deptford. 18in gauge.

[115] Owned by the Ebbw Vale Co., which had leased the WSMR, and provided as a substitute while *Pontypool* was under repair. The name is sometimes given as *Esperenza*.

[116] 18in gauge.

[117] Built by the London & South Western Railway to Robert Urie's design. Nameplates fitted 1925 by Southern Railway.

[118] Formerly no. 23 *Mersey* of the Birkenhead, Lancashire & Cheshire Junction Railway.

[119] Built for South Devon Railway.

[120] Renamed *Colwyn Bay* in 1937 and rebuilt with taper boiler in August 1948.

[121] Nameless until 1937, when this name was applied. Rebuilt with taper boiler in December 1948.

[122] *Eugenie* was designed by J.E. McConnell of the London & North Western Railway and built by Fairbairns of Manchester for the Paris Exhibition of 1855. It broadly followed the design of McConnell's 'Large Bloomer' 2-2-2, with 7ft driving wheels. It was tried out on L&NWR tracks, but remained the property of its builders. See *The Illustrated London News*, 30 June 1855.

[123] Originally named *Shooting Star*, renamed *Eupatoria* in August 1906.

[124] Purchased from the Manchester, Sheffield & Lincolnshire Railway in June 1854. The London, Brighton & South Coast Railway had a shortage of goods locomotives while the MSLR needed the money for re-tooling and extending Gorton Works! Built in February 1854 and thus brand new, it had been MSLR no. 121 *Europa*, and so kept both its name and its number.

[125] Preserved at the National Railway Museum, York.

[126] Transferred to Engineer's Department 1921–January 1932 and renamed *Engineer South Wales*.

[127] Previously no. 14 *Loch*. Renamed and renumbered in November 1897.

[128] Rebuilt in July 1939 to Castle class, no. 5085.

[129] Rebuilt from Star class.

[130] Named, and painted royal blue, for a short period only in 1876.

[131] Built by the London & South Western Railway to Robert Urie's design. Nameplates fitted 1925 by the Southern Railway.

British Railways 9F class 2–10–0 no. 92220 *Evening Star*, on a railtour at Princes Risborough on 3 April 1960. (*Photo: LCGB Ken Nunn Collection*)

Name	Number	Class	Date	Railway	Name	Number	Class	Date	Railway
Excelsior	141	Peel	7/1859	Stockton & Darlington Rly	*Expedition*	51908	cSentinel	1928	London & North Eastern Rly
Exe	–	Wolf	9/1838	Great Western Rly (bg) [132]	*Experiment*	6	0–4–0	2/1828	Stockton & Darlington Rly [137]
Exe	–	2–2–2	7/1844	London & South Western Rly (bg) [133]	*Experiment*	32	2–2–0	1833	Liverpool & Manchester Rly
Exe	72	River	8/1895	Great Western Rly [134]	*Experiment*	66	1Experiment	1882	London & North Western Rly
Exe	E760	2–6–2T	12/1897	Southern Rly [135]	*Experiment*	66	2Experiment	4/1905	London & North Western Rly
Exeter	3357	Bulldog	6/1900	Great Western Rly [136]	**(*Experiment*)**	**24061**	**24**	**1960**	**British Railways**
Exeter	21C101	rWC	5/1945	Southern Rly	*Express*	–	Steam Railcar	10/1847	Eastern Counties Rly
Exeter	**50044**	**50**	**1968**	**British Railways**	*Express*	520	1Experiment	1883	London & North Western Rly
Exeter	43025	43	8/1976	British Railways	*Express*	811	2Precursor	9/1905	London & North Western Rly
Exmoor	3279	Duke	1/1897	Great Western Rly	*Express*	5706	Jubilee	1936	London Midland & Scottish Rly
Exmoor	3279	Bulldog	12/1907	Great Western Rly	*Eydon Hall*	4924	Hall	5/1929	Great Western Rly
Exmoor	21C122	rWC	1/1946	Southern Rly	*Eynsham Hall*	4925	Hall	5/1929	Great Western Rly
Exmouth	21C115	WC	11/1945	Southern Rly	*Eyton Hall*	4998	Hall	3/1931	Great Western Rly

[132] Previously named *Snake*. Renamed *Exe* in 1846, original name restored in 1851.

[133] Thought to be the locomotive built for the Bristol & Gloucester Railway as their no. 6 *Berkeley*. Broad gauge. In April 1856 it was sold to Thomas Brassey for working the North Devon Railway, and is thought to have become their *Exe*.

[134] Rebuilt from 2–2–2 no. 72 of 1855.

[135] Built for the Lynton & Barnstaple Railway. 1ft 11½in gauge.

[136] Temporarily renamed *Royal Sovereign* to work a Royal Train on 7 March 1902, and renamed *Smeaton* in October 1903.

[137] Probably rebuilt to 0–6–0 in July 1828. May originally have been no. 7.

F

Name	Number	Class	Date	Railway
Faerie Queen	837	Problem	c.1860	London & North Western Rly
Faerie Queene	1433	2Precursor	4/1906	London & North Western Rly
Fairbairn	338	bCrewe	5/1854	London & North Western Rly
Fairbairn	870	Precedent	6/1877	London & North Western Rly
Fairbairn	210	B2	11/1897	London, Brighton & South Coast Rly [1]
Fairbairn	870	rPrecedent	3/1898	London & North Western Rly
Fairey Battle	5077	Castle	8/1938	Great Western Rly [2]
Fairfield	–	0-4-0	1838	Manchester & Bolton Rly
Fairfield	–	Steam Railcar	1848	Bristol & Exeter Rly (bg)
(Fairfield)	F82	4wBE	1940	Bo'ness & Kinneil Rly
Fairleigh Hall	4926	Hall	5/1929	Great Western Rly
Fairlight	331	G	7/1881	London, Brighton & South Coast Rly
Fair Maid	32	cSentinel	1929	London & North Eastern Rly
Fair Rosamund	1473	517	5/1883	Great Western Rly [3]
Fair Rosamund	47836	47/8		British Railways
Fairway	2746	A3	10/1928	London & North Eastern Rly
Fairy	–	?		Brecon & Merthyr Rly [4]
Fakenham	–	4-4-0T	6/1879	Lynn & Fakenham Rly
Falaba	1324	Prince/W	4/1916	London & North Western Rly
Falcon	5	2-2-2	1837	Grand Junction Rly
Falcon	–	2-2-0	8/1839	London & South Western Rly
Falcon	–	Priam	11/1840	Great Western Rly (bg)
Falcon	5	aCrewe	4/1844	London & North Western Rly
Falcon	29	1Eagle	12/1844	London & South Western Rly
Falcon	2102	4-4-0ST	9/1852	Great Western Rly (bg) [5]
Falcon	5	bCrewe	11/1855	London & North Western Rly [6]
Falcon	109	Peel	6/1856	Stockton & Darlington Rly
Falcon	3	Tiger	8/1861	London, Chatham & Dover Rly
Falcon	29	Falcon	6/1863	London & South Western Rly
Falcon	4484	A4	2/1937	London & North Eastern Rly
Falcon	7	4wDM	1939	Leighton Buzzard Rly [7]
Falcon	DO280	Co-Co	12/1961	Brush Electrical Engineering Co. Ltd
Falkirk	239	233	1867	North British Rly [8]
Falkland Islands	5606	Jubilee	1935	London Midland & Scottish Rly
Falloden	2816	B17/2	10/1930	London & North Eastern Rly [9]
Falloden	1616	B2	11/1945	London & North Eastern Rly [10]
Falmer	294	D1	11/1877	London, Brighton & South Coast Rly [11]
Falmouth	1384	2-4-0	8/1855	Great Western Rly [12]
Falmouth	3280	Duke	1/1897	Great Western Rly
Falmouth	3280	Bulldog	1/1909	Great Western Rly
Falstaff	358	bCrewe	3/1855	London & North Western Rly
Falstaff	358	DX	c.1860	London & North Western Rly
Falstaff	795	Samson	3/1864	London & North Western Rly
Falstaff	795	Whitworth	6/1893	London & North Western Rly
Falstaff	2203	Prince/W	11/1915	London & North Western Rly
Fame	197	bCrewe	3/1848	London & North Western Rly
Fame	427	1Precursor	10/1874	London & North Western Rly
Fame	2578	2Precursor	12/1905	London & North Western Rly
Fanny	–	0-6-0	?	Sirhowy Rly [13]
Faraday	1487	Newton	5/1866	London & North Western Rly
Faraday	1487	rPrecedent	1887	London & North Western Rly
Faraday	1553	2Experiment	1/1909	London & North Western Rly
Farewell	210	0-4-0ST	8/1861	Midland Rly [14]
Farleigh Castle	5027	Castle	4/1934	Great Western Rly
Farlington	382	D3	10/1893	London, Brighton & South Coast Rly
Farmer's Friend	–	0-6-0ST	12/1875	Garstang & Knott End Rly
Farnborough Hall	4927	Hall	5/1929	Great Western Rly
Farncombe	572	E5	1/1903	London, Brighton & South Coast Rly
Farnley Hall	6943	Hall	8/1942	Great Western Rly [15]
Father Ambrose	498	Scott	11/1920	North British Rly
Faversham	63	Sondes	2/1858	London, Chatham & Dover Rly
Fawley Court	2942	Saint	5/1912	Great Western Rly
Fay Gate	472	E4	6/1898	London, Brighton & South Coast Rly
Feanor	18	4wDM	1956	Leighton Buzzard Rly [16]
Fearless	5723	Jubilee	1936	London Midland & Scottish Rly
Fearless	50050	50	1967	British Railways
Featherstonehaugh	43	0-6-0	9/1857	Newcastle & Carlisle Rly [17]
Felicia Hemans	1400	Prince/W	1/1914	London & North Western Rly
Felstead	2743	A3	8/1928	London & North Eastern Rly
Fenchurch	72	A1	9/1872	London, Brighton & South Coast Rly
Fenchurch	30	Class 1	1884	London, Tilbury & Southend Rly
Fenchurch	413	E6	7/1905	London, Brighton & South Coast Rly
Fenella	8	2-4-0T	1894	Isle of Man Rly [18]
Fenton	–	Hawthorn	7/1865	Great Western Rly (bg)
Fernhill	–	0-6-0ST	1875	Snailbeach District Rly [19]
Fernhurst	405	E5	1/1904	London, Brighton & South Coast Rly
Ferret	11	0-4-0DM	1940	Welshpool & Llanfair Light Rly [20]
Ferrybridge 'C' Power Station	56006	56	1977	British Railways
Ferrybridge C Power Station	56089	56	1981	British Railways
Festoon	21	4wPM	1929	Leighton Buzzard Rly [21]
Fiddlers Ferry Power Station	56099	56	1981	British Railways
Fidget	–	0-4-0ST	4/1874	Chatham Dockyard [22]
Fife	7	Seafield	8/1858	Highland Rly [23]
Fife	82	Clyde Bogie	9/1886	Highland Rly [24]
Fighter Command	21C164	BB	7/1947	Southern Rly
Fighter Pilot	21C155	BB	2/1947	Southern Rly
Fiji	5607	Jubilee	1934	London Midland & Scottish Rly
Fillongley Hall	6941	Hall	8/1942	Great Western Rly [25]
Fina Energy	31201	31	1960	British Railways
Financial Times	90005	90/0	3/1988	British Railways
Fingolfin	22			Leighton Buzzard Rly [26]
Finsbury Park	47408	47/4	1963	British Railways
Firdaussi	2503	A3	9/1924	London & North Eastern Rly
Fire Ball	–	Wolf	5/1840	Great Western Rly (bg)
Fireball	73	Fireball	12/1846	London & South Western Rly
Fireball	73	Clyde	6/1864	London & South Western Rly
Firebrand	23	2-2-0	4/1840	Midland Counties Rly
Fire Brand	–	Priam	5/1840	Great Western Rly (bg)
Firebrand	74	Fireball	12/1846	London & South Western Rly
Firebrand	74	Clyde	6/1864	London & South Western Rly
Firecrest	47218	47/0	1965	British Railways
Firefly	31	2-2-0	1833	Liverpool & Manchester Rly
Fire Fly	–	Priam	3/1840	Great Western Rly (bg)

---

[1] Rebuilt to class B2x, February 1909.

[2] *Eastnor Castle* until October 1940.

[3] The only 517 class locomotive to be named, when it hauled a Royal special on the Woodstock branch. The name commemmorates Rosamund Clifford, a resident of Woodstock. She is said to have been a mistress of Henry II, and to have been murdered by order of his Queen, Eleanor of Aquitaine, in the twelfth century.

[4] A tender engine, acquired c. 1865 (source unknown) and disposed of in 1870 (destination also unknown!)

[5] Built for the South Devon Railway.

[6] Originally no. 378 *Palmerston*.

[7] 2ft gauge.

[8] Ex-Edinburgh & Glasgow Railway, absorbed by NBR in 1865. Later renamed *Stonehaven*.

[9] Rebuilt to class B2, November 1945.

[10] Date rebuilt from class B17/2 to class B2.

[11] Named *Rosebery* prior to March 1897.

[12] Built for the West Cornwall Railway.

[13] Built some time between 1832 and 1853.

[14] Taken over from the Staveley Coal & Iron Co. in 1866.

[15] Nameplates fitted in June 1947.

[16] 2ft gauge.

[17] Became North Eastern Railway no. 491 in 1862.

[18] 3ft gauge.

[19] 2ft 4½in gauge.

[20] 2ft 6in gauge.

[21] 2ft gauge.

[22] 18in gauge.

[23] Renamed *Dingwall* and altered from 2-4-0 to 4-4-0 in May 1875.

[24] Renamed *Durn* in 1900.

[25] Nameplates fitted in April 1946.

[26] Under construction at the time of writing. 2ft gauge.

Name	Number	Class	Date	Railway
Firefly	76	Fireball	2/1847	London & South Western Rly
Firefly	231	aCrewe	11/1848	London & North Western Rly
Firefly	6	2-2-2	7/1849	Liverpool, Crosby & Southport Rly
Firefly	231	0-4-2	10/1858	London & North Western Rly [27]
Firefly	231	Samson	2/1865	London & North Western Rly
Firefly	76	Standard	2/1872	London & South Western Rly
Firefly	231	Whitworth	6/1890	London & North Western Rly
Firefly	–	0-4-0ST	1896	**Rutland Railway Museum**
FIRE FLY	47609	47/4	1965	British Railways
Fire Fly	–	Priam		**Great Western Rly (bg)** [28]
Fire King	–	Wolf	5/1840	Great Western Rly (bg)
Fireking	75	Fireball	2/1847	London & South Western Rly
Fire King	40	Phaeton	7/1849	East Lancashire Rly
Fireking	75	Clyde	12/1864	London & South Western Rly
Fire King	3010	3001	3/1892	Great Western Rly [29]
Fire Queen	–	0-4-0	1848	**Pardarn Rly** [30]
Fire Queen	1360	George V	7/1911	London & North Western Rly
Firth of Clyde	70050	Britannia	8/1954	British Railways
Firth of Forth	70051	Britannia	8/1954	British Railways
Firth of Tay	70052	Britannia	8/1954	British Railways
Fishbourne	W9	A1x	12/1876	**Southern Rly** [31]
Fishbourne	91	E1	10/1883	London, Brighton & South Coast Rly
Fishbourne	W14	O2	12/1889	Southern Rly [32]
Fisher	5669	Jubilee	1935	London Midland & Scottish Rly
Fishergate	487	E4	6/1899	London, Brighton & South Coast Rly
Fittleworth	381	D3	10/1893	London, Brighton & South Coast Rly
FitzHerbert Wright	1249	B1	10/1947	London & North Eastern Rly [33]
Fitzwilliam	3	0-4-2	1849	South Yorkshire Rly [34]
Fitzwilliam	–	0-6-0ST	1939	Southport Railway Centre
Flamboyant	60153	A1	8/1949	British Railways (Eastern Region)
Flamingo	160	bCrewe	5/1853	London & North Western Rly [35]
Flamingo	3	0-4-2T	1885	Longmoor Military Rly [36]
Flamingo	3735	Bulldog	5/1909	Great Western Rly
Flamingo	2749	A3	1/1929	London & North Eastern Rly
"Flannel Jacket"	21C1	MN	6/1941	Southern Rly [37]
Fledborough Hall	6944	Hall	9/1942	Great Western Rly [38]
Fleetwood	–	2-4-0	?	Preston & Wyre Railway, Harbour & Dock Co.
Fleetwood	5546	Patriot	3/1934	London Midland & Scottish Rly
Fletching	480	E4	12/1898	London, Brighton & South Coast Rly
Fleur-de-Lis	–	Metro	7/1863	Great Western Rly (bg)
Flintshire	1658	2Experiment	1/1910	London & North Western Rly
Flirt	–	Caesar	5/1852	Great Western Rly (bg)
Flirt	30	Echo	5/1862	London, Chatham & Dover Rly
Flora	78	2-2-2WT	8/1849	Manchester, Sheffield & Lincolnshire Rly
Flora	–	Caesar	2/1854	Great Western Rly (bg)
Flora	29	Echo	4/1862	London, Chatham & Dover Rly
Flora MacIvor	2674	D11/2	8/1924	London & North Eastern Rly

Name	Number	Class	Date	Railway
Floreat Salopia	31147	31/1	1959	British Railways
Florence	–	Caesar	11/1851	Great Western Rly (bg)
Florence	1217	Newton	4/1872	London & North Western Rly
Florence	117	E1	8/1877	London, Brighton & South Coast Rly
Florence	1217	rPrecedent	6/1891	London & North Western Rly
Florence	2	0-6-0ST	1953	**Battlefield Steam Rly**
(Florence)	08764	08	1961	**British Railways**
Florence Nightingale	17	Bo-Bo	1922	Metropolitan Rly [39]
Florence Nightingale	60035	60	9/1991	British Railways
Flosh	–	0-4-0T	?	Cockermouth & Workington Rly
Flower of Yarrow	31	cSentinel	1928	London & North Eastern Rly
Fluff	16	0-4-0DM	1937	**Lakeside & Haverthwaite Rly**
Fly	40	Summers	6/1839	London & South Western Rly
Fly	302	bCrewe	2/1853	London & North Western Rly
Fly	–	0-4-0ST	1891	Lancashire & Yorkshire Rly
Flying Dutchman	81	Mails	1/1866	South Eastern Rly [40]
Flying Dutchman	3009	3001	3/1892	Great Western Rly [41]
Flying Dutchman	70018	Britannia	6/1951	British Railways
Flying Fox	1920	Jubilee	8/1899	London & North Western Rly
Flying Fox	4475	A3	4/1923	London & North Eastern Rly
Flying Scotsman	4472	A3	2/1923	**London & North Eastern Rly**
Flying Scotsman	70216	0-6-0DE	1935	Martin Mill Military Rly [42]
Flying Scotsman	4472	4-6-2	1976	**Bressingham Museum** [43]
Fobbing	77	69	1908	London, Tilbury & Southend Rly
Foch	608	C	8/1888	North British Rly
Foggia	5041	J94	12/1943	**Longmoor Military Rly** [44]
Foinaven	60079	60	1/1992	British Railways
Foligno	135	E1	1/1879	London, Brighton & South Coast Rly
Foligno	5277	J94	1945	Longmoor Military Rly
Folly	–	4wDM	1937	**Gwili Rly**
Folkington	376	D3	5/1893	London, Brighton & South Coast Rly
Folkstone	136	4-2-0	4/1851	South Eastern Rly [45]
Fonmon	–	0-6-0ST	1924	**Avon Valley Rly**
Ford Castle	2817	B17/2	11/1930	London & North Eastern Rly [46]
Ford Castle	1617	B2	12/1946	London & North Eastern Rly [47]
Fordcombe	403	E5	10/1904	London, Brighton & South Coast Rly
Foremarke Hall	7903	M/Hall	4/1949	**British Railways (Western Region)**
Forerunner	13	0-6-0	3/1849	Birkenhead, Lancashire & Cheshire Junction Rly [48]
Forester	10	0-4-0	11/1844	London, Brighton & South Coast Rly [49]
Forester	5	0-6-0ST	6/1886	Severn & Wye & Severn Bridge Rly [50]
Forest Gate	39	37	1897	London, Tilbury & Southend Rly
Forest Hill	471	E4	6/1898	London, Brighton & South Coast Rly
Forfarshire	266	D49/1	12/1927	London & North Eastern Rly
Formby	2	0-4-2	7/1848	Liverpool, Crosby & Southport Rly
Formidable	1953	Alfred	2/1902	London & North Western Rly
Formidable	D802	Warship	12/1958	British Railways
Formidable	50038	50	1968	British Railways
Forres	21	S/Goods	8/1863	Highland Rly

---

[27] Built for the Birkenhead, Lancashire & Cheshire Junction Railway.

[28] Replica. Under construction at Didcot at the time of writing.

[29] Rebuilt to 4-2-2 in September 1894.

[30] 4ft gauge.

[31] Formerly London, Brighton & South Coast Railway no. 50 *Whitechapel*. Rebuilt to class A1x, May 1920. Went to Isle of Wight as W9 *Fishbourne* in May 1930. Returned to the mainland in May 1936 as no. 515S in the Service Stock list, mainly acting as Lancing Carriage Works pilot. Returned to capital stock as no. 32650 in November 1953. It was withdrawn in November 1963 and is preserved by the London Borough of Sutton, who named it *Sutton*. Currently on long-term loan to Kent & East Sussex Railway as their no. 10 *Sutton*.

[32] Originally London & South Western Railway no. 178. Name applied by the Southern Railway on transfer to the Isle of Wight.

[33] Nameplates fitted in December 1947.

[34] Became Manchester, Sheffield & Lincolnshire Railway no. 154 in 1864.

[35] Formerly Grand Junction Railway. Became London & North Western Railway no. 160 in 1846.

[36] 18in gauge. Came, in 1906, from the Admiralty Dockyard, Chatham, who in turn had obtained it from the Royal Arsenal Railway at Woolwich.

[37] This was the Cockney enginemen's nickname for *Channel Packet*!

[38] Nameplates fitted in March 1947.

[39] Nominally a rebuild of an earlier, unnamed locomotive. However, it incorporated few if any of the parts of the original.

[40] Named, and painted royal blue, for a short period only in 1876.

[41] Rebuilt to 4-2-2 in November 1894.

[42] Originally London Midland & Scottish Railway no. 7063.

[43] 15in gauge.

[44] Preserved as no. 107 *Barbara*.

[45] This Crampton-type locomotive, with the name as spelt here, was exhibited at the Great Exhibition of 1851.

[46] Rebuilt to class B2, December 1946.

[47] Date rebuilt from class B17/2.

[48] Originally named *Mersey*.

[49] Built for London & Brighton and South Eastern joint stock.

[50] Became no. 1126A of the Midland Railway, and converted to side tank.

Name	Number	Class	Date	Railway
Forres	29	Glenbarry	10/1863	Highland Rly [51]
Forrester	–	2-2-0	7/1837	Manchester & Bolton Rly
Fort-George	16	Lochgorm	10/1874	Highland Rly [52]
Forth	13	?	1852	St Helens Canal & Rly
Forth	–	Caesar	8/1858	Great Western Rly (bg)
Forth	**10**	**0-4-0ST**	**1926**	**Strathspey Rly**
Forthampton Grange	6837	Grange	9/1937	Great Western Rly
Fortrose	15	Yankee	10/1893	Highland Rly
Fortuna	1435	Problem	c.1860	London & North Western Rly
Fortuna	887	2Experiment	1/1909	London & North Western Rly
Fort William	37073	37/0	1962	British Railways
Foster	–	Hawthorn	8/1865	Great Western Rly (bg)
Foulis	15	14	10/1862	Highland Rly [53]
Foulis Castle	59	Castle	1917	Highland Rly
Fountains Hall	7904	M/Hall	4/1949	British Railways (Western Region)
Fowey	1394	0-6-0T	1873	Great Western Rly [54]
Fowey	3281	Duke	1/1897	Great Western Rly
Fowey Castle	7019	Castle	5/1949	British Railways (Western Region)
Fowey Hall	7905	M/Hall	4/1949	British Railways (Western Region)
Fowler	7	2-4-0	9/1864	London & South Western Rly (ed) [55]
Fowler	2158	Sir Watkin	9/1866	Great Western Rly (bg) [56]
"Fowler's Ghost"	–	2-4-0	1861	Metropolitan Rly [57]
Fox	46	0-4-2	5/1840	Midland Counties Rly
Fox	149	Panther	4/1860	Stockton & Darlington Rly
Fox	1391	0-4-0ST	1872	Great Western Rly [58]
Fox	6	I	1/1886	Mersey Rly
Foxcote Manor	**7822**	**Manor**	**12/1950**	**British Railways (Western Region)**
Foxhound	1628	George V	5/1911	London & North Western Rly
Foxhound	D817	Warship	3/1960	British Railways
Foxhunter	60134	A1	11/1948	British Railways (Eastern Region)
Frachtverbindungen	90129	90/1	4/1989	British Railways
Framfield	559	E4	10/1901	London, Brighton & South Coast Rly
Framlingham	2803	B17/1	12/1928	London & North Eastern Rly [59]
Framlingham	1602	B2	10/1946	London & North Eastern Rly [60]
France	145	E1	10/1880	London, Brighton & South Coast Rly
Francis Baily of Thatcham	**251**	**0-4-0DM**	**1956**	**Admiralty [61]**
Francis Mildmay	3707	Bulldog	6/1906	Great Western Rly [62]
Francis Stevenson	1960	Alfred	3/1902	London & North Western Rly
Franconia CLS	40020	40	7/1959	British Railways [63]
Frank Bibby	3416	Bulldog	2/1903	Great Western Rly [64]
Frank Hornby	86614	86/6	3/1966	British Railways
Franklin	1520	Newton	11/1866	London & North Western Rly
Franklin	1520	rPrecedent	5/1891	London & North Western Rly
(Franklyn D. Roosevelt)	701	S160	1944	United States Army Transportation Corps [65]
Frankton Grange	6816	Grange	12/1936	Great Western Rly
Fratton	270	2-4-0T	3/1873	London, Brighton & South Coast Rly [66]
Fratton	174	Gladstone	1/1891	London, Brighton & South Coast Rly
(Fred)	71480	J94	1945	War Department
Frederick Baynes	2239	Claughton	9/1914	London & North Western Rly
Frederick Saunders	3042	3031	10/1894	Great Western Rly
Freightconnection	90022	90/0	1/1989	British Railways
Freightliner 1995	47376	47/3	1965	British Railways
Freightliner Birmingham	47301	47/3	1964	British Railways
Freightliner Coatbridge	90143	90/1	6/1990	British Railways
Freight Transport Association	37672	37/5	1/1964	British Railways
Fremantle	193	Gladstone	11/1888	London, Brighton & South Coast Rly
French	176	C	4/1890	North British Rly
French Line C.G.T.	21C19	MN	6/1945	Southern Rly [67]
Frensham Hall	5981	Hall	10/1938	Great Western Rly
Freshford Manor	7813	Manor	1/1939	Great Western Rly
Freshwater	207	Belgravia	1/1876	London, Brighton & South Coast Rly
Freshwater	**W8**	**A1**	**1/1877**	**Southern Rly [68]**
Freshwater	W35	O2	5/1890	Southern Rly [69]
Freshwater	567	E5	11/1902	London, Brighton & South Coast Rly
Fretconnection	90130	90/1	5/1989	British Railways
Frewin Hall	6909	Hall	11/1940	Great Western Rly
Friar	178	aCrewe	11/1849	London & North Western Rly
Friar	1116	1Experiment	1884	London & North Western Rly
Friar	837	2Precursor	2/1906	London & North Western Rly
Friar Tuck	1122A	0-6-0T	12/1870	Midland Rly [70]
Friary	08645	08	1959	British Railways
Frilford Grange	6815	Grange	12/1936	Great Western Rly
Frilsham Manor	7816	Manor	1/1939	Great Western Rly
Fringford Manor	7814	Manor	1/1939	Great Western Rly
Fritwell Manor	7815	Manor	1/1939	Great Western Rly
Frobisher	1528	Newton	11/1866	London & North Western Rly
Frobisher	1528	rPrecedent	2/1888	London & North Western Rly
Frobisher	2268	Claughton	3/1920	London & North Western Rly
Frobisher	5640	Jubilee	1934	London Midland & Scottish Rly
Frog	–	0-4-0ST	1887	Caldon Low Quarry
Frolic	36	Dawn	11/1862	London, Chatham & Dover Rly

[51] Originally named *Highlander*. Altered from 2–2–2 to 2–4–0 in August 1871, and renamed *Forres* in May 1879.

[52] Previously named *St Martins*. Renamed *Fort-George* in 1899.

[53] Previously named *Dunkeld*, and before that *Sutherland*.

[54] Built for the Cornwall Minerals Railway as their no. 3.

[55] Ex-Somerset & Dorset Railway. Transferred to Engineer's Department in December 1878. Withdrawn 1890.

[56] This locomotive was sold to the South Devon Railway in July 1872, retaining its name and still unnumbered. In 1876 the Great Western absorbed the South Devon, and the SDR engines received numbers, *Fowler* becoming no. 2158. It ceased work in June 1887.

[57] A broad gauge 2–4–0 tender locomotive with the boiler heated by hot bricks in place of a conventional firebox, in an attempt to avoid smoke in the Metropolitan Railway's tunnels. The engine could barely move itself, let alone haul a train.

[58] Built for the West Cornwall Railway.

[59] Rebuilt to class B2, October 1946.

[60] Date of rebuilding from class B17/1.

[61] Built for the United States Air Force; transferred to the Admiralty Dept in 1973.

[62] Renamed *Lord Mildmay of Flete* in July 1923.

[63] Originally no. D220 *Franconia*.

[64] Originally named *Bibby*. Renamed in April 1903.

[65] After the war, it was with FS (Italian Railways). Sold to Hellenic Railways (Greece) and numbered 575. USATC no. was 3278. Now on the Mid-Hants Railway.

[66] Originally no. 53. Renumbered 270 in November 1875 and named *Bishopstone*. Renamed *Fratton* in May 1878 and sent to the Hayling Island branch. Renumbered 357 in April 1880 and 497 in April 1886, it was withdrawn in September 1890.

[67] The initials in the name stood for Compagnie Générale Transatlantique – the company's name in French.

[68] This engine was built as London, Brighton & South Coast Railway no. 46 *Newington*. It was sold to the London & South Western Railway in March 1903, becoming their no. 734, for the Axminster–Lyme Regis branch (where it was not a success), and then re-sold in December 1913 to the Freshwater, Yarmouth & Newport Railway. It returned to the Southern Railway in 1923 and took up its old number in the LB&SCR duplicate list, 2646. It later became BR no. 32646 and was finally withdrawn in November 1963.

[69] Originally London & South Western Railway (and Southern Railway) no. 181.

[70] Built for the Severn & Wye & Severn Bridge Railway.

Name	Number	Class	Date	Railway	Name	Number	Class	Date	Railway
Frome	114	Rocklia	12/1849	London & South Western Rly	*Fury*	21	2–2–0	1831	Liverpool & Manchester Rly
Frome	114	Volcano	7/1869	London & South Western Rly	*Fury*	–	Fury	12/1846	Great Western Rly (bg)
Fron Hall	7906	M/Hall	12/1949	British Railways (Western Region)	*Fury*	32	2–4–0	1/1847	Manchester, Sheffield &
Fryerage	87	0–4–0	1845	Stockton & Darlington Rly [71]					Lincolnshire Rly
F.S.P. Wolferstan	1294	George V	11/1911	London & North Western Rly	*Fury*	307	bCrewe	3/1853	London & North Western Rly
Fulham	44	A1	6/1877	London, Brighton & South Coast Rly	*Fury*	6138	Royal Scot	9/1927	London Midland & Scottish Rly [72]
Fulmar	47360	47/3	1965	British Railways	*Fury*	6399	Royal Scot	12/1929	London Midland & Scottish Rly [73]
Fulton	–	Victoria	1/1864	Great Western Rly (bg)	*Fusee*	R.L.4	0–4–0ST	7/1884	Woolwich Arsenal [74]
Furious	5729	Jubilee	1936	London Midland & Scottish Rly	*F.W. Webb*	238	George V*	10/1910	London & North Western Rly
Furious	50034	50	1968	British Railways	*Fylde*	16	2–4–0	1857	Lancaster & Carlisle Rly

---

[71] Purchased from the Manchester & Leeds Railway in 1854.

[72] Renamed *The London Irish Rifleman* in October 1929.

[73] Experimental ultra-high pressure locomotive. A three-cylinder compound, its boiler was in three sections, with 1800, 900 and 250lb per square inch pressure in each. On test, a boiler tube burst and an inspector in the cab was killed. The engine never hauled a revenue-earning train. It was rebuilt with a taper boiler in November 1935 and became no. 6170 *British Legion*, forming the prototype of the 'Converted Royal Scots' class.

[74] 18in gauge. The name means 'Rocket' in French!

G

Name	Number	Class	Date	Railway
Gadfly	–	2-2-0	?	London, Chatham & Dover Rly [1]
Gadie	–	0-4-0ST	1920	Nidd Valley Light Rly [2]
Gadie	–	0-6-0ST	1925	Nidd Valley Light Rly
Gadlys	19	0-6-0	5/1850	Taff Vale Rly
Gadwall	4469	A4	3/1938	London & North Eastern Rly [3]
Gaelic	1312	Teutonic	6/1890	London & North Western Rly
Gaelic	802	2Precursor	7/1907	London & North Western Rly
Gainford	97	Peel	6/1855	Stockton & Darlington Rly
Gainsborough	2597	A3	4/1930	London & North Eastern Rly
Galashiels	488	Abbotsford	1878	North British Rly
Galatea	**5699**	**Jubilee**	**1936**	**London Midland & Scottish Rly**
Gallia	224	DFG	4/1866	London & South Western Rly
Gallipoli	95	Prince/W	3/1916	London & North Western Rly
Gallo	–	0-4-0ST	1898	Fishguard & Rosslare Railways & Harbours
Galloway Princess	47673	47/4	11/1965	British Railways
Galltfaenan	–	0-4-2	1859	Vale of Clwyd Rly
Galopin	2575	A3	10/1924	London & North Eastern Rly
Galtee More	2548	A3	9/1924	London & North Eastern Rly
Gamma	**75256**	**0-6-0ST**	**6/1945**	**Tanfield Rly**
Gannet	4900	A4	5/1938	London & North Eastern Rly
Gannymede	45	0-4-0	8/1840	Stockton & Darlington Rly [4]
Ganymede	5	1Sussex	9/1839	London & South Western Rly
Ganymede	–	Priam	7/1842	Great Western Rly (bg)
Ganymede	5	2Hercules	12/1854	London & South Western Rly
Ganymede	1670	Newton	3/1868	London & North Western Rly
Ganymede	5	Volcano	3/1873	London & South Western Rly
Ganymede	1670	rPrecedent	1887	London & North Western Rly
Ganymede	2579	2Precursor	12/1905	London & North Western Rly
Garden Festival Wales 1992	43016	43	6/1976	British Railways [5]
Gardenia	4108	Flower	6/1908	Great Western Rly
Gardner	–	0-4-0ST	12/1856	Preston & Longridge Rly
Gareloch	89	157	7/1877	North British Rly [6]
Garganey	4500	A4	4/1938	London & North Eastern Rly [7]
Garnet	–	Rennie	6/1838	London & South Western Rly [8]
Garrett	**11**	**4wDM**	**1939**	**Llanberis Lake Rly [9]**
Garsington Manor	7817	Manor	1/1939	Great Western Rly
Gartcosh	37784	37/7	11/1963	British Railways
Gasbag	**–**	**4wVB**	**1923**	**Steamtown, Carnforth [10]**
Gascony	126	E1	8/1878	London, Brighton & South Coast Rly
Gas-Oil	**–**	**0-4-0DM**	**1957**	**Foxfield Steam Rly**
Gatacre Hall	4928	Hall	5/1929	Great Western Rly
Gateshead	**47402**	**47**	**1962**	**British Railways**
Gatwick	395	D3	5/1896	London, Brighton & South Coast Rly
Gatwick Express	73206	73/2	5/1966	British Railways
Gaul	140	Saxon	10/1857	London & South Western Rly

Name	Number	Class	Date	Railway
Gaveller	1353	0-6-0T	3/1891	Great Western Rly [11]
Gay Crusader	4477	A3	6/1923	London & North Eastern Rly
Gayton Hall	2841	B17/1	5/1933	London & North Eastern Rly
Gazelle	–	Wolf	3/1841	Great Western Rly (bg)
Gazelle	26	1Sussex	7/1842	London & South Western Rly [12]
Gazelle	5	2-2-2	8/1848	Liverpool, Crosby & Southport Rly [13]
Gazelle	49	Venus	4/1850	East Lancashire Rly
Gazelle	26	2Hercules	8/1854	London & South Western Rly
Gazelle	370	aCrewe	6/1855	London & North Western Rly
Gazelle	30	2-4-0	1856	Newport, Abergavenny & Hereford Rly
Gazelle	125	Peel	2/1858	Stockton & Darlington Rly
Gazelle	2110	4-4-0ST	5/1859	Great Western Rly (bg) [14]
Gazelle	40	0-6-0	1872	Taff Vale Rly
Gazelle	26	Volcano	7/1872	London & South Western Rly
Gazelle	**–**	**0-4-2T**	**1896**	**Shropshire & Montgomeryshire Rly [15]**
Gazelle	1003	B1	11/1943	London & North Eastern Rly
G B Keeling	**4**	**J94**	**12/1953**	**Dean Forest Rly [16]**
GEFCO	47049	47/0	1964	British Railways
Gelert	**–**	**0-4-2T**	**1953**	**Welsh Highland Rly [17]**
Gelly Gaer	50	0-6-0	1860	Taff Vale Rly
Gem	37	Commerce	6/1847	Stockton & Darlington Rly
Gem	107	107	10/1847	London & South Western Rly
Gem	107	Gem	12/1862	London & South Western Rly
Gemini	–	Leo	9/1841	Great Western Rly (bg)
Gemsbok	1020	B1	2/1947	London & North Eastern Rly
General	174	bCrewe	10/1847	London & North Western Rly
General	1170	Precedent	9/1878	London & North Western Rly
General Don	?4	0-4-2ST	9/1877	Jersey Rly [18]
General Don	?	2-4-0T	1879	Jersey Rly [19]
General Joffre	27	Prince/W	10/1915	London & North Western Rly
General Lord Robertson	**610**	**0-8-0DH**	**1963**	**War Department**
General Steam Navigation	**21C11**	**MN**	**12/1944**	**Southern Rly**
General Wood	1	0-6-0	5/1865	Manchester & Milford Rly
Geneva	86	E1	3/1883	London, Brighton & South Coast Rly
Genoa	305	Lyons	12/1877	London, Brighton & South Coast Rly
Geoffrey Chaucer	70002	Britannia	3/1951	British Railways
Geoffrey Gibbs	1248	B1	10/1947	London & North Eastern Rly [20]
Geoffrey H. Kitson	1237	B1	9/1947	London & North Eastern Rly [21]
George	**–**	**4wVB**	**1955**	**South Yorkshire Rly [22]**
George A. Wallis	185	Gladstone	7/1889	London, Brighton & South Coast Rly
George A. Wills	3061	3031	5/1897	Great Western Rly [23]
George A. Wills	3705	Bulldog	5/1906	Great Western Rly
George B	**–**	**0-4-0ST**	**1898**	**Gloucestershire Warwickshire Rly [24]**

[1] Bury-type locomotive purchased from the LNWR; built in either 1838 or 1845.

[2] Later renamed *Craven*.

[3] Renamed *Sir Ralph Wedgwood* in March 1939.

[4] Bury type. Ex-Midland Counties Railway no. 41 *Ganymede* or *Gannymede*. Sold to the Stockton & Darlington Railway in November 1844.

[5] Originally named *Songs of Praise*. Also named (on the other side) *Gwyl Gerddi Cymru 1992*.

[6] Later renamed *Ladybank*.

[7] Renamed *Sir Ronald Matthews* in March 1939.

[8] Unsuccessful in service. Sent to Fairbairns for rebuilding, February 1841. It returned as no. 17 *Queen*.

[9] 1ft 11½in gauge.

[10] Sentinel vertical-boiler geared steam locomotive.

[11] Built for the Severn & Wye & Severn Bridge Railway.

[12] Originally *Thetis*, unnumbered, of April 1838. Unsatisfactory in service, it was rebuilt by Fairbairns in 1842 and returned to the LSWR as no. 26 *Gazelle*.

[13] Originally named *Southport* or *Waterloo*. It is uncertain whether *Southport* was renamed *Antelope* and *Waterloo* became *Gazelle* by October 1850, or *vice versa*.

[14] Built for the South Devon Railway.

[15] Built by Dodman of King's Lynn as a 2-2-2T for a railway director, the mayor of King's Lynn, who, unusually, had the right to operate his own locomotive over the parent system. On purchase by the Shropshire & Montgomeryshire Railway it was altered to 0-4-2T for working the Criggion branch. It survived the line's closure and take-over by the Army, and spent some years on display outside the Officers' Mess at Longmoor, before going to the Army Transport Museum at Beverley. It is now with the Kent & East Sussex Railway. Fitted with wooden wheels, it was reputed to be the smallest standard gauge locomotive built in this country.

[16] Later renamed *W.P. Awdrey*.

[17] 1ft 11½in gauge.

[18] 3ft 6in gauge. The Jersey Railway started off as a standard gauge line, then changed to the 3ft 6in gauge.

[19] Later *Clevedon* of the Weston, Clevedon & Portishead Railway.

[20] Nameplates only fitted in December 1947.

[21] Nameplates only fitted in December 1947.

[22] The modern, preserved South Yorkshire Railway.

[23] Originally named *Alexandra*; renamed in October 1911.

[24] 2ft gauge.

Name	Number	Class	Date	Railway
George Davidson	45	F	6/1921	Great North of Scotland Rly
George Edwards	33	4wDM	1943	**Scottish Mining Museum – Prestongrange**
George Eliot	92027	92		British Railways
George Findlay	2051	G.Britain	1894	London & North Western Rly
George Findlay	1406	2Experiment	4/1909	London & North Western Rly
George Henry	–	0–4–0VB	1877	**Narrow Gauge Museum, Tywyn** [25]
George Jackson Churchward	D1664	47	1965	British Railways
George Macpherson	511	Claughton	7/1916	London & North Western Rly
(George Mason)	08123	08	1955	**British Railways**
George Romney	11	Bo-Bo	1921	Metropolitan Rly [26]

Metropolitan Railway electric locomotive no. 11 *George Romney*, at Baker Street with a through train to Aylesbury in 1959. (*Photo: Author*)

Name	Number	Class	Date	Railway
George Sholto	–	0–4–0ST	1909	**Bressingham Steam Museum** [27]
George Stephenson	–	?	1831	Garnkirk & Glasgow Rly [28]
(George Stephenson)	4767	5	1947	**London Midland & Scottish Rly**
George the Fifth	2663	George V	7/1910	London & North Western Rly
George Waddell	–	0–6–0T	8/1907	Llanelly & Mynydd Mawr Rly [29]
George Whale	896	George V*	10/1910	London & North Western Rly
Georgina	20906	20	11/1967	Hunslet-Barclay Ltd
Gerald Loder	317	B2	5/1896	London, Brighton & South Coast Rly [30]
Gerard Powys Dewhurst	507	11F	2/1920	Great Central Rly
Germanic	333	1Experiment	1884	London & North Western Rly
Germanic	372	2Experiment	6/1905	London & North Western Rly [31]
Gert	169	GWR2301	4/1896	War Department [32]
Geryon	–	Caesar	12/1854	Great Western Rly (bg)
Ghana	45610	Jubilee	1934	British Railways [33]
Gheber	14	0–6–0	3/1849	Birkenhead, Lancashire & Cheshire Junction Rly [34]
G.H. Stratton	08649	08	1959	British Railways
G.H. Wood	10	2–4–0T	1905	**Isle of Man Rly** [35]
Giaour	–	Caesar	5/1852	Great Western Rly (bg)
Gibraltar	3401	Atbara	8/1901	Great Western Rly

Name	Number	Class	Date	Railway
Gibraltar	3401	City	2/1907	Great Western Rly
Gibraltar	2291	George V	7/1911	London & North Western Rly
Gibraltar	5608	Jubilee	1934	London Midland & Scottish Rly
Gibraltar	–	0–4–0ST	1948	**Buckinghamshire Railway Centre**
Giffard	680	1Precursor	1/1879	London & North Western Rly
Giggleswick	5538	Patriot	7/1933	London Midland & Scottish Rly
Gilbert and Ellice Islands	5609	Jubilee	1934	London Midland & Scottish Rly
Gilwell Park	2846	B17/1	8/1935	London & North Eastern Rly
Gipsyhill	43	A1	6/1877	London, Brighton & South Coast Rly [36]
Giraffe	–	Wolf	9/1841	Great Western Rly (bg)
Giraffe	22	1Sussex	4/1842	London & South Western Rly [37]
Giraffe	242	bCrewe	5/1849	London & North Western Rly
Giraffe	65	Giraffe	7/1857	East Lancashire Rly
Giraffe	2112	4–4–0ST	6/1859	Great Western Rly (bg) [38]
Giraffe	22	Lion	7/1871	London & South Western Rly
Giraffe	2182	Precedent	3/1875	London & North Western Rly
Giraffe	2182	rPrecedent	2/1895	London & North Western Rly
Gisland	–	?	?	Brampton Rly
G.J. Churchward	7017	Castle	8/1948	British Railways (Western Region) [39]
Gladiateur	2569	A3	9/1924	London & North Eastern Rly
Gladiator	–	Caesar	3/1861	Great Western Rly (bg)
Gladiator	1685	Newton	5/1868	London & North Western Rly
Gladiator	1685	rPrecedent	11/1888	London & North Western Rly
Gladiator	–	0–6–0ST	1922	**Yorkshire Dales Rly**
Gladiator	5076	Castle	8/1938	Great Western Rly [40]
Gladstone	171	Panther	12/1863	Stockton & Darlington Rly
Gladstone	53	Small Pass	10/1865	Cambrian Railways
Gladstone	1521	Newton	11/1866	London & North Western Rly
Gladstone	214	Gladstone	12/1882	**London, Brighton & South Coast Rly**
Gladstone	4	I	12/1885	Mersey Rly
Gladstone	1521	rPrecedent	8/1889	London & North Western Rly
Gladys	58	2–4–0T	5/1866	Cambrian Railways
Gladys	–	0–4–0ST	1894	**Midland Railway Centre**
Glandovey	42	Small Pass	3/1864	Cambrian Railways

London, Brighton & South Coast Railway 0–4–2 no. 214 *Gladstone*, as restored for preservation, at Battersea Yard on 21 May 1927. (*Photo: LCGB Ken Nunn Collection*)

[25] 1ft 11½in gauge.

[26] Nominally a rebuild of an earlier, unnamed locomotive. However, it incorporated few if any of its parts, and is best considered as a replacement.

[27] 2ft gauge.

[28] 4ft 6in gauge.

[29] Became Great Western Railway no. 312.

[30] Rebuilt to class B2x, October 1908.

[31] Renamed *Belgic* during the First World War. The old nameplate was left in place, with the name defaced, and the new name mounted above – so that nobody should miss the point!

[32] Originally Great Western Railway no. 2479.

[33] Built by the London Midland & Scottish Railway and originally named *Gold Coast*.

[34] Originally named *Dee*. Later passed to the London & North Western Railway.

[35] 3ft gauge.

[36] Became Weston, Clevedon & Portishead Railway no. 2 *Portishead*, and then Great Western Railway no. 5. Withdrawn by British Railways in 1954.

[37] Built in April 1842 by Tayleur as *Renown* (no number). The design was unsatisfactory in service, and in 1842 the engine was rebuilt by Fairbairns, returning to the LSWR as no. 22 *Giraffe*.

[38] Originally built for the South Devon Railway.

[39] After the engine had been in service for a few days, the nameplates were removed until the naming ceremony on 29 October 1948.

[40] *Drysllwyn Castle* until January 1941.

Name	Number	Class	Date	Railway
Glansevern	11	0–4–2	11/1859	Brecon & Merthyr Rly [41]
Glansevern	15	S/Goods	9/1875	Cambrian Railways
Glasfryn Hall	6945	Hall	9/1942	Great Western Rly [42]
Glasgow	–	0–4–0T	1915	Woolwich Arsenal [43]
Glasgow 1990 Cultural Capital of Europe	90012	90/0	11/1988	British Railways
Glasgow Yeomanry	5158	5	1935	London Midland & Scottish Rly
Glaslyn	**1**	**4wDM**	**1952**	**Welsh Highland Rly [44]**
Glasshoughton	**4**	**0–6–0ST**	**1954**	**Southport Railway Centre**
Glastonbury	3336	Bulldog	12/1899	Great Western Rly
Glastonbury Abbey	4061	Star	5/1922	Great Western Rly
Glastonbury Tor	60039	60	9/1991	British Railways
Glatton	1928	Jubilee	4/1900	London & North Western Rly
Glen Aladale	504	Glen	4/1920	North British Rly
Glenalmond	4	1A	6/1913	Great Central Rly
Glen Arklet	503	Glen	5/1920	North British Rly
Glen Auldyn	**–**	**8wDH**	**1986**	**Mull Rail [45]**
Glenbarry	28	Glenbarry	9/1863	Highland Rly [46]
Glen Beasdale	407	Glen	12/1913	North British Rly
Glenbruar	100	Strath	6/1892	Highland Rly
Glen Cona	505	Glen	5/1920	North British Rly
Glen Croe	406	Glen	12/1913	North British Rly
Glendarrock	37403	37/4	1965	British Railways
Glen Dessary	490	Glen	5/1920	North British Rly
Glen Dochart	100	Glen	5/1917	North British Rly
Glen Douglas	**256**	**Glen**	**9/1913**	**North British Rly**
Glendower	280	aCrewe	4/1852	London & North Western Rly
Glendower	280	DX	c.1860	London & North Western Rly
Glendower	1987	2Experiment	9/1906	London & North Western Rly
(Glendower)	**–**	**J94**	**1954**	**South Devon Rly [47]**
Glen Falloch	266	Glen	10/1913	North British Rly
Glenfiddich	86241	86/2	1965	British Railways
Glenfinnan	149	Glen	9/1913	North British Rly
Glen Fintaig	502	Glen	5/1920	North British Rly
Glen Fruin	153	Glen	6/1917	North British Rly
Glengarnock	37111	37/0	1963	British Railways
Glen Garry	270	Glen	3/1919	North British Rly
Glen Garvin	34	Glen	6/1920	North British Rly
Glen Gau	492	Glen	7/1920	North British Rly [48]
Glen Gloy	35	Glen	6/1920	North British Rly
Glen Gour	9492	D34	7/1920	London & North Eastern Rly [See Note 48 below]
Glen Grant	52	F	10/1920	Great North of Scotland Rly
Glen Gyle	287	Glen	4/1919	North British Rly [49]
Glen Loy	494	Glen	8/1920	North British Rly
Glen Luss	493	Glen	7/1920	North British Rly
Glen Lyon	278	Glen	4/1919	North British Rly
Glen Mallie	495	Glen	8/1920	North British Rly
Glen Mamie	242	Glen	3/1919	North British Rly
Glen Moidart	496	Glen	9/1920	North British Rly
Glenmore	97	Strath	6/1892	Highland Rly
Glen Murran	281	Glen	4/1919	North British Rly
Glen Nevis	307	Glen	12/1913	North British Rly
Glen Ogle	241	Glen	7/1917	North British Rly
Glen Orchy	221	Glen	9/1913	North British Rly
Glen Quoich	291	Glen	5/1917	North British Rly
Glen Roy	258	Glen	9/1913	North British Rly
Glen Sheil	298	Glen	5/1917	North British Rly
Glenside	3018	3001	4/1892	Great Western Rly [50]
Glen Sloy	408	Glen	12/1913	North British Rly
Glen Spean	405	Glen	12/1913	North British Rly
Glentilt	96	Strath	6/1892	Highland Rly
Glentromie	99	Strath	6/1892	Highland Rly
Glentruim	98	Strath	6/1892	Highland Rly
Globe	9	0–4–0	10/1830	Stockton & Darlington Rly
Globe	27	0–6–0	1836	Newcastle & Carlisle Rly [51]
Glo Cymru	37800	37/7	5/1963	British Railways
Glorious	5719	Jubilee	1936	London Midland & Scottish Rly
Glorious	**50033**	**50**	**1968**	**British Railways**
Glorious Devon	47824	47/4	10/1964	British Railways
Glorious Devon	43027	43	9/1976	British Railways [52]
Glory	D818	Warship	3/1960	British Railways
Glossidae	47324	47/3	1965	British Railways
Gloucester	10	4–2–0	6/1840	Birmingham & Gloucester Rly [53]
Gloucester	261	2–2–2	7/1844	Midland Rly (bg) [54]
Gloucester	10	0–6–0	?	Joint Board of Management [55]
Gloucester	–	Swindon	3/1866	Great Western Rly (bg)
Gloucester Castle	7020	Castle	5/1949	British Railways (Western Region)
Glowworm	359	bCrewe	3/1855	London & North Western Rly
Glowworm	359	DX	c.1860	London & North Western Rly
Glowworm	752	Samson	5/1863	London & North Western Rly
Glowworm	752	Whitworth	3/1892	London & North Western Rly
Glowworm	1745	rPrecedent	4/1892	London & North Western Rly [56]
Glyder Fawr	60012	60	11/1991	British Railways
Glyn	267	bCrewe	4/1851	London & North Western Rly
Glyn	768	S/Bloomer	1854	London & North Western Rly
Glyn	3	0–4–2T	1892	Glyn Valley Tramway [57]
Glyncorrwg	–	0–4–2ST	5/1864	South Wales Mineral Rly
Glynde	194	2–2–2	10/1864	London, Brighton & South Coast Rly
Glynde	375	D3	4/1893	London, Brighton & South Coast Rly
Glynllivvon	–	2–4–0	1867	Caernarvonshire Rly
Gnat	301	bCrewe	2/1853	London & North Western Rly
Gnat	–	Metro	7/1862	Great Western Rly (bg)
Gnome	109	0–6–0	3/1849	Great Western Rly [58]
Gnu	1018	B1	2/1947	London & North Eastern Rly
Goat	2174	0–4–0WT	2/1873	Great Western Rly (bg) [59]
Goat Fell	60052	60	9/1991	British Railways
Godalming	486	E4	5/1899	London, Brighton & South Coast Rly
Godolphin	3358	Bulldog	10/1900	Great Western Rly
Godshill	W25	O2	11/1890	Southern Rly [60]
Goethe	92040	92		European Passenger Services

[41] Ran for a time as no. 6 of the Cambrian Railways. Davies & Savin, contractors, supplied locomotives to both lines.
[42] Nameplates fitted in September 1946.
[43] 18in gauge.
[44] 1ft 11½in gauge.
[45] 10¼in gauge.
[46] Altered from 2–2–2 to 2–4–0 in August 1872, and renamed *Grantown* in May 1896.
[47] The modern, preserved South Devon Railway.
[48] There was no such place as Glen Gau. The London & North Eastern Railway renamed the engine *Glen Gour* in July 1925.
[49] Ran as *Glen Lyon* for a few weeks during November and December 1941.

[50] Originally named *Racer*. Rebuilt to 4–2–2 in August 1894. Renamed *Glenside* in September 1911.
[51] Became North Eastern Railway no. 455 in 1862.
[52] Later named *Westminster Abbey*.
[53] Later sold to the Taff Vale Railway, one of three sold to that company. The others were *Columbia* and *W.S. Moorsom*.
[54] Built for the Bristol & Gloucester Railway as their no. 5. Broad gauge. In November 1855 it was sold to Thomas Brassey for working the North Devon Railway, a broad gauge line which later became part of the London & South Western Railway. On the NDR it is thought to have become their *Barnum*.

[55] Birmingham & Gloucester and Bristol & Gloucester Railways, formed on 14 January 1845. Standard gauge. The locomotives passed to the Midland Railway on 3 August 1846, and were renumbered into Midland stock wef February 1847.
[56] Originally named *John Bright*; renamed in July 1914.
[57] 2ft 4½in gauge.
[58] Originally built for the Birkenhead, Lancashire & Cheshire Junction Railway, and named *Chester*.
[59] Built for the South Devon Railway.
[60] Formerly London & South Western Railway no. 190.

Southern Railway O2 class 0–4–4T no. W25 *Godshill*, at Ryde depot in the Isle of Wight between the two world wars. The locomotive has the enlarged coal bunker peculiar to Isle of Wight locomotives, which were also numbered in a separate series. It will be noted that the 'W' of the number did not actually appear on the locomotives. (*Photo: Lens of Sutton*)

Name	Number	Class	Date	Railway
Gog	9	0–4–0	12/1843	London, Brighton & South Coast Rly [61]
Gogar	419	418	1873	North British Rly
Gold Coast	5610	Jubilee	1934	London Midland & Scottish Rly [62]
Golden Eagle	4482	A4	12/1936	London & North Eastern Rly
Golden Fleece	4495	A4	8/1937	London & North Eastern Rly [63]
Golden Plover	4497	A4	10/1937	London & North Eastern Rly
Golden Shuttle	4496	A4	9/1937	London & North Eastern Rly [64]
Goldfinch	151	bCrewe	10/1853	London & North Western Rly
Goldfinch	151	aCrewe	8/1857	London & North Western Rly [65]
Goldfinch	3736	Bulldog	11/1909	Great Western Rly
Goldsmid	363	D3	6/1892	London, Brighton & South Coast Rly
Goldsmid	316	B2	7/1895	London, Brighton & South Coast Rly [66]
Goliah	–	?	?	Eastern Union Rly [67]
Goliah	15	0–4–0	1831	Liverpool & Manchester Rly
Goliah	68	0–4–2	1839	Liverpool & Manchester Rly [68]
Goliah	–	Fury	8/1842	Great Western Rly (bg)
Goliah	122	bCrewe	9/1847	London & North Western Rly
Goliah	2141	0–6–0ST	9/1855	Great Western Rly (bg) [69]
Goliath	–	?	?	Eastern Union Rly [70]
Goliath	–	0–4–0	3/1833	Leicester & Swannington Rly
Goliath	6	0–6–0	1836	Newcastle & Carlisle Rly [71]
Goliath	32	0–6–0	2/1843	South Eastern Rly
Goliath	24	Goliath	5/1848	East Lancashire Rly
Goliath	25	?	1854	St Helens Canal & Rly
Goliath	127	Saxon	6/1855	London & South Western Rly
Goliath	1927	Jubilee	3/1900	London & North Western Rly
(Goliath)	**5239**	**42XX**	**8/1924**	**Great Western Rly**

Name	Number	Class	Date	Railway
Goliath	6136	Royal Scot	9/1927	London Midland & Scottish Rly [72]
Goliath	D819	Warship	4/1960	British Railways
Gollum	**8**	**4wDM**	**1942**	**Leighton Buzzard Rly [73]**
Golspie	9	Seafield	8/1858	Highland Rly [74]
Golspie	19	S/Goods	8/1863	Highland Rly [75]
Golspie	53	Glenbarry	9/1864	Highland Rly [76]
Gooch	–	Hawthorn	5/1865	Great Western Rly (bg)
Gooch	1130	Queen	7/1875	Great Western Rly
Gooch	8	No.7	5/1894	Great Western Rly
Good Hope	–	?	?	Brassey [77]
Good Hope	1970	Alfred	3/1903	London & North Western Rly
Goodmoor Grange	6838	Grange	9/1937	Great Western Rly
Goodrich Castle	5014	Castle	6/1932	Great Western Rly
Goodwood	202	Belgravia	7/1872	London, Brighton & South Coast Rly
Goodwood	71	B4	9/1901	London, Brighton & South Coast Rly [78]
Goonbarrow	1388	0–6–0ST	9/1893	Great Western Rly [79]
Gordon	RCD5	0–4–0ST	3/1886	Woolwich Arsenal [80]
Gordon	19	0–6–2T	1897	Longmoor Military Rly [81]
Gordon	**600**	**WD2–10–0**	**1943**	**War Department**
Gordon Castle	118	Special Tank	8/1870	Highland Rly [82]
Gordon Castle	143	Castle	1900	Highland Rly
Gordon Highlander	**49**	**F**	**10/1920**	**Great North of Scotland Rly**
Gordon Highlander	6106	Royal Scot	8/1927	London Midland & Scottish Rly
Gordon Highlander	**55016**	**Deltic**	**10/1961**	**British Railways**
Gordon-Lennox	191	Gladstone	12/1888	London, Brighton & South Coast Rly
Gorgon	41	0–4–2	1838	Grand Junction Rly
Gorgon	–	Priam	11/1841	Great Western Rly (bg)
Gorgon	41	aCrewe	3/1847	London & North Western Rly
Gorgon	44	0–6–0	6/1849	Manchester, Sheffield & Lincolnshire Rly
Gorgon	52	John Bull	5/1850	East Lancashire Rly
Gorgon	17	Tiger	12/1861	London, Chatham & Dover Rly
Gorgon	2122	4–4–0ST	9/1866	Great Western Rly (bg) [83]
Gorilla	14	Tiger	11/1861	London, Chatham & Dover Rly
Goring	272	D1	5/1880	London, Brighton & South Coast Rly [84]
Gossington Hall	6910	Hall	12/1940	Great Western Rly
Goth	136	Saxon	12/1857	London & South Western Rly
Gothenburg	**32**	**0–6–0T**	**9/1903**	**East Lancashire Rly [85]**
Gough	659	C	8/1891	North British Rly
Gournay	131	E1	11/1878	London, Brighton & South Coast Rly [86]
Gowrie	–	0–6–4T	1908	North Wales Narrow Gauge Rly [87]
Goytrey Hall	4929	Hall	5/1929	Great Western Rly
G.P. Bidder	322	B2	11/1896	London, Brighton & South Coast Rly [88]
G.P. Neele	2520	Prince/W	3/1914	London & North Western Rly
Graffham	409	E6	12/1904	London, Brighton & South Coast Rly
Graf Schwerin-Lorwitz	**99.3353**	**0–6–2T**	**1908**	**Brecon Mountain Rly [89]**
Graham	2	Times	7/1849	Stockton & Darlington Rly
Graham Alexander	**7**	**B-B DM**	**1990**	**Ruislip Lido Rly [90]**

[61] Built for London & Brighton and South Eastern joint stock.

[62] Later renamed *Ghana* by British Railways.

[63] Originally named *Great Snipe*. Renamed in September 1937.

[64] Renamed *Dwight D. Eisenhower* in September 1945.

[65] Formerly Liverpool & Manchester Railway no. 93.

[66] Rebuilt to class B2x, July 1916.

[67] It is not clear whether this locomotive's name is *Goliah* or *Goliath*; contemporary records use both spellings indiscriminately.

[68] Rebuilt as a 2–4–0 and became London & North Western Railway no. 122 in 1846.

[69] Built for the South Devon Railway.

[70] It is not clear whether this locomotive's name is *Goliah* or *Goliath*; contemporary records use both spellings indiscriminately.

[71] Became NER no. 455 in 1862.

[72] Renamed *The Border Regiment* in May 1936.

[73] 1ft 11½in gauge.

[74] Originally named *Aultnaskiah*.

[75] Originally no. 18 *Inverness*, becoming no. 19 *Dingwall*, then renamed *Golspie*.

[76] Previously named *Stafford*. Altered from 2–2–2 to 2–4–0 in November 1873, and renamed *Golspie* in 1886.

[77] Thomas Brassey contracted to maintain the tracks of the London & South Western Railway from 4 November 1839 to December 1853. He provided his own locomotives, of which *Good Hope* was one. Beyond their names, very little is known of them.

[78] Name removed 1905. Rebuilt to class B4x, June 1923.

[79] Built for the Cornwall Minerals Railway.

[80] Name applied, c. 1901. 18in gauge.

[81] Formerly Taff Vale Railway no. 78.

[82] Purchased from the Duke of Sutherland in 1895, who had previously named it *Dunrobin*. Rebuilt from 2–4–0T to 4–4–0T in 1896.

[83] Built for the South Devon Railway.

[84] Originally *Nevill*. Renamed in July 1897.

[85] The modern, preserved, East Lancashire Railway.

[86] Transferred to the Isle of Wight in June 1933 by the Southern Railway as no. W4 *Wroxall*.

[87] 1ft 11½in gauge.

[88] Rebuilt to class B2x, September 1908.

[89] 1ft 11¾in gauge.

[90] 12in gauge.

Name	Number	Class	Date	Railway
Grahamston	284	165	11/1875	North British Rly [91]
Grainflow	37068	37/0	1962	British Railways
Granada Telethon	31410	31/4	1960	British Railways
Grand Parade	2744	A3	8/1928	London & North Eastern Rly
Grandtully	90	Strath	5/1892	Highland Rly [92]
Grange	72	Duke	7/1884	Highland Rly [93]
Granite City	43040	43	12/1976	British Railways
Grant	–	0–4–0ST	1862	Cockermouth & Workington Rly
Grantham	218	0–4–0WT	11/1850	Great Northern Rly [94]
Grantley Hall	6924	Hall	8/1941	Great Western Rly [95]
Granton	29	165	3/1878	North British Rly
Grantown	28	Glenbarry	9/1863	Highland Rly [96]
Granville	113	E1	5/1877	London, Brighton & South Coast Rly [97]
Granville	216	Gladstone	1/1884	London, Brighton & South Coast Rly
Granville	**102**	**B4**	**12/1893**	**London & South Western Rly**
Granville Manor	7818	Manor	1/1939	Great Western Rly

Highland Railway Strath class 4–4–0 no. 90 *Grandtully*, pictured at Dingwall. (*Photo: RAS Marketing*)

Name	Number	Class	Date	Railway
Grasmere	–	2–4–0T	1851	Kendal & Windermere Rly
Grasmere	532	DX	c.1860	London & North Western Rly
Grasshopper	6	0–4–0ST	11/1857	Birkenhead, Lancashire & Cheshire Junction Rly [98]
Gravesend	2	Class 1	1880	London, Tilbury & Southend Rly
Grays	10	Class 1	1880	London, Tilbury & Southend Rly
Graythwaite Hall	6976	M/Hall	10/1947	Great Western Rly
Great Britain	38	0–6–0ST	6/1845	Birmingham & Gloucester Rly
Great Britain	–	Iron Duke	7/1847	Great Western Rly (bg)
Great Britain	–	Rover	9/1880	Great Western Rly (bg)
Great Britain	3013	3001	3/1892	Great Western Rly [99]
Great Central	**39**	**0–6–0T**	**1938**	**Steamtown, Carnforth**
Great Central	60156	A1	10/1949	British Railways (Eastern Region)
Great Central	08749	08	1960	British Railways
Great Eastern	60157	A1	11/1949	British Railways (Eastern Region)
Great Eastern	37216	37/0	1964	British Railways
Great Eastern	47581	47/4	1964	British Railways
Greater Britain	2053	G.Britain	10/1891	London & North Western Rly
Greater Britain	884	2Experiment	12/1908	London & North Western Rly

Name	Number	Class	Date	Railway
Greater Manchester The Life and Soul of Britain	86259	86/2	1966	British Railways
Great Gable	**44004**	**Peak**	**1959**	**British Railways**
Great Gable	60006	60	9/1991	British Railways
Great Ilford	43	37	1898	London, Tilbury & Southend Rly
Great Mountain	–	0–6–0T	4/1902	Llanelly & Mynydd Mawr Rly [100]
Great Northern	4470	A1	4/1922	London & North Eastern Rly [101]
Great Northern	113	A1	4/1922	London & North Eastern Rly [102]
Great North Run	91027	91	12/1990	British Railways
Great Rocks	37688	37/5	9/1963	British Railways
Great Snipe	4495	A4	8/1937	London & North Eastern Rly [103]
Great Snipe	4462	A4	11/1937	London & North Eastern Rly [104]
Great Snipe	47401	47/4	1964	British Railways
Great Western	–	Iron Duke	4/1846	Great Western Rly (bg) [105]
Great Western	–	Rover	5/1888	Great Western Rly (bg)
Great Western	3012	3001	3/1892	Great Western Rly [106]
Great Western	7007	Castle	7/1946	Great Western Rly [107]
Great Western	47500	47/4	1966	British Railways
Great Western	43185	43	3/1982	British Railways
Great Whernside	60020	60	1/1991	British Railways
Great Yarmouth	–	4–4–0T	10/1881	Yarmouth & North Norfolk Rly
Grecian	50	2–4–0	7/1847	Manchester, Sheffield & Lincolnshire Rly
Green Arrow	**4771**	**V2**	**6/1936**	**London & North Eastern Rly**
Greenbank	2586	0–4–0T	1884	London & North Western Rly
Green Dragon	13	0–6–0ST	1/1862	Cambrian Railways [108]
Green Goddess	**1**	**4–6–2**	**1925**	**Romney, Hythe & Dymchurch Rly [109]**
Greensleeves	1444	J94	3/1945	War Department
Greenwich	7	0–4–0	2/1838	London & Greenwich Rly
Grenade	R.L.6	0–4–0ST	1887	Woolwich Arsenal [110]
Grenadier Guardsman	6110	Royal Scot	9/1927	London Midland & Scottish Rly
Grenville	1	2–4–2T	1900	Bideford, Westward Ho! & Appledore Rly
Grenville	D820	Warship	5/1960	British Railways
Gresham Hall	5991	Hall	12/1939	Great Western Rly
Greta	119	Peel	12/1856	Stockton & Darlington Rly

London & North Eastern Railway V2 class 2–6–2 no. 4771 *Green Arrow*, at Belle Isle on 8 July 1936. (*Photo: LCGB Ken Nunn Collection*)

---

[91] Originally named *Airdrie*.
[92] Originally named *Tweeddale*. Renamed *Grandtully* in 1897.
[93] Originally named *Bruce*. Renamed *Grange* in 1886.
[94] Built for the Nottingham & Grantham Railway & Canal.
[95] Nameplates fitted May 1947.
[96] Originally named *Glenbarry*. Altered from 2–2–2 to 2–4–0 in August 1872, and renamed *Grantown* in May 1896.

[97] Later renamed *Durdans*.
[98] Later became Great Western Railway no. 95.
[99] Rebuilt to 4–2–2 in November 1894.
[100] Later became Great Western Railway no. 944.
[101] Great Northern Railway no. 1470. The first Gresley 4–6–2.
[102] Rebuild by Edward Thompson in September 1945 of Gresley no. 4470 *Great Northern*.
[103] Renamed *Golden Fleece* in September 1937.
[104] Renamed *William Whitelaw* in July 1941.

[105] Originally built as a 2–2–2. Rebuilt to 4–2–2 after a few months.
[106] Rebuilt to 4–2–2 in June 1894.
[107] *Ogmore Castle* until January 1948.
[108] Originally named *Whixall*.
[109] 15in gauge.
[110] Name applied in about 1901. 18in gauge. In spite of its somewhat ominous name, there is no record of *Grenade* exploding!

Name	Number	Class	Date	Railway	Name	Number	Class	Date	Railway
Gretna	49	165	5/1878	North British Rly [111]	*Guernsey*	3316	Duke	3/1899	Great Western Rly [118]
Greyfriars Bobby	47711	47/7	1966	British Railways	*Guglielmo Marconi*	20128	20/0	1/1966	British Railways
Greyhound	–	Priam	1/1841	Great Western Rly (bg)	*Guide Dog*	91028	91	12/1990	British Railways
Greyhound	323	aCrewe	11/1853	London & North Western Rly	*Guildford*	274	D1	12/1879	London, Brighton & South Coast Rly
Greyhound	2059	Dreadnought	1885	London & North Western Rly	*Guild Hall*	5927	Hall	6/1933	Great Western Rly
Greyhound	3011	3001	3/1892	Great Western Rly [112]	*Guillemot*	4465	A4	12/1937	London & North Eastern Rly [119]
Greyhound	302	2Precursor	7/1905	London & North Western Rly	*Guillemot*	47009	47/0	1963	British Railways
Greyhound	**D821**	**Warship**	**5/1960**	**British Railways**	*Guinevere*	3257	Duke	8/1895	Great Western Rly
Greystock	81	Samson	1/1865	London & North Western Rly [113]	*Guisbro'*	36	Commerce	5/1847	Stockton & Darlington Rly
Greystoke	81	bCrewe	4/1846	Grand Junction Rly	**(Gunby)**	**–**	**J94**	**1941**	**East Anglian Railway Museum**
Greystoke	23	2–2–2	1857	Lancaster & Carlisle Rly	*Gunton*	2808	B17/1	12/1928	London & North Eastern Rly
Greystoke	81	Samson	1/1865	London & North Western Rly [114]	*Gurth*	17	0–6–0	1863	Whitehaven & Furness Junction Rly
Greystoke	81	Whitworth	1/1892	London & North Western Rly	*Guy*	–	4–6–0T	1916	Ashover Rly
Greystoke	2116	2Experiment	1/1909	London & North Western Rly	*Guy*	–	4–6–0T	1917	Ashover Rly [120]
Grierson	3058	3031	4/1895	Great Western Rly [115]	*Guy Calthrop*	1093	Claughton	7/1916	London & North Western Rly [121]
Griffon	33019	33/0	1961	British Railways	*GUY FAWKES*	47705	47/7	1967	British Railways
Grimesthorpe 41B	08878	08	1960	British Railways	*Guy Mannering*	2984	Saint	7/1905	Great Western Rly [122]
Grimsby Town	2850	B17/4	3/1936	London & North Eastern Rly	*Guy Mannering*	360	Scott	12/1911	North British Rly
Grinstead	280	D1	11/1879	London, Brighton & South Coast Rly	*Guy Mannering*	60129	A1	6/1949	British Railways (Eastern Region)
Grisi	70	2–2–2	3/1849	Manchester, Sheffield & Lincolnshire Rly	*Gwalior*	5589	Jubilee	1934	London Midland & Scottish Rly
					Gwenddwr Grange	6817	Grange	12/1936	Great Western Rly
G.R. Jebb	37	Claughton	2/1917	London & North Western Rly	*Gwendraeth*	–	0–4–0ST	1868	Burry Port & Gwendraeth Valley Rly
Grongar	–	0–6–0	1870	Llanelly Rly [116]					
Groombridge	278	D1	12/1879	London, Brighton & South Coast Rly	*Gwendraeth*	6	0–6–0ST	1906	Burry Port & Gwendraeth Valley Rly [123]
Grosvenor	151	B	12/1874	London, Brighton & South Coast Rly	**Gwril**	**–**	**4wBE**	**1987**	**Fairbourne & Barmouth Steam Rly [124]**
Grosvenor	3298	Badminton	6/1898	Great Western Rly					
Grotrian Hall	5926	Hall	6/1933	Great Western Rly	**(Gwyneth)**	**D3019**	**08**	**1953**	**British Railways**
Grouse	1733	George V	10/1911	London & North Western Rly	**Gwynnedd**	**–**	**0–4–0ST**	**1883**	**Bressingham Steam Museum [125]**
Grundisburgh Hall	6977	M/Hall	11/1947	Great Western Rly	*Gwyl Gerddi Cymru 1992*	43016	43	6/1976	British Railways [126]
Guardbridge	151	165	5/1877	North British Rly [117]					
Guernsey	106	E1	10/1876	London, Brighton & South Coast Rly	*Gyfeillon*	–	Caesar	6/1856	Great Western Rly (bg)
Guernsey	176	B4	10/1893	London & South Western Rly	*GYPSUM QUEEN II*	60008	60	12/1992	British Railways [127]

[111] Previously named *Sunnyside*.

[112] Rebuilt to 4–2–2 in October 1894.

[113] Renamed *Greystoke* in March 1884.

[114] Originally named *Greystock*; renamed in March 1884.

[115] Originally named *Ulysses*; renamed in May 1895.

[116] Became Great Western Railway no. 911.

[117] Previously named *Dalmuir*.

[118] Renamed *Isle of Guernsey* in January 1904.

[119] As BR no. 60020, was renamed *Dominion of Pakistan*.

[120] The second *Guy* was purchased from the War Department to replace the first one when it needed heavy repairs. These engines were built by the Baldwin Locomotive Company (USA) for service in France with the British and French Armies in the First World War. 2ft gauge.

[121] Renamed *Sir Guy Calthrop* when the General Manager of the London & North Western Railway received his baronetcy in 1918 for wartime services as Controller of Coal Mines at the Board of Trade.

[122] Originally named *Churchill*; altered to *Viscount Churchill* in 1906, and became *Guy Mannering* in 1907.

[123] Replacement for the earlier locomotive of the same name, shown above. Became Great Western Railway no. 2196.

[124] 12¼in gauge.

[125] 2ft gauge.

[126] Originally named *Songs of Praise*. Also named (on the other side) *Garden Festival Wales 1992*.

[127] Later became *Moel Fammau*.

Name	Number	Class	Date	Railway
Hackbridge	484	E4	4/1899	London, Brighton & South Coast Rly
Hackness Hall	6925	Hall	8/1941	Great Western Rly [1]
Hackworth	71	2–4–0	3/1851	Stockton & Darlington Rly
Hackworth	–	Hawthorn	5/1865	Great Western Rly (bg)
Hackworth	205	B2	5/1897	London, Brighton & South Coast Rly [2]
Hackworth	2328	Remembrance	2/1936	Southern Rly [3]
Haddington	20	165	11/1877	North British Rly
Haddon Hall	5928	Hall	5/1929	Great Western Rly
Hades	–	Caesar	8/1861	Great Western Rly (bg)
Hadleigh	–	?	?	Eastern Union Rly
Hadleigh	72	69	1903	London, Tilbury & Southend Rly
Hagley Hall	**4930**	**Hall**	**5/1929**	**Great Western Rly**
Haig	650	C	4/1891	North British Rly
Haig	65311	J36	3/1899	British Railways (Scottish Region) [4]
Haileybury	924	Schools	12/1933	Southern Rly
Hailsham	76	A1	6/1877	London, Brighton & South Coast Rly
H.A. Ivatt	60123	A1	2/1949	British Railways (Eastern Region)
Halesworth	2	2–4–0T	1879	Southwold Rly [5]
Halewood Silver Jubilee 1988	47241	47/0	1966	British Railways
Halifax	29	2–2–2	2/1841	Manchester & Leeds Rly
Halifax	3402	Atbara	8/1901	Great Western Rly
Halifax	3402	City	12/1908	Great Western Rly
Haliotidae	47196	47/0	1965	British Railways
Halley's Comet	86217	86/2	1965	British Railways
Hallgarth	59	Woodlands	10/1848	Stockton & Darlington Rly
Hal o'the Wind	363	Scott	10/1912	North British Rly
Hal o'the Wind	60116	A1	10/1948	British Railways (Eastern Region)
Hal o'the Wynd	87031	87/0	1974	British Railways
Halstead	–	2–4–0T	1863	Colne Valley & Halstead Rly
Halstead	–	2–4–2T	1887	Colne Valley & Halstead Rly
Halton	321	2–4–0	5/1864	Lancashire & Yorkshire Rly
Hambledon	254	D1	2/1882	London, Brighton & South Coast Rly
Hamburg	**31**	**0–6–0T**	**9/1903**	**Keighley & Worth Valley Rly**
Hamilton	108	165	6/1878	North British Rly [6]
Hamilton	299	72	8/1880	North British Rly
Hampden	1532	Newton	11/1866	London & North Western Rly
Hampden	220	Gladstone	12/1887	London, Brighton & South Coast Rly
Hampden	1532	rPrecedent	6/1892	London & North Western Rly
Hampden	974	Prince/W	3/1919	London & North Western Rly
Hampden	5074	Castle	7/1938	Great Western Rly [7]
Hampshire	5	0–6–0ST	1906	Longmoor Military Rly [8]
Hampton	–	2–2–2	7/1839	Birmingham & Derby Junction Rly
Hampton Court	2943	Saint	5/1912	Great Western Rly
Hanbury Hall	4931	Hall	5/1929	Great Western Rly
Handcombe	583	E5	11/1903	London, Brighton & South Coast Rly
Handcross	233	D1	3/1883	London, Brighton & South Coast Rly
Handel	92011	92		British Railways
Handyman	**–**	**0–4–0ST**	**1900**	**Midland Railway Centre** [9]
Hangleton	491	E4	9/1899	London, Brighton & South Coast Rly
Hanham Hall	5929	Hall	5/1929	Great Western Rly
Hannibal	57	Rossendale	7/1853	East Lancashire Rly
Hannibal	–	0–4–0ST	1885	Woolwich Arsenal [10]
Hannington Hall	5930	Hall	5/1929	Great Western Rly
Happy Knight	60533	A2	4/1948	British Railways (Eastern Region)
Harbinger	284	bCrewe	4/1852	London & North Western Rly
Harbinger	2146	1Precursor	8/1874	London & North Western Rly
Harbinger	1395	2Precursor	3/1904	London & North Western Rly
Hardham	404	E5	10/1904	London, Brighton & South Coast Rly
Hardicanute	10	2–2–2	5/1842	South Eastern Rly
Hardinge	333	bCrewe	4/1854	London & North Western Rly
Hardinge	85	Peel	7/1854	Stockton & Darlington Rly
Hardinge	333	aCrewe	3/1858	London & North Western Rly
Hardman	355	bCrewe	2/1855	London & North Western Rly
Hardman	355	DX	c.1860	London & North Western Rly
Hardman	758	Samson	5/1863	London & North Western Rly
Hardman	758	Whitworth	1/1890	London & North Western Rly
Hardwicke	292	bCrewe	11/1852	London & North Western Rly
Hardwicke	790	Newton	8/1873	London & North Western Rly
Hardwicke	**790**	**rPrecedent**	**4/1892**	**London & North Western Rly**
Hardwicke	86225	86/2	1965	British Railways
Hardwick Grange	6818	Grange	12/1936	Great Western Rly
Hardy	5675	Jubilee	1935	London Midland & Scottish Rly
Hare	–	2–2–2	1848	Oxford, Worcester & Wolverhampton Rly
Hare	302	2–4–0	12/1861	Lancashire & Yorkshire Rly
Hare	670	627	9/1881	Lancashire & Yorkshire Rly
Haren	244	0–4–0ST	1916	War Department
Harewood House	2828	B17/1	3/1931	London & North Eastern Rly
Hark Forward	2139	cSentinel	1928	London & North Eastern Rly
Harlaxton	**–**	**0–6–0T**	**1941**	**North Norfolk Rly**
Harlaxton Manor	2836	B17/1	7/1931	London & North Eastern Rly
Harlech	52	S/Goods	5/1865	Cambrian Railways
Harlech Castle	4095	Castle	6/1926	Great Western Rly
(Harlech Castle)	25265	25/3	1966	**British Railways**
Harlech Castle	**–**	**0–6–0DH**	**1983**	**Festiniog Rly** [11]
Harlequin	44	2–2–2	1838	Grand Junction Rly
Harlequin	40	0–4–0	8/1840	Midland Counties Rly [12]
Harlequin	44	aCrewe	9/1846	London & North Western Rly
Harlequin	44	Problem	c.1860	London & North Western Rly
Harlequin	496	2Experiment	9/1907	London & North Western Rly
Haro Haro	1	2–4–0T	9/1870	Jersey Rly
Harold	12	2–2–2	8/1842	South Eastern Rly
Harold	130	Canute	1/1856	London & South Western Rly
Harold	–	0–6–0ST	?1872	Weston, Clevedon & Portishead Rly
Harold	–	0–6–0T	1872	Alexandra (Newport & South Wales) Docks & Rly
Harold MacMillan	86218	86/2	1965	British Railways
Haroldstone Hall	6978	M/Hall	11/1947	Great Western Rly
Harpy	25	2–2–2	1837	Grand Junction Rly
Harpy	–	Priam	8/1841	Great Western Rly (bg)
Harpy	34	2–2–0	8/1841	Midland Counties Rly
Harpy	22	2–2–2	12/1845	Manchester, Sheffield & Lincolnshire Rly
Harpy	25	aCrewe	1/1846	London & North Western Rly
Harpy	79	Fireball	7/1847	London & South Western Rly
Harpy	893	L/Bloomer	1851	London & North Western Rly
Harpy	20	Tiger	2/1862	London, Chatham & Dover Rly
Harpy	79	Falcon	12/1865	London & South Western Rly
Harpy	2061	Dreadnought	1885	London & North Western Rly
Harpy	1396	2Precursor	11/1905	London & North Western Rly
Harrier	1394	George V	8/1911	London & North Western Rly
Harrier	47005	47/0	1963	British Railways
Harriet	–	0–6–0ST	1876	Swansea Harbour Trust [13]
Harringay	56	51	1900	London, Tilbury & Southend Rly
Harrington Hall	5982	Hall	10/1938	Great Western Rly
Harris	8	0–4–2	1845	Maryport & Carlisle Rly
Harrison	9	2–4–0	9/1864	London & South Western Rly (ed) [14]

---

[1] Nameplates fitted in August 1946.

[2] Rebuilt to class B2x, March 1910.

[3] Rebuilt from London, Brighton & South Coast Railway L class 4–6–4T no. 328 of September 1914.

[4] Named unofficially in 1953, and perpetuated by Inverurie Works in June 1955. Class J36 was the North British Railway's C class.

[5] 3ft gauge.

[6] Later renamed St Andrews.

[7] Denbigh Castle until January 1941.

[8] This may be the same Hampshire that worked on the Swansea & Mumbles Railway in about 1918–19.

[9] 3ft gauge.

[10] 18in gauge.

[11] 1ft 11½in gauge.

[12] Renamed Shark in 1842–3.

[13] Formerly Derby of the Port Talbot Railway. It was named Harriet for a short while only.

[14] Formerly no. 201 of the Locomotive Department.

Name	Number	Class	Date	Railway
Harrogate	12	0–4–2	1839	Manchester & Leeds Rly [15]
Harrow	919	Schools	6/1933	Southern Rly
Harrowby	322	bCrewe	5/1854	London & North Western Rly
Harrowby	697	1Precursor	10/1878	London & North Western Rly
Harrowby	315	2Precursor	7/1905	London & North Western Rly
Harry	–	**0–4–0ST**	**1926**	**Pontypool & Blaenavon Rly**
Harry	71499	J94	11/1944	War Department
(Harry A. Frith)	**828**	**S15**	**7/1927**	**Southern Rly**
Harry Hinchliffe	1240	B1	10/1947	London & North Eastern Rly [16]
Hartebeeste	1009	B1	6/1944	London & North Eastern Rly
Hartfield	26	D1	3/1876	London, Brighton & South Coast Rly
Hart Hall	7907	M/Hall	1/1950	British Railways (Western Region)
Hartington	17	4–4–0	8/1878	Cambrian Railways
Hartington	212	Richmond	3/1880	London, Brighton & South Coast Rly
Hartland	**34101**	**rWC**	**2/1950**	**British Railways (Southern Region)**
Hartland Point	2039	H1	1/1906	Southern Rly [17]
Hartlebury Castle	7033	Castle	7/1950	British Railways (Western Region)
Hartlepool	43105	43	1961	British Railways
Hartlepool Pipe Mill	37718	37/7	12/1962	British Railways
Harvester	2573	A3	10/1924	London & North Eastern Rly
"Harvey Combe"	–	2–2–2	1835	? [18]
Harworth Colliery	56095	56	1981	British Railways
Haslemere	398	D3	11/1896	London, Brighton & South Coast Rly
Hassocks	244	D1	12/1881	London, Brighton & South Coast Rly
Hastings	255	Victoria	12/1868	London, Brighton & South Coast Rly [19]
Hastings	182	Gladstone	1/1890	London, Brighton & South Coast Rly
Hatcham	66	A1	8/1874	London, Brighton & South Coast Rly
Hatfield House	2821	B17/1	11/1930	London & North Eastern Rly
Hatherley Hall	5931	Hall	6/1933	Great Western Rly
Hatherton Hall	4932	Hall	6/1929	Great Western Rly
Hatton Castle	50	F	10/1920	Great North of Scotland Rly
Hatton Castle	08855	08	1961	British Railways
Haughley	1	0–6–0T	1904	Mid Suffolk Light Rly [20]
Haughton Grange	6874	Grange	4/1939	Great Western Rly
Haulwen	–	**J94**	**1945**	**Caerphilly Railway Society**
Haulwen 2	**75282**	**J94**	**1945**	**War Department** [21]
Havant	161	2–2–2	9/1863	London, Brighton & South Coast Rly [22]
Havelock	150	Canute	7/1858	London & South Western Rly
Havelock	818	Problem	c.1860	London & North Western Rly
Havelock	184	2Precursor	5/1905	London & North Western Rly
Haverfordwest Castle	7021	Castle	6/1949	British Railways (Western Region)
Haverhill		0–6–0T	1873	Colne Valley & Halstead Rly [23]
Havre	146	E1	10/1880	London, Brighton & South Coast Rly
Havre	86	B4	12/1891	London & South Western Rly
Hawarden	–	**0–4–0ST**	**1899**	**Penrhyn Castle Industrial Railway Museum** [24]
Hawarden	–	**0–4–0ST**	**1940**	**Foxfield Steam Rly** [25]
Hawick	489	Abbotsford	1878	North British Rly
Hawk	37	2–2–2	1838	Grand Junction Rly
Hawk	3	2–2–0	4/1839	Midland Counties Rly
Hawk	–	2–2–0	6/1839	London & South Western Rly
Hawk	–	Priam	10/1840	Great Western Rly (bg)

Name	Number	Class	Date	Railway
Hawk	28	1Eagle	8/1844	London & South Western Rly
Hawk	37	aCrewe	7/1847	London & North Western Rly
Hawk	110	Peel	6/1856	Stockton & Darlington Rly
Hawk	–	2–4–0	1/1858	Swansea Vale Rly
Hawk	2108	4–4–0ST	4/1859	Great Western Rly (bg) [26]
Hawk	28	2Eagle	12/1862	London & South Western Rly
Hawk	–	Hawthorn	12/1865	Great Western Rly (bg)
Hawke	5652	Jubilee	1935	London Midland & Scottish Rly
Hawkenbury	588	E5	12/1903	London, Brighton & South Coast Rly
Hawkinge	21C169	BB	10/1947	Southern Rly
Hawkins	5649	Jubilee	1935	London Midland & Scottish Rly
Hawkshaw	1	2–4–0	3/1857	London & South Western Rly (ed)
Hawkstone	236	aCrewe	4/1849	London & North Western Rly
Hawkstone	236	DX	c.1860	London & North Western Rly
Hawthorn	82	0–6–0	2/1846	Stockton & Darlington Rly [27]
Hawthorn	40	0–6–0	1848	Edinburgh & Glasgow Rly
Hawthorn	–	Hawthorn	4/1865	Great Western Rly (bg)
Haydn Taylor	**10**	**4wDM**	**1945**	**Leighton Buzzard Rly** [28]
Haydock	–	**0–6–0T**	**1879**	**Penrhyn Castle Industrial Railway Museum**
Haydon Hall	5932	Hall	6/1933	Great Western Rly
Hayle	–	2–4–0T	1853	West Cornwall Rly

Kent & East Sussex Railway *Hecate*, here shown as Southern Railway no. 949 at Nine Elms, 14 September 1946. (*Photo: LCGB Ken Nunn Collection*)

Name	Number	Class	Date	Railway
Hayling	177	2–4–0	7/1864	London, Brighton & South Coast Rly [29]
Hayling	175	Gladstone	12/1890	London, Brighton & South Coast Rly
Hayling Island	115	2–4–0T	9/1869	London, Brighton & South Coast Rly [30]
Haymarket	211	211	3/1861	North British Rly [31]
Haymarket	47715	47/7	1966	British Railways
Haystoun of Bucklaw	2682	D11/2	10/1924	London & North Eastern Rly
Haywards Heath	370	D3	10/1892	London, Brighton & South Coast Rly
Hazeldean	878	H	8/1906	North British Rly

---

[15] Some sources show this locomotive's name as *Leeds*. It is not clear whether no. 8 was named *Leeds* and no. 12 *Harrogate*, or *vice versa*.

[16] Nameplates only fitted in December 1947.

[17] Built for the London, Brighton & South Coast Railway, who named it *La France* in June 1913 for a special train carrying the French President, M. Raymond Poincaré. It was renamed *Hartland Point* by the Southern Railway in January 1926.

[18] Built by Stephensons and mentioned by E.L. Ahrons, *The British Steam Locomotive 1825–1925*. A close contemporary of Stephenson's *Patentee* locomotive, it does not seem to have worked on any railway, and its ultimate fate is a mystery.

[19] Name applied in June 1871.

[20] Extant photographs do not show the name actually carried.

[21] Named *Insein* on the Longmoor Military Railway.

[22] Modified by Stroudley and named *Havant*, October 1871.

[23] Purchased in 1879 from the Cornwall Minerals Railway.

[24] Built by Hudswell Clarke of Leeds in 1899, their Works no. 526.

[25] Built by Bagnalls of Stafford in 1940, their Works no. 2623.

[26] Built for the South Devon Railway.

[27] Purchased from the Edinburgh & Glasgow Railway in 1854.

[28] 1ft 11½in gauge.

[29] Name applied in May 1872.

[30] Originally 2–4–0T no. 96, and named *Kemptown*. Renumbered 115 and renamed *Hayling Island* in September 1874. Renumbered 359 in June 1877, and 499 in January 1886. It was then altered by William Stroudley in January 1890 to a 2–4–2T with a small inspection saloon mounted on the back, renumbered 4481 and renamed *Inspector*. Stroudley died in December 1889 while the alteration was still in progress, and the locomotive saw little use before withdrawal in March 1898.

[31] Ex-Edinburgh & Glasgow Railway, absorbed by the NBR in 1865.

Name	Number	Class	Date	Railway
Hazeley Grange	6840	Grange	9/1937	Great Western Rly
Hazel Hall	5901	Hall	5/1931	Great Western Rly
Headbourne Grange	6852	Grange	11/1937	Great Western Rly
Heatherden Hall	6946	Hall	12/1942	Great Western Rly [32]
Heathfield	227	D1	1/1885	London, Brighton & South Coast Rly
Heaton Traincare Depot	47771	47/7		British Railways
Hebe	–	Caesar	5/1852	Great Western Rly (bg)
Hebe	2148	0–6–0ST	4/1860	Great Western Rly (bg) [33]
Hebe	175	Undine	6/1860	London & South Western Rly
Hebe	–	0–4–2ST	1870	Garstang & Knott End Rly
Hecate	4	2–2–2	1837	Grand Junction Rly
Hecate	6	2–2–0	6/1839	Midland Counties Rly
Hecate	2	0–4–2ST	1840	Shropshire & Montgomeryshire Rly [34]
Hecate	–	Priam	11/1841	Great Western Rly (bg)
Hecate	4	aCrewe	1/1846	London & North Western Rly
Hecate	3	Medusa	5/1846	East Lancashire Rly
Hecate	78	Fireball	6/1847	London & South Western Rly
Hecate	84	2–4–0	10/1849	Manchester, Sheffield & Lincolnshire Rly
Hecate	848	L/Bloomer	1851	London & North Western Rly
Hecate	78	Gem	5/1863	London & South Western Rly
Hecate	4	0–6–0ST	5/1876	Kent & East Sussex Rly [35]
Hecate	7	A1	7/1880	Shropshire & Montgomeryshire Rly [36]
Hecate	1113	1Experiment	1884	London & North Western Rly
Hecate	–	2–4–0	1902	Woolwich Arsenal [37]
Hecate	949	KES	12/1904	Southern Rly [38]
Hecate	688	2Precursor	7/1905	London & North Western Rly
Hecla	2	2–2–2	1837	Grand Junction Rly
Hecla	–	Leo	4/1841	Great Western Rly (bg)
Hecla	2	bCrewe	10/1844	London & North Western Rly
Hecla	77	Fireball	5/1847	London & South Western Rly [39]
Hecla	105	0–6–0	5/1852	Manchester, Sheffield & Lincolnshire Rly
Hecla	120	1Vesuvius	6/1852	London & South Western Rly
Hecla	2	0–4–2	11/1856	Whitehaven & Furness Junction Rly
Hecla	2	DX	c.1860	London & North Western Rly
Hecla	2133	4–4–0ST	6/1864	Great Western Rly (bg) [40]
Hecla	732	Samson	7/1864	London & North Western Rly
Hecla	120	Lion	1/1870	London & South Western Rly
Hecla	732	Whitworth	1/1895	London & North Western Rly
Hector	–	0–6–0	10/1840	Leicester & Swannington Rly
Hector	–	Priam	7/1841	Great Western Rly (bg)
Hector	34	0–6–0	7/1847	Manchester, Sheffield & Lincolnshire Rly
Hector	35	Goliath	3/1849	East Lancashire Rly
Hector	304	bCrewe	2/1853	London & North Western Rly
Hector	2117	4–4–0ST	8/1860	Great Western Rly (bg) [41]
Hector	304	Newton	9/1870	London & North Western Rly
Hector	–	0–4–0ST	1885	Woolwich Arsenal [42]
Hector	304	rPrecedent	6/1892	London & North Western Rly
Hector	6140	Royal Scot	10/1927	London Midland & Scottish Rly [43]
Hector	26048	EM1	9/1952	British Railways [44]
Hecuba	–	Caesar	11/1853	Great Western Rly (bg)
Hedingham	4	2–4–2T	1894	Colne Valley & Halstead Rly
(Hedingham Castle)	**190**	**J94**	**1/1953**	**Colne Valley Rly [45]**
Hedley	–	Hawthorn	6/1865	Great Western Rly (bg)
Helen	**–**	**4wDM**	**1924**	**Foxfield Steam Rly**
Helena	–	0–4–0	1/1839	Llanelly Rly [46]
Helena	86	2–4–0	11/1849	Manchester, Sheffield & Lincolnshire Rly
Helena	195	Peel	10/1866	Stockton & Darlington Rly
Helen Kathryn	**14**	**0–4–0T**	**1948**	**South Tynedale Rly [47]**
Helen MacGregor	338	Scott	10/1911	North British Rly
Helensburgh	88	157	7/1877	North British Rly [48]
Helensburgh	496	Helensburgh	5/1879	North British Rly
(Helen Turner)	**24032**	**24**	**1959**	**British Railways**
Helicon	119	0–6–0	12/1853	Manchester, Sheffield & Lincolnshire Rly
Hellingly	483	E4	3/1899	London, Brighton & South Coast Rly
Helmingham Hall	2847	B17/4	9/1935	London & North Eastern Rly
Helmingham Hall	6947	Hall	12/1942	Great Western Rly [49]
Helmsdale	6	Seafield	5/1858	Highland Rly [50]
Helmsdale	49	Glenbarry	7/1864	Highland Rly [51]
Helmster Hall	6912	Hall	1/1941	Great Western Rly
Helperley Hall	6979	M/Hall	11/1947	Great Western Rly
Helston	917	2–4–0ST	1860	Great Western Rly [52]
Helvellyn	–	2–2–0	3/1838	North British Rly [53]
Helvellyn	94	aCrewe	11/1846	London & North Western Rly
Helvellyn	890	L/Bloomer	1851	London & North Western Rly
Helvellyn	1149	1Precursor	9/1878	London & North Western Rly
Helvellyn	2023	2Precursor	4/1904	London & North Western Rly
Helvellyn	D2	Peak	9/1959	British Railways
Helvellyn	60037	60	9/1991	British Railways
Helvetia	151	E1	12/1880	London, Brighton & South Coast Rly
Hem Heath	**3D**	**0–6–0DM**	**1956**	**Chatterley Whitfield Mining Museum**
Henbury	**S9**	**0–6–0ST**	**1937**	**Bristol Industrial Museum**
Hendon	**–**	**0–4–0CT**	**1940**	**Tanfield Rly**
Henfield	358	D1	11/1886	London, Brighton & South Coast Rly
Hengist	1	2–2–2	12/1841	South Eastern Rly
Hengrave Hall	5970	Hall	4/1937	Great Western Rly
Henley Hall	5983	Hall	10/1938	Great Western Rly
Henrietta	814	Samson	1/1866	London & North Western Rly
Henrietta	814	Whitworth	1/1890	London & North Western Rly
Henry	**–**	**0–4–0ST**	**1901**	**Birmingham Railway Museum**
Henry Bessemer	527	G.Britain	1894	London & North Western Rly
Henry Bessemer	1014	2Experiment	9/1907	London & North Western Rly
Henry Cort	838	1Precursor	1/1879	London & North Western Rly

---

[32] Nameplates fitted in March 1946.

[33] Built for the South Devon Railway.

[34] Reputed to contain parts of a Bury 0–4–0 built in 1840 for the Shrewsbury & Hereford Railway and named *Severn*. Purchased by the Griff Colliery Co. and rebuilt as 0–4–2T. Briefly renamed *Hecate* on arrival on the Shropshire & Montgomeryshire Railway, but very soon reverted to its original name.

[35] London & South Western Railway no. 335, which became no. 0335 in 1907 and Southern Railway no. E0335 in 1923. See footnote 38 for further details. This *Hecate* was taken over by British Railways in 1948, but was scrapped at Ashford in August of the same year. It was the last survivor of the 330 class.

[36] Built as London, Brighton & South Coast Railway no. 81 *Beulah*. Sold to the Admiralty in January 1918, and to the Shropshire &

Montgomeryshire Railway in July 1921.

[37] Paraffin/mechanical. 18in gauge.

[38] Purchased by the Kent & East Sussex Railway from makers Hawthorn, Leslie & Co. in January 1905 for a proposed (but never built) extension to Maidstone. So *Hecate*, K&ESR's no. 4, was something of a white elephant, and was taken over by the Southern Railway in July 1932 in exchange for ex-LSWR 0–6–0ST no. E0335 (which the K&ESR named *Hecate*) and some items of rolling stock. As Southern Railway no. 949 and retaining its name, it then spent most of the rest of its career shunting at Nine Elms and Clapham Junction.

[39] Renamed *Wildfire* in June 1852.

[40] Built for the South Devon Railway.

[41] Built for the South Devon Railway.

[42] 18in gauge.

[43] Renamed *The King's Royal Rifle Corps* in May 1936.

[44] A cab from this locomotive is preserved at the Museum of Science and Industry in Manchester.

[45] Or *Castle Hedingham*.

[46] Originally *Princess Helena*. Renamed *Helena* on rebuilding in 1857.

[47] 2ft gauge.

[48] Later renamed *Kirkcaldy*.

[49] Nameplates fitted in November 1946.

[50] Originally named *Bruce*. Renamed in about 1874.

[51] Originally named *Belladrum*. Altered from 2–2–2 to 2–4–0 in April 1879.

[52] Built for the Llynvi & Ogmore Railway.

[53] Said to be ex-London & North Western Railway, who in turn had inherited it from the London & Birmingham Railway.

Name	Number	Class	Date	Railway
Henry Cort	1512	John Hick	1898	London & North Western Rly
Henry Cort	–	0-4-0ST	**1903**	**Foxfield Steam Rly**
Henry Cort	1413	2Experiment	4/1909	London & North Western Rly
Henry Crosfield	2001	Newton	4/1871	London & North Western Rly
Henry Crosfield	2001	rPrecedent	11/1890	London & North Western Rly
Henry Crosfield	2279	George V	3/1913	London & North Western Rly
Henry de Lacy II	–	0-4-0ST	**1917**	**Middleton Rly**
Henry Fletcher	203	B2	5/1897	London, Brighton & South Coast Rly [54]
Henry Ford	47310	47/3	1965	British Railways
Henry Maudslay	1535	John Hick	1898	London & North Western Rly
Henry Maudslay	2168	George V	1/1911	London & North Western Rly
Henry Oakley	**990**	**C2**	**1898**	**Great Northern Rly**
Henry Pease	364	Precedent	2/1882	London & North Western Rly
Henry Pease	364	rPrecedent	10/1894	London & North Western Rly
Henry Pease	20165	20	1966	British Railways
Henry Ward	1583	George V	11/1910	London & North Western Rly
Henry W. Longfellow	321	Prince/W	11/1913	London & North Western Rly
Henshall Hall	7908	M/Hall	1/1950	British Railways (Western Region)
Herald	263	bCrewe	2/1851	London & North Western Rly
Herald	765	S/Bloomer	1854	London & North Western Rly
Herald	34	Dawn	10/1862	London, Chatham & Dover Rly
Herald	2062	Dreadnought	1885	London & North Western Rly
Herald	911	2Precursor	9/1905	London & North Western Rly
Herbert	–	0-4-0ST	**1941**	**Royal Ordnance** [55]
Herbert Austin	47200	47/0	1965	British Railways
Hercules	–	0-4-2	12/1833	Leicester & Swannington Rly
Hercules	39	0-4-0	1835	Liverpool & Manchester Rly
Hercules	4	0-4-0	1/1836	Newcastle & Carlisle Rly [56]
Hercules	7	0-4-2	5/1839	London & Croydon Rly
Hercules	2	2-2-2	4/1840	Midland Counties Rly
Hercules	48	1Hercules	8/1840	London & South Western Rly
Hercules	–	Fury	7/1842	Great Western Rly (bg)
Hercules	21	0-6-0T	1844	Edinburgh & Glasgow Rly
Hercules	37	0-6-0ST	7/1844	Birmingham & Gloucester Rly
Hercules	30	0-6-0	2/1847	Manchester, Sheffield & Lincolnshire Rly
Hercules	19	Samson	5/1847	East Lancashire Rly
Hercules	261	bCrewe	10/1850	London & North Western Rly
Hercules	48	2Hercules	8/1851	London & South Western Rly
Hercules	9	2-2-2T	1852	London & Blackwall Rly
Hercules	32	0-6-0	1853	Taff Vale Rly
Hercules	4	0-6-0T	1856	St Helens Canal & Rly
Hercules	4	?	9/1857	Newcastle & Carlisle Rly [57]
Hercules	–	0-4-2	?	Brassey [58]
Hercules	5	0-6-0ST	1860	Whitehaven, Cleator & Egremont Rly [59]
Hercules	–	0-6-0	8/1860	London, Chatham & Dover Rly
Hercules	261	DX	c.1860	London & North Western Rly
Hercules	19	S/Goods	11/1862	Cambrian Railways
Hercules	18	A	8/1864	Metropolitan Rly
Hercules	27	0-6-0ST	6/1871	Brecon & Merthyr Rly
Hercules	2163	0-6-0ST	8/1872	Great Western Rly (bg) [60]
Hercules	1105	Precedent	5/1877	London & North Western Rly

Name	Number	Class	Date	Railway
Hercules	–	0-6-0	?	Boultons
Hercules	3043	3031	1/1895	Great Western Rly
Hercules	1105	rPrecedent	12/1897	London & North Western Rly
Hercules	1	0-4-0ST	1900	British Railways [61]
Hercules	16	0-6-4CT	4/1922	Great Western Rly [62]
Hercules	5	4-8-2	**1926**	**Romney, Hythe & Dymchurch Rly** [63]
Hercules	–	4wDM	**1946**	**Foxfield Steam Rly**
Hercules	D822	Warship	6/1960	British Railways
Hercules	**50007**	**50**	**1968**	**British Railways** [64]
Hereford	16	0-6-0ST	5/1862	Brecon & Merthyr Rly [65]
Hereford	15	(?)	?	Cambrian Railways [66]
Hereford	–	Swindon	3/1866	Great Western Rly (bg)
Hereford Castle	7022	Castle	6/1949	British Railways (Western Region)
Herefordshire	1455	2Experiment	11/1909	London & North Western Rly
Hereward the Wake	70037	Britannia	12/1952	British Railways
Hermes	D823	Warship	7/1960	British Railways
Hermeuric	40	2-2-2	12/1843	South Eastern Rly
Hermit	4478	A3	6/1923	London & North Eastern Rly
Hermoine	2359	Prince/W	12/1911	London & North Western Rly
Hero	192	aCrewe	1/1848	London & North Western Rly
Hero	85	2-4-0	11/1849	Manchester, Sheffield & Lincolnshire Rly
Hero	–	Caesar	12/1851	Great Western Rly (bg)
Hero	23	0-6-0T	1853	St Helens Canal & Rly
Hero	2144	0-6-0ST	4/1860	Great Western Rly (bg) [67]
Hero	192	DX	c.1860	London & North Western Rly
Hero	901	Samson	1/1864	London & North Western Rly
Hero	901	Whitworth	10/1890	London & North Western Rly
Hero	272	aSentinel	1928	London & North Eastern Rly
Herod	63	2-2-2	6/1840	Grand Junction Rly
Herod	81	Fireball	8/1847	London & South Western Rly
Herod	63	bCrewe	9/1855	London & North Western Rly
Herod	81	Falcon	12/1865	London & South Western Rly
Heron	130	aCrewe	5/1852	London & North Western Rly [68]
Heron	130	DX	c.1860	London & North Western Rly
Heron	2134	4-4-0ST	1861	Great Western Rly (bg) [69]
Heron	5	Tiger	8/1861	London, Chatham & Dover Rly
Herringbone	524	A2/3	9/1947	London & North Eastern Rly
Herring Gull	4466	A4	1/1938	London & North Eastern Rly [70]
Herschel	156	Panther	2/1861	Stockton & Darlington Rly
Herschel	1482	Newton	5/1866	London & North Western Rly
Herschel	1482	rPrecedent	1/1890	London & North Western Rly
Herschel	1571	2Experiment	1/1909	London & North Western Rly
Herschell	3376	Atbara	4/1900	Great Western Rly
Hertfordshire	1611	2Experiment	11/1909	London & North Western Rly
Hertfordshire	256	D49/1	12/1927	London & North Eastern Rly
Hertfordshire Rail Tours	33116	33/1	**1961**	**British Railways**
Hesiod	–	Bogie	3/1855	Great Western Rly (bg)
Hesketh	7	2-4-0	12/1859	London & South Western Rly (ed)
Hesketh Park	10	0-4-0T	1884	West Lancashire Rly
Hesperus	–	Wolf	1/1841	Great Western Rly (bg)
Hesperus	15	2-2-2	5/1845	Manchester, Sheffield & Lincolnshire Rly

[54] Rebuilt to class B2x, February 1909.

[55] Preserved on the Battlefield Steam Railway.

[56] Replaced in September 1857 by a new locomotive with the same name and number.

[57] Probably an 0–6–0. Became North Eastern Railway no. 453 in 1862.

[58] Thomas Brassey contracted to maintain the track of the London & South Western Railway from 4 November 1839 to December 1853. He provided his own locomotives, of which *Hercules* was one. Beyond their names, very little is known of them.

[59] Became Furness Railway no. 101.

[60] Built for the South Devon Railway.

[61] This locomotive came from industrial service with the Ystalyfera Tinplate Works. It was purchased from the Liquidator by British Railways (Western Region), and was thus never a Great Western Railway locomotive.

[62] Date into service. Built April 1921.

[63] 15in gauge.

[64] Renamed *Sir Edward Elgar* on 25 February 1984.

[65] Renamed *Lady Cornelia* in 1869.

[66] Built pre-1866, when the Cambrian first numbered its locomotives. Almost certainly the same locomotive as Brecon & Merthyr no. 16 above.

[67] Built for the South Devon Railway.

[68] Formerly Liverpool & Manchester Railway no. 71. Became London & North Western Railway property in 1846.

[69] Built for the South Devon Railway.

[70] Renamed *Sir Ralph Wedgwood* in January 1944. The original *Sir Ralph Wedgwood*, no. 4469, was destroyed by enemy action at York Motive Power Depot in June 1942.

Name	Number	Class	Date	Railway
Hesperus	–	0–4–2ST	1872	West Sussex Light Rly [71]
Hesperus	3	Ilfracombe	4/1875	Shropshire & Montgomeryshire Rly [72]
Hesperus	4	2–4–0T	1876	Weston, Clevedon & Portishead Rly [73]
Hesperus	8	0–6–0ST	1876	Kent & East Sussex Rly [74]
Hetton Loco	–	**0–4–0**	**1822**	**Beamish Museum** [75]
Heveningham Hall	7909	M/Hall	1/1950	British Railways (Western Region)
Hewell Grange	6839	Grange	9/1937	Great Western Rly
Hexham	34	0–6–0	7/1850	Newcastle & Carlisle Rly [76]
H G Wells	92002	92		British Railways
Hibernia	225	DFG	5/1866	London & South Western Rly
Hibernia	1749	Newton	11/1869	London & North Western Rly
Hibernia	1749	rPrecedent	1/1888	London & North Western Rly
Hibernia	2063	Prince/W	11/1915	London & North Western Rly
Hickstead	571	E5	1/1903	London, Brighton & South Coast Rly
Highclere Castle	4096	Castle	6/1926	Great Western Rly
High Flyer	210	aSentinel	1928	London & North Eastern Rly
Highflyer	D824	Warship	7/1960	British Railways
Highgate	60	51	1900	London, Tilbury & Southend Rly
Highgate Road	60	51	1900	London, Tilbury & Southend Rly
Highland Chief	902	I	7/1911	North British Rly
Highland Chieftain	33	cSentinel	1929	London & North Eastern Rly
Highland Chieftain	507	A2/1	9/1944	London & North Eastern Rly
Highland Enterprise	37427	37/4	1965	British Railways
Highlander	29	Glenbarry	10/1863	Highland Rly [77]
Highlander	59	Jones Tank	6/1879	Highland Rly [78]
Highland Light	46121	Royal Scot	10/1927	British Railways [79]
Infantry, City of Glasgow Regiment				
Highland Region	37417	37/4	1965	British Railways
High Marnham	58018	58	1977	British Railways
Power Station				
Highnam Court	2944	Saint	5/1912	Great Western Rly
Highnam Grange	6819	Grange	12/1936	Great Western Rly
High Sheriff	627	627	7/1881	Lancashire & Yorkshire Rly
High Sheriff	90006	90/0	9/1988	British Railways
High Willhays	60041	60	6/1991	British Railways
Hilda	–	0–6–0ST	1917	Llanelly & Mynydd Mawr Rly [80]
Hilda	–	**0–4–0ST**	**1936**	**Great Central Rly** [81]
Hill	–	Railcar	1905	Nidd Valley Light Rly [82]
Hillingdon Court	2945	Saint	6/1912	Great Western Rly
Hillington	–	4–4–0T	11/1878	Lynn & Fakenham Rly
Hilsea	249	D1	12/1881	London, Brighton & South Coast Rly
Himalaya	37	0–6–0	1852	Oxford, Worcester & Wolverhampton Rly [83]
Himalaya	303	2Precursor	1/1905	London & North Western Rly
Himley Hall	4933	Hall	6/1929	Great Western Rly
Hinchingbrooke	2834	B17/1	6/1931	London & North Eastern Rly

Name	Number	Class	Date	Railway
Hinderton Hall	5900	Hall	3/1931	**Great Western Rly**
Hindford Grange	6875	Grange	4/1939	Great Western Rly
Hindlip Hall	4934	Hall	6/1929	Great Western Rly
Hindostan	1972	Alfred	7/1903	London & North Western Rly [84]
Hinton Manor	7819	Manor	2/1939	**Great Western Rly**
Hirola	1023	B1	4/1947	London & North Eastern Rly
Hirondelle	5	2–2–2	12/1840	Chester & Birkenhead Rly
Hirondelle	–	Iron Duke	12/1848	Great Western Rly (bg)
Hirondelle	–	Rover	5/1873	Great Western Rly (bg)
Hirondelle	3045	3031	1/1895	Great Western Rly
His Majesty	42	B4	6/1902	London, Brighton & South Coast Rly
Hither Green	58021	58	1984	British Railways
H.L.I.	6121	Royal Scot	10/1927	London Midland & Scottish Rly [85]
HMS Endeavour	20156	20	1966	British Railways
Hoathly	250	D1	12/1881	London, Brighton & South Coast Rly
Hobart	3403	Atbara	9/1901	Great Western Rly
Hobart	3403	City	2/1909	Great Western Rly
Hobbie Elliott	2683	D11/2	10/1924	London & North Eastern Rly
Hogue	156	Nile	5/1859	London & South Western Rly
Hogue	5683	Jubilee	1936	London Midland & Scottish Rly
Holbeck	47634	47/4	1964	British Railways
Holbrook Hall	6948	Hall	12/1942	Great Western Rly [86]
Holdsworth	1	4–4–0T	6/1866	Nidd Valley Light Rly [87]
Holker Hall	6911	Hall	1/1941	Great Western Rly
Holkham	2801	B17/1	12/1928	London & North Eastern Rly
Holkham Hall	6926	Hall	11/1941	Great Western Rly [88]
Holland-Afrika Line	35023	MN	11/1948	British Railways (Southern Region)
Holland-America Line	35022	MN	10/1948	British Railways (Southern Region)
Holland Hibbert	163	Claughton	6/1913	London & North Western Rly
Hollington	593	E5	5/1904	London, Brighton & South Coast Rly
Holloway	59	51	1900	London, Tilbury & Southend Rly
Holloway Road	59	51	1900	London, Tilbury & Southend Rly
(Holman F. Stephens)	91	**J94**	**1/1953**	**Kent & East Sussex Rly** [89]
Holmbury	289	D1	7/1879	London, Brighton & South Coast Rly
Holme	335	2–4–0	2/1865	Lancashire & Yorkshire Rly [90]
Holmwood	285	D1	9/1879	London, Brighton & South Coast Rly
Holmwood	7	1813	9/1882	Pembroke & Tenby Rly [91]
Holsworthy	34097	rWC	11/1949	British Railways (Southern Region)
Holt Pioneer	D5386	**27**	**1962**	**North Norfolk Rly** [92]
Holyhead	2106	George V	7/1916	London & North Western Rly
Holyhead	5514	Patriot	9/1932	London Midland & Scottish Rly [93]
Holyrood	70	B4	9/1901	London, Brighton & South Coast Rly [94]
Holyrood	904	I	8/1911	North British Rly
Holyrood	60152	A1	7/1949	British Railways (Eastern Region)
Holyrood	47707	47/7	1966	British Railways
Holy War	–	**0–4–0ST**	**1902**	**Bala Lake Rly** [95]

[71] Built as a narrow gauge 0–4–0ST for the East Cornwall Mineral Railway, this engine was purchased by the Plymouth, Devonport & South Western Junction Railway in June 1891. It was no. 2 *Pensilva*, and was rebuilt as a standard gauge 0–4–2ST. In August 1912 it went to the West Sussex Light Railway (also known as the Selsey Tramway), where it worked until 1927.

[72] Built for the London & South Western Railway as no. 324, later duplicated as no. 0324. It was withdrawn in May 1939 but not broken up until November 1941 – the last of the Ilfracombe Goods class to survive.

[73] Formerly no. 2 of the Watlington & Princes Risborough Railway (unnamed).

[74] Formerly *Ringing Rock* on the North Pembrokeshire & Fishguard Railways. This later became part of the Great Western Railway, the locomotive becoming their no.

1380. The name was changed in 1920 by the K&ESR.

[75] Built by George Stephenson.

[76] Became North Eastern Railway no. 482 in 1862. Rebuilt to 2–4–0 in 1872.

[77] Altered from 2–2–2 to 2–4–0 in August 1871, and renamed *Forres* in May 1879.

[78] Altered from 2–4–0T to 4–4–0T in June 1887.

[79] Built by the London Midland & Scottish Railway and originally named *H.L.I.* Renamed in January 1949.

[80] Became Great Western Railway no. 359.

[81] The modern, preserved Great Central Railway.

[82] Formerly Great Western Railway steam railcar no. 15.

[83] Purchased from the Manchester, Sheffield & Lincolnshire Railway. It became Great Western Railway no. 237.

[84] Some sources give *Hindustan*, but the

nameplate preserved at the NRM, York, confirms that *Hindostan* is correct.

[85] Renamed *Highland Light Infantry, City of Glasgow Regiment* in January 1949.

[86] Nameplates fitted January 1948.

[87] Formerly Metropolitan Railway no. 20.

[88] Nameplates fitted November 1946.

[89] Originally War Department no. 191 *Black Knight*.

[90] The name may not have actually been carried.

[91] Built at Swindon as Great Western Railway no. 1813, an 0–6–0T, and purchased by the Pembroke & Tenby Railway in June 1883. In 1896, when the GWR took over the P&TR, it resumed its original GWR number.

[92] Built for British Railways.

[93] Rebuilt with taper boiler in March 1947.

[94] Renamed *Devonshire* in March 1907. Rebuilt to class B4x, May 1923.

[95] 2ft gauge.

Holy War, an 0–4–0ST built in 1902 for the Padarn Quarries in North Wales, and seen here on the Bala Lake Railway. (*Photo: R.G. Pike*)

Name	Number	Class	Date	Railway
Home Guard	5543	Patriot	3/1934	London Midland & Scottish Rly [96]
Homer	–	Bogie	8/1854	Great Western Rly (bg)
Honegger	92042	92		British Railways
Honeyway	519	A2/3	2/1947	London & North Eastern Rly
Honfleur	97	E1	10/1874	London, Brighton & South Coast Rly
Honfleur	95	B4	11/1893	London & South Western Rly
Hong Kong	5611	Jubilee	1934	London Midland & Scottish Rly
Honingham Hall	2810	B17/1	8/1930	London & North Eastern Rly
Honiton	21C134	rWC	7/1946	Southern Rly
Honor Oak	466	E4	4/1898	London, Brighton & South Coast Rly [97]
Honourable Artillery Company	6144	Royal Scot	10/1927	London Midland & Scottish Rly [98]
Honourable Artillery Company	D89	Peak	3/1961	British Railways
Hood	–	2–2–2?	?	Leeds & Selby Rly
Hood	145	Nelson	8/1858	London & South Western Rly
Hood	1973	Alfred	7/1903	London & North Western Rly
Hood	5654	Jubilee	1935	London Midland & Scottish Rly
Hood	**50031**	**50**	**1968**	**British Railways**
Hook Norton	1337	0–6–0ST	11/1889	Great Western Rly [99]
Hook Norton Manor	7823	Manor	12/1950	British Railways (Western Region)
Hope	2	Locomotion	11/1825	Stockton & Darlington Rly [100]
Hope	273	bCrewe	8/1851	London & North Western Rly
Hope	1	2–4–0T	1879	East & West Junction Rly
Hope	–	0–6–0ST	11/1883	Garstang & Knott End Rly
Hope	2136	cSentinel	1928	London & North Eastern Rly
Hopeman	17	0–4–0T	5/1863	Highland Rly [101]
Hopetown	5	Tory	8/1841	Stockton & Darlington Rly
Hopewell	205	0–4–0ST	1851	Midland Rly [102]
Hopton Grange	6865	Grange	3/1939	Great Western Rly
Horace	–	Bogie	9/1854	Great Western Rly (bg)
Horden	–	**0–6–0ST**	**1904**	**Tanfield Rly**
Horley	507	E4	12/1900	London, Brighton & South Coast Rly

Name	Number	Class	Date	Railway
Hornby Castle	1	0–4–0	4/1850	North Western Rly
Hornchurch	20	Class 1	1884	London, Tilbury & Southend Rly
Horndean	582	E4	9/1903	London, Brighton & South Coast Rly
Horne	660	C	8/1891	North British Rly
Hornet	50	2–2–2	1838	Grand Junction Rly
Hornet	28	2–2–0	7/1840	Midland Counties Rly
Hornet	–	2–2–0	1845	London, Chatham & Dover Rly
Hornet	80	Fireball	5/1847	London & South Western Rly
Hornet	50	bCrewe	5/1848	London & North Western Rly
Hornet	–	Metro	6/1862	Great Western Rly (bg)
Hornet	80	Falcon	12/1865	London & South Western Rly
Hornet	–	**0–4–0ST**	**1937**	**Southport Railway Centre**
Hornets Beauty	60535	A2	5/1948	British Railways (Eastern Region)
Hornsey	58	51	1900	London, Tilbury & Southend Rly
Hornsey Road	58	51	1900	London, Tilbury & Southend Rly
Horsa	2	2–2–2	12/1841	South Eastern Rly
Horsebridge	578	E4	6/1903	London, Brighton & South Coast Rly
Horsham	233	2–2–2	10/1866	London, Brighton & South Coast Rly [103]
Horsham	231	D1	7/1884	London, Brighton & South Coast Rly
Horsted Keynes	378	D3	5/1893	London, Brighton & South Coast Rly
Horton Hall	5992	Hall	12/1939	Great Western Rly
Horwich Enterprise	47491	47/4	1964	British Railways
Hotspur	277	bCrewe	11/1851	London & North Western Rly
Hotspur	631	Samson	10/1874	London & North Western Rly
Hotspur	631	Whitworth	1896	London & North Western Rly
Hotspur	3300	Badminton	7/1898	Great Western Rly
Hotspur	2300	Prince/W	12/1915	London & North Western Rly
Hotspur	70011	Britannia	5/1951	British Railways
Hotwheels	–	**0–6–0DM**	**1958**	**South Yorkshire Rly [104]**
Houghton Hall	2812	B17/1	10/1930	London & North Eastern Rly
Hove	248	2–4–0	2/1868	London, Brighton & South Coast Rly
Howard of Effingham	854	Lord Nelson	10/1928	Southern Rly
Howard of Effingham	5670	Jubilee	1935	London Midland & Scottish Rly
Howard of Effingham	87015	87/0	1974	British Railways
Howe	144	Nelson	8/1858	London & South Western Rly
Howe	1974	Alfred	7/1903	London & North Western Rly
Howe	5644	Jubilee	1934	London Midland & Scottish Rly
Howe	50023	50	1968	British Railways
Howick Hall	5902	Hall	5/1931	Great Western Rly
Hown Hall	7910	M/Hall	1/1950	British Railways (Western Region)
Hubbard	3299	Badminton	6/1898	Great Western Rly [105]
Hucknall Colliery	3	**4wDM**	**1961**	**Midland Railway Centre [106]**
Hucknall Colliery	1	**4wDM**	**1963**	**Midland Railway Centre [107]**
Huddersfield	89	0–4–0	1845	Stockton & Darlington Rly [108]
Huddersfield	–	2–2–2	1847	Huddersfield & Manchester Railway & Canal
Huddersfield	–	0–6–0ST	7/1876	Metropolitan Rly [109]
Huddersfield Town	2853	B17/4	4/1936	London & North Eastern Rly
Hudson	–	2–2–2	1840	York & North Midland Rly
Hugh Myddleton	1536	John Hick	1898	London & North Western Rly
Hugh Myddleton	1477	2Experiment	5/1909	London & North Western Rly
Hugh Napier	–	**0–4–0ST**	**1904**	**Penrhyn Castle Industrial Railway Museum [110]**
Huish	309	bCrewe	5/1853	London & North Western Rly
Hull	10	0–4–2	9/1839	Manchester & Leeds Rly

---

[96] Name applied in July 1940; the engine was originally nameless.

[97] Rebuilt to class E4x, February 1909.

[98] Originally named *Ostrich*. Renamed in January 1933.

[99] Built for Hook Norton Ironstone Partnership Ltd.

[100] According to some accounts, may have been named *Bedlington*.

[101] Originally an 0–4–0T built in 1863 for the Inverness & Aberdeen Junction Railway, who numbered it 17 and named it *Hopeman*. In 1865 it became Highland Railway property.

In 1867 William Stroudley altered it to 0–4–2T, renamed it *Needlefield*, and deleted the number. It was later numbered 1A.

[102] Taken over from the Staveley Coal & Iron Co. in 1866.

[103] Name applied in October 1872. Renumbered 487 in August 1881, it was sold to the West Lancashire Railway in January 1883, becoming its no. 5 *Horsham*.

[104] The modern, preserved South Yorkshire Railway.

[105] Renamed *Alexander Hubbard* in August 1903.

[106] 2ft 6in gauge.

[107] 2ft gauge.

[108] Purchased from the Manchester & Leeds Railway in 1854.

[109] Ex-Wotton Tramway. This had started as the Oxford & Aylesbury Tramroad, but never reached either town. It started from the Metropolitan Railway at Quainton Road, and reached the quiet market town of Brill, just over 6 miles away. The line was later absorbed by the Metropolitan Railway.

[110] 1ft 10¾in gauge.

Name	Number	Class	Date	Railway
Hull City	2860	B17/4	6/1936	London & North Eastern Rly
Humber	15	2–2–2	9/1840	Manchester & Leeds Rly
Humber	–	Caesar	6/1857	Great Western Rly (bg)
Humber	278	4	1909	Great Central Rly [111]
Hummy	–	4–6–0T	1917	Ashover Rly [112]
Humorist	2751	A3	3/1929	London & North Eastern Rly
Humphrey Davy	945	Precedent	11/1880	London & North Western Rly
Humphrey Davy	945	rPrecedent	6/1895	London & North Western Rly
Humphry Davy	60069	60	9/1991	British Railways
Hun	137	Saxon	5/1857	London & South Western Rly
Hungary	152	E1	10/1880	London, Brighton & South Coast Rly [113]
Huntingdonshire	322	D49/3	7/1928	London & North Eastern Rly [114]
Huntingtower	62	Duke	6/1874	Highland Rly [115]
Hurricane	–	2–2–2	10/1838	Great Western Rly (bg) [116]
Hurricane	22	2–2–0	3/1840	Midland Counties Rly
Hurricane	39	Goliath	5/1849	East Lancashire Rly
Hurricane	330	bCrewe	3/1854	London & North Western Rly
Hurricane	3044	3031	1/1895	Great Western Rly
Hurricane	1988	2Experiment	9/1906	London & North Western Rly
Hurricane	**8**	**4–6–2**	**1926**	**Romney, Hythe & Dymchurch Rly [117]**
Hurricane	5072	Castle	6/1938	Great Western Rly [118]
Hurricane	21C165	BB	7/1947	Southern Rly
Hurricane	37077	37/0	1962	British Railways
Hurst Grange	6851	Grange	11/1937	Great Western Rly
Hurst Green	465	E4	4/1898	London, Brighton & South Coast Rly
Hurstmonceaux	344	G	1/1882	London, Brighton & South Coast Rly
Hurstpierpoint	377	D3	5/1893	London, Brighton & South Coast Rly
Hurstpierpoint	918	Schools	6/1933	Southern Rly
Huskisson	169	aCrewe	9/1847	London & North Western Rly
Huskisson	2063	Dreadnought	1885	London & North Western Rly
Huskisson	638	2Precursor	12/1904	London & North Western Rly
Hutchinson	14	2–4–0	4/1866	London & South Western Rly (ed) [119]
Hutchinson	**12**	**2–4–0T**	**1908**	**Isle of Man Rly [120]**
Hutton	130	Peel	5/1858	Stockton & Darlington Rly
Hutton Hall	8	0–6–0ST	1907	Cleator & Workington Junction Rly
Huz	133	0–6–0	7/1873	London, Chatham & Dover Rly
H W Robinson	**–**	**0–4–0DM**	**1946**	**Yorkshire Dales Rly**
Hyacinth	43	Bluebell	6/1863	London, Chatham & Dover Rly
Hyacinth	4113	Flower	6/1908	Great Western Rly [121]
Hycilla	516	A2/3	11/1946	London & North Eastern Rly
Hyderabad	5585	Jubilee	1934	London Midland & Scottish Rly
Hydra	33	2–2–0	8/1841	Midland Counties Rly
Hydra	–	Priam	4/1842	Great Western Rly (bg)
Hydra	95	aCrewe	11/1846	London & North Western Rly
Hydra	888	L/Bloomer	1851	London & North Western Rly
Hydra	303	1Experiment	1883	London & North Western Rly
Hydra	1617	2Precursor	8/1905	London & North Western Rly
Hylton	**–**	**0–4–0DH**	**1961**	**Northamptonshire Ironstone Railway Trust**
Hyperion	62	2–2–2	7/1840	Grand Junction Rly
Hyperion	62	bCrewe	11/1850	London & North Western Rly
Hyperion	1787	2Precursor	5/1906	London & North Western Rly
Hyperion	2502	A3	7/1934	London & North Eastern Rly

[111] 0–6–0ST. Acquired 1911. Used on the construction of Immingham Dock and the Barton–Immingham line.

[112] Ex-War Department. These engines were built by the Baldwin Locomotive Company (USA) for service in France with the Allied Armies in the First World War. 2ft gauge.

[113] Transferred to the Isle of Wight in June 1932 by the Southern Railway as no. W2 *Yarmouth.*

[114] As originally built with Lentz Oscillating Cam poppet valves. In November 1938 it was altered to piston valves and integrated into class D49/1.

[115] Originally named *Perthshire.* Became *Stemster* in 1889, *Huntingtower* in 1899 and *Ault Wharrie* in 1903.

[116] *Hurricane* was a 2–2–2 with 10ft driving wheels. The boiler was mounted on a trailing six-wheeled frame, and the tender came behind that. The result was that the adhesive weight was about 6 tons. It ceased 'work' at the end of 1839.

[117] 15in gauge.

[118] *Compton Castle* until November 1940.

[119] Formerly no. 228 of the Locomotive Department.

[120] 3ft gauge.

[121] Originally spelt *Hyacinthe* and not corrected until May 1916.

Name	Number	Class	Date	Railway
Iago	–	Banking	10/1852	Great Western Rly (bg)
Ian Allan	91007	91	7/1988	British Railways
Iarll Meirionnydd	–	**0–4–4–0F**	**1885**	**Festiniog Rly** [1]
Ibstock	–	**4wDM**	**1951**	**Amberley Chalk Pits Museum** [2]
ICI Diamond Jubilee	47365	47/3	1965	British Railways
Ida	311	bCrewe	5/1853	London & North Western Rly
Ida	311	aCrewe	1/1858	London & North Western Rly [3]
Idas	98	2–4–0	3/1850	Manchester, Sheffield & Lincolnshire Rly
Idris	–	**4wDM**	**1941**	**Gwili Rly**
Iford Manor	7824	Manor	12/1950	British Railways (Western Region)
Ignifer	–	0–4–0ST	1871	Aberford Rly
Ilfracombe	3445	Bulldog	9/1903	Great Western Rly
Ilfracombe	21C117	rWC	12/1945	Southern Rly
Ilion	1669	Newton	3/1868	London & North Western Rly
Ilion	1669	rPrecedent	3/1880	London & North Western Rly
Ilion	526	2Precursor	3/1906	London & North Western Rly
Ilkeston	–	0–6–0T	?	Alexandra (Newport & South Wales) Docks & Rly
Illustrious	150	Claughton	3/1921	London & North Western Rly [4]
Illustrious	5532	Patriot	4/1933	London Midland & Scottish Rly [5]
Illustrious	50037	50	1968	British Railways
Imberhorne	327	G	12/1880	London, Brighton & South Coast Rly
Immingham	1097	8F	6/1906	Great Central Rly
Immingham	47380	47/3	1965	British Railways
Impala	1002	B1	9/1943	London & North Eastern Rly
Imperial	37343	37/3	8/1962	British Railways
Implacable	1915	Jubilee	6/1899	London & North Western Rly
Implacable	5709	Jubilee	1936	London Midland & Scottish Rly
Implacable	50039	50	1968	British Railways
Impney Hall	6951	Hall	2/1943	Great Western Rly [6]
Impregnable	5721	Jubilee	1936	London Midland & Scottish Rly
Ince Castle	7034	Castle	8/1950	British Railways (Western Region)
Inchcape	3720	Bulldog	8/1906	Great Western Rly
Independent	2270	cSentinel	1929	London & North Eastern Rly
India	868	George V	6/1911	London & North Western Rly
India	5574	Jubilee	1934	London Midland & Scottish Rly
Indian Runner	–	**4wDM**	**1940**	**Bala Lake Rly** [7]
Indomitable	5720	Jubilee	1936	London Midland & Scottish Rly
Indomitable	**50026**	**50**	**1968**	**British Railways**
Indore	5592	Jubilee	1934	London Midland & Scottish Rly
Industry	2	2–4–0	9/1844	Bristol & Gloucester Rly (bg) [8]
Industry	2271	cSentinel	1929	London & North Eastern Rly
Inflexible	1917	Jubilee	7/1899	London & North Western Rly
Inflexible	5727	Jubilee	1936	London Midland & Scottish Rly
Ingestre	85	aCrewe	5/1846	London & North Western Rly
Ingestre	856	L/Bloomer	1851	London & North Western Rly
Ingestre	682	0–4–4ST	1860	Great Northern Rly [9]
Ingestre	2420	Claughton	6/1917	London & North Western Rly
Ingleboro	14	2–4–0	1857	Lancaster & Carlisle Rly
Ingleboro	24	2–2–2	1857	Lancaster & Carlisle Rly [10]
Ingleborough	–	2–2–0	1838	North Western Rly [11]
Ingleborough	D7	Peak	11/1959	British Railways
Ingleborough	60022	60	1/1991	British Railways
Inglewood	607	S/Bloomer	1854	London & North Western Rly
Inglewood	13	2–4–0	1857	Lancaster & Carlisle Rly
Inkerman	35	0–6–0	1855	Taff Vale Rly
Inkermann	–	Iron Duke	3/1855	Great Western Rly (bg)
Inkermann	–	Rover	10/1878	Great Western Rly (bg)
Insein	**5282**	**J94**	**1945**	**Longmoor Military Rly** [12]
Inspector	481	2–4–2T	9/1869	London, Brighton & South Coast Rly [13]
Institution of Civil Engineers	47975	47/4	3/1964	British Railways
Institution of Railway Signal Engineers	37411	37/4	1965	British Railways
Integrity	2135	aSentinel	1928	London & North Eastern Rly
INTERCITY	43154	43	1/1981	British Railways
Intercontainer	86405	86/6	10/1965	British Railways
Intrepid	1922	Jubilee	2/1900	London & North Western Rly
Intrepid	D825	Warship	8/1960	British Railways
Inveravon	–	0–4–0ST	1879	Llanelly & Mynydd Mawr Rly
Inverdon	**15**	**4wDM**	**1957**	**Strathspey Rly**
Inveresk	**14**	**0–4–0DM**	**1950**	**Strathspey Rly**
Invergordon	24	S/Goods	10/1863	Highland Rly [14]
Invergordon	55	Glenbarry	10/1864	Highland Rly [15]
Inverness	18	S/Goods	8/1863	Highland Rly [16]
Inverness	63	Duke	7/1874	Highland Rly [17]
Inverness-shire	63	Duke	7/1874	Highland Rly [18]
Inverness-shire	329	D49/3	8/1928	London & North Eastern Rly [19]
Inverness TMD Quality Approved	37025	37/0	1961	British Railways
Invicta	–	**0–4–0**	**4/1830**	**Canterbury & Whitstable Rly**
Invicta	–	**0–4–0ST**	**1946**	**Chatham Dockyard**
Invincible	1914	Jubilee	6/1899	London & North Western Rly
Invincible	**37**	**0–4–0ST**	**1915**	**Woolwich Arsenal** [20]
Invincible	5715	Jubilee	1936	London Midland & Scottish Rly
Invincible	50025	50	1968	British Railways
Inyala	1016	B1	1/1947	London & North Eastern Rly
Iona	81	Scotchmen	4/1866	London, Chatham & Dover Rly
Iona	20905	20	1/1968	Hunslet-Barclay Ltd [21]
Ionic	1306	Teutonic	6/1890	London & North Western Rly
Ionic	1312	2Precursor	2/1906	London & North Western Rly
Ipswich	2	2–2–2	5/1846	Eastern Union Rly

[1] 1ft 11½in gauge. Originally named *Livingston Thompson*, and renamed *Taliesin* in 1930. Later renamed *Earl of Merioneth*, with the Welsh *Iarll Meirionnydd* on the other side. The title Earl of Merioneth, incidentally, is held by HRH the Duke of Edinburgh, while Taliesin was a chief of the bards, flourishing in about AD 570.

[2] 2ft gauge.

[3] Replacement of previous engine, which was sold to the Lancaster & Carlisle Railway.

[4] Nameless until May 1923.

[5] Rebuilt with taper boiler in July 1948.

[6] Nameplates fitted in April 1948.

[7] 2ft gauge.

[8] Later taken over by the Midland Railway, who renumbered it 269. In 1856 it was sold to Thomas Brassey for working the North Devon Railway, a broad gauge line which later passed to the London & South Western Railway. It is thought to have become the NDR's *Venus*.

[9] Built as 0–4–2ST in 1860 by Beyer Peacock of Manchester for the North London Railway, becoming their no. 41. Purchased by Stamford & Uttoxeter Railway in 1868 and rebuilt to 0–4–4ST. Became GNR no. 682.

[10] Originally named *Belted Will*.

[11] Said to be formerly London & North Western Railway no. 178 *Friar*. But this locomotive was a 2–4–0, built in November 1849. The North Western's 2–2–0 was probably a Bury type, with bar frames.

[12] As no. 75282, was earlier named *Haulwen 2*.

[13] Originally 2–4–0T no. 96, and named *Kemptown*. Renumbered 115 and named *Hayling Island* in September 1874. Renumbered 359 in June 1877, and 499 in January 1886. Then altered by Stroudley in January 1890 to a 2–4–2T with a small inspection saloon mounted on the back, renumbered 481 and renamed *Inspector*. Stroudley died in December 1889 while the alteration was still in progress, and the locomotive saw little use before withdrawal in March 1898.

[14] Later renamed *Lairg*.

[15] Originally named *Cluny*. Became *Sutherland* in 1874, and *Invergordon* in 1884.

[16] Later became no. 19 *Dingwall*, and further renamed *Golspie*.

[17] Previously named *Inverness-shire*.

[18] Renamed *Inverness* in 1890s.

[19] As originally built with Lentz Oscillating Cam poppet valves. In September 1938 altered to piston valves and integrated into class D49/1.

[20] Preserved on the Isle of Wight Railway.

[21] Built for British Railways.

Name	Number	Class	Date	Railway
Ipswich WRD Quality Assured	37379	37/3	2/1964	British Railways
Ireland	202	0–6–0	6/1867	Stockton & Darlington Rly
Iris	–	Caesar	3/1854	Great Western Rly (bg)
Iris	**420**	**0–6–0DH**	**1952**	**Chinnor & Princes Risborough Rly**
Irish Elegance	60534	A2	4/1948	British Railways (Eastern Region)
Irish Free State	5572	Jubilee	1934	London Midland & Scottish Rly
Irish Guardsman	6116	Royal Scot	9/1927	London Midland & Scottish Rly
Irish Mail	**3**	**0–4–0ST**	**1903**	**West Lancashire Light Rly [22]**
Irk	27	2–2–2	2/1841	Manchester & Leeds Rly
Iron Age	187	Panther	12/1864	Stockton & Darlington Rly
Ironbridge No 1	**–**	**0–4–0ST**	**1933**	**Foxfield Steam Rly**
Ironbridge No 3	**–**	**0–4–0ST**	**1940**	**Telford Horsehay Steam Trust**
Ironbridge Power Station	58042	58		British Railways
Ironbridge Power Station	58005	58	1983	British Railways

Canterbury & Whitstable Railway 0–4–0 *Invicta*, as preserved at Canterbury, 29 September 1959. (*Photo: LCGB Ken Nunn Collection*)

Name	Number	Class	Date	Railway
Iron Duke	–	Iron Duke	4/1847	Great Western Rly (bg)
Iron Duke	46	Iron Duke	1/1850	East Lancashire Rly
Iron Duke	–	Rover	8/1873	Great Western Rly (bg)
Iron Duke	RCD3	0–4–0ST	1878	Woolwich Arsenal [23]
Iron Duke	3014	3001	4/1892	Great Western Rly [24]
Iron Duke	1903	Jubilee	1899	London & North Western Rly
Iron Duke	70014	Britannia	6/1951	British Railways
Iron Duke	87017	87/0	1974	British Railways
Iron Duke	**–**	**Iron Duke**	**1985**	**Great Western Rly (bg) [25]**
Ironside	11	2–2–2	7/1842	South Eastern Rly
Ironside	458	0–4–0ST	7/1890	London & South Western Rly [26]
Ironsides	–	?	1852	West Cornwall Rly [27]
Ironsides	134	Canute	12/1855	London & South Western Rly
Irresistable	1916	Jubilee	1899	London & North Western Rly
Irresistable	5710	Jubilee	1936	London Midland & Scottish Rly

Name	Number	Class	Date	Railway
Irresistable	47778	47/7		British Railways
Irwell	31	2–2–2	2/1841	Manchester & Leeds Rly
Irwell	282	bCrewe	3/1852	London & North Western Rly
Irwell	3	?	?	St Helens Canal & Rly
Irwell	**–**	**0–4–0ST**	**1937**	**Tanfield Rly**
Isabel	**–**	**0–4–0ST**	**1897**	**Amerton Rly [28]**
Isabel	**–**	**0–6–0ST**	**1919**	**West Somerset Rly**
Isabella	403	Newton	8/1873	London & North Western Rly
Isabella	403	rPrecedent	4/1892	London & North Western Rly
Isambard Kingdom Brunel	5069	Castle	6/1938	Great Western Rly
ISAMBARD KINGDOM BRUNEL	47484	47/4	1965	British Railways
(Isebrook No 2)	**49**	**4wVB**	**1926**	**Great Western Rly [29]**
Iseult	749	King Arthur	9/1922	Southern Rly [30]
Iseult	73116	5MT	11/1955	British Railways
Isfield	28	D1	4/1876	London, Brighton & South Coast Rly
Isibutu	**5**	**4–4–0T**	**1946**	**Gloucestershire Warwickshire Rly [31]**
Isinglass	2562	A3	6/1925	London & North Eastern Rly
Isis	310	bCrewe	5/1853	London & North Western Rly
Isis	147	Tweed	12/1858	London & South Western Rly
Isis	147	2–4–0	9/1864	London & South Western Rly [32]
Isis	2153	Samson	11/1874	London & North Western Rly
Isis	2153	Whitworth	6/1893	London & North Western Rly
Isis	73	River	10/1895	Great Western Rly [33]
Isla Bank	35	Glenbarry	11/1863	Highland Rly [34]
Islay	85	Scotchmen	7/1866	London, Chatham & Dover Rly
Isle of Grain	33050	33/0	1961	British Railways
Isle of Grain	56051	56	1978	British Railways
Isle of Guernsey	3316	Duke	3/1899	Great Western Rly [35]
Isle of Guernsey	3316	Bulldog	2/1908	Great Western Rly
Isle of Iona	47781	47/7		British Railways
Isle of Jersey	3317	Duke	4/1899	Great Western Rly [36]
Isle of Man	5511	Patriot	8/1932	London Midland & Scottish Rly
Isle of Mull	37424	37/4	1965	British Railways
Isle of Tresco	3288	Duke	3/1897	Great Western Rly [37]
Italian Monarch	4025	Star	7/1909	Great Western Rly [38]
Itchingfield	481	E4	12/1898	London, Brighton & South Coast Rly
I.T. Williams	155	Claughton	3/1917	London & North Western Rly
Ivanhoe	–	Abbot	3/1855	Great Western Rly (bg)
Ivanhoe	675	Problem	c.1860	London & North Western Rly
Ivanhoe	2981	Saint	6/1905	Great Western Rly [39]
Ivanhoe	222	2Experiment	11/1906	London & North Western Rly
Ivanhoe	339	Scott	10/1911	North British Rly
Ivernia CLS	40021	40	7/1959	British Railways [40]
Ivor	08600	08	1959	British Railways
Ixion	–	Priam	10/1841	Great Western Rly (bg)
Ixion	31	2–2–2	3/1847	Manchester, Sheffield & Lincolnshire Rly
Ixion	232	bCrewe	11/1848	London & North Western Rly
Ixion	2105	4–4–0ST	4/1853	Great Western Rly (bg) [41]
Ixion	17	A	8/1864	Metropolitan Rly
Ixion	445	Samson	9/1873	London & North Western Rly
Ixion	445	Whitworth	4/1893	London & North Western Rly
Ixion	**D172**	**46**	**1962**	**British Railways**

[22] 2ft gauge.
[23] Name applied in about 1891. 18in gauge.
[24] Rebuilt to 4–2–2 in October 1894.
[25] Built for the National Railway Museum, York.
[26] Built for Southampton Dock Co.
[27] Date of purchase, probably second-hand.
[28] 2ft gauge. Ex-Cliff Hill Quarry, Leicestershire.
[29] Sentinel-type shunter, returned to the makers and subsequently sold into industrial service.
[30] Built for the London & South Western Railway to Robert Urie's design. Nameplates fitted by the Southern Railway in 1925.

[31] 2ft gauge.
[32] Built for the Somerset & Dorset Railway. Became no. 2 *Brunel* (the second of that name and number) of the London & South Western Railway's Engineering Department.
[33] Rebuilt from 2–2–2 no. 73 of 1856.
[34] Originally named *Kingsmills*. Renamed *Isla Bank* in 1888 and rebuilt from 2–2–2 to 2–4–0 in July 1892.
[35] Originally named *Guernsey*. Renamed in January 1904.
[36] Originally named *Jersey*. Renamed in

January 1904.
[37] Originally named *Tresco*. Renamed in February 1904.
[38] Originally named *King Charles*. Renamed *The Italian Monarch* in June or July 1927. Further renamed *Italian Monarch* in October or November 1927. Name removed June 1940 and the words STAR CLASS were painted on the splashers.
[39] Nameplates fitted in 1907.
[40] Originally no. D221 *Ivernia*.
[41] Built for the South Devon Railway.

Name	Number	Class	Date	Railway
J.A. Bright	250	Claughton	8/1914	London & North Western Rly
Jack	–	0–4–0WT	11/1898	**John Knowles & Co. (Wooden Box) Ltd** [1]
Jack	–	0–4–0T	1925	**Groudle Glen Rly** [2]
Jackall	19	Tiger	1/1862	London, Chatham & Dover Rly
Jackdaw	3737	Bulldog	12/1909	Great Western Rly
Jackdaw	47200	47/0	1965	British Railways
Jacks Green	–	0–6–0ST	1939	**Nene Valley Rly**
Jack Stirk	60093	60	2/1992	British Railways [3]
Jacob	680	0–4–0P	1916	**Beamish Open Air Museum**
Jacomb-Hood	192	Gladstone	11/1888	London, Brighton & South Coast Rly
J.A.F. Aspinall	2395	Claughton	9/1916	London & North Western Rly
Jairou	1037	B1	11/1947	London & North Eastern Rly
Jamaica	3464	Bulldog	3/1904	Great Western Rly
Jamaica	5612	Jubilee	1934	London Midland & Scottish Rly
(007 James)	08077	08	1955	**British Railways**
James Bishop	1345	Claughton	8/1916	London & North Western Rly
James Clerk-Maxwell	60067	60	9/1991	British Railways
James Fitzjames	2694	D11/2	11/1924	London & North Eastern Rly
James Fryars	1	D1	7/1886	Whittingham Light Rly [4]
James Kennedy GC	86242	86/2	1966	British Railways
James Mason	3041	3031	10/1894	Great Western Rly [5]
James Mason	3703	Bulldog	4/1906	Great Western Rly
James Murray	60063	60	9/1991	British Railways
James Nightall G.C.	47579	47/4	1964	British Railways
James Spooner	8	0–4–4–0F	1872	Festiniog Rly [6]
Jamestown	317	317	1859	North British Rly [7]
James Watt	60060	60	9/1991	British Railways
Jane	–	0–6–0	?	Sirhowy Rly [8]
"Jane"	5	0–4–0T	1857	**Wantage Tramway** [9]
"Jane"	–	4wDM	1940	Festiniog Rly [10]
Jane Austen	92004	92		British Railways
Janis	20904	20	11/1961	Hunslet-Barclay Ltd [11]
Janus	–	Caesar	5/1854	Great Western Rly (bg)
Janus	28	0–6–0DE	1962	**Rutland Railway Museum**
Japan	991	L/Bloomer	1851	London & North Western Rly
Japanese Monarch	4026	Star	9/1909	Great Western Rly [12]
Jason	40	2–2–2	1838	Grand Junction Rly
Jason	–	Fury	5/1847	Great Western Rly (bg)
Jason	40	bCrewe	5/1847	London & North Western Rly
Jason	56	2–4–0	6/1848	Manchester, Sheffield & Lincolnshire Rly
Jason	40	aCrewe	8/1856	London & North Western Rly [13]
Jason	718	1Precursor	2/1879	London & North Western Rly
Jason	2064	2Precursor	3/1905	London & North Western Rly
Jason	26049	EM1	10/1952	British Railways
Javelin	–	Wolf	7/1841	Great Western Rly (bg)
Jay	2179	0–4–0ST	2/1875	Great Western Rly (bg) [14]
Jay	47123	47/0	1964	British Railways
J.B. Earle	2	2–6–4T	1904	Leek & Manifold Light Rly [15]
J B Priestley OM	86234	86/2	1966	British Railways
J. Bruce Ismay	209	Claughton	9/1914	London & North Western Rly
J.C. Parkinson	5	0–6–0T	1868	Alexandra (Newport & South Wales) Docks & Rly
Jeanie Deans	1304	Teutonic	7/1890	London & North Western Rly
Jeanie Deans	2161	2Experiment	10/1907	London & North Western Rly
Jeanie Deans	899	Scott	8/1909	North British Rly
Jeannie Waddell	–	0–6–0ST	?1888	Llanelly & Mynydd Mawr Rly
Jellicoe	5667	Jubilee	1935	London Midland & Scottish Rly
Jennifer	20	0–6–0T	1942	**West Somerset Rly**
Jenny Lind	21	2–2–2	1847	Midland Rly [16]
Jenny Lind	319	2–2–2	1848	North Eastern Rly
Jenny Lind	60	2–2–2	1848	London, Brighton & South Coast Rly
Jenny Lind	61	2–2–2	7/1848	Manchester, Sheffield & Lincolnshire Rly
Jenny Lind	6146	Royal Scot	10/1927	London Midland & Scottish Rly [17]
Jenny Sharp	2	2–2–2	10/1847	Manchester, Sheffield & Lincolnshire Rly
Jerome K. Jerome	31423	31/4	1960	British Railways
Jerry M	38	0–4–0ST	1895	**Hollycombe Steam Collection** [18]
Jersey	108	E1	11/1876	London, Brighton & South Coast Rly
Jersey	81	B4	11/1893	London & South Western Rly
Jersey	3317	Duke	4/1899	Great Western Rly [19]
Jersey No. 1	–	0–4–0	1880	Torrington & Marland Rly
Jersey No. 2	–	0–4–0	1880	Torrington & Marland Rly [20]
Jervis	5663	Jubilee	1935	London Midland & Scottish Rly
Jessie	408	0–4–0ST	9/1876	London & South Western Rly
Jessie	–	0–6–0ST	1937	**Dean Forest Rly**
Jevington	492	E4	10/1899	London, Brighton & South Coast Rly

[1] This firm produced aluminous fireclay bricks. The 'Wooden Box' of the company's title refers to a wooden sentry box on a former toll road in the vicinity of the firm's premises. These were at Mount Pleasant, near Woodville, Leics. *Jack*, by Hunslet and of 18in gauge, was followed by two more industrial locomotives, *Scout* (by Bagnall, 1909), and *Gwen* (Hunslet, 1920, and very similar to *Jack*). At the closure in 1958 *Gwen* was sold for £100 for preservation on the Wild Cat Railroad, California, while *Jack* went to the Leeds Industrial Museum at Armley Mills. *Scout* was purchased second-hand in May 1913. It was not very successful and was sold in 1921.

[2] 2ft gauge.

[3] Originally named *Ben More Assynt*.

[4] Originally no. 357 *Riddlesdown* of the London, Brighton & South Coast Railway. In February 1948, as no. 2357, it was sold for £745 to Lancashire County Council for use on the Whittingham Light Railway, connecting Grimsargh with the Mental Hospital at Whittingham. There it worked until the line closed on 30 June 1957.

[5] Originally named *Emlyn*. Renamed *The Queen* in 1897 and *James Mason* in June 1910.

[6] 1ft 11½in gauge.

[7] Ex-Edinburgh & Glasgow Railway, absorbed by the NBR in 1865.

[8] Built some time between 1832 and 1853.

[9] Originally built for the Sandy & Potton Railway, which was owned by Capt William Peel RN (a brother of Sir Robert Peel, the politician), and was named *Shannon* after the gallant gentleman's ship. In 1862 the locomotive was sold, with the rest of the railway, to the London & North Western Railway, and numbered 1104 on their duplicate list. After a couple of weeks' unsuccessful trials on the Cromford & High Peak Railway, the engine returned to Crewe and served as works shunter, renumbered to 1863 in 1872. It was sold to the Wantage Tramway in May 1878 for £365 8s 1d! On the Wantage Tramway no name was carried. The engine was colloquially known as *"Jane"*; but since restoration for preservation the name *Shannon* has been restored. When the tramway closed in 1946 the locomotive was purchased for £100 by the Great Western Railway and overhauled at Swindon Works. It was then placed on display on a pedestal at Wantage Road station, until closure in 1965 when the nameplates disappeared. *Shannon*, as the engine was now known, changed storage site a few times before coming to rest, one hopes permanently, with the Great Western Society at Didcot.

[10] 1ft 11½in gauge.

[11] Built for British Railways.

[12] Originally named *King Richard*. Renamed *The Japanese Monarch* in June or July 1927, and further renamed *Japanese Monarch* in October or November 1927. Name removed in January 1941 and the words STAR CLASS were painted on the splashers.

[13] Later renumbered 42 and renamed *Sunbeam*.

[14] Built for the South Devon Railway.

[15] 2ft 6in gauge.

[16] It is not certain that this engine actually carried the name. Jenny Lind was a Swedish opera singer.

[17] Renamed *The Rifle Brigade* in May 1936.

[18] 2ft gauge.

[19] Renamed *Isle of Jersey* in January 1904.

[20] *Jersey No. 1* and *Jersey No. 2* were both 3ft gauge. The Torrington & Marland Railway was rebuilt to standard gauge and formed part of the Southern Railway's Halwill–Torrington line.

Name	Number	Class	Date	Railway
J. Gay	315	B2	7/1895	London, Brighton & South Coast Rly [21]
Jim Crow	–	0–4–2ST	3/1894	London & North Western Rly [22]
Jimmy Milne	47635	47/4	1964	British Railways
Jimmy Shand	37188	37/0	1964	British Railways
Jingling Geordie	421	Scott	10/1914	North British Rly
J.N. Derbyshire	–	**0–4–0ST**	**1929**	**Steamtown, Carnforth**
Joan	–	4–6–0T	1917	Ashover Rly [23]
Joan	12	**0–6–2T**	**1927**	**Welshpool & Llanfair Light Rly [24]**
(Joem)	69023	J72	1951	British Railways
Joffre	682	C	2/1892	North British Rly
Johann Strauss	92039	92		British Railways
John	–	**0–4–0ST**	**1939**	**Gloucestershire Warwickshire Rly**
(John Alcock)	7051	0–6–0DM	1933	Hunslet Engine Co. [25]
John Anthony	–	4–6–2	1915	Ravenglass & Eskdale Rly [26]
John Bateson	1725	George V	11/1910	London & North Western Rly
John Blenkinsop	–	**0–4–0ST**	**1941**	**Middleton Rly**
John Bright	1745	Newton	10/1869	London & North Western Rly
John Bright	1745	rPrecedent	4/1892	London & North Western Rly [27]
John Bull	4	0–4–0	4/1836	Dundee & Newtyle Rly [28]
John Bull	44	John Bull	12/1849	East Lancashire Rly
John Bunyan	70003	Britannia	3/1951	British Railways
John Dixon	174	Panther	6/1864	Stockton & Darlington Rly
(John F. Kennedy)	25173	25/2	**1965**	**British Railways**
John Flamsteed	60028	60	11/1990	British Railways
John Fowler	319	B2	10/1896	London, Brighton & South Coast Rly [29]
John G. Griffiths	3060	3031	4/1895	Great Western Rly [30]
John G. Griffiths	3702	Bulldog	4/1906	Great Western Rly
John Gray	–	Hawthorn	5/1865	Great Western Rly (bg)
John Grooms	43020	43	7/1976	British Railways

Name	Number	Class	Date	Railway
John Hampden	5	**Bo-Bo**	**1922**	**Metropolitan Rly [31]**
John Hawkshaw	324	B2	12/1896	London, Brighton & South Coast Rly [32]
John Hick	20	John Hick	1898	London & North Western Rly
John Hick	752	George V	2/1913	London & North Western Rly
John Howard	60058	60	9/1991	British Railways
John Howe	5	**0–4–0ST**	**1908**	**Steamtown, Carnforth**
John Keats	1081	Prince/W	10/1913	London & North Western Rly
John Logie Baird	60066	60	9/1991	British Railways
John Loudon McAdam	60070	60	10/1991	British Railways
John Lyon	1	Bo-Bo	1921	Metropolitan Rly [33]
John Mayall	1747	rPrecedent	5/1891	London & North Western Rly [34]
John Mayall	89	George V	3/1913	London & North Western Rly
John Milton	9	Bo-Bo	1921	Metropolitan Rly [35]
John Milton	70005	Britannia	4/1951	British Railways
Johnnie Walker	–	**4wDM**	**1959**	**Scottish Industrial Railway Centre**
Johnnie Walker	47283	47/0	1966	British Railways
John of Gaunt	70012	Britannia	5/1951	British Railways
John o'Gaunt	–	2–2–0	1840	Lancaster & Preston Junction Rly
John o'Gaunt	250	bCrewe	11/1849	London & North Western Rly
John O'Gaunt	74	2–2–2	1859	Lancaster & Carlisle Rly
John O'Gaunt	1163	Samson	10/1874	London & North Western Rly
John o'Gaunt	1163	Whitworth	1895	London & North Western Rly
John O'Gaunt	87013	87/0	1974	British Railways
John o'Groat	252	bCrewe	11/1849	London & North Western Rly
John o'Groat	487	Samson	10/1874	London & North Western Rly
John o'Groat	487	Whitworth	8/1895	London & North Western Rly
John O'Groat	1599	Claughton	2/1920	London & North Western Rly
John Owen	1385	0–6–0ST	1872	Great Western Rly [36]
John Peel	144	**0–4–0DM**	**1938**	**Air Ministry**
John Penn	1548	John Hick	1898	London & North Western Rly
John Penn	1566	2Experiment	5/1909	London & North Western Rly
John Ramsbottom	1211	Newton	3/1872	London & North Western Rly
John Ramsbottom	1211	rPrecedent	11/1888	London & North Western Rly
John Reith	60053	60	6/1991	British Railways
John Rennie	1147	1Precursor	10/1878	London & North Western Rly
John Rennie	321	B2	11/1896	London, Brighton & South Coast Rly [37]
John Rennie	1549	John Hick	1898	London & North Western Rly
John Rennie	2124	George V	2/1913	London & North Western Rly
John Ruskin	2198	Prince/W	11/1913	London & North Western Rly
Johnson Stevens Agency	47157	47/0	1964	British Railways
John Smith	6	?	1855	St Helens Canal & Rly [38]
John Southland	12	**Bo-Bo D**	**1983**	**Romney, Hythe & Dymchurch Rly [39]**
John Waddell	–	0–4–0T	11/1881	Llanelly & Mynydd Mawr Rly
John Waddell	–	0–6–0ST	1912	Llanelly & Mynydd Mawr Rly [40]
John Wakefield	126	Peel	5/1858	Stockton & Darlington Rly
John Wesley	43103	43	10/1978	British Railways
John W. Wilson	3059	3031	4/1895	Great Western Rly [41]
John W. Wilson	3706	Bulldog	6/1906	Great Western Rly
John Wycliffe	19	Bo-Bo	1922	Metropolitan Rly [42]
Jonas Levy	197	Gladstone	5/1888	London, Brighton & South Coast Rly

British Railways J72 class 0–6–0T no. 69023 at Didcot. Built by British Railways in 1951 to a North Eastern Railway design of 1898, the locomotive was named *Joem* in preservation. (*Photo: Author*)

[21] Originally named *Duncannon*. Renamed *J. Gay* in October 1906. Rebuilt to class B2x in March 1909.

[22] Diggle Tunnel Works. 2ft 6in gauge.

[23] Ex-War Department. These engines were built by the Baldwin Locomotive Company (USA) for service in France with the Allied Armies in the First World War. 2ft gauge.

[24] 2ft 6in gauge.

[25] Preserved on the Middleton Railway.

[26] 15in gauge. From Capt J.E.P. Howey's estate railway at Staughton Manor. On transfer to the R&ER it was immediately renamed *Colossus*. Chassis reused to construct the first *River Mite*.

[27] Renamed *Glowworm* in 1914.

[28] 4ft 6in gauge.

[29] Renamed *Leconfield* in October 1906, and rebuilt to class B2x in June 1914.

[30] Originally named *Warlock*; renamed *John G. Griffiths* in March 1909 and name removed in March 1914.

[31] Officially a rebuild of a previous, unnamed locomotive, but incorporating few if any of its parts.

[32] Rebuilt to class B2x, May 1913.

[33] Officially a rebuild of a previous, unnamed locomotive, but incorporating few if any of its parts.

[34] Originally named *Tennyson*; renamed in 1885.

[35] Officially a rebuild of a previous, unnamed

locomotive, but incorporating few if any of its parts.

[36] Built for the Whitland & Taff Vale Railway.

[37] Rebuilt to class B2x, October 1907.

[38] Described as 'four-coupled, Bury type'. This makes it possibly an 0–4–2, but more likely an 0–4–0.

[39] 15in gauge.

[40] Not to be confused with the earlier engine of the same name noted above.

[41] Originally named *Voltigeur*; renamed *John W. Wilson* in March 1908.

[42] Officially a rebuild of an earlier, unnamed locomotive; however, little if any of the original was incorporated.

Name	Number	Class	Date	Railway
Jonathan	–	0–4–0ST	**1898**	**West Lancashire Light Rly** [43]
Jonathan Oldbuck	2676	D11/2	8/1924	London & North Eastern Rly
Jonathon	6	4wDM	**1959**	**Welsh Highland Rly** [44]
Joseph	–	0–6–0ST	**1944**	**Chatterley Whitfield Mining Museum**
Joseph Banks	60027	60	2/1991	British Railways
Josephine Butler	60045	60	3/1991	British Railways
Joseph Chamberlain	86215	86/2	1965	British Railways
Joseph Lister	60025	60	12/1990	British Railways
Joseph Shaw	3724	Bulldog	8/1906	Great Western Rly
Joshua Radcliffe	1193	Precedent	8/1878	London & North Western Rly
Joshua Radcliffe	1193	rPrecedent	8/1896	London & North Western Rly
(Josiah Wedgwood)	52	J94	**1952**	**War Department**
Josiah Wedgwood	86236	86/2	1965	British Railways
MASTER POTTER 1736–1795				
Jostinot	47145	47/0	1964	British Railways
Joyous Gard	741	King Arthur	5/1919	Southern Rly [45]
Joyous Gard	73088	5MT	9/1955	British Railways
J.P. Bickersteth	2271	George V*	11/1910	London & North Western Rly
J.R. Maclean	3	0–6–0ST	1848	Alexandra (Newport & South Wales) Docks & Rly [46]
J S Bach	92024	92		British Railways
J.T. Daly	3	0–4–0ST	**1931**	**Alderney Rly**
Jubilee	724	721	1896	Caledonian Rly
Jubilee	1901	Jubilee	6/1897	London & North Western Rly
Jubilee	–	0–4–0ST	**1936**	**East Anglian Railway Museum**
Jubilee 1897	–	0–4–0ST	**1897**	**Narrow Gauge Museum, Tywyn** [47]
Jubilee Queen	–	0–6–0ST	7/1897	Garstang & Knott End Rly [48]
Jules Verne	92008	92		British Railways
(Julia V)	75115	J94	**5/1944**	**War Department**
Jullundur	5042	J94	12/1943	War Department
Jumbo	458	0–6–0ST	4/1862	London & South Western Rly [49]
Jumbo	–	0–4–0ST	?	Swansea Harbour Trust
Juna	83	Scotchmen	4/1866	London, Chatham & Dover Rly
Junction	5	0–4–2	5/1839	Manchester & Leeds Rly
Juno	72	2–2–2WT	7/1850	Manchester, Sheffield & Lincolnshire Rly
Juno	–	Banking	10/1852	Great Western Rly (bg) [50]
Juno	3	A	6/1864	Metropolitan Rly
Juno	2153	0–6–0ST	12/1864	Great Western Rly (bg) [51]
Juno	113	Craven	10/1871	Lancashire & Yorkshire Rly [52]
Juno	9	Ilfracombe	2/1873	Kent & East Sussex Rly [53]
Juno	5	0–6–02T	1911	Shropshire & Montgomeryshire Rly
Juno	27004	EM2	9/1954	British Railways
Juno	–	J94	**1958**	**Buckinghamshire Railway Centre**
Jupiter	14	2–2–0	1831	Liverpool & Manchester Rly
Jupiter	12	Venus	12/1838	London & South Western Rly

Name	Number	Class	Date	Railway
Jupiter	24	?	1840	Newcastle & Carlisle Rly [54]
Jupiter	46	2–2–2	12/1840	London & Brighton Rly
Jupiter	–	Priam	4/1841	Great Western Rly (bg)
Jupiter	8	Bacchus	6/1846	East Lancashire Rly
Jupiter	3	0–6–0	9/1847	Manchester, Sheffield & Lincolnshire Rly
Jupiter	12	Tartar	6/1852	London & South Western Rly
Jupiter	154	Panther	11/1860	Stockton & Darlington Rly
Jupiter	16	A	1861	Rhymney Rly [55]
Jupiter	14	0–6–0ST	11/1863	Brecon & Merthyr Rly
Jupiter	1	A	6/1864	Metropolitan Rly
Jupiter	12	Lion	2/1871	London & South Western Rly
Jupiter	608	Craven	5/1876	Lancashire & Yorkshire Rly [56]
Jupiter	1299	2–4–0T	12/1878	Great Western Rly [57]
Jupiter	3318	Bulldog	4/1899	Great Western Rly
Jupiter	1975	Alfred	7/1903	London & North Western Rly
Jupiter	3318	Bulldog	2/1908	Great Western Rly
Jupiter	–	0–6–0ST	**1950**	**Colne Valley Rly**
Jupiter	D826	Warship	9/1960	British Railways
Jurassic	–	0–6–0ST	**1903**	**Bala Lake Rly** [58]
Justin	19	2–4–0	5/1853	South Staffordshire Rly
Justine	–	0–4–0WT	**1906**	**Gloucestershire Warwickshire Rly** [59]
Jutland	504	11F	11/1922	Great Central Rly
Jutland	5684	Jubilee	1936	London Midland & Scottish Rly
Juvenal	–	Bogie	11/1854	Great Western Rly (bg)

British Railways (ex-LMS) Jubilee class 4–6–0 no. 45684 *Jutland* at Crewe North Shed in August 1953. (*Photo: RAS Marketing*)

[43] 2ft gauge.
[44] 1ft 11½in gauge.
[45] Built for the London & South Western Railway to Robert Urie's design. Nameplates fitted by the Southern Railway in 1925.
[46] Built in 1848 for the London & North Western Railway, and subsequently purchased by the Alexandra (Newport & South Wales) Docks and Railway.
[47] 1ft 11½in gauge.
[48] Became LMS no. 11300.
[49] Previously Cambrian Railways no. 14 *Nantclwyd*.

[50] Rebuilt in March 1869; its wheelbase was reduced and tank capacity increased. In September 1872 it was sold to the South Devon Railway, who renamed it *Stromboli*. In 1876 it reverted to the Great Western, retained its name and became no. 2138.
[51] Built for the South Devon Railway.
[52] Built for the East Lancashire Railway.
[53] Built for the London & South Western Railway as their no. 284, later duplicated as no. 0284. An Ilfracombe Goods class engine, it was withdrawn by the Kent & East Sussex in

March 1935, but not scrapped until October 1939.
[54] Either 0–6–0 or 0–4–2. Became NER no. 472 in 1862.
[55] Class A consisted of four 2–4–0 passenger locomotives by Vulcan Foundry. No. 16 became class E in 1906, and was scrapped in the same year.
[56] Built for the East Lancashire Railway.
[57] Built for the South Devon Railway. Name may not have been carried.
[58] 2ft gauge.
[59] 2ft gauge.

K

Name	Number	Class	Date	Railway
Kaiser	–	Metro	9/1862	Great Western Rly (bg)
Karen	–	**0–4–2T**	**1942**	**Welsh Highland Rly** [1]
Karour	77	0–6–0ST	1921	War Department
Kashmir	5588	Jubilee	1934	London Midland & Scottish Rly
Katerfelto	3319	Duke	4/1899	Great Western Rly
Katherine	9	**4wDM**	**1968**	**Welsh Highland Rly** [2]
Katie	–	0–4–0T	1896	Fairbourne Miniature Rly [3]
Keekle	4	0–6–0ST	1858	Whitehaven, Cleator & Egremont Rly [4]
Keele Hall	5903	Hall	5/1931	Great Western Rly
Keighley and Worth Valley Railway	31444	31/4	1959	British Railways
Keith	40	M/Goods	5/1864	Highland Rly
Keith	5655	Jubilee	1934	London Midland & Scottish Rly
Kekewich	3383	Atbara	7/1900	Great Western Rly
Kelham Hall	5904	Hall	5/1931	Great Western Rly
Kellingley Colliery	56074	56	1980	British Railways
Kelly	2	0–4–2ST	1871	Plymouth, Devonport & South Western Junction Rly [5]
Kelly	D827	Warship	10/1960	British Railways
Kelpie	11	0–4–2	1855	Whitehaven & Furness Junction Rly [6]
Kelton Fell	13	**0–4–0ST**	**1876**	**Bo'ness & Kinneil Rly**
Kelvin	89	Scotchmen	8/1866	London, Chatham & Dover Rly
Kempenfelt	5662	Jubilee	1934	London Midland & Scottish Rly
Kempsey	34	2–2–0	6/1842	Birmingham & Gloucester Rly
Kemptown	96	2–4–0T	9/1869	London, Brighton & South Coast Rly [7]
Kemptown	64	A1	6/1874	London, Brighton & South Coast Rly
Ken	67	**0–6–0DH**	**1964**	**South Yorkshire Rly** [8]
Kendal	134	Peel	12/1858	Stockton & Darlington Rly
Kendal	77	2–2–2	7/1859	Lancaster & Carlisle Rly
Kenilworth	3337	Bulldog	12/1899	Great Western Rly
Kenilworth	422	Scott	10/1914	North British Rly
Kenilworth	60124	A1	3/1949	British Railways (Eastern Region)
Kenilworth	87032	87/0	1974	British Railways
Kenilworth Castle	4097	Castle	6/1926	Great Western Rly
Kenley	21C168	BB	10/1947	Southern Rly
Kennet	3015	3001	4/1892	Great Western Rly [9]
Kenneth J. Painter	59005	59/0	6/1989	Foster-Yeoman
Kensington	205	Belgravia	7/1892	London, Brighton & South Coast Rly
Kensington	569	E5	12/1902	London, Brighton & South Coast Rly
Kent	4	2–2–2	2/1839	London & Croydon Rly
Kent	–	0–4–0ST	1915	Woolwich Arsenal [10]
Kent & East Sussex Railway	73126	73/1	1966	British Railways
Kentish Man	16	2–2–2	2/1843	London & Brighton Rly [11]
Kentish Mercury	73119	73/1	1966	British Railways
Kentish Town	61	51	1900	London, Tilbury & Southend Rly

Name	Number	Class	Date	Railway
Kenton	2	0–6–0T	1905	Mid Suffolk Light Rly [12]
Kent Youth Music	73136	73/1	1966	British Railways
Kenya	5613	Jubilee	1934	London Midland & Scottish Rly
Kenyon	2	0–4–2	5/1839	Manchester & Leeds Rly
Kenyon	2	0–6–0ST	1862	Wrexham, Mold & Connah's Quay Rly [13]
Keppel	5673	Jubilee	1935	London Midland & Scottish Rly
"Kerosene Castle"	18100	Co-Co	1951	British Railways (Western Region) [14]
Kertch	–	Iron Duke	4/1855	Great Western Rly (bg)
Kestrel	344	aCrewe	8/1854	London & North Western Rly
Kestrel	122	Peel	3/1857	Stockton & Darlington Rly
Kestrel	–	2–4–0	2/1860	Swansea Vale Rly [15]
Kestrel	852	Samson	5/1879	London & North Western Rly
Kestrel	852	Whitworth	1895	London & North Western Rly
Kestrel	90	Prince/W	12/1915	London & North Western Rly
Kestrel	4485	A4	2/1937	London & North Eastern Rly [16]
Kestrel	44	**4wDM**	**1941**	**Leighton Buzzard Rly** [17]
Kestrel	60130	A1	9/1948	British Railways (Eastern Region)
Kestrel	47298	47/0	1966	British Railways
Kestrel	–	Co-Co	1967	Hawker Siddeley Brush Electric [18]
Keswick	165	Saltburn	1862	Stockton & Darlington Rly
Ketley Hall	4935	Hall	6/1929	Great Western Rly
Kettledrummle	425	Scott	7/1915	North British Rly
Kettering	47527	47/4	1967	British Railways
Kettering Furnaces No 3	–	**0–4–0ST**	**1885**	**Penrhyn Castle Industrial Railway Museum** [19]
Keyes	5658	Jubilee	1934	London Midland & Scottish Rly
Keymer	353	D1	1/1886	London, Brighton & South Coast Rly
Khan	–	Metro	9/1862	Great Western Rly (bg)
Khartoum	3378	Atbara	5/1900	Great Western Rly
Khartum	–	0–4–0ST	2/1899	Chatham Dockyard [20]
Kidbrooke	362	D1	3/1887	London, Brighton & South Coast Rly
Kidwelly	5	0–6–0ST	1872	Burry Port & Gwendraeth Valley Rly [21]
Kidwelly	4	0–6–0T	1903	Burry Port & Gwendraeth Valley Rly [22]
Kidwelly	1	0–6–0ST	1905	Gwendraeth Valleys Rly [23]
KIDWELLY	08995	08	10/1959	British Railways
Kidwelly Castle	4098	Castle	7/1926	Great Western Rly
Kilbagie	DS2	**4wDM**	**1949**	**Bo'ness & Kinneil Rly**
Kildale	197	Roseberry	11/1866	Stockton & Darlington Rly
Kilgerran Castle	4099	Castle	8/1926	Great Western Rly
Killarney	3408	City	5/1907	Great Western Rly [24]
Kilmar	1312	0–6–0ST	1869	Great Western Rly [25]
Kilmarnock 400	20906	20/9	11/1967	British Railways
Kilmersdon	–	**0–4–0ST**	**1929**	**West Somerset Rly**
Kilverstone Hall	2842	B17/1	5/1933	London & North Eastern Rly
Kimberley	3379	Atbara	5/1900	Great Western Rly

---

[1] 1ft 11½in gauge.

[2] 1ft 11½in gauge.

[3] 15in gauge Heywood-type locomotive, formerly on the Duffield Bank Railway, and then on the Ravenglass & Eskdale Railway.

[4] Became Furness Railway no. 102.

[5] Originally built as an 0–4–0ST on the 3ft 6in gauge, and was purchased by the Plymouth, Devonport & South Western Junction Railway. They rebuilt it as a standard gauge 0–4–2ST and named it *Kelly*. They sold it to the West Sussex Railway in 1912, where it became *Chichester*, a replacement for an earlier locomotive of that name.

[6] Originally no. 3 *Sefton* on the Liverpool, Crosby & Southport Railway, and sold to the Whitehaven & Furness Junction Railway in 1855.

[7] Originally 2–4–0T no. 96, and named *Kemptown*. Renumbered 115 and renamed *Hayling Island* in September 1874. Renumbered 359 in June 1877, and 499 in January 1886. It was then altered by William Stroudley in January 1890 to a 2–4–2T with a small inspection saloon mounted on the back, renumbered 481 and renamed *Inspector*. Stroudley died in December 1889 while the alteration was still in progress, and the locomotive saw little use before withdrawal in March 1898.

[8] The modern, preserved South Yorkshire Railway.

[9] Rebuilt to 4–2–2 in August 1894.

[10] 18in gauge.

[11] Built for London & Brighton and South Eastern Railways joint stock.

[12] Extant photographs do not show the name actually carried.

[13] Built for the Buckley Railway.

[14] Gas turbine locomotive.

[15] Later rebuilt to 0–4–2ST.

[16] Renamed *Miles Beevor* in November 1947.

[17] 1ft 11½in gauge.

[18] 4,000 horsepower diesel locomotive built by makers as a private venture. After extensive trials on British Railways, it was sold to the Soviet Union in 1971. Its subsequent fate is unknown.

[19] 3ft gauge.

[20] 18in gauge.

[21] Built for the Gwendraeth Valleys Railway.

[22] Became Great Western Railway no. 2194.

[23] Later renamed *Velindre*, and became Great Western Railway no. 26.

[24] Originally named *Ophir*. Renamed *Killarney* in September 1907, on a temporary basis for an excursion train to Killarney (via Fishguard), but the original name was never restored.

[25] Built for the Liskeard & Looe Railway.

Name	Number	Class	Date	Railway
Kimberley	60	B4	8/1901	London, Brighton & South Coast Rly [26]
Kimberley Hall	6952	Hall	2/1943	Great Western Rly [27]
Kimbolton Castle	2833	B17/1	5/1931	London & North Eastern Rly
Kincardine	234	233	1859	North British Rly
Kincardineshire	307	D49/1	3/1928	London & North Eastern Rly
Kincraig	38	M/Goods	4/1864	Highland Rly
Kinder Low	60065	60	9/1991	British Railways
Kinder Scout	60080	60	11/1991	British Railways
Kineton	1	0–6–0T	1866	East & West Junction Rly [28]
King	2171	2–4–0T	1/1871	Great Western Rly (bg) [29]
King Arthur	3258	Duke	8/1895	Great Western Rly [30]
King Arthur	453	King Arthur	2/1925	Southern Rly
King Arthur	87010	87/0	1973	British Railways
King Charles	4025	Star	7/1909	Great Western Rly [31]
King Charles I	6010	King	4/1928	Great Western Rly
King Charles II	6009	King	3/1928	Great Western Rly
King Edward	4021	Star	6/1909	Great Western Rly [32]
King Edward I	**6024**	**King**	**6/1930**	**Great Western Rly**
King Edward II	**6023**	**King**	**6/1930**	**Great Western Rly**
King Edward III	6022	King	6/1930	Great Western Rly
King Edward IV	6017	King	6/1928	Great Western Rly
King Edward V	6016	King	6/1928	Great Western Rly
King Edward VI	6012	King	4/1928	Great Western Rly
King Edward VII	259	8D	2/1906	Great Central Rly
King Edward VII	6001	King	7/1927	Great Western Rly
King Edward VIII	6029	King	8/1930	Great Western Rly [33]
King Feisal	**5118**	**J94**	**5/1944**	**War Department** [34]
King Feisal	195	J94	2/1953	War Department
Kingfisher	131	bCrewe	5/1851	London & North Western Rly [35]
Kingfisher	3738	Bulldog	12/1909	Great Western Rly
Kingfisher	4483	A4	12/1936	London & North Eastern Rly
Kingfisher	47217	47/0	1965	British Railways
King George	4023	Star	6/1909	Great Western Rly [36]
King George	**–**	**0–6–0ST**	**1942**	**Gloucestershire Warwickshire Rly**
King George I	6006	King	2/1928	Great Western Rly
King George II	6005	King	7/1927	Great Western Rly
King George III	6004	King	7/1927	Great Western Rly
King George IV	6003	King	7/1927	Great Western Rly
King George V	110	11C	5/1904	Great Central Rly [37]
King George V	**6000**	**King**	**6/1927**	**Great Western Rly**
King George VI	6028	King	7/1930	Great Western Rly [38]
King George VI	6244	Duchess	7/1940	London Midland & Scottish Rly [39]
King Haakon VII	**377**	**21c**	**1919**	**Norwegian State Rly** [40]
King Harold	4030	Star	9/1909	Great Western Rly [41]
King Henry	4027	Star	9/1909	Great Western Rly [42]

Name	Number	Class	Date	Railway
King Henry II	6028	King	7/1930	Great Western Rly [43]
King Henry III	6025	King	7/1930	Great Western Rly
King Henry IV	6020	King	5/1930	Great Western Rly
King Henry V	6019	King	7/1928	Great Western Rly
King Henry VI	6018	King	6/1928	Great Western Rly
King Henry VII	6014	King	5/1928	Great Western Rly
King Henry VIII	6013	King	5/1928	Great Western Rly
King James	4024	Star	6/1909	Great Western Rly [44]
King James I	6011	King	4/1928	Great Western Rly
King James II	6008	King	3/1928	Great Western Rly
King John	4028	Star	9/1909	Great Western Rly [45]
King John	6026	King	7/1930	Great Western Rly
King Lear	37	2–2–2	9/1843	South Eastern Rly
King Lear	9	0–6–0	1854	Whitehaven & Furness Junction Rly
King Leodegrance	739	King Arthur	2/1919	Southern Rly [46]
King Leodegrance	73118	5MT	12/1955	British Railways

Great Western Railway King class 4–6–0 no. 6028 *King Henry II*, at Old Oak Common in April 1933. This locomotive was later renamed *King George VI*. (Photo: RAS Marketing)

Name	Number	Class	Date	Railway
King of Italy	185	Prince/W	11/1915	London & North Western Rly
King of Serbia	160	Prince/W	11/1915	London & North Western Rly
King of the Belgians	122	Prince/W	11/1915	London & North Western Rly
King Pellinore	738	King Arthur	12/1918	Southern Rly [47]
King Pellinore	73115	5MT	11/1955	British Railways
King Richard	4026	Star	9/1909	Great Western Rly [48]
King Richard I	6027	King	7/1930	Great Western Rly

[26] Name removed in May 1906. Rebuilt to class B4x, September 1922.

[27] Nameplates fitted in September 1948.

[28] Built by Manning Wardle of Leeds as a contractor's engine, and worked on the Stratford-on-Avon & Midland Junction Railway where it was named *Crampton*. Sold in 1910 to the Shropshire & Montgomery-shire Railway and renamed *Morous*, and in 1924 transferred to the West Sussex Light Railway (previously the Hundred of Manhood & Selsey Tramway). It was scrapped when that line closed in 1936.

[29] Built for the South Devon Railway.

[30] Name removed in May 1927 in case of confusion with 'King' class locomotives.

[31] Renamed *The Italian Monarch* in June or July 1927. Further renamed *Italian Monarch* in October or November 1927. Name removed June 1940 and the words STAR CLASS were painted on the splashers.

[32] Renamed *The British Monarch* in June or July 1927, and then *British Monarch* in October or November 1927.

[33] Originally *King Stephen*. Renamed *King Edward VIII* on 14 May 1936.

[34] Preserved as no. S134 *Wheldale*.

[35] Rebuilt from Liverpool & Manchester Railway 2–2–2 no. 72; became London & North Western property in 1846.

[36] Renamed *The Danish Monarch* in June or July 1927, and *Danish Monarch* in October or November 1927. Name removed November 1940 and the words STAR CLASS painted on the splashers.

[37] Built May 1904 to class 11B. Rebuilt to class 11C in 1907, and named in 1911.

[38] Originally *King Henry II*. Renamed *King George VI* on 12 January 1937.

[39] Originally named *City of Leeds*. Renamed in April 1941.

[40] A 2–6–0 with light axle load, used on branch lines in Norway.

[41] Renamed *The Swedish Monarch* in July 1927, and *Swedish Monarch* in November 1927.

[42] Renamed *The Norwegian Monarch* in July

1927, and *Norwegian Monarch* in November 1927.

[43] Renamed *King George VI* on 12 January 1937.

[44] Renamed *The Dutch Monarch* in June or July 1927, and further renamed *Dutch Monarch* in October or November 1927.

[45] Renamed *The Roumanian Monarch* in June or July 1927, and *Roumanian Monarch* in November 1927. The name was removed in November 1940 and the words STAR CLASS painted on the splashers.

[46] Built by London & South Western Railway to Robert Urie's design. Nameplates fitted by Southern Railway in 1925.

[47] Built by London & South Western Railway to Robert Urie's design. Nameplates fitted by Southern Railway in 1925.

[48] Renamed *The Japanese Monarch* in June or July 1927, and further renamed *Japanese Monarch* in October or November 1927. Name removed in January 1941 and the words STAR CLASS were painted on the splashers.

Name	Number	Class	Date	Railway
King Richard II	6021	King	6/1930	Great Western Rly
King Richard III	6015	King	6/1928	Great Western Rly
Kingsbridge	3359	Bulldog	10/1900	Great Western Rly
Kingsbury	–	0–4–2	1841	Birmingham & Derby Junction Rly
King's Canterbury	933	Schools	2/1935	Southern Rly
King's Courier	60144	A1	3/1949	British Railways (Eastern Region)
Kingsland Grange	6876	Grange	4/1939	Great Western Rly
Kingsley	10	4–4–0T	1880	Longmoor Military Rly [49]
Kingsley	2	2–4–2T	1900	Bideford, Westward Ho! & Appledore Rly
King's Lynn	–	4–4–0T	10/1881	Lynn & Fakenham Rly
King's Lynn	47576	47/4	1964	British Railways
Kingsmills	35	Glenbarry	11/1863	Highland Rly [50]
King's Own Yorkshire Light Infantry	4843	V2	4/1939	London & North Eastern Rly
King's Shropshire Light Infantry	D50	Peak	5/1962	British Railways
King Stephen	4029	Star	10/1909	Great Western Rly [51]
King Stephen	6029	King	8/1930	Great Western Rly [52]
Kingsthorpe Hall	6950	Hall	12/1942	Great Western Rly [53]
Kingston	5	2–2–2	11/1839	London & Brighton Rly [54]
Kingstone Grange	6820	Grange	1/1937	Great Western Rly
Kingsway Hall	5933	Hall	6/1933	Great Western Rly
Kingswear Castle	5015	Castle	7/1932	Great Western Rly
King's Wimbledon	931	Schools	12/1934	Southern Rly
Kingswood	512	E4	2/1901	London, Brighton & South Coast Rly
Kingswood	–	0–4–0DM	1959	Avon Valley Rly
Kingussie	41	M/Goods	5/1864	Highland Rly
Kingussie	46	Glenbarry	6/1864	Highland Rly [55]
King Uther	737	King Arthur	10/1918	Southern Rly [56]
King Uther	73111	5MT	10/1955	British Railways
King William	4022	Star	6/1909	Great Western Rly [57]
King William III	6007	King	3/1928	Great Western Rly
King William IV	–	0–4–0	9/1830	Liverpool & Manchester Rly [58]
King William IV	6002	King	7/1927	Great Western Rly
Kinlet Hall	4936	Hall	6/1929	Great Western Rly
Kinmundy	6	N	2/1887	Great North of Scotland Rly
Kinnerley	2	4wDM	1953	Welsh Highland Rly [59]
Kinross	110	72	1880	North British Rly
Kinross-shire	310	D49/1	5/1928	London & North Eastern Rly
Kipling	92034	92		British Railways
Kirby Hall	5993	Hall	12/1939	Great Western Rly
Kirkby Stephen	133	Peel	9/1858	Stockton & Darlington Rly

Name	Number	Class	Date	Railway
Kirkcaldy	88	157	7/1877	North British Rly [60]
Kirkland	2978	Saint	4/1905	Great Western Rly [61]
Kissack	13	2–4–0T	1910	Isle of Man Rly [62]
Kitchener	–	0–6–2T	1886	Longmoor Military Rly [63]
Kitchener	3374	Atbara	4/1900	Great Western Rly [64]
Kitchener	3377	Atbara	5/1900	Great Western Rly
Kitchener	58	B4	8/1901	London, Brighton & South Coast Rly [65]
Kitchener	21	0–6–2T	1938	Longmoor Military Rly
Kitchener	601	WD2–10–0	1944	Longmoor Military Railway [66]
Kite	–	0–6–0ST	11/1863	Swansea Vale Rly
Kittiwake	60120	A1	12/1948	British Railways (Eastern Region)
Klipspringer	1007	B1	4/1944	London & North Eastern Rly
Kneller Hall	5934	Hall	6/1933	Great Western Rly
Knight Commander	4020	Star	5/1908	Great Western Rly
Knight of Liege	4017	Star	4/1908	Great Western Rly [67]
Knight of St. John	4015	Star	3/1908	Great Western Rly
Knight of St. Patrick	4013	Star	3/1908	Great Western Rly
Knight of the Bath	4014	Star	3/1908	Great Western Rly
Knight of the Black Eagle	4017	Star	4/1908	Great Western Rly [68]
Knight of the Garter	4011	Star	3/1908	Great Western Rly
Knight of the Golden Fleece	4016	Star	4/1908	Great Western Rly [69]
Knight of the Grand Cross	4018	Star	4/1908	Great Western Rly
Knight of the Thistle	4012	Star	3/1908	Great Western Rly
Knight of the Thistle	87014	87/0	1974	British Railways
Knight of Thistle	2564	A3	7/1924	London & North Eastern Rly [70]
Knighton	–	0–4–2ST	1861	Knighton Rly
Knight Templar	4019	Star	5/1908	Great Western Rly
Knothole Worker	–	4wDM	1959	Moseley Railway Museum [71]
Knott End	–	0–6–0T	1909	Garstang & Knott End Rly
Knowle	78	A1	7/1880	London, Brighton & South Coast Rly [72]
Knowsley	91	aCrewe	10/1846	London & North Western Rly
Knowsley	887	L/Bloomer	1851	London & North Western Rly
Knowsley	306	1Experiment	1883	London & North Western Rly
Knowsley	1114	2Precursor	9/1905	London & North Western Rly
Knowsley Hall	5905	Hall	5/1931	Great Western Rly
Kolhapur	5593	Jubilee	1934	London Midland & Scottish Rly
Konigswinter	1	2–8–0	1972	Cleethorpes Coast Light Rly [73]
Kudu	1008	B1	5/1944	London & North Eastern Rly
Kynite	–	0–4–2T	1901	Corringham Light Rly

---

[49] Formerly Midland & Great Northern Joint Railway. Before that, was *Norwich* of the Lynn & Fakenham Railway.

[50] Renamed *Isla Bank* in 1888. Altered from 2–2–2 to 2–4–0 in July 1892.

[51] Originally named *King Stephen* until July 1927. Renamed *The Spanish Monarch* in June or July 1927, and further renamed *Spanish Monarch* in November 1927. Nameplates were removed in November 1940, and the words STAR CLASS were painted on the splashers.

[52] Renamed *King Edward VIII* on 14 May 1936.

[53] Nameplates fitted in April 1947.

[54] Later renumbered 44.

[55] Originally named *Clachnacuddin*. Altered from 2–2–2 to 2–4–0 in May 1880, and renamed *Kingussie* in 1883.

[56] Built by the London & South Western Railway to Robert Urie's design. Nameplates fitted by Southern Railway in 1925.

[57] Originally named *King William* until June 1927. Renamed *The Belgian Monarch* in June or July 1927, and *Belgian Monarch* in October 1927. Nameplates were removed in May 1940, and the words STAR CLASS were painted on the splashers.

[58] Built by Braithwaite & Ericsson. Sometimes referred to as *William IV*. Its trials were unsatisfactory and the Liverpool & Manchester declined to purchase it, hence the absence of a number.

[59] 1ft 11½in gauge.

[60] Originally named *Helensburgh*.

[61] Renamed *Charles J. Hambro* in May 1935.

[62] 3ft gauge.

[63] Previously Taff Vale Railway no. 168. Later renamed *Wellington*.

[64] Originally named *Baden Powell*. Temporarily renamed *Pretoria* for City Imperial Volunteers' Special Train on 29 October 1900, *Britannia* for Royal Trains on 7 and 10 March 1902, and *Kitchener* for special train on 12 July 1902.

[65] Name removed in May 1906.

[66] Formerly named *Sapper*.

[67] Originally *Knight of the Black Eagle* until August 1914.

[68] Renamed *Knight of Liege* in August 1914.

[69] Rebuilt to Castle class in October 1925 and was renamed *The Somerset Light Infantry (Prince Albert's)* in 1938.

[70] Originally *Knight of the Thistle*. New nameplates reading *Knight of Thistle* were fitted at an overhaul in December 1932, an error never corrected.

[71] 2ft gauge.

[72] Transferred to the Isle of Wight by the Southern. Renumbered W4 (later W14) and renamed *Bembridge*, May 1929. In May 1964 it was sold to Butlins Holiday Camp, Minehead.

[73] 14¼in gauge.

L

Name	Number	Class	Date	Railway
Lablanche	–	0–4–0	1847	Midland Rly [1]
Lachesis	–	0–4–0	1896	Woolwich Arsenal [2]
Laconia CLS	40022	40	8/1959	British Railways [3]
Lacy	158	Clyde	2/1859	London & South Western Rly
Ladas	1	0–4–2T	1895	Snowdon Mountain Rly [4]
Ladas	2566	A3	8/1924	London & North Eastern Rly
Lady Angela	**1690**	**0–4–0ST**	**1926**	**South Devon Rly [5]**
Lady Armstrong	–	0–4–0DE	?	North Sunderland Rly
Ladybank	89	157	7/1877	North British Rly [6]
Lady Beatrice	2190	Precedent	4/1875	London & North Western Rly [7]
Lady Cornelia	16	0–6–0ST	5/1862	Brecon & Merthyr Rly [8]
Lady Diana Spencer	47712	47/7	1966	British Railways
Lady Disdain	2907	Saint	5/1906	Great Western Rly [9]
Lady Elizabeth	3	2–4–0	1866	Manchester & Milford Rly
Lady Faringdon	364	8E	12/1906	Great Central Rly [10]
Lady Godiva	1976	Alfred	7/1903	London & North Western Rly
Lady Godiva	2904	Saint	5/1906	Great Western Rly [11]
Lady Godiva	110	Claughton	9/1920	London & North Western Rly
Lady Godiva	5519	Patriot	2/1933	London Midland & Scottish Rly
LADY GODIVA	47710	47/7	1966	British Railways
Lady Hamilton	224	DE Railcar	1934	London & North Eastern Rly
Lady Henderson	364	8E	12/1906	Great Central Rly [12]
Lady Macbeth	2905	Saint	5/1906	Great Western Rly [13]
Lady Madcap	**–**	**4wDM**	**1949**	**Bala Lake Rly [14]**
Lady Margaret	1308	2–4–0T	1902	Great Western Rly [15]
Lady Margaret Hall	7911	M/Hall	2/1950	British Railways (Western Region)
Lady Nan	**1719**	**0–4–0ST**	**1920**	**East Somerset Rly**
Lady of Avenal	340	Scott	11/1911	North British Rly
Lady of Lynn	2906	Saint	5/1906	Great Western Rly
Lady of Lyons	2903	Saint	5/1906	Great Western Rly [16]
Lady of Provence	2909	Saint	5/1906	Great Western Rly [17]
Lady of Quality	2908	Saint	5/1906	Great Western Rly [18]
Lady of Shalott	2910	Saint	5/1906	Great Western Rly [19]
Lady of the Isles	**–**	**2–6–2T**	**1981**	**Mull Rail [20]**
Lady of the Lake	–	0–4–2T	1850	Kendal & Windermere Rly
Lady of the Lake	494	DX	c.1860	London & North Western Rly
Lady of the Lake	531	Problem	c.1860	London & North Western Rly
Lady of the Lake	2902	Saint	5/1906	Great Western Rly [21]
Lady of the Lake	1989	2Experiment	10/1906	London & North Western Rly
Lady of the Lake	6149	Royal Scot	11/1927	London Midland & Scottish Rly [22]
Lady of the Lakes	**5**	**B-B DM**	**1985**	**Ruislip Lido Rly [23]**
Lady Patricia	6210	Princess	9/1935	London Midland & Scottish Rly
Lady Portsmouth	392	0–6–0ST	6/1862	London & South Western Rly
Lady Rowena	424	Scott	6/1915	North British Rly
Lady Sale	–	0–6–0	?	Sirhowy Rly [24]
Ladysmith	3380	Atbara	5/1900	Great Western Rly
Ladysmith	61	B4	8/1901	London, Brighton & South Coast Rly [25]

Name	Number	Class	Date	Railway
Lady Superior	2901	Saint	5/1906	Great Western Rly [26]
Lady Tredegar	6	0–6–0ST	1848	Alexandra (Newport & South Wales) Docks & Rly
Lady Victoria	**3**	**0–6–0ST**	**1916**	**Bo'ness & Kinneil Rly**
Lady Wakefield	**–**	**Bo-Bo**	**1980**	**Ravenglass & Eskdale Rly [27]**
La France	1926	Jubilee	3/1900	London & North Western Rly
La France	102	4–4–2	10/1903	Great Western Rly
La France	39	H1	1/1906	London, Brighton & South Coast Rly [28]
(La France)	**231K55**	**231K**	**1914**	**Société Nationale des Chemins de fer Français [29]**
Lagoon	–	Caesar	3/1861	Great Western Rly (bg)
Laindon	23	Class 1	1884	London, Tilbury & Southend Rly
Laira	3338	Bulldog	1/1900	Great Western Rly
Laird of Balmawhapple	2691	D11/2	11/1924	London & North Eastern Rly
Laird o'Monkbarns	412	Scott	4/1914	North British Rly
Lairg	24	S/Goods	10/1863	Highland Rly [30]
Lake	–	Sondes	11/1857	London, Chatham & Dover Rly
Laleham	–	0–6–0ST	1923	South Shields, Marsden & Whitburn Colliery Rly [31]
Lalla Rookh	–	Abbott	2/1855	Great Western Rly (bg)
Lalla Rookh	2982	Saint	6/1905	Great Western Rly
Lambeth	29	D1	4/1876	London, Brighton & South Coast Rly
Lambert	3055	3031	3/1895	Great Western Rly [32]
Lambton Castle	2823	B17/1	2/1931	London & North Eastern Rly
La Moye	5	2–4–0T	1907	Jersey Rly [33]
La Moye	3	Sentinel	3/1925	Jersey Rly [34]
Lampeter	4	0–6–0ST	11/1867	Manchester & Milford Rly
Lamphey Castle	5054	Castle	6/1936	Great Western Rly [35]
Lamphey Castle	5078	Castle	5/1939	Great Western Rly [36]
Lamphey Castle	7005	Castle	6/1946	Great Western Rly [37]
Lamport No 3	**–**	**0–6–0ST**	**1942**	**Battlefield Steam Rly**
Lamport & Holt Line	35026	MN	12/1948	British Railways (Southern Region)
Lanarkshire	265	D49/1	12/1927	London & North Eastern Rly
Lanarkshire Steel	37108	37/0	1963	British Railways
Lanarkshire Yeomanry	5154	5	1935	London Midland & Scottish Rly
Lancashire	1616	2Experiment	11/1909	London & North Western Rly
Lancashire	236	D49/1	1/1928	London & North Eastern Rly
Lancashire Fusilier	6119	Royal Scot	10/1927	London Midland & Scottish Rly
Lancashire Witch	–	0–4–0	7/1828	Bolton & Leigh Rly
Lancashire Witch	6125	Royal Scot	8/1927	London Midland & Scottish Rly [38]
Lancashire Witch	86213	86/2	1965	British Railways
Lancaster	4	0–4–0	5/1839	Manchester & Leeds Rly
Lancaster	–	2–2–2	1840	Lancaster & Preston Junction Rly
Lancaster Castle	5	0–4–0	8/1850	North Western Rly
Lancastria CLS	40023	40	8/1959	British Railways [39]
Lance	–	Wolf	8/1841	Great Western Rly (bg)

[1] A locomotive built to T.R. Crampton's patent. It was an 0–4–0 express engine with an intermediate oscillating drive shaft. The boiler was oval in section. It underwent extensive trials on the Birmingham & Gloucester Railway, but the Midland Railway did not purchase it. After a total rebuild by E.B. Wilson & Co., it ended its days as a more or less orthodox 2–4–0 on contractor's work.

[2] Paraffin/mechanical. 18in gauge.

[3] Originally no. D222 *Laconia*.

[4] 800mm gauge rack and pinion locomotive.

[5] The modern, preserved South Devon Railway.

[6] Originally named *Gareloch*.

[7] Originally named *Beatrice*. Renamed *Lady Beatrice*, and then *Princess Beatrice*, in 1888.

[8] Originally named *Hereford*. Renamed *Lady Cornelia* in 1869.

[9] Nameplates fitted in April 1907.

[10] Originally named *Lady Henderson*; renamed in 1917 *Lady Faringdon*.

[11] Nameplates fitted in April 1907.

[12] Renamed *Lady Faringdon* in 1917.

[13] Nameplates fitted in April 1907.

[14] 2ft gauge.

[15] Built for the Liskeard & Looe Railway.

[16] Nameplates fitted in April 1907.

[17] Nameplates fitted in May 1907.

[18] Nameplates fitted in May 1907.

[19] Nameplates fitted in May 1907.

[20] 10¼in gauge.

[21] Nameplates fitted in April 1907.

[22] Renamed *The Middlesex Regiment* in May 1936.

[23] 12in gauge.

[24] Built between 1832 and 1853.

[25] Name removed in May 1906.

[26] Nameplates fitted in October 1906.

[27] 15in gauge.

[28] Named in June 1913 for a special train carrying the French President, M. Raymond Poincaré. The Southern Railway renamed the engine *Hartland Point* in January 1926.

[29] A 4–6–2 express passenger locomotive, built for the PLM (Chemin de Fer de Paris à Lyon et à la Méditerranée). 231K55 is its SNCF number.

[30] Originally named *Invergordon*.

[31] Borrowed from Boldon Colliery, 1929–38.

[32] Originally named *Trafalgar*; renamed *Lambert* in July 1901.

[33] 3ft 6in gauge.

[34] Sentinel-Cammell steam railcar. 3ft 6in gauge.

[35] Renamed *Earl of Ducie* in September 1937.

[36] Renamed *Beaufort* in January 1941.

[37] Renamed *Sir Edward Elgar* in 1957.

[38] Renamed *3rd Carabinier* in June 1936.

[39] Originally no. D223 *Lancastria*.

Name	Number	Class	Date	Railway
Lance	–	4–4–0ST	10/1851	South Devon Rly [40]
Lance	2130	4–4–0ST	2/1875	Great Western Rly (bg) [41]
Lancing	146	Lancing	7/1861	London, Brighton & South Coast Rly
Lancing	354	D1	5/1886	London, Brighton & South Coast Rly
Lancing	904	Schools	5/1930	Southern Rly
Landrail	1417	George V	9/1911	London & North Western Rly
Lanelay Hall	4937	Hall	6/1929	Great Western Rly
(Langbaurgh)	07005	07	1962	British Railways
Langdale	–	0–4–0T	10/1850	Kendal & Windermere Rly
Langdale	603	S/Bloomer	1854	London & North Western Rly
Langdale Pikes	60016	60	2/1993	British Railways
Langford Court	2946	Saint	6/1912	Great Western Rly
Langholm	22	165	3/1878	North British Rly
Langley	40	0–6–0	1855	Newcastle & Carlisle Rly [42]
Lang Meg	73	2–2–2	1859	Lancaster & Carlisle Rly
Lang Meg	1150	1Precursor	10/1878	London & North Western Rly
Lang Meg	1387	2Precursor	3/1906	London & North Western Rly
Langston	264	D1	5/1882	London, Brighton & South Coast Rly
Langton Hall	6914	Hall	2/1941	Great Western Rly
Langwith	08308	08	1957	British Railways
Lanwercost	42	0–6–0	1855	Newcastle & Carlisle Rly [43]
Lapford	34102	WC	3/1950	British Railways (Southern Region)
Lapwing	143	bCrewe	10/1853	London & North Western Rly [44]
Lapwing	18	0–6–0T	?	St Helens Canal & Rly
Lapwing	1151	1Precursor	10/1878	London & North Western Rly
Lapwing	1642	2Precursor	3/1906	London & North Western Rly
Larchfield	64	Birkbeck	2/1849	Stockton & Darlington Rly
Lark	–	2–2–0	2/1839	London & South Western Rly
Lark	184	Windsor	3/1866	Stockton & Darlington Rly
Lark	2178	0–4–0ST	12/1874	Great Western Rly (bg) [45]
Lartington	116	Woodlands	7/1856	Stockton & Darlington Rly
La Savoie	–	0–6–0	?	East & West Junction Rly [46]
Latona	364	aCrewe	4/1855	London & North Western Rly [47]
Latona	11	A	7/1864	Metropolitan Rly
Laughton	562	E4	12/1901	London, Brighton & South Coast Rly
Launceston	3360	Bulldog	10/1900	Great Western Rly
Launceston	21C112	rWC	10/1945	Southern Rly
Launceston Castle	5000	Castle	9/1926	Great Western Rly
Laurel	–	Metro	10/1864	Great Western Rly (bg)
Laurence Olivier	86233	86/2	1965	British Railways
Lavant	352	D1	1/1886	London, Brighton & South Coast Rly
Lavington	260	D1	3/1882	London, Brighton & South Coast Rly
Lawrence	514	Precedent	11/1880	London & North Western Rly
Lawrence	514	rPrecedent	10/1895	London & North Western Rly [48]
Lawton Hall	5906	Hall	5/1931	Great Western Rly
Laxfield	3	0–6–0T	1909	Mid Suffolk Light Rly [49]
Lazonby	25	2–2–2	1857	Lancaster & Carlisle Rly
Lazonby	512	Precedent	11/1880	London & North Western Rly
L/Corpl. J.A. Christie, V.C.	1407	Claughton	2/1920	London & North Western Rly
Lea & Perrins	37185	37/0	1964	British Railways
Leadenhall	48	A1	12/1876	London, Brighton & South Coast Rly
Leader	8	Tory	4/1842	Stockton & Darlington Rly [50]
Leader	–	**0–4–2ST**	**1905**	**Sittingbourne & Kemsley Light Rly** [51]

Name	Number	Class	Date	Railway
"Leader"	36001	Leader	6/1949	British Railways (Southern Region)
Leamington Spa	104	George V	6/1916	London & North Western Rly
Leander	196	aCrewe	2/1848	London & North Western Rly
Leander	93	2–4–0	1/1850	Manchester, Sheffield & Lincolnshire Rly
Leander	–	Caesar	12/1852	Great Western Rly (bg)
Leander	196	Problem	c.1860	London & North Western Rly
Leander	291	2Experiment	11/1906	London & North Western Rly
Leander	5690	**Jubilee**	**1936**	**London Midland & Scottish Rly**
Leatherhead	59	2–4–0T	6/1860	London, Brighton & South Coast Rly [52]
Leatherhead	178	Gladstone	7/1890	London, Brighton & South Coast Rly
Leatherhead	939	Schools	7/1935	Southern Rly
Leaton Grange	6921	Grange	1/1937	Great Western Rly
Lec	–	**4wDM**	**1960**	**Bodmin & Wenford Rly**
Lechlade Manor	7825	Manor	12/1950	British Railways (Western Region)
Leconfield	360	D1	1/1887	London, Brighton & South Coast Rly
Leconfield	319	B2	10/1896	London, Brighton & South Coast Rly [53]
Leeds	30	2–2–0	1833	Liverpool & Manchester Rly
Leeds	31	Fenton	6/1839	London & South Western Rly
Leeds	8	0–4–2	8/1839	Manchester & Leeds Rly [54]
Leeds	31	2Hercules	7/1852	London & South Western Rly
Leeds	31	Volcano	3/1873	London & South Western Rly
Leeds	–	0–4–0T	1916	Woolwich Arsenal [55]
Leeds United	2856	B17/4	5/1936	London & North Eastern Rly
Leeds United	43054	43	5/1977	British Railways
Leeward Islands	5614	Jubilee	1934	London Midland & Scottish Rly
Leghorn	122	E1	8/1878	London, Brighton & South Coast Rly
Leicester	22	0–4–0	5/1832	Birmingham & Gloucester Rly [56]
Leicester City	2865	B17/4	1/1937	London & North Eastern Rly
Leicestershire	1624	2Experiment	11/1909	London & North Western Rly
Leicestershire	352	D49/2	3/1929	London & North Eastern Rly [57]
Leicestershire and Derbyshire Yeomanry	D163	Peak	4/1962	British Railways
Leigh	14	Class 1	1881	London, Tilbury & Southend Rly
Leigham	292	D1	11/1877	London, Brighton & South Coast Rly
Leighton	8	0–4–2	12/1860	Cambrian Railways
Leinster	5741	Jubilee	1936	London Midland & Scottish Rly
Leith	297	165	1/1916	North British Rly [58]
Lemberg	2544	A3	7/1924	London & North Eastern Rly
Lennoxtown	174	72	2/1883	North British Rly
Lentran	42	M/Goods	5/1864	Highland Rly
Lenzie	214	211	1856	North British Rly
Leo	–	Leo	10/1841	Great Western Rly (bg)
Leo	902	0–8–0T	1858	Great Western Rly [59]
Leon	–	?	?	Brecon & Merthyr Rly [60]
Leonard	1	**0–4–0ST**	**1919**	**Birmingham Museum of Science and Industry** [61]
Leopard	62	2–2–2	1838	Liverpool & Manchester Rly
Leopard	11	2–2–0	1/1840	Midland Counties Rly
Leopard	–	Priam	5/1840	Great Western Rly (bg)
Leopard	105	Bison	10/1848	London & South Western Rly
Leopard	147	Panther	2/1860	Stockton & Darlington Rly
Leopard	18	Tiger	12/1861	London, Chatham & Dover Rly

[40] Destroyed in a collision between Menheniot and St Germans on 2 December 1873, and never became a Great Western engine.
[41] Built for the South Devon Railway.
[42] Became North Eastern Railway no. 488 in 1862.
[43] Became North Eastern Railway no. 490 in 1862.
[44] Previously Liverpool & Manchester Railway no. 85. Became London & North Western property in 1846.
[45] Built for the South Devon Railway.
[46] Built by André Koechlin for the Chemin de Fer du Rhône et Loire, and sold to

contractors on 1 August 1858. In 1885 it became Cardiff Railway no. 25, nameless, and by then was an 0–6–0ST. It disappeared some time after 1907.
[47] Built for the Birkenhead, Lancashire & Cheshire Junction Railway.
[48] Renamed *Puck* in 1913.
[49] Extant photographs do not show the name actually carried.
[50] Rebuilt in 1842 from no. 25 *Enterprise*.
[51] 2ft 6in gauge.
[52] Originally a 2–4–0, rebuilt as a 2–4–0T in May 1872 by Stroudley and named *Leatherhead*.

[53] Originally named *John Fowler*. Renamed *Leconfield* in October 1906. Rebuilt to class B2x, in June 1914.
[54] It is not clear whether no. 8 was named *Leeds* and no. 12 *Harrogate*, or *vice versa*.
[55] 18in gauge.
[56] Originally *Comet* on the Leicester & Swannington Railway.
[57] Renamed *The Meynell* in June 1932.
[58] Originally named *Penicuik*.
[59] Built for the Llanelly Railway.
[60] Probably a small contractor's tank engine, c. 1865.
[61] Originally named *Victory*. 2ft gauge.

Name	Number	Class	Date	Railway
Leopard	2128	4–4–0ST	12/1872	Great Western Rly (bg) [62]
Leopold	–	Victoria	9/1856	Great Western Rly (bg)
Leslie Runciman	1238	B1	9/1947	London & North Eastern Rly [63]
Lethe	–	Priam	4/1842	Great Western Rly (bg)
Lethe	–	Tiger	5/1862	London, Chatham & Dover Rly [64]
Leuchars	107	165	7/1878	North British Rly [65]
Levens	15	2–4–0	1857	Lancaster & Carlisle Rly
Levens	338	1Precursor	2/1879	London & North Western Rly
Levens	2513	2Precursor	3/1906	London & North Western Rly
Levens Hall	6913	Hall	2/1941	Great Western Rly
Leviathan	244	bCrewe	9/1849	London & North Western Rly
Leviathan	1001	L/Bloomer	1851	London & North Western Rly
Leviathan	510	Dreadnought	1885	London & North Western Rly
Leviathan	301	2Precursor	10/1904	London & North Western Rly
Leviathan	5704	Jubilee	1936	London Midland & Scottish Rly
Leviathan	50040	50	1968	British Railways
Lew	E188	2–6–2T	7/1925	Southern Rly [66]
Lewes	232	D1	7/1884	London, Brighton & South Coast Rly
Lewis Carroll	146	Prince/W	1/1914	London & North Western Rly
LEWIS CARROLL	47703	47/7	1967	British Railways
Lewisham	–	**0–6–0ST**	**1927**	**Foxfield Steam Rly**
Leyton	32	Class 1	1892	London, Tilbury & Southend Rly
Leytonstone	41	37	1897	London, Tilbury & Southend Rly
Liathach	60075	60	12/1991	British Railways
Libert Dickinson	08578	08	1959	British Railways
Liberty	267	aSentinel	1928	London & North Eastern Rly
Libra	–	Leo	2/1842	Great Western Rly (bg)
Lichfield	4	2–2–2	5/1849	South Staffordshire Rly
Liddesdale	877	H	8/1906	North British Rly
Liddington Hall	4938	Hall	6/1929	Great Western Rly [67]
Liffey	–	Caesar	8/1857	Great Western Rly (bg)
Lifford	30	4–2–0	8/1841	Birmingham & Gloucester Rly
Lightning	10	0–4–0	1/1837	Newcastle & Carlisle Rly
Lightning	20	2–2–0	3/1840	Midland Counties Rly
Lightning	–	Iron Duke	8/1847	Great Western Rly (bg)
Lightning	26	Venus	6/1848	East Lancashire Rly
Lightning	114	aCrewe	11/1849	London & North Western Rly [68]
Lightning	1219	Newton	4/1872	London & North Western Rly
Lightning	–	Rover	9/1878	Great Western Rly (bg)
Lightning	1219	rPrecedent	1/1888	London & North Western Rly
Lightning	3016	3001	4/1892	Great Western Rly [69]
Lightning	1781	2Experiment	5/1909	London & North Western Rly
Lightning	70019	Britannia	6/1951	British Railways
Lilford Hall	6927	Hall	11/1941	Great Western Rly [70]
Lilian	–	**0–4–0ST**	**1883**	**Launceston Steam Rly [71]**
Lilian Walter	–	**A1–1AD**	**1985**	**Fairbourne & Barmouth Steam Rly [72]**
Lilleshall	21	0–4–0ST	12/1862	Cambrian Railways
Lily	222	aCrewe	9/1848	London & North Western Rly
Lily	222	Problem	c.1860	London & North Western Rly
Lily	–	Metro	5/1864	Great Western Rly (bg)
Lily	188	Panther	8/1865	Stockton & Darlington Rly
Lily of the Valley	–	**0–4–0DM**	**1943**	**Scottish Industrial Railway Centre**
Limpsfield	517	E4	6/1901	London, Brighton & South Coast Rly
Lincolnshire	245	D49/1	2/1928	London & North Eastern Rly
Lincolnshire Regiment	2805	B17/1	12/1928	London & North Eastern Rly [73]
Linda	–	**2–4–0TT**	**1893**	**Festiniog Rly [74]**
Linda	–	**0–4–0ST**	**1941**	**Battlefield Steam Rly**
Linda	26	**J94**	**11/1952**	**Kent & East Sussex Rly [75]**
(Linda)	03119	**03**	**1959**	**British Railways**
Linden Hall	5984	Hall	10/1938	Great Western Rly
Lindfield	238	D1	11/1881	London, Brighton & South Coast Rly
Lindisfarne	47789	47/7		British Railways
Lindsay	–	**0–6–0ST**	**1887**	**Steamtown, Carnforth**
Lingfield	511	E4	2/1901	London, Brighton & South Coast Rly
Linnet	150	aCrewe	8/1853	London & North Western Rly [76]
Linette	752	King Arthur	12/1922	Southern Rly [77]
Linette	73087	5MT	8/1955	British Railways
Linlithgow	427	418	1873	North British Rly
Lion	–	2–2–2	5/1838	Great Western Rly (bg)
Lion	57	**0–4–2**	**7/1838**	**Liverpool & Manchester Rly [78]**
Lion	7	2–2–0	6/1839	Midland Counties Rly
Lion	101	Bison	7/1848	London & South Western Rly
Lion	112	Peel	8/1856	Stockton & Darlington Rly
Lion	116	bCrewe	8/1856	London & North Western Rly
Lion	2113	4–4–0ST	6/1859	Great Western Rly (bg) [79]
Lion	101	Lion	12/1863	London & South Western Rly
Lion	–	**0–4–0ST**	**1914**	**Chasewater Light Rly**
(Lion)	–	**4–6–0T**	**1917**	**Amberley Chalk Pits Museum [80]**
Lion	6142	Royal Scot	10/1927	London Midland & Scottish Rly [81]
(Lion)	08022	**08**	**1953**	**British Railways**
Lion	DO260	Co-Co	5/1962	Birmingham Railway Carriage & Wagon Co. [82]
Lion	50027	**50**	**1968**	**British Railways**
Lioness	102	Bison	7/1848	London & South Western Rly
Lioness	102	Lion	6/1864	London & South Western Rly

Great Western Railway broad gauge Iron Duke class 4–2–2 *Lightning*. In 1878 this engine was renewed as a member of the Rover class. (*Photo: RAS Marketing*)

[62] Built for the South Devon Railway.
[63] Nameplates only fitted in December 1947.
[64] Renamed *Sphynx* in August 1862. Later became no. 24.
[65] Originally named *Uddingston*.
[66] For the Lynton & Barnstaple section. 1ft 11½in gauge.
[67] The nameplates may have been removed for a time during the Second World War.
[68] Previously Liverpool & Manchester Railway 2–2–2 no. 45. Became London & North Western property in 1846.
[69] Rebuilt to 4–2–2 in November 1894.

[70] Nameplates fitted in June 1948.
[71] 1ft 11½in gauge.
[72] 12¼in gauge.
[73] Originally *Burnham Thorpe*. Renamed *Lincolnshire Regiment* in April 1938.
[74] Formerly 0–4–0ST on the Penrhyn Railway. 1ft 11½in gauge.
[75] This is the same locomotive (Hunslet Engine Co. no. 3781 of 1952) as *Thomas* on the Mid Hants Railway.
[76] Previously Liverpool & Manchester Railway no. 92. Became London & North Western property in 1846.

[77] Built by the London & South Western Railway to Robert Urie's designs. Nameplates applied by the Southern Railway in 1925.
[78] Became London & North Western Railway no. 116 in 1846.
[79] Built for the South Devon Railway.
[80] 2ft gauge.
[81] Renamed *The York and Lancaster Regiment* in May 1936.
[82] 2,750 horsepower prototype diesel locomotive, built as a speculative venture. It operated for only a few months.

Liverpool & Manchester Railway 0–4–2 no. 57 *Lion*, as restored, at Wavertree Park, Liverpool, on 16 September 1930. (*Photo: LCGB Ken Nunn Collection*)

Name	Number	Class	Date	Railway
Lionheart	08682	08	1959	British Railways
Lisieux	5079	J94	1943	Longmoor Military Rly [83]
Liskeard	–	0–6–0T?	?	Liskeard & Looe Rly [84]
Little Barford	**–**	**0–4–0ST**	**1939**	**Foxfield Steam Rly**
"Little Dick"	889	5	1897	Great Central Rly [85]
Little England	–	2–2–2WT	1857	Sandy & Potton Rly [86]
Little Giant	6	0–4–0TT	1863	Festiniog Rly [87]
Littlehampton	31	2–2–2	12/1862	London, Brighton & South Coast Rly [88]
Littlehampton	172	Gladstone	4/1891	London, Brighton & South Coast Rly
Little Ilford	48	Class 37	1898	London, Tilbury & Southend Rly
"Little Jim"	30072	USA	1943	Southern Rly [89]
Little John	2	0–4–0WT	6/1865	Severn & Wye & Severn Bridge Rly
Little John	1123A	0–6–0T	11/1874	Midland Rly [90]
Little Lady	**1903**	**0–4–0ST**	**1936**	**Gwili Rly**
Little Linford Hall	7912	M/Hall	3/1950	British Railways (Western Region)
Littleton	565	E4	5/1902	London, Brighton & South Coast Rly
Littleton Colliery	58049	58	12/1986	British Railways
Littleton Hall	4939	Hall	7/1929	Great Western Rly
Littleton No 5	**–**	**0–6–0ST**	**1922**	**Avon Valley Rly**
Little Wonder	7	0–4–4–0F	7/1869	Festiniog Rly [91]
Little Wyrley Hall	7913	M/Hall	3/1950	British Railways (Western Region)
Liver	26	2–2–0	1832	Liverpool & Manchester Rly
Liver	262	bCrewe	11/1850	London & North Western Rly
Liver	2155	Samson	11/1874	London & North Western Rly
Liver	2155	Whitworth	1895	London & North Western Rly
Liverpool	–	0–4–0	5/1831	Bolton & Leigh Rly
Liverpool	2	2–2–0	1835	Cromford & High Peak Rly
Liverpool	–	0–4–0	7/1835	Leicester & Swannington Rly
Liverpool	13	0–4–0	5/1840	Manchester & Leeds Rly
Liverpool	–	6–2–0	1848	London & North Western Rly

Name	Number	Class	Date	Railway
Liverpool	3021	Special Tank	1/1876	London & North Western Rly
Liverpool	7	I	1/1886	Mersey Rly
Liverpool	3446	Bulldog	9/1903	Great Western Rly [92]
Liverpool	–	0–4–0T	1915	Woolwich Arsenal [93]
Liverpool	6130	Royal Scot	8/1927	London Midland & Scottish Rly [94]
Liverpool	2864	B17/4	1/1937	London & North Eastern Rly
Liverpool Street Pilot	08833	08	1960	British Railways
Livingstone	1680	Newton	5/1868	London & North Western Rly
Livingstone	1680	rPrecedent	6/1891	London & North Western Rly
Livingstone	173	Prince/W	10/1915	London & North Western Rly
Livingston Thompson	**11**	**0–4–4–0F**	**1885**	**Festiniog Rly [95]**
Lizard	3258	Duke	9/1895	Great Western Rly [96]
Lizzie	–	0–4–0ST	1868	Burry Port & Gwendraeth Valley Rly
Llancaiach	–	0–4–2	1841	Taff Vale Rly
Llancaiach	5	0–6–0	1861	Taff Vale Rly [97]
Llandaff	–	0–6–0	1846	Taff Vale Rly
Llandaff	11	0–6–0	1861	Taff Vale Rly
Llandinam	–	0–6–0ST	10/1861	Pembroke & Tenby Rly
Llandovery Castle	5001	Castle	9/1926	Great Western Rly
Llandrindod	2153	George V	7/1916	London & North Western Rly
Llandudno	363	George V	6/1916	London & North Western Rly
Llandudno	5520	Patriot	2/1933	London Midland & Scottish Rly
Llanelli	**19**	**4wDM**	**1961**	**Llanberis Lake Rly [98]**
Llanerchydol	7	0–4–2	12/1860	Cambrian Railways
Llanfrechfa Grange	6827	Grange	2/1937	Great Western Rly
Llangedwyn Hall	4941	Hall	7/1929	Great Western Rly
Llanstephan Castle	5004	Castle	6/1927	Great Western Rly
Llantilio Castle	5028	Castle	5/1934	Great Western Rly
Llanthony Abbey	4068	Star	1/1923	Great Western Rly [99]
Llanthony Abbey	5088	Castle	2/1939	Great Western Rly [100]
Llanfair Grange	6877	Grange	4/1939	Great Western Rly
Llanidloes	–	?	c.1858	Cambrian Railways [101]
Llanrumney Hall	6980	M/Hall	11/1947	Great Western Rly
Llantwit	–	0–4–2	1838	Taff Vale Rly [102]
Llantwit	8	0–4–0	1859	Taff Vale Rly
Llanvair Grange	6825	Grange	2/1937	Great Western Rly
Llewellyn	225	bCrewe	10/1848	London & North Western Rly
Llewellyn	869	Precedent	6/1877	London & North Western Rly
Llewellyn	869	rPrecedent	11/1896	London & North Western Rly
Llewellyn	180	Claughton	4/1921	London & North Western Rly
Llewelyn	–	?	?	Llanidloes & Newtown Rly [103]
Lleweni Hall	7914	M/Hall	3/1950	British Railways (Western Region)
Lloyd George	1167	9P	9/1920	Great Central Rly
Lloyds	100A1	Castle	4/1925	Great Western Rly [104]
LLOYD'S LIST 250TH ANNIVERSARY	86222	86/2	1965	British Railways
LLOYD'S LIST 250TH ANNIVERSARY	86502	86/2	1/1966	British Railways
Llywelyn	**8**	**2–6–2T**	**7/1923**	**British Railways [105]**
Load Star	–	Priam	1/1841	Great Western Rly (bg)

[83] Originally named *Sir John French*.

[84] Date of construction uncertain. It was hired from the contractor, James Murphy of Newport, Mon., who had built the line, in December 1860 and purchased outright in September 1861.

[85] Originally 0–6–0ST, converted to 0–6–2ST and fitted with a crane for use in Gorton Works. Conversion was approved in January 1903, but when the actual work was done is not known.

[86] It has been suggested that this locomotive may be ex-London & Blackwall Railway's *Pigmy Giant* (of which no trace has so far been found), but confirmation is lacking.

[87] 1ft 11½in gauge.

[88] Name applied in about 1863.

[89] This nickname was bestowed on the engine when it was shed pilot at Guildford in the 1950s.

[90] Built for the Severn & Wye & Severn Bridge Railway as a replacement for the 1865 engine.

[91] 1ft 11½in gauge.

[92] Renamed *Swindon* in October 1903.

[93] 18in gauge.

[94] Renamed *The West Yorkshire Regiment* in June 1935.

[95] Later renamed *Taliesin* and renumbered 3, and then further renamed *Earl of Merioneth* on one side and *Iarll Meirionnydd* on the other. 1ft 11½in gauge. (Earl of Merioneth is a title held by HRH the Duke of Edinburgh, and Taliesin was a Chief of the Bards, who flourished around AD 570.)

[96] Renamed *The Lizard* in January 1904.

[97] Name removed in about 1866, and rebuilt to 0–4–4T in 1878.

[98] 1ft 11½in gauge.

[99] Rebuilt to Castle class, February 1939, as no. 5088.

[100] Rebuilt from Star class no. 4068.

[101] Formerly Llanidloes & Newtown Railway.

[102] Purchased in 1845.

[103] Used at the opening of the railway in 1859, may have gone to the Cambrian Railways.

[104] No. 4009 *Shooting Star* until 1936. Rebuilt to Castle class in April 1925. In service, it was always referred to simply as no. 100.

[105] 1ft 11½in gauge. Built by the Great Western Railway; name applied by British Railways in June 1956.

Name	Number	Class	Date	Railway
Loadstone	288	bCrewe	8/1852	London & North Western Rly
Loadstone	2154	Samson	11/1874	London & North Western Rly
Loadstone	2154	Whitworth	3/1894	London & North Western Rly
Loadstone	2175	Prince/W	11/1915	London & North Western Rly
Loard	139	Saxon	4/1857	London & South Western Rly
Lobelia	4109	Flower	6/1908	Great Western Rly
Loch	14	14	9/1862	Highland Rly [106]
Loch	**4**	**2–4–0T**	**1874**	**Isle of Man Rly** [107]
Lochalsh	78	Clyde Bogie	6/1886	Highland Rly
Loch andorb	123	Loch	8/1896	Highland Rly [108]
Loch Arkaig	4764	K2	7/1918	Great Northern Rly [109]
Loch Ashie	70	Loch	3/1917	Highland Rly
Loch Awe	37026	37/4	9/1961	British Railways
Lochee	314	157	6/1877	North British Rly [110]
Loch Eil	4692	K2	7/1921	Great Northern Rly [111]
Loch Eil Outward Bound	37027	37/4	9/1961	British Railways
Loch Ericht	121	Loch	8/1896	Highland Rly
Loch Fannich	130	Loch	9/1896	Highland Rly
Loch Garry	127	Loch	8/1896	Highland Rly
Loch Garry	4684	K2	6/1921	Great Northern Rly [112]
Loch Garve	71	Loch	3/1917	Highland Rly
Lochgorm	57	Lochgorm	11/1872	Highland Rly
Loch Insh	119	Loch	7/1896	Highland Rly
Loch Laggan	124	Loch	8/1896	Highland Rly
Loch Laggan	4701	K2	8/1921	Great Northern Rly [113]
Loch Laidon	4699	K2	8/1921	Great Northern Rly [114]
Loch Laochal	14393	Loch	9/1896	London Midland & Scottish Rly [115]
Loch Laoghal	133	Loch	9/1896	Highland Rly
Loch Leven	162	165	5/1877	North British Rly [116]
Loch Lochy	4682	K2	6/1921	Great Northern Rly [117]
Loch Lomond	4700	K2	8/1921	Great Northern Rly [118]
Loch Lomond	37043	37	6/1962	British Railways
Loch Long	61993	K4	1/1937	London & North Eastern Rly
Loch Long	37081	37/4	11/1962	British Railways
Loch Luichart	128	Loch	8/1896	Highland Rly
Loch Maree	129	Loch	9/1896	Highland Rly
Loch Morar	4691	K2	7/1921	Great Northern Rly [119]
Loch Moy	122	Loch	8/1896	Highland Rly
Lochnagar	60004	60	9/1991	British Railways
Loch Naver	132	Loch	9/1896	Highland Rly
Loch Ness	120	Loch	7/1896	Highland Rly
Loch Oich	4704	K2	9/1921	Great Northern Rly [120]
Loch Quoich	4697	K2	8/1921	Great Northern Rly [121]
Loch Rannoch	4698	K2	8/1921	Great Northern Rly [122]
Loch Rannoch	37012	37/4	3/1961	British Railways
Loch Ruthven	72	Loch	3/1917	Highland Rly
Loch Sheil	4693	K2	7/1921	Great Northern Rly [123]
Loch Shin	131	Loch	9/1896	Highland Rly
Loch Tay	125	Loch	8/1896	Highland Rly
Loch Treig	4685	K2	6/1921	Great Northern Rly [124]
Loch Tummel	126	Loch	8/1896	Highland Rly
Locke	4	1Sussex	8/1838	London & South Western Rly
Locke	278	aCrewe	4/1852	London & North Western Rly

Name	Number	Class	Date	Railway
Locke	4	2Sussex	8/1852	London & South Western Rly
Locke	278	DX	c.1860	London & North Western Rly
Locke	762	Problem	c.1860	London & North Western Rly
Locke	4	2–4–0	2/1861	London & South Western Rly (ed)
Locke	–	Victoria	6/1863	Great Western Rly (bg)
Locke	4	2Vesuvius	12/1870	London & South Western Rly
Locke	1011	2Precursor	7/1907	London & North Western Rly
Lockheed Hudson	5081	Castle	5/1939	Great Western Rly [125]
Locomotion	**1**	**0–4–0**	**9/1825**	**Stockton & Darlington Rly**
Locomotion	**1**	**0–4–0**	**1975**	**Stockton & Darlington Rly Replica** [126]
Locust	–	Metro	8/1862	Great Western Rly (bg)
Lode Star	**4003**	**Star**	**2/1907**	**Great Western Rly**
Lodsworth	590	E5	4/1904	London, Brighton & South Coast Rly
Lombardy	139	E1	3/1879	London, Brighton & South Coast Rly
London	–	Rennie	10/1838	London & South Western Rly

Stockton & Darlington Railway 0–4–0 no. 1 *Locomotion*, seen at Darlington at the Railway Centenary of 1925. (*Photo: LCGB Ken Nunn Collection*)

Name	Number	Class	Date	Railway
London	42	0–4–0	1839	Stockton & Darlington Rly
London	5	2–2–2	3/1839	London & Croydon Rly
London	34	0–4–0	5/1841	Manchester & Leeds Rly
London	4	2–2–2WT	1848	London & Blackwall Rly
London	162	2–2–2	9/1863	London, Brighton & South Coast Rly
London	173	Panther	6/1864	Stockton & Darlington Rly
London	–	Swindon	12/1865	Great Western Rly (bg)
London	339	G	12/1881	London, Brighton & South Coast Rly
London	–	0–4–0ST	1915	Woolwich Arsenal [127]
London Rifle Brigade	6166	Royal Scot	10/1930	London Midland & Scottish Rly
London School of Economics	86621	86/6	7/1966	British Railways
London Scottish	6124	Royal Scot	11/1927	London Midland & Scottish Rly
Longford Grange	6878	Grange	5/1939	Great Western Rly
Long Hull	131	Peel	5/1858	Stockton & Darlington Rly
Longmoor	6	0–4–4T	1890	Longmoor Military Rly [128]

[106] Later no. 32 *Evanton* (November 1897).

[107] 3ft gauge.

[108] Name subsequently rendered *Loch an Dorb* by the London Midland & Scottish Railway, and the engine renumbered 14383.

[109] Name applied in March 1933 by the London & North Eastern Railway.

[110] Originally named *Craigendoran*.

[111] Name applied in February 1933 by the London & North Eastern Railway.

[112] Name applied in July 1933 by the London & North Eastern Railway.

[113] Name applied in May 1933 by the London & North Eastern Railway.

[114] Name applied in June 1934 by the London & North Eastern Railway.

[115] *Loch Laoghal* (Highland Railway no. 133) was wrongly painted on the engine as *Loch Laochal* from about 1925.

[116] Previously named *Milngarvie*.

[117] Name applied in May 1933 by the London & North Eastern Railway.

[118] Name applied in December 1933 by the London & North Eastern Railway.

[119] Name applied in August 1933 by the London & North Eastern Railway.

[120] Name applied in June 1933 by the London & North Eastern Railway.

[121] Name applied in June 1933 by the London & North Eastern Railway.

[122] Name applied in July 1933 by the London & North Eastern Railway.

[123] Name applied in March 1933 by the London & North Eastern Railway.

[124] Name applied in December 1933 by the London & North Eastern Railway.

[125] Originally named *Penrice Castle*; renamed in January 1941.

[126] Preserved at Beamish.

[127] 18in gauge.

[128] Formerly Great Western Railway no. 34.

Battle of Britain class no. 34054 *Lord Beaverbrook*, slowing to 60 mph for the crossovers at Worting Junction, with an Up West of England express. (*Photo: Author*)

Name	Number	Class	Date	Railway
Longmoor	73755	WD2–10–0	1945	Dutch State Rly [129]
Longton	2	0–4–2	1877	West Lancashire Rly [130]
Longworth Manor	7826	Manor	12/1950	British Railways (Western Region)
Lonsdale	1	2–4–0	1846	Whitehaven & Furness Junction Rly
Lonsdale	78	bCrewe	2/1846	Grand Junction Rly
Lonsdale	3	2–4–0	9/1847	Whitehaven & Furness Junction Rly [131]
Lonsdale	78	2–4–0	1849	Stockton & Darlington Rly [132]
Lonsdale	840	S/Bloomer	1854	London & North Western Rly
Lonsdale	11	2–4–0	1857	Lancaster & Carlisle Rly
Lonsdale	19	0–6–0	1864	Whitehaven & Furness Junction Rly [133]
Looe	–	0–6–0ST	4/1901	Liskeard & Looe Rly
Lord Aberconway	94	G	12/1915	Metropolitan Rly [134]
Lord Anson	861	Lord Nelson	9/1929	Southern Rly
Lord Balfour of Burleigh	1246	B1	10/1947	London & North Eastern Rly [135]
Lord Barrymore	2974	Saint	3/1905	Great Western Rly [136]
Lord Beaverbrook	21C154	BB	1/1947	Southern Rly
Lord Brougham	17	Majestic	1831	Stockton & Darlington Rly
Lord Burghley	1247	B1	10/1947	London & North Eastern Rly [137]
Lord Byron	1679	Prince/W	12/1913	London & North Western Rly
Lord Byron	4	Bo-Bo	1921	Metropolitan Rly [138]
Lord Collingwood	862	Lord Nelson	10/1929	Southern Rly
Lord Dowding	21C152	rBB	12/1946	Southern Rly
Lord Duncan	858	Lord Nelson	1/1929	Southern Rly
Lord Durham	22	Director	1832	Stockton & Darlington Rly
Lord Faber	1131	Claughton	8/1914	London & North Western Rly
Lord Faringdon	1169	9P	11/1917	Great Central Rly
Lord Faringdon	4903	A4	7/1938	London & North Eastern Rly [139]
Lord Fisher	125	0–4–0ST	1915	East Somerset Rly [140]
Lord Glenallan	2679	D11/2	10/1924	London & North Eastern Rly
Lord Glenarthur	384	4–4–0	1897	Glasgow & South Western Rly
Lord Glenvarloch	427	Scott	8/1915	North British Rly
Lord Granby	–	0–4–0T	1902	Armley Mills Industrial Museum, Leeds [141]
Lord Hawke	860	Lord Nelson	4/1929	Southern Rly
Lord Hood	859	Lord Nelson	3/1929	Southern Rly
Lord Howe	857	Lord Nelson	12/1928	Southern Rly
Lord Hurcomb	70001	Britannia	2/1951	British Railways
Lordington	584	E5	11/1903	London, Brighton & South Coast Rly
Lord James of Douglas	2687	D11/2	10/1924	London & North Eastern Rly

[129] Preserved at the Netherlands Railway Museum, Utrecht.
[130] Originally named *Sir T. Hesketh*. Renamed in 1880.
[131] Later renamed *Phoenix*.
[132] Purchased in 1854 from the Whitehaven & Furness Junction Railway. It is not clear whether this was no. 1 or no. 3 of the W&FJR, and in any case there is a discrepancy in the building dates – which have been taken from what one can only hope are reliable sources.
[133] Became Furness Railway no. 42.
[134] Sold to the London & North Eastern Railway in November 1937, becoming their no. 6154 of class M2.
[135] Nameplates only fitted in December 1947.
[136] Previously named *Barrymore* until May 1905.
[137] Nameplates only fitted in December 1947.
[138] Officially rebuilt from an earlier, unnamed, locomotive, but incorporating few if any of its components.
[139] Originally named *Peregrine*. Renamed in March 19 48.
[140] The author has fond childhood memories of this little industrial locomotive at Blackwater Gasworks, Hants, in the 1940s and 1950s.
[141] 3ft gauge.

Southern Railway Lord Nelson class 4–6–0 no. 862 *Lord Collingwood*, at Nine Elms Shed. (*Photo: RAS Marketing*)

Name	Number	Class	Date	Railway
Lord Kenyon	968	Claughton	7/1916	London & North Western Rly
Lord King	–	0–4–0ST	**1926**	**Bo'ness & Kinneil Rly**
Lord Kitchener	2401	Claughton	10/1914	London & North Western Rly
Lord Kitchener	70043	Britannia	6/1953	British Railways
Lord Loch	1059	George V	11/1910	London & North Western Rly
Lord Marshall of Goring	392	0–4–0DM	**1954**	**Dean Forest Rly**
Lord Mayor	–	0–4–0ST	**1893**	**Vintage Carriages Trust**
Lord Mildmay of Flete	3707	Bulldog	6/1906	Great Western Rly [142]
Lord Nelson	850	Lord Nelson	**8/1926**	**Southern Rly**
Lord Nelson	87018	87/0	1974	British Railways
Lord of Dunvegan	3446	K4	1/1939	London & North Eastern Rly [143]
Lord of the Isles	–	Iron Duke	3/1851	Great Western Rly (bg)
Lord of the Isles	665	Problem	c.1860	London & North Western Rly
Lord of the Isles	3046	3031	1/1895	Great Western Rly
Lord of the Isles	2623	2Experiment	2/1909	London & North Western Rly
Lord of the Isles	61996	K4	12/1938	London & North Eastern Rly
Lord of the Isles	87024	87/0	1974	British Railways
Lord Palmer	2975	Saint	3/1905	Great Western Rly [144]
Lord President	2003	P2	6/1936	London & North Eastern Rly
Lord President	503	A2/2	12/1944	London & North Eastern Rly [145]
Lord President	87028	87/0	1974	British Railways
Lord Raglan	–	0–4–0ST	3/1871	Woolwich Arsenal [146]
Lord Rathmore	650	Claughton	6/1913	London & North Western Rly
Lord Rathmore	5533	Patriot	4/1933	London Midland & Scottish Rly
Lord Richard	4	0–6–0ST	1863	Wrexham, Mold & Connah's Quay Rly
Lord Robartes	–	0–6–0	1847	– [147]
Lord Roberts	70042	Britannia	4/1953	British Railways
Lord Rodney	863	Lord Nelson	10/1929	Southern Rly

Name	Number	Class	Date	Railway
Lord Rodney	–	0–6–0	?	Sirhowy Rly [148]
Lord Rowallan	70045	Britannia	6/1954	British Railways
Lord Rutherford of Nelson	5665	Jubilee	1935	London Midland & Scottish Rly
Lord St. Levan	758	757	12/1907	Southern Rly [149]
Lord St. Vincent	856	Lord Nelson	11/1928	Southern Rly
Lord Stalbridge	2428	George V	5/1913	London & North Western Rly
Lord Stamp	90007	90/0	4/1988	British Railways
Lord Stuart of Wortley	1168	9P	10/1920	Great Central Rly
Lord Tredegar	2	0–6–0ST	1848	Alexandra (Newport & South Wales) Docks & Rly
Lord Trenchard	–	0–4–0DM	**1956**	**Steamtown, Carnforth**
Lord Wharncliffe	–	0–2–4	9/1833	Dundee & Newtyle Rly [150]
Lorna	20902	20	5/1961	Hunslet-Barclay Ltd [151]
Lorna Doone	3047	3031	2/1895	Great Western Rly
Lorna Doone	56	0–4–0ST	**1922**	**Birmingham Museum of Science and Industry** [152]
Lorraine	115	E1	7/1877	London, Brighton & South Coast Rly
Lothair	52	Enigma	9/1870	London, Chatham & Dover Rly [153]
Lotherton Hall	6954	Hall	3/1943	Great Western Rly [154]
Loughborough Grammar School	47146	47/0	1964	British Railways
Loughor	901	2–4–0ST	8/1865	Great Western Rly [155]
Louisa	904	0–6–0	1860	Great Western Rly [156]
Louis Armand	92006	92		Société Nationale des Chemins de fer Français
Lovat	13	Belladrum	5/1862	Highland Rly [157]
Lovat	47	Glenbarry	6/1864	Highland Rly [158]
Lovat	77	Clyde Bogie	5/1886	Highland Rly
Lovett Eames	–	4–4–2	1880	The Eames Vacuum Brake Co. [159]
Lowca	7	0–4–2	1845	Maryport & Carlisle Rly
Lowes Water	9	0–6–0ST	1867	Whitehaven, Cleator & Egremont Rly [160]
Low Street	16	Class 1	1881	London, Tilbury & Southend Rly
Lowther	1	0–4–2	8/1846	Whitehaven & Furness Junction Rly
Lowther	90	bCrewe	9/1846	London & North Western Rly
Lowther	21	2–2–2	1857	Lancaster & Carlisle Rly
Lowther	161	Brougham	10/1860	Stockton & Darlington Rly
Lowther	2186	Precedent	4/1875	London & North Western Rly
Lowther	2186	rPrecedent	2/1896	London & North Western Rly
Loyalty	1680	George V	4/1913	London & North Western Rly
L.S. Lowry	86239	86/2	1965	British Railways
L.S. Lowry	86507	86/2	6/1965	British Railways
Lucan	–	Bogie	3/1855	Great Western Rly (bg)
Lucania CLS	40024	40	8/1959	British Railways [161]
Luccombe	95	E1	11/1883	London, Brighton & South Coast Rly
Lucerne	149	E1	10/1880	London, Brighton & South Coast Rly
Lucifer	55	2–2–2	1839	Grand Junction Rly
Lucifer	21	2–2–0	3/1840	Midland Counties Rly
Lucifer	–	Priam	8/1841	Great Western Rly (bg)

[142] *Francis Mildmay* until July 1923.

[143] Renamed *MacLeod of MacLeod* in March 1939.

[144] Previously *Viscount Churchill*; renamed *Sir Ernest Palmer* (February 1924) and *Lord Palmer* (October 1933).

[145] Rebuild of no. 2003 above.

[146] 18in gauge.

[147] Built for Peto, Brassey & Betts, contractors, and employed on the construction of the Portland Breakwater, the Schleswig Railway and in Jutland. It returned to the UK and, after a few years at Stratford, East London, was named *Lord Robartes* and worked on the construction of the Cornwall Minerals Railway. It was bought by Boulton in 1875 and eventually scrapped at Ashton. It was never a Cornwall Minerals Railway locomotive.

[148] Built between 1832 and 1853.

[149] Built for the Plymouth, Devonport & South Western Junction Railway.

[150] 4ft 6in gauge.

[151] Built for British Railways.

[152] 2ft gauge.

[153] Name removed by W. Kirtley when number applied.

[154] Nameplates fitted in August 1948.

[155] Built for the Llanelly Railway.

[156] Built for the Llanelly Railway.

[157] Later renamed *Thurso* (1874).

[158] Originally named *Bruce*, renamed *Lovat* and then, in 1886, *Beauly*. Altered from 2–2–2 to 2–4–0 in July 1880.

[159] This locomotive was built by the Baldwin Locomotive Works for the Philadelphia & Reading Railroad, but never went into that company's service. Instead it was sold to the Eames Vacuum Brake Co. in 1881 and named *Lovett Eames*. It was fitted with the Eames brake, and shipped to England for demonstration purposes. It was re-erected at the Miles Platting works of the Lancashire & Yorkshire Railway, and suitably modified to fit the British loading gauge. It ran demonstration trials on the L&YR and on the Great Northern, in the Leeds area. In the summer of 1882 it was exhibited at Alexandra Palace and, having failed to evince the slightest interest among British railway companies, was sold for scrap and broken up at Wood Green, North London, rather more than a year after its arrival in England. Its American locomotive bell is preserved at the National Railway Museum, York.

[160] Became Furness Railway no. 105.

[161] Originally no. D224 *Lucania*.

Name	Number	Class	Date	Railway
Lucifer	55	bCrewe	5/1848	London & North Western Rly
Lucifer	28	Venus	9/1848	East Lancashire Rly
Lucifer	1004	L/Bloomer	1851	London & North Western Rly
Lucifer	114	0–6–0	5/1853	Manchester, Sheffield & Lincolnshire Rly
Lucinidae	47193	47/0	1965	British Railways
Luckie Mucklebackit	2678	D11/2	9/1924	London & North Eastern Rly
Lucknow	1673	Newton	4/1868	London & North Western Rly
Lucknow	1673	rPrecedent	5/1891	London & North Western Rly
Lucknow	1290	Prince/W	7/1919	London & North Western Rly
Luck of Edenhall	8	2–4–0	1857	Lancaster & Carlisle Rly
Luck of Edenhall	90	Samson	10/1874	London & North Western Rly
Luck of Edenhall	90	Whitworth	1894	London & North Western Rly
Lucretius	–	Bogie	12/1854	Great Western Rly (bg)
Lucy Ashton	2680	D11/2	10/1924	London & North Eastern Rly
Ludford Hall	4940	Hall	7/1929	Great Western Rly
Ludlow Castle	5002	Castle	9/1926	Great Western Rly
Lullington	348	G	4/1882	London, Brighton & South Coast Rly
Lulworth Castle	5003	Castle	5/1927	Great Western Rly
Lumley Castle	2824	B17/1	2/1931	London & North Eastern Rly
Lundy	21C129	rWC	5/1946	Southern Rly
Luna	–	Caesar	2/1863	Great Western Rly (bg)
Lune	28	?	?	St Helens Canal & Rly
Lune	88	bCrewe	8/1846	London & North Western Rly
Lune	615	S/Bloomer	1854	London & North Western Rly
Lune	6	2–4–0	1857	Lancaster & Carlisle Rly
Lune	158	Panther	10/1861	Stockton & Darlington Rly
Lupus	6	2–2–2	9/1840	Chester & Birkenhead Rly
Lusitania	1100	Prince/W	3/1916	London & North Western Rly
Lusitania CLS	40025	40	8/1959	British Railways [162]
Lybster	53	Strathpeffer	5/1890	Highland Rly [163]
Lydcott Hall	6955	Hall	3/1943	Great Western Rly [164]

Name	Number	Class	Date	Railway
Lydford	34106	WC	3/1950	British Railways (Southern Region)
Lydford Castle	5055	Castle	6/1936	Great Western Rly [165]
Lydford Castle	5079	Castle	5/1939	Great Western Rly [166]
Lydford Castle	7006	Castle	6/1946	Great Western Rly
Lydham Manor	**7827**	**Manor**	**12/1950**	**British Railways (Western Region)**
Lyme Regis	21C109	rWC	9/1945	Southern Rly
Lyn	–	2–4–2T	7/1898	Lynton & Barnstaple Rly [167]
Lynett	47245	47/0	1966	British Railways
Lynmouth	34099	WC	12/1949	British Railways (Southern Region)
Lynton	21C138	WC	9/1946	Southern Rly
Lynx	16	2–2–2	1837	Grand Junction Rly
Lynx	–	Priam	7/1840	Great Western Rly (bg)
Lynx	31	2–2–0	9/1840	Midland Counties Rly
Lynx	16	aCrewe	1846	London & North Western Rly
Lynx	18	Medusa	5/1847	East Lancashire Rly
Lynx	2109	4–4–0ST	4/1859	Great Western Rly (bg) [168]
Lynx	13	Tiger	11/1861	London, Chatham & Dover Rly
Lynx	2005	Newton	4/1871	London & North Western Rly
Lynx	2005	rPrecedent	1/1894	London & North Western Rly
Lyonnesse	3361	Bulldog	10/1900	Great Western Rly
Lyonnesse	743	King Arthur	7/1919	Southern Rly [169]
Lyonnesse	73113	5MT	10/1955	British Railways
Lyons	300	Lyons	9/1876	London, Brighton & South Coast Rly
Lyonshall Castle	5036	Castle	5/1935	Great Western Rly
Lysander	5079	Castle	5/1939	Great Western Rly [170]
Lytham	–	0–6–0	?	Preston & Wyre Railway, Harbour & Dock Co.
Lytham No 1	–	**0–4–0ST**	**1949**	**Midland Railway Centre**
Lytham St. Annes	5548	Patriot	4/1934	London Midland & Scottish Rly
Lytham St. Annes	D60	Peak	1962	British Railways [171]
Lyttelton	3404	City	10/1907	Great Western Rly [172]

[162] Originally no. D225 *Lusitania*.
[163] Originally named *Strathpeffer*. Renamed *Lybster* in May 1903.
[164] Nameplates fitted in June 1947.
[165] Renamed *Earl of Eldon* in August 1937.
[166] Renamed *Lysander* in November 1940.
[167] Built by the Baldwin Locomotive Company, USA. Became Southern Railway no. E762.
[168] Built for the South Devon Railway.
[169] Built for the London & South Western Railway to Robert Urie's design. Nameplates fitted by the Southern Railway in 1925.
[170] Originally named *Lydford Castle*. Renamed in November 1940.
[171] Later no. 45022.
[172] Spelt *Lyttleton* until June 1920.

M

US Army Transportation Corps S160 class 2–8–0 *Maj.Gen. Carl R.Gray Jnr* at Longmoor Downs, Longmoor Military Railway. The station is decked with flags for an Open Day. (*Photo: Author*)

A close-up of the motion and nameplate of US Army Transportation Corps S160 class 2–8–0 *Maj.Gen. Carl R.Gray Jnr* (*Photo: Author*)

Name	Number	Class	Date	Railway
Mabel	619	Precedent	10/1880	London & North Western Rly
Mabel	619	rPrecedent	2/1896	London & North Western Rly
Maberley	327	bCrewe	2/1854	London & North Western Rly
Maberley	1871	ELBloomer	1861	London & North Western Rly
Mablona	–	2–4–0T	?	Cambrian Railways
MacCailein Mor	**3442**	**K4**	**7/1938**	**London & North Eastern Rly** [1]
MacCailin Mor	3445	K4	1/1939	London & North Eastern Rly [2]
Macduff	54	Glenbarry	10/1864	Highland Rly [3]
Macedon	67	Charon	5/1859	East Lancashire Rly
MacIver	3421	Bulldog	2/1903	Great Western Rly [4]
MacLeod of MacLeod	61998	K4	1/1939	London & North Eastern Rly [5]
Macon	138	E1	1/1879	London, Brighton & South Coast Rly
Madden	5668	Jubilee	1935	London Midland & Scottish Rly
Madge	2002	Newton	4/1871	London & North Western Rly
Madge	2002	rPrecedent	6/1891	London & North Western Rly
Madge	**9**	**4wDM**	**1935**	**Leighton Buzzard Rly** [6]
Madge Wildfire	244	Scott	10/1911	North British Rly
Madge Wildfire	60135	A1	11/1948	British Railways (Eastern Region)
Madoqua	1027	B1	5/1947	London & North Eastern Rly
Madras	3469	Bulldog	4/1904	Great Western Rly
Madras	5575	Jubilee	1934	London Midland & Scottish Rly
Madresfield Court	2947	Saint	6/1912	Great Western Rly
Madrid	154	E1	3/1881	London, Brighton & South Coast Rly [7]
Mafeking	3382	Atbara	5/1900	Great Western Rly
Mafeking	62	B4	8/1901	London, Brighton & South Coast Rly
Magdala	1744	Newton	10/1869	London & North Western Rly
Magdala	1744	rPrecedent	4/1892	London & North Western Rly
Magi	–	Caesar	5/1856	Great Western Rly (bg)
Magistrate	107	bCrewe	6/1847	London & North Western Rly
Maglona	57	2–4–0T	5/1866	Cambrian Railways
Magnet	24	0–6–0	7/1835	Stockton & Darlington Rly
Magnet	294	bCrewe	11/1852	London & North Western Rly
Magnet	–	0–4–2T	7/1860	London, Chatham & Dover Rly [8]

Name	Number	Class	Date	Railway
Magnet	2979	Saint	4/1905	Great Western Rly [9]
Magnificent	D828	Warship	10/1960	British Railways
Magnus	–	0–4–0T	7/1860	London, Chatham & Dover Rly [10]
Magog	39	0–4–0	12/1843	South Eastern Rly
Magpie	2135	4–4–0ST	1861	Great Western Rly (bg) [11]
(Magpie)	**4806**	**5**	**1944**	**London Midland & Scottish Rly**
Magpie	D829	Warship	11/1960	British Railways
Maid Marian	1357	0–6–0T	12/1872	Great Western Rly [12]
Maid Marian	**–**	**0–4–0ST**	**1903**	**Bala Lake Rly** [13]
Maid of Astolat	744	King Arthur	9/1919	Southern Rly [14]
Maid of Astolat	73089	5MT	9/1955	British Railways
Maid of Lorn	2689	D11/2	11/1924	London & North Eastern Rly
Mail	6143	Royal Scot	10/1927	London Midland & Scottish Rly [15]
Maindy Hall	**4942**	**Hall**	**7/1929**	**Great Western Rly**
Maine	3373	Atbara	4/1900	Great Western Rly [16]
Maine	3381	Atbara	5/1900	Great Western Rly
Maitland	**11**	**2–4–0T**	**1905**	**Isle of Man Rly** [17]
Majestic	10	0–2–2	1830	Liverpool & Manchester Rly
Majestic	12	Majestic	1831	Stockton & Darlington Rly [18]
Majestic	50	2–2–2	1836	Liverpool & Manchester Rly
Majestic	368	aCrewe	6/1855	London & North Western Rly
Majestic	368	DX	c.1860	London & North Western Rly
Majestic	564	Problem	c.1860	London & North Western Rly
Majestic	3048	3031	2/1895	Great Western Rly
Majestic	1020	2Experiment	1/1909	London & North Western Rly
Majestic	D830	Warship	1/1961	British Railways
Maj.Gen. Carl R.Gray Jnr	3257	S160		Longmoor Military Rly
Maj.Gen. Frank S.Ross	4382	USA0–6–0T		Longmoor Military Rly
Major-General McMullen	9250	WD2–8–0		Longmoor Military Rly
Malay States	5615	Jubilee	1934	London Midland & Scottish Rly

[1] Renamed *The Great Marquess* within a fortnight of introduction.

[2] Rebuilt by Thompson to class K1 in December 1945, and renumbered 1997 in 1946. It was the prototype for Edward Thompson's K1 class, of which seventy were built after nationalization. This engine, however, was the only one to carry a name.

[3] Altered from 2–2–2 to 2–4–0 in August 1873.

[4] Renamed *David MacIver* in April 1903.

[5] Originally named *Lord of Dunvegan*. Renamed in March 1939.

[6] 1ft 11½in gauge.

[7] Transferred to the Isle of Wight by the Southern Railway in July 1932 as no. W3 *Ryde*.

[8] Formerly an 0–4–0T named *Magnus*.

[9] Renamed *Quentin Durward* in March 1907.

[10] Later rebuilt as an 0–4–2T and renamed *Magnet*.

[11] Built for the South Devon Railway.

[12] Built for the Severn & Wye & Severn Bridge Railway.

[13] 2ft gauge.

[14] Built for the London & South Western Railway, to Robert Urie's design. Nameplates fitted by the Southern Railway in 1925.

[15] Renamed *The South Staffordshire Regiment* in July 1934.

[16] Originally named *Atbara*. Temporarily renamed *Maine* for a City Imperial Volunteers' Special Train on 29 October 1900, and *Royal Sovereign* for Queen Victoria's funeral train on 2 February 1901.

[17] 3ft gauge.

[18] Originally entered service as no. 2 *Bedlington*.

Name	Number	Class	Date	Railway
Malcolm Graeme	2685	D11/2	10/1924	London & North Eastern Rly
Mallard	**4468**	**A4**	**3/1938**	**London & North Eastern Railway**
Malmesbury Abbey	4062	Star	5/1922	Great Western Rly
Malta	3407	Atbara	9/1901	Great Western Rly
Malta	3407	City	11/1908	Great Western Rly
Malta	2177	George V	7/1911	London & North Western Rly
Malta G.C.	5616	Jubilee	1934	London Midland & Scottish Rly
Maltby Colliery	56012	56	1977	British Railways
Maltby Colliery	56114	56	1983	British Railways
Malton	181	Windsor	12/1865	Stockton & Darlington Rly
Malvern	929	Schools	7/1934	Southern Rly
Malvern Abbey	4066	Star	12/1922	Great Western Rly [19]
Mammoth	61	0–4–2	1838	Liverpool & Manchester Rly

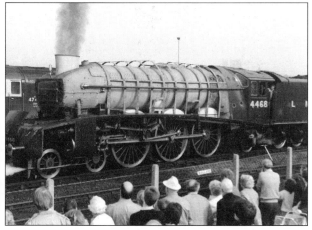

An unusual photograph of LNER A4 class no. 4468 *Mallard* without streamlining. The locomotive was undergoing steam trials after extensive restoration at the National Railway Museum, York, in 1988. (*Photo: Author*)

Name	Number	Class	Date	Railway
Mammoth	45	0–4–0	6/1841	Midland Counties Rly
Mammoth	–	Caesar	4/1848	Great Western Rly (bg)
Mammoth	247	cCrewe	10/1849	London & North Western Rly
Mammoth	978	S/Bloomer	1854	London & North Western Rly
Mammoth	513	Dreadnought	1885	London & North Western Rly
Mammoth	645	2Precursor	1/1905	London & North Western Rly
Mam Tor	60082	60	12/1991	British Railways
Manchester	–	0–4–0	1838	Manchester & Bolton Rly
Manchester	53	2–2–2	10/1840	Stockton & Darlington Rly
Manchester	30	2–2–2	2/1841	Manchester & Leeds Rly
Manchester	–	0–4–0T	1916	Woolwich Arsenal [20]
Manchester City	2870	B17/4	5/1937	London & North Eastern Rly [21]
Manchester City	2871	B17/4	6/1937	London & North Eastern Rly [22]
Manchester City	2871	B2	8/1945	London & North Eastern Rly [23]
Manchester United	2862	B17/4	1/1937	London & North Eastern Rly
Manipur Road	5290	J94	1945	Longmoor Military Rly
Manitoba	5558	Jubilee	1934	London Midland & Scottish Rly

Name	Number	Class	Date	Railway
Manna	2553	A3	12/1924	London & North Eastern Rly [24]
Manna	2596	A3	2/1930	London & North Eastern Rly
(Mannertreu)	**–**	**4–6–2**	**1937**	**Bressingham Steam Museum [25]**
Mannin	**16**	**2–4–0T**	**1926**	**Isle of Man Rly [26]**
Man of Kent	27	2–2–2	12/1842	South Eastern Rly
Manorbier Castle	5005	Castle	6/1927	Great Western Rly
Mansion House	63	51	1903	London, Tilbury & Southend Rly
Manston	**21C170**	**BB**	**11/1947**	**Southern Rly**
Manton Colliery	58047	58	10/1986	British Railways
Manton Grange	6822	Grange	1/1937	Great Western Rly
Maplehurst	586	E5	12/1903	London, Brighton & South Coast Rly [27]
Mappa Mundi	31405	31/4	1960	British Railways
Marathon	517	Precedent	9/1878	London & North Western Rly
Marathon	1542	Prince/W	11/1919	London & North Western Rly
Marazion	3340	Bulldog	1/1900	Great Western Rly
Marble Hall	5907	Hall	5/1931	Great Western Rly
Marchioness	10	S/Goods	8/1873	Cambrian Railways
Marchioness of Stafford	507	Dreadnought	1885	London & North Western Rly
Marchwood Military Port	47213	47/0	1965	British Railways
Marcia	**12**	**0–4–0T**	**1923**	**Kent & East Sussex Rly**
Marco Polo	3339	Bulldog	1/1900	Great Western Rly
Maresfield	267	D1	5/1882	London, Brighton & South Coast Rly
Margam Abbey	4069	Star	1/1923	Great Western Rly [28]
Margaret	**1378**	**0–6–0ST**	**11/1878**	**Great Western Rly [29]**
Margaret	**–**	**0–4–0ST**	**1894**	**Groudle Glen Rly [30]**
(Margaret Ethel – Thomas Alfred Naylor)	**D4067**	**10**	**1961**	**British Railways**
Marguerite	4114	Flower	7/1908	Great Western Rly
Marigold	4115	Flower	7/1908	Great Western Rly
Maristow	3282	Duke	2/1897	Great Western Rly
Maristowe	3282	Bulldog	7/1907	Great Western Rly [31]
(Mark)	**08195**	**08**	**1956**	**British Railways**
Markham Colliery	58003	58	1983	British Railways
Markinch	157	157	6/1877	North British Rly [32]
Mark Lane	68	51	1903	London, Tilbury & Southend Rly
Mark Twain	86	Prince/W	1/1914	London & North Western Rly
Marland	2	0–6–0T	1910	Torrington & Marland Rly [33]
Marlas Grange	6841	Grange	9/1937	Great Western Rly
Marlborough	1523	Newton	11/1866	London & North Western Rly
Marlborough	1523	rPrecedent	4/1893	London & North Western Rly
Marlborough	3303	Badminton	7/1894	Great Western Rly
Marlborough	68	B4	9/1901	London, Brighton & South Coast Rly
Marlborough	2022	2Experiment	5/1909	London & North Western Rly
Marlborough	20	0–6–2T	c.1923	Longmoor Military Rly [34]
Marlborough	922	Schools	11/1933	Southern Rly
Marmion	152	Canute	7/1858	London & South Western Rly
Marmion	667	Problem	c.1863	London & North Western Rly
Marmion	152	SFG	4/1878	London & South Western Rly
Marmion	469	2Precursor	6/1907	London & North Western Rly
Marmion	60132	A1	10/1948	British Railways (Eastern Region)
Marne	666	C	10/1891	North British Rly
Marne	511	11F	12/1922	Great Central Rly
Marquis	102	bCrewe	3/1847	London & North Western Rly
Marquis	470	0–6–0T	12/1863	Great Northern Rly [35]

[19] Renamed *Sir Robert Horne* in May 1935 and *Viscount Horne* in August 1937.

[20] 18in gauge.

[21] Renamed *Tottenham Hotspur* in May 1937. In September 1937 it was further renamed *City of London*, and was streamlined for working the 'East Anglian' express.

[22] Rebuilt to class B2, August 1945.

[23] Date rebuilt from class B17/4. Renamed *Royal Sovereign* in April 1946.

[24] Renamed *Prince of Wales* in December 1926.

[25] 15in gauge. Built by Krupp for a German miniature railway.

[26] 3ft gauge.

[27] Rebuilt to class E5x, January 1911.

[28] Renamed *Westminster Abbey* in May 1923 and rebuilt to Castle class as no. 5089.

[29] Built for the North Pembrokeshire & Fishguard Railway. The Gwendraeth Valleys Railway purchased no. 1378 *Margaret* from the GWR in 1910 or 1911 as their no. 2. They sold it to the Kidwelly Tinplate Co. Ltd in 1923. It survived the closure of the works in 1941 and has lasted into preservation.

[30] 2ft gauge.

[31] To correct a spelling error, the name was changed to *Maristow* by about 1908.

[32] Formerly named *Dumbarton*.

[33] 3ft gauge. The Torrington & Marland Railway was rebuilt to standard gauge and formed part of the Southern Railway's Halwill–Torrington line.

[34] Formerly North Stafford Railway class New L, no. 158. Rebuilt by LMS in 1925.

[35] Reputed to have carried this name on the West Yorkshire Railway, for which it was built.

Name	Number	Class	Date	Railway
Marquis	6	S/Goods	7/1873	Cambrian Railways
Marquis	1143	1Precursor	8/1874	London & North Western Rly
Marquis Douro	–	0-4-2	1838	Bolton & Leigh Rly [36]
Marquis Douro	124	aCrewe	3/1850	London & North Western Rly
Marquis Douro	124	Samson	2/1865	London & North Western Rly
Marquis Douro	124	Whitworth	3/1893	London & North Western Rly
Marrington Hall	4943	Hall	7/1929	Great Western Rly
Marron	3	0-4-2	8/1847	Cockermouth & Workington Rly
Marron	12	2-4-0T	1850	Whitehaven, Cleator & Egremont Rly [37]
Mars	12	2-2-0	1830	Liverpool & Manchester Rly
Mars	15	Venus	12/1838	London & South Western Rly
Mars	23	?	1840	Newcastle & Carlisle Rly [38]
Mars	–	2-2-2	4/1840	Great Western Rly (bg)
Mars	–	2-2-2	1/1841	London & Brighton Rly [39]
Mars	–	Priam	7/1841	Great Western Rly (bg)
Mars	39	0-4-2	6/1848	Manchester, Sheffield & Lincolnshire Rly
Mars	15	2Sussex	5/1852	London & South Western Rly
Mars	27	0-6-0	7/1853	Taff Vale Rly
Mars	3	0-4-2	7/1857	Whitehaven & Furness Junction Rly
Mars	153	Panther	10/1860	Stockton & Darlington Rly
Mars	2	A	6/1864	Metropolitan Rly
Mars	1386	0-6-0ST	12/1866	Great Western Rly [40]
Mars	15	2Vesuvius	8/1870	London & South Western Rly
Mars	1	0-4-2T	1885	Longmoor Military Rly [41]
Mars	3341	Bulldog	1/1900	Great Western Rly
Mars	1977	Alfred	7/1903	London & North Western Rly
Mars	5698	Jubilee	1936	London Midland & Scottish Rly
Mars	HMF 13.915	0-6-0DH	1944	Longmoor Military Rly [42]
Mars II	–	0-4-0ST	1948	Snibston Discovery Park
Marseilles	98	E1	10/1874	London, Brighton & South Coast Rly
Marshall	286	2-4-0	4/1861	Lancashire & Yorkshire Rly
Marske	101	Pierremont	9/1855	Stockton & Darlington Rly
Martello	62	A1	10/1875	London, Brighton & South Coast Rly
Martham	–	4-4-0T	3/1879	Yarmouth & North Norfolk Rly
Martin	129	aCrewe	11/1850	London & North Western Rly [43]
Martin	129	DX	c.1860	London & North Western Rly
Martin	793	Samson	2/1864	London & North Western Rly
Martin	793	Whitworth	5/1894	London & North Western Rly [44]
Mary	1	0-6-0ST	1880	Torrington & Marland Rly [45]
Mary	–	0-4-0DM	1932	Middleton Rly
Mary Ann	–	4wDM	1917	Festiniog Rly [46]
Maryport	4	2-4-0	9/1847	Whitehaven & Furness Junction Rly [47]
Mary Queen of Scots	37401	37/4	1965	British Railways
Mary Somerville	60051	60	9/1991	British Railways
M.A. SMITH	08790	08	1960	British Railways
Mastiff	44	0-4-0	11/1840	Midland Counties Rly
Mastiff	150	Panther	5/1860	Stockton & Darlington Rly
Mastodon	119	bCrewe	3/1849	London & North Western Rly [48]
Mastodon	625	S/Bloomer	1854	London & North Western Rly
Mastodon	479	Samson	5/1879	London & North Western Rly
Mastodon	479	Whitworth	3/1892	London & North Western Rly
Matruh	5275	J94	1945	Longmoor Military Rly
Matthew Murray	–	0-4-0ST	1943	Middleton Rly
Matt. Plummer	21	0-6-0	12/1839	Newcastle & Carlisle Rly
Maude	673	C	12/1891	North British Rly
(Maunsell)	22	USA	1943	Kent & East Sussex Rly [49]
Mauretania CL	40011	40	5/1959	British Railways [50]
Mauritius	3405	Atbara	9/1901	Great Western Rly
Mauritius	3405	City	9/1902	Great Western Rly
Mauritius	5617	Jubilee	1934	London Midland & Scottish Rly
Mawddwy	–	0-6-0ST	1865	Mawddwy Rly [51]
May	–	0-4-0ST	1915	Steamtown, Carnforth
May	2	0-4-0DM	1957	Swanage Rly
Mayfield	23	D1	8/1875	London, Brighton & South Coast Rly
(Mayflower)	1306	B1	4/1948	British Railways (Eastern Region) [52]
Mayflower	61397	B1	6/1951	British Railways (Eastern Region)
Mayflower	47558	47/4	1964	British Railways
Mayor	108	bCrewe	7/1847	London & North Western Rly
Mazda	–	0-4-0DE	1950	Airfield Line
Mazeppa	–	Priam	3/1841	Great Western Rly (bg)
Mazeppa	53	Mazeppa	3/1847	London & South Western Rly
Mazeppa	33	Venus	2/1849	East Lancashire Rly
Mazeppa	234	aCrewe	3/1849	London & North Western Rly
Mazeppa	2111	4-4-0ST	5/1859	Great Western Rly (bg) [53]
Mazeppa	28	Small Pass	3/1863	Cambrian Railways
Mazeppa	234	Problem	c.1863	London & North Western Rly
Mazeppa	53	Lion	7/1865	London & South Western Rly
Mazeppa	667	2Experiment	11/1906	London & North Western Rly
McConnell	26	0-6-0	1858	South Staffordshire Rly
McMurdo	71438	J94	1/1945	Longmoor Military Rly [54]
Meadowbank	158	165	5/1877	North British Rly [55]
Meaford No 4	–	0-6-0DH	1964	Foxfield Steam Rly
Medea	46	2-2-2	1838	Grand Junction Rly
Medea	–	Priam	3/1842	Great Western Rly (bg)
Medea	54	Mazeppa	5/1847	London & South Western Rly
Medea	46	bCrewe	4/1848	London & North Western Rly
Medea	623	S/Bloomer	1854	London & North Western Rly
Medea	54	Lion	8/1865	London & South Western Rly
Medea	995	Samson	5/1879	London & North Western Rly
Medea	995	Whitworth	1895	London & North Western Rly
Medina	W1	E1	1/1879	Southern Rly [56]
Medina	340	G	12/1881	London, Brighton & South Coast Rly
Medina	W1	0-6-0ST	1902	Southern Rly [57]
Medite	37079	37/0	1962	British Railways
Medusa	54	2-2-2	1838	Grand Junction Rly
Medusa	–	Priam	6/1842	Great Western Rly (bg)
Medusa	54	aCrewe	6/1846	London & North Western Rly
Medusa	1	Medusa	9/1846	East Lancashire Rly
Medusa	55	Mazeppa	2/1847	London & South Western Rly

[36] The name is sometimes given as *Marquis of Douro*.

[37] Became Furness Railway no. 108.

[38] Either 0-6-0 or 0-4-2. Became North Eastern Railway no. 471 in 1862.

[39] On the dissolution of the locomotive pool between the London & Brighton and the South Eastern Railways, became SER no. 55.

[40] Built for the West Cornwall Railway.

[41] 18in gauge. Came from the School of Military Engineering, Chatham, who in turn obtained it from the Royal Arsenal Railway at Woolwich. The boiler was retained for instructional purposes, and went to the Museum of Army Transport, Beverley.

[42] 750mm gauge. Built by Gmeinder & Co. of Mosbach (works no. 4177), 1944. Originally used in Germany for hauling V2 rockets.

[43] Previously Liverpool & Manchester Railway 2-2-2 no. 70. Became a London & North Western engine in 1846.

[44] Transferred to Engineer's Department, May 1923–April 1936, and renamed *Engineer Watford*.

[45] 3ft gauge. The Torrington & Marland Railway was rebuilt to standard gauge and formed part of the Southern Railway's Halwill–Torrington line.

[46] 1ft 11½in gauge.

[47] Later renamed *Petrel*.

[48] Rebuilt from Liverpool & Manchester Railway 0-4-2 no. 63. Became London & North Western property in 1846.

[49] Formerly BR no. 30065 and Southern Railway no. 65.

[50] Originally no. D211 *Mauretania*.

[51] Became Cambrian Railways no. 30.

[52] Originally no. 61306 and unnamed.

[53] Built for the South Devon Railway.

[54] Also named *Sapper* at WD Bicester.

[55] Originally named *North-Berwick* (with a hyphen).

[56] Formerly London, Brighton & South Coast Railway no. 136 *Brindisi*.

[57] Formerly Freshwater, Yarmouth & Newport Railway no. 1. Named *Medina* by the Southern Railway after 1928. Previously owned by Pauling & Co., contractors (their no. 56 *Northolt*), and purchased by FYNR in 1913. Built in 1902, it was the most modern steam locomotive ever to work in the Isle of Wight (apart from the loco part of a steam railcar).

Name	Number	Class	Date	Railway	Name	Number	Class	Date	Railway
Medusa	47	0–6–0	11/1849	Manchester, Sheffield & Lincolnshire Rly	*Mercury*	14	2Sussex	5/1852	London & South Western Rly
Medusa	999	L/Bloomer	1851	London & North Western Rly	*Mercury*	371	aCrewe	6/1855	London & North Western Rly
Medusa	55	Gem	6/1863	London & South Western Rly	*Mercury*	42	0–6–0	1857	Taff Vale Rly
Medusa	6	A	6/1864	Metropolitan Rly	*Mercury*	151	Panther	6/1860	Stockton & Darlington Rly
Medusa	2058	Dreadnought	1885	London & North Western Rly	*Mercury*	4	A	6/1864	Metropolitan Rly
Medusa	366	2Precursor	5/1905	London & North Western Rly	*Mercury*	14	2Vesuvius	8/1870	London & South Western Rly
Medway	6	2–2–0	11/1842	London, Brighton & South Coast Rly [58]	*Mercury*	749	Precedent	9/1878	London & North Western Rly
Megaera	–	0–4–0	1914	Woolwich Arsenal [59]	*Mercury*	1300	2–4–0ST	12/1878	Great Western Rly [64]
Megatherium	212	aCrewe	5/1848	London & North Western Rly	*Mercury*	749	rPrecedent	5/1895	London & North Western Rly
Meg Dods	410	Scott	4/1914	North British Rly	*Mercury*	3321	Duke	4/1899	Great Western Rly
Meg Merrilies	243	Scott	9/1911	North British Rly	*Mercury*	70020	Britannia	7/1951	British Railways
Meg Merrilies	60115	A1	9/1948	British Railways (Eastern Region)	*(Mercury)*	**25185**	**25/2**	**1965**	**British Railways** [65]
Meirionydd	**–**	**Bo-Bo**	**1973**	**Bala Lake Rly** [60]	**Merddyn Emrys**	**10**	**0–4–4–0F**	**1879**	**Festiniog Rly** [66]
Melbourne	3406	Atbara	9/1901	Great Western Rly	*Merddyn Emrys*	47281	47/0	1965	British Railways
Melbourne	3406	City	1/1908	Great Western Rly	*Mere Hall*	7915	M/Hall	3/1950	British Railways (Western Region)
Meld	D9003	Deltic	3/1961	British Railways	*Merehead*	56031	56	1977	British Railways
Melior	**–**	**0–4–2ST**	**1924**	**Sittingbourne & Kemsley Light Rly** [61]	*Merevale Hall*	5971	Hall	4/1937	Great Western Rly
Melisande	753	King Arthur	1/1923	Southern Rly [62]	*Meridian*	–	Wolf	8/1840	Great Western Rly (bg)
Melisande	73085	5MT	8/1955	British Railways	*Merion*	17	0–6–0ST	8/1862	Cambrian Railways
Melling	–	Hawthorn	5/1865	Great Western Rly (bg)	*Merkland*	–	0–6–0T	1912	Llanelly & Mynydd Mawr Rly [67]
Melmerby Hall	6982	M/Hall	1/1948	Great Western Rly	*Merlin*	27	2–2–2	1838	Grand Junction Rly
Melrose	478	Abbotsford	6/1877	North British Rly	*Merlin*	–	0–4–2	5/1842	Swansea Vale Rly [68]
Melton	2543	A3	6/1924	London & North Eastern Rly	*Merlin*	27	aCrewe	10/1843	London & North Western Rly
Melton Constable	1	0–6–0T	1874	Lynn & Fakenham Rly [63]	*Merlin*	27	bCrewe	10/1854	London & North Western Rly
Melton Hall	2838	B17/1	3/1933	London & North Eastern Rly	*Merlin*	3260	Duke	9/1895	Great Western Rly
Memnon	356	bCrewe	2/1855	London & North Western Rly	*Merlin*	1978	Alfred	7/1903	London & North Western Rly
Memnon	62	Ulysses	8/1856	East Lancashire Rly	*Merlin*	740	King Arthur	3/1919	Southern Rly [69]
Memnon	356	DX	c.1860	London & North Western Rly	*Merlin*	4486	A4	3/1937	London & North Eastern Rly
Memnon	736	Samson	7/1864	London & North Western Rly	**Merlin**	**1371**	**0–4–0ST**	**1939**	**Swindon & Cricklade Rly** [70]
Memnon	736	Whitworth	1/1892	London & North Western Rly	**Merlin**	**231**	**0–6–0DM**	**1951**	**Keighley & Worth Valley Rly**
Menai	206	DX	c.1860	London & North Western Rly	*Merlin*	73080	5MT	6/1955	British Railways
Mendelssohn	92035	92		British Railways	*(Merlin)*	**73096**	**5MT**	**11/1955**	**British Railways** [71]
Mendip	3323	Duke	6/1899	Great Western Rly	*Merlin*	33046	33/0	1961	British Railways
(Mendip)	**08032**	**08**	**1953**	**British Railways**	*Merlin*	47100	47/0	1963	British Railways
Menelaus	29	2–2–2	12/1846	Manchester, Sheffield & Lincolnshire Rly	*Mermaid*	51	Enigma	6/1870	London, Chatham & Dover Rly [72]
Menelaus	**–**	**0–6–0ST**	**1935**	**Pontypool & Blaenavon Rly**	*Mermaid*	–	0–4–0ST	1898	Fishguard & Rosslare Railways & Harbours Co.
Mentone	141	E1	3/1879	London, Brighton & South Coast Rly	*Merrie Carlisle*	72	2–2–2	1859	Lancaster & Carlisle Rly
Mentor	–	Priam	8/1841	Great Western Rly (bg)	*Merrie Carlisle*	860	Precedent	5/1877	London & North Western Rly
Mentor	56	Mazeppa	3/1847	London & South Western Rly	*Merrie Carlisle*	860	rPrecedent	11/1894	London & North Western Rly
Mentor	37	0–4–2	4/1848	Manchester, Sheffield & Lincolnshire Rly	*Merry Hampton*	2565	A3	7/1924	London & North Eastern Rly
Mentor	56	Gem	6/1863	London & South Western Rly	*Mersey*	16	0–6–0	?	St Helens Canal & Rly
Mentor	26051	EM1	1/1953	British Railways	*Mersey*	16	2–2–2	9/1840	Manchester & Leeds Rly
Merchant	90	Peel	2/1855	Stockton & Darlington Rly	*Mersey*	77	aCrewe	11/1845	Grand Junction Rly
Merchant Taylors	910	Schools	12/1932	Southern Rly	*Mersey*	13	0–6–0	3/1849	Birkenhead, Lancashire & Cheshire Junction Rly [73]
Merchant Venturer	43125	43	4/1979	British Railways	*Mersey*	–	?	?	Midland Counties Rly
Mercury	11	2–2–0	1830	Liverpool & Manchester Rly	*Mersey*	23	2–4–0	8/1852	Birkenhead, Lancashire & Cheshire Junction Rly [74]
Mercury	14	Venus	12/1838	London & South Western Rly					
Mercury	–	2–2–2	9/1839	Great Western Rly (bg)	*Mersey*	–	Caesar	1/1857	Great Western Rly (bg)
Mercury	–	2–2–2	1841	London, Brighton & South Coast Rly	*Mersey*	77	Problem	c.1860	London & North Western Rly
Mercury	57	2–2–2	7/1841	South Eastern Rly	*Mersey*	23	0–6–0ST	3/1868	Brecon & Merthyr Rly
Mercury	–	Priam	10/1841	Great Western Rly (bg)	*Mersey*	10	II	12/1887	Mersey Rly
Mercury	11	Bacchus	8/1846	East Lancashire Rly	*Mersey*	3322	Duke	4/1899	Great Western Rly
Mercury	88	2–2–2	12/1849	Manchester, Sheffield & Lincolnshire Rly	*Mersey*	3322	Bulldog	11/1904	Great Western Rly
					Mersey	665	2Precursor	6/1907	London & North Western Rly
					Merseysider	**8**	**0–4–0DM**	**1964**	**Talyllyn Rly** [75]
					Merstham	3	2–2–2	7/1839	London & Brighton Rly

[58] Built for London & Brighton and South Eastern joint stock.

[59] Date of purchase. Petrol/mechanical. 18in gauge.

[60] 2ft gauge.

[61] 2ft 6in gauge.

[62] Nameplates fitted in 1925.

[63] Built for the Cornwall Minerals Railway.

[64] Built for the South Devon Railway.

[65] Occasionally carries the number D7535.

[66] 1ft 11½in gauge.

[67] Allotted no. 937 by GWR, but never actually carried.

[68] Originally Liverpool & Manchester Railway no. 76 *Bat*, and the name was retained on sale to the Swansea Vale Railway in January 1856. Renamed *Merlin* in 1861.

[69] Built for the London & South Western Railway to Robert Urie's design. Nameplates fitted by the Southern Railway in 1925.

[70] Also named *Myrddin*, in Welsh.

[71] Restored as no. 73080.

[72] Name removed by W. Kirtley when number applied.

[73] Later renamed *Forerunner*, and passed to the London & North Western Railway.

[74] Later renamed *Etna*, and passed to the London & North Western Railway.

[75] 2ft 3in gauge.

Name	Number	Class	Date	Railway
Merstone	W27	O2	6/1890	Southern Rly [76]
Merthyr	–	0-4-2	1841	Taff Vale Rly
Merthyr	6	0-6-0	1861	Taff Vale Rly
Merton	14	2-2-2WT	5/1852	London, Brighton & South Coast Rly [77]
Merton	45	A1	6/1877	London, Brighton & South Coast Rly
Merton	4	0-4-0	1880	Torrington & Marland Rly [78]
Messenger	324	aCrewe	11/1853	London & North Western Rly
Messenger	1111	1Experiment	1884	London & North Western Rly
Messenger	519	2Precursor	5/1905	London & North Western Rly
Met	–	0-4-0ST	1909	**Darlington Railway Centre and Museum**
Meteor	3	0-2-2	1830	Liverpool & Manchester Rly [79]
Meteor	3	0-4-0	9/1835	Newcastle & Carlisle Rly
Meteor	–	Wolf	11/1840	Great Western Rly (bg)
Meteor	50	2-2-2	6/1843	Stockton & Darlington Rly [80]
Meteor	57	Mazeppa	4/1847	London & South Western Rly
Meteor	115	aCrewe	5/1849	London & North Western Rly [81]
Meteor	2098	4-4-0ST	11/1851	Great Western Rly (bg) [82]
Meteor	–	2-2-2	6/1860	London, Chatham & Dover Rly [83]
Meteor	57	Gem	6/1863	London & South Western Rly
Meteor	863	Precedent	5/1877	London & North Western Rly
Meteor	3320	Duke	4/1899	Great Western Rly
Meteor	2242	George V	5/1913	London & North Western Rly
Meteor	6128	Royal Scot	8/1927	London Midland & Scottish Rly [84]
Meteor	5734	Jubilee	1936	London Midland & Scottish Rly
Meteor	31	0-6-0T	1950	**South Devon Rly [85]**
Meteor	37178	37/0	1963	British Railways
Meteor	86216	86/2	1965	British Railways
Metis	–	Caesar	3/1855	Great Western Rly (bg)
Meuse	45	0-4-2	4/1843	Manchester & Leeds Rly
Mexborough 41F	08880	08	1960	British Railways
Meynell	115	Edward Pease	8/1856	Stockton & Darlington Rly
Michael Faraday	18	Bo-Bo	1922	Metropolitan Rly [86]
Michael Faraday	91013	91	4/1990	British Railways
Mickleham	4	D1	1/1874	London, Brighton & South Coast Rly
Midas	23	2-2-2	1/1846	Manchester, Sheffield & Lincolnshire Rly
Midas	–	Caesar	11/1854	Great Western Rly (bg)
Middlesbro'	9	Tory	8/1839	Stockton & Darlington Rly
Middlesbrough	2855	B17/4	4/1936	London & North Eastern Rly
Middlesex	1652	2Experiment	11/1909	London & North Western Rly
Middleton	96	Peel	6/1855	Stockton & Darlington Rly
Middleton	399	E5	7/1904	London, Brighton & South Coast Rly
Middleton Hall	4944	Hall	7/1929	Great Western Rly
Midge	–	0-4-0T	11/1870	London & North Western Rly
Midget	–	0-4-0ST	1899	Lancashire & Yorkshire Rly
Midhurst	468	E4	5/1898	London, Brighton & South Coast Rly
Midland	08434	08	1958	British Railways
Midlander	5	0-4-0DM	1940	**Talyllyn Rly [87]**

North Bristol Railway H class 4-4-2 no. 875 *Midlothian*, at Edinburgh on 20 September 1910. (*Photo: LCGB Ken Nunn Collection*)

Name	Number	Class	Date	Railway
Midland Railway Centre	37248	37/0	1964	British Railways
Midlothian	875	H	8/1906	North British Rly
Midlothian	60151	A1	6/1949	British Railways (Eastern Region)
Miers	3	0-6-0WT	6/1862	Neath & Brecon Rly [88]
Mignonette	4116	Flower	7/1908	Great Western Rly
Milan	303	Lyons	1/1878	London, Brighton & South Coast Rly
Mile End	54	51	1900	London, Tilbury & Southend Rly
Miles	–	Sir Watkin	8/1866	Great Western Rly (bg)
Miles Beevor	4485	A4	2/1937	London & North Eastern Rly [89]
Miles McInnes	2507	George V*	11/1910	London & North Western Rly
Milford	3	0-4-2ST	3/1858	Cambrian Railways
Milford	–	?	?	Llanidloes & Newtown Rly [90]
Milford	2	2-2-2T	1863	Pembroke & Tenby Rly [91]
Militades	–	0-4-0ST	1889	Woolwich Arsenal [92]
Miller	81	0-6-0	2/1846	Stockton & Darlington Rly [93]
Millfield	–	0-4-0CT	1942	**Bressingham Steam Museum**
Millgrove	9	0-6-0ST	1913	Cleator & Workington Junction Rly
Millhouses 41C	08870	08	1960	British Railways
Milligan Hall	4945	Hall	8/1929	Great Western Rly
Mill Reef	27	4wDM	1939	**West Lancashire Light Rly [94]**
Millwall	38	A1	6/1878	London, Brighton & South Coast Rly [95]
Milner	2	4-4-0T	1879	Nidd Valley Light Rly [96]
Milner	–	0-6-0T	1909	Nidd Valley Light Rly [97]
Milngarvie	162	165	5/1877	North British Rly [98]
Milngavie	326	317	1862	North British Rly [99]
Milngavie	225	72	1882	North British Rly
Milo	25	0-4-0	1832	Liverpool & Manchester Rly
Milo	47	2-2-2	1836	Liverpool & Manchester Rly
Milo	–	Priam	6/1841	Great Western Rly (bg)

[76] Formerly London & South Western Railway (and Southern Railway) no. 184. Name applied by the Southern Railway on transfer to the Isle of Wight.

[77] Name applied in May 1871.

[78] 3ft gauge. The Torrington & Marland Railway was rebuilt to standard gauge and formed part of the Southern Railway's Halwill–Torrington line.

[79] Originally named *Wildfire*, but renamed before entering service.

[80] May have been delivered in July 1843.

[81] Formerly Liverpool & Manchester Railway 2-2-2 no. 54. Became a London & North Western engine in 1846.

[82] Built for the South Devon Railway.

[83] Date purchased from R. & W. Hawthorn & Co., builders. There is a suggestion that

it and a sister engine *Eclipse* were built to Government order for use in the Crimea, and were left uncompleted when that conflict ended. Both had seen previous service, for *Meteor* had received a new firebox, while *Eclipse*'s firebox had been patched.

[84] Renamed *The Lovat Scouts* in April 1936.

[85] The modern, preserved South Devon Railway.

[86] Officially rebuilt from an earlier, unnamed, locomotive, but incorporating few if any of its components.

[87] 2ft 3in gauge.

[88] Originally *Anglesea* on the Anglesey Railway. Later became no. 42 of the Waterford & Limerick Railway in Ireland (5ft 3in gauge).

[89] Originally named *Kestrel*. Renamed in November 1947.

[90] Used at the opening of the line, 1859. May have gone to the Cambrian Railways.

[91] In 1896 became Great Western Railway no. 1360.

[92] 18in gauge.

[93] Edinburgh & Glasgow Railway no. 41, sold to the S&DR in 1854.

[94] 2ft gauge.

[95] Sold to the Admiralty in February 1918, and resold in November 1923 to the Shropshire & Montgomeryshire Railway as their no. 8 *Dido*.

[96] Formerly Metropolitan Railway no. 34.

[97] Replacement for previous engine in 1909.

[98] Later renamed *Loch Leven*.

[99] Previously named *Renton*.

Name	Number	Class	Date	Railway
Milo	43	1Hercules	11/1841	London & South Western Rly
Milo	16	2–2–2	5/1845	Manchester, Sheffield & Lincolnshire Rly
Milo	36	Phaeton	3/1849	East Lancashire Rly
Milo	43	2Hercules	12/1851	London & South Western Rly
Milo	43	2Vesuvius	1/1875	London & South Western Rly
Milton	1515	Newton	10/1866	London & North Western Rly
Milton	1515	rPrecedent	5/1890	London & North Western Rly
Milton	2055	Prince/W	1/1916	London & North Western Rly
Milton	2835	B17/1	7/1931	London & North Eastern Rly
Milton	92020	92		British Railways
Mina	8	0–4–0ST	5/1865	London & South Western Rly (ed)
Miner	29	Miner	6/1845	Stockton & Darlington Rly
Miner	–	0–4–0ST	11/1854	Redruth & Chasewater Rly [100]
Minerva	11	Venus	6/1838	London & South Western Rly
Minerva	87	2–4–0	12/1849	Manchester, Sheffield & Lincolnshire Rly
Minerva	–	Caesar	8/1853	Great Western Rly (bg)
Minerva	11	Minerva	5/1856	London & South Western Rly
Minerva	31	Small Pass	3/1863	Cambrian Railways
Minerva	9	A	7/1864	Metropolitan Rly
Minerva	1681	Newton	5/1868	London & North Western Rly
Minerva	11	Volcano	3/1873	London & South Western Rly
Minerva	1681	rPrecedent	2/1888	London & North Western Rly
Minerva	136	Prince/W	10/1915	London & North Western Rly
Minerva	27005	EM2	12/1954	British Railways
Minories	79	A1	7/1880	London, Brighton & South Coast Rly
Minoru	2561	A3	5/1925	London & North Eastern Rly
Minos	–	Priam	9/1841	Great Western Rly (bg)
Minos	46	1Hercules	2/1842	London & South Western Rly
Minos	46	2Hercules	9/1851	London & South Western Rly
Minotaur	51	2–4–0	9/1847	Manchester, Sheffield & Lincolnshire Rly
Minotaur	271	bCrewe	8/1851	London & North Western Rly
Minotaur	271	Newton	9/1870	London & North Western Rly
Minotaur	271	rPrecedent	6/1887	London & North Western Rly
Minotaur	5695	Jubilee	1936	London Midland & Scottish Rly
Mirage	**37032**	**37/0**	**1962**	**British Railways**
Miranda	341	aCrewe	7/1854	London & North Western Rly
Miranda	1194	Precedent	9/1878	London & North Western Rly
Miranda	1194	rPrecedent	2/1897	London & North Western Rly
Mirrlees Pioneer	37901	37/9	7/1963	British Railways
Mirvale	–	**0–4–0ST**	**8/1955**	**Middleton Rly**
Misterton Hall	6916	Hall	6/1941	Great Western Rly [101]
Mistlethrush	47284	47/0	1966	British Railways [102]
Mitcham	33	D1	5/1876	London, Brighton & South Coast Rly
Mobberley Hall	7916	M/Hall	4/1950	British Railways (Western Region)
Moel Fammau	60008	60	12/1992	British Railways [103]
Moel Hebog	–	**0–4–0DM**	**1955**	**Festiniog Rly [104]**
Moel Siabod	**5**	**0–4–2T**	**1896**	**Snowdon Mountain Rly [105]**
Moel Siabod	60018	60	10/1990	British Railways
Moel Tryfan	–	0–6–4T	1875	North Wales Narrow Gauge Rly [106]
Moel Tryfan	–	**0–4–2T**	**1953**	**Welsh Highland Rly [107]**
Moelwyn	–	**2–4–0DM**	**1918**	**Festiniog Rly [108]**
Mogul	–	Metro	8/1862	Great Western Rly (bg)
Mogul	527	2–6–0	1878	Great Eastern Rly
Mole	–	2–2–2	12/1884	London & South Western Rly (bg) [109]
Moliere	92010	92		Société Nationale des Chemins de fer Français
Molly	6909	0–4–0VB	1927	War Department
Moltke	456	4	6/1871	Manchester, Sheffield & Lincolnshire Rly [110]
Momus	14	2–2–2	4/1845	Manchester, Sheffield & Lincolnshire Rly
Mona	99	L/Scotchmen	3/1873	London, Chatham & Dover Rly
Mona	**5**	**2–4–0T**	**1874**	**Isle of Man Rly [111]**
Monarch	230	aCrewe	11/1848	London & North Western Rly
Monarch	–	Caesar	12/1853	Great Western Rly (bg)
Monarch	230	Problem	c.1860	London & North Western Rly
Monarch	3301	Badminton	7/1898	Great Western Rly
Monarch	419	2Precursor	6/1907	London & North Western Rly
Monarch	–	**0–4–4–0T**	**1953**	**Festiniog Rly [112]**
Monarch	D831	Warship	1/1961	British Railways
Monarch	50010	50	1968	British Railways
Monckton	**1**	**J94**	**1953**	**Yorkshire Dales Rly [113]**
Monk	8	2–2–2	4/1845	Chester & Birkenhead Rly [114]
Monkland	83	Clyde Bogie	10/1886	Highland Rly [115]
Monkton No 1	–	**0–6–0ST**	**1953**	**Yorkshire Dales Rly**
Monmouth Castle	5037	Castle	5/1935	Great Western Rly
Monmouthshire	1689	2Experiment	12/1909	London & North Western Rly
Monro	621	C	10/1889	North British Rly
Mons	648	C	2/1891	North British Rly
Mons	501	11F	9/1922	Great Central Rly
Mons Meg	2004	P2	7/1936	London & North Eastern Rly
Mons Meg	504	A2/2	11/1944	London & North Eastern Rly [116]
Montalban	**34**	**0–4–0WT**	**1913**	**West Lancashire Light Rly [117]**
Montgomery	5	0–4–2	10/1859	Cambrian Railways
Montgomery Castle	5016	Castle	7/1932	Great Western Rly
Mont Orgueil	–	0–4–2T	1886	Jersey Eastern Rly
Montpelier	111	E1	4/1877	London, Brighton & South Coast Rly
Montreal	3460	Bulldog	2/1904	Great Western Rly
Montrose	151	Canute	7/1858	London & South Western Rly
Montrose	151	SFG	4/1878	London & South Western Rly
Montrose	487	Abbotsford	10/1878	North British Rly [118]
Montrose	103	72	6/1881	North British Rly
(Monty)	6	4wDM	1936	Amberley Chalk Pits Museum [119]
Monty	**3**	**4wPetrol**	**1944**	**London & North Eastern Rly**
Moonstone	2583	2Precursor	1/1906	London & North Western Rly [120]
Moorbarrow	**47**	**0–6–0T**	**1955**	**Peak Rail plc**
Moor Hen	1472	George V	9/1911	London & North Western Rly

[100] 4ft gauge. First steamed on 1 December 1854. Altered to 0–4–2ST in the winter of 1855/6. Substantially rebuilt as 0–6–0ST in 1868, but a plate on the engine stated REDRUTH & CHASEWATER RAILWAY. MANUFACTURED AT DEVORAN WORKS 1869.

[101] Nameplates fitted in April 1946.

[102] Named *Mistlethrush* on one side and *Storm Cock* on the other.

[103] Originally named *Gypsum Queen II*.

[104] 1ft 11½in gauge.

[105] 800mm gauge rack and pinion locomotive.

[106] 1ft 11½in gauge, later no. 11 of the Welsh Highland Railway.

[107] 1ft 11½in gauge.

[108] 1ft 11½in gauge.

[109] Originally no. 9(?) *Stroud* of the Bristol & Gloucester Railway, a broad gauge concern which was later taken over by the Midland Railway; it was renumbered 265. In November 1855 it was sold to Thomas Brassey for working the North Devon Railway, another broad gauge line which afterwards passed to the London & South Western Railway. There it is thought to have become their *Mole*.

[110] 0–6–0ST. Built for Logan & Hemingway, contractors, who named it *Moltke*. Purchased by the MS&LR in May 1880.

[111] 3ft gauge.

[112] Meyer-type articulated locomotive built by Bagnalls of Stafford for Bowaters Lloyd Pulp & Paper Mills Ltd. Later went to the Welshpool & Llanfair Railway, where it was not a success, and from where it was bought privately for the Festiniog Railway.

[113] Originally built for the War Department.

[114] Formerly named *Birkenhead*.

[115] Originally named *Cadboll*. Renamed *Monkland* in 1900.

[116] Rebuild of no. 2004 above.

[117] 2ft gauge.

[118] Later renamed *Waverley* in 1880 on transfer to the Carlisle route following the fall of the first Tay Bridge.

[119] 3ft 2¼in gauge.

[120] Originally named *Teutonic*. Renamed *The Czar* in 1914, and again renamed *Moonstone* in October 1915 when 'Prince of Wales' class 4–6–0 no. 88 *Czar of Russia* was built.

Name	Number	Class	Date	Railway
Moorsom	–	4-2-0	1840	Taff Vale Rly [121]
Moray Firth	70053	Britannia	9/1954	British Railways
Morayshire	64	Duke	7/1874	Highland Rly [122]
Morayshire	246	D49/1	2/1928	London & North Eastern Rly
Morden	35	A1	6/1878	London, Brighton & South Coast Rly
Morecambe	82	2-4-0	1859	Lancaster & Carlisle Rly
Morecambe	163	Saltburn	1862	Stockton & Darlington Rly
Morecambe and Heysham	5526	Patriot	3/1933	London Midland & Scottish Rly [123]
Morehampton Grange	6853	Grange	11/1937	Great Western Rly
Moreton Hall	5908	Hall	6/1931	Great Western Rly
Morfa Grange	6866	Grange	3/1939	Great Western Rly
Morgan le Fay	750	King Arthur	10/1922	Southern Rly [124]
Morgan le Fay	73112	5MT	10/1955	British Railways
Morlais Castle	5038	Castle	6/1935	Great Western Rly
Morlaix	105	E1	9/1876	London, Brighton & South Coast Rly
Morning Star	–	Priam	1/1839	Great Western Rly (bg)
Morning Star	381	Sir Daniel	10/1866	Great Western Rly
Morning Star	4004	Star	2/1907	Great Western Rly
Morning Star	70021	Britannia	8/1951	British Railways
(Morning Star)	92207	9F	6/1959	British Railways
Morous	4	0-6-0ST	1866	Shropshire & Montgomeryshire Rly [125]
Morpeth	72	72	1880	North British Rly
Morthoe	34094	WC	10/1949	British Railways (Southern Region)
Mortimer	3302	Badminton	7/1898	Great Western Rly [126]
Moseley	16	4-2-0	2/1840	Birmingham & Gloucester Rly
Moseley	–	4wDM	1936	Moseley Railway Museum [127]
Moseley Hall	4946	Hall	8/1929	Great Western Rly
Mosquito	–	Metro	8/1862	Great Western Rly (bg)
Moss Bay	–	0-4-0ST	1920	Foxfield Steam Rly
Mostyn Hall	5985	Hall	10/1938	Great Western Rly
"Mother Shuter"	243	0-6-0	1852	Great Western Rly [128]
Mottram Hall	6956	Hall	3/1943	Great Western Rly [129]
Mountaineer	37	0-4-0ST	6/1863	Cambrian Railways
Mountaineer	3	0-4-0TT	1864	Festiniog Rly [130]
Mountaineer	–	0-4-4-0F	1866	Neath & Brecon Rly
Mountaineer	–	0-4-4-0F	1870	Burry Port & Gwendraeth Valley Rly [131]

Name	Number	Class	Date	Railway
Mountaineer	–	2-6-2T	1917	Festiniog Rly [132]
Mount Edgcumbe	3261	Duke	9/1895	Great Western Rly
Mount's Bay	6	2-4-0	1853	Llynvi & Ogmore Rly [133]
Mounts Bay	3283	Duke	2/1897	Great Western Rly
Mountsorrel	56062	56	1979	British Railways
Mouse	–	0-4-0ST	1899	Lancashire & Yorkshire Rly
Mozart	92005	92		British Railways
MR Mercury	1	4wDM	1950	East Lancashire Rly [134]
"Mrs Jonson"	53	2-2-2WT	1859	Oxford, Worcester & Wolverhampton Rly
Mudlark	–	?	?	Brassey [135]
Mudlark	F	?	c.1852	Oxford, Worcester & Wolverhampton Rly [136]
Muirtown	68	Duke	8/1874	Highland Rly [137]
Mulciber	–	0-4-0ST	1870	Aberford Rly [138]
Munich	156	E1	3/1881	London, Brighton & South Coast Rly
Munlochy	102	Yankee	10/1893	Highland Rly [139]
Munster	5740	Jubilee	1936	London Midland & Scottish Rly
Murdock	–	Hawthorn	5/1865	Great Western Rly (bg)
Murdock	1488	Newton	5/1866	London & North Western Rly
Murdock	1488	rPrecedent	11/1888	London & North Western Rly
Muricidae	47195	47/0	1965	British Railways
Muriel	–	0-8-0T	1894	Duffield Bank Rly [140]
Muriel	–	0-4-0DH	1966	Nene Valley Rly
Murray B. Hofmeyr	20137	20	1966	British Railways
Murray of Elibank	1245	B1	10/1947	London & North Eastern Rly [141]
Mursley Hall	6915	Hall	2/1941	Great Western Rly
Murthly	23	S/Goods	10/1863	Highland Rly [142]
Murthly Castle	145	Castle	1900	Highland Rly
Musselburgh	313	165	1/1878	North British Rly [143]
Musketeer	–	0-4-0TG	1946	Northamptonshire Ironstone Railway Trust
Mutual Improvement	56101	56	1981	British Railways
Myrddin	1371	0-4-0ST	1939	Swindon & Cricklade Rly [144]
Myrtle	78	Rose	8/1863	London, Chatham & Dover Rly
Myrtle	–	Metro	5/1864	Great Western Rly (bg)
Mysore	5586	Jubilee	1934	London Midland & Scottish Rly
Mytton Hall	5996	Hall	6/1940	Great Western Rly

[121] Norris-type locomotive, built in the USA between 1839 and 1842, and one of three purchased in 1845 (*Columbia* in 1846) from the Birmingham & Gloucester Railway. The others were *Columbia* and *Gloucester*.

[122] Renamed *Seafield* in about 1889.

[123] Rebuilt with taper boiler in February 1947.

[124] Built for the London & South Western Railway to Robert Urie's design. Nameplates fitted by the Southern Railway in 1925.

[125] Built by Manning Wardle of Leeds as a contractor's engine, and worked on the Stratford-on-Avon & Midland Junction Railway, where it was named *Crampton*. Sold in 1910 to the Shropshire & Montgomery-shire, and in 1924 transferred to the West Sussex Light Railway (previously the Hundred of Manhood & Selsey Tramway). It was scrapped when the line closed in 1936.

[126] Renamed *Charles Mortimer* in August 1904.

[127] 2ft gauge.

[128] Built for the West Midland Railway.

[129] Nameplates fitted in January 1947.

[130] 1ft 11½in gauge.

[131] Originally named *Pioneer*. These two Fairlies were quite separate engines. Neither was very successful.

[132] Ex-First World War locomotive by Alco (USA). 1ft 11½in gauge.

[133] Later became Great Western Railway no. 915.

[134] The modern, preserved East Lancashire Railway.

[135] Thomas Brassey contracted to maintain the track of the London & South Western Railway from 4 November 1839 to December 1853. He provided his own locomotives, of which *Mudlark* was one. Beyond their names, very little is known of them.

[136] Purchased for the opening of the OWWR on 1 May 1852 from contractors to the Great Northern Railway at Welwyn. It had disappeared by 1854.

[137] Originally named *Caithness-shire*, then *Caithness*, and finally *Muirtown*.

[138] Sold before 1912 to industrial service at Low Staithes Colliery, where it may have been renamed *Tiger*.

[139] Date taken into stock. Originally built by Dubs & Co. in 1891 for the Uruguay Eastern Railway, who could not pay for it. The Highland Railway bought all five engines at the bargain price of £1,500 each.

[140] 15in gauge. *Muriel* later went to the Ravenglass & Eskdale Railway, where it was rebuilt as an 0-8-2 tender engine and renamed *River Irt*.

[141] Nameplate only fitted in December 1947.

[142] Later renamed *Dalcross*.

[143] Originally named *Clydebank*.

[144] Also named *Merlin*.

Name	Number	Class	Date	Railway
Nab Gill	–	0–6–0T	1874	Ravenglass & Eskdale Rly [1]
Naiad	174	Undine	6/1860	London & South Western Rly
Nairn	36	M/Goods	4/1864	Highland Rly
Nairnshire	65	Duke	7/1874	Highland Rly [2]
(Naklo)	**10**	**0–6–0TT**	**1957**	**South Tynedale Rly** [3]
Namur	81	4–2–0	2/1847	South Eastern Rly
Nancy	20901	20	11/1959	Hunslet-Barclay Ltd [4]
Nanhoran Hall	4947	Hall	8/1929	Great Western Rly
Nannerth Grange	6826	Grange	2/1937	Great Western Rly
Nantclwyd	14	0–6–0ST	4/1862	Cambrian Railways [5]
Napier		0–4–0	?	Edinburgh & Glasgow Rly
Napier	917	S/Bloomer	1854	London & North Western Rly
Napier	5646	Jubilee	1934	London Midland & Scottish Rly
Naples	306	Lyons	4/1878	London, Brighton & South Coast Rly
Napoleon	380	bCrewe	11/1855	London & North Western Rly [6]
Napoleon	–	Victoria	8/1856	Great Western Rly (bg)
Napoleon	149	Canute	7/1858	London & South Western Rly
Napoleon	565	Problem	c.1860	London & North Western Rly
Napoleon	1311	2Precursor	3/1906	London & North Western Rly
Napoleon III	894	2–4–0	1868	Great Western Rly [7]
Narcissus	186	bCrewe	11/1847	London & North Western Rly
Narcissus	79	Rose	8/1863	London, Chatham & Dover Rly
Narcissus	604	Samson	9/1873	London & North Western Rly
Narcissus	604	Whitworth	11/1890	London & North Western Rly
Narcissus	4117	Flower	7/1908	Great Western Rly
Nasmyth	339	bCrewe	5/1854	London & North Western Rly
Nasmyth	919	Precedent	9/1878	London & North Western Rly
Nasmyth	919	rPrecedent	12/1893	London & North Western Rly
Natal Colony	3458	Bulldog	1/1904	Great Western Rly [8]
National Garden Festival Gateshead 1990	43114	43	3/1979	British Railways
National Railway Museum The First Ten Years 1975–1985	43038	43	12/1976	British Railways
Navarre	125	E1	7/1878	London, Brighton & South Coast Rly
Navvie	1	?	?	St Helens Canal & Rly
Naworth	36	0–6–0	1853	Newcastle & Carlisle Rly [9]
Naworth	**4**	**0–6–0DM**	**1952**	**South Tynedale Rly** [10]
Naworth Castle	2829	B17/1	4/1931	London & North Eastern Rly
Neath	1	2–4–0	?	Neath & Brecon Rly
Neath Abbey	–	0–4–2	1848	Taff Vale Rly
Neath Abbey	4070	Star	2/1923	Great Western Rly [11]
Neath Abbey	5090	Castle	4/1939	Great Western Rly [12]
Neath Abbey	**–**	**4wDM**	**1964**	**Moseley Railway Museum** [13]
Nederland Line	21C14	MN	2/1945	Southern Rly
Needlefield	1A	0–4–2T	5/1863	Highland Rly [14]
Neil Gow	2581	A3	11/1924	London & North Eastern Rly
(Nellie)	**D2875**	**0–4–0DE**	**1960**	**Gwili Rly**
Nelson	–	2–2–0	1833	Bolton & Leigh Rly
Nelson	15	0–4–0	1838	Newcastle & Carlisle Rly
Nelson	219	aCrewe	8/1848	London & North Western Rly
Nelson	–	Caesar	4/1853	Great Western Rly (bg)
Nelson	143	Nelson	7/1858	London & South Western Rly

Name	Number	Class	Date	Railway
Nelson	3017	3001	4/1892	Great Western Rly [15]
Nelson	3049	3031	2/1895	Great Western Rly [16]
Nelson	1979	Alfred	7/1903	London & North Western Rly
Nelson	5664	Jubilee	1935	London Midland & Scottish Rly
Nemesis	60	2–4–0	6/1848	Manchester, Sheffield & Lincolnshire Rly
Nemesis	–	Caesar	1/1855	Great Western Rly (bg)
Nene Valley Railway	31558	31/5		British Railways
Neptune	–	2–2–2	3/1838	Great Western Rly (bg)
Neptune	94	2–2–2	1847	Stockton & Darlington Rly [17]
Neptune	41	0–4–2	11/1848	Manchester, Sheffield & Lincolnshire Rly
Neptune	94	0–6–0	5/1867	Stockton & Darlington Rly
Neptune	1980	Alfred	8/1903	London & North Western Rly
Neptune	265	aSentinel	1928	London & North Eastern Rly

London & North Eastern Railway Sentinel steam railcar no. 265 *Neptune*, at Darlington on 12 November 1933. (*Photo: RAS Marketing*)

Name	Number	Class	Date	Railway
Neptune	5687	Jubilee	1936	London Midland & Scottish Rly
Neptune	50006	50	1968	British Railways
Neritidae	47368	47/3	1965	British Railways
Nero	–	Caesar	1/1855	Great Western Rly (bg)
Nestor	1387	0–6–0	c.1846	Great Western Rly [18]
Nestor	120	0–6–0	2/1854	Manchester, Sheffield & Lincolnshire Rly [19]
Nestor	366	aCrewe	5/1855	London & North Western Rly
Nestor	61	Ulysses	8/1856	East Lancashire Rly
Nestor	124	Acis	10/1862	London, Chatham & Dover Rly
Nestor	26052	EM1	1/1953	British Railways
Netherby	493	Abbotsford	1879	North British Rly
Nettle	35	cSentinel	1928	London & North Eastern Rly
Nettlestone	564	E4	12/1901	London, Brighton & South Coast Rly
Nevill	272	D1	5/1880	London, Brighton & South Coast Rly [20]

---

1. The name is sometimes given as *Nab Gyll*, but photographic evidence shows that *Nab Gill* was the name actually carried. The original Ravenglass & Eskdale Railway was officially 2ft 9in gauge, but 3ft according to a tape measure, and according to recently excavated sleeper blocks!
2. Later renamed *Dalraddy*.
3. 2ft gauge. Built in 1957 by Chrzanow, Poland (works no. 3459).
4. Built for British Railways.
5. Later became London & South Western Railway no. 458 *Jumbo*.
6. Later sold to the Lancaster & Carlisle

Railway; became London & North Western Railway no. 156 *Redstart*.
7. Built for the Llanelly Railway.
8. Said to have been named *Natal* at first, but this is not confirmed.
9. Became North Eastern Railway no. 484 in 1862.
10. 2ft gauge.
11. Rebuilt to Castle class as no. 5090, February 1923.
12. Rebuilt from Star class no. 4070.
13. 2ft gauge.
14. Originally an 0–4–0T built in 1863 for the Inverness & Aberdeen Junction Rly, who numbered it 17 and named it *Hopeman*. In

1865 it became Highland Railway property. In 1867 William Stroudley altered it to 0–4–2T, renamed it *Needlefield*, and deleted the number. It was later numbered 1A.
15. Rebuilt to 4–2–2 in September 1894; renamed *Prometheus* in May 1895.
16. Originally named *Prometheus*; renamed *Nelson* in May 1895.
17. Purchased from the Edinburgh & Glasgow Railway in 1855.
18. Built for the West Cornwall Railway.
19. Date to stock. Delivered December 1853.
20. Renamed *Goring* in July 1897.

Name	Number	Class	Date	Railway
Nevill	171	B2	6/1897	London, Brighton & South Coast Rly [21]
Neville Hill	43049	43	4/1977	British Railways
Neville Hill 1st	08950	08	1962	British Railways
Newbridge	–	0–6–0	1846	Taff Vale Rly
Newbridge	12	0–6–0	1862	Taff Vale Rly
New Brunswick	5557	Jubilee	1934	London Midland & Scottish Rly
Newby	2	2–4–0	1857	Lancaster & Carlisle Rly
Newcastle	11	0–6–0	5/1837	Newcastle & Carlisle Rly
Newcastle	37	0–4–2	10/1841	Manchester & Leeds Rly
Newcastle	215	211	1856	North British Rly [22]
Newcastle	–	0–4–0T	1915	Woolwich Arsenal [23]
Newcastleton	492	Abbotsford	2/1879	North British Rly
Newcastle United	2858	B17/1	5/1936	London & North Eastern Rly [24]
New Century	–	0–6–0ST	1900	Garstang & Knott End Rly
Newcomen	1483	Newton	5/1866	London & North Western Rly
Newcomen	1483	rPrecedent	3/1890	London & North Western Rly
Newcomen	2151	George V*	11/1910	London & North Western Rly
New Cross	36	D1	6/1876	London, Brighton & South Coast Rly
New Fly	2219	cSentinel	1929	London & North Eastern Rly
Newfoundland	5573	Jubilee	1934	London Midland & Scottish Rly
Newhaven	330	G	6/1881	London, Brighton & South Coast Rly
New Hebrides	5618	Jubilee	1934	London Midland & Scottish Rly
Newick	478	E4	11/1898	London, Brighton & South Coast Rly [25]
Newington	**46**	**A1**	**1/1877**	**London, Brighton & South Coast Rly [26]**
Newlands	167	Panther	11/1862	Stockton & Darlington Rly
Newlyn	3362	Bulldog	11/1900	Great Western Rly
Newmarket	65	Priam	1850	Stockton & Darlington Rly [27]
Newport	–	2–2–2T	1860	Isle of Wight (Newport Junction) Rly [28]
Newport	489	2–2–2	8/1864	London, Brighton & South Coast Rly [29]
Newport	–	Swindon	3/1866	Great Western Rly (bg)
Newport	166	165	1875	North British Rly [30]
Newport	**W11**	**A1x**	**3/1878**	**Southern Rly [31]**
Newport	6	4–4–0T	1890	Isle of Wight Central Rly [32]
Newport	W34	O2	7/1891	Southern Rly [33]
Newport	368	D3	8/1892	London, Brighton & South Coast Rly
Newport	3447	Bulldog	9/1903	Great Western Rly
Newport Castle	5058	Castle	5/1937	Great Western Rly [34]
Newport Castle	5065	Castle	7/1937	Great Western Rly [35]
Newquay	2355	0–6–0T	1873	Great Western Rly [36]
Newquay	3284	Duke	2/1897	Great Western Rly
New South Wales	5564	Jubilee	1934	London Midland & Scottish Rly
New Star	–	**4wPM**	**1931**	**Cadeby Light Rly [37]**
Newtimber	482	E4	12/1898	London, Brighton & South Coast Rly
Newton	–	2–2–0	9/1831	Warrington & Newton Rly
Newton	1480	Newton	4/1866	London & North Western Rly

Name	Number	Class	Date	Railway
Newton	1480	rPrecedent	11/1888	London & North Western Rly
Newton Hall	5909	Hall	6/1931	Great Western Rly
Newton Manor	11	0–6–0ST	1870	Whitehaven, Cleator & Egremont Rly [38]
New York	32	4–2–0	5/1842	Birmingham & Gloucester Rly
New Zealand	3454	Bulldog	1/1904	Great Western Rly
New Zealand	2081	George V	6/1911	London & North Western Rly
New Zealand	5570	Jubilee	1934	London Midland & Scottish Rly
New Zealand Line	35021	MN	9/1948	British Railways (Southern Region)
Niagara	31	4–2–0	5/1842	Birmingham & Gloucester Rly
Niagara	515	Dreadnought	1885	London & North Western Rly
Niagara	40	2Precursor	3/1905	London & North Western Rly
Nice	304	Lyons	12/1877	London, Brighton & South Coast Rly
Nick the Greek	–	**4wDM**	**1944**	**Moseley Railway Centre [39]**
Niddrie	**6**	**0–6–0ST**	**1924**	**Strathspey Rly**
Nigeria	5619	Jubilee	1934	London Midland & Scottish Rly
Night Hawk	2577	A3	10/1924	London & North Eastern Rly
Nightingale	367	aCrewe	5/1855	London & North Western Rly
Nightingale	3739	Bulldog	12/1909	Great Western Rly
Night Mail	47476	47/4	1964	British Railways
Nile	154	Nile	4/1859	London & South Western Rly
Nilghai	1019	B1	2/1947	London & North Eastern Rly
Nimbus	55020	Deltic	2/1962	British Railways
Nimrod	–	Caesar	11/1854	Great Western Rly (bg)
Ningwood	W18	O2	9/1892	Southern Rly [40]
Ninian	**9**	**0–4–0DH**	**1986**	**Snowdon Mountain Rly [41]**
Niobe	58	2–2–2	6/1848	Manchester, Sheffield & Lincolnshire Rly
Nipper	–	0–4–0T	1/1867	London & North Western Rly
Nipper	–	0–4–0ST	1903	Fishguard & Rosslare Railways & Harbours Co.
Nith	93	Scotchmen	12/1866	London, Chatham & Dover Rly
Nora	**5**	**0–4–0ST**	**1920**	**Pontypool & Blaenavon Rly**
Nora Creina	–	Caesar	11/1851	Great Western Rly (bg)
Norbury	293	D1	10/1877	London, Brighton & South Coast Rly
Norfolk	213	Richmond	3/1880	London, Brighton & South Coast Rly
Norfolk	64	B4	8/1901	London, Brighton & South Coast Rly [42]
Norfolk	2279	cSentinel	1930	London & North Eastern Rly
Norfolk and Norwich Festival	86232	86/2	1965	British Railways
Norma	–	0–6–2T	1912	Longmoor Military Rly [43]
(Norma)	–	**J94** •	**1952**	**Oswestry Cycle & Railway Museum**
Norman	125	Saxon	6/1855	London & South Western Rly
Normanby	20	0–6–0	1861	Stockton & Darlington Rly [44]
Normandy	103	E1	9/1876	London, Brighton & South Coast Rly
Normandy	**96**	**B4**	**11/1893**	**London & South Western Rly**
Normandy	4	Sentinel	1927	Jersey Rly [45]

[21] Rebuilt to class B2x, August 1910.

[22] Ex-Edinburgh & Glasgow Railway, absorbed in 1865.

[23] 18in gauge.

[24] Renamed *The Essex Regiment* in June 1936.

[25] Rebuilt to class E4x, May 1909.

[26] This engine was built as London, Brighton & South Coast Railway no. 46 *Newington*. It was sold to the London & South Western Railway in March 1903, becoming their no. 734, for the Axminster–Lyme Regis branch (where it was not a success), and then re-sold in December 1913 to the Freshwater, Yarmouth & Newport Railway. It returned to the Southern Railway in 1923 and took up its old number in the LBSC duplicate list, 2646. It later became BR no. 32646 and was finally withdrawn in November 1963. It has since been preserved.

[27] Named *Stephenson*. May have been named *Newmarket* originally, according to one source.

[28] Formerly *Queen Mab* of the Whitehaven & Furness Junction Railway, and later Furness Railway no. 46. Sold to the Isle of Wight (Newport Junction) Railway in 1876, as their *Newport*. They did not number it – as it was their sole locomotive! It passed to the Isle of Wight Central Railway as their no. 6, and was scrapped in 1895.

[29] Originally no. 199. Named *Paris* in April 1870, and renumbered 489 in November 1887. Renamed *Newport* in September 1883, and withdrawn in June 1892.

[30] Originally named *Bothwell*.

[31] Formerly London, Brighton & South Coast Railway no. 40 *Brighton*, the Gold Medal engine of 1878. Sold to Isle of Wight Central Railway in January 1902, becoming their no. 11 (without name). In 1923 it became Southern Railway property, becoming no. W11 *Newport*.

[32] Became Southern Railway no. W6. Scrapped in 1926.

[33] Originally London & South Western Railway (and Southern Railway) no. 201. Name applied by the Southern Railway on transfer to the Isle of Wight.

[34] Renamed *Earl of Clancarty* in September 1937.

[35] *Upton Castle* until September 1937.

[36] Built for the Cornwall Minerals Railway.

[37] 2ft gauge.

[38] Became Furness Railway no. 107.

[39] 2ft gauge.

[40] Originally London & South Western Railway no. 220.

[41] 800mm gauge, rack and pinion locomotive.

[42] Renamed *Norfolk* in December 1908. Originally named *Windsor*.

[43] Great Northern Railway no. 1587. Stayed at Longmoor for one year during which it was experimentally armour-plated. Returned to GNR in 1922.

[44] Ex-West Hartlepool Harbour & Railway, absorbed by the North Eastern Railway in 1865.

[45] Sentinel-Cammell steam railcar. Built for the Jersey Eastern Railway (a standard gauge line), and sold in 1930 to the Jersey Railway. They altered it to 3ft 6in gauge.

Name	Number	Class	Date	Railway
Norman Ramsey	RCD2	0–4–0ST	3/1876	Woolwich Arsenal [46]
Norman Tunna G.C.	47471	47/4	1964	British Railways
Norna	426	Scott	7/1915	North British Rly
Norsk Hydro	47319	47/3	1965	British Railways
Northamptonshire	47676	47/4	10/1964	British Railways
North Aston Hall	7917	M/Hall	4/1950	British Railways (Western Region)
North-Berwick	158	165	5/1877	North British Rly [47]
North Borneo	5620	Jubilee	1934	London Midland & Scottish Rly
North British	90773	WD2–10–0	1945	War Department
North British	90774	WD2–10–0	1945	War Department
North British	60161	A1	12/1949	British Railways (Eastern Region)
North Briton	2276	cSentinel	1930	London & North Eastern Rly
North Briton	87020	87/0	1974	British Railways
Northcote	217	Gladstone	2/1884	London, Brighton & South Coast Rly
North Downs	**3**	**0–6–0T**	**1955**	**North Downs Steam Rly**
North Eastern	60147	A1	4/1949	British Railways (Eastern Region)
(North Eastern)	**47401**	**47/4**	**1962**	**British Railways**
North Eastern	47443	47/4	1964	British Railways
North Elmham	**–**	**0–4–0DH**	**1963**	**County School**
Northern	2	2–4–0T	1879	Manx Northern Rly [48]
Northern Chief	**2**	**4–6–2**	**1925**	**Romney, Hythe & Dymchurch Rly [49]**
Northern Electric	91014	91	5/1990	British Railways
Northern Lights	08680	08	1959	British Railways
Northern Rhodesia	5621	Jubilee	1934	London Midland & Scottish Rly
Northern Rock	**–**	**2–6–2**	**1976**	**Ravenglass & Eskdale Rly [50]**
Northern Rock	91010	91	4/1989	British Railways
North Foreland	2422	H2	7/1911	Southern Rly [51]
Northiam	2	2–4–0T	1899	Kent & East Sussex Rly [52]
(Northiam)	**25**	**J94**	**3/1953**	**Kent & East Sussex Rly [53]**
Northlands	557	E4	9/1901	London, Brighton & South Coast Rly
North Star	8	0–2–2	1830	Liverpool & Manchester Rly
North Star	11	Planet	3/1831	Stockton & Darlington Rly
North Star	–	Wolf	11/1838	Great Western Rly (bg)
North Star	–	2–2–2	1840	Lancaster & Preston Junction Rly
North Star	934	Samson	1/1866	London & North Western Rly
North Star	380	Sir Daniel	3/1866	Great Western Rly
North Star	934	Whitworth	3/1893	London & North Western Rly
North Star	3072	3031	6/1898	Great Western Rly [54]
North Star	4000	Star	4/1906	Great Western Rly [55]
North Star	**–**	**Wolf**	**1925**	**Great Western Rly (bg) [56]**
North Star	263	aSentinel	1928	London & North Eastern Rly
North Star	4000	Castle	11/1929	Great Western Rly [57]
North Star	47613	47/4	1965	British Railways
North Star	47840	47/4	3/1965	British Railways
Northumberland	16	0–4–0	10/1838	Newcastle & Carlisle Rly
Northumberland	1703	2Experiment	12/1909	London & North Western Rly
Northumberland	2758	D49/1	3/1929	London & North Eastern Rly
Northumbria	47526	47/4	1967	British Railways
Northumbrian	7	0–2–2	1830	Liverpool & Manchester Rly
Northumbrian	15	Majestic	1831	Stockton & Darlington Rly

Name	Number	Class	Date	Railway
Northumbrian	232	DE Railcar	1934	London & North Eastern Rly
North Walsham	–	4–4–0T	9/1878	Yarmouth & North Norfolk Rly
North Western	171	bCrewe	9/1847	London & North Western Rly
North Western	?	2–4–0T	1871	Jersey Eastern Rly [58]
North Western	1132	Newton	8/1873	London & North Western Rly
North Western	1132	rPrecedent	6/1887	London & North Western Rly
North Western	1990	2Experiment	10/1906	London & North Western Rly
North Western Gas Board	**–**	**0–4–0ST**	**1941**	**Southport Railway Centre**
North West Frontier	5584	Jubilee	1934	London Midland & Scottish Rly
North Yorkshire Moors Railway	31439	31/4	1960	British Railways
Norton Hall	5935	Hall	7/1933	Great Western Rly
Norwegian Monarch	4027	Star	9/1909	Great Western Rly [59]
Norwich	–	4–4–0T	10/1880	Lynn & Fakenham Rly [60]
Norwich Cathedral	86215	86/2	1965	British Railways
Norwich City	2839	B17/2	5/1933	London & North Eastern Rly [61]
Norwich City	2859	B17/4	6/1936	London & North Eastern Rly [62]
Norwich City	1639	B2	1/1946	London & North Eastern Rly [63]
Norwich Festival	86232	86/2	1965	British Railways
Norwich Union	86223	86/2	1966	British Railways
Norwood	127	2–2–2	6/1871	London, Brighton & South Coast Rly
Norwood	367	D3	7/1892	London, Brighton & South Coast Rly
Norwood	**77**	**0–6–0ST**	**1948**	**Bowes Rly**
Nottingham Forest	2866	B17/4	2/1937	London & North Eastern Rly
Nottingham Playhouse	43066	43	10/1977	British Railways
Nottinghamshire	327	D49/3	7/1928	London & North Eastern Rly [64]
Nova Scotia	5556	Jubilee	1934	London Midland & Scottish Rly
Novar	25	S/Goods	10/1863	Highland Rly
Novelty		(Rainhill trials 1830) [65]		
Novelty	1682	Newton	5/1868	London & North Western Rly
Novelty	1682	rPrecedent	6/1892	London & North Western Rly
Novelty	6127	Royal Scot	8/1927	London Midland & Scottish Rly [66]
Novelty		**replica**	**1929**	[67]
Novelty	5733	Jubilee	1936	London Midland & Scottish Rly
Novelty	86235	86/2	1965	British Railways
Novelty		**replica**	**1980**	
Nubian	1623	George V	8/1911	London & North Western Rly
Nun	179	aCrewe	11/1849	London & North Western Rly
Nunhold Grange	6842	Grange	9/1937	Great Western Rly
Nunlow	**–**	**0–6–0T**	**1938**	**Keighley & Worth Valley Rly**
Nunney Castle	**5029**	**Castle**	**5/1934**	**Great Western Rly**
Nunthorpe	117	Woodlands	8/1856	Stockton & Darlington Rly
Nuremberg	143	E1	3/1879	London, Brighton & South Coast Rly
Nutbourne	573	E5	2/1903	London, Brighton & South Coast Rly
Nutty	**–**	**0–4–0VB**	**1929**	**Narrow Gauge Museum, Tywyn [68]**
Nyala	1030	B1	6/1947	London & North Eastern Rly
Nyasaland	5622	Jubilee	1934	London Midland & Scottish Rly
Nymph	173	Undine	6/1860	London & South Western Rly

---

[46] Name applied in about 1891. 18in gauge.

[47] With a hyphen. Later renamed *Meadowbank*.

[48] 3ft gauge. The MNR was absorbed by the Isle of Man Railway in 1905, who allocated no. 17 to *Northern*. However, this number was never carried, for the engine was withdrawn soon afterwards.

[49] 15in gauge.

[50] 15in gauge.

[51] Built for the London, Brighton & South Coast Railway. Named by the Southern Railway in June 1925.

[52] Appeared in the Will Hay comedy film *Oh, Mr Porter* in 1937, for which purpose it was given a tall spiked chimney and renamed *Gladstone*. It was scrapped soon afterwards.

[53] At WD Bicester, this locomotive was no. 197 *Sapper*.

[54] Name removed in 1906. Renamed *Bulkeley* in September 1906.

[55] Originally 4–4–2 no. 40 (unnamed). Nameplates added September 1906. Altered to 4–6–0 in November 1909, and renumbered 4000 in December 1912.

[56] Replica, built by GWR at Swindon and incorporating some of the original parts.

[57] Rebuild of Star class no. 4000 *North Star*.

[58] Originally built for the Jersey Railway.

[59] Originally named *King Henry* until July 1927. Renamed *The Norwegian Monarch* in July 1927, and *Norwegian Monarch* in November 1927.

[60] Became no. 10 *Kingsley* of the Longmoor Military Railway.

[61] Originally *Rendelsham Hall*. Renamed *Norwich City* in January 1938. Rebuilt to class B2, January 1946.

[62] In September 1937 this locomotive was renamed *East Anglian*, and streamlined for working the 'East Anglian' express.

[63] Date rebuilt from class B17/2.

[64] As originally built with Lentz Oscillating Cam poppet valves. In June 1938 altered to piston valves and integrated into class D49/1.

[65] At the Science Museum, South Kensington.

[66] Renamed *The Old Contemptibles* in June 1936.

[67] Incorporating some original parts. At Greater Manchester Museum of Science & Industry.

[68] 2ft 6in gauge.

Name	Number	Class	Date	Railway
Oakley Grange	6823	Grange	1/1937	Great Western Rly
Oakley Hall	5936	Hall	7/1933	Great Western Rly
Oakwood	488	E4	6/1899	London, Brighton & South Coast Rly
Oberon	48	2–2–2	1838	Grand Junction Rly
Oberon	48	bCrewe	10/1848	London & North Western Rly
Oberon	4	2–2–2WT	1851	Whitehaven & Furness Junction Rly
Oberon	425	1Precursor	10/1874	London & North Western Rly
Oberon	2164	2Precursor	4/1904	London & North Western Rly
Ocean	28	Tory	8/1840	Stockton & Darlington Rly [1]
Ocean	5730	Jubilee	1936	London Midland & Scottish Rly
Oceanic	1302	Teutonic	5/1889	London & North Western Rly
Oceanic	807	2Precursor	8/1907	London & North Western Rly
Ocean Swell	517	A2/3	11/1946	London & North Eastern Rly
Ockendon	24	Class 1	1884	London, Tilbury & Southend Rly
Octa	24	2–2–2	1/1843	London & Brighton Rly [2]
Octane	8	0–4–0DE	1960	North Downs Steam Rly
Octavia	–	Caesar	2/1855	Great Western Rly (bg)
Oddson	–	4wVB	1970	Midland Railway Centre [3]
Odin	64	2–2–2	7/1840	Grand Junction Rly
Odin	847	L/Bloomer	1851	London & North Western Rly
Odin	64	aCrewe	11/1851	London & North Western Rly
Odin	1	Clio	1/1867	East Lancashire Rly
Odin	1164	Samson	5/1879	London & North Western Rly
Odin	1164	Whitworth	1895	London & North Western Rly
Odin	2442	Prince/W	2/1916	London & North Western Rly
Odin	47606	47/4	1965	British Railways
Odney Manor	7828	Manor	12/1950	British Railways (Western Region)
Ogmore Castle	5056	Castle	6/1936	Great Western Rly [4]
Ogmore Castle	5080	Castle	5/1939	Great Western Rly [5]
Ogmore Castle	7007	Castle	7/1946	Great Western Rly [6]
Ogmore Castle	7035	Castle	8/1950	British Railways (Western Region)
Ogmore Castle	56034	56	1977	British Railways [7]
Okehampton	21C113	rWC	10/1945	Southern Rly
Old Blue	2283	bSentinel	1930	London & North Eastern Rly
Oldham	39	0–4–2	5/1842	Manchester & Leeds Rly
Oldham	–	2–2–2	1847	Huddersfield & Manchester Railway & Canal
Oldham	–	0–6–0T	5/1888	Cockermouth, Keswick & Penrith Rly [8]
Old Joe	70213	0–6–0DE	5/1936	Martin Mill Military Rly [9]
Old John Bull	2281	bSentinel	1930	London & North Eastern Rly
Oldlands Hall	6917	Hall	6/1941	Great Western Rly [10]
Old Oak Common 1882–1982	08480	08	1958	British Railways
Old Oak Common Traction & Rolling Stock Depot	47004	47/0	1963	British Railways
Old Oak Common Traction & Rolling Stock Depot	47701	47/7	1966	British Railways
Old Yep	5199	J94	1944	War Department
Ole Bill	661	C	11/1891	North British Rly
Oliver Bury	1251	B1	11/1947	London & North Eastern Rly [11]
Oliver Cromwell	2	Bo-Bo	1921	Metropolitan Rly [12]
Oliver Cromwell	70013	Britannia	5/1951	British Railways
Oliver Goldsmith	2040	Prince/W	11/1913	London & North Western Rly
Oliver Goldsmith	16	Bo-Bo	1921	Metropolitan Rly [13]
Olton Hall	5972	Hall	4/1937	Great Western Rly
Olwen	1144	0–4–0ST	1942	Gwili Rly
Olympus	103	0–6–0	4/1852	Manchester, Sheffield & Lincolnshire Rly
Olympus	–	Caesar	10/1861	Great Western Rly (bg)
Omdurman	3384	Atbara	7/1900	Great Western Rly
One and All	3363	Bulldog	11/1900	Great Western Rly
Onslaught	D832	Warship	2/1961	British Railways
Ontario	5554	Jubilee	1934	London Midland & Scottish Rly
Onward	240	F	2/1889	South Eastern Rly [14]
Onyx	211	aCrewe	5/1848	London & North Western Rly
Onyx	211	DX	c.1860	London & North Western Rly
Onyx	65	Ruby	8/1861	London, Chatham & Dover Rly
Onyx	902	Samson	2/1864	London & North Western Rly
Onyx	902	Whitworth	4/1893	London & North Western Rly
Onyx	810	Prince/W	1/1916	London & North Western Rly
Oor Wullie	37275	37/0	1965	British Railways [15]
Oor Wullie	37402	37/4	1965	British Railways
Ophir	–	2–2–0ST	?	Edenham & Little Bytham Rly [16]
Ophir	3408	Atbara	10/1901	Great Western Rly
Ophir	3408	City	5/1907	Great Western Rly [17]
Oregon	353	1Experiment	1884	London & North Western Rly
Oregon	2007	2Precursor	11/1905	London & North Western Rly
Orestes	117	0–6–0	9/1853	London, Brighton & South Coast Rly [18]
Oribi	1014	B1	12/1946	London & North Eastern Rly
Orient Line	21C8	MN	6/1942	Southern Rly
Oriole	47098	47/0	1963	British Railways
Orion	35	0–4–0	1834	Liverpool & Manchester Rly
Orion	13	Venus	12/1838	London & South Western Rly
Orion	–	2–2–2	1841	London & Brighton Rly
Orion	58	2–2–2	8/1841	South Eastern Rly
Orion	–	Wolf	3/1842	Great Western Rly (bg)
Orion	223	2–2–2	1846	North British Rly [19]
Orion	67	Priam	4/1848	Stockton & Darlington Rly
Orion	31	Venus	12/1848	East Lancashire Rly
Orion	89	2–2–2	1/1850	Manchester, Sheffield & Lincolnshire Rly
Orion	13	Tartar	6/1852	London & South Western Rly
Orion	31	0–6–0	1853	Taff Vale Rly
Orion	2103	4–4–0ST	2/1853	Great Western Rly (bg) [20]
Orion	7	A	6/1864	Metropolitan Rly
Orion	13	Lion	7/1871	London & South Western Rly
Orion	3342	Bulldog	2/1900	Great Western Rly
Orion	5691	Jubilee	1936	London Midland & Scottish Rly

---

[1] Later renumbered 13, then 12.

[2] Built for London & Brighton and South Eastern Railways joint stock.

[3] 2ft gauge.

[4] Renamed Earl of Powis in September 1937.

[5] Renamed Defiant in January 1941, and preserved as such.

[6] Renamed Great Western in January 1948.

[7] Also named (on the other side) Castell Ogwr.

[8] Built as Oldham by Manning Wardle, Leeds, for industrial service. It was bought by the CKPR in 1901 for permanent way work, and was by them named Strachan No. 7. The London & North Western, who had agreed with the CKPR to supply motive power to the latter, took grave exception to Strachan No. 7, and insisted that it be disposed of at once. In the event, it was June 1913 before Strachan No. 7 departed for further industrial service.

[9] Built for the London Midland & Scottish Railway as their no. 7059, and transferred to the War Department in 1939 on the outbreak of war.

[10] Nameplates fitted in December 1946.

[11] Nameplates fitted in December 1947.

[12] Officially a rebuild of an earlier, unnamed, locomotive, but incorporated few if any of the original parts.

[13] Officially a rebuild of an earlier, unnamed, locomotive, but incorporated few if any of the original parts.

[14] Carried the name at the Paris Exhibition of 1889 but did not carry it in service. It was the only F class engine to carry a name, if only for a few months! Rebuilt to class F1 in October 1913.

[15] This may be no. 37402, with a different diesel engine and other alterations.

[16] Rebuilt by Boltons as 0–4–0ST and sold in April 1867 for industrial use.

[17] Renamed Killarney in September 1907, originally on a temporary basis but the original name was never reinstated.

[18] Purchased from the Manchester, Sheffield & Lincolnshire Railway (also their no. 117 Orestes) in June 1854. The LB&SCR was short of goods engines, and the MS&LR was short of cash to re-equip and extend its Gorton Works! The engine was nearly new (19,464 miles), so everyone was satisfied.

[19] Built for the Edinburgh & Glasgow Railway.

[20] Built for the South Devon Railway.

British Railways Britannia class 4–6–2 no. 70013 *Oliver Cromwell* at Liverpool Street on 12 June 1951. The engine was brand new only the previous month. (*Photo: LCGB Ken Nunn Collection*)

Name	Number	Class	Date	Railway	Name	Number	Class	Date	Railway
Orion	**15**	**2–6–2T**	**1948**	**Welshpool & Llanfair Rly [21]**	*Osborne*	296	D1	10/1877	London, Brighton & South Coast Rly [23]
Orion	47633	47/4	1965	British Railways	*Osborne*	W19	O2	9/1891	Southern Rly [24]
Orleans	101	E1	4/1875	London, Brighton & South Coast Rly	*Osborne*	67	B4	9/1901	London, Brighton & South Coast Rly [25]
Orleton	18	S/Goods	9/1875	Cambrian Railways					
Ormonde	2556	A3	1/1925	London & North Eastern Rly	*Oscar*	–	Victoria	9/1856	Great Western Rly (bg)
Orpheus	76	2–4–0	9/1849	Manchester, Sheffield & Lincolnshire Rly	*Oscar Wilde*	92025	92		British Railways
					Osiris	–	Caesar	5/1855	Great Western Rly (bg)
Orpheus	–	Caesar	9/1861	Great Western Rly (bg)	*Osiris*	2131	4–4–0ST	3/1875	Great Western Rly (bg) [26]
Orsett	74	69	1903	London, Tilbury & Southend Rly	*Osiris*	–	0–4–2T	1885	Woolwich Arsenal [27]
Orson	–	Caesar	6/1854	Great Western Rly (bg)	*Osprey*	703	S/Bloomer	1854	London & North Western Rly
Orwell	5	2–2–2	10/1846	Eastern Union Rly	*Osprey*	163	bCrewe	5/1856	London & North Western Rly [28]
Oryx	1004	B1	12/1943	London & North Eastern Rly	*Osprey*	34	Chaplin	8/1856	London & South Western Rly
Osborne	177	Windsor	5/1865	Stockton & Darlington Rly	*Osprey*	–	0–6–0ST	6/1865	Swansea Vale Rly
Osborne	–	0–4–0ST	9/1866	Southampton Dock Co.	*Osprey*	34	Standard	5/1874	London & South Western Rly
Osborne	5	2–4–0T	1876	Isle of Wight Central Rly [22]	***Osprey***	**60009**	**A4**	**6/1937**	**British Railways [29]**

[21] 2ft 6in gauge.
[22] Became Southern Railway no. W5. Scrapped in 1926.
[23] Renamed *Peckham* in December 1901.
[24] Originally London & South Western Railway no. 206.
[25] Name removed in May 1906, and rebuilt to class B4x in October 1923.
[26] Built for the South Devon Railway.
[27] 18in gauge.
[28] Built for the Grand Junction Railway.
[29] Originally named *Union of South Africa*. Its name changed temporarily while in preservation but the original name was later restored.

Name	Number	Class	Date	Railway
Osprey	4494	A4	8/1937	London & North Eastern Rly [30]
Osprey	60131	A1	10/1948	British Railways (Eastern Region)
Osprey	47120	47/0	1964	British Railways
Osram	–	**0–4–0DM**	**1933**	**Buckinghamshire Railway Centre**
Ostrich	–	Priam	12/1840	Great Western Rly (bg)
Ostrich	2104	4–4–0ST	8/1852	Great Western Rly (bg) [31]
Ostrich	133	bCrewe	5/1854	London & North Western Rly [32]
Ostrich	146	Panther	2/1860	Stockton & Darlington Rly
Ostrich	10	Tiger	10/1861	London, Chatham & Dover Rly

Merchant Navy class no. 35008 *Orient Line* passing Farnborough with an Up express. The locomotive is seen in its original air-smoothed condition. (*Photo: Author*)

Name	Number	Class	Date	Railway
Ostrich	–	Hawthorn	12/1865	Great Western Rly (bg)
Ostrich	632	Samson	12/1865	London & North Western Rly
Ostrich	–	0–6–0ST	11/1868	Swansea Vale Rly
Ostrich	–	0–4–2T	1885	Woolwich Arsenal [33]

Name	Number	Class	Date	Railway
Ostrich	632	Whitworth	6/1890	London & North Western Rly
Ostrich	739	Whitworth	4/1893	London & North Western Rly [34]
Ostrich	6144	Royal Scot	10/1927	London Midland & Scottish Rly [35]
Oswald Gilkes	166	Woodlands	11/1860	Stockton & Darlington Rly
Otho	–	Victoria	11/1856	Great Western Rly (bg)
Ottawa	3461	Bulldog	2/1904	Great Western Rly
Otterhound	1513	George V	5/1911	London & North Western Rly
Otterington Hall	6983	M/Hall	2/1948	Great Western Rly
Ottery St Mary	21C145	rWC	10/1946	Southern Rly
Ourebi	1026	B1	4/1947	London & North Eastern Rly
Ouse	25	2–2–2	1/1841	Manchester & Leeds Rly
Ousel	155	bCrewe	11/1854	London & North Western Rly
Outram	719	Problem	c.1860	London & North Western Rly
Overton Grange	6879	Grange	5/1939	Great Western Rly
Ovid	–	Bogie	10/1854	Great Western Rly (bg)
Ovingdean	243	D1	11/1881	London, Brighton & South Coast Rly
OVS BULLEID C.B.E.	73128	73/1	1966	British Railways
1937–1949 C.M.E. SOUTHERN RAILWAY				
Owain Glyndwr	**7**	**2–6–2T**	**7/1923**	**British Railways** [36]
Owen	4	0–6–0	1865	Pembroke & Tenby Rly [37]
Owen Glendower	70010	Britannia	5/1951	British Railways
Owen Tudor	520	A2/3	3/1947	London & North Eastern Rly
Owl	134	aCrewe	11/1853	London & North Western Rly [38]
Owl	134	Problem	c.1860	London & North Western Rly
Owl	–	0–6–0ST	1872	Swansea Vale Rly
Owl	2172	0–4–0WT	1/1873	Great Western Rly (bg) [39]
Owl	–	0–4–2T	1885	Woolwich Arsenal [40]
Owsden Hall	**6984**	**M/Hall**	**2/1948**	**Great Western Rly**
Owzell	155	2–4–0	11/1845	London & North Western Rly [41]
Oxburgh Hall	6958	Hall	4/1943	Great Western Rly [42]
Oxcroft Opencast	58044	58	8/1986	British Railways
Oxford	–	Swindon	1/1866	Great Western Rly (bg)
Oxford	3304	Badminton	9/1898	Great Western Rly
Oxfordshire	71	2Experiment	12/1909	London & North Western Rly
Oxfordshire	253	D49/1	11/1927	London & North Eastern Rly
Oxted	262	D1	4/1882	London, Brighton & South Coast Rly
Oystermouth	56040	56	1978	British Railways

---

[30] Renamed *Andrew K. McCosh* in October 1942.
[31] Built for the South Devon Railway.
[32] Rebuilt from Liverpool & Manchester Railway 2–2–2 no. 74. Became a London & North Western engine in 1846.
[33] 18in gauge.

[34] Originally named *Sutherland*. Renamed in 1913.
[35] Renamed *Honourable Artillery Company* in January 1933.
[36] Built by the Great Western Railway for the Vale of Rheidol line; name applied by British Railways. 1ft 11½in gauge.
[37] Became Great Western Railway no. 1362.

[38] Rebuilt from Liverpool & Manchester Railway 2–4–0 no. 75; became a London & North Western engine in 1846.
[39] Built for the South Devon Railway.
[40] 18in gauge.
[41] Built for the Grand Junction Railway.
[42] Nameplates fitted in August 1947.

Name	Number	Class	Date	Railway
Pacific	976	2Precursor	8/1907	London & North Western Rly
Packwood Hall	4949	Hall	8/1929	Great Western Rly
Padarn	**6**	**0-4-2T**	**1922**	**Snowdon Mountain Rly [1]**
Paddington	3448	Bulldog	9/1903	Great Western Rly
Padstow	21C108	rWC	9/1945	Southern Rly
Palace of Holyroodhouse	91030	91		British Railways
Palestine	5623	Jubilee	1934	London Midland & Scottish Rly
Pallah	1025	B1	4/1947	London & North Eastern Rly
Pallas	64	2-2-2	8/1848	Manchester, Sheffield & Lincolnshire Rly
Pallas	–	Caesar	5/1856	Great Western Rly (bg)
Palmerston	378	bCrewe	11/1855	London & North Western Rly [2]
Palmerston	562	Problem	c.1860	London & North Western Rly
Palmerston	4	0-4-0TT	1864	Festiniog Rly [3]
Palmerston	54	Small Pass	10/1865	Cambrian Railways
Palmerston	1991	2Experiment	10/1906	London & North Western Rly
(Pamela)	**–**	**J94**	**3/1956**	**Vale of Neath Railway, Cadoxton [4]**
P & O Containers	37358	37/0	1/1963	British Railways
Pandora	–	0-4-2	1838	Bolton & Leigh Rly [5]
Pandora	10	2-2-2	12/1844	Manchester, Sheffield & Lincolnshire Rly
Pandora	1430	Problem	c.1860	London & North Western Rly
Pandora	–	Caesar	1/1863	Great Western Rly (bg)
Pandora	13	0-6-0ST	11/1863	Brecon & Merthyr Rly
Pandora	1116	2Precursor	9/1905	London & North Western Rly
Pandora	27006	EM2	12/1954	British Railways
Panopea	1432	Problem	c.1860	London & North Western Rly
Panopea	520	2Precursor	3/1905	London & North Western Rly
Panthea	–	Caesar	3/1856	Great Western Rly (bg)
Panther	64	2-2-2	1839	Liverpool & Manchester Rly
Panther	12	2-2-0	5/1840	Midland Counties Rly
Panther	–	Priam	6/1840	Great Western Rly (bg)
Panther	106	Bison	10/1848	London & South Western Rly
Panther	145	Panther	1/1860	Stockton & Darlington Rly
Panther	21	Tiger	2/1862	London, Chatham & Dover Rly
Panther	D833	Warship	7/1960	British Railways
Papyrus	2750	A3	2/1929	London & North Eastern Rly
Paridae	47146	47/0	1964	British Railways
Paris	199	2-2-2	8/1864	London, Brighton & South Coast Rly [6]
Paris	313	Lyons	10/1883	London, Brighton & South Coast Rly
Park Hall	5910	Hall	6/1931	Great Western Rly
Parkhurst	341	G	1/1882	London, Brighton & South Coast Rly
Parkside	6	0-6-0ST	1862	Whitehaven, Cleator & Egremont Rly [7]
Parnassus	122	0-6-0	1854	Manchester, Sheffield & Lincolnshire Rly
Parthia CLS	40027	40	8/1959	British Railways [8]
Partick	161	165	4/1877	North British Rly [9]
Partridge	617	S/Bloomer	1854	London & North Western Rly
Partridge	126	bCrewe	5/1854	London & North Western Rly [10]
Partridge	1713	George V	9/1911	London & North Western Rly
Partridge Green	475	E4	10/1898	London, Brighton & South Coast Rly
Parwick Hall	6985	M/Hall	2/1948	Great Western Rly
Pasha	–	Iron Duke	11/1847	Great Western Rly (bg)
Patcham	239	D1	11/1881	London, Brighton & South Coast Rly
Patentee	33	2-2-2	1834	Liverpool & Manchester Rly
Pathfinder	1691	Prince/W	11/1911	London & North Western Rly
Pathfinder	D834	Warship	7/1960	British Railways
Patience	2179	Precedent	3/1875	London & North Western Rly
Patience	2179	rPrecedent	5/1897	London & North Western Rly
Patience	2499	Claughton	2/1920	London & North Western Rly
Patrick Stirling	60119	A1	11/1948	British Railways (Eastern Region)
Patriot	1914	Claughton	1/1920	London & North Western Rly
Patriot	5500	Patriot	11/1930	London Midland & Scottish Rly [11]
Patriot	87003	87/0	1973	British Railways
Patshull Hall	4950	Hall	8/1929	Great Western Rly
Patterdale	5	2-4-0	1857	Lancaster & Carlisle Rly
Patterdale	381	Newton	12/1869	London & North Western Rly
Patterdale	381	rPrecedent	4/1893	London & North Western Rly
Paviland Grange	6845	Grange	10/1937	Great Western Rly
Paxman	**11**	**0-4-0DE**	**1958**	**North Downs Steam Rly**
P.C. Allen	**11**	**0-4-0WT**	**1912**	**Leighton Buzzard Rly [12]**
Peacock	305	bCrewe	2/1853	London & North Western Rly
Peacock	–	Hawthorn	2/1866	Great Western Rly (bg)
Peacock	3740	Bulldog	12/1909	Great Western Rly
Peak	1	0-4-0	1833	Cromford & High Peak Rly
Peak National Park	37684	37/6	4/1963	British Railways
Pearl	193	aCrewe	2/1848	London & North Western Rly
Pearl	–	Caesar	5/1852	Great Western Rly (bg)
Pearl	70	Ruby	10/1861	London, Chatham & Dover Rly
Pearl	1180	1Precursor	2/1879	London & North Western Rly
Pearl	234	2Precursor	3/1906	London & North Western Rly
Pearl	38	cSentinel	1929	London & North Eastern Rly
Pearl Diver	E529	A2	2/1948	British Railways (Eastern Region) [13]
Peatling Hall	6959	M/Hall	3/1944	Great Western Rly [14]
Pebble Mill	86256	86/2	1966	British Railways
Peckham	69	A1	7/1874	London, Brighton & South Coast Rly [15]
Peckham	296	D1	10/1887	London, Brighton & South Coast Rly [16]
Pectin	**–**	**0-4-0ST**	**1921**	**Bulmer Railway Centre**
Pectinidae	37418	37/4	1965	British Railways
Pectinidae	47190	47/0	1965	British Railways
Pedemoura	**–**	**0-6-0WT**	**1924**	**Welsh Highland Rly [17]**
Pedigree	47280	47/0	1965	British Railways
Peebles	325	317	1862	North British Rly [18]
Peebles-shire	311	D49/1	5/1928	London & North Eastern Rly
Peel	–	0-4-2	1840	Bolton & Leigh Rly
Peel	240	bCrewe	5/1849	London & North Western Rly [19]
Peel	127	aCrewe	5/1850	London & North Western Rly
Peel	72	Peel	10/1852	Stockton & Darlington Rly
Peel	127	Problem	c.1860	London & North Western Rly
Peel	2581	2Precursor	12/1905	London & North Western Rly
Peel Castle	6	0-4-0	7/1851	North Western Rly
Peer Gynt	**5865**	**52**	**1944**	**Deutsches Reichsbahn [20]**
Peerless	190	aCrewe	1/1848	London & North Western Rly

[1] Formerly *Sir Harmood*. 800mm gauge rack and pinion locomotive.

[2] Later renumbered 5 and renamed *Falcon*.

[3] 1ft 11½in gauge.

[4] Hunslet Engine Co. works no. 3840, built for the National Coal Board's Maesteg Deep Colliery, South Wales.

[5] Later passed to the Joint Board of Management of the Birmingham & Gloucester and Bristol & Gloucester Railways, formed on 14 January 1845, retaining its name and becoming their no. 60. Standard gauge. The locomotives passed to the Midland Railway on 3 August 1846, and were renumbered into Midland stock wef February 1847.

[6] Name applied in April 1870. The locomotive was renumbered 489 in November 1887. It was renamed *Newport* in September 1883, and was withdrawn in June 1892.

[7] Later became Furness Railway no. 102.

[8] Originally no. D227 *Parthia*.

[9] Later renamed *Buckhaven*.

[10] Rebuilt from Liverpool & Manchester Railway 2-2-2 no. 83; became a London & North Western engine in 1846.

[11] Date of rebuilding from Claughton class no. 5971. Originally named *Croxteth*; renamed *Patriot* in February 1937.

[12] 2ft gauge.

[13] Soon renumbered 60529.

[14] Nameplates fitted in December 1946.

[15] On transfer to the Isle of Wight by the Southern Railway, became their no. W10 *Cowes*.

[16] Originally named *Osborne*; renamed *Peckham* in December 1901.

[17] 1ft 11½in gauge.

[18] Ex-Edinburgh & Glasgow Railway, absorbed by NBR in 1865.

[19] Charged in current A/C as *Peel*, but entered service as *Bee*.

[20] Ex-German Reichsbahn 2-10-0, 52 class Kriegslokomotiv, which after 1945 went to the Dutch State Railways, and is now preserved at Bressingham.

Name	Number	Class	Date	Railway
Pegasus	31	2–2–2	1838	Grand Junction Rly
Pegasus	–	1Sussex	3/1839	London & South Western Rly [21]
Pegasus	31	2–2–2	11/1842	Grand Junction Rly
Pegasus	–	Priam	12/1842	Great Western Rly (bg)
Pegasus	16	Pegasus	4/1847	East Lancashire Rly
Pegasus	35	4–2–0	12/1847	Manchester, Sheffield & Lincolnshire Rly
Pegasus	97	Fireball	8/1848	London & South Western Rly
Pegasus	31	aCrewe	11/1853	London & North Western Rly
Pegasus	22	Tiger	3/1862	London, Chatham & Dover Rly
Pegasus	29	Small Pass	3/1863	Cambrian Railways
Pegasus	97	Clyde	9/1868	London & South Western Rly
Pegasus	16	Craven	1/1872	East Lancashire Rly
Pegasus	482	Precedent	11/1880	London & North Western Rly
Pegasus	482	rPrecedent	1/1894	London & North Western Rly
Pegasus	3343	Bulldog	2/1900	Great Western Rly
Pegasus	–	0–4–0ST	1902	Woolwich Arsenal [22]
Pegasus	446	Prince/W	11/1915	London & North Western Rly
Pegasus	D835	Warship	8/1960	British Railways
Pegasus	47298	47/0	1966	British Railways
Peggy	–	4–6–0T	1917	Ashover Rly
Peldon	–	4wDM	1936	**Amberley Chalk Pits Museum** [23]
Pelham	253	D1	1/1882	London, Brighton & South Coast Rly
Pelican	132	bCrewe	5/1852	London & North Western Rly [24]
Pelican	12	Tiger	11/1861	London, Chatham & Dover Rly
Pelican	–	0–4–2T	1885	Woolwich Arsenal [25]
Pelican	3741	Bulldog	1/1910	Great Western Rly
Pelops	–	Caesar	5/1855	Great Western Rly (bg)
Pelsall	12	0–6–0	1/1851	South Staffordshire Rly [26]
Pembrey	7	0–6–0ST	1907	Burry Port & Gwendraeth Valley Rly [27]
Pembroke	3	2–4–0	1866	Pembroke & Tenby Rly [28]
Pembroke	3386	Atbara	8/1900	Great Western Rly
Pembroke Castle	4078	Castle	2/1924	Great Western Rly
Pembury	560	E4	11/1901	London, Brighton & South Coast Rly
Penarth	46	0–6–0	1858	Taff Vale Rly
Pendarves	–	?	c.1838	West Cornwall Rly
Pendeford Hall	4951	Hall	7/1929	Great Western Rly
Pendennis Castle	3253	Duke	5/1895	Great Western Rly [29]
Pendennis Castle	3253	Bulldog	11/1908	Great Western Rly
Pendennis Castle	4079	**Castle**	2/1924	**Great Western Rly** [30]
Pender	3	**2–4–0T**	1873	**Isle of Man Rly** [31]
Pendragon	3364	Bulldog	11/1900	Great Western Rly
Pendragon	746	King Arthur	6/1922	Southern Rly [32]
Pendragon	73083	5MT	7/1955	British Railways
Pendyffryn	–	**0–4–0VB**	1894	**Brecon Mountain Rly** [33]
Penfold	65	0–4–0	4/1845	Upper Medway Navigation Co. [34]

Name	Number	Class	Date	Railway
Penge	133	2–2–2	10/1859	London, Brighton & South Coast Rly [35]
Penguin	148	aCrewe	11/1853	London & North Western Rly [36]
Penguin	1117	1Experiment	1884	London & North Western Rly
Penguin	2012	2Precursor	11/1905	London & North Western Rly
Penguin	3742	Bulldog	1/1910	Great Western Rly
Penicuick	105	72	5/1881	North British Rly
Penicuik	241	165	1/1876	North British Rly [37]
Penicuik	297	165	1/1876	North British Rly [38]
Peninsular and Oriental S.N. Co.	21C6	**MN**	12/1941	**Southern Rly**
Penmaenmawr	295	bCrewe	11/1852	London & North Western Rly
Penmaenmawr	295	Newton	9/1870	London & North Western Rly
Penmaenmawr	295	rPrecedent	4/1893	London & North Western Rly
Penmaenmawr	1188	George V	4/1913	London & North Western Rly
Penn	–	Hawthorn	1/1866	Great Western Rly (bg)
Penn Green	54	**0–6–0ST**	1941	**East Anglian Railway Museum**
Penny Black	90019	90/0	1/1989	British Railways
Penrhos Grange	6868	Grange	3/1939	Great Western Rly
Penrice Castle	5057	Castle	6/1936	Great Western Rly [39]
Penrice Castle	5081	Castle	5/1939	Great Western Rly [40]
Penrice Castle	7023	Castle	6/1949	British Railways (Western Region)
Penrith	140	Peel	4/1859	Stockton & Darlington Rly
Penrith Beacon	75	2–2–2	7/1859	Lancaster & Carlisle Rly
Penrith Beacon	2187	Precedent	4/1875	London & North Western Rly
Penrith Beacon	2187	rPrecedent	12/1896	London & North Western Rly
Penrith Beacon	86255	86/2	1966	British Railways
Pensilva	2	0–4–0ST	1872	East Cornwall Mineral Rly [41]
Pentewan	–	0–6–0	1873	Pentewan Rly [42]
Penwith	–	2–4–0	1853	West Cornwall Rly
Penwith	2136	2–4–0ST	1853	Great Western Rly (bg) [43]
Penwithers	08954	08	1962	British Railways
Penydd Grange	6844	Grange	10/1937	Great Western Rly
Penyghent	4	2–2–2WT	6/1850	North Western Rly
Penyghent	44008	**Peak**	1959	**British Railways**
Pen-y-Ghent	60021	60	12/1990	British Railways
Penylan	–	0–6–0ST	8/1886	Port Talbot Rly [44]
Penzance	–	2–4–0T	4/1851	West Cornwall Rly
Penzance	–	0–4–0ST	1860	Llynvi & Ogmore Rly [45]
Penzance	1300	2–4–0	5/1860	Great Western Rly [46]
Penzance	3429	Bulldog	5/1903	Great Western Rly
Peplow Hall	4952	Hall	8/1929	Great Western Rly
(Percy)	68009	**J94**	1954	**North Norfolk Rly**
Percy Bysshe Shelley	2293	Prince/W	2/1914	London & North Western Rly
Peregrine	4903	A4	7/1938	London & North Eastern Rly [47]
Peregrine	60146	A1	4/1949	British Railways (Eastern Region)
Peri	–	Priam	11/1846	Great Western Rly (bg)

[21] An unsatisfactory design, the locomotive was reconstructed by Fairbairns in June 1842 and returned to traffic as no. 25 *Reindeer*.

[22] 18in gauge.

[23] 2ft gauge.

[24] Rebuilt from Liverpool & Manchester Railway 2–2–2 no. 73. Became a London & North Western engine in 1846.

[25] 18in gauge.

[26] Became LNWR no. 909 in 1862, and was sold to the Wrexham, Mold & Connah's Quay Railway in 1876. By then it was nameless.

[27] Became Great Western Railway no. 2176.

[28] Became Great Western Railway no. 1361.

[29] Name removed in May 1923 to avoid confusion with new Castle class locomotive.

[30] Preserved at Hammersley Iron Co., Australia.

[31] 3ft gauge. Sectioned and preserved at the Museum of Science and Industry at Manchester.

[32] Built for the London & South Western Railway to Robert Urie's design. Nameplates applied by the Southern Railway in 1925.

[33] 1ft 11½in gauge. De Winton vertical-boilered locomotive.

[34] Date of purchase by the Upper Medway Navigation Co. from unknown source. Bury type. UMN's railway ran from the river wharf at Tonbridge to Paddock Wood. It competed directly with the South Eastern Railway, and closed on 17 April 1847. The two locomotives, *Penfold* and *Polyphemus*, were sold to the South Eastern and given numbers as shown here. *Polyphemus* was used as a stationary boiler from October 1849, while *Penfold* continued in service. Both were withdrawn in 1851.

[35] Name applied by Stroudley in November 1871.

[36] Rebuilt from Liverpool & Manchester Railway 2–4–0 no. 90; became a London & North Western engine in 1846.

[37] Originally named *Roslin* and later renamed *Bervie*.

[38] Later renamed *Leith*.

[39] Renamed *Earl Waldegrave* in October 1937.

[40] Renamed *Lockheed Hudson* in January 1941.

[41] 3ft gauge. In June 1891 it was purchased by the Plymouth, Devonport & South Western Junction Railway and rebuilt as a standard gauge 0–4–2ST. In August 1912 it went to the West Sussex Light Railway, who renamed it *Hesperus*. It worked there until 1927.

[42] 2ft 6in gauge.

[43] Built for the South Devon Railway, to standard gauge. Converted to broad gauge in January 1872.

[44] Built for the Cefn & Pyle Railway, which the Port Talbot took over on 1 January 1897. It may have been Port Talbot Railway no. 16, but evidence that the number was in fact carried is lacking.

[45] Became Great Western Railway no. 916.

[46] Built for the West Cornwall Railway.

[47] Renamed *Lord Faringdon* in March 1948.

Name	Number	Class	Date	Railway
Perkins	–	0–4–4DM	1929	**Ravenglass & Eskdale Rly** [48]
Perseus	57	2–4–0	6/1848	Manchester, Sheffield & Lincolnshire Rly
Perseus	–	Iron Duke	6/1850	Great Western Rly (bg)
Perseus	3345	Bulldog	2/1900	Great Western Rly
Perseus	2494	George V	8/1911	London & North Western Rly
Perseus	26053	EM1	3/1953	British Railways
Perseverance	–	0–4–0	1830	Rainhill Trials Competitor
Perseverance	–	0–4–2	10/1830	London & South Western Rly
Perseverance	14	0–4–2T	1854	Wrexham, Mold & Connah's Quay Rly [49]
Perseverance	2180	Precedent	3/1875	London & North Western Rly
Perseverance	2180	rPrecedent	3/1897	London & North Western Rly
Perseverance	255	aSentinel	1928	London & North Eastern Rly
Perseverance	5731	Jubilee	1936	London Midland & Scottish Rly
Pershore	28	4–2–0	6/1841	Birmingham & Gloucester Rly
Pershore Plum	3353	Bulldog	11/1900	Great Western Rly [50]
Persia	280	2Vesuvius	2/1873	London & South Western Rly
Persia	2276	Prince/W	4/1916	London & North Western Rly
Persil	–	0–4–0DM	1952	**Southport Railway Centre**
Persimmon	2549	A3	10/1924	London & North Eastern Rly
Perthshire	34	Glenbarry	10/1863	Highland Rly [51]
Perthshire	62	Duke	6/1874	Highland Rly [52]
Perthshire	250	D49/1	3/1928	London & North Eastern Rly
Pertinax	131	Adrian	9/1866	London, Chatham & Dover Rly
Pet	–	0–4–0T	6/1865	**London & North Western Rly** [53]
Petain	627	C	1/1890	North British Rly
Peter	3	0–4–0T	c.1870	Torrington & Marland Rly [54]
Peter	–	0–6–0ST	1896	**Telford Horsehay Steam Trust**
Peter	–	0–4–0ST	1918	**Amberley Chalk Pits Museum** [55]
Peter	–	0–4–0DM	1940	**Bodmin & Wenford Rly**
(Peter)	02003	02	1960	**British Railways**
Peterborough Depot	58023	58	1984	British Railways
Peter Pan	–	0–4–0ST	1922	**Leighton Buzzard Rly** [56]
Peter Pan	86259	86/2	1966	British Railways
Peter Pan	86045	86/0	1/1966	British Railways
Peter Poundtext	497	Scott	12/1920	North British Rly
Peterston Grange	6867	Grange	3/1939	Great Western Rly
Petrel	4	2–4–0	9/1847	Whitehaven & Furness Junction Rly [57]
Petrel	838	S/Bloomer	1854	London & North Western Rly
Petrel	149	bCrewe	11/1855	London & North Western Rly [58]
Petrel	11	Tiger	10/1861	London, Chatham & Dover Rly
Petrel	209	Samson	5/1879	London & North Western Rly [59]
Petrel	209	Whitworth	8/1895	London & North Western Rly [60]
Petrel	1744	Prince/W	1/1916	London & North Western Rly
Petrolea	760	T19	1886	Great Eastern Rly
Petrolea	–	0–4–0ST	1914	Woolwich Arsenal [61]
Petrolea	37888	37/7	4/1963	British Railways
Petrolea	58042	58	5/1986	British Railways
Petteril	12	2–4–0	1857	Lancaster & Carlisle Rly
Petunia	4110	Flower	6/1908	Great Western Rly
Petworth	334	G	7/1881	London, Brighton & South Coast Rly

Name	Number	Class	Date	Railway
Pevensey	196	2–2–2	12/1865	London, Brighton & South Coast Rly [62]
Pevensey	176	Gladstone	11/1890	London, Brighton & South Coast Rly
Peveril	6	2–4–0T	1875	**Isle of Man Rly** [63]
Peveril of the Peak	2985	Saint	7/1905	Great Western Rly [64]
Peveril Point	2041	H1	2/1906	Southern Rly [65]
Phaeton	104	aCrewe	5/1847	London & North Western Rly
Phaeton	30	Phaeton	11/1848	East Lancashire Rly
Phaeton	1218	Newton	4/1872	London & North Western Rly
Phaeton	1218	rPrecedent	11/1890	London & North Western Rly
Phaeton	–	0–4–0ST	1901	Woolwich Arsenal [66]
Phaeton	2086	George V	4/1913	London & North Western Rly
(Phaeton)	45149	45	1961	**British Railways**
Phalaris	15	2–2–2	1837	Grand Junction Rly
Phalaris	15	bCrewe	4/1844	London & North Western Rly
Phalaris	285	Samson	9/1873	London & North Western Rly
Phalaris	285	Whitworth	3/1893	London & North Western Rly

Great Eastern Railway T19 class 2–4–0 no. 760 *Petrolea*. (Photo: LCGB Ken Nunn Collection)

Name	Number	Class	Date	Railway
Phalaris	1297	2Precursor	8/1907	London & North Western Rly
Phantom	56	2–2–2	1839	Grand Junction Rly
Phantom	19	2–2–0	6/1840	Midland Counties Rly
Phantom	56	bCrewe	11/1848	London & North Western Rly
Phantom	38	Aurora	4/1849	East Lancashire Rly
Phantom	38	Craven	4/1876	East Lancashire Rly
Phantom	883	Precedent	5/1877	London & North Western Rly
Phantom	883	rPrecedent	8/1894	London & North Western Rly
Phanton	37209	37/0	1964	British Railways
Pheasant	141	aCrewe	5/1851	London & North Western Rly [67]
Pheasant	666	S/Bloomer	1854	London & North Western Rly
Pheasant	263	Samson	5/1879	London & North Western Rly
Pheasant	263	Whitworth	1895	London & North Western Rly
Pheasant	2076	2Experiment	1/1909	London & North Western Rly

[48] 15in gauge.

[49] Built by Dodds & Co. of Rotherham as an 0–4–2 tender engine. Rebuilt as 0–4–2T by Newport, Abergavenny & Hereford Railway, 1860. Became West Midland Railway no. 92 in 1861 and Great Western no. 227 in 1863. Sold to Bishops Castle Railway in 1870 and named *Perseverance*. Sold in 1887 to the Wrexham, Mold & Connah's Quay Railway as their no. 14, and disposed of in 1895.

[50] Originally named *Plymouth* until May 1927. Its original number was 3365.

[51] Originally named *Seafield*. Altered from 2–2–2 to 2–4–0 in December 1883, and renamed *Perthshire* in about 1889.

[52] Later renamed *Stemster* (1889), *Huntingtower* (1899) and *Ault Wharrie* (1903).

[53] 18in gauge.

[54] 3ft gauge. The Torrington & Marland Railway was rebuilt to standard gauge and formed part of the Southern Railway's Halwill–Torrington line.

[55] 2ft gauge.

[56] 2ft gauge.

[57] Originally named *Maryport*.

[58] Previously Liverpool & Manchester Railway no. 91; became a London & North Western engine in 1846 as no. 379 *Combermere*.

[59] Transferred to Engineers Department from 1902 to 1923 and renamed *Engineer Northampton*.

[60] Transferred to Engineers Department from 1914 to 1932 and renamed *Engineer Crewe*. Between January and August 1932 it was renamed *Engineer South Wales*.

[61] 18in gauge.

[62] Name applied by Stroudley in February 1871.

[63] 3ft gauge.

[64] Named *Winterstoke* in February 1906, and renamed *Peveril of the Peak* in April 1907.

[65] Built for the London, Brighton & South Coast Railway. Nameplates applied by Southern Railway in March 1925.

[66] 18in gauge.

[67] Previously Liverpool & Manchester Railway no. 82. Became a London & North Western engine in 1846.

Name	Number	Class	Date	Railway
Phenomena	2291	dSentinel	1930	London & North Eastern Rly
Philadelphia	13	4–2–0	5/1840	Birmingham & Gloucester Rly
Philip Rose	187	Gladstone	6/1889	London, Brighton & South Coast Rly
Phillips-Imperial	31233	31/1	1960	British Railways
Phlegethon	72	2–2–2	7/1841	Grand Junction Rly
Phlegethon	–	Priam	5/1842	Great Western Rly (bg)
Phlegethon	72	bCrewe	4/1853	London & North Western Rly
Phlegethon	–	Hawthorn	1/1866	Great Western Rly (bg)
Phlegon	36	4–2–0	1/1848	Manchester, Sheffield & Lincolnshire Rly
Phlegon	99	Fireball	9/1848	London & South Western Rly
Phlegon	7	0–6–0	4/1858	Manchester, Sheffield & Lincolnshire Rly
Phlegon	99	Clyde	9/1868	London & South Western Rly
P.H. Chambres	445	George V	1/1911	London & North Western Rly
Phoebus	34	2–2–2	1838	Grand Junction Rly
Phoebus	34	2–2–2	8/1841	Grand Junction Rly
Phoebus	34	aCrewe	5/1850	London & North Western Rly
Phoebus	34	DX	c.1860	London & North Western Rly
Phoenix	6	0–2–2	1830	Liverpool & Manchester Rly
Phoenix	–	0–4–0	8/1832	Leicester & Swannington Rly
Phoenix	49	2–2–2	1836	Liverpool & Manchester Rly
Phoenix	33	Fenton	5/1840	London & South Western Rly
Phoenix	–	Priam	8/1842	Great Western Rly (bg)
Phoenix	3	2–4–0	9/1847	Whitehaven & Furness Junction Rly [68]
Phoenix	77	2–4–0	11/1849	Manchester, Sheffield & Lincolnshire Rly
Phoenix	43	Iron Duke	12/1849	East Lancashire Rly
Phoenix	33	Tartar	7/1852	London & South Western Rly
Phoenix	?	2–4–0	?	Whitehaven & Furness Junction Rly
Phoenix	33	Standard	2/1872	London & South Western Rly
Phoenix	–	0–4–0ST	1902	Woolwich Arsenal [69]
Phoenix	**70**	**0–6–0T**	**1921**	**East Lancashire Rly [70]**
Phoenix	6132	Royal Scot	9/1927	London Midland & Scottish Rly [71]
Phoenix	254	aSentinel	1928	London & North Eastern Rly
Phoenix	5736	Jubilee	1936	London Midland & Scottish Rly
Phoenix	**1**	**4wDM**	**1941**	**South Tynedale Rly [72]**
Phoenix	**–**	**4wDM**	**1958**	**Rutland Railway Museum**
Phoenix	31160	31	1960	British Railways
Phoenix	86219	86/2	1965	British Railways
Phosphorus	61	2–2–2	6/1840	Grand Junction Rly
Phosphorus	61	aCrewe	11/1850	London & North Western Rly
Phosphorus	61	Problem	c.1860	London & North Western Rly
Phosphorus	830	2Experiment	9/1907	London & North Western Rly
Picardy	133	E1	12/1878	London, Brighton & South Coast Rly
Piccadilly	41	A1	6/1877	London, Brighton & South Coast Rly
Piccadilly	414	E6	10/1905	London, Brighton & South Coast Rly
Piccadilly	08673	08	1960	British Railways
Pierremont	98	Pierremont	5/1855	Stockton & Darlington Rly
Pilkington	334	2–4–0	2/1865	Lancashire & Yorkshire Rly
Pilkington	668	627	7/1881	Lancashire & Yorkshire Rly
Pillar	60097	60	12/1992	British Railways
Pilot	–	0–6–0	1836	Clarence Rly
Pilot	26	Tory	6/1840	Stockton & Darlington Rly

Name	Number	Class	Date	Railway
Pilot	3	2–4–0	9/1844	Bristol & Gloucester Rly (bg)
Pilot	181	bCrewe	11/1847	London & North Western Rly
Pilot	864	Precedent	5/1877	London & North Western Rly
Pilot	864	rPrecedent	6/1896	London & North Western Rly
Pilot	2121	Clayton	1927	London & North Eastern Rly
Pimlico	13	D1	12/1874	London, Brighton & South Coast Rly
Pinza	55007	Deltic	6/1961	British Railways
Pioneer	36	0–4–2	6/1841	Manchester & Leeds Rly
Pioneer	1	2–2–2T	1861	Isle of Wight Central Rly [73]
Pioneer	–	Caesar	7/1861	Great Western Rly (bg)
Pioneer	17	0–6–0ST	12/1861	Brecon & Merthyr Rly [74]
Pioneer	35	Dawn	10/1862	London, Chatham & Dover Rly
Pioneer	–	0–4–4–0F	1870	Burry Port & Gwendraeth Valley Rly [75]
Pioneer	1212	Newton	3/1872	London & North Western Rly
Pioneer	407	0–4–0ST	3/1876	London & South Western Rly
Pioneer	–	0–4–0WT	11/1877	Campbeltown & Machrihanish Rly [76]
Pioneer	1212	rPrecedent	11/1888	London & North Western Rly
Pioneer	–	2–6–2T	1893	Pentewan Rly [77]
Pioneer	–	0–4–0ST	1897	Fishguard & Rosslare Railways & Harbours Co.
Pioneer	8	0–6–0T	3/1909	Burry Port & Gwendraeth Valley Rly [78]
Pirate	–	Abbott	5/1855	Great Western Rly (bg)
Pisces	–	Leo	7/1842	Great Western Rly (bg)
Pitchford Hall	**4953**	**Hall**	**8/1929**	**Great Western Rly**
Pitsea	12	Class 1	1880	London, Tilbury & Southend Rly
Pitsford	**–**	**0–6–0ST**	**1923**	**Steamtown, Carnforth**
Pitt	1522	Newton	11/1866	London & North Western Rly
Pitt	1522	rPrecedent	1/1888	London & North Western Rly
Pivot	17	4–2–0	7/1840	Birmingham & Gloucester Rly
Pixie	**–**	**0–4–0ST**	**1919**	**Cadeby Light Rly [79]**
Pixie	**2**	**0–4–0ST**	**1922**	**Leighton Buzzard Rly [80]**
Plaish Hall	4954	Hall	8/1929	Great Western Rly
Plaistow	5	Class 1	1880	London, Tilbury & Southend Rly
Planet	9	2–2–0	1830	Liverpool & Manchester Rly
Planet	10	Planet	11/1830	Stockton & Darlington Rly
Planet	–	2–2–2	8/1839	Great Western Rly (bg)
Planet	28	0–6–0	1846	Newcastle & Carlisle Rly [81]
Planet	157	Panther	8/1861	Stockton & Darlington Rly
Planet	935	Samson	1/1866	London & North Western Rly
Planet	935	Whitworth	4/1893	London & North Western Rly
Planet	2197	George V	4/1913	London & North Western Rly
Planet	6131	Royal Scot	9/1927	London Midland & Scottish Rly [82]
Planet	**–**	**4wPM**	**1931**	**Leicestershire Museum [83]**
Planet	45545	Patriot	3/1934	British Railways [84]
Planet	86218	86/2	1965	British Railways
Planet	**9**	**replica**	**1992**	**Liverpool & Manchester Rly [85]**
Plasfynnon	36	0–4–0ST	6/1863	Cambrian Railways
Plaspower Hall	4955	Hall	8/1929	Great Western Rly
Plato	–	Banking	9/1854	Great Western Rly (bg)
Plews	180	2–2–2	1848	North Eastern Rly [86]
Plowden	–	2–4–0	?	Bishops Castle Rly [87]
Plowden Hall	4956	Hall	9/1929	Great Western Rly
Pluck	2178	Precedent	3/1875	London & North Western Rly
Pluck	2178	rPrecedent	1/1894	London & North Western Rly

[68] Originally named *Lonsdale*.

[69] 18in gauge.

[70] The modern, preserved East Lancashire Railway.

[71] Renamed *The King's Regiment, Liverpool* in May 1936.

[72] 2ft gauge.

[73] Formerly the Cowes & Newport Railway.

[74] Renamed *Blanche* by 1871.

[75] Later renamed *Mountaineer*.

[76] 2ft 3in gauge. Later altered to 0–4–2WT. It was delivered by steamer on 11 November 1877, maker unknown, for use at Argyll Coal & Cannel Co. Ltd's colliery. It was out of use by 1906 and was never included in Campbeltown & Machrihanish Light Railway stock, but is included here for the sake of completeness.

[77] 2ft 6in gauge. Purchased in 1913 from the Chattenden & Upnor Naval Tramway.

[78] Later became Great Western Railway no. 2197.

[79] 2ft gauge. Built by Bagnall of Stafford, works no. 2090.

[80] 2ft gauge. Built by Kerr Stuart, Stoke on Trent, in 1922. Works no. 4260.

[81] Became North Eastern Railway no. 476 in 1862, and was rebuilt to 0–6–0ST in 1873.

[82] Renamed *The Royal Warwickshire Regiment* in May 1936.

[83] 1ft 11½in gauge.

[84] Built for the London Midland & Scottish Railway. Name applied by British Railways in November 1948, when the engine was rebuilt with a taper boiler.

[85] At the Greater Manchester Museum of Science & Industry.

[86] Ex-York & North Midland Railway.

[87] Actually an 0–6–0 minus the front coupling rods! Said to be ex-St Helens Railway.

Name	Number	Class	Date	Railway
Plumer	657	C	7/1891	North British Rly
Plumpton	345	G	3/1882	London, Brighton & South Coast Rly
Plutarch	–	Caesar	9/1862	Great Western Rly (bg)
Pluto	27	2–2–0	1832	Liverpool & Manchester Rly [88]
Pluto	–	Priam	8/1841	Great Western Rly (bg)
Pluto	44	1Hercules	12/1841	London & South Western Rly
Pluto	11	2–2–2	3/1845	Manchester, Sheffield & Lincolnshire Rly
Pluto	47	Pluto	3/1850	East Lancashire Rly
Pluto	276	bCrewe	11/1851	London & North Western Rly
Pluto	44	2Hercules	11/1854	London & South Western Rly
Pluto	44	0–6–0	1857	Taff Vale Rly
Pluto	8	A	6/1864	Metropolitan Rly
Pluto	2123	4–4–0ST	10/1866	Great Western Rly (bg) [89]
Pluto	276	Newton	9/1870	London & North Western Rly
Pluto	44	Standard	10/1875	London & South Western Rly
Pluto	276	rPrecedent	11/1888	London & North Western Rly
Pluto	3344	Bulldog	2/1900	Great Western Rly
Pluto	–	0–4–0ST	1901	Woolwich Arsenal [90]
Pluto	745	Prince/W	1/1916	London & North Western Rly
Pluto	70214	0–6–0DE	6/1936	Martin Mill Military Rly
Pluto	26054	EM1	4/1953	British Railways
Plutus	98	Fireball	8/1848	London & South Western Rly
Plutus	43	0–4–2	11/1849	Manchester, Sheffield & Lincolnshire Rly
Plutus	–	Caesar	2/1855	Great Western Rly (bg)
Plutus	98	Clyde	6/1868	London & South Western Rly
Plym	–	Caesar	6/1859	Great Western Rly (bg)
Plymouth	–	0–4–2	1841	Taff Vale Rly
Plymouth	3	0–6–0	1862	Taff Vale Rly
Plymouth	3365	Bulldog	11/1900	Great Western Rly [91]
Plymouth	21C103	rWC	6/1945	Southern Rly
Plymouth	08953	08	1962	British Railways
Plymouth SPIRIT OF DISCOVERY	43193	43	6/1982	British Railways [92]
Plynlimmon	1183	Precedent	9/1878	London & North Western Rly
Plynlimmon	2	2–4–2T	1891	Manchester & Milford Rly [93]
Plynlimmon	1183	rPrecedent	8/1896	London & North Western Rly
Plynlimmon	257	Prince/W	11/1915	London & North Western Rly
Plynlimon	43	Small Pass	3/1864	Cambrian Railways
Plynlimon	60010	60	1/1991	British Railways [94]
Pochard	4499	A4	4/1938	London & North Eastern Rly [95]
Pochard	47121	47/0	1964	British Railways
Polam	127	Peel	6/1858	Stockton & Darlington Rly
Polar Bear	–	2–4–0T	1905	Groudle Glen Rly [96]
Polar Star	–	Wolf	7/1840	Great Western Rly (bg)
Polar Star	4005	Star	2/1907	Great Western Rly
Polar Star	70026	Britannia	12/1952	British Railways
Polegate	239	2–2–2	5/1867	London, Brighton & South Coast Rly [97]
Polegate	392	D3	6/1894	London, Brighton & South Coast Rly
Polesden	92	E1	11/1883	London, Brighton & South Coast Rly
Pollux	–	Priam	7/1842	Great Western Rly (bg)
Pollux	200	bCrewe	3/1848	London & North Western Rly
Pollux	118	0–6–0	1853	Oxford, Worcester & Wolverhampton Rly [98]
Pollux	2120	4–4–0ST	5/1865	Great Western Rly (bg) [99]
Pollux	–	Hawthorn	2/1866	Great Western Rly (bg)
Polmont	213	211	1856	North British Rly [100]
Polton	240	165	1/1878	North British Rly [101]
Polumephus	–	0–4–0ST	1901	Woolwich Arsenal [102]
Polyanthus	4118	Flower	7/1908	Great Western Rly
Polyphemus	–	0–6–0VB	12/1844	Upper Medway Navigation Co. [103]
Polyphemus	96	aCrewe	11/1846	London & North Western Rly
Polyphemus	53	2–4–0	1/1848	Manchester, Sheffield & Lincolnshire Rly
Polyphemus	892	L/Bloomer	1851	London & North Western Rly
Polyphemus	1929	Jubilee	4/1900	London & North Western Rly
Polyphemus	5688	Jubilee	1936	London Midland & Scottish Rly
Pommern	60133	A1	10/1948	British Railways (Eastern Region)
Pompey	–	0–4–0ST	1912	Woolwich Arsenal [104]
Ponsonby Hall	7	0–6–0ST	1896	Cleator & Workington Junction Rly
Pontyberem	**2**	**0–6–0ST**	**1900**	**Burry Port & Gwendraeth Valley Rly**
Pontypool	–	0–6–0ST	2/1866	West Somerset Mineral Rly
Pontypridd	7	0–6–2ST	1857	Alexandra (Newport & South Wales) Docks & Rly
Pontypridd	9	0–6–0T	8/1866	Alexandra (Newport & South Wales) Docks & Rly [105]
Pony	**–**	**0–4–0ST**	**1912**	**County School**
Poplar	**70**	**A1**	**12/1872**	**London, Brighton & South Coast Rly [106]**
Poppy	**27**	**4wDM**	**1957**	**Leighton Buzzard Rly [107]**
Porchester	518	E4	6/1901	London, Brighton & South Coast Rly
Portbury	**S3**	**0–6–0ST**	**1917**	**Bristol Industrial Museum**
Portelet	2	Sentinel	1/1924	Jersey Rly [108]
PORTERBROOK	47810	47/4	1/1966	British Railways
Portessie	14	Yankee	10/1893	Highland Rly
Portfield	519	E4	6/1901	London, Brighton & South Coast Rly
Porth	9	0–6–0	1859	Taff Vale Rly
Portishead	2	0–6–0T	6/1877	Weston, Clevedon & Portishead Rly [109]
Portishead	–	0–6–0T	1887	Weston, Clevedon & Portishead Rly [110]
Portishead	2	0–6–0ST	1890	Weston, Clevedon & Portishead Rly [111]
Portland Bill	2038	H1	12/1905	Southern Rly [112]
Port Line	**35027**	**MN**	**12/1948**	**British Railways (Southern Region)**
Port of Liverpool	47286	47/0	1966	British Railways
Port of Tilbury	37059	37/0	1962	British Railways
Port of Tyne Authority	56135	56	1984	British Railways
Portslade	160	E1	7/1891	London, Brighton & South Coast Rly

[88] In 1846 became London & North Western Railway no. 127.

[89] Built for the South Devon Railway.

[90] 18in gauge.

[91] Renamed *Pershore Plum* in May 1927, and renumbered 3353.

[92] Later renamed *Yorkshire Post*.

[93] Became Great Western Railway no. 1304.

[94] Also named (on the other side) *Pumlumon*.

[95] Renamed *Sir Murrough Wilson* in April 1939.

[96] 2ft gauge. Preserved at the Amberley Chalk Pits Museum.

[97] Name applied in May 1870.

[98] Purchased from the Manchester, Sheffield & Lincolnshire Railway.

[99] Built for the South Devon Railway.

[100] Ex-Edinburgh & Glasgow Railway, absorbed by the NBR in 1865.

[101] Originally named *Coatbridge*.

[102] 18in gauge.

[103] At any rate, this was the date of the boiler! It was built for the Upper Medway Navigation Co., whose railway ran from the river wharf at Tonbridge to Paddock Wood. It competed directly with the South Eastern Railway, and closed on 17 April 1847. The two locomotives, *Penfold* and *Polyphemus*, were sold to the South Eastern and given numbers as shown here. *Polyphemus* was used as a stationary boiler from October 1849, while *Penfold* continued in service. Both were withdrawn in 1851.

[104] 18in gauge.

[105] Said to have carried the name. Formerly London, Brighton & South Coast Railway no. 228.

[106] Sold to the Kent & East Sussex Railway in May 1901 as their no. 3 *Bodiam*. Taken into British Railways stock on nationalization in 1948 as no. 32670.

[107] 2ft gauge.

[108] Sentinel-Cammell steam railcar. 3ft 6in gauge. Originally named *The Pioneer No 2*.

[109] Purchased by the WC&PR from the Southern Railway in December 1925 or January 1926, their SR no. B643. Originally it was London, Brighton & South Coast Railway no. 43 *Gipsy Hill*, an A1x class 0–6–0T. Became Great Western Railway no. 5, retaining the name *Portishead*.

[110] Purchased (source unknown), c. 1889. Ran for a while without front coupling rods as a 2–4–0T. Sold in 1900.

[111] Purchased (source unknown) in 1907.

[112] Built for the London, Brighton & South Coast Railway. Nameplates applied by the Southern Railway in May 1925.

Name	Number	Class	Date	Railway
Portsmouth	195	2–2–2	7/1864	London, Brighton & South Coast Rly [113]
Portsmouth	385	D3	12/1893	London, Brighton & South Coast Rly
Poste Restante	47774	47/7		British Railways
Post Haste	73138	73/1	1966	British Railways
Post Haste	86319	86/3	1965	British Railways
150 YEARS OF TRAVELLING POST OFFICES				
Post Haste	86419	86/4		British Railways
150 YEARS OF TRAVELLING POST OFFICES				
Postlip Hall	4957	Hall	9/1929	Great Western Rly
Postman's Pride	08888	08	1962	British Railways
Potiers	127	E1	10/1878	London, Brighton & South Coast Rly
Poulton	–	0–6–0	?	Preston & Wyre Railway, Harbour & Dock Co.
Poulton Grange	6843	Grange	10/1937	Great Western Rly
Powderham	3262	Duke	4/1896	Great Western Rly [114]
Powderham	3262	Bulldog	10/1906	Great Western Rly
Powderham Castle	4080	Castle	3/1924	Great Western Rly
Powerful	1924	Jubilee	3/1900	London & North Western Rly
Powerful	3385	Atbara	7/1900	Great Western Rly
Powerful	3392	Atbara	9/1900	Great Western Rly [115]
Powerful	D836	Warship	9/1960	British Railways
Powis	239	bCrewe	4/1849	London & North Western Rly
Powis Castle	5059	Castle	5/1937	Great Western Rly [116]
Powis Castle	5082	Castle	6/1939	Great Western Rly [117]
Powis Castle	7024	Castle	6/1949	British Railways (Western Region)
Poynings	477	E4	10/1898	London, Brighton & South Coast Rly [118]
Precedent	2175	Precedent	12/1874	London & North Western Rly
Precedent	2175	rPrecedent	11/1894	London & North Western Rly
Precedent	1749	Prince/W	11/1915	London & North Western Rly
Precelly	1379	0–6–0ST	1/1875	Great Western Rly [119]
Precursor	255	bCrewe	3/1850	London & North Western Rly
Precursor	2	2–2–2T	1861	Isle of Wight Central Rly [120]
Precursor	2145	1Precursor	4/1874	London & North Western Rly
Precursor	513	2Precursor	3/1904	London & North Western Rly
Premier	–	2–2–2	11/1837	Great Western Rly (bg)
Premier	–	Fury	2/1846	Great Western Rly (bg)
Premier	93	aCrewe	10/1846	London & North Western Rly
Premier	1216	Newton	4/1872	London & North Western Rly
Premier	8	0–6–0ST	1880	Wrexham, Mold & Connah's Quay Rly [121]
Premier	1216	rPrecedent	11/1888	London & North Western Rly
Premier	**–**	**0–4–2ST**	**1905**	**Sittingbourne & Kemsley Light Rly** [122]
Premier	1694	Prince/W	11/1919	London & North Western Rly
President	20	4–2–0	12/1840	Birmingham & Gloucester Rly
President	238	bCrewe	5/1849	London & North Western Rly
President	1007	L/Bloomer	1851	London & North Western Rly
President	103	4–4–2	6/1905	Great Western Rly [123]
President	1992	2Experiment	10/1906	London & North Western Rly
President Garfield	253	Precedent	1/1882	London & North Western Rly
President Garfield	253	rPrecedent	2/1895	London & North Western Rly
President Lincoln	254	Precedent	1/1882	London & North Western Rly

Name	Number	Class	Date	Railway
President Lincoln	254	rPrecedent	2/1895	London & North Western Rly
President Lincoln	2627	2Experiment	3/1909	London & North Western Rly
President Washington	256	Precedent	1/1882	London & North Western Rly
President Washington	256	rPrecedent	8/1894	London & North Western Rly
Prestatyn	5522	Patriot	3/1933	London Midland & Scottish Rly [124]
Preston	–	2–2–2	?	Preston & Wyre Railway, Harbour & Dock Co.
Preston	76	2–2–2	7/1859	Lancaster & Carlisle Rly
Preston	8	2–4–0	2/1862	West Lancashire Rly [125]
Preston	63	A1	10/1875	London, Brighton & South Coast Rly
Prestongrange	**7**	**0–4–2ST**	**1914**	**Scottish Mining Museum – Prestongrange**
Preston Guild *1328–1992*	86212	86/2	1966	British Railways
Preston Hall	5911	Hall	6/1931	Great Western Rly
Pretoria	**–**	**0–4–0T**	**1866**	**Talyllyn Rly** [126]
Pretoria	3374	Atbara	4/1900	Great Western Rly [127]
Pretoria	3389	Atbara	8/1900	Great Western Rly [128]
Pretoria	63	B4	8/1901	London, Brighton & South Coast Rly
Pretty Polly	2560	A3	3/1925	London & North Eastern Rly
Priam	–	Priam	3/1842	Great Western Rly (bg)
Priam	66	Priam	11/1847	Stockton & Darlington Rly
Priam	2100	4–4–0ST	11/1851	Great Western Rly (bg) [129]
Priam	20	0–6–0	1855	South Staffordshire Rly
Pride of Laira	43179	43	11/1981	British Railways
Primrose	4119	Flower	7/1908	Great Western Rly
Primrose	**27**	**P**	**2/1910**	**Bluebell Rly** [130]
Primrose No 2	**–**	**0–6–0ST**	**1952**	**Yorkshire Dales Rly**
Prince	21	Fairbairn	12/1841	London & South Western Rly [131]
Prince	7	Tory	3/1843	Stockton & Darlington Rly
Prince	73	2–2–2	6/1845	Grand Junction Rly
Prince	–	Priam	8/1846	Great Western Rly (bg)
Prince	21	2Hercules	4/1853	London & South Western Rly
Prince	2	0–4–0TT	1863	Festiniog Rly [132]
Prince	30	Glenbarry	10/1863	Highland Rly [133]
Prince	2137	2–4–0ST	6/1871	Great Western Rly (bg) [134]
Prince	21	2Vesuvius	12/1871	London & South Western Rly
Prince Albert	–	0–6–0	?	Sirhowy Rly [135]
Prince Albert	73	aCrewe	6/1845	London & North Western Rly
Prince Albert	65	2–2–2	8/1848	Manchester, Sheffield & Lincolnshire Rly
Prince Albert	1214	Newton	4/1872	London & North Western Rly
Prince Albert	1214	rPrecedent	11/1890	London & North Western Rly
Prince Albert	4042	Star	5/1913	Great Western Rly
Prince Albert	1178	Prince/W	9/1919	London & North Western Rly
Prince Albert	509	11F	3/1920	Great Central Rly
Prince Alfred	–	0–4–0	9/1839	Llanelly Rly [136]
Prince Alfred	622	Problem	c.1860	London & North Western Rly
Prince Arthur	315	aCrewe	7/1853	London & North Western Rly
Prince Christian	1118	Queen	3/1875	Great Western Rly
Prince Edward Island	5560	Jubilee	1934	London Midland & Scottish Rly

[113] Name applied by Stroudley in August 1870.

[114] Nameplates removed in May 1923 to avoid confusion with new Castle class locomotive.

[115] Originally named *White*. Temporarily renamed *Powerful* for a City Imperial Volunteers' Special Train on 29 October 1900.

[116] Renamed *Earl St. Aldwyn* in October 1937.

[117] Renamed *Swordfish* in January 1941.

[118] Rebuilt to class E4x, April 1911.

[119] Built for the North Pembrokeshire & Fishguard Railway.

[120] Formerly the Cowes & Newport Railway.

[121] After absorption by the Great Central Railway in 1904, it was renumbered 401. Then it was successively renumbered 405 in 1910 and 405C in 1912. Scrapped in September 1922.

[122] 2ft 6in gauge.

[123] Name not fitted until 1907.

[124] Rebuilt with taper boiler in February 1949.

[125] Originally LBSCR no. 150, renumbered 455 in October 1880. Sold to the WLR in April 1883, becoming their no. 8 *Preston*.

[126] *Dolgoch* (numbered 2 in Preservation Society days) was named *Pretoria* for a while during the Boer War.

[127] Originally named *Baden Powell*. Temporarily renamed *Pretoria* for City Imperial Volunteers' Special Train on 29 October 1900, *Britannia* for Royal Trains on 7 and 10 March 1902, and *Kitchener* for a Special Train on 12 July 1902.

[128] Originally named *Sir Daniel* until November 1900.

[129] Formerly the South Devon Railway.

[130] Formerly Southern Railway no. 1027 and British Railways 31027. Carried the name *Primrose* in 1961–2.

[131] Originally *Reed* (no number), of November 1838. An unsatisfactory design, the class was despatched to Fairbairns for total rebuilding. On return, *Reed* had become no. 21 *Prince*.

[132] 1ft 11½in gauge.

[133] Altered from 2–2–2 to 2–4–0 in September 1891.

[134] Built for the South Devon Railway.

[135] Built some time between 1832 and 1853.

[136] Renamed *Alfred* in 1862. Became Great Western Railway no. 897, and altered to 0–4–2.

Name	Number	Class	Date	Railway
Prince Edward of Wales	–	4–4–2	1915	Fairbourne Miniature Rly [137]
Prince Ernest	313	aCrewe	6/1853	London & North Western Rly
Prince Eugene	316	aCrewe	8/1853	London & North Western Rly
Prince George	2052	G.Britain	1894	London & North Western Rly
Prince George	1135	2Experiment	9/1907	London & North Western Rly
Prince George	4044	Star	5/1913	Great Western Rly
Prince George	437	11E	11/1913	Great Central Rly [138]
Prince Henry	4043	Star	5/1913	Great Western Rly
Prince Henry	429	11E	11/1913	Great Central Rly [139]
Prince Henry	47799	47/7		British Railways
Prince John	4045	Star	6/1913	Great Western Rly
Prince Leopold	857	Precedent	4/1877	London & North Western Rly
Prince Leopold	671	627	9/1881	Lancashire & Yorkshire Rly
Prince Leopold	857	rPrecedent	7/1897	London & North Western Rly
Prince of Wales	–	0–6–0	5/1843	Llanelly Rly [140]
Prince of Wales	13	2–2–2	9/1847	Shrewsbury & Chester Rly [141]
Prince of Wales	291	aCrewe	11/1852	London & North Western Rly
Prince of Wales	76	Peel	2/1854	Stockton & Darlington Rly
Prince of Wales	291	Problem	c.1860	London & North Western Rly
Prince of Wales	12	S/Goods	12/1861	Cambrian Railways
Prince of Wales	1132	Queen	7/1875	Great Western Rly
Prince of Wales	865	863	6/1885	Lancashire & Yorkshire Rly
Prince of Wales	**2**	**2–6–2T**	**1/1902**	**Vale of Rheidol Rly** [142]
Prince of Wales	46	B4	9/1902	London, Brighton & South Coast Rly
Prince of Wales	819	Prince/W	10/1911	London & North Western Rly
Prince of Wales	4041	Star	6/1913	Great Western Rly
Prince of Wales	508	11F	3/1920	Great Central Rly
Prince of Wales	2553	A3	12/1924	London & North Eastern Rly [143]
Prince Oscar	561	Problem	c.1860	London & North Western Rly
Prince Palatine	2551	A3	11/1924	London & North Eastern Rly
Prince Regent	310	cSentinel	1929	London & North Eastern Rly
Prince Rupert	5671	Jubilee	1935	London Midland & Scottish Rly

Name	Number	Class	Date	Railway
Princess	20	Fairbairn	11/1841	London & South Western Rly [144]
Princess	19	aCrewe	7/1845	Grand Junction Rly
Princess	20	2Sussex	12/1852	London & South Western Rly
Princess	**1**	**0–4–0TT**	**1863**	**Festiniog Rly** [145]
Princess	–	0–6–0ST	5/1863	South Wales Mineral Rly [146]
Princess	31	Glenbarry	10/1863	Highland Rly [147]
Princess	193	Peel	8/1866	Stockton & Darlington Rly
Princess	2006	Newton	4/1871	London & North Western Rly
Princess	20	2Vesuvius	7/1871	London & South Western Rly
Princess	2006	rPrecedent	11/1890	London & North Western Rly
Princess	–	0–4–2T	1900	Campbeltown & Machrihanish Rly [148]
Princess	**14**	**0–6–0ST**	**1942**	**Lakeside & Haverthwaite Rly**
Princess Alexandra	618	Problem	c.1860	London & North Western Rly
Princess Alexandra	1603	2Experiment	5/1909	London & North Western Rly
Princess Alexandra	4053	Star	6/1914	Great Western Rly
Princess Alexandra	6224	Duchess	7/1937	London Midland & Scottish Rly
Princess Alice	–	0–4–0	7/1839	Llanelly Rly
Princess Alice	612	Problem	c.1860	London & North Western Rly
Princess Alice	937	2Experiment	9/1907	London & North Western Rly
Princess Alice	4050	Star	6/1914	Great Western Rly
Princess Alice	6223	Duchess	7/1937	London Midland & Scottish Rly
Princess Anne	46202	Princess	6/1935	British Railways [149]
Princess Arthur of Connaught	6207	Princess	8/1935	London Midland & Scottish Rly
Princess Augusta	4058	Star	7/1914	Great Western Rly
Princess Beatrice	2190	Precedent	4/1875	London & North Western Rly [150]
Princess Beatrice	3076	3031	2/1899	Great Western Rly
Princess Beatrice	4052	Star	6/1914	Great Western Rly
Princess Beatrice	6209	Princess	8/1935	London Midland & Scottish Rly
Princess Charlotte	4054	Star	6/1914	Great Western Rly
Princess Elizabeth	4057	Star	7/1914	Great Western Rly
Princess Elizabeth	**6201**	**Princess**	**11/1933**	**London Midland & Scottish Rly**
Princess Elizabeth	**6201**	**4–6–2DM**	**1938**	**Midland Railway Centre** [151]
Princess Eugenie	4060	Star	7/1914	Great Western Rly
Princess Helena	–	0–4–0	1/1839	Llanelly Rly [152]
Princess Helena	1517	Newton	11/1866	London & North Western Rly
Princess Helena	1517	rPrecedent	11/1888	London & North Western Rly
Princess Helena	3074	3031	6/1898	Great Western Rly [153]
Princess Helena	4051	Star	6/1914	Great Western Rly
Princess Helena Victoria	6208	Princess	8/1935	London Midland & Scottish Rly
Princess Louise	1177	Precedent	4/1877	London & North Western Rly
Princess Louise	1177	rPrecedent	3/1896	London & North Western Rly
Princess Louise	3075	3031	7/1898	Great Western Rly
Princess Louise	4047	Star	5/1914	Great Western Rly
Princess Louise	42	Claughton	8/1920	London & North Western Rly
Princess Louise	6204	Princess	7/1935	London Midland & Scottish Rly
Princess Marie Louise	6206	Princess	8/1935	London Midland & Scottish Rly
Princess Margaret	4056	Star	7/1914	Great Western Rly
Princess Margaret	**6**	**0–4–0DM**	**1948**	**North Downs Steam Rly**
Princess Margaret Rose	**6203**	**Princess**	**7/1935**	**London Midland & Scottish Rly**

Vale of Rheidol 2–6–2T no. 9 *Prince of Wales*, seen at Aberystwyth soon after receiving its name and being painted in BR express passenger livery in the 1950s. (*Photo: Author*)

[137] 15in gauge Bassett-Lowke scale model.

[138] Originally named *Charles Stuart-Wortley*. Renamed *Prince George* in 1920.

[139] Originally named *Sir Alexander Henderson*. Renamed *Sir Douglas Haig* in 1917 and *Prince Henry* in 1920.

[140] Name later abbreviated to *Wales*.

[141] Name applied in November 1852, to act as pilot to a Royal Train from Chester to Wolverhampton.

[142] Became Great Western Railway (and British Railways) no. 9 after a very thorough rebuild in 1923–4; it is sometimes considered to be a new locomotive.

[143] Originally named *Manna*; name changed December 1926.

[144] Originally *Victoria* (no number), of November 1838. An unsatisfactory design, the class was despatched to Fairbairns for total rebuilding. On return, *Victoria* had become no. 20 *Princess*.

[145] 1ft 11½in gauge. Originally named *The Princess*.

[146] Built as a broad gauge 0–4–0ST, then may have been altered to 0–4–2ST while still on the broad gauge. It was then rebuilt, emerging as a standard gauge 0–6–0ST.

[147] Altered from 2–2–2 to 2–4–0 in May 1884.

[148] 2ft 3in gauge. Built for the Campbeltown Coal Co. and taken into Campbeltown & Machrihanish Railway stock in 1906.

[149] Built by the London Midland & Scottish Railway. Originally turbine-driven and unnamed, although semi-officially nicknamed the "Turbomotive". Rebuilt by British Railways as a four-cylinder conventional locomotive in August 1952, and named *Princess Anne*. Destroyed in the Harrow and Wealdstone accident on 8 October 1952.

[150] Originally named *Beatrice*, and after a short period renamed *Lady Beatrice*. Became *Princess Beatrice* in 1888.

[151] 21in gauge.

[152] Rebuilt in 1857 and renamed *Helena*.

[153] Name removed in April 1914.

London & North Western Railway Problem class 2–2–2 no. 610 *Princess Royal*, at Crewe on 11 August 1902. (*Photo: LCGB Ken Nunn Collection*)

Name	Number	Class	Date	Railway
Princess Margaret Rose	6203	4–6–2DM	1938	**Midland Railway Centre** [154]
Princess Mary	4048	Star	5/1914	Great Western Rly [155]
Princess Mary	510	11F	5/1920	Great Central Rly
Princess Maud	4049	Star	5/1914	Great Western Rly
Princess May	1129	Queen	6/1875	Great Western Rly
Princess May	525	G.Britain	1894	London & North Western Rly
Princess May	3077	3031	2/1899	Great Western Rly
Princess May	1709	2Experiment	11/1906	London & North Western Rly
Princess of Wales	1119	Queen	4/1875	Great Western Rly
Princess of Wales	866	863	6/1885	Lancashire & Yorkshire Rly
Princess of Wales	2601	Princess	1899	Midland Rly
Princess Patricia	4059	Star	7/1914	Great Western Rly
Princess Royal	–	0–6–0	1842	Llanelly Rly [156]
Princess Royal	610	Problem	c.1860	London & North Western Rly
Princess Royal	3073	3031	6/1898	Great Western Rly
Princess Royal	54	B4	5/1900	London, Brighton & South Coast Rly [157]
Princess Sophia	4055	Star	7/1914	Great Western Rly
Princess Victoria	4048	Star	5/1914	Great Western Rly [158]
Princess Victoria	6205	Princess	7/1935	London Midland & Scottish Rly
Prince William	47798	47/7		British Railways
Priory Hall	4958	Hall	9/1929	Great Western Rly
Prittlewell	44	37	1898	London, Tilbury & Southend Rly
Private E. Sykes, V.C.	2035	Claughton	4/1921	London & North Western Rly

Name	Number	Class	Date	Railway
Private E. Sykes V.C.	5537	Patriot	7/1933	London Midland & Scottish Rly
Private W. Wood, V.C.	1097	Claughton	4/1921	London & North Western Rly
Private W. Wood, V.C.	5536	Patriot	5/1933	London Midland & Scottish Rly [159]
Problem	184	aCrewe	2/1848	London & North Western Rly
Problem	184	Problem	c.1860	London & North Western Rly
Problem	2580	2Precursor	12/1905	London & North Western Rly
Progress	5	2–4–0	1861	Bishops Castle Rly [160]
Progress	–	0–4–4–0F	12/1865	Robt Fairlie [161]
Progress	–	0–4–0ST	1923	**Bodmin & Wenford Rly**
Progress	–	0–4–0DM	1945	**Bodmin & Wenford Rly**
Progress	–	0–6–0ST	1946	**Tanfield Rly**
Progress	47726	47/7		British Railways
Prometheus	28	2–2–2	1838	Grand Junction Rly
Prometheus	28	2–2–2	1841	Grand Junction Rly
Prometheus	21	Aurora	9/1847	East Lancashire Rly
Prometheus	71	2–2–2	7/1849	Manchester, Sheffield & Lincolnshire Rly
Prometheus	28	aCrewe	11/1849	London & North Western Rly
Prometheus	–	Iron Duke	3/1850	Great Western Rly (bg)
Prometheus	28	Problem	c.1860	London & North Western Rly
Prometheus	38	0–4–0ST	6/1863	Cambrian Railways
Prometheus	–	Rover	4/1888	Great Western Rly (bg)
Prometheus	3017	3001	4/1892	Great Western Rly [162]
Prometheus	3049	3031	2/1895	Great Western Rly [163]

[154] 21in gauge.

[155] Carried this name for a royal wedding on 28 February 1922; renamed *Princess Victoria*.

[156] Originally named *Dryslwyn*. Later renamed *Royal*. Became Great Western Railway no. 909.

[157] Originally named *Empress*. Renamed in August 1906.

[158] Temporarily named *Princess Mary* for a royal wedding on 28 February 1922.

[159] Rebuilt with taper boiler in November 1948.

[160] Ex-Somerset & Dorset Railway no. 1, where it was unnamed.

[161] A double-bogie 0–4–4–0 Fairlie articulated locomotive. It was built by James Cross at St Helens, and worked on the Neath &

Brecon Railway until 1869. It then worked on the Brecon & Merthyr Railway till June 1870, when it went to the Monmouthshire Railway & Canal Co. The rest of its history and ultimate fate is unknown.

[162] Originally named *Nelson*; renamed *Prometheus* in May 1895.

[163] Renamed *Nelson* in May 1895.

Name	Number	Class	Date	Railway
Prometheus	–	0–4–0ST	1902	Woolwich Arsenal [164]
Prometheus	1304	2Experiment	11/1906	London & North Western Rly
Prometheus	26055	EM1	6/1953	British Railways
Prompt	–	0–4–0ST	2/1899	Chatham Dockyard [165]
Pronghorn	1035	B1	10/1947	London & North Eastern Rly
Proserpine	–	Priam	6/1842	Great Western Rly (bg)
Proserpine	45	0–6–0	5/1846	Joint Board of Management [166]
Prosperine	90	2–2–2	3/1850	Manchester, Sheffield & Lincolnshire Rly
Prosperine	1006	L/Bloomer	1851	London & North Western Rly
Prosperine	376	bCrewe	11/1855	London & North Western Rly
Prosperine	871	Precedent	6/1877	London & North Western Rly
Prosperine	871	rPrecedent	5/1894	London & North Western Rly
Prospero	13	2–2–2	1837	Grand Junction Rly
Prospero	13	aCrewe	12/1843	London & North Western Rly
Prospero	102	2–2–2	10/1850	Manchester, Sheffield & Lincolnshire Rly
Prospero	13	bCrewe	11/1854	London & North Western Rly
Prospero	414	Samson	9/1873	London & North Western Rly [167]
Prospero	414	Whitworth	1896	London & North Western Rly
Prospero	1361	2Experiment	10/1907	London & North Western Rly
Protector	39	cSentinel	1929	London & North Eastern Rly
Proteus	52	2–4–0	12/1847	Manchester, Sheffield & Lincolnshire Rly
Provence	120	E1	8/1877	London, Brighton & South Coast Rly
(Prudence)	08164	08	1956	British Railways
Prudhoe	35	0–6–0	12/1852	Newcastle & Carlisle Rly [168]
Psyche	–	Caesar	10/1853	Great Western Rly (bg)
Psyche	164	Undine	12/1859	London & South Western Rly
Psyche	1431	Problem	c.1860	London & North Western Rly
Psyche	1510	2Precursor	9/1905	London & North Western Rly [169]
Ptarmigan	334	bCrewe	5/1854	London & North Western Rly
Ptarmigan	1681	George V	9/1911	London & North Western Rly

Name	Number	Class	Date	Railway
Puccini	92013	92		British Railways
Puck	819	Samson	1/1866	London & North Western Rly
Puck	819	Whitworth	3/1893	London & North Western Rly
Puck	514	rPrecedent	10/1895	London & North Western Rly [170]
"Puffing Billy"	–	0–4–0	1813	Wylam Colliery [171]
Puku	1012	B1	11/1946	London & North Eastern Rly
Pulborough	374	D3	12/1892	London, Brighton & South Coast Rly
Pumlumon	60010	60	1/1991	British Railways [172]
Punjab	5579	Jubilee	1934	London Midland & Scottish Rly
Purcell	92021	92		EPS
Purdon Viccars	430	11E	9/1913	Great Central Rly
Purfleet	9	Class 1	1880	London, Tilbury & Southend Rly
Purfleet	51	51	1900	London, Tilbury & Southend Rly
Purley	263	D1	4/1882	London, Brighton & South Coast Rly
Purley Hall	4959	Hall	9/1929	Great Western Rly
Puttenham	500	E4	6/1900	London, Brighton & South Coast Rly
Pyle Hall	4960	Hall	9/1929	Great Western Rly
Pyracmon	–	Caesar	11/1847	Great Western Rly (bg)
Pyramus	5	Ilfracombe	7/1874	Shropshire & Montgomeryshire Rly [173]
Pyramus	–	0–6–2T	1911	Shropshire & Montgomeryshire Rly
Pyrland Hall	4961	Hall	11/1929	Great Western Rly
Pyrrhus	92	0–6–0	8/1849	Manchester, Sheffield & Lincolnshire Rly
Python	69	2–2–2	4/1841	Grand Junction Rly
Python	1	0–4–2	10/1841	Manchester, Sheffield & Lincolnshire Rly
Python	100	Fireball	9/1848	London & South Western Rly
Python	69	bCrewe	5/1853	London & North Western Rly
Python	100	Clyde	12/1868	London & South Western Rly
Python	2168	0–6–0ST	3/1874	Great Western Rly (bg) [174]
Python	413	1Precursor	10/1874	London & North Western Rly
Python	1784	2Precursor	10/1905	London & North Western Rly
Python	47538	47	1964	British Railways

[164] 18in gauge.
[165] 18in gauge.
[166] Birmingham & Gloucester and Bristol & Gloucester Railways, formed on 14 January 1845. Standard gauge. The locomotives passed to the Midland Railway on 3 August 1846, and were renumbered into Midland stock wef February 1847.
[167] Transferred to Engineer's Department 1903–February 1924, and renamed *Engineer Lancaster*.
[168] Became North Eastern Railway no. 483 in 1862.
[169] This locomotive's name is said to have given many enginemen problems. Pronounciations were variously 'Pish', 'Fish', and 'Physic'!
[170] No. 514 was named *Lawrence* from October 1895 until August 1913.[171] Built by William Hedley. At the Science Museum, South Kensington.
[172] Also named (on the other side) *Plynlimon*.
[173] Built for the London & South Western Railway as no. 300, later duplicated as no. 0300. This Ilfracombe Goods class engine was purchased for the Shropshire & Montgomeryshire Railway in December 1914 and named. It was laid aside in October 1930, and broken up in March 1932.
[174] Built for the South Devon Railway.

Q

London Midland & Scottish Railway Duchess class streamlined 4–6–2 no. 6222 *Queen Mary* near Wembley with the Down Euston–Glasgow Coronation Scot express on 8 July 1937. (*Photo: LCGB Ken Nunn Collection*)

Name	Number	Class	Date	Railway	Name	Number	Class	Date	Railway
Quail	335	bCrewe	5/1854	London & North Western Rly	*Queen*	29	0–4–0	2/1837	Stockton & Darlington Rly [3]
Quail	–	0–4–2T	1885	Woolwich Arsenal [1]	*Queen*	17	Fairbairn	9/1841	London & South Western Rly [4]
Quail	1371	George V	9/1911	London & North Western Rly	*Queen*	6	0–6–0ST	1846	Wrexham, Mold & Connah's Quay Rly [5]
Quantock	3324	Duke	6/1899	Great Western Rly	*Queen*	–	Priam	2/1847	Great Western Rly (bg)
Quantock	3324	Bulldog	12/1908	Great Western Rly	*Queen*	109	aCrewe	7/1847	London & North Western Rly
Quarryman	–	**0–4–0P**	**1928**	**Ravenglass & Eskdale Rly [2]**	*Queen*	–	0–6–0ST	c.1847	Boulton's Siding [6]
Quebec	3409	Atbara	10/1901	Great Western Rly	*Queen*	62	2–2–2	8/1848	Manchester, Sheffield &
Quebec	3409	City	11/1907	Great Western Rly					Lincolnshire Rly [7]
Quebec	5555	Jubilee	1934	London Midland & Scottish Rly	*Queen*	–	0–4–0WT	1852	Torbay & Brixham Rly (bg) [8]

[1] 18in gauge.

[2] 15in gauge.

[3] Some sources give the date of building as 1838. Later no. 40, and rebuilt to 0–4–2.

[4] Originally *Garnet* (no number), of June 1838. An unsatisfactory design, the entire class was despatched to Fairbairns for total rebuilding. On return, *Garnet* had become no. 17 *Queen*.

[5] Built as 0–6–0 for the London & North Western Railway. Rebuilt as 0–6–0ST by

LNWR in 1858 (their no. 1829). Acquired by the Wrexham, Mold & Connah's Quay Railway in 1872 as no. 6 *Queen*, and rebuilt as 0–8–0ST in 1880, as 0–6–2ST in 1888, and as 0–8–0ST in 1903. Renumbered 400 by Great Central in 1904, and as 400B in 1907. Scrapped in October 1923.

[6] Originally a London & North Western Railway 0–6–0 'Wolverton Goods', altered in 1873 to 0–6–0ST. Went to Cowbridge Railway and in 1876 to the Severn & Wye

Railway. In 1881 or 1882 was sold to Ilkeston Colliery Co.

[7] Rebuilt from 2–2–2 to 2–4–0, June 1864.

[8] Included in South Devon Railway stock from July 1870, but continued to work on the Torbay and Brixham until that company was purchased by the Great Western Railway on 1 January 1883. It was then added to Great Western stock, but simultaneously withdrawn. It is said to have spent some years in a scrap siding at Swindon before being cut up.

Name	Number	Class	Date	Railway
Queen	17	Tartar	7/1852	London & South Western Rly
Queen	11	S/Goods	12/1861	Cambrian Railways
Queen	17	2Vesuvius	12/1871	London & South Western Rly
Queen	55	Queen	1873	Great Western Rly
Queen Adelaide	–	0–4–0	9/1830	Liverpool & Manchester Rly [9]
Queen Adelaide	4034	Star	11/1910	Great Western Rly
Queen Alexandra	104	11B	3/1904	Great Central Rly [10]
Queen Alexandra	4032	Star	10/1910	Great Western Rly [11]
Queen Alexandra	4032	Castle	4/1926	Great Western Rly [12]
Queen Anne	**20**	**4wDM**	**1948**	**Strathspey Rly**
Queen Berengaria	4038	Star	1/1911	Great Western Rly
Queen Boadicea	4040	Star	3/1911	Great Western Rly
Queen Charlotte	4035	Star	11/1910	Great Western Rly
Queen Elizabeth	4036	Star	11/1910	Great Western Rly
Queen Elizabeth	6221	Duchess	6/1937	London Midland & Scottish Rly
Queen Elizabeth II	91029	91	1/1991	British Railways
Queen Empress	2054	G.Britain	5/1893	London & North Western Rly
Queen Empress	2027	2Experiment	11/1906	London & North Western Rly
Queen Guinevere	454	King Arthur	3/1925	Southern Rly
Queen Mab	10	2–2–2WT	12/1860	Whitehaven & Furness Junction Rly [13]
Queen Mary	1021	11B	2/1902	Great Central Rly [14]
Queen Mary	2664	George V*	7/1910	London & North Western Rly
Queen Mary	4031	Star	10/1910	Great Western Rly
Queen Mary	6222	Duchess	6/1937	London Midland & Scottish Rly
Queen Matilda	4039	Star	2/1911	Great Western Rly
Queen Maud	6211	Princess	9/1935	London Midland & Scottish Rly
Queen of Beauty	314	cSentinel	1931	London & North Eastern Rly
Queen of the Belgians	2395	Prince/W	12/1915	London & North Western Rly
Queen Philippa	4037	Star	12/1910	Great Western Rly [15]

Name	Number	Class	Date	Railway
Queen Philippa	4037	Castle	6/1926	Great Western Rly [16]
Queen Victoria	4033	Star	11/1910	Great Western Rly
Queen Victoria's Rifleman	6160	Royal Scot	8/1930	London Midland & Scottish Rly
Queensferry	259	165	11/1875	North British Rly [17]
Queen's Hall	5912	Hall	6/1931	Great Western Rly [18]
Queensland	49	B4	7/1901	London, Brighton & South Coast Rly [19]
Queensland	3471	Bulldog	4/1904	Great Western Rly
Queensland	5566	Jubilee	1934	London Midland & Scottish Rly
Queen's Own Highlander	55004	Deltic	5/1961	British Railways
Queen's Westminster Rifleman	6162	Royal Scot	9/1930	London Midland & Scottish Rly
Quentin Durward	2979	Saint	4/1905	Great Western Rly [20]
Quentin Durward	423	Scott	10/1914	North British Rly
Quernmore	4	2–4–0	1857	Lancaster & Carlisle Rly
Quernmore	380	Newton	12/1869	London & North Western Rly
Quernmore	380	rPrecedent	6/1891	London & North Western Rly
Quickspeed	–	0–4–0	1829	Stockton & Darlington Rly [21]
Quicksilver	293	bCrewe	11/1852	London & North Western Rly
Quicksilver	293	DX	c.1860	London & North Western Rly
Quicksilver	3025	3001	8/1891	Great Western Rly [22]
Quicksilver	2972	Saint	2/1905	Great Western Rly [23]
Quicksilver	31073	cSentinel	1929	London & North Eastern Rly
Quicksilver	2510	A4	9/1935	London & North Eastern Rly
Quidenham	2809	B17/1	12/1928	London & North Eastern Rly
Quinag	60090	60	2/1992	British Railways
Qwag	**1**	**4wDM**	**1954**	**Great Central Rly [24]**

[9] Built by Braithwaite & Ericsson to Liverpool & Manchester Railway order. However, the locomotive was unsatisfactory, and the railway declined to purchase it. Hence the absence of a number.

[10] Rebuilt to class 11C in 1907 and named *Queen Alexandra* in 1911.

[11] Rebuilt to Castle class, April 1926.

[12] Rebuilt from Star class no. 4032.

[13] Became Furness Railway no. 46. Sold to the Isle of Wight (Newport Junction) Railway in 1876, as their *Newport*. They did not number it; it was their sole locomotive! It passed to the Isle of Wight Central Railway as their no. 6, and was scrapped in 1895.

[14] Named *Queen Mary* in 1913.

[15] Rebuilt to Castle class, June 1926.

[16] Renamed *The South Wales Borderers* in March 1937 and fitted with plaques of the regimental crest.

[17] Previously named *Bellshill*.

[18] Originally named *Queens Hall* (without an apostrophe) until May 1935.

[19] Renamed *Duchess of Norfolk*, December 1904.

[20] Originally named *Magnet*. Renamed *Quentin Durward* in March 1907.

[21] The evidence is that this locomotive was planned but may never have been built.

[22] Built as a broad gauge convertible. Originally named *St George*; rebuilt to 4–2–2 in October 1894 and renamed *Quicksilver* in May 1907.

[23] Renamed *The Abbot* in March 1907.

[24] The modern, preserved Great Central Railway.

R

Name	Number	Class	Date	Railway
Raby Castle	30	2–2–2	10/1839	Stockton & Darlington Rly
Raby Castle	2825	B17/1	2/1931	London & North Eastern Rly
Racehorse	1631	George V	8/1911	London & North Western Rly
Racer	3018	3001	4/1892	Great Western Rly [1]
Rachel	**9**	**4wDM**	**1924**	**Lakeside & Haverthwaite Rly**
Radcliffe	190	0–6–0ST	1876	Taff Vale Rly [2]
Radio Highland	37260	37/0	2/1965	British Railways
Radley	930	Schools	12/1934	Southern Rly
RAF Biggin Hill	**5110**	**5**	**1935**	**London Midland & Scottish Rly**
RAF Stanbridge	**28**	**4wDM**	**1949**	**Leighton Buzzard Rly** [3]
Raglan	996	L/Bloomer	1851	London & North Western Rly
Raglan	352	bCrewe	10/1854	London & North Western Rly
Raglan Castle	5008	Castle	6/1927	Great Western Rly
Ragley Hall	4962	Hall	11/1929	Great Western Rly
Raigmore	1	Raigmore	9/1855	Highland Rly [4]
Raigmore (II)	1	2Raigmore	11/1877	Highland Rly
RAIL Celebrity	37055	37/0	1962	British Railways
Rail Express	90017	90/0	12/1988	British Railways
Systems Quality Assured				
Rail Riders	47488	47/4	1964	British Railways
Railway	43303	Clayton	1928	London & North Eastern Rly
RAILWAY HERITAGE	43189	43	4/1982	British Railways
TRUST				
275 Railway	90010	90/0	10/1988	British Railways
Squadron (Volunteers)				
Rainbow	24	2–2–0	4/1840	Midland Counties Rly
Rainham	8	Class 1	1880	London, Tilbury & Southend Rly
Raleigh	1527	Newton	11/1866	London & North Western Rly
Raleigh	1527	rPrecedent	2/1888	London & North Western Rly
Raleigh	5639	Jubilee	1934	London Midland & Scottish Rly
Ralph	**7**	**0–4–2T**	**1923**	**Snowdon Mountain Rly** [5]
Ralph Assheton	1036	B1	11/1947	London & North Eastern Rly
Ralph Brocklebank	1159	Claughton	5/1913	London & North Western Rly
Ralph Easby	08867	08	1960	British Railways
Ralph L. Lopes	196	Gladstone	6/1888	London, Brighton & South Coast Rly
Ramillies	1930	Jubilee	4/1900	London & North Western Rly
Ramillies	D837	Warship	11/1960	British Railways
Ramillies	**50019**	**50**	**1968**	**British Railways**
Ramsbury Manor	7829	Manor	12/1950	British Railways (Western Region)
Ramsey	1	2–4–0T	1879	Manx Northern Rly [6]
(Ranald)	**–**	**4wVB**	**1957**	**Bo'ness & Kinneil Rly**
Ranger	1358	0–6–0ST	?	Great Western Rly [7]
Ranmore	286	D1	7/1879	London, Brighton & South Coast Rly
Rapid	37	2–2–2	1835	Liverpool & Manchester Rly
Rapid	1	0–6–0	3/1835	Newcastle & Carlisle Rly
Rapid	285	Clayton	1928	London & North Eastern Rly
Rapid	D838	Warship	10/1960	British Railways
Rastrick	320	B2	10/1896	London, Brighton & South Coast Rly [8]
Ratcliffe Power Station	58041	58	3/1986	British Railways
Ratho	428	418	1873	North British Rly
Ravel	92023	92		Société Nationale des Chemins de fer Français
Ravelston	–	0–6–0T	1911	Llanelly & Mynydd Mawr Rly [9]
Raven	47	2–2–0	6/1839	London & South Western Rly
Raven	144	aCrewe	11/1853	London & North Western Rly [10]
Raven	–	0–6–0ST	1872	Swansea Vale Rly
Raven	2175	0–4–0ST	11/1874	Great Western Rly (bg) [11]
Raven	–	0–6–0ST	6/1876	Severn & Wye & Severn Bridge Rly
Raven	643	Dreadnought	1888	London & North Western Rly
Raven	47310	47/3	1965	British Railways
Raveningham Hall	**6960**	**M/Hall**	**3/1944**	**Great Western Rly** [12]
Ravenswood	9362	Scott	12/1911	North British Rly
Rawlinson	620	C	10/1889	North British Rly
Raymond Poincare	877	Prince/W	11/1915	London & North Western Rly
Raynham Hall	2811	B17/1	8/1930	London & North Eastern Rly
R.B. Sheridan	307	Prince/W	1/1914	London & North Western Rly
Reader 125	43011	43	4/1976	British Railways
Reading	–	Swindon	1/1866	Great Western Rly (bg)
Reading	3449	Bulldog	10/1903	Great Western Rly
Reading Abbey	4064	Star	12/1922	Great Western Rly [13]
Reading Abbey	5084	Castle	4/1937	Great Western Rly [14]
Reading Evening Post	43161	43	6/1981	British Railways
Ready	–	0–4–0ST	1913	Chatham Dockyard [15]
Recovery	2267	cSentinel	1929	London & North Eastern Rly
Redbreast	157	bCrewe	5/1851	London & North Western Rly [16]
Redcar	31	Miner	9/1845	Stockton & Darlington Rly
Redcar	**12139**	**0–6–0DE**	**1948**	**North York Moors Rly**
Red Gauntlet	–	Abbot	6/1855	Great Western Rly (bg)
Red Gauntlet	802	Problem	c.1860	London & North Western Rly
Redgauntlet	2983	Saint	7/1905	Great Western Rly [17]
Red Gauntlet	1483	2Experiment	1/1909	London & North Western Rly
Redgauntlet	897	Scott	9/1909	North British Rly
Redgauntlet	60137	A1	12/1948	British Railways (Eastern Region)
Redgauntlet	PW3	4wPM	1975	Romney, Hythe & Dymchurch Rly [18]
Redhill 1844–1994	73107	73/1	1966	British Railways
Redland	**–**	**0–4–0DM**	**1929**	**Buckinghamshire Railway Centre** [19]
Redland	**–**	**4wDM**	**1937**	**Amberley Chalk Pits Museum** [20]
Redmire	20172	20	1966	British Railways
Red Rover	253	aSentinel	1928	London & North Eastern Rly
Red Rum	**29**	**4wDM**	**1936**	**West Lancashire Light Rly** [21]
Redruth	37	?	1852	West Cornwall Rly
Redruth	2156	0–6–0ST	1865	Great Western Rly (bg) [22]
Red Star	–	Wolf	8/1840	Great Western Rly (bg)
Red Star	4006	Star	4/1907	Great Western Rly
Red Star	47567	47/4	1964	British Railways
Redstart	156	bCrewe	11/1855	London & North Western Rly [23]

[1] Rebuilt to 4–2–2 in August 1894; renamed *Glenside* in September 1911.

[2] Purchased from contractors in 1892. It is not known if it retained its name.

[3] 2ft gauge.

[4] Altered from 2–2–2 to 2–4–0 in 1869.

[5] 800mm gauge rack and pinion locomotive.

[6] 3ft gauge. In 1905 the Manx Northern was absorbed by the Isle of Man Railway, who allocated no. 16 to *Ramsey*. However, the number was never carried for the engine was withdrawn soon afterwards.

[7] The origins of this engine are obscure. The Severn & Wye Railway purchased an 0–6–0 tender engine from the Northampton & Banbury Junction Railway in November 1875; it is thought to have been either LNWR no. 1827 or no. 1849. If this hypothesis is correct, then the engine must have been rebuilt as a saddle tank somewhere in its career. It eventually passed to the Great Western Railway.

[8] Rebuilt to class B2x, July 1910.

[9] Became Great Western Railway no. 803.

[10] Previously Liverpool & Manchester Railway 2–4–0 no. 86; became a London & North Western engine in 1846.

[11] Built for the South Devon Railway. Sold by the GWR in 1877 to the Torbay & Brixham Railway, and returned to the GWR when that company purchased the T&BR on 1 January 1883. It was converted to standard gauge in 1892, becoming no. 1329. It was sold in March 1910 to the Wantage Tramway. There it was prone to derailments, and was scrapped at Wantage in 1919.

[12] Nameplates fitted in June 1947.

[13] Rebuilt to Castle class no. 5084, April 1937.

[14] Rebuilt from Star class no. 4064.

[15] 18in gauge.

[16] Built for the Grand Junction Railway.

[17] Named *Red Gauntlet* in September 1906. Altered to *Redgauntlet* in June 1915.

[18] 15in gauge.

[19] Standard gauge. Built by Kerr Stuart, Stoke on Trent, in 1929, works no. K4428.

[20] 2ft gauge. Built by Orenstein & Koppel, Berlin, 1937, works no. 6193.

[21] 2ft gauge.

[22] Built for the South Devon Railway.

[23] Originally no. 380 *Napoleon* of the Grand Junction Railway. Later sold to the Lancaster & Carlisle Railway.

Name	Number	Class	Date	Railway
Redstart	156	cCrewe	3/1857	London & North Western Rly [24]
Redstone	–	**0–4–0VB**	**1905**	**Brecon Mountain Rly** [25]
Redwing	146	bCrewe	5/1854	London & North Western Rly [26]
Reed	–	Rennie	11/1838	London & South Western Rly [27]
Reedbuck	1031	B1	7/1947	London & North Eastern Rly
Reepham	2	0–6–0T	1874	Lynn & Fakenham Rly [28]
Reginald Munns	60092	60	1/1992	British Railways [29]
Regulus	–	Caesar	10/1862	Great Western Rly (bg)
Regulus	–	0–4–0ST	1912	Woolwich Arsenal [30]
Reigate	237	2–2–2	4/1867	London, Brighton & South Coast Rly [31]
Reims	676	C	12/1891	North British Rly [32]
Reindeer	13	2–2–0	7/1840	Midland Counties Rly
Reindeer	25	Fairbairn	6/1842	London & South Western Rly [33]
Reindeer	54	Venus	11/1850	East Lancashire Rly
Reindeer	28	2–4–0	1855	Newport, Abergavenny & Hereford Rly
Reindeer	44	Reindeer	7/1865	London, Chatham & Dover Rly
Reindeer	25	Volcano	7/1872	London & South Western Rly
Reitbok	1021	B1	3/1947	London & North Eastern Rly
Relentless	D839	Warship	11/1960	British Railways
Reliance	170	Panther	1/1864	Stockton & Darlington Rly
R.E.M.E.	45528	Patriot	4/1933	British Railways [34]
Remus	–	Caesar	11/1853	Great Western Rly (bg)
Remus	2154	0–6–0ST	11/1866	Great Western Rly (bg) [35]
Remembrance	333	L	4/1922	London, Brighton & South Coast Rly [36]
Renard	318	bCrewe	9/1853	London & North Western Rly
Rendelsham Hall	2839	B17/2	5/1933	London & North Eastern Rly [37]
Rennes	130	E1	11/1878	London, Brighton & South Coast Rly
Rennes	75189	J94	1944	Longmoor Military Rly
Rennie	–	Victoria	4/1864	Great Western Rly (bg)
Renown	–	1Sussex	6/1839	London & South Western Rly [38]
Renown	1918	Jubilee	7/1899	London & North Western Rly
Renown	5713	Jubilee	1936	London Midland & Scottish Rly
Renown	**50029**	**50**	**1968**	**British Railways**
Renton	326	317	1862	North British Rly [39]
REPTA 1893–1993	47085	47/0	1965	British Railways
Repton	**926**	**Schools**	**5/1934**	**Southern Rly**
Repulse	5725	Jubilee	1936	London Midland & Scottish Rly
(Repulse)	–	**J94**	**1950**	**Lakeside & Haverthwaite Rly**
Repulse	**50030**	**50**	**1968**	**British Railways**
Rescue	–	?	6/1867	Llynvi & Ogmore Rly [40]
Reserved	47770	47/7		British Railways
Reservist	47773	47/7		British Railways
Res Gestae	47524	47/4	1966	British Railways
Resilient	47597	47/4	1964	British Railways
Resilient	47741	47/7		British Railways
Resistance	D840	Warship	2/1961	British Railways
Resolute	203	0–6–0ST	1876	Great Eastern Rly [41]

Name	Number	Class	Date	Railway
Resolute	47642	47/4	9/1964	British Railways [42]
Resolute	47766	47/7		British Railways
Resolution	1919	Jubilee	8/1899	London & North Western Rly
Resolution	5708	Jubilee	1936	London Midland & Scottish Rly
Resolution	50018	50	1968	British Railways
Resolve	47769	47/7		British Railways
Resolven Grange	6869	Grange	3/1939	Great Western Rly
Resonant	47768	47/7		British Railways
Resounding	47764	47/7		British Railways
Resourceful	47594	47/4	1964	British Railways
Resourceful	47739	47/7		British Railways
Respected	47776	47/7		British Railways
Respite	47775	47/7		British Railways
(Respite)	–	**J94**	**10/1950**	**Foxfield Rly**
Resplendent	47625	47/4	1965	British Railways
Responsive	47565	47/4	1964	British Railways
Res Publica	47747	47/7		British Railways
Ressaldar	47765	47/7		British Railways
Restitution	47757	47/7		British Railways
Restive	47475	47/4	1964	British Railways
Restless	47760	47/7		British Railways
Restored	47777	47/7		British Railways
Restormel	3366	Bulldog	11/1900	Great Western Rly
Restormel	47732	47/7		British Railways
Restormel Castle	5010	Castle	7/1927	Great Western Rly
Resurgent	47737	47/7		British Railways
Retaliator	312	cSentinel	1929	London & North Eastern Rly
Revenge	5714	Jubilee	1936	London Midland & Scottish Rly
Revenge	50020	50	1968	British Railways
Reverend W Awdry	91024	91	10/1990	British Railways
Reynard	2184	Precedent	3/1875	London & North Western Rly
Reynard	2184	rPrecedent	5/1897	London & North Western Rly
R.H. Dutton	169	Clyde	9/1859	London & South Western Rly
Rhea	–	Caesar	4/1855	Great Western Rly (bg)
Rheidol	44	Small Pass	3/1864	Cambrian Railways [43]
Rheidol	3	2–4–0T	1896	Vale of Rheidol Rly [44]
Rheims	676	C	12/1891	North British Rly [45]
Rhiewport	45	S/Goods	8/1864	Cambrian Railways
Rhine	43	0–4–2	12/1842	Manchester & Leeds Rly
Rhine	88	E1	4/1883	London, Brighton & South Coast Rly
Rhinoceros	52	Bison	6/1846	London & South Western Rly
Rhinoceros	167	aCrewe	8/1847	London & North Western Rly
Rhinoceros	52	Lion	7/1865	London & South Western Rly
Rhondda	–	2–2–2	1840	Taff Vale Rly
Rhondda	4	0–6–0ST	1849	Alexandra (Newport & South Wales) Docks & Rly
Rhondda	2	2–4–0	1859	Taff Vale Rly

[24] Replacement for previous engine.
[25] 1ft 11½in gauge.
[26] Previously Liverpool & Manchester Railway 2–2–2 no. 88; became a London & North Western engine in 1846.
[27] An unsatisfactory design, this engine, with the rest of the class, was sent to Fairbairns for total reconstruction. On return in December 1841, the engine had become no. 21 *Prince*.
[28] Purchased from Cornwall Minerals Railway.
[29] Originally named *Boar of Badenoch*.
[30] 18in gauge.
[31] Name applied by Stroudley in January 1872.
[32] This is the official spelling; contemporary observers recorded it wrongly as *Rheims*.
[33] Originally *Pegasus* (no number), of March 1839. An unsatisfactory design, the engine was reconstructed by Fairbairns in June 1842 and returned to traffic as no. 25 *Reindeer*.
[34] Built by the London Midland & Scottish Railway. Name applied by British Railways in October 1959; engine previously nameless. Rebuilt with taper boiler in August 1947.
[35] Built for the South Devon Railway.
[36] Rebuilt by the Southern Railway as a 4–6–0 tender engine, renumbered 2333, and reclassified Remembrance class or N15x, keeping its name and commemorative plates.
[37] Renamed *Norwich City* in January 1938, and rebuilt to class B2 in January 1946.
[38] An unsatisfactory design, this engine was sent to Fairbairns for total reconstruction. It returned in April 1842 as no. 22 *Giraffe*.
[39] Built for the Edinburgh & Glasgow Railway, absorbed by the NBR in 1865. Later renamed *Milngavie*.
[40] Date of purchase. It shunted at Porthcawl until November 1871, when it was sold to W. Hanson.
[41] Built for the Wivenhoe & Brightlingsea Railway.
[42] Also named *Strathisla*.
[43] Later altered to 2–4–0T.
[44] Built by Bagnalls of Stafford for Collier Antures & Co., to 2ft 5½in gauge, and was to be named *Treze de Maio* ('Thirteenth of May' in Portuguese). Actually named *Talybont*, it was bought by the Hafan & Talybont Tramway and altered to 2ft 3in gauge. It worked until closure in 1900, when it was sold to Messrs Pethick Bros, contractors, who were building the Vale of Rheidol Railway, and who had *Talybont* rebuilt by its makers and regauged to 1ft 11½in. It was then renamed *Rheidol*, and was a most effective machine, so much so that it was purchased by the VofR, numbered 3, and worked until 1923. The GWR gave it the number 1198, which was possibly never actually carried.
[45] The official spelling is *Reims*. Contemporary observers recorded it wrongly as *Rheims*.

Name	Number	Class	Date	Railway
Rhondda	–	Caesar	6/1859	Great Western Rly (bg)
Rhone	311	Lyons	7/1883	London, Brighton & South Coast Rly
Rhos	–	**0–6–0ST**	**1918**	**Nene Valley Rly**
Rhose Wood Hall	7918	M/Hall	4/1950	British Railways (Western Region)
Rhuddlan Castle	5039	Castle	6/1935	Great Western Rly
Rhydychen	–	**4wDM**	**1961**	**Brecon Mountain Rly** [46]
Rhyl	5521	Patriot	3/1933	London Midland & Scottish Rly [47]
Rhymney	34	2–4–0	1854	Taff Vale Rly
Ribble	10	?	?	St Helens Canal & Rly
Ribble	–	?	?1846	Preston & Wyre Harbour, Dock & Rly Co.
Ribble	630	S/Bloomer	1854	London & North Western Rly
Ribble	258	bCrewe	5/1856	London & North Western Rly
Ribble	19	2–4–0	1857	Lancaster & Carlisle Rly
Rich	13	2–4–0	4/1866	London & South Western Rly (ed) [48]
Richard Arkwright	1505	John Hick	1898	London & North Western Rly
Richard Arkwright	2282	George V	2/1913	London & North Western Rly
Richard Cobden	974	Newton	8/1873	London & North Western Rly
Richard Cobden	974	rPrecedent	1/1890	London & North Western Rly
Richard Cobden	940	Prince/W	1/1919	London & North Western Rly
Richard Francis Roberts	311	1Experiment	1884	London & North Western Rly
Richard Moon	528	G.Britain	1894	London & North Western Rly
Richard Moon	1993	2Experiment	10/1906	London & North Western Rly
Richard Trevithick	772	G.Britain	1894	London & North Western Rly
Richard Trevithick	1650	2Precursor	5/1906	London & North Western Rly
Richard Trevithick	–	**0–4–0ST**	**1955**	**Swindon & Cricklade Rly**
Richard Trevithick	56037	56	1978	British Railways
Richboro	–	**0–6–0T**	**1917**	**Llangollen Rly**
Richmond	208	Richmond	10/1878	London, Brighton & South Coast Rly
Richmond	53	B4	1/1900	London, Brighton & South Coast Rly [49]
Rickerby	1	2–4–0	1857	Lancaster & Carlisle Rly
Riddlesdown	357	D1	7/1886	London, Brighton & South Coast Rly [50]
Ridgewood	502	E4	6/1900	London, Brighton & South Coast Rly
Rignall Hall	4963	Hall	11/1929	Great Western Rly
Ring Haw	–	**0–6–0ST**	**1940**	**North Norfolk Rly**
Ringing Rock	1380	0–6–0ST	1876	Great Western Rly [51]
Ringing Rock	–	0–6–0ST	5/1883	West Sussex Rly [52]
Ringmer	242	D1	11/1881	London, Brighton & South Coast Rly
Ringwell	207	0–4–0ST	12/1855	Midland Rly [53]
Ripon Hall	5914	Hall	7/1931	Great Western Rly
Ripple Lane	37892	37/7	6/1963	British Railways
Rippleside	79	79	1909	London, Tilbury & Southend Rly
Rishra	3	**0–4–0T**	**1921**	**Leighton Buzzard Rly** [54]
Rising Star	–	Wolf	3/1841	Great Western Rly (bg)
Rising Star	4007	Star	4/1907	Great Western Rly [55]
Rising Star	70027	Britannia	10/1952	British Railways
Rising Sun	51912	cSentinel	1929	London & North Eastern Rly
Ritzebuttel	110	0–4–0ST	12/1879	London & South Western Rly [56]
Rival	51913	cSentinel	1929	London & North Eastern Rly
River Adur	A791	River	5/1925	Southern Rly

Name	Number	Class	Date	Railway
River Arun	A792	River	5/1925	Southern Rly
River Avon	A790	River	6/1917	Southern Rly [57]
River Axe	A807	River	11/1926	Southern Rly
River Camel	A805	River	10/1926	Southern Rly
River Char	A808	River	11/1926	Southern Rly
River Cray	A800	River	7/1926	Southern Rly
River Cuckmere	A802	River	8/1926	Southern Rly
River Darenth	A801	River	7/1926	Southern Rly
River Dart	A809	River	12/1926	Southern Rly
River Eden	400	**0–4–0DH**	**1955**	**War Department**
River Esk	–	**2–8–2**	**1923**	**Ravenglass & Eskdale Rly** [58]
River Fal	3431	Bulldog	5/1903	Great Western Rly
River Frome	A890	River	12/1925	Southern Rly
River Irt	–	**0–8–2**	**1928**	**Ravenglass & Eskdale Rly** [59]
River Itchen	A803	River	8/1926	Southern Rly
River Medway	A795	River	6/1925	Southern Rly

Southern Railway's unique three-cylinder River class 2–6–4T no. 890 *River Frome*. (Photo: LCGB Ken Nunn Collection)

Name	Number	Class	Date	Railway
River Mite	–	4–6–6–4	1928	Ravenglass & Eskdale Rly [60]
River Mite	–	**2–8–2**	**1966**	**Ravenglass & Eskdale Rly** [61]
River Mole	A797	River	6/1925	Southern Rly
River Ness	70	River	1915	Highland Rly
River Ouse	A793	River	5/1925	Southern Rly
River Plym	3428	Bulldog	5/1903	Great Western Rly
River Rother	A794	River	5/1925	Southern Rail
River Spey	71	River	1915	Highland Rly
River Stour	A796	River	6/1925	Southern Rly
River Tamar	3268	Duke	6/1896	Great Western Rly [62]
River Tamar	3268	Bulldog	6/1907	Great Western Rly [63]
River Tamar	A804	River	9/1926	Southern Rly
River Tawe	3430	Bulldog	5/1903	Great Western Rly
River Test	A799	River	6/1925	Southern Rly
River Torridge	A806	River	10/1926	Southern Rly

[46] 1ft 11½in gauge.

[47] Rebuilt with taper boiler in October 1946.

[48] Originally no. 227 of Loco Dept.

[49] Originally named *Sirdar*. Renamed *Richmond* in November 1906.

[50] Sold by British Railways in February 1948 for £745 to the Whittingham Light Railway, Lancashire, where it became their no. 1 *James Fryars*.

[51] Built for the North Pembrokeshire & Fishguard Railway. The GWR sold it to the Bute Works Supply Co. in 1912, and it then became no. 8 *Hesperus* on the Kent & East Sussex Railway. It lasted until 1941.

[52] Originally named *Vida* and in industrial service. Date of purchase by the West Sussex Railway unknown.

[53] Taken over from the Staveley Coal & Iron Co. in 1866.

[54] 2ft gauge.

[55] Renamed *Swallowfield Park* in May 1937.

[56] Date purchased by LSWR from Alexander Shanks & Son of Arbroath, Scotland. It shunted at Southampton Docks, and was sold in December 1915 to Kynock Ltd, Birmingham. It is thought to have been broken up in 1919.

[57] Class prototype, built by the South Eastern & Chatham Railway. Named by the Southern Railway after 1923, when more of the class were introduced.

[58] 15in gauge. Fitted with an 0–8–0 steam tender from 1928 to 1931.

[59] 15in gauge. Rebuilt from *Muriel*, Duffield Bank Railway.

[60] 15in gauge. Rebuilt in 1927–8 from the chassis of *Colossus* and *Sir Aubrey Brocklebank*. Laid aside in 1937.

[61] 15in gauge. Re-used an 0–8–0 chassis formerly used for a few years under the tender of *River Esk*.

[62] Originally named *Tamar*. Renamed in December 1903.

[63] Originally named *Tamar*, renamed in December 1903. Rebuild of previous engine.

Southern Railway Lord Nelson class 4–6–0 no. E855 *Robert Blake* on the Down 'Golden Arrow' near Chelsfield on 30 March 1930. (*Photo: LCGB Ken Nunn Collection*)

Name	Number	Class	Date	Railway
(River Torridge)	31806	U	10/1926	**British Railways** [64]
River Wey	A798	River	6/1925	Southern Rly
River Yealm	3432	Bulldog	5/1903	Great Western Rly
Roach	2	Roach	10/1846	East Lancashire Rly
(Robert)	75091	J94	1943	**Railway Age, Crewe**
Robert	3	0–4–4PM	1973	**Ruislip Lido Rly** [65]
Robert Adam	60007	60	2/1992	British Railways
Robert Adley	91022	91	9/1990	British Railways
Robert A Riddles	86102	86/1	1966	British Railways
Robert Benson	2176	Precedent	2/1875	London & North Western Rly
Robert Benson	2176	rPrecedent	4/1896	London & North Western Rly
Robert Blake	855	Lord Nelson	10/1928	Southern Rly
Robert Boyle	60013	60	2/1993	British Railways
Robert Burns	2075	Prince/W	11/1913	London & North Western Rly
Robert Burns	70006	Britannia	4/1951	British Railways
Robert Burns	87035	87/0	1974	British Railways
Robert Fairlie	2	0–4–4T	1876	East & West Junction Rly [66]

Name	Number	Class	Date	Railway
Robert F. Fairlie	37422	37/4	1965	British Railways
Locomotive Engineer 1831–1885				
Robert H. Selbie	95	G	1/1916	Metropolitan Rly
Robert L. Stevenson	2283	Prince/W	12/1913	London & North Western Rly
Robert Louis Stevenson	91018	91	8/1990	British Railways
Robert Nelson No 4	–	0–6–0ST	1936	**Gloucestershire Warwickshire Rly**
Robert Owen	60047	60	7/1991	British Railways
Roberts	429	DX	c.1860	London & North Western Rly
Roberts	737	Samson	7/1864	London & North Western Rly
Roberts	–	Hawthorn	6/1865	Great Western Rly (bg)
Roberts	737	Whitworth	5/1894	London & North Western Rly [67]
Roberts	3387	Atbara	8/1900	Great Western Rly
Roberts	56	B4	7/1901	London, Brighton & South Coast Rly [68]
Robertson	2987	Saint	8/1905	Great Western Rly [69]
Robert Southey	362	Prince/W	10/1913	London & North Western Rly
Robert the Bruce	510	A2/1	1/1945	London & North Eastern Rly

[64] Built as River class 2–6–4T no. A806 *River Torridge* by Southern Railway. Rebuilt to 2–6–0 U class in June 1928; ran nameless until purchased for preservation.

[65] 12in gauge.

[66] Single boiler Fairlie articulated locomotive. Purchased in 1876 from the builders, the Yorkshire Engine Co., who had built it for a Mexican railway but had left it on their hands.

[67] Transferred to Engineer's Department

February 1924–1935 and renamed *Engineer Lancaster*.

[68] Name removed in about May 1906. Rebuilt to class B4x in August 1923.

[69] Renamed *Bride of Lammermoor* in April 1907.

Name	Number	Class	Date	Railway
Robert the Bruce	87021	87/0	1974	British Railways
Robert the Devil	4479	A3	7/1923	London & North Eastern Rly
Robin	–	0–4–0ST	1887	Lancashire & Yorkshire Rly [70]
Robin	–	**4wVB**	**1957**	**Summerlee Heritage Trust**
Robin Hood	–	Abbot	3/1855	Great Western Rly (bg)
Robin Hood	1121A	0–6–0T	11/1868	Midland Rly [71]
Robin Hood	1906	Jubilee	4/1899	London & North Western Rly
Robin Hood	2986	Saint	7/1905	Great Western Rly
Robin Hood	70038	Britannia	1/1953	British Railways
Robin Hood	47480	47/4	1964	British Railways
Robin Hood	47901	47/9	1964	British Railways
Robins Bolitho	2973	Saint	3/1905	Great Western Rly
Rob Roy	47	2–2–2	7/1839	Midland Counties Rly
Rob Roy	–	Abbot	4/1855	Great Western Rly (bg)
Rob Roy	1904	Jubilee	3/1899	London & North Western Rly
Rob Roy	2988	Saint	8/1905	Great Western Rly
Rob Roy	895	Scott	7/1909	North British Rly
Rob Roy	250	aSentinel	1928	London & North Eastern Rly
Rochdale	7	0–4–2	7/1839	Manchester & Leeds Rly
Rochdale Pioneers	47539	47/4	1964	British Railways
Rochelle	119	E1	8/1877	London, Brighton & South Coast Rly
Rocket	7	0–6–0	9/1829	Stockton & Darlington Rly
Rocket	1	**0–2–2**	**10/1829**	**Liverpool & Manchester Rly [72]**
Rocket	–	Wolf	11/1841	Great Western Rly (bg)
Rocket	2097	4–4–0ST	10/1851	Great Western Rly (bg) [73]
Rocket	290	aCrewe	8/1852	London & North Western Rly
Rocket	RL2	0–4–0ST	4/1875	Woolwich Arsenal [74]
Rocket	193	Precedent	9/1878	London & North Western Rly
Rocket	193	rPrecedent	3/1897	London & North Western Rly
Rocket	1	**replica**	**1929**	**Liverpool & Manchester Rly [75]**
Rocket	1	**replica**	**1979**	**Liverpool & Manchester Rly [76]**
Rockingham	29	aSentinel	1928	London & North Eastern Rly
Rocklia	109	Rocklia	10/1848	London & South Western Rly
Rocklia	109	Lion	2/1869	London & South Western Rly
Roderic	118	aCrewe	9/1847	London & North Western Rly [77]
Roderick Dhu	2693	D11/2	11/1924	London & North Eastern Rly
Rodney	237	aSentinel	1928	London & North Eastern Rly
Rodney	5643	Jubilee	1934	London Midland & Scottish Rly
Rodney	50021	**50**	**1968**	**British Railways**
Rodwell Hall	4964	Hall	11/1929	Great Western Rly
Roebuck	182	aCrewe	11/1847	London & North Western Rly
Roebuck	–	?	?	Cornwall Minerals Rly
Roebuck	1644	George V	1/1911	London & North Western Rly
Roebuck	D841	Warship	12/1960	British Railways
Roedeer	1040	B1	4/1946	London & North Eastern Rly
Roehampton	579	E4	7/1903	London, Brighton & South Coast Rly
ROF Bridgwater No. 1	–	**0–4–0DH**	**1972**	**War Department [78]**
ROF Bridgwater No. 2	–	**0–4–0DH**	**1972**	**War Department**
Rokeby	59	2–2–2	1838	Liverpool & Manchester Rly [79]
Rokeby	38	Rokeby	6/1847	Stockton & Darlington Rly
Roker	–	**0–4–0CT**	**1940**	**Foxfield Steam Rly**
Rolleston Hall	5973	Hall	5/1937	Great Western Rly
Rolvenden	5	A1x	9/1872	Kent & East Sussex Rly [80]

Name	Number	Class	Date	Railway
(Rolvenden)	27	**J94**	**1943**	**Kent & East Sussex Rly [81]**
Romford	28	Class 1	1884	London, Tilbury & Southend Rly
Rom River	–	**6wDM**	**1929**	**Foxfield Steam Rly**
Romulus	91	0–6–0	8/1849	Manchester, Sheffield & Lincolnshire Rly
Romulus	–	Caesar	11/1853	Great Western Rly (bg)
Romulus	2155	0–6–0ST	11/1866	Great Western Rly (bg) [82]
Rood Ashton Hall	4965	Hall	11/1929	Great Western Rly
Rook	2176	0–4–0ST	11/1874	Great Western Rly (bg) [83]
Rook	47096	47/0	1963	British Railways
Rooke	5660	Jubilee	1934	London Midland & Scottish Rly
(Rorke's Drift)	240	**0–4–0DM**	**1934**	**War Department [84]**
Rosa	2145	0–6–0ST	1863	Great Western Rly (bg) [85]
Rose	223	aCrewe	9/1848	London & North Western Rly
Rose	75	Rose	7/1863	London, Chatham & Dover Rly
Rose	–	Metro	8/1863	Great Western Rly (bg)

British Railways (ex-LNER) B1 class 4–6–0 no. 61040 *Roedeer*, passing Manor Park with a Liverpool Street–Norwich express on 9 July 1948. (*Photo: LCGB Ken Nunn Collection*)

Name	Number	Class	Date	Railway
Roseberry	196	Roseberry	11/1866	Stockton & Darlington Rly
Roseberry Topping	60050	60	3/1991	British Railways
Rosebery	294	D1	11/1877	London, Brighton & South Coast Rly [86]
Rosebery	201	B2	3/1897	London, Brighton & South Coast Rly [87]
Rosehaugh	73	Duke	1/1885	Highland Rly [88]
Roseneath	480	157	6/1877	North British Rly [89]
Roseneath	495	Helensburgh	4/1879	North British Rly
Rosenkavalier	–	**4–6–2**	**1937**	**Bressingham Steam Museum [90]**
Roslin	241	165	1/1876	North British Rly [91]
Roslin	104	72	5/1881	North British Rly
Rossendale	55	Rossendale	11/1852	East Lancashire Rly
Ross-shire	66	Duke	7/1874	Highland Rly [92]
Rosyth No 1	1	**0–4–0ST**	**1914**	**Gwili Rly**
Rotary International	86615	86/6	10/1965	British Railways
Rothbury	73	72	1880	North British Rly
Rother	34	2–2–0	7/1843	South Eastern Rly

[70] 18in gauge.
[71] Built for the Severn & Wye & Severn Bridge Railway.
[72] The remains of the original locomotive. Normally based at the Science Museum, South Kensington.
[73] Built for the South Devon Railway.
[74] 18in gauge. Nameless until about 1901.
[75] Sectioned replica at the National Railway Museum.
[76] Working replica at the National Railway Museum.
[77] Formerly Liverpool & Manchester Railway

no. 60; became a London & North Western engine in 1846.
[78] Both this locomotive and the next are preserved on the West Somerset Railway.
[79] In 1846 became London & North Western Railway no. 123.
[80] Originally London, Brighton & South Coast Railway no. 71 *Wapping*. Sold to K&ESR in January 1905.
[81] Also occasionally carries the number 75050.
[82] Built for the South Devon Railway.
[83] Built for the South Devon Railway.
[84] LMS no. 7050 of 1934. Now at the

Museum of Army Transport, Beverley.
[85] Built for the South Devon Railway.
[86] Later renamed *Falmer*.
[87] Rebuilt to class B2x, January 1909.
[88] Originally named *Thurlow*. Renamed *Rosehaugh* in 1898.
[89] Later renamed *Burntisland*.
[90] 15in gauge. Built by Krupp in 1937 for a German miniature railway. Now at Bressingham.
[91] Later renamed *Penicuik*, and then *Bervie*.
[92] Later renamed *Ardvuela*.

Name	Number	Class	Date	Railway
Rother	7	Ilfracombe	12/1880	Kent & East Sussex Rly [93]
Rotherfield	25	D1	3/1876	London, Brighton & South Coast Rly
Rotherham	**2**	**0–4–0DE**	**1950**	**South Yorkshire Rly [94]**
Rotherham Enterprise	43047	43	3/1977	British Railways
Rotherhithe	51	A1	12/1876	London, Brighton & South Coast Rly
Rotherwood	08543	08	1959	British Railways
Rothschild	318	B2	6/1896	London, Brighton & South Coast Rly [95]
Rotterdam Lloyd	21C15	MN	3/1945	Southern Rly
Rottingdean	234	D1	10/1881	London, Brighton & South Coast Rly
Rouen	101	2–4–0	9/1858	London, Brighton & South Coast Rly [96]
Rougemont	–	Iron Duke	10/1848	Great Western Rly (bg)
Rougemont	3022	3001	5/1891	Great Western Rly [97]
Rougemont Castle	5007	Castle	6/1927	Great Western Rly
Rough Pup	**–**	**0–4–0ST**	**1891**	**Narrow Gauge Museum, Tywyn [98]**
Rough Tor	21C125	WC	3/1946	Southern Rly [99]
Roumanian Monarch	4028	Star	9/1909	Great Western Rly [100]
Roundhill Grange	6854	Grange	11/1937	Great Western Rly
Rover	–	Iron Duke	9/1850	Great Western Rly (bg)
Rover	–	Rover	8/1871	Great Western Rly (bg)
Rover	3019	3001	4/1892	Great Western Rly [101]
ROVER GROUP QUALITY ASSURED	47323	47/3	1965	British Railways
Rowcliffe	–	0–6–0ST	1857	West Somerset Mineral Rly
Rowfant	282	D1	10/1879	London, Brighton & South Coast Rly
Rowland Hill	1008	L/Bloomer	1851	London & North Western Rly
Rowland Hill	326	bCrewe	2/1854	London & North Western Rly
Rowland Hill	659	Dreadnought	1886	London & North Western Rly
Rowland Hill	2582	2Precursor	12/1905	London & North Western Rly
Roxburgh	99	72	1882	North British Rly
Roxburghshire	306	D49/1	3/1928	London & North Eastern Rly
Royal	–	0–6–0	10/1842	Llanelly Rly [102]
Royal	909	0–6–0	1870	Great Western Rly [103]
Royal Adelaide	2	2–2–0	c.1834	London & Greenwich Rly
Royal Air Force Regiment	91005	91	5/1988	British Railways
Royal Albert	10	2–2–2	1886	Great Western Rly [104]
Royal Anchor	**–**	**B-B DH**	**1956**	**Ravenglass & Eskdale Rly [105]**
Royal Anglian Regiment	86246	86/2	1966	British Railways
Royal Armouries	91021	91	9/1990	British Railways
Royal Army Ordnance Corps	**45112**	**Peak**	**1962**	**British Railways**
Royal Army Service Corps	6126	Royal Scot	8/1927	London Midland & Scottish Rly [106]
Royal Artilleryman	D67	Peak	1962	British Railways
Royal Charlotte	2217	cSentinel	1929	London & North Eastern Rly
Royal Corps of Transport	D84	Peak	12/1960	British Railways
Royal Eagle	36	cSentinel	1929	London & North Eastern Rly
Royal Engineer	6109	Royal Scot	9/1927	London Midland & Scottish Rly
Royal Engineer	70217	0–6–0DE	?	Martin Mill Military Rly
Royal Engineer	**198**	**J94**	**1953**	**War Department [107]**

Name	Number	Class	Date	Railway
Royal Engineer	45059	Peak	1961	British Railways
Royal Engineers Postal & Courier Services	47568	47/4	1964	British Railways
Royal Forrester	51914	cSentinel	1929	London & North Eastern Rly
Royal Fusilier	6111	Royal Scot	9/1927	London Midland & Scottish Rly
Royal Fusilier	45046	Peak	1960	British Railways
Royal George	5	0–6–0	10/1827	Stockton & Darlington Rly [108]
Royal George	1908	Jubilee	4/1899	London & North Western Rly
Royal Highland Fusilier	**55019**	**Deltic**	**12/1961**	**British Railways**
5th Royal Inniskilling Dragoon Guards	45143	Peak	1962	British Railways
Royal Inniskilling Fusilier	6120	Royal Scot	10/1927	London Midland & Scottish Rly
Royal Inniskilling Fusilier	45044	Peak	1962	British Railways
Royal Irish Fusilier	6123	Royal Scot	10/1927	London Midland & Scottish Rly
Royal Irish Fusilier	45004	Peak	1960	British Railways
Royal Lancer	4476	A3	5/1923	London & North Eastern Rly
Royal London Society for the Blind	47745	47/7		British Railways
Royal Mail	21C3	MN	9/1941	Southern Rly
Royal Mail	47549	47/4	1964	British Railways
Royal Mail Cheltenham	47750	47/7		British Railways
Royal Mail Midlands	86226	86/2	1965	British Railways
Royal Mail Tyneside	47756	47/7		British Railways
Royal Marines	D70	Peak	11/1960	British Railways
Royal Naval Division	5502	Patriot	7/1932	London Midland & Scottish Rly
Royal Naval Reserve 1859–1959	D812	Warship	11/1959	British Railways [109]
Royal Oak	D842	Warship	12/1960	British Railways
Royal Oak	**50017**	**50**	**1968**	**British Railways**
Royal Observer Corps	21C150	rBB	12/1946	Southern Rly
Royal Observer Corps	73202	73/2	9/1966	British Railways
Royal Philharmonic	43046	43	3/1977	British Railways
Royal Pioneer	75078	J94	1943	War Department
Royal Pioneer	75186	J94	1944	War Department
Royal Sailor	287	Clayton	1928	London & North Eastern Rly
Royal Scot	**6100**	**Royal Scot**	**7/1927**	**London Midland & Scottish Rly**
Royal Scot	87001	87/0	1973	British Railways
Royal Scots Fusilier	6103	Royal Scot	8/1927	London Midland & Scottish Rly
Royal Scots Grey	**55002**	**Deltic**	**2/1961**	**British Railways**
Royal Scots Greys	6101	Royal Scot	8/1927	London Midland & Scottish Rly
Royal Show	90009	90/0	9/1988	British Railways
Royal Signals	5504	Patriot	7/1932	London Midland & Scottish Rly
Royal Signals	45144	Peak	1962	British Railways
Royal Society of Edinburgh	47578	47/4	1964	British Railways
Royal Sovereign	3050	3031	2/1895	Great Western Rly

[93] Originally London & South Western Railway no. 349, later duplicated as no. 0349. This Ilfracombe Goods class engine was withdrawn by the LSWR in May 1909 and sold to the Kent & East Sussex Railway in April 1910. They named it *Rother*, after a local river. Laid aside in October 1932, it was finally scrapped in October 1938.

[94] The modern, preserved South Yorkshire Railway.

[95] Rebuilt to class B2x in July 1910.

[96] Name applied by Stroudley in May 1872.

[97] Built as a broad gauge convertible. Rebuilt to 4–2–2 in July 1894 and renamed *Bessemer* in 1898.

[98] 1ft 11½in gauge.

[99] This name was carried from 11 April 1948 to 23 April 1948. The locomotive was renamed *Whimple* as from 3 May 1948.

[100] Originally named *King John*. Renamed *The Roumanian Monarch* in July 1927, and *Roumanian Monarch* in November 1927. The name was removed in November 1940 and the words STAR CLASS painted on the splashers.

[101] Rebuilt to 4–2–2 in August 1894.

[102] Originally named *Drysllwyn*. Later renamed *Princess Royal* and became Great Western Railway no. 909.

[103] Built for the Llanelly Railway and named originally *Drysllwyn*, and then *Princess Royal*.

[104] This 2–2–2 passenger locomotive was assembled from parts for a second 4–2–4 express tank locomotive. It lasted until January 1906. See footnote to *Victoria*, no. 9 of September 1884, for the rest of the story.

[105] 15in gauge. From the Royal Anchor Hotel, Liss, Hants.

[106] Originally named *Sanspareil*; renamed in June 1936.

[107] Preserved on the Isle of Wight Railway.

[108] Probably incorporated the boiler shell of "*Chittaprat*", with possibly the wheels and other parts.

[109] The name *Despatch* was originally allocated, but never carried.

Name	Number	Class	Date	Railway
Royal Sovereign	3373	Atbara	4/1900	Great Western Rly [110]
Royal Sovereign	3357	Bulldog	6/1900	Great Western Rly [111]
Royal Sovereign	1936	Jubilee	10/1900	London & North Western Rly
Royal Sovereign	246	bSentinel	1932	London & North Eastern Rly
Royal Sovereign	1671	B2	8/1945	London & North Eastern Rly [112]
Royal Sovereign	61632	B2	7/1946	British Railways (Eastern Region) [113]
Royal Sovereign	87002	87/0	1973	British Railways
Royal Star	–	Priam	11/1841	Great Western Rly (bg)
Royal Star	4008	Star	5/1907	Great Western Rly
Royal Star	70028	Britannia	10/1952	British Railways
Royal Tank Corps	5507	Patriot	8/1932	London Midland & Scottish Rly
Royal Tank Regiment	**45041**	**Peak**	**1962**	**British Railways**
Royal Ulster Rifleman	6122	Royal Scot	10/1927	London Midland & Scottish Rly
Royal Welch Fusilier	6118	Royal Scot	10/1927	London Midland & Scottish Rly
Royal William	1	2–2–0	_c._1834	London & Greenwich Rly
Royal Worcester	47821	47/4	4/1964	British Railways
Roy Castle OBE	47786	47/7		British Railways
Roydon Hall	5994	Hall	12/1939	Great Western Rly
Ruby	39	Rokeby	6/1847	Stockton & Darlington Rly
Ruby	108	107	10/1847	London & South Western Rly
Ruby	194	aCrewe	2/1848	London & North Western Rly
Ruby	–	Caesar	1/1854	Great Western Rly (bg)
Ruby	68	Ruby	8/1861	London, Chatham & Dover Rly
Ruby	108	Lion	1/1869	London & South Western Rly
Ruby	2145	cSentinel	1928	London & North Eastern Rly
Ruckley Grange	6846	Grange	10/1937	Great Western Rly
Rudgwick	276	D1	12/1879	London, Brighton & South Coast Rly
Rudyard Kipling	70035	Britannia	12/1952	British Railways
Rufus	131	Canute	2/1856	London & South Western Rly
Rugby	920	Schools	10/1933	Southern Rly
Rugeley Power Station	58039	58	3/1986	British Railways
Rumney	28	0–6–0ST	9/1872	Brecon & Merthyr Rly
Runter Hall	7919	M/Hall	5/1950	British Railways (Western Region)
Rupert	**–**	**4wDM**	**1944**	**National Tramway Museum**
Rupert Guinness	668	Claughton	9/1914	London & North Western Rly
Rushton Hall	5913	Hall	6/1931	Great Western Rly

Name	Number	Class	Date	Railway
Ruskin College	47714	47/7	1966	British Railways
Ruskin College Oxford	47587	47/4	1965	British Railways
Russell	111	aCrewe	7/1847	London & North Western Rly
Russell	111	Problem	_c._1860	London & North Western Rly
Russell	**–**	**2–6–2T**	**1906**	**North Wales Narrow Gauge Rly [114]**
Russell	**–**	**2–6–2T**	**1985**	**Fairbourne & Barmouth Steam Rly [115]**
Rustington	516	E4	4/1901	London, Brighton & South Coast Rly
Ruston	**–**	**4wPM**	**1941**	**Leicestershire Museum [116]**
Ruthin	2	0–4–0	10/1860	Cambrian Railways
Rutland	219	0–4–0WT	11/1850	Great Northern Rly [117]
Rutlandshire	2754	D49/1	4/1929	London & North Eastern Rly
Rydal Hall	6986	M/Hall	3/1948	Great Western Rly
Ryde	148	2–4–0	4/1862	London, Brighton & South Coast Rly [118]
Ryde	–	2–4–0T	1864	Isle of Wight Rly [119]
Ryde	W3	E1	3/1881	Southern Rly [120]

London Midland & Scottish Railway (ex-London & North Western Railway) Claughton class 4–6–0 no. 5915 _Rupert Guinness_, at Camden Shed in May 1932. (_Photo: RAS Marketing_)

[110] Originally named _Atbara_. Temporarily renamed _Maine_ for a City Imperial Volunteers' Special Train on 29 October 1900, and _Royal Sovereign_ for Queen Victoria's funeral train on 2 February 1901.

[111] Originally named _Exeter_. Temporarily renamed _Royal Sovereign_ to work a Royal Train on 7 March 1902, and renamed _Smeaton_ in October 1903.

[112] Originally class B17/4 no. 2871 _Manchester City_. Rebuilt to class B2, August 1945, and renamed _Royal Sovereign_ in April 1946.

[113] Originally class B17/2 no. 2832 _Belvoir Castle_. Rebuilt to class B2, July 1946. Renamed _Royal Sovereign_ in October 1958 on the withdrawal of no. 61671.

[114] 1ft 11½in gauge. Later no. 12 of the Welsh Highland Railway.

[115] 12¼in gauge.

[116] 1ft 11½in gauge.

[117] Built for the Nottingham & Grantham Railway & Canal.

[118] Name applied by Stroudley in October 1871.

[119] Became Southern Railway no. W13. Withdrawn in 1932.

[120] Formerly London, Brighton & South Coast Railway no. 154 _Madrid_. Transferred to the Isle of Wight in July 1932, painted in passenger green and named _Ryde_.

S

Name	Number	Class	Date	Railway
Sabrina	1125A	0–6–0T	7/1882	Midland Rly [1]
Saddleback	–	2–2–0	6/1840	North Western Rly
Saddleback	84	aCrewe	4/1846	London & North Western Rly
Saddleback	10	2–4–0	1857	Lancaster & Carlisle Rly
Saddleback	1162	Samson	5/1879	London & North Western Rly
Saddleback	1162	Whitworth	6/1893	London & North Western Rly
Saddleback	845	George V	3/1913	London & North Western Rly
Saddleback	60048	60	6/1991	British Railways
Saddlescombe	167	E3	12/1894	London, Brighton & South Coast Rly
Saddleworth	–	2–2–2	1847	Huddersfield & Manchester Railway & Canal
Safety	15	2–4–0T	1853	South Staffordshire Rly
Sagittarius	–	Leo	4/1842	Great Western Rly (bg)
Saighton Grange	6855	Grange	11/1937	Great Western Rly
Saint Agatha	2911	Saint	8/1907	Great Western Rly
St Agnes	3287	Duke	3/1897	Great Western Rly
Saint Aidan	47535	47/4	1965	British Railways
St. Alban's Head	2426	H2	1/1912	Southern Rly [2]
Saint Ambrose	2912	Saint	8/1907	Great Western Rly
Saint Andrew	2913	Saint	8/1907	Great Western Rly
Saint Andrew	47624	47/4	1965	British Railways
St. Andrews	108	165	6/1878	North British Rly [3]
St Anthony	3264	Duke	5/1896	Great Western Rly
St Anthony	3264	Bulldog	12/1907	Great Western Rly
St. Arnaud	353	bCrewe	11/1854	London & North Western Rly
St. Arnaud	353	aCrewe	3/1858	London & North Western Rly [4]
St Aubyn	3367	Bulldog	11/1900	Great Western Rly
St Aubyns	2	2–4–0T	3/1884	Jersey Rly [5]
Saint Augustine	2914	Saint	8/1907	Great Western Rly
St Austell	3326	Duke	7/1899	Great Western Rly
Saint Bartholomew	2915	Saint	8/1907	Great Western Rly
Saint Bede	47721	47/7		British Railways
Saint Benedict	2916	Saint	8/1907	Great Western Rly
Saint Benets Hall	5947	Hall	3/1935	Great Western Rly [6]
Saint Bernard	2917	Saint	8/1907	Great Western Rly
Saint Blaise Church 1445–1995	37674	37/5	8/1963	British Railways
St. Blazey T&RS Depot	37670	37/5	10/1963	British Railways
St. Boswell's	490	Abbotsford	1878	North British Rly
St Brelades	4	2–4–0T	1/1896	Jersey Rly [7]
Saint Brides Hall	4972	Hall	1/1930	Great Western Rly [8]
Saint Catherine	2918	Saint	8/1907	Great Western Rly
St. Catherine's Point	2040	H1	2/1906	Southern Rly [9]
Saint Cecilia	2919	Saint	9/1907	Great Western Rly [10]
St. Christopher's Railway Home	47348	47/3	1965	British Railways
St Columb	3325	Duke	6/1899	Great Western Rly
St Columb	3325	Bulldog	12/1908	Great Western Rly
Saint Cuthbert	2919	Saint	9/1907	Great Western Rly [11]
Saint Cuthbert	47792	47/7		British Railways
St. David	–	0–6–0	?	Sirhowy Rly [12]
St. David	–	0–4–2	1841	Bolton & Leigh Rly [13]
St. David	205	bCrewe	5/1848	London & North Western Rly
St. David	740	S/Bloomer	1854	London & North Western Rly
Saint David	2920	Saint	9/1907	Great Western Rly
Saint David	47790	47/7		British Railways [14]
St. Donats Castle	5017	Castle	7/1932	Great Western Rly [15]
Saint Dunstan	2921	Saint	9/1907	Great Western Rly
St. Dunstan's	5501	Patriot	11/1930	London Midland & Scottish Rly [16]
Saint Edwin	47744	47/7		British Railways
St Erth	3285	Duke	2/1897	Great Western Rly
St. Fagans Castle	5067	Castle	7/1937	Great Western Rly
St. Frusquin	2574	A3	10/1924	London & North Eastern Rly
Saint Gabriel	2922	Saint	9/1907	Great Western Rly
St. Gatien	2572	A3	10/1924	London & North Eastern Rly
St. George	–	0–4–0	7/1835	London & South Western Rly
St. George	203	bCrewe	4/1848	London & North Western Rly
St. George	121	1Vesuvius	1/1853	London & South Western Rly
St. George	121	2Vesuvius	12/1869	London & South Western Rly
St. George	469	Samson	10/1874	London & North Western Rly
St. George	3025	3001	8/1891	Great Western Rly [17]
St. George	469	Whitworth	6/1893	London & North Western Rly
Saint George	2923	Saint	9/1907	Great Western Rly
St. George	681	George V	3/1913	London & North Western Rly
St. Germain	331	bCrewe	3/1854	London & North Western Rly
St Germans	3265	Duke	5/1896	Great Western Rly
Saint Helena	2924	Saint	9/1907	Great Western Rly
St. Helena	5624	Jubilee	1934	London Midland & Scottish Rly
St Heliers	1	2–4–0T	3/1884	Jersey Rly [18]
St. Ives	918	2–4–0ST	1855	Great Western Rly [19]
St Ives	3266	Duke	5/1896	Great Western Rly
St. John Ambulance	86608	86/6	10/1965	British Railways
St Johns	3411	Atbara	10/1901	Great Western Rly
St. Johnstoun	901	I	7/1911	North British Rly
Saint Johnstoun	60162	A1	12/1949	British Railways (Eastern Region)
St. Just	–	0–6–0	6/1863	West Cornwall Rly [20]
St Just	3286	Duke	2/1897	Great Western Rly

Southern Railway H1 class 4–4–2 no. B40 *St Catherine's Point*, at East Croydon on 4 September 1926. (*Photo: LCGB Ken Nunn Collection*)

[1] Formerly the Severn & Wye & Severn Bridge Railway.
[2] Built by the London, Brighton & South Coast Railway. Name applied by the Southern Railway in June 1925.
[3] Originally named *Hamilton*.
[4] Considered as a replacement for the previous engine, which was sold to the Lancaster & Carlisle Railway.
[5] 3ft 6in gauge.
[6] Renamed *Saint Benet's Hall* (with apostrophe) in May 1935.
[7] 3ft 6in gauge.
[8] Renamed *Saint Bride's Hall* (with apostrophe) later in January 1930.
[9] Built for the London, Brighton & South Coast Railway. Nameplates applied by the Southern Railway in July 1925.
[10] Renamed *Saint Cuthbert* in October 1907.
[11] Named *Saint Cecilia* until October 1907.
[12] Built between 1832 and 1853.
[13] May have been a 2–2–2.
[14] Also named (on the other side) *Dewi Sant*.
[15] Renamed *The Gloucestershire Regiment 28th 61st* in 1954.
[16] Date of rebuilding from Claughton class no. 5902. Originally named *Sir Frank Ree*, renamed *St. Dunstan's* in April 1937.
[17] Built as broad gauge convertible. Rebuilt to 4–2–2 in October 1894 and renamed *Quicksilver* in May 1907.
[18] 3ft 6in gauge.
[19] Built for the Llynvi & Ogmore Railway.
[20] Became Great Western Railway no. 1385.

Name	Number	Class	Date	Railway
St Just	3286	Bulldog	9/1908	Great Western Rly
St. Lawrence	342	G	1/1882	London, Brighton & South Coast Rly
St. Lawrence	934	Schools	3/1935	Southern Rly
St. Leonards	240	2–2–2	6/1867	London, Brighton & South Coast Rly [21]
St. Leonards	390	D3	5/1894	London, Brighton & South Coast Rly
St. Malo	93	B4	12/1892	London & South Western Rly
Saint Margaret	37201	37/0	1963	British Railways
Saint Martin	2925	Saint	9/1907	Great Western Rly [22]
Saint Martin	4900	Hall	12/1924	Great Western Rly [23]
St. Martins	3	Raigmore	8/1856	Highland Rly
St Martins	16	Lochgorm	10/1874	Highland Rly [24]
St. Mawes Castle	5018	Castle	7/1932	Great Western Rly
St. Michael	457	0–4–0ST	1/1872	London & South Western Rly
St Michael	3267	Duke	6/1896	Great Western Rly
St. Michael	3201	3200	4/1936	Great Western Rly [25]
St Mirren	**3**	**0–4–0DE**	**1958**	**Bo'ness & Kinneil Rly**
St Monans	**–**	**4wVB**	**1947**	**Southport Railway Centre**
Saint Mungo	873	H	7/1906	North British Rly
Saint Mungo	60145	A1	3/1949	British Railways (Eastern Region)
Saint Mungo	86425	86/6	10/1965	British Railways
Saint Mungo	47703	47/7	1967	British Railways
Saint Nicholas	2926	Saint	9/1907	Great Western Rly
Saint Nicholas	91009	91	8/1988	British Railways
St. Olave's	938	Schools	7/1935	Southern Rly
St. Paddy	55001	Deltic	2/1961	British Railways
St. Pancras	31	Class 1	1892	London, Tilbury & Southend Rly
St. Patrick	208	bCrewe	5/1848	London & North Western Rly
St. Patrick	434	Samson	10/1874	London & North Western Rly
St. Patrick	434	Whitworth	4/1893	London & North Western Rly
Saint Patrick	2927	Saint	9/1907	Great Western Rly
St. Paul's	909	Schools	7/1930	Southern Rly
Saint Peter	47783	47/7		British Railways
Saint Peter's Hall	7900	M/Hall	4/1949	British Railways (Western Region)

Name	Number	Class	Date	Railway
St. Peter's School, York, A.D. 627	4818	V2	3/1939	London & North Eastern Rly
St Peter's School York AD 627	43152	43	6/1981	British Railways
St. Quentin	605	C	8/1888	North British Rly
St. Rollox	–	?	1831	Garnkirk & Glasgow Rly [26]
Saint Saens	92028	92		Société Nationale des Chemins de fer Français
Saint Sebastian	2928	Saint	9/1907	Great Western Rly
St. Simon	4481	A3	8/1923	London & North Eastern Rly
Saint Stephen	2929	Saint	9/1907	Great Western Rly
St. Vincent	115	2–2–2	8/1844	South Eastern Rly [27]
Saint Vincent	2930	Saint	9/1907	Great Western Rly
St. Vincent	5686	Jubilee	1936	London Midland & Scottish Rly
St Vincent	50004	50	1967	British Railways
Salamander	–	2–2–0	5/1831	Bolton & Leigh Rly [28]
Salamander	6	Roach	12/1846	East Lancashire Rly
Salford	44	0–4–2	1/1843	Manchester & Leeds Rly
Salford Hall	7922	M/Hall	9/1950	British Railways (Western Region)
Salisbury	16	Minerva	6/1856	London & South Western Rly
Salisbury	16	Lion	8/1872	London & South Western Rly [29]
Salisbury	215	Gladstone	12/1883	London, Brighton & South Coast Rly
Salisbury	15	Il	1/1888	Mersey Rly
Salisbury	16	0–6–0T	1914	Longmoor Military Rly
Salisbury	21C102	WC	6/1945	Southern Rly
Salmon	**8410/39**	**0–6–0ST**	**1942**	**Rutland Railway Museum**
Salmon Trout	2506	A3	12/1934	London & North Eastern Rly
Salopian	54	2–2–2	6/1849	Great Western Rly [30]
Salopian	248	bCrewe	10/1849	London & North Western Rly
Salopian	2193	Precedent	5/1875	London & North Western Rly
Salopian	2193	rPrecedent	2/1896	London & North Western Rly
Saltburn	162	Saltburn	1862	Stockton & Darlington Rly
Saltburn by the Sea	20118	20	1962	British Railways
Saltley Depot Quality Approved	47326	47/3	1965	British Railways
Salus	–	Caesar	8/1854	Great Western Rly (bg)
Salzberg	96	E1	12/1883	London, Brighton & South Coast Rly
(Sam)	**D2868**	**02**	**1961**	**British Railways**
Samaria CLS	40028	40	8/1959	British Railways [31]
Sambo	459	0–6–0ST	5/1863	London & South Western Rly
Sampson	–	Fury	7/1842	Great Western Rly (bg)
Sampson	2142	0–6–0ST	9/1855	Great Western Rly (bg) [32]
Sam Slick	–	1Sussex	3/1839	London & South Western Rly [33]
Samson	13	0–4–0	1831	Liverpool & Manchester Rly
Samson	–	0–4–0	1/1833	Leicester & Swannington Rly
Samson	31	0–6–0	2/1843	South Eastern Rly
Samson	22	0–6–0T	1844	Edinburgh & Glasgow Rly
Samson	12	Samson	3/1847	East Lancashire Rly
Samson	120	bCrewe	11/1847	London & North Western Rly [34]
Samson	8	2–2–2T	1852	London & Blackwall Rly
Samson	128	Saxon	6/1855	London & South Western Rly
Samson	120	DX	c.1860	London & North Western Rly
Samson	633	Samson	5/1863	London & North Western Rly
Samson	26	0–6–0ST	4/1871	Brecon & Merthyr Rly
Samson	633	Whitworth	1/1892	London & North Western Rly
Samson	3305	Badminton	9/1898	Great Western Rly

Southern Region Schools class 4–4–0 no. 30909 *St. Paul's*, near Blackwater with a Reading–Redhill service. (*Photo: Author*)

[21] Name applied by Stroudley, November 1870.

[22] Rebuilt in December 1924 with 6ft driving wheels, as a prototype of the Hall class, and renumbered 4900.

[23] Rebuilt from Saint class in December 1924 with 6ft driving wheels, as a prototype of the Hall class, and renumbered 4900.

[24] Renamed *Fort-George* in 1899.

[25] Name removed in May 1936; renamed *Earl of Dunraven* in June 1936.

[26] 4ft 6in gauge.

[27] Built for the Gravesend & Rochester Railway. Passed to the South Eastern Railway on absorption, 1846.

[28] Sometimes said to be an 0–4–0.

[29] Renamed *Stonehenge* in August 1877, at the request of the Traffic Dept. Passengers apparently mistook the engine's name for the train's destination. Presumably no one wanted to go to Stonehenge!

[30] Built for the Shrewsbury & Birmingham Railway.

[31] Originally no. D228 *Samaria*.

[32] Originally built for the South Devon Railway.

[33] Not a satisfactory design; the engine was sent to Fairbairns for total reconstruction. It returned in April 1842 as no. 23 *Antelope*. Sam Slick, by the way, was a character in a series of comic stories written by Judge J.C. Halliburton of Nova Scotia, popular in England during the 1830s.

[34] Previously Liverpool & Manchester Railway 0–4–2 no. 66; became a London & North Western engine in 1846.

Name	Number	Class	Date	Railway
Samson	2339	Prince/W	1/1916	London & North Western Rly
Samson	**6**	**4–8–2**	**1926**	**Romney, Hythe & Dymchurch Rly** [35]
Samson	6135	Royal Scot	9/1927	London Midland & Scottish Rly [36]
Samson	5738	Jubilee	1936	London Midland & Scottish Rly
Samson	47088	47	1965	British Railways
Samuel Johnson	60062	60	6/1991	British Railways
Samuel Laing	199	Gladstone	1/1888	London, Brighton & South Coast Rly
Samuel Plimsoll	60059	60	9/1991	British Railways [37]
Sanderstead	379	D3	7/1893	London, Brighton & South Coast Rly
Sandon	86	aCrewe	6/1846	London & North Western Rly
Sandon	855	L/Bloomer	1851	London & North Western Rly
Sandon Hall	6918	Hall	6/1941	Great Western Rly [38]
Sandown	163	2–2–2	10/1863	London, Brighton & South Coast Rly [39]
Sandown	–	2–4–0T	1864	Isle of Wight Rly
Sandown	179	Gladstone	6/1890	London, Brighton & South Coast Rly
Sandown	W21	O2	9/1891	Southern Rly [40]
Sandpiper	47219	47/0	1965	British Railways
Sandringham	65	B4	8/1901	London, Brighton & South Coast Rly
Sandringham	2800	B17/1	12/1928	London & North Eastern Rly
Sandwich	5641	Jubilee	1934	London Midland & Scottish Rly
Sandwich	2504	A3	9/1934	London & North Eastern Rly
Sandy River	**2**	**2–6–2**	**1989**	**Bure Valley Rly** [41]
San Justo	**4**	**0–4–2ST**	**1903**	**Brecon Mountain Rly** [42]
Sankey	8	?	?	St Helens Canal & Rly
Sankey	–	0–4–0ST	1888	Edge Hill Light Rly
Sansovino	2552	A3	11/1924	London & North Eastern Rly
Sanspareil	**–**	**0–4–0**	**1829**	**Liverpool & Manchester Rly** [43]
Sanspareil	832	Samson	1/1866	London & North Western Rly
Sanspareil	832	Whitworth	4/1893	London & North Western Rly
Sanspareil	1526	2Experiment	10/1907	London & North Western Rly
Sans Pareil	–	4–4–2	1912	Ravenglass & Eskdale Rly [44]
Sanspareil	6126	Royal Scot	8/1927	London Midland & Scottish Rly [45]
Sanspareil	5732	Jubilee	1936	London Midland & Scottish Rly
Sans Pareil	86214	86/2	1965	British Railways
Sanspareil	**–**	**replica**	**1980**	**Liverpool & Manchester Rly**
Sanspareil 2	–	2–2–2	1849	York, Newcastle & Berwick Rly
Santa Ana	**–**	**0–4–2ST**	**1903**	**Brecon Mountain Rly** [46]
Sao Domingos	**3**	**0–6–0WT**	**1928**	**South Tynedale Rly** [47]
Sapper	222	0–4–0ST	1900	War Department
Sapper	601	WD2-10-0	1943	War Department [48]
Sapper	5039	J94	12/1943	War Department
Sapper	5113	J94	4/1944	War Department
Sapper	1438	J94	1/1945	War Department [49]
Sapper	202	J94	1953	War Department
Sapper	**197**	**J94**	**3/1953**	**War Department** [50]
Sappho	60	Mazeppa	10/1847	London & South Western Rly
Sappho	–	Bogie	6/1854	Great Western Rly (bg)
Sappho	60	Lion	8/1866	London & South Western Rly
Saracen	1	2–2–2	1837	Grand Junction Rly
Saracen	1	0–4–2	2/1842	Grand Junction Rly
Saracen	85	Fireball	11/1847	London & South Western Rly
Saracen	1	aCrewe	4/1852	London & North Western Rly
Saracen	12	?	1858	St Helens Canal & Rly
Saracen	1	Problem	c.1860	London & North Western Rly
Saracen	85	Falcon	10/1866	London & South Western Rly
Saracen	2624	2Experiment	2/1909	London & North Western Rly
Sarah Siddons	**12**	**Bo-Bo**	**1922**	**Metropolitan Rly** [51]
Sarawak	5625	Jubilee	1934	London Midland & Scottish Rly
Sardinian	381	bCrewe	11/1855	London & North Western Rly [52]
Sarmatian	310	1Experiment	1884	London & North Western Rly
Sarmatian	507	2Experiment	6/1905	London & North Western Rly
Sarum Castle	5060	Castle	6/1937	Great Western Rly [53]
Sarum Castle	5097	Castle	7/1939	Great Western Rly
Saskatchewan	5561	Jubilee	1934	London Midland & Scottish Rly
Sassaby	1022	B1	3/1947	London & North Eastern Rly
Satellite	13	2–2–2	12/1841	London & Brighton Rly
Saturn	16	2–2–0	1831	Liverpool & Manchester Rly
Saturn	–	2–2–2	1841	London & Brighton Rly
Saturn	26	?	4/1841	Newcastle & Carlisle Rly [54]
Saturn	–	Priam	6/1841	Great Western Rly (bg)
Saturn	56	2–2–2	7/1841	South Eastern Rly
Saturn	17	2–2–2	12/1845	Manchester, Sheffield & Lincolnshire Rly
Saturn	89	Fireball	12/1847	London & South Western Rly
Saturn	155	Panther	1/1861	Stockton & Darlington Rly
Saturn	89	Volcano	12/1867	London & South Western Rly
Saturn	1298	2–4–0T	12/1878	Great Western Rly [55]
Satyr	23	Tiger	4/1862	London, Chatham & Dover Rly
Saunders	–	Sir Watkin	9/1866	Great Western Rly (bg) [56]
Saunton	34093	rWC	10/1949	British Railways (Southern Region)
Savernake	3308	Badminton	12/1898	Great Western Rly
Saxon	124	Saxon	6/1855	London & South Western Rly
Saxonia CLS	40029	40	9/1959	British Railways [57]
Sayajirao	E530	A2	3/1948	British Railways (Eastern Region)
Scafell	60049	60	9/1991	British Railways
Scafell Pike	D1	Peak	4/1959	British Railways
Scaldwell	**–**	**0–6–0ST**	**1913**	**Amberley Chalk Pits Museum** [58]
Scarborough	11	0–4–2	9/1839	Manchester & Leeds Rly
Sceptre	2568	A3	9/1924	London & North Eastern Rly
Scheldt	46	0–4–2	6/1843	Manchester & Leeds Rly
Schiehallion	60086	60	1/1992	British Railways
Schubert	92007	92		British Railways
Scipio	–	0–4–0ST	1885	Woolwich Arsenal [59]
Scorpio	–	Leo	2/1842	Great Western Rly (bg)
Scorpion	15	?	?	St Helens Canal & Rly
Scorpion	7	2–2–2	1837	Grand Junction Rly
Scorpion	27	2–2–0	7/1840	Midland Counties Rly
Scorpion	7	0–4–2	2/1842	Grand Junction Rly
Scorpion	7	aCrewe	4/1852	London & North Western Rly
Scorpion	7	Problem	c.1860	London & North Western Rly
Scorpion	1723	2Precursor	8/1905	London & North Western Rly
Scotia	221	DFG	3/1866	London & South Western Rly
Scotia	395	Newton	9/1870	London & North Western Rly
Scotia	100	L/Scotchmen	3/1873	London, Chatham & Dover Rly
Scotia	395	rPrecedent	6/1892	London & North Western Rly
Scotia	1584	Prince/W	3/1919	London & North Western Rly

[35] 15in gauge.
[36] Renamed *The East Lancashire Regiment* in May 1936.
[37] Originally named *Swinden Dalesman*.
[38] Nameplates fitted in April 1946.
[39] Modified by Stroudley and named *Brighton* in February 1873. Renamed *Sandown* in 1878.
[40] Originally London & South Western Railway no. 205. Name applied by the Southern Railway on transfer to the Isle of Wight.
[41] 15in gauge.
[42] 1ft 11½in gauge.
[43] The Rainhill competitor. Now at the Science Museum, South Kensington. Purchased by the Liverpool & Manchester, and transferred to the Bolton & Leigh Railway.
[44] 15in gauge. Said to have been built for an exhibition railway in Geneva, then moved to a similar line in Oslo and named *Prins Olaf*.
[45] Renamed *Royal Army Service Corps* in June 1936.
[46] 1ft 11½in gauge.
[47] 2ft gauge.
[48] Originally WD no. 73797. Later renamed *Kitchener*.
[49] Later named *McMurdo* on Longmoor Military Railway.
[50] At WD Bicester. Now Kent & East Sussex Railway no. 25 *Northiam*.
[51] Officially a rebuild of an earlier, unnamed, locomotive, but incorporating few if any of its parts.
[52] Later renumbered 21 and renamed *Wizard*.
[53] Renamed *Earl of Berkeley* in October 1937.
[54] Either 0–6–0 or 0–4–2. Became North Eastern Railway no. 474 in 1862.
[55] Built for the South Devon Railway.
[56] Sold to the South Devon Railway in 1872; returned to the Great Western in 1876 and numbered 2159.
[57] Originally no. D229 *Saxonia*.
[58] 3ft gauge.
[59] 18in gauge.

Name	Number	Class	Date	Railway
Scots Guardsman	6115	Royal Scot	9/1927	London Midland & Scottish Rly
Scott	21	2–4–0T	12/1861	London & South Western Rly (ed)
Scott	1514	Newton	10/1866	London & North Western Rly
Scott	1514	rPrecedent	11/1890	London & North Western Rly
Scott	1132	Prince/W	1/1916	London & North Western Rly
Scott	–	0–4–0ST	1932	Buckinghamshire Railway Centre
Scottie	1	4wDM	1957	North Downs Steam Rly
Scottish Borderer	6104	Royal Scot	8/1927	London Midland & Scottish Rly
Scottish Chief	526	G.Britain	1894	London & North Western Rly
Scottish Chief	1994	2Experiment	10/1906	London & North Western Rly
Scottish Enterprise	91019	91	8/1990	British Railways
Scottish National Orchestra	86030	86/0	1965	British Railways
Scottish National Orchestra	86430	86/4	6/1965	British Railways
Scottish Union	60125	A1	4/1949	British Railways (Eastern Region)

British Railways (ex-LMS) Royal Scot class 4-6-0 no. 46115 *Scots Guardsman* passing Kings Langley with a Euston–Holyhead express on 20 July 1950. (*Photo: LCGB Ken Nunn Collection*)

Name	Number	Class	Date	Railway
Scunthorpe Steel Centenary	56102	56	1981	British Railways
Scythia CLS	40030	40	9/1959	British Railways [60]
Sea Eagle	4487	A4	4/1937	London & North Eastern Rly [61]
Sea Eagle	60139	A1	12/1948	British Railways (Eastern Region)
Sea Eagle	47002	47/0	1963	British Railways
Seafield	5	Seafield	2/1858	Highland Rly [62]
Seafield	34	Glenbarry	10/1863	Highland Rly [63]
Seafield	64	Duke	7/1874	Highland Rly [64]
Seafire	33026	33/0	1961	British Railways
Seaford	98	2–2–2T	12/1859	London, Brighton & South Coast Rly [65]
Seaford	228	D1	12/1884	London, Brighton & South Coast Rly
Seaforth Highlander	6108	Royal Scot	8/1927	London Midland & Scottish Rly
Seagull	3743	Bulldog	1/1910	Great Western Rly
Seagull	4902	A4	6/1938	London & North Eastern Rly
Seagull	33057	33/0	1961	British Railways
Seagull	47226	47/0	1965	British Railways
Seaham	59	2–4–0T	5/1866	Cambrian Railways
Seahawk	43191	43	5/1982	British Railways
Seahorse	5705	Jubilee	1936	London Midland & Scottish Rly

Name	Number	Class	Date	Railway
Sea King	33002	33/0	1961	British Railways
Sea Lion	–	2–4–0T	1896	Groudle Glen Rly [66]
Sealion	33065	33/0	1961	British Railways
Seaton	21C120	WC	12/1945	Southern Rly
Seaview	W17	O2	12/1891	Southern Rly [67]
Sebastopol	–	Iron Duke	7/1855	Great Western Rly (bg)
Sebastopol	–	Rover	10/1880	Great Western Rly (bg)
Second East Anglian Regiment	D6704	37/0	1/1961	British Railways
Secundus	–	0–6–0WT	1874	Birmingham Museum of Science & Industry [68]
Sedbergh	78	2–2–2	1859	Lancaster & Carlisle Rly
Sedgemoor	3351	Bulldog	3/1900	Great Western Rly
Sedgewick	3	2–4–0	1857	Lancaster & Carlisle Rly
Sedgwick	379	Newton	12/1869	London & North Western Rly
Sedgwick	379	rPrecedent	10/1888	London & North Western Rly
Sedley	2124	4–4–0ST	10/1866	Great Western Rly (bg) [69]
Sefton	3	0–4–2	7/1848	Liverpool, Crosby & Southport Rly [70]
Sefton	285	aCrewe	5/1852	London & North Western Rly
Sefton	–	4wDM	1963	Southport Railway Centre
Seine	123	E1	8/1878	London, Brighton & South Coast Rly
Selborne	18	0–6–0T	1922	Longmoor Military Rly
Selby	26	2–2–2	1/1841	Manchester & Leeds Rly
Selby Coalfield	56080	56	1980	British Railways
Selhurst	11	D1	6/1874	London, Brighton & South Coast Rly
Selhurst	73210	73/2	3/1966	British Railways
Selkirkshire	2756	D49/1	3/1929	London & North Eastern Rly
Selsey	–	2–4–2T	1897	West Sussex Light Rly
Selsey Bill	2037	H1	12/1905	Southern Rly [71]
Semster	62	Duke	6/1874	Highland Rly [72]
Senator	106	bCrewe	5/1847	London & North Western Rly
Senator	406	1Precursor	9/1874	London & North Western Rly
Senator	305	2Precursor	11/1904	London & North Western Rly
Seneca	–	Bogie	11/1854	Great Western Rly (bg)
Senhouse	6	0–4–2	1845	Maryport & Carlisle Rly
Serapis	–	0–4–2T	1885	Woolwich Arsenal [73]
Serlby Hall	2831	B17/1	5/1931	London & North Eastern Rly
Serpent	62	Mazeppa	12/1847	London & South Western Rly
Serpent	374	bCrewe	8/1855	London & North Western Rly

West Sussex Railway 2-4-2T no. 2 *Selsey*, at Chichester on 12 June 1915. (*Photo: LCGB Ken Nunn Collection*)

[60] Originally no. D230 *Scythia*.
[61] Renamed *Walter K. Wigham* in October 1947.
[62] Renamed *Tain* in 1875.
[63] Renamed *Perthshire, c.* 1889. Altered from 2–2–2 to 2–4–0 in December 1883.
[64] Originally named *Morayshire*. Renamed *Seafield, c.* 1889.
[65] Name applied by Stroudley in May 1873.
[66] 2ft gauge.
[67] Originally London & South Western Railway no. 208. Name applied by the Southern Railway on transfer to the Isle of Wight.
[68] 2ft 8in gauge. From the Furzebrook Railway, Dorset.
[69] Built for the South Devon Railway.
[70] Sold to the Whitehaven & Furness Junction Railway in 1855, becoming their no. 11 *Kelpie*.
[71] Built for the London, Brighton & South Coast Railway. Nameplates applied by the Southern Railway in March 1926.
[72] Originally named *Perthshire*. Renamed *Semster* in 1889, *Huntingtower* in 1899, and *Ault Wharrie* in 1903.
[73] 18in gauge.

Name	Number	Class	Date	Railway
Serpent	62	Volcano	7/1869	London & South Western Rly
Serpent	2158	Samson	11/1874	London & North Western Rly
Serpent	2158	Whitworth	1/1895	London & North Western Rly [74]
Servia	321	1Experiment	1884	London & North Western Rly
Servia	2115	2Precursor	11/1905	London & North Western Rly
Sestostris	63	Ulysses	8/1856	East Lancashire Rly
Sevenoaks	935	Schools	5/1935	Southern Rly
Severn	–	0–4–2ST	1840	Shropshire & Montgomeryshire Rly [75]
Severn	13	0–6–0	7/1846	Taff Vale Rly
Severn	–	Caesar	2/1857	Great Western Rly (bg)
Severn	19	0–6–0	1859	St Helens Canal & Rly
Severn	162	Tweed	6/1859	London & South Western Rly
Severn	22	0–6–0ST	3/1868	Brecon & Merthyr Rly
Severn	162	SFG	5/1878	London & South Western Rly
Severn	3328	Duke	7/1899	Great Western Rly
Severn	47513	47/4	1967	British Railways

Wantage Tramway 0–4–0WT no. 5, at Wantage on 26 April 1924. Originally named *Shannon*, she was nameless at Wantage, though colloquially referred to as *Jane*. (Photo: LCGB Ken Nunn Collection)

Name	Number	Class	Date	Railway
Severn Bridge	1354	0–6–0T	1880	Great Western Rly [76]
Severn Valley Railway	31233	31/1	1960	British Railways
Severn Valley Railway	31413	31/4	1961	British Railways
Severus	–	Caesar	6/1861	Great Western Rly (bg)
Seychelles	5626	Jubilee	1934	London Midland & Scottish Rly
Seymour	–	0–6–0	1836	Clarence Rly
Seymour	209	0–4–0ST	5/1861	Midland Rly [77]

Name	Number	Class	Date	Railway
Seymour Clarke	969	0–6–0ST	1875	Llanelly & Mynydd Mawr Rly [78]
Sgt Murphy	–	**0–6–2T**	**1917**	**Penrhyn Rly [79]**
Sgurr Na Ciche	60036	60	9/1991	British Railways
Shadwell	2	2–2–2WT	1848	London & Blackwall Rly
Shadwell	74	A1	10/1872	London, Brighton & South Coast Rly
Shaftesbury	21C135	WC	7/1946	Southern Rly
Shah	–	Metro	6/1862	Great Western Rly (bg)
Shah of Persia	942	Newton	8/1873	London & North Western Rly
Shah of Persia	942	rPrecedent	4/1893	London & North Western Rly
Shakenhurst Hall	4966	Hall	11/1929	Great Western Rly
Shakespeare	1513	Newton	10/1866	London & North Western Rly
Shakespeare	1513	rPrecedent	2/1890	London & North Western Rly
Shakespeare	3309	Badminton	12/1898	Great Western Rly
Shakespeare	1676	2Experiment	11/1906	London & North Western Rly
Shakespeare	92017	92		British Railways
Shakespeare Cliff	33051	33/0	1961	British Railways
Shakspear	36	2–2–2	9/1843	South Eastern Rly
Shamrock	–	?	c.1839	Brassey [80]
Shamrock	76	Rose	7/1863	London, Chatham & Dover Rly
Shamrock	–	Metro	11/1863	Great Western Rly (bg)
Shamrock	1671	Newton	3/1868	London & North Western Rly
Shamrock	1671	rPrecedent	6/1891	London & North Western Rly
Shamrock	–	0–4–0ST	1904	Chatham Dockyard [81]
Shamrock	1309	2Precursor	8/1907	London & North Western Rly
Shanklin	126	Ventnor	7/1857	London, Brighton & South Coast Rly [82]
Shanklin	–	2–4–0T	1864	Isle of Wight Rly [83]
Shanklin	332	G	7/1881	London, Brighton & South Coast Rly
Shanklin	W20	O2	3/1892	Southern Rly [84]
Shannon	**5**	**0–4–0T**	**5/1857**	**Sandy & Potton Rly [85]**
Shannon	–	Caesar	8/1857	Great Western Rly (bg)
Shannon	22	0–6–0	1859	St Helens Canal & Rly
Shannon	161	Tweed	6/1859	London & South Western Rly
Shap	20	2–4–0	1857	Lancaster & Carlisle Rly
Shap	764	Samson	2/1864	London & North Western Rly
Shap	764	Whitworth	3/1893	London & North Western Rly
Shap Fell	37026	37/0	1961	British Railways
Shark	3	2–2–2	1837	Grand Junction Rly
Shark	40	0–4–0	8/1840	Midland Counties Rly [86]
Shark	3	aCrewe	1/1845	London & North Western Rly
Shark	86	Fireball	11/1847	London & South Western Rly
Shark	3	bCrewe	11/1854	London & North Western Rly
Shark	86	Falcon	11/1867	London & South Western Rly
Shark	2159	Samson	11/1874	London & North Western Rly
Shark	2159	Whitworth	1894	London & North Western Rly
Sharp	–	Hawthorn	2/1866	Great Western Rly (bg)
Sharpness	1124A	0–6–0T	3/1880	Midland Rly [87]

[74] Later renamed *Sister Dora*.

[75] Reputed to contain parts of a Bury 0–4–0 built in 1840 for the Shrewsbury & Hereford Railway. Purchased by the Griff Colliery Co. and rebuilt as 0–4–2T. Briefly renamed *Hecate* on arrival on the Shropshire & Montgomeryshire Railway, but very soon reverted to its original name.

[76] Built for the Severn & Wye & Severn Bridge Railway.

[77] Taken over from the Staveley Coal & Iron Co. in 1866.

[78] Originally unnumbered. Allocated GWR no. 969 in 1923, but never carried.

[79] Built as an 0–6–0T for the Admiralty; then Penrhyn Quarries. Privately owned. 1ft 11½in gauge.

[80] Thomas Brassey contracted to maintain the permanent way of the London & Southampton Railway (later London & South Western Railway) on 4 November 1839. In the next year or so he made use of engines named *Good Hope*, *Taurus*, *Shamrock*, *Mudlark*, *Defiant* and *Hercules*. Apart from *Hercules*, an 0–4–2 built by Jones and later sold to the LSWR, nothing is known of these locomotives.

[81] 18in gauge.

[82] Name applied by Stroudley in January 1872.

[83] Later Southern Railway no. W14; scrapped 1927.

[84] Originally London & South Western Railway no. 211. Name applied by the Southern Railway on transfer to the Isle of Wight.

[85] The Sandy & Potton Railway was owned by Capt William Peel RN (a brother of Sir Robert Peel, the politician), and the locomotive was named *Shannon* after the gallant gentleman's ship. In 1862 the locomotive was sold, with the rest of the railway, to the London & North Western Railway, and numbered 1104 on their duplicate list. After a couple of weeks' unsuccessful trials on the Cromford & High Peak Railway, the engine returned to Crewe and served as works shunter, renumbered 1863 in 1872. It was sold to the Wantage Tramway in May 1878 for £365 8s 1d! On the Wantage Tramway, no name was carried. The engine was colloquially known as *"Jane"*; but since restoration for preservation the name *Shannon* has been reinstated. When the tramway closed in 1946 the locomotive was purchased for £100 by the Great Western Railway and overhauled at Swindon Works. It was then placed on a pedestal at Wantage Road station, until it closed in 1965 when the nameplates disappeared. *Shannon* changed storage site a few times before coming to rest, one hopes permanently, with the Great Western Society at Didcot.

[86] Originally named *Harlequin*. Renamed in 1842 or 1843.

[87] Built for the Severn & Wye & Severn Bridge Railway.

Name	Number	Class	Date	Railway
Sharpshooter	D843	Warship	1/1961	British Railways
Sharpthorn	–	**0-6-0ST**	**1877**	**Bluebell Rly**
Shaw Savill	**21C9**	**MN**	**6/1942**	**Southern Rly**
Sheffield	–	?	?	Sheffield & Rotherham Rly [88]
Sheffield	23	2-2-2	1/1841	Manchester & Leeds Rly
Sheffield	198	Gladstone	1/1888	London, Brighton & South Coast Rly
Sheffield	–	0-4-0T	1916	Woolwich Arsenal [89]
Sheffield Children's Hospital	09009	09	1959	British Railways
Sheffield Children's Hospital	08879	08	1960	British Railways
Sheffield Star	43055	43	6/1977	British Railways
Sheffield United	2849	B17/4	3/1936	London & North Eastern Rly
Sheffield Wednesday	2861	B17/4	6/1936	London & North Eastern Rly
Shelagh of Eskdale	–	**4-6-4DH**	**1969**	**Ravenglass & Eskdale Rly [90]**
Shelburne	3306	Badminton	9/1898	Great Western Rly

Name	Number	Class	Date	Railway
Shooting Star	519	1Experiment	1883	London & North Western Rly
Shooting Star	3078	3031	2/1899	Great Western Rly [94]
Shooting Star	2166	2Precursor	10/1905	London & North Western Rly
Shooting Star	4009	Star	5/1907	Great Western Rly [95]
Shooting Star	4009	Castle	4/1925	Great Western Rly [96]
Shooting Star	70029	Britannia	11/1952	British Railways
Shoreditch	56	A1	11/1875	London, Brighton & South Coast Rly
Shoreham	–	0-4-2	4/1839	London & Brighton Rly [97]
Shoreham	238	2-2-2	5/1867	London, Brighton & South Coast Rly [98]
Shoreham	389	D3	5/1894	London, Brighton & South Coast Rly
Shortbridge	594	E5	6/1904	London, Brighton & South Coast Rly
Shorwell	94	E1	11/1883	London, Brighton & South Coast Rly
Shorwell	W30	O2	9/1892	Southern Rly [99]
Shotley	56	Shotley	1/1852	Stockton & Darlington Rly [100]
Shotover	2580	A3	11/1924	London & North Eastern Rly

Rebuilt Merchant Navy class no. 35009 *Shaw Savill* approaching Andover Junction under adverse signals with the Up 'Atlantic Coast Express' in 1956. (*Photo: Author*)

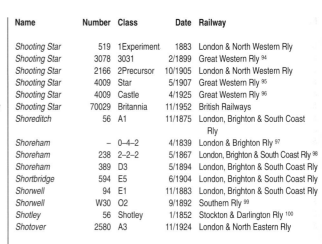

Southern Railway O2 class 0-4-4T no W30 *Shorwell*, pictured at Newport, Isle of Wight, on 15 July 1956. The engine is in British Railways livery, although retaining its Southern Railway number. (*Photo: RAS Marketing*)

Name	Number	Class	Date	Railway
Shepcote	09014	09	1961	British Railways
Sherborne	906	Schools	6/1930	Southern Rly
Sherlock Holmes	8	Bo-Bo	1921	Metropolitan Rly [91]
Shermanbury	580	E4	7/1903	London, Brighton & South Coast Rly
Sherpa	–	**0-4-0STT**	**1978**	**Fairbourne & Barmouth Steam Rly [92]**
Sherrington Hall	6987	M/Hall	3/1948	Great Western Rly
Sherwood Forester	6112	Royal Scot	9/1927	London Midland & Scottish Rly
Sherwood Forester	**45060**	**45**	**1961**	**British Railways**
Shildon	18	Majestic	1831	Stockton & Darlington Rly
Shildon	33	Miner	2/1846	Stockton & Darlington Rly
Shining Tor	60083	60	3/1992	British Railways
Shirburn Castle	5030	Castle	5/1934	Great Western Rly
Shirebrook Colliery	58019	58	1984	British Railways
Shirenewton Hall	4967	Hall	12/1929	Great Western Rly
Shoeburyness	45	37	1898	London, Tilbury & Southend Rly
Sholto	–	**4wDM**	**1941**	**Teifi Valley Rly [93]**
Shooting Star	–	Wolf	8/1841	Great Western Rly (bg)

Name	Number	Class	Date	Railway
Shotton Hall	4968	Hall	12/1929	Great Western Rly
Shotton Paper Mill	56033	56	1977	British Railways
Shovell	5651	Jubilee	1935	London Midland & Scottish Rly
Shrapnel	RL3	0-4-0ST	6/1876	Woolwich Arsenal [101]
Shrewsbury	–	Swindon	2/1866	Great Western Rly (bg)
Shrewsbury	3307	Badminton	11/1898	Great Western Rly
Shrewsbury	921	Schools	10/1933	Southern Rly
Shrewsbury and Talbot	683	2-4-0T	1868	Great Northern Rly [102]
Shrewsbury Castle	5009	Castle	6/1927	Great Western Rly
Shrigley	–	2-2-0	12/1831	Warrington & Newton Rly
Shropshire	275	2Experiment	12/1909	London & North Western Rly
(Shropshire)	**93**	**J94**	**1953**	**Steamport, Southport**
Shrugborough Hall	4969	Hall	12/1929	Great Western Rly
Sibyl	–	Caesar	8/1854	Great Western Rly (bg)
Sidlesham	–	0-6-0ST	1861	West Sussex Light Rly
Sidmouth	**21C110**	**rWC**	**9/1945**	**Southern Rly**
Siemens	52	B4	12/1899	London, Brighton & South Coast Rly [103]
Sierra Leone	5627	Jubilee	1934	London Midland & Scottish Rly

[88] See *The Locomotive* of 15 June 1943 for an article describing a contrivance for coupling wheels of unequal diameter, which was applied to this unfortunate locomotive. It was invented by Mr Vickers, Chairman of the S&RR, and ought to have been an awful warning to locomotive superintendents not to let the chairman tinker with the engines!

[89] 18in gauge.

[90] 15in gauge.

[91] Officially a rebuild of an earlier, unnamed, locomotive, but incorporating few if any of its parts.

[92] 12¼in gauge. Model of a Darjeeling–Himalaya locomotive, with added tender.

[93] 2ft gauge.

[94] Renamed *Eupatoria* in August 1906.

[95] Rebuilt to Castle class, April 1925.

[96] Rebuilt from Star class. Later renumbered 100A1 and named *Lloyds*.

[97] Later sold to the South Eastern Railway, becoming their no. 46.

[98] Name applied by Stroudley in December 1871.

[99] Originally London & South Western Railway no. 219. Name applied by the Southern Railway on transfer to the Isle of Wight.

[100] Some sources show this engine as no. 57.

[101] 18in gauge.

[102] Built for the Stafford & Uttoxeter Railway.

[103] Renamed *Sussex* in September 1908. Rebuilt to class B4x in May 1923.

Name	Number	Class	Date	Railway
Silurian	60121	A1	12/1948	British Railways (Eastern Region)
Silver Fox	2512	A4	12/1935	London & North Eastern Rly
Silver Jubilee	5552	Jubilee	1934	London Midland & Scottish Rly
Silver Jubilee	–	**DMU**	**1977**	**Ravenglass & Eskdale Rly** [104]
Silver King	2511	A4	11/1935	London & North Eastern Rly
Silver Link	2509	A4	9/1935	London & North Eastern Rly
Simon	–	**4wDM**	**1936**	**Teifi Valley Rly** [105]
Simon Glover	501	Scott	12/1920	North British Rly
Simoom	329	bCrewe	3/1854	London & North Western Rly
Simoom	408	1Precursor	9/1874	London & North Western Rly
Simoom	2	2Precursor	6/1904	London & North Western Rly
Singapore	3412	Atbara	10/1901	Great Western Rly
Singapore	2507	A3	12/1934	London & North Eastern Rly
Singapore	440	**0–4–0ST**	**1936**	**Rutland Railway Museum**
Singleton	251	D1	12/1881	London, Brighton & South Coast Rly
Sir Aglovale	781	King Arthur	7/1925	Southern Rly

London & North Eastern Railway A4 class 4–6–2 no. 2509 *Silver Link*, in original livery, at King's Cross Shed on 21 May 1935. (*Photo: LCGB Ken Nunn Collection*)

Name	Number	Class	Date	Railway
Sir Agravaine	775	King Arthur	6/1925	Southern Rly
Sir Alexander	999	Queen	3/1875	Great Western Rly
Sir Alexander	1014	11B	10/1901	Great Central Rly [106]
Sir Alexander Cockburn	506	Precedent	11/1880	London & North Western Rly
Sir Alexander Cockburn	506	rPrecedent	7/1896	London & North Western Rly
Sir Alexander Erskine-Hill	1221	B1	8/1947	London & North Eastern Rly [107]
Sir Alexander Henderson	429	11E	8/1913	Great Central Rly [108]
Sir Archibald Sinclair	21C159	**rBB**	**4/1947**	**Southern Rly**
Sir Arthur Lawley	695	Claughton	7/1916	London & North Western Rly
Sir Arthur Yorke	3708	Bulldog	6/1906	Great Western Rly
Sir Aubrey Brocklebank	–	4–6–2	1919	Ravenglass & Eskdale Rly [109]
Sir Balan	769	King Arthur	6/1925	Southern Rly
Sir Balin	768	King Arthur	6/1925	Southern Rly
Sir Bedivere	457	King Arthur	4/1925	Southern Rly
Sir Berkeley	–	**0–6–0ST**	**1891**	**Vintage Carriages Trust**
Sir Berkeley Sheffield	436	11E	11/1913	Great Central Rly
Sir Bevis	–	0–4–0ST	1/1872	Southampton Dock Co.

Name	Number	Class	Date	Railway
Sir Blamor de Ganis	797	King Arthur	6/1926	Southern Rly
Sir Bors de Ganis	763	King Arthur	5/1925	Southern Rly
Sir Brian	782	King Arthur	7/1925	Southern Rly
Sir Brian Robertson	D800	Warship	8/1958	British Railways
Sir Cador of Cornwall	804	King Arthur	12/1926	Southern Rly
Sir Charles	–	0–6–0WT	1863	Ludlow & Clee Hill Rly
Sir Charles	–	**0–4–0Fs**	**1919**	**Swansea Maritime & Industrial Museum**
Sir Charles Cust	207	Claughton	5/1921	London & North Western Rly
Sir Charles Halle	86237	86/2	1965	British Railways
Sir Charles Newton	4901	A4	6/1938	London & North Eastern Rly [110]
Sir Charles Wheatstone	20187	20/0	1/1967	British Railways
Sir Christopher Wren	20	Bo-Bo	1922	Metropolitan Rly [111]
Sir Christopher Wren	70039	Britannia	2/1953	British Railways
Sir Clement Royds	435	11E	11/1913	Great Central Rly
Sir Clwyd	86248	86/2	1965	British Railways [112]
Sir Colgrevance	779	King Arthur	7/1925	Southern Rly
Sir Constantine	805	King Arthur	1/1927	Southern Rly
Sir Daniel	378	Sir Daniel	9/1866	Great Western Rly
Sir Daniel	3389	Atbara	8/1900	Great Western Rly [113]
Sir Daniel Gooch	5070	Castle	6/1938	Great Western Rly
Sir Daniel Gooch	47628	47	1965	British Railways
Sirdar	53	B4	1/1900	London, Brighton & South Coast Rly [114]
Sir David Stewart	47	F	9/1920	Great North of Scotland Rly

British Railways 47 class diesel no. 47628 *Sir Daniel Gooch*, at Didcot. (*Photo: Author*)

Name	Number	Class	Date	Railway
Sir De Morgannwg	56032	56	1977	British Railways [115]
Sir Dinadan	795	King Arthur	4/1926	Southern Rly
Sir Dodinas le Savage	796	King Arthur	5/1926	Southern Rly
Sir Douglas Haig	429	11E	8/1913	Great Central Rly [116]
Sir Drefaldwyn	10	**0–8–0T**	**1944**	**Welshpool & Llanfair Light Rly** [117]
Sir Durnore	802	King Arthur	10/1926	Southern Rly
Sir Dyfed	37180	37/7	10/1963	British Railways [118]
Sir Ector de Maris	794	King Arthur	3/1926	Southern Rly
Sir Edward Elgar	3414	Bulldog	5/1906	Great Western Rly [119]
Sir Edward Elgar	7005	Castle	6/1946	Great Western Rly [120]
Sir Edward Elgar	50007	**50**	**1968**	**British Railways** [121]

[104] 15in gauge.

[105] 2ft gauge.

[106] Name removed in 1913.

[107] Nameplates only applied in December 1947.

[108] Renamed *Sir Douglas Haig* in 1917, and *Prince Henry* in 1920.

[109] 15in gauge. Chassis re-used to construct the first *River Mite*.

[110] Originally named *Capercailie*; renamed *Charles H. Newton* in September 1942, and further renamed in June 1943.

[111] Officially a rebuild of an earlier, unnamed, locomotive, but incorporating few if any of its components.

[112] Also named (on the other side) *County of Clwyd*.

[113] Renamed *Pretoria* in November 1900.

[114] Renamed *Richmond* in November 1906.

[115] Also named (on the other side) *County of South Glamorgan*.

[116] Originally named *Sir Alexander Henderson*. Renamed *Sir Douglas Haig* in 1917, and *Prince Henry* in 1920.

[117] 2ft 6in gauge.

[118] Also named, in English, *County of Dyfed*.

[119] Originally no. 3704 *A.H. Mills*. Renamed in August 1932.

[120] *Lamphey Castle* until 1957.

[121] Originally named *Hercules*.

Name	Number	Class	Date	Railway
Sir Edward Fraser	432	11E	10/1913	Great Central Rly
Siren	37	2–2–0	5/1841	Midland Counties Rly
Siren	83	Fireball	9/1847	London & South Western Rly
Siren	58	bCrewe	6/1848	London & North Western Rly
Siren	25	Tiger	7/1862	London, Chatham & Dover Rly
Siren	83	Falcon	9/1866	London & South Western Rly
Siren	446	Samson	9/1873	London & North Western Rly
Siren	446	Whitworth	4/1893	London & North Western Rly
Sir Ernest Palmer	3420	Bulldog	2/1903	Great Western Rly [122]
Sir Ernest Palmer	2975	Saint	3/1905	Great Western Rly [123]
Sir Eustace	34090	rBB	2/1949	British Railways (Southern Region)
Missenden Southern Railway				
Sir Felix Pole	5066	Castle	7/1937	Great Western Rly [124]
Sir Felix Pole	43131	43	7/1979	British Railways
Sir Francis Dent	2221	Claughton	8/1916	London & North Western Rly
Sir Francis Drake	3053	3031	3/1895	Great Western Rly
Sir Francis Drake	851	Lord Nelson	5/1928	Southern Rly
Sir Francis Drake	43186	43	3/1982	British Railways
Sir Frank Ree	1191	Claughton	5/1913	London & North Western Rly
Sir Frank Ree	5501	Patriot	11/1930	London Midland & Scottish Rly [125]
Sir Frank Ree	5530	Patriot	4/1933	London Midland & Scottish Rly [126]
Sir Frederick Banbury	1471	A1	7/1922	Great Northern Rly
Sir Frederick Harrison	1319	Claughton	5/1913	London & North Western Rly
Sir Frederick Harrison	5524	Patriot	3/1933	London Midland & Scottish Rly [127]
Sir Frederick Harrison	5531	Patriot	4/1933	London Midland & Scottish Rly [128]
Sir Frederick Pile	**21C158**	**rBB**	**3/1947**	**Southern Rly**
Sir Gaheris	774	King Arthur	6/1925	Southern Rly
Sir Galagars	776	King Arthur	6/1925	Southern Rly
Sir Galahad	456	King Arthur	4/1925	Southern Rly
Sir Galleron	806	King Arthur	1/1927	Southern Rly
Sir Gareth	765	King Arthur	5/1925	Southern Rly
Sir Gawain	764	King Arthur	5/1925	Southern Rly
Sir George	89	Strath	5/1892	Highland Rly
Sir George Elliot	1	0–6–0ST	1848	Alexandra (Newport & South Wales) Docks & Rly [129]
Sir George Elliot	23	0–6–0ST	1900	Alexandra (Newport & South Wales) Docks & Rly [130]
Sir Geraint	766	King Arthur	5/1925	Southern Rly
Sir Gilbert Claughton	2222	Claughton	1/1913	London & North Western Rly
Sir Gillemere	783	King Arthur	8/1925	Southern Rly
Sir Gomer	**–**	**0–6–0ST**	**1932**	**Butetown Historic Railway Society**
Sir Gorllewin	37899	37/7	7/1963	British Railways
Morgannwg				
Sir Guy	789	King Arthur	9/1925	Southern Rly
Sir Guy Calthrop	1093	Claughton	7/1916	London & North Western Rly [131]
Sir Guy Williams	7337	WD2–8–0	1943	Longmoor Military Rly
Sir Gwynedd	47537	47/4	1965	British Railways [132]
Sir Gyles Isham	**764**	**0–4–0DM**	**1953**	**Northampton & Lamport Rly**
Sir Hardman Earle	890	Precedent	4/1877	London & North Western Rly
Sir Hardman Earle	890	rPrecedent	2/1895	London & North Western Rly
Sir Harmood	**6**	**0–4–2T**	**1922**	**Snowdon Mountain Rly [133]**
Sir Harold Mitchell	1243	B1	10/1947	London & North Eastern Rly [134]
Sir Harry le Fise Lake	803	King Arthur	11/1926	Southern Rly

Name	Number	Class	Date	Railway
Sir Haydn	**3**	**0–4–2ST**	**1878**	**Talyllyn Rly [135]**
Sir Hectimere	798	King Arthur	6/1926	Southern Rly
Sir Henry Johnson	86227	86/2	1965	British Railways
Sir Henry Royce	91031	91	2/1991	British Railways
Sir Herbert Walker	2204	Claughton	8/1916	London & North Western Rly [136]
Sir Herbert Walker	73003	73/0	1962	British Railways
Sir Herbert Walker K.C.B.	5529	Patriot	4/1933	London Midland & Scottish Rly [137]
Sir Herbert Walker K.C.B.	5535	Patriot	5/1933	London Midland & Scottish Rly [138]
Sir Hervis de Revel	792	King Arthur	10/1925	Southern Rly
Sir Hugo	2582	A3	12/1924	London & North Eastern Rly
Sir Ironside	799	King Arthur	7/1926	Southern Rly
Sirius	30	0–4–2	1838	Grand Junction Rly
Sirius	–	2–2–2	8/1841	London & Brighton Rly [139]
Sirius	30	aCrewe	9/1844	London & North Western Rly

Southern Railway N15 class 4–6–0 no. 764 *Sir Gawain*, at Stewarts Lane in 1935. The engine is one of those of the class to have a six-wheeled tender instead of the usual eight-wheeled type. (*Photo: RAS Marketing*)

Name	Number	Class	Date	Railway
Sirius	88	Fireball	12/1847	London & South Western Rly
Sirius	224	2–2–2	1848	North British Rly [140]
Sirius	30	bCrewe	1/1855	London & North Western Rly
Sirius	13	0–4–2	7/1857	Whitehaven & Furness Junction Rly
Sirius	–	Caesar	6/1861	Great Western Rly (bg)
Sirius	88	Falcon	12/1867	London & South Western Rly
Sirius	424	Samson	9/1873	London & North Western Rly
Sirius	424	Whitworth	7/1895	London & North Western Rly
Sir Ivor	25	0–6–0ST	12/1870	Brecon & Merthyr Rly
Sir James	69	Duke	8/1874	Highland Rly [141]
Sir James	**21**	**0–6–0F**	**1917**	**Lakeside & Haverthwaite Rly**
Sir James King	909	908	1906	Caledonian Rly
Sir James Milne	7001	Castle	5/1946	Great Western Rly [142]
Sir James Thompson	50	49	1903	Caledonian Rly

[122] Originally named *Ernest Palmer*, renamed in February 1916.

[123] Named *Viscount Churchill* in 1907; renamed *Sir Ernest Palmer* (February 1924) and *Lord Palmer* (1933).

[124] *Wardour Castle* until 1956.

[125] Date of rebuilding from Claughton class no. 5902 (originally no. 1191). Renamed *St. Dunstan's* in April 1937.

[126] Rebuilt with taper boiler in October 1946.

[127] Renamed *Blackpool* in March 1936.

[128] Name applied in 1937; engine previously nameless. Rebuilt with taper boiler in December 1947.

[129] Ex-London & North Western Railway.

[130] Rebuilt from nos 1 and 2.

[131] Originally named *Guy Calthrop*. Renamed when the General Manager of the LNWR received his baronetcy in 1918 for wartime services as Controller of Coal Mines at the Board of Trade.

[132] Also named (on the other side) *County of Gwynedd*.

[133] 800mm gauge. Later renamed *Padarn*.

[134] Nameplates only fitted December 1947.

[135] 2ft 3in gauge. This engine was successively Corris Railway no. 3, Great Western Railway no. 3, British Railways no. 3, and Talyllyn Railway no. 3!

[136] Renamed *Sir Herbert Walker K.C.B.* in 1917.

[137] Rebuilt with taper boiler in July 1947, and renamed *Stephenson* in July 1948.

[138] Name applied in 1937; engine previously nameless. Rebuilt with taper boiler in September 1948.

[139] Later became South Eastern Railway no. 59. Rebuilt to 2–4–0 in October 1855, and withdrawn in 1879.

[140] Ex-Edinburgh & Glasgow Railway, absorbed by the NBR in 1865.

[141] Originally named *The Lord Provost*, and later renamed *Aldourie*.

[142] *Denbigh Castle* until February 1948.

Name	Number	Class	Date	Railway
Sir John Betjeman	86229	86/2	1965	British Railways
Sir John de Graeme	47636	47/4	1/1966	British Railways
Sir John French	8	0–6–2T	1914	Longmoor Military Rly
Sir John French	1333	Prince/W	11/1915	London & North Western Rly
Sir John French	5079	J94	1943	Longmoor Military Rly [143]
Sir John Hawkins	865	Lord Nelson	11/1929	Southern Rly
Sir John Llewelyn	3422	Bulldog	3/1903	Great Western Rly
Sir John Moore	70041	Britannia	3/1953	British Railways
Sir Joshua Reynolds	47559	47/4	1964	British Railways
Sir Kay	450	King Arthur	6/1925	Southern Rly
Sir Keith Park	**21C153**	**rBB**	**1/1947**	**Southern Rly**
Sir Lamiel	**777**	**King Arthur**	**6/1925**	**Southern Rly**
Sir Lamorak	451	King Arthur	6/1925	Southern Rly
Sir Lancelot	3263	Duke	4/1896	Great Western Rly
Sir Lancelot	3263	Bulldog	7/1907	Great Western Rly
Sir Launcelot	455	King Arthur	3/1925	Southern Rly
Sir Lavaine	773	King Arthur	6/1925	Southern Rly
Sir Lionel	786	King Arthur	8/1925	Southern Rly
Sir Mador de la Porte	785	King Arthur	8/1925	Southern Rly
Sir Martin Frobisher	864	Lord Nelson	11/1929	Southern Rly
Sir Massey Lopes	3423	Bulldog	3/1903	Great Western Rly [144]
Sir Meleaus de Lile	800	King Arthur	9/1926	Southern Rly
Sir Meliagrance	452	King Arthur	7/1925	Southern Rly
Sir Meliot de Logres	801	King Arthur	10/1926	Southern Rly
Sir Menadeuke	787	King Arthur	9/1925	Southern Rly
Sir Morgannwg Ganol	56053	56	1978	British Railways [145]
Sir Murray Morrison Pioneer of British Aluminium Industry	37423	37/4	1965	British Railways [146]
Sir Murrough Wilson	4499	A4	4/1938	London & North Eastern Rly [147]
Sir Nerovens	784	King Arthur	8/1925	Southern Rly
Sir Nigel	3424	Bulldog	3/1903	Great Western Rly [148]
Sir Nigel Gresley	**4498**	**A4**	**11/1937**	**London & North Eastern Rly**
Sir N. Kingscote	3424	Bulldog	3/1903	Great Western Rly [149]
Sirocco	24	2–2–2	1837	Grand Junction Rly
Sirocco	25	2–2–0	4/1840	Midland Counties Rly
Sirocco	24	2–2–2	11/1842	Grand Junction Rly
Sirocco	59	Mazeppa	9/1847	London & South Western Rly
Sirocco	100	2–2–2	7/1850	Manchester, Sheffield & Lincolnshire Rly
Sirocco	24	bCrewe	5/1854	London & North Western Rly
Sirocco	59	Lion	8/1866	London & South Western Rly
Sirocco	1153	1Precursor	9/1874	London & North Western Rly
Sirocco	643	2Precursor	11/1904	London & North Western Rly
Sir Ontzlake	793	King Arthur	3/1926	Southern Rly
Sir Pelleas	778	King Arthur	6/1925	Southern Rly
Sir Percivale	772	King Arthur	6/1925	Southern Rly
Sir Persant	780	King Arthur	7/1925	Southern Rly
Sir Powis	37431	37/4	1965	British Railways [150]
Sir Prianius	770	King Arthur	6/1925	Southern Rly
Sir Ralph Verney	3	Bo-Bo	1921	Metropolitan Rly [151]
Sir Ralph Wedgwood	4466	A4	1/1938	London & North Eastern Rly [152]
Sir Ralph Wedgwood	4469	A4	3/1938	London & North Eastern Rly [153]
Sir Redvers	3388	Atbara	8/1900	Great Western Rly
Sir Richard Arkwright	87026	87/0	1974	British Railways
Sir Richard Grenville	3054	3031	3/1895	Great Western Rly
Sir Richard Grenville	853	Lord Nelson	9/1928	Southern Rly
Sir Robert Horne	4066	Star	12/1922	Great Western Rly [154]
Sir Robert McAlpine	37425	37/4	1965	British Railways [155]
Sir Robert Peel	**8**	**J94**	**9/1952**	**Gloucestershire Warwickshire Rly**
Sir Robert Peel	**3776**	**J94**	**1953**	**East Lancashire Rly**
Sir Robert Turnbull	1161	Claughton	5/1913	London & North Western Rly
Sir Robert Turnbull	5540	Patriot	8/1933	London Midland & Scottish Rly [156]
Sir Rowland Hill	47474	47/4	1964	British Railways
Sir Ronald Matthews	4500	A4	4/1938	London & North Eastern Rly [157]
Sir Sagramore	771	King Arthur	6/1925	Southern Rly
Sir Salar Jung	858	Precedent	5/1877	London & North Western Rly
Sir Salar Jung	858	rPrecedent	5/1897	London & North Western Rly
Sir Sam Fay	423	1	12/1912	Great Central Rly
Sir Stafford	3368	Bulldog	11/1900	Great Western Rly
Sir Stephen	5	0–6–0ST	1863	Wrexham, Mold & Connah's Quay Rly [158]
Sir Theodore	2	0–4–2T	1888	Glyn Valley Tramway [159]
Sir T. Hesketh	2	0–4–2	1877	West Lancashire Rly [160]
Sir Thomas	**–**	**0–6–0T**	**1918**	**Buckinghamshire Railway Centre**
Sir Thomas Brooke	2025	George V	12/1910	London & North Western Rly
Sir Thomas Royden	**–**	**0–4–0ST**	**1940**	**Rutland Railway Museum**
Sir Thomas Williams	155	Claughton	3/1917	London & North Western Rly
Sir Torre	449	King Arthur	6/1925	Southern Rly
Sir Trafford Leigh-Mallory	34109	rBB	5/1950	British Railways (Southern Region)
Sir Tristram	448	King Arthur	5/1925	Southern Rly
Sir Urre of the Mount	788	King Arthur	9/1925	Southern Rly
Sir Uwaine	791	King Arthur	9/1925	Southern Rly
Sir Valence	767	King Arthur	6/1925	Southern Rly
Sir Villiars	790	King Arthur	9/1925	Southern Rly
Sir Vincent	**8800**	**0–4–0GT**	**1917**	**Northamptonshire Ironstone Railway Trust [161]**
Sir Vincent Raven	60126	A1	4/1949	British Railways (Eastern Region)
Sir Visto	68	A10	8/1924	London & North Eastern Rly
Sir Walter Raleigh	3052	3031	3/1895	Great Western Rly
Sir Walter Raleigh	852	Lord Nelson	7/1928	Southern Rly
Sir Walter Scott	898	895	8/1909	North British Rly
Sir Walter Scott	60143	A1	2/1949	British Railways (Eastern Region)
Sir Walter Scott	47710	47/7	1966	British Railways
Sir Watkin	39	S/Goods	6/1863	Cambrian Railways
Sir Watkin	–	Sir Watkin	9/1866	Great Western Rly (bg)
Sir Watkin	471	Sir Daniel	6/1869	Great Western Rly
Sir Watkin Wynn	3427	Bulldog	5/1903	Great Western Rly
Sir W.H. Wills	3425	Bulldog	5/1903	Great Western Rly [162]
Sir William Arrol	37693	37/5	11/1963	British Railways
Sir William A. Stanier, F.R.S.	6256	Duchess	12/1947	London Midland & Scottish Rly
Sir William A. Stanier FRS	86101	86/1	1965	British Railways

[143] Later renamed *Lisieux*.

[144] Originally named *Sir Massey*; renamed in October 1903.

[145] Also named (on the other side) *County of Mid Glamorgan*.

[146] Later renamed *Sir Murray Morrison 1874–1948*.

[147] Originally named *Pochard*; renamed April 1939.

[148] Renamed *Sir N. Kingscote* in December 1903.

[149] Originally named *Sir Nigel*; renamed in December 1903.

[150] Name carried on one side only. On the other side, the locomotive is *County of Powis*.

[151] Officially a rebuild of an earlier, unnamed, locomotive, but incorporating very few if any parts thereof.

[152] Originally named *Herring Gull*; renamed January 1944. Sir Ralph was the company's Chief General Manager.

[153] No. 4469 *Sir Ralph Wedgwood* was damaged beyond repair in an air raid on York in June 1942. It was previously named *Gadwall* and renamed in March 1939.

[154] Previously named *Malvern Abbey*. Renamed *Sir Robert Horne* in May 1935, and *Viscount Horne* on 8 August 1937.

[155] Named *Sir Robert McAlpine* on one side, and *Concrete Bob* on the other. Sir Robert was a pioneer of the use of reinforced concrete as a building material;

Glenfinnan Viaduct on the West Highland line is a good example of his work.

[156] Rebuilt with taper boiler in November 1947.

[157] Originally named *Garganey*; renamed March 1939.

[158] Rebuilt as 0–6–0T in 1884, as 2–4–0T in 1893, as 0–6–0T in 1898, and scrapped by the Great Central Railway in February 1905.

[159] 2ft 4½in gauge.

[160] Renamed *Longton* in 1880.

[161] Built by Aveling & Porter, Rochester. Rather like a traction engine on railway wheels!

[162] Renamed *Sir William Henry* in January 1906. The original choice of *Sir William Henry Wills* was too long to fit the standard GWR nameplate.

Name	Number	Class	Date	Railway
Sir William Burrell	47672	47/4	9/1964	British Railways
Sir William Cooke	20075	20/0	7/1961	British Railways
Sir William Gray	1189	B1	8/1947	London & North Eastern Rly [163]
Sir William Henry	3425	Bulldog	5/1903	Great Western Rly [164]
Sir William Pollitt	365	8E	12/1906	Great Central Rly
Sir Winston Churchill	87019	87/0	1974	British Railways
Sir W.S. Gilbert	985	Prince/W	2/1914	London & North Western Rly
Sister Dora	2158	Whitworth	1/1895	London & North Western Rly [165]
Sister Dora	31530	31/5		British Railways
Sister Dora	37116	37/0	1963	British Railways
Sisyphus	48	0–6–0	12/1849	Manchester, Sheffield & Lincolnshire Rly
Sisyphus	1683	Newton	5/1868	London & North Western Rly
Sisyphus	1683	rPrecedent	4/1891	London & North Western Rly
Sisyphus	1649	2Experiment	5/1909	London & North Western Rly
Sittingbourne	–	Sondes	3/1861	London, Chatham & Dover Rly
Skelton Castle	24	Tory	5/1846	Stockton & Darlington Rly
Sketty Hall	4970	Hall	12/1929	Great Western Rly
Skibo	11	Seafield	10/1859	Highland Rly [166]
Skibo Castle	146	Castle	1900	Highland Rly
Skiddaw	–	2–2–0	8/1840	North Western Rly
Skiddaw	83	bCrewe	4/1846	London & North Western Rly
Skiddaw	9	2–4–0	1857	Lancaster & Carlisle Rly
Skiddaw	486	Samson	10/1874	London & North Western Rly
Skiddaw	486	Whitworth	6/1893	London & North Western Rly
Skiddaw	D3	Peak	9/1959	British Railways
Skiddaw	60005	60	9/1991	British Railways
Skiddaw Lodge	10	0–6–0ST	1920	Cockermouth & Workington Rly
Skipton Castle	3	0–4–0	1850	North Western Rly
Skylark	3744	Bulldog	1/1910	Great Western Rly
Skylark	47376	47/3	1965	British Railways
Slamannan	106	165	7/1878	North British Rly [167]
Slamannan	147	72	6/1882	North British Rly
Slaughter	–	Hawthorn	12/1865	Great Western Rly (bg) [168]
Slinfold	277	D1	12/1879	London, Brighton & South Coast Rly
Slioch	60087	60	12/1991	British Railways
Slough Estates No 5	–	0–6–0ST	1939	**Yorkshire Dales Rly**
Smeaton	5	2–4–0	4/1861	London & South Western Rly (ed)
Smeaton	–	Victoria	8/1863	Great Western Rly (bg)
Smeaton	1485	Newton	5/1866	London & North Western Rly
Smeaton	1485	rPrecedent	12/1887	London & North Western Rly
Smeaton	206	B2	5/1897	London, Brighton & South Coast Rly [169]
Smeaton	3357	Bulldog	6/1900	Great Western Rly [170]
Smeaton	1484	Prince/W	1/1916	London & North Western Rly
Smelter	–	0–4–0ST	11/1854	Redruth & Chasewater Rly [171]
Smiths Dock Co Ltd	–	0–4–0DM	1947	**Darlington Railway Centre**
Snaigow	74	Snaigow	1916	Highland Rly
Snake	–	Wolf	9/1838	Great Western Rly (bg) [172]
Snake	61	Mazeppa	11/1847	London & South Western Rly
Snake	373	bCrewe	8/1855	London & North Western Rly
Snake	373	aCrewe	5/1858	London & North Western Rly [173]
Snake	61	Volcano	7/1869	London & South Western Rly
Snake	1115	1Experiment	1884	London & North Western Rly
Snake	127	2Precursor	11/1905	London & North Western Rly

Name	Number	Class	Date	Railway
Snipe	337	bCrewe	5/1854	London & North Western Rly
Snipe	1730	George V	10/1911	London & North Western Rly
Snowdon	227	bCrewe	9/1848	London & North Western Rly
Snowdon	51	S/Goods	4/1865	Cambrian Railways
Snowdon	2191	Precedent	4/1875	London & North Western Rly
Snowdon	4	0–4–2T	1896	**Snowdon Mountain Rly** [174]
Snowdon	D9	Peak	12/1959	British Railways
Snowdon	86257	86/2	1966	British Railways
Snowdon Ranger	–	0–6–4T	1875	North Wales Narrow Gauge Rly [175]

North Wales Narrow Gauge Railway 0–6–4T *Snowdon Ranger*, at Dinas Junction on 23 June 1909. (*Photo: LCGB Ken Nunn Collection*)

Name	Number	Class	Date	Railway
Snowdrop	40	Bluebell	5/1863	London, Chatham & Dover Rly
Soho	–	0–4–2	1838	Bolton & Leigh Rly
Soho	125	aCrewe	5/1850	London & North Western Rly
Soho	125	DX	c.1860	London & North Western Rly
Sol	2125	4–4–0ST	11/1866	Great Western Rly (bg) [176]
Solario	4473	A3	3/1923	London & North Eastern Rly
Solent	197	2–2–2	7/1864	London, Brighton & South Coast Rly [177]
Solomon Islands	5603	Jubilee	1935	London Midland & Scottish Rly
Solway	1	2–4–0T	1854	Carlisle & Silloth Bay Railway & Dock Co. [178]
Solway	–	0–4–0ST	1856	Cockermouth & Workington Rly
Solway	4	2–4–0	?	Cockermouth & Workington Rly
Solway Firth	70049	Britannia	7/1954	British Railways
Somaliland	5628	Jubilee	1934	London Midland & Scottish Rly
Somerleyton Hall	2840	B17/1	5/1933	London & North Eastern Rly
Somerset	3327	Duke	7/1899	Great Western Rly
Somerset	3327	Bulldog	5/1908	Great Western Rly
Somme	646	C	2/1891	North British Rly
Somme	503	11F	11/1922	Great Central Rly
Sondes	–	Sondes	12/1857	London, Chatham & Dover Rly
Songs of Praise	43016	43	6/1976	British Railways [179]
Soughton Hall	6962	M/Hall	4/1944	Great Western Rly [180]
Soult	804	Problem	c.1860	London & North Western Rly

[163] Nameplates fitted only in December 1947.

[164] Originally named *Sir W.H. Wills*; renamed in January 1906. The original choice of *Sir William Henry Wills* was too long to fit the standard GWR nameplate!

[165] Originally named *Serpent*; renamed in 1895. Sister Dorothy Pattison was a nurse whose devotion to the sick during a smallpox epidemic in Walsall in 1878 led to her own death. The London & North Western Railway commemmorated her by the name by which she was generally known in the town.

[166] Previously named *Stafford*.

[167] Later renamed *Tayport*.

[168] Soon renamed *Avonside*. *Slaughter* was a reference to one of the partners of Slaughter, Gruning & Co. (which in late 1865 became the Avonside Engine Co.), the builders, and not to the railway's safety record!

[169] Rebuilt to class B2x, January 1909.

[170] Originally named *Exeter*. Temporarily renamed *Royal Sovereign* to work a Royal Train on 7 March 1902, and renamed *Smeaton* in October 1903.

[171] 4ft gauge. First steamed on 1 December 1854. Altered to 0–4–2ST during winter of 1855/6.

[172] Renamed *Exe* in 1846. Original name restored in 1851.

[173] Considered as a replacement for the previous engine, sold to the Lancaster & Carlisle Railway.

[174] 800mm gauge rack and pinion locomotive.

[175] Cannibalized to keep sister engine *Moel Tryfan* running. 1ft 11½in gauge.

[176] Built for the South Devon Railway.

[177] Name applied by Stroudley in June 1871.

[178] Became North British Railway no. 100. Withdrawn and sold in 1877, its subsequent history is unknown.

[179] Later named *Gwyl Gerddi Cymru 1992/Garden Festival Wales 1992*.

[180] Nameplates fitted in October 1946.

Name	Number	Class	Date	Railway
South Africa	2212	George V	6/1911	London & North Western Rly
South Africa	5571	Jubilee	1934	London Midland & Scottish Rly
Southam	–	**0–4–0DM**	**1936**	**Airfield Line**
Southampton	–	0–4–2	5/1837	London & South Western Rly [181]
Southampton	–	?	3/1839	Birmingham & Gloucester Rly
Southampton	–	Summers	8/1839	London & South Western Rly
Southampton	–	2–2–2	?	Sheffield & Rotherham Rly
Southampton	109	0–4–0ST	9/1876	London & South Western Rly
South Australia	5567	Jubilee	1935	London Midland & Scottish Rly
Southbourne	350	G	5/1882	London, Brighton & South Coast Rly
Southborough	168	E3	12/1894	London, Brighton & South Coast Rly
Southchurch	46	37	1898	London, Tilbury & Southend Rly
Southdown	37	A1	5/1878	London, Brighton & South Coast Rly
South Durham Malleable	**5**	**0–4–0ST**	**c.1880**	**Beamish Museum**
Southend	62	Cleveland	2/1849	Stockton & Darlington Rly
Southend	1	Class 1	1880	London, Tilbury & Southend Rly
Southend-on-Sea	80	79	1909	London, Tilbury & Southend Rly

Name	Number	Class	Date	Railway
South Yorkshire Metropolitan County	43122	43	4/1979	British Railways
(Sovereign)	**4871**	**5**	**1945**	**London Midland & Scottish Rly**
Spanish Monarch	4029	Star	10/1909	Great Western Rly [190]
Sparkford Hall	5997	Hall	6/1940	Great Western Rly
Sparrow Hawk	4463	A4	12/1937	London & North Eastern Rly
Spartan	D844	Warship	3/1961	British Railways
Spearmint	2796	A3	5/1930	London & North Eastern Rly
Speedwell	–	0–4–0	1830	Sirhowy Rly
Speedwell	38	2–2–2	1835	Liverpool & Manchester Rly
Speedwell	206	0–4–0ST	1851	Midland Rly [191]
Speedy	**126**	**A7**	**1942**	**War Department [192]**
Speke	1684	Newton	5/1868	London & North Western Rly
Speke	1684	rPrecedent	6/1891	London & North Western Rly
Speke Hall	7923	M/Hall	9/1950	British Railways (Western Region)
Spetchley	24	4–2–0	1/1841	Birmingham & Gloucester Rly
Spey	90	Scotchmen	11/1866	London, Chatham & Dover Rly
Sphinx	–	Caesar	9/1854	Great Western Rly (bg)
Sphinx	60	Ulysses	7/1856	East Lancashire Rly
Sphinx	2156	Samson	11/1874	London & North Western Rly
Sphinx	1466	Prince/W	1/1916	London & North Western Rly
Sphynx	70	0–4–2	5/1841	Grand Junction Rly
Sphynx	49	0–6–0	7/1850	Manchester, Sheffield & Lincolnshire Rly
Sphynx	70	bCrewe	5/1851	London & North Western Rly
Sphynx	24	Tiger	5/1862	London, Chatham & Dover Rly [193]
Sphynx	2156	Whitworth	2/1895	London & North Western Rly [194]
Spion Kop	2752	A3	4/1929	London & North Eastern Rly
Spit Fire	–	Priam	4/1840	Great Western Rly (bg)
Spitfire	4	Roach	12/1846	East Lancashire Rly
Spitfire	91	Fireball	1/1848	London & South Western Rly

Romney, Hythe & Dymchurch Railway no. 3 *Southern Maid* at Dungeness. (Photo: Author)

Name	Number	Class	Date	Railway
Southern Maid	**3**	**4–6–2**	**1925**	**Romney, Hythe & Dymchurch Rly [182]**
Southern Rhodesia	5595	Jubilee	1935	London Midland & Scottish Rly
Southesk	54	F	10/1920	Great North of Scotland Rly
South Foreland	2421	H2	6/1911	Southern Rly [183]
Southover	509	E4	12/1900	London, Brighton & South Coast Rly
Southport	5	2–2–2	8/1848	Liverpool, Crosby & Southport Rly [184]
Southport	1	0–4–2	1877	West Lancashire Rly [185]
Southport	5527	Patriot	3/1933	London Midland & Scottish Rly [186]
Southsea	154	2–2–2	8/1862	London, Brighton & South Coast Rly [187]
Southsea	177	Gladstone	11/1890	London, Brighton & South Coast Rly
Southwark	35	D1	6/1876	London, Brighton & South Coast Rly
Southwater	162	E1	11/1891	London, Brighton & South Coast Rly
Southwick	163	E1	12/1891	London, Brighton & South Coast Rly
Southwick	–	**0–4–0CT**	**1942**	**Keighley & Worth Valley Rly**
Southwold	1	2–4–0T	1879	Southwold Rly [188]
Southwold	1	2–4–2T	1893	Southwold Rly [189]

Southern Region H2 class 4–4–2 no. 32421 *South Foreland* passing Kensington (Olympia) with a through train for the London Midland Region on a summer Saturday in 1955. (Photo: Author)

[181] Later sold to the Birmingham & Gloucester Railway, becoming their no. 23 and retaining its name.
[182] 15in gauge.
[183] Built by the London, Brighton & South Coast Railway. Nameplates applied by the Southern Railway in February 1926.
[184] Renamed *Antelope* or *Gazelle* by October 1850.
[185] Originally named *Edward Holden*; renamed in 1880.
[186] Rebuilt with taper boiler in September 1948.
[187] Name applied by Stroudley in November 1871.
[188] 3ft gauge. Returned to manufacturers (Sharp Stewart & Co.) in 1883.
[189] 3ft gauge. Replacement of previous engine.
[190] Originally named *King Stephen*. Renamed *The Spanish Monarch* in July 1927, and *Spanish Monarch* in November 1927. The name was removed in November 1940 and the words STAR CLASS painted on the splashers.
[191] Taken over from the Staveley Coal & Iron Co. in 1866.
[192] 0–4–0DM now on the South Yorkshire Railway.
[193] Originally named *Lethe*. Renamed *Sphynx* in August 1862.
[194] Transferred to Engineer's Department 1914–October 1927, and renamed *Engineer Manchester*.

Name	Number	Class	Date	Railway
Spitfire	–	?	10/1850	Liverpool, Crosby & Southport Rly [195]
Spitfire	215	bCrewe	8/1856	London & North Western Rly
Spitfire	–	0–6–0ST	9/1859	Redruth & Chasewater Rly [196]
Spitfire	215	DX	c.1860	London & North Western Rly
Spitfire	742	Samson	7/1864	London & North Western Rly
Spitfire	91	Volcano	2/1868	London & South Western Rly
Spitfire	742	Whitworth	3/1893	London & North Western Rly [197]
Spitfire	**–**	**4wPM**	**1937**	**North Gloucestershire Rly [198]**
Spitfire	5071	Castle	6/1938	Great Western Rly [199]
Spitfire	**S112**	**J94**	**1942**	**Yorkshire Dales Rly**
Spitfire	**39**	**4wDM**	**1946**	**Northamptonshire Ironstone Railway Trust**
Spitfire	21C166	BB	9/1947	Southern Rly
Spitfire	**33035**	**33/0**	**1961**	**British Railways**
Spithead	153	2–2–2	8/1862	London, Brighton & South Coast Rly [200]
Spithead	164	E1	12/1891	London, Brighton & South Coast Rly
Splugen	309	Lyons	7/1883	London, Brighton & South Coast Rly
Spondon No 2	**–**	**4wBE**	**1939**	**Foxfield Steam Rly**
Sprightly	D845	Warship	4/1961	British Railways
Spring	189	Panther	9/1865	Stockton & Darlington Rly
Springbok	1000	B1	12/1942	London & North Eastern Rly
(Springbok)	**4112**	**GMAM**	**1956**	**South African Railways [201]**
Springfield	13	0–6–0ST	1871	Whitehaven, Cleator & Egremont Rly [202]
Springwell	208	0–4–0ST	1856	Midland Rly [203]
Spyck	5040	J94	12/1943	Longmoor Military Rly
17 Squadron	21C162	rBB	5/1947	Southern Rly
25 Squadron	21C160	rBB	4/1947	Southern Rly
41 Squadron	34076	BB	6/1948	British Railways (Southern Region)
46 Squadron	34074	BB	5/1948	British Railways (Southern Region)
66 Squadron	34110	BB	1/1951	British Railways (Southern Region)
73 Squadron	21C161	BB	4/1947	Southern Rly
74 Squadron	34080	BB	8/1948	British Railways (Southern Region)
92 Squadron	**34081**	**BB**	**9/1948**	**British Railways (Southern Region)**
141 Squadron	34079	BB	7/1948	British Railways (Southern Region)
145 Squadron	34087	rBB	12/1948	British Railways (Southern Region)
213 Squadron	34088	rBB	12/1948	British Railways (Southern Region)
219 Squadron	34086	BB	12/1948	British Railways (Southern Region)
222 Squadron	34078	BB	7/1948	British Railways (Southern Region)
229 Squadron	21C163	rBB	5/1947	Southern Rly
249 Squadron	**34073**	**BB**	**5/1948**	**British Railways (Southern Region)**
253 Squadron	34084	BB	11/1948	British Railways (Southern Region)
257 Squadron	**34072**	**BB**	**4/1948**	**British Railways (Southern Region)**
264 Squadron	34075	BB	6/1948	British Railways (Southern Region)
501 Squadron	34085	rBB	11/1948	British Railways (Southern Region)
601 Squadron	34071	rBB	4/1948	British Railways (Southern Region) [204]
602 Squadron	34089	rBB	12/1948	British Railways (Southern Region)
603 Squadron	34077	rBB	7/1948	British Railways (Southern Region)
605 Squadron	34083	BB	10/1948	British Railways (Southern Region)
615 Squadron	34071	rBB	4/1948	British Railways (Southern Region) [205]
615 Squadron	34082	BB	9/1948	British Railways (Southern Region)
Squirrel	–	?	1858	Cambrian Railways [206]
S.R. Graves	1141	Newton	8/1873	London & North Western Rly
S.R. Graves	1141	rPrecedent	11/1888	London & North Western Rly
S.R. Graves	132	George V	3/1913	London & North Western Rly

Name	Number	Class	Date	Railway
s.s. Great Britain	47508	47/4	1966	British Railways
Stackpole Court	2948	Saint	6/1912	Great Western Rly
Stac Polliadh	60078	60	11/1991	British Railways
Staffa	86	Scotchmen	8/1866	London, Chatham & Dover Rly
Stafford	6	2–2–2	5/1849	South Staffordshire Rly
Stafford	11	Seafield	10/1859	Highland Rly [207]
Stafford	53	Glenbarry	9/1864	Highland Rly [208]
Stafford	80	Clyde Bogie	7/1886	Highland Rly
Staffordshire	677	2Experiment	12/1909	London & North Western Rly
Stag	–	Priam	9/1840	Great Western Rly (bg)
Stag	17	0–6–0	1/1853	South Staffordshire Rly
Stag	111	Peel	8/1856	Stockton & Darlington Rly
Stag	39	0–6–0	1857	Taff Vale Rly
Stag	–	?	c.1865	Brecon & Merthyr Rly [209]
Stag	2129	4–4–0ST	12/1872	Great Western Rly (bg) [210]
Staghound	1792	George V	5/1911	London & North Western Rly
Stagshaw	**–**	**0–6–0ST**	**1923**	**Tanfield Rly**
Staindrop	106	Peel	2/1856	Stockton & Darlington Rly
Stainless Pioneer	37717	37/7	8/1962	British Railways
Stamford	**–**	**0–6–0ST**	**1927**	**Bluebell Rly**
Standedge	–	0–6–0	1846	Huddersfield & Manchester Railway & Canal
Standford	256	D1	3/1882	London, Brighton & South Coast Rly
Stanford	11	Class 1	1880	London, Tilbury & Southend Rly
Stanford Court	2949	Saint	5/1912	Great Western Rly
Stanford Hall	5937	Hall	7/1933	Great Western Rly
Stanhope	16	Tory	4/1845	Stockton & Darlington Rly
Stanley	1	0–4–2	5/1839	Manchester & Leeds Rly
Stanley	257	bCrewe	5/1850	London & North Western Rly
Stanley	129	Peel	4/1858	Stockton & Darlington Rly
Stanley Baldwin	3701	Bulldog	4/1906	Great Western Rly
Stanley Hall	5938	Hall	7/1933	Great Western Rly
Stanlow No 4	**4**	**0–4–0DM**	**1966**	**Southport Railway Centre**
Stanmer	241	D1	11/1881	London, Brighton & South Coast Rly
Stanton	**24**	**0–4–0CT**	**1925**	**Midland Railway Centre**
Stanton	**44**	**0–4–0DE**	**1956**	**North Yorkshire Moors Rly**
Stanton	**50**	**0–6–0DE**	**1958**	**Rutland Railway Museum**
Staplefield	461	E3	12/1895	London, Brighton & South Coast Rly
Star	14	?	?	St Helens Canal & Rly
Star	41	2–2–2	1836	Liverpool & Manchester Rly [211]
Star	20	0–4–2	11/1839	Newcastle & Carlisle Rly
Star	–	2–2–2	7/1844	London & South Western Rly (bg) [212]
Star	165	aCrewe	5/1847	London & North Western Rly
Star	61	Cleveland	1/1849	Stockton & Darlington Rly
Star	165	Problem	c.1860	London & North Western Rly
Star Construction	**–**	**4wDM**	**c.1941**	**Amberley Chalk Pits Museum [213]**
Starlight Express	86231	86/2	1965	British Railways
Starling	154	bCrewe	11/1854	London & North Western Rly [214]
Starling	3745	Bulldog	1/1910	Great Western Rly
Star of the East	47401	47/4	1962	British Railways
Statius	–	Bogie	1/1855	Great Western Rly (bg)
Steadfast	D846	Warship	4/1961	British Railways
Steadfast	60001	60	9/1991	British Railways
Steady Aim	512	A2/3	8/1946	London & North Eastern Rly
Stedham Hall	6961	M/Hall	3/1944	Great Western Rly [215]
Steep Holm	08919	08	1962	British Railways

---

[195] A four-wheeled patent locomotive built by G. Forrester. It was later rebuilt as a conventional 2–2–2.

[196] 4ft gauge.

[197] Transferred to Engineer's Department 1921–October 1932 and renamed *Engineer Liverpool*.

[198] 2ft gauge.

[199] *Clifford Castle* until September 1940.

[200] Name applied by Stroudley in May 1872.

[201] 3ft 6in gauge. 4–8–2 + 2–8–4 Beyer-Garratt articulated locomotive from South African Railways.

[202] Became Furness Railway no. 109.

[203] Taken over from Staveley Coal & Iron Co. in 1866.

[204] Originally *615 Squadron*; renamed in August 1948.

[205] Renamed *601 Squadron* in August 1948.

[206] Date of purchase. Date of construction unknown.

[207] Later renamed *Skibo*.

[208] Altered from 2–2–2 to 2–4–0 in November 1873. Renamed *Golspie* in 1886.

[209] Probably a small contractor's tank engine.

[210] Built for the South Devon Railway.

[211] Became London & North Western Railway no. 124 in 1846.

[212] Thought to be the locomotive built for Bristol & Gloucester Railway as their no. 4 *Bristol*. In June 1855 it was sold to Thomas Brassey for working the North Devon Railway and renamed *Star*.

[213] 2ft gauge.

[214] Built for the Grand Junction Railway.

[215] Nameplates fitted July 1948.

Name	Number	Class	Date	Railway
Stefcomatic	–	2–2–0DH	**1956**	**Festiniog Rly** [216]
Steinbok	1039	B1	12/1947	London & North Eastern Rly
Stella	8	2–4–0	12/1884	Pembroke & Tenby Rly [217]
Stembok	1032	B1	8/1947	London & North Eastern Rly
Stemster	62	Duke	6/1874	Highland Rly [218]
Stendhal	92018	92		Société Nationale des Chemins de fer Français
Stentor	6	2–2–2	1837	Grand Junction Rly
Stentor	–	Priam	12/1842	Great Western Rly (bg)
Stentor	6	aCrewe	1/1844	London & North Western Rly
Stentor	87	Fireball	11/1847	London & South Western Rly
Stentor	45	0–6–0	10/1849	Manchester, Sheffield & Lincolnshire Rly
Stentor	6	bCrewe	11/1854	London & North Western Rly
Stentor	87	Falcon	11/1867	London & South Western Rly
Stentor	522	Prince/W	6/1919	London & North Western Rly
Stentor	26050	EM1	11/1952	British Railways
Stephanotis	4120	Flower	7/1908	Great Western Rly
Stephenson	3	0–4–2	5/1839	Manchester & Leeds Rly
Stephenson	65	Priam	4/1850	Stockton & Darlington Rly [219]
Stephenson	279	aCrewe	12/1851	London & North Western Rly
Stephenson	279	Problem	c.1860	London & North Western Rly
Stephenson	3	2–4–0	9/1864	London & South Western Rly (ed) [220]
Stephenson	–	Victoria	6/1863	Great Western Rly (bg)
Stephenson	3	2–4–0	9/1864	London & South Western Rly (ed) [221]
Stephenson	329	G	5/1881	London, Brighton & South Coast Rly
Stephenson	2052	2Experiment	12/1906	London & North Western Rly
Stephenson	329	L	10/1921	London, Brighton & South Coast Rly [222]
Stephenson	45529	Patriot	4/1933	British Railways [223]
Stephenson	2329	N15x	12/1934	Southern Rly [224]

Name	Number	Class	Date	Railway
STEPHENSON	87101	87/1	1975	British Railways
Stepney	1	2–2–2WT	1848	London & Blackwall Rly
Stepney	55	**A1**	**12/1875**	**London, Brighton & South Coast Rly**
Stepney	29	Class 1	1884	London, Tilbury & Southend Rly
Stepney Green	53	51	1900	London, Tilbury & Southend Rly
Steropes	–	Caesar	1/1848	Great Western Rly (bg)
Steropes	18	0–6–4CT	4/1901	Great Western Rly
Stewart	568	DX	c.1860	London & North Western Rly
Stewart	–	Hawthorn	1/1866	Great Western Rly (bg)
Stewart	1189	Precedent	5/1877	London & North Western Rly
Stewart	1189	rPrecedent	6/1897	London & North Western Rly
Stewarts Lane 1860–1985	73204	73/2	5/1966	British Railways
Stewarts Lane Traction Maintenance Depot	73114	73/1	1966	British Railways
Steyning	387	D3	4/1894	London, Brighton & South Coast Rly
Stifford	25	Class 1	1884	London, Tilbury & Southend Rly
Stiletto	–	Wolf	12/1841	Great Western Rly (bg)
Stirling	233	233	1859	North British Rly [225]
Stirlingshire	264	D49/1	12/1927	London & North Eastern Rly
Stoats Nest	501	E4	6/1900	London, Brighton & South Coast Rly
Stobart	100	Pierremont	7/1855	Stockton & Darlington Rly
Stocksbridge	–	0–6–0T	1923	Stocksbridge Rly [226]
Stockton	4	Tory	7/1841	Stockton & Darlington Rly
Stockton Haulage	37511	37/5	1/1963	British Railways
Stockwell	18	D1	5/1875	London, Brighton & South Coast Rly
Stokesay Castle	5040	Castle	6/1935	Great Western Rly
Stonehaven	239	233	1867	North British Rly [227]
Stonehenge	16	Lion	8/1872	London & South Western Rly [228]
Stork	992	L/Bloomer	1851	London & North Western Rly
Stork	136	bCrewe	5/1852	London & North Western Rly [229]
Stork	6	Tiger	8/1861	London, Chatham & Dover Rly
Stork	1379	Dreadnought	1886	London & North Western Rly
Stork	229	2Precursor	11/1905	London & North Western Rly
Storm Cock	47284	47/0	1966	British Railways [230]
Storm Force	43160	43	4/1981	British Railways
Storm King	3024	3001	7/1891	Great Western Rly [231]
Stormy Petrel	3051	3031	2/1895	Great Western Rly
Storrington	454	E3	4/1895	London, Brighton & South Coast Rly
Stour	24	2–2–0	12/1842	London & Brighton & South Eastern Railways Joint Committee
Stour	6	2–2–2	10/1846	Eastern Union Rly
Stour	113	Rocklia	5/1849	London & South Western Rly
Stour	113	Lion	2/1869	London & South Western Rly
Stour	74	River	3/1897	Great Western Rly [232]
Stowe	**928**	**Schools**	**6/1934**	**Southern Rly**
Stowe Grange	6856	Grange	11/1937	Great Western Rly

Great Western Railway 0–6–4 crane tank no. 18 *Steropes*, at Swindon in 1932. (*Photo: RAS Marketing*)

[216] 1ft 11½in gauge.

[217] It was bought, new, from the Great Western Railway as Pembroke & Tenby Railway no. 8, and named *Stella*. On absorption of the P&TR by the GWR in July 1896, no. 8 resumed its original number, 3201, but kept its name.

[218] Originally named *Perthshire*. Renamed *Stemster* in 1889, *Huntingtower* in 1899, and finally *Ault Wharrie* in 1903.

[219] May originally have been named *Newmarket*, according to one source.

[220] Formerly *Colne* of the Somerset & Dorset Railway, later no. 148 of the London & South Western Railway.

[221] Replacement of previous engine.

[222] In December 1934 it was rebuilt by the Southern Railway as a 4–6–0 with separate tender, reclassified Remembrance class or N15x class, and renumbered 2329. It retained its name.

[223] Built by the London Midland & Scottish Railway and originally named *Sir Herbert Walker, K.C.B.* Rebuilt with taper boiler in July 1947, and renamed *Stephenson* in July 1948.

[224] Built for the London, Brighton & South Coast Railway in October 1921 as L class 4–6–4T no. 329 *Stephenson*. In December 1934 it was rebuilt by the Southern Railway as a 4–6–0 with separate tender, reclassified N15x, and renumbered 2329. It retained its name.

[225] Ex-Edinburgh & Glasgow Railway, absorbed by NBR in 1865.

[226] Line opened in 1874 from Deepcar, near Sheffield, to the Stocksbridge steelworks of Samuel Fox & Co. A passenger service ran for a while for workpeople. The line is now closed and dismantled.

[227] Originally named *Falkirk*, of the Edinburgh & Glasgow Railway. Absorbed by the NBR in 1865.

[228] Originally named *Salisbury*. Renamed in August 1877 at Traffic Dept's request, due, it is said, to passengers mistaking the locomotive's name for the train's destination. Presumably no one wanted to go to Stonehenge!

[229] Previously Liverpool & Manchester Railway no. 191.

[230] On one side only. On the other side, the locomotive is named *Mistlethrush*.

[231] Built as a broad gauge convertible. Rebuilt to 4–2–2 in December 1894.

[232] Rebuilt from 2–2–2 no. 74 of 1856.

Name	Number	Class	Date	Railway
Strachan No. 7	–	0–6–0T	5/1888	Cockermouth, Keswick & Penrith Rly [233]
Stradey	910	0–6–0	1870	Great Western Rly [234]
Straight Deal	522	A2/3	6/1947	London & North Eastern Rly
Straits Settlements	5629	Jubilee	1934	London Midland & Scottish Rly
Strang Steel	1244	B1	10/1947	London & North Eastern Rly [235]
Strasbourg	109	E1	3/1877	London, Brighton & South Coast Rly
Stratford	22	2–2–2	1/1846	Joint Board of Management [236]
Stratford	47	37	1898	London, Tilbury & Southend Rly
Stratford	47007	47/0	1963	British Railways
Stratford Major Depot	31165	31/1	1960	British Railways
Stratford TMD Quality Approved	37023	37/0	1961	British Railways
Strathcarron	95	Strath	6/1892	Highland Rly
Strathclyde Region	37405	37/4	1965	British Railways
Strathdearn	92	Strath	6/1892	Highland Rly
Strathendrick	19	72	1882	North British Rly
Strathisla	47642	47/4	9/1964	British Railways [237]
Strathspey	91	Strath	5/1892	Highland Rly
Strathpeffer	12	Belladrum	5/1862	Highland Rly [238]
Strathpeffer	13	0–4–4ST	5/1890	Highland Rly [239]
Strathpeffer	25	W	1905	Highland Rly
Strathnairn	93	Strath	6/1892	Highland Rly
Strathtay	94	Strath	6/1892	Highland Rly
Streatham	5	D1	1/1874	London, Brighton & South Coast Rly
"Stretcher"	2	0–6–0T	c.1902	Powesland & Mason Ltd [240]
Strettington	498	E4	5/1900	London, Brighton & South Coast Rly
Strombidae	37421	37/4	1965	British Railways
Strombidae	47233	47/0	1965	British Railways
Stromboli	–	Leo	4/1841	Great Western Rly (bg)
Stromboli	116	1Vesuvius	12/1850	London & South Western Rly
Stromboli	2138	0–6–0ST	10/1852	Great Western Rly (bg) [241]
Stromboli	116	Volcano	8/1869	London & South Western Rly
Strongbow	D847	Warship	4/1961	British Railways
Stroud	9?	2–2–2	12/1844	Bristol & Gloucester Rly (bg) [242]
Stroudley	184	Gladstone	10/1889	London, Brighton & South Coast Rly [243]
Stroudley	2332	Remembrance	11/1935	Southern Rly [244]
Struan	37	M/Goods	4/1864	Highland Rly
Stuart	18	0–6–0	1860	Taff Vale Rly
Stuart	288	2–4–0	5/1861	Lancashire & Yorkshire Rly
Sturdee	5647	Jubilee	1935	London Midland & Scottish Rly
(Sturdee)	**601**	**WD2–10–0**	**1943**	**War Department**
Styx	8	2–2–2	12/1843	Manchester, Sheffield & Lincolnshire Rly
Styx	84	Fireball	9/1847	London & South Western Rly
Styx	84	Falcon	10/1866	London & South Western Rly
Sudeley Castle	5061	Castle	6/1937	Great Western Rly [245]
Sudeley Castle	7025	Castle	8/1949	British Railways (Western Region)

Name	Number	Class	Date	Railway
"Sue"	11218	04	1956	British Railways
Suffolk (?)	9 or 10	0–4–2	1846	Eastern Union Rly
Sugar Palm	526	A2	1/1948	British Railways (Eastern Region)
Suilven	60076	60	11/1991	British Railways
Sulis Minerva	43130	43	7/1979	British Railways
Sullivan	92037	92		British Railways
Sultan	57	2–2–2	1839	Grand Junction Rly
Sultan	38	2–2–0	5/1841	Midland Counties Rly
Sultan	58	Mazeppa	8/1847	London & South Western Rly
Sultan	–	Iron Duke	11/1847	Great Western Rly (bg)
Sultan	57	bCrewe	5/1848	London & North Western Rly
Sultan	977	S/Bloomer	1854	London & North Western Rly
Sultan	58	Lion	7/1866	London & South Western Rly
Sultan	–	Rover	9/1876	Great Western Rly (bg)
Sultan	3020	3001	4/1892	Great Western Rly [246]
Sultan	1938	Jubilee	10/1900	London & North Western Rly
Sultan	D848	Warship	4/1961	British Railways
Sultan	33025	33/0	1961	British Railways
Sultan	33114	33/1	1961	British Railways [247]
Sultana	82	Fireball	8/1847	London & South Western Rly
Sultana	82	Falcon	6/1866	London & South Western Rly
Summer	190	Panther	9/1865	Stockton & Darlington Rly
Sun	17	2–2–0	1831	Liverpool & Manchester Rly
Sun	53	2–2–2	1837	Liverpool & Manchester Rly
Sun	44	2–2–0	4/1839	Stockton & Darlington Rly [248]
Sun	19	0–4–2	11/1839	Newcastle & Carlisle Rly

London & North Eastern Railway B17/4 class 4–6–0 no. 2854 *Sunderland*, at Marylebone on 23 May 1936. (*Photo: LCGB Ken Nunn Collection*)

[233] Built as *Oldham* by Manning Wardle, Leeds, for industrial service. It was bought by the CKPR in 1901 for permanent way work, and was by then named *Strachan No. 7*. The London & North Western, who had agreed with the CKPR to supply motive power to the latter, took grave exception to *Strachan No. 7*, and insisted that it be disposed of at once. In the event, it was June 1913 before *Strachan No. 7* departed for further industrial service.

[234] Built for the Llanelly Railway.

[235] Nameplates only fitted in December 1947.

[236] Birmingham & Gloucester and Bristol & Gloucester Railways, formed on 14 January 1845. Standard gauge. The locomotives passed to the Midland Railway on 3 August 1846, and were renumbered into Midland stock wef February 1847.

[237] Also named *Resolute*.

[238] Originally named *Belladrum*, then *Breadalbane* (1871) and *Strathpeffer* (1885).

[239] Although officially a member of the Strathpeffer class, it was in fact the only member! Renamed *Lybster* in May 1903. Withdrawn by the London Midland & Scottish Railway in 1929.

[240] Nicknamed on account of its long stovepipe chimney. Built in Chesterfield, it was in use for some years from 1902, and replaced by another no. 2 early in 1913.

[241] Built by the Great Western Railway and named *Juno*, a member of the Banking class of 0–6–0ST. Rebuilt in March 1869: the wheelbase was reduced and tank capacity increased. In September 1872 it was sold to the South Devon Railway, who renamed it *Stromboli*. In 1876 it reverted to the Great Western, retained its name and became no. 2138.

[242] Later Midland Railway no. 265. In November 1855 this locomotive was sold to Thomas

Brassey for working the North Devon Railway, a broad gauge concern which afterwards passed to the London & South Western Railway. There is thought to have become their *Mole*.

[243] Originally *Carew D. Gilbert*. Renamed *Stroudley* in September 1906.

[244] Rebuilt from London, Brighton & South Coast Railway L class 4–6–4T no. 332, of March 1922.

[245] Renamed *Earl of Birkenhead* in October 1937.

[246] Rebuilt to 4–2–2 in September 1894.

[247] The name was transferred from 33114 (formerly no. D6532) to 33025 (formerly no. D6543) when 33114 was renamed *Ashford 150*.

[248] Bury type. Formerly Midland Counties Railway no. 4, purchased October 1844. May have been named *Sunbeam*, and renamed to avoid confusion with an existing S&DR locomotive of that name.

Name	Number	Class	Date	Railway
Sun	–	Wolf	4/1840	Great Western Rly (bg)
Sun	164	aCrewe	5/1847	London & North Western Rly
Sun	20	0–6–0	?1859	St Helens Canal & Rly
Sunbeam	28	2–2–0	1837	Stockton & Darlington Rly
Sunbeam	42	2–2–2	1838	Grand Junction Rly
Sunbeam	4	2–2–0	4/1839	Midland Counties Rly [249]
Sunbeam	–	Wolf	5/1840	Great Western Rly (bg)
Sunbeam	37	Aurora	4/1849	East Lancashire Rly
Sunbeam	42	aCrewe	4/1856	London & North Western Rly [250]
Sunbeam	1104	1Experiment	1884	London & North Western Rly
Sunbeam	–	0–4–0ST	1903	Chatham Dockyard [251]
Sunbeam	2062	2Precursor	8/1905	London & North Western Rly
Sunbrite	**8**	**0–6–0ST**	**1944**	**South Yorkshire Rly [252]**
Sun Castle	523	A2/3	8/1947	London & North Eastern Rly
Sun Chariot	E527	A2	1/1948	British Railways (Eastern Region)
Sunderland	2854	B17/4	4/1936	London & North Eastern Rly
Sunnyside	49	165	5/1878	North British Rly [253]
Sunnyside	75	72	6/1882	North British Rly
Sunstar	2571	A3	9/1924	London & North Eastern Rly
Sun Stream	515	A2/3	10/1946	London & North Eastern Rly
Superb	1937	Jubilee	10/1900	London & North Western Rly
Superb	**–**	**0–6–2T**	**1940**	**Sittingbourne & Kemsley Light Rly [254]**
Superb	D849	Warship	5/1961	British Railways
Superb	**50002**	**50**	**1967**	**British Railways**
Surprise	2200	cSentinel	1929	London & North Eastern Rly
Surrey	1	2–2–2	7/1838	London & Croydon Rly
Surrey	52	A1	2/1876	London, Brighton & South Coast Rly
(Susan)	**P400D**	**08**	**1957**	**British Railways [255]**
Sussex	1	1Sussex	4/1838	London & South Western Rly
Sussex	3	2–2–2	9/1838	London & Croydon Rly
Sussex	1	2Sussex	9/1852	London & South Western Rly
Sussex	203	2–2–2	11/1864	London, Brighton & South Coast Rly [256]
Sussex	1	2Vesuvius	7/1870	London & South Western Rly
Sussex	52	B4	12/1899	London, Brighton & South Coast Rly [257]
Sussex	72	B4	9/1901	London, Brighton & South Coast Rly [258]
Sutherland	266	bCrewe	2/1851	London & North Western Rly
Sutherland	266	DX	c.1860	London & North Western Rly
Sutherland	15	14	10/1862	Highland Rly [259]
Sutherland	32	Glenbarry	10/1863	Highland Rly [260]
Sutherland	739	Samson	7/1864	London & North Western Rly
Sutherland	55	Glenbarry	10/1864	Highland Rly [261]
Sutherland	**1**	**2–4–0T**	**1873**	**Isle of Man Rly [262]**
Sutherland	60	Duke	6/1874	Highland Rly [263]
Sutherland	328	G	2/1881	London, Brighton & South Coast Rly
Sutherland	739	Whitworth	4/1893	London & North Western Rly [264]
Sutherlandshire	61	Duke	6/1874	Highland Rly [265]
Sutton	61	A1	10/1875	London, Brighton & South Coast Rly
(Sutton)	**32650**	**A1X**	**12/1876**	**Kent & East Sussex Rly [266]**
Sutton Nelthorpe	439	1A	7/1914	Great Central Rly
Suvla Bay	833	Prince/W	3/1916	London & North Western Rly
Swale	–	0–6–0	8/1860	London, Chatham & Dover Rly [267]
Swallow	9	2–4–0	?	St Helens Canal & Rly [268]
Swallow	–	Iron Duke	6/1849	Great Western Rly (bg)
Swallow	128	aCrewe	11/1849	London & North Western Rly [269]
Swallow	9	Tiger	10/1861	London, Chatham & Dover Rly
Swallow	185	Windsor	4/1866	Stockton & Darlington Rly
Swallow	–	Rover	9/1871	Great Western Rly (bg)
Swallow	3023	3001	7/1891	Great Western Rly [270]
Swallow	91001	91	4/1988	British Railways
Swallowfield Park	4007	Star	4/1907	Great Western Rly [271]
Swan	5	?	1848	St Helens Canal & Rly
Swan	138	bCrewe	5/1853	London & North Western Rly [272]
Swan	629	S/Bloomer	1854	London & North Western Rly
Swan	5	?	1855	St Helens Canal & Rly
Swanage	**34105**	**WC**	**3/1950**	**British Railways (Southern Region)**
Swan Hunter	43004	43	3/1976	British Railways
Swanmore	515	E4	4/1901	London, Brighton & South Coast Rly
Swanscombe	**–**	**0–4–0ST**	**1891**	**Buckinghamshire Railway Centre**
Swansea	3450	Bulldog	10/1903	Great Western Rly
Swansea	–	0–6–0ST	?	Swansea & Mumbles Rly
(Swansea)	**2**	**0–6–0ST**	**1909**	**Powlesland & Mason [273]**
Swansea Castle	7008	Castle	5/1948	British Railways (Western Region)
Swansea Jack	**–**	**4wDM**	**1955**	**Gwili Rly**
Swansea Vale	**1**	**4wVB**	**1958**	**Gwili Rly**
Swaziland	5630	Jubilee	1934	London Midland & Scottish Rly
Swedish Monarch	4030	Star	10/1909	Great Western Rly [274]
Sweelinck	92046	92		EPS
Sweeney Hall	4973	Hall	1/1930	Great Western Rly
Sweyn	8	2–2–2	3/1842	South Eastern Rly
Swift	27	0–4–0	1836	Stockton & Darlington Rly [275]
Swift	30	0–4–2	1847	Newcastle & Carlisle Rly [276]
Swift	274	bCrewe	11/1851	London & North Western Rly
Swift	717	S/Bloomer	1854	London & North Western Rly
Swift	7	Tiger	9/1861	London, Chatham & Dover Rly
Swift	3350	Bulldog	3/1900	Great Western Rly
Swift	2231	cSentinel	1929	London & North Eastern Rly
Swift	D850	Warship	6/1961	British Railways
Swiftsure	36	2–2–0	1835	Liverpool & Manchester Rly
Swiftsure	648	Dreadnought	1888	London & North Western Rly
Swiftsure	806	2Precursor	1/1905	London & North Western Rly
Swiftsure	5716	Jubilee	1936	London Midland & Scottish Rly

[249] In October 1844 it was sold to the Stockton & Darlington Railway, becoming their no. 44 *Sun*.

[250] Originally no. 40 *Jason*.

[251] 18in gauge.

[252] The modern, preserved South Yorkshire Railway.

[253] Later renamed *Gretna*.

[254] 2ft 6in gauge.

[255] Formerly no. 08320. Named on sale to English China Clay, Blackpool Dries.

[256] Rebuilt by Stroudley in April 1871 and named *Sussex*.

[257] Originally named *Siemens*. Renamed *Sussex* in September 1908, and rebuilt to class B4x in May 1923.

[258] Name removed in May 1906. Rebuilt to class B4x in January 1924.

[259] Later renamed *Dunkeld*, and then *Foulis*.

[260] Renamed *Cluny* in 1874. Altered from 2–2–2 to 2–4–0 in May 1884.

[261] Originally named *Cluny*. Renamed *Sutherland* in 1874, and *Invergordon* in 1884. Altered from 2–2–2 to 2–4–0 in September 1874.

[262] 3ft gauge.

[263] Originally named *Bruce*. Renamed *Sutherland* in June 1884.

[264] Renamed *Ostrich* in 1913.

[265] Renamed *Duke* in January 1877.

[266] Built for the London, Brighton & South Coast Railway as no. 50, and originally named *Whitechapel*. It was renamed *Sutton* in the preservation era, its restoration having been financed by the Borough of Sutton. The genuine *Sutton*, no. 61, had meanwhile been scrapped.

[267] Date purchased from Messrs Brotherhood of Chippenham. Its previous history is unknown.

[268] Said to have been obtained from the Liverpool & Manchester Railway.

[269] Previously Liverpool & Manchester Railway 2–2–2 no. 69; became a London & North Western engine in 1846. Renewed in 1849.

[270] Built as a broad gauge convertible. Rebuilt as 4–2–2 in September 1894.

[271] Previously named *Rising Star*. Renamed in May 1937.

[272] Previously Liverpool & Manchester Railway 2–2–2 no. 79; became a London & North Western engine in 1846. Renewed in 1853.

[273] Recorded in 1962 as being with the Middleton Railway.

[274] Originally named *King Harold*. Renamed *The Swedish Monarch* in July 1927, and *Swedish Monarch* in November 1927. The name was removed in November 1940 and the words STAR CLASS painted on the splashers.

[275] Some sources show this engine as no. 26.

[276] Became North Eastern Railway no. 478.

Name	Number	Class	Date	Railway	Name	Number	Class	Date	Railway
Swiftsure	75008	J94	5/1943	**War Department** [277]	*Sybil*	–	0–4–0ST	1906	**Launceston Steam Rly** [283]
Swiftsure	50047	50		British Railways	*(Sybila)*	25278	25/3	1965	**British Railways** [284]
Swinden Dalesman	60059	60	9/1991	British Railways [278]	Sydenham	8	2–2–2	7/1839	London & Croydon Rly
Swindon	–	Swindon	11/1865	Great Western Rly (bg)	Sydenham	1	D1	11/1873	London, Brighton & South Coast Rly
Swindon	3446	Bulldog	9/1903	Great Western Rly [279]	*Sydenham*	–	4wTG	1895	**Buckinghamshire Railway Centre** [285]
Swindon	7037	Castle	8/1950	British Railways (Western Region) [280]	Sydney	3410	Atbara	10/1901	Great Western Rly
Swithland Hall	6988	M/Hall	3/1948	Great Western Rly	*Sydney*	4	2–4–2	1963	**Bure Valley Rly** [286]
Swordfish	5082	Castle	6/1939	Great Western Rly [281]	Sydney Smith	1089	Prince/W	10/1913	London & North Western Rly
Swordfish	–	0–6–0ST	1941	**Rutland Railway Museum**	Sylla	–	Caesar	12/1862	Great Western Rly (bg)
Sybil	45	2–2–2	1838	Grand Junction Rly	Sylph	–	Priam	3/1847	Great Western Rly (bg)
Sybil	90	Fireball	12/1847	London & South Western Rly	Sylph	14	2–4–0T	7/1851	South Staffordshire Rly
Sybil	45	aCrewe	4/1849	London & North Western Rly	Sylph	171	Undine	6/1860	London & South Western Rly
Sybil	90	Volcano	1/1868	London & South Western Rly	Sylph	31	Echo	5/1862	London, Chatham & Dover Rly
Sybil	2152	Samson	11/1874	London & North Western Rly	Sylvania CLS	40031	40	9/1959	British Railways [287]
Sybil	2152	Whitworth	1894	London & North Western Rly	*Synolda*	–	4–4–2	1909	**Ravenglass & Eskdale Rly** [288]
Sybil	–	0–4–0ST	1903	**Brecon Mountain Rly** [282]	Syren	58	2–2–2	1839	Grand Junction Rly

[277] Preserved on the Bodmin Steam Railway.

[278] Later renamed *Samuel Plimsoll*.

[279] Originally named *Liverpool*; renamed *Swindon* in October 1903.

[280] Ran nameless until a naming ceremony on 15 November 1950.

[281] Originally *Powis Castle*. Renamed in January 1941.

[282] 1ft 11½in gauge. Built by Hunslet Engine Co., Leeds, 1903. Works no. 827.

[283] 1ft 11½in gauge. Built by Bagnalls of Stafford, 1906. Works no. 1760.

[284] Named on sale to the North Yorkshire Moors Railway.

[285] Built by Aveling & Porter, Rochester, 1895. A geared steam locomotive, it was basically a traction engine on railway wheels!

[286] 15in gauge.

[287] Originally no. D231 *Sylvania*.

[288] 15in gauge. Originally built for Sir Robert Walker's Sand Hutton Railway; then various exhibitions, ending with Belle Vue Zoo, Manchester. Restored to working order.

Name	Number	Class	Date	Railway
Tacita	125	Acis	10/1862	London, Chatham & Dover Rly
Tadworth	556	E4	8/1901	London, Brighton & South Coast Rly
Taff	–	2–2–2	1839	Taff Vale Rly
Taff	1	2–4–0	1859	Taff Vale Rly [1]
Taff	29	0–6–0ST	9/1872	Brecon & Merthyr Rly
Taff Merthyr	37702	37/7	7/1961	British Railways
Tagalie	2563	A3	7/1924	London & North Eastern Rly [2]
Tain	5	Seafield	2/1858	Highland Rly [3]
Talavera	1672	Newton	3/1868	London & North Western Rly
Talavera	1672	rPrecedent	2/1890	London & North Western Rly
Talbot	213	aCrewe	5/1848	London & North Western Rly
Talbot	–	Caesar	3/1861	Great Western Rly (bg)
Talerddig	34	S/Goods	12/1861	Cambrian Railways [4]
Talerddig	13	0–6–0T	2/1875	Cambrian Railways
Talgarth Hall	4974	Hall	1/1930	Great Western Rly
Taliesin	9	0–4–4T	1876	Festiniog Rly [5]
Taliesin	**–**	**0–4–4–0F**	**1885**	**Festiniog Rly [6]**
Talisman	35	2–2–2	1838	Grand Junction Rly
Talisman	35	2–2–2	1841	Grand Junction Rly
Talisman	35	aCrewe	9/1849	London & North Western Rly
Talisman	35	Samson	2/1865	London & North Western Rly
Talisman	48	Reindeer	7/1865	London, Chatham & Dover Rly
Talisman	35	Whitworth	10/1890	London & North Western Rly
Talisman	2989	Saint	9/1905	Great Western Rly
Talisman	9419	D30	9/1914	London & North Eastern Rly [7]
Talisman	12	Claughton	4/1920	London & North Western Rly
Tally-Ho	26	aSentinel	1928	London & North Eastern Rly
Talybont	–	2–4–0T	1897	Hafan & Talybont Tramway [8]
Talyllyn	**1**	**0–4–2ST**	**1865**	**Talyllyn Rly**

Name	Number	Class	Date	Railway
Talyllyn – The First Preserved Railway	86258	86/2	1966	British Railways
Tamar	–	Caesar	6/1859	Great Western Rly (bg)
Tamar	3268	Bulldog	6/1907	Great Western Rly [9]
Tamar	47832	47/4	8/1964	British Railways
Tamar Valley	21C124	rWC	2/1946	Southern Rly
Tamarlane	32	2–2–2	1838	Grand Junction Rly
Tame	–	2–2–2	11/1839	Birmingham & Derby Junction Rly
Tamerlane	32	aCrewe	10/1843	London & North Western Rly
Tamerlane	34	Phaeton	3/1849	East Lancashire Rly
Tamerlane	1003	L/Bloomer	1851	London & North Western Rly

'It'll never run again!' Talyllyn Railway 0–4–2T *Talyllyn* of 1865, no. 1 in the Preservation Society's list, dumped in a barn at Tywyn Pendre in 1955. But this 'Sleeping Beauty' did receive the kiss of life! (*Photo: Author*)

Festiniog Railway Fairlie articulated locomotive *Taliesin*, at Penrhyndeudraeth in 1957. (*Photo: Author*)

[1] Not to be confused with earlier, unnumbered locomotive of the same name, for which no. 1 was a replacement.

[2] Originally named *William Whitelaw*. Renamed in 1941.

[3] Originally named *Seafield*. Renamed *Tain* in 1875.

[4] Later renamed *Cader Idris*.

[5] 1ft 11½in gauge. Single power bogie Fairlie articulated locomotive. Later renumbered 7. At the time of writing (1999), a replica is under construction by the Festiniog Railway at Boston Lodge Works.

[6] Originally named *Livingston Thompson*, and renamed *Taliesin* in 1930. Later renamed *Earl of Merioneth*. Taliesin, incidentally, was a chief of the bards, and flourished *c.* AD 570, while Earl of Merioneth is one of the titles held by HRH the Duke of Edinburgh.

[7] Originally North British Railway Scott class no. 419 *The Talisman*. Ran as *Talisman* from December 1931 to February 1938, and again from May 1940 to March 1947. 9419 is the 1924 number. Became no. 2428 in November 1946, and British Railways no. 62428 in September 1949.

[8] Later *Rheidol* on the Vale of Rheidol Railway. Built by Bagnalls of Stafford for Collier Antures & Co., to 2ft 5½in gauge, and was to be named *Treze de Maio* ('Thirteenth of May' in Portuguese). Actually named *Talybont*, it was bought by the Hafan & Talybont Tramway and altered to 2ft 3in gauge. It worked until closure in 1900, when it was sold to Messrs Pethick Bros, contractors, who were building the Vale of Rheidol Railway, and who had *Talybont* rebuilt by its makers and regauged to 1ft 11½in. It was then renamed *Rheidol*, and was a most effective machine, so much so that it was purchased by the VofR, numbered 3, and worked until 1923. The Great Western Railway gave it the number 1198, which was possibly never actually carried.

[9] Renamed *River Tamar* in December 1903.

Name	Number	Class	Date	Railway
Tamerlane	32	bCrewe	5/1854	London & North Western Rly
Tamerlane	545	Dreadnought	1886	London & North Western Rly
Tamerlane	1419	2Precursor	3/1904	London & North Western Rly
Tamworth	–	2-2-2	7/1839	Birmingham & Derby Junction Rly
(Tamworth Castle)	**D7672**	**25**	**1967**	**British Railways**
Tandridge	412	E6	7/1905	London, Brighton & South Coast Rly
Tanfield	**20**	**J94**	**6/1945**	**War Department** [10]
Tanganyika	5631	Jubilee	1934	London Midland & Scottish Rly
Tangley Hall	5939	Hall	7/1933	Great Western Rly
Tangmere	**21C167**	**BB**	**9/1947**	**Southern Rly**
Tantalus	60	2-2-2	2/1840	Grand Junction Rly
Tantalus	59	2-2-2	6/1848	Manchester, Sheffield & Lincolnshire Rly
Tantalus	253	bCrewe	11/1849	London & North Western Rly [11]
Tantalus	60	aCrewe	11/1850	London & North Western Rly
Tantalus	60	Problem	c.1860	London & North Western Rly
Tantalus	–	Caesar	11/1862	Great Western Rly (bg)
Tantalus	1469	2Precursor	3/1905	London & North Western Rly
Tantivy	248	bSentinel	1932	London & North Eastern Rly
Taplow Court	2950	Saint	5/1912	Great Western Rly
Tara	2340	Prince/W	4/1916	London & North Western Rly
Tarleton	4	0-6-0ST	1882	West Lancashire Rly
Tarmac	**–**	**0-4-0DM**	**1955**	**Buckinghamshire Railway Centre**
Tarndune	–	0-6-0T	1913	Llanelly & Mynydd Mawr Rly [12]
Tarquin	130	Adrian	9/1886	London, Chatham & Dover Rly
Tartar	2	1Sussex	5/1838	London & South Western Rly
Tartar	–	Iron Duke	7/1848	Great Western Rly (bg)
Tartar	2	Tartar	5/1852	London & South Western Rly
Tartar	2	2Vesuvius	12/1870	London & South Western Rly
Tartar	–	Rover	8/1876	Great Western Rly (bg)
Tartar	3057	3031	4/1895	Great Western Rly [13]
Tartar	202	0-4-0ST	1899	War Department
Tartaras	39	2-2-2	1838	Grand Junction Rly
Tartarus	39	DX	c.1860	London & North Western Rly
Tartarus	628	Samson	2/1864	London & North Western Rly
Tartarus	628	Whitworth	4/1893	London & North Western Rly
Tasmania	50	B4	7/1901	London, Brighton & South Coast Rly [14]
Tasmania	3457	Bulldog	1/1904	Great Western Rly
Tasmania	5569	Jubilee	1934	London Midland & Scottish Rly
Tattoo	**4**	**0-4-2T**	**1921**	**Corris Rly** [15]
Taunton	3451	Bulldog	10/1903	Great Western Rly
Taunton Castle	7036	Castle	8/1950	British Railways (Western Region)
Taurus	–	?	?	Brassey [16]
Taurus	–	Leo	7/1841	Great Western Rly (bg)
Taurus	42	0-4-2	9/1849	Manchester, Sheffield & Lincolnshire Rly
Taurus	47	2Hercules	12/1851	London & South Western Rly
Taurus	2170	0-6-0ST	5/1869	Great Western Rly (bg) [17]
Tavistock	21C111	WC	10/1945	Southern Rly
Tavy	3346	Bulldog	2/1900	Great Western Rly
Taw	–	2-2-2	1838	London & South Western Rly [18]
Taw	–	2-6-2T	12/1897	Lynton & Barnstaple Rly [19]

Name	Number	Class	Date	Railway
Tawd	**2**	**4wDM**	**1943**	**West Lancashire Light Rly** [20]
Tawstock Court	2951	Saint	3/1913	Great Western Rly
Taw Valley	**21C127**	**rWC**	**4/1946**	**Southern Rly**
Tay	–	Caesar	9/1858	Great Western Rly (bg)
Tay	92	Scotchmen	12/1866	London, Chatham & Dover Rly
Taymouth Castle	140	Castle	1900	Highland Rly

Haworth Motive Power Dept, Keighley & Worth Valley Railway, with two visitors to the line. Rebuilt West Country class 4-6-2 no. 34027 *Taw Valley* and *Sir Berkeley*, an 0-6-0ST of 1891 preserved by the Vintage Carriages Trust. (*Photo: Author*)

Name	Number	Class	Date	Railway
Tayport	106	165	7/1878	North British Rly [21]
Teazle	283	aSentinel	1928	London & North Eastern Rly
Tebay	136	Peel	11/1858	Stockton & Darlington Rly
Tebay	79	2-2-2	1859	Lancaster & Carlisle Rly
Tees	14	Enterprise	7/1837	Stockton & Darlington Rly [22]
Teesdale	105	Peel	12/1855	Stockton & Darlington Rly
Teesside Steelmaster	37078	37/7	10/1962	British Railways
Tehran	518	A2/3	12/1946	London & North Eastern Rly
Teign	–	Wolf	8/1838	Great Western Rly (bg) [23]
Teign	75	River	12/1895	Great Western Rly [24]
Teilo	912	0-6-0	1870	Great Western Rly [25]
Teise	25	2-2-0	12/1842	London & Brighton & South Eastern Railways joint stock
Telegraph	2218	cSentinel	1929	London & North Eastern Rly
Telemon	**9**	**0-4-0DM**	**1955**	**North Downs Steam Rly**
Telford	6	2-4-0	4/1861	London & South Western Rly (ed)
Telford	–	Victoria	4/1864	Great Western Rly (bg)
Telford	1484	Newton	5/1866	London & North Western Rly
Telford	259	D1	3/1882	London, Brighton & South Coast Rly [26]
Telford	1484	rPrecedent	11/1890	London & North Western Rly
Telford	204	B2	5/1897	London, Brighton & South Coast Rly [27]
Telford	621	Prince/W	2/1919	London & North Western Rly
Telica	–	Fury	10/1846	Great Western Rly (bg)

[10] Preserved on the Tanfield Railway. WD no. 75256.

[11] See footnote for no. 253 *Bucephalus*.

[12] Became Great Western Railway no. 339.

[13] Renamed *Walter Robinson* in July 1901.

[14] Name removed in about 1906. Rebuilt to class B4x in June 1923.

[15] It is not certain whether this name, the manufacturer's code name for the design, was in fact carried. The locomotive was nameless until it became Talyllyn Railway no. 4 *Edward Thomas*. In more recent years, it has carried the name *Peter Sam*, a character in a children's book by the Revd W. Audrey. It has successively been Corris Railway no. 4, Great

Western Railway no. 4, (briefly) British Railways no. 4, and Talyllyn Railway no. 4!

[16] Thomas Brassey contracted to maintain the track of the London & South Western Railway from 4 November 1839 to December 1853. He provided his own locomotives, of which *Taurus* was one. Beyond their names, very little is known of them.

[17] Built for the South Devon Railway.

[18] Rebuilt from a locomotive built *c.* 1838–40 for the Birmingham & Gloucester Railway. Purchased by Thomas Brassey, the contractor, it was converted to a broad gauge 2–2–2, possibly a tank engine, and used on the

North Devon Railway. After the London & South Western Railway took over the North Devon in 1865, it was offered for sale as scrap.

[19] Became Southern Railway no. E761 in 1923. 1ft 11½in gauge.

[20] 2ft gauge.

[21] Previously named *Slamannan*.

[22] Rebuilt to Tory class in May 1848.

[23] Originally named *Viper*, renamed in 1846. Original name restored in 1851.

[24] Rebuilt from 2–2–2 no. 75 of 1856.

[25] Built for the Llanelly Railway.

[26] Renamed *Barnham* in April 1898.

[27] Rebuilt to class B2x in March 1911.

Name	Number	Class	Date	Railway
Telscombe	493	E4	11/1899	London, Brighton & South Coast Rly
Temeraire	1939	Jubilee	1900	London & North Western Rly
Temeraire	D851	Warship	7/1961	British Railways
Temeraire	50003	50	1968	British Railways
Tempest	101	2–2–2	9/1850	Manchester, Sheffield & Lincolnshire Rly
Templar	47	Reindeer	7/1865	London, Chatham & Dover Rly
Templecombe	34098	rWC	12/1949	British Railways (Southern Region)
Templecombe	33112	33/1	1961	British Railways
Templecombe	47315	47/3	1965	British Railways
Templecombe	47708	47/7	10/1965	British Railways
Tenacious	D852	Warship	7/1961	British Railways
Tenby	1	2–2–2T	1863	Pembroke & Tenby Rly
Tenby	6	0–6–0	1863	Pembroke & Tenby Rly [28]
Tenby Castle	5062	Castle	6/1937	Great Western Rly [29]
Tenby Castle	7026	Castle	8/1949	British Railways (Western Region)
Tennyson	1747	Newton	11/1869	London & North Western Rly [30]
Tennyson	396	Newton	9/1870	London & North Western Rly [31]
Tennyson	396	rPrecedent	5/1891	London & North Western Rly [32]
Tennyson	2373	Claughton	5/1917	London & North Western Rly
Tennyson	70032	Britannia	12/1952	British Railways
Tenterden	1	2–4–0T	1899	Kent & East Sussex Rly
(Terence)	08331	08	1957	British Railways [33]
Terence Cuneo	91011	91	2/1990	British Railways
Teribus	906	901	8/1911	North British Rly
Terrible	3390	Atbara	8/1900	Great Western Rly
Terrier	357	bCrewe	2/1855	London & North Western Rly
Terrier	357	DX	c.1860	London & North Western Rly
Terrier	738	Samson	5/1863	London & North Western Rly
Terrier	738	Whitworth	1890	London & North Western Rly
Terrier	2629	2Experiment	3/1909	London & North Western Rly
Terror	54	2–4–0	7/1848	Manchester, Sheffield & Lincolnshire Rly
Test	111	Rocklia	12/1848	London & South Western Rly
Test	111	Lion	2/1869	London & South Western Rly
Teutonic	1301	Teutonic	3/1889	London & North Western Rly
Teutonic	2583	2Precursor	1/1906	London & North Western Rly [34]
Tewkesbury	2	2–2–2	9/1839	Birmingham & Gloucester Rly
Texaco	–	0–4–0DM	1958	Bo'ness & Kinneil Rly
Thakeham Tiles No 3	–	4wDM	1941	Amberley Chalk Pits Museum [35]
Thakeham Tiles No 4	–	4wDM	1948	Amberley Chalk Pits Museum [36]
Thalaba	36	2–2–2	1838	Grand Junction Rly
Thalaba	36	2–2–2	8/1841	Grand Junction Rly
Thalaba	36	aCrewe	11/1850	London & North Western Rly
Thalaba	36	Samson	2/1865	London & North Western Rly
Thalaba	36	Whitworth	10/1890	London & North Western Rly
Thalaba	30	Claughton	8/1920	London & North Western Rly
Thames	8	?	3/1838	London & Greenwich Rly
Thames	13	2–2–0	10/1842	London & Brighton & South Eastern Railways joint stock [37]
Thames	6	2–2–2WT	1848	London & Blackwall Rly

Name	Number	Class	Date	Railway
Thames	–	Caesar	2/1854	Great Western Rly (bg)
Thames	160	Tweed	6/1859	London & South Western Rly
Thames	57	A1	1/1876	London, Brighton & South Coast Rly
Thames	160	SFG	5/1878	London & South Western Rly
Thames	3027	3001	8/1891	Great Western Rly [38]
Thames	3329	Duke	7/1899	Great Western Rly
Thames	**3**	**0–4–0ST**	**1951**	**Cholsey & Wallingford Rly**
Thames Haven	17	Class 1	1881	London, Tilbury & Southend Rly
Thane of Fife	871	H	7/1906	North British Rly
Thane of Fife	2005	P2	8/1936	London & North Eastern Rly
Thane of Fife	505	A2/2	1/1943	London & North Eastern Rly [39]
Thane of Fife	87033	87/0	1974	British Railways
Thanet	96	L/Scotchmen	2/1873	London, Chatham & Dover Rly
The Abbot	2972	Saint	2/1905	Great Western Rly [40]
The Abbot	420	Scott	10/1914	North British Rly
The Albrighton	205	D49/2	7/1934	London & North Eastern Rly
The Artists' Rifleman	6164	Royal Scot	9/1930	London Midland & Scottish Rly
The Atherstone	214	D49/2	7/1934	London & North Eastern Rly
The Auditor	1173	Precedent	8/1878	London & North Western Rly
The Auditor	1173	rPrecedent	1/1894	London & North Western Rly
The Badsworth	232	D49/2	5/1932	London & North Eastern Rly
The Bedale	235	D49/2	6/1932	London & North Eastern Rly
The Bedfordshire and Hertfordshire Regiment	5516	Patriot	10/1932	London Midland & Scottish Rly
The Bedfordshire and Hertfordshire Regiment (T.A.)	D56	Peak	10/1962	British Railways
The Belgian Monarch	4022	Star	6/1909	Great Western Rly [41]
The Belvoir	217	D49/2	7/1934	London & North Eastern Rly
The Berkeley	222	D49/2	7/1934	London & North Eastern Rly
The Bilsdale	226	D49/2	7/1934	London & North Eastern Rly
The Birmingham Post	86251	86/2	1965	British Railways
The Birmingham Royal Ballet	90008	90/0	5/1988	British Railways
The Blackcountryman	31106	31/1	1959	British Railways
The Black Horse	43034	43	11/1976	British Railways
The Black Prince	87011	87/0	1974	British Railways
The Black Watch	55013	Deltic	9/1961	British Railways
The Blankney	247	D49/2	7/1932	London & North Eastern Rly
The Bluebell Railway	73133	73/1	1966	British Railways
The Bobby	47746	47/7		British Railways
The Border Regiment	6136	Royal Scot	9/1927	London Midland & Scottish Rly [42]
The Boys' Brigade	86243	86/2	1965	British Railways
The Boy Scout	6169	Royal Scot	11/1930	London Midland & Scottish Rly
The Braes of Derwent	255	D49/2	8/1932	London & North Eastern Rly
The Bramham Moor	201	D49/2	4/1932	London & North Eastern Rly
The British Monarch	4021	Star	6/1909	Great Western Rly [43]
The Brocklesby	230	D49/2	8/1934	London & North Eastern Rly
The Brontes of Haworth	47424	47/4	1963	British Railways
"The Bug"	733	F9	6/1899	London & South Western Rly [44]

[28] Originally named *Cambria*. Renamed when the original *Tenby*, no. 1, was withdrawn in 1886. In 1896 it became Great Western Railway no. 1364.

[29] Renamed *Earl of Shaftesbury* in November 1937.

[30] Renamed *John Mayall* in 1885.

[31] Originally named *Dunrobin*; renamed in 1885.

[32] Later became no. 1747 *John Mayall*.

[33] Formerly no. 08331. Named on sale to RFS (E) Ltd, Doncaster.

[34] Renamed *The Czar* in 1914, and again renamed *Moonstone* when Prince of Wales class 4–6–0 no. 88 was named *Czar of Russia* in October 1915.

[35] 2ft gauge.

[36] 2ft gauge.

[37] On the break-up of the Joint Committee, became London & Brighton Railway no. 4.

[38] Built as a broad gauge convertible. Rebuilt to 4–2–2 in November 1894 and renamed *Worcester* in December 1895.

[39] Rebuild of previous engine.

[40] Named *Quicksilver* until March 1907.

[41] Originally named *King William* until June 1927. Renamed *The Belgian Monarch* in June or July 1927, and *Belgian Monarch* in October 1927. Nameplates removed in May 1940, and the words STAR CLASS were painted on the splashers.

[42] Originally named *Goliath*; renamed in May 1936.

[43] Originally named *King Edward*. Renamed *The British Monarch* in June or July 1927, and then *British Monarch* in October or November 1927.

[44] This was a 4–2–4T with an inspection saloon mounted over the rear bogie, and used by Mr Dugald Drummond, the LSWR's Chief Mechanical Engineer. The sight of it approaching, apparently, could cause terror! It is said that signalmen passed word of its coming: 'Watch out for the Bug – 'er's round again!' After Drummond's death in 1912 the car fell into disuse, but found employment carrying VIPs on tours of inspection of Southampton Docks. There was talk of preservation, but it was dismantled during the Second World War. The saloon body survived, first as a mess room, and now in private preservation.

Name	Number	Class	Date	Railway
The Bug	4	0-4-0TT	1925	**Romney, Hythe & Dymchurch Rly** [45]
The Burma Star	33056	33/0	1961	**British Railways**
The Burma Star	33202	33/2	1961	British Railways [46]
The Burton	238	D49/2	8/1934	London & North Eastern Rly
The Canary	08869	08	1960	British Railways
The Cardiff Rod Mill	37229	37/7	2/1964	British Railways
The Cardiff Rod Mill	56060	56	1979	British Railways
The Cattistock	258	D49/2	8/1934	London & North Eastern Rly
The Chartered Institute of Transport	90011	90/0	9/1988	British Railways
The Cheshire Regiment	6134	Royal Scot	9/1927	London Midland & Scottish Rly [47]
The Cheviot	60023	60	11/1990	British Railways
The Cleveland	269	D49/2	8/1932	London & North Eastern Rly
The Coal Merchants' Association of Scotland	37332	37/3	8/1964	British Railways
The Colonel	–	4wDM	1943	**Festiniog Rly** [48]
The Commonwealth Spirit	47555	47/4	1964	British Railways
The Cotswold	279	D49/2	9/1934	London & North Eastern Rly
The Cottesmore	297	D49/2	8/1933	London & North Eastern Rly
The Countess	–	0-6-0T	9/1902	**Welshpool & Llanfair Rly** [49]
The Craftsman	5151	J94	1944	War Department
The Craven	274	D49/2	8/1934	London & North Eastern Rly
The Cub	3	B-B DH	1954	**Cleethorpes Coast Light Rly** [50]
The Czar	2583	2Precursor	1/1906	London & North Western Rly [51]
The Danish Monarch	4023	Star	6/1909	Great Western Rly [52]
The Derbyshire Yeomanry	45509	Patriot	8/1932	British Railways [53]
The Derwent	353	D49/2	9/1934	London & North Eastern Rly
(The Diana)	25191	25/2	1965	British Railways [54]
The Doncaster Postman	08562	08	1959	British Railways
The Dougal Cratur	400	Scott	9/1912	North British Rly
The D'Oyly Carte Opera Company	90004	90/0	4/1988	British Railways
The Duke	123	1Vesuvius	12/1853	London & South Western Rly
The Duke	80	The Duke	5/1854	Stockton & Darlington Rly
The Duke	67	Duke	8/1874	Highland Rly [55]
The Duke	7	0-4-0ST	3/1876	Wrexham, Mold & Connah's Quay Rly
The Duke	144	J94	1944	**War Department** [56]
The Duke and Duchess of York	43051	43	4/1977	British Railways
The Duke of Edinburgh	1481	Newton	6/1866	London & North Western Rly

Name	Number	Class	Date	Railway
The Duke of Edinburgh	1481	rPrecedent	10/1888	London & North Western Rly
The Duke of Edinburgh's Award	47716	47/7	1966	British Railways
The Duke of Wellington	86230	86/2	1965	British Railways
The Duke of Wellington's Regiment	55014	Deltic	9/1961	British Railways
The Duke of Wellington's Regt. (West Riding)	6145	Royal Scot	10/1927	London Midland & Scottish Rly [57]
The Durham Light Infantry	60964	V2	1/1943	British Railways [58]
The Durham Light Infantry	55017	Deltic	11/1961	British Railways
The Dutch Monarch	4024	Star	6/1909	Great Western Rly [59]

Welshpool & Llanfair Light Railway 0-6-0T *The Earl* at Didcot. The 2ft 6in gauge locomotive is mounted on a standard gauge well wagon. (*Photo: Author*)

Name	Number	Class	Date	Railway
The Earl	–	0-6-0T	9/1902	**Welshpool & Llanfair Rly** [60]
The Earl of Chester	609	Samson	1/1866	London & North Western Rly
The Earl of Chester	609	Whitworth	4/1893	London & North Western Rly [61]
The Earl of Dumfries	36	2-4-2T	1/1879	Cardiff Rly [62]
The Earl of Kerry	434	11E	11/1913	Great Central Rly
The East Lancashire Regiment	6135	Royal Scot	9/1927	London Midland & Scottish Rly [63]
The Economist	90009	90/0	9/1988	British Railways
The Enginemen's Fund	31468	31/4	1962	British Railways

45 15in gauge.
46 33056 was the original *The Burma Star*, being named with 33027 *Earl Mountbatten of Burma* to haul the great man's funeral train on 5 September 1979. On 33056's withdrawal (and sale for preservation) in February 1991 the name was transferred to 33202. 33056 was originally D6574, and 33202 was originally D6587.
47 Originally named *Atlas*; renamed in May 1936.
48 1ft 11½in gauge.
49 Built for the Welshpool & Llanfair Railway. Name changed to *Countess* by Great Western Railway, who numbered it 823; original name now restored. 2ft 6in gauge.
50 14¼in gauge.
51 Originally named *Teutonic*. Renamed *The Czar* in 1914, and again renamed *Moonstone* when Prince of Wales class 4-6-0 no. 88 was named *Czar of Russia* in October 1915.
52 Originally named *King George* until July 1927. Renamed *Danish Monarch* in October 1927. Nameplates removed in November 1940, and the words STAR CLASS were painted on the splashers.
53 Built by the London Midland & Scottish Railway. Name applied in November 1951.
54 Named on sale to North Yorkshire Moors Railway.
55 Renamed *Cromartie* in January 1877.
56 Preserved on Peak Railway, Darley Dale.
57 Originally named *Condor*.
58 Built by the London & North Eastern Railway. Name applied by British Railways, 29 April 1958.
59 Originally named *King James*. Renamed *The Dutch Monarch* in June or July 1927, and further renamed *Dutch Monarch* in October or November 1927.
60 Built for the Welshpool & Llanfair Railway. Name changed to *Earl* by the Great Western Railway, who numbered it 822; original name now restored. 2ft 6in gauge.
61 In June 1923, as London Midland & Scottish Railway no. 5094, it was transferred to the Engineer's Department and renamed *Engineer Walsall*.
62 Built by the London & North Western Railway at Crewe Works as a 2-4-0T; their no. 1181, it was converted to a 2-4-2T at Crewe in March 1898. It was sold to the Cardiff Railway in March 1914 and was the only Cardiff Railway locomotive to carry a name. It was allocated Great Western no. 1327, but went to Swindon and was promptly scrapped without ever being renumbered. The official date of withdrawal is May 1922.
63 Originally named *Samson*; renamed in May 1936.

Name	Number	Class	Date	Railway
The Enterprising Scot	47492	47/4	1964	British Railways
The Enterprising Scot	47742	47/7		British Railways
The Essex Regiment	2858	B17/1	5/1936	London & North Eastern Rly [64]
The Fair Maid	900	Scott	9/1909	North British Rly
The Fernie	357	D49/2	9/1934	London & North Eastern Rly
The Fiery Cross	2686	D11/2	10/1924	London & North Eastern Rly
The Fife and Forfar Yeomanry	55006	Deltic	6/1961	British Railways
The Fitzwilliam	359	D49/2	9/1934	London & North Eastern Rly
"The Flying Flogger"	32	2–2–2	11/1852	Shrewsbury & Chester Rly
The Garth	361	D49/2	10/1934	London & North Eastern Rly
(The Gauge O Guild)	**48151**	**8F**	**1942**	**London Midland & Scottish Rly**
The Geordie	47503	47/4	1966	British Railways
The Girl Guide	6168	Royal Scot	10/1930	London Midland & Scottish Rly
The Girls' Brigade	90002	90/0	4/1988	British Railways
The Glasgow Herald	86250	86/2	1965	British Railways
The Glasgow Highlander	5157	5	1935	London Midland & Scottish Rly
The Gloucestershire Regiment	47569	47/4	1964	British Railways

Name	Number	Class	Date	Railway
The Grove	364	D49/2	11/1934	London & North Eastern Rly
The Gunner	–	0–4–0ST	1/1875	Woolwich Arsenal [70]
The Halewood Transmission	47309	47/3	1965	British Railways
THE HERALD	90003	90/0	4/1988	British Railways
The Hertfordshire Regiment	6167	Royal Scot	10/1930	London Midland & Scottish Rly
The Holderness	273	D49/2	10/1932	London & North Eastern Rly
The Hurworth	282	D49/2	10/1932	London & North Eastern Rly

Great Western Railway 4–6–2 no. 111 *The Great Bear*, at Paddington. (*Photo: RAS Marketing*)

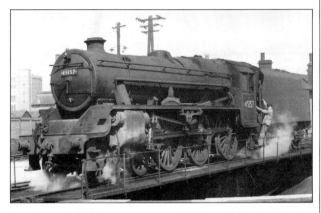

British Railways (ex-LMS) class 5 4–6–0 no. 45157 *The Glasgow Highlander*, at Haymarket Shed on 16 August 1958. (*Photo: RAS Marketing*)

Name	Number	Class	Date	Railway
The Gloucestershire Regiment 28th 61st	5017	Castle	7/1932	Great Western Rly [65]
The Goathland	362	D49/2	10/1934	London & North Eastern Rly
The Grafton	363	D49/2	11/1934	London & North Eastern Rly
The Grammar School Doncaster AD 1350	43045	43	3/1977	British Railways
The Great Bear	111	4–6–2	2/1908	Great Western Rly [66]
The Great Marquess	**3442**	**K4**	**7/1938**	**London & North Eastern Rly [67]**
The Green Howard, Alexandra, Princess of Wales's Own Yorkshire Regiment	4806	V2	9/1938	London & North Eastern Rly
The Green Howards	6133	Royal Scot	9/1927	London Midland & Scottish Rly [68]
The Green Howards	55008	Deltic	7/1961	British Railways
The Green Knight	754	King Arthur	2/1923	Southern Rly [69]
(The Green Knight)	**75029**	**4MT**	**1954**	**British Railways**
The Green Knight	73086	5MT	8/1955	British Railways

Name	Number	Class	Date	Railway
The Hussar	6154	Royal Scot	7/1930	London Midland & Scottish Rly
The Industrial Society	86627	86/6	6/1965	British Railways
The Institute of Export	47245	47/0	1966	British Railways
The Institution of Civil Engineers	47540	47/4	1964	British Railways
The Institution of Electrical Engineers	86607	86/6	8/1965	British Railways
The Institution of Mechanical Engineers	47841	47/4	3/1964	British Railways
The Institution of Mining Engineers	56093	56	1981	British Railways
The Institution of Railway Signal Engineers	37232	37/0	1964	British Railways
The Italian Monarch	4025	Star	7/1909	Great Western Rly [71]
The Japanese Monarch	4026	Star	9/1909	Great Western Rly [72]
The King	–	**0–4–0WT**	**1906**	**Battlefield Steam Rly**
The King's Dragoon Guardsman	6152	Royal Scot	7/1930	London Midland & Scottish Rly
The Kingsman	37421	37/4	1965	British Railways
The Kingsman	86317	86/3	1965	British Railways
The Kingsman	86417	86/4	1966	British Railways
The King's Own	6161	Royal Scot	9/1930	London Midland & Scottish Rly
The King's Own Royal Border Regiment	D58	Peak	2/1962	British Railways
The King's Own Scottish Borderer	55010	Deltic	7/1961	British Railways

[64] Originally *Newcastle United*. Renamed *The Essex Regiment* in June 1936.

[65] *St. Donats Castle* until 1954.

[66] On 7 January 1924 a start was made with dismantling the engine. The front part of the chassis was reused to produce a new Castle class locomotive, no. 111 *Viscount Churchill*.

[67] Originally named *MacCailein Mor*. Renamed within a fortnight.

[68] Originally named *Vulcan*; renamed in May 1936.

[69] Nameplates fitted in 1925.

[70] Name said to have been carried. Later sold to Wantage Tramway for £600, and renamed *Driver*. It was not successful, being unable to maintain steam pressure (one old driver is quoted as saying 'She was only a good engine as long as she was standing still'). It was broken up at Wantage in 1920, after less than a year's service.

[71] Originally named *King Charles*. Renamed *The Italian Monarch* in June or July 1927. Further renamed *Italian Monarch* in October or November 1927. Name removed June 1940 and the words STAR CLASS were painted on the splashers.

[72] Originally named *King Richard*. Renamed *The Japanese Monarch* in June or July 1927, and further renamed *Japanese Monarch* in October or November 1927. Name removed in January 1941 and the words STAR CLASS were painted on the splashers.

Name	Number	Class	Date	Railway
The King's Own Yorkshire Light Infantry	55002	Deltic	3/1961	**British Railways**
The King's Regiment Liverpool	6132	Royal Scot	9/1927	London Midland & Scottish Rly [73]
The King's Royal Rifle Corps	6140	Royal Scot	10/1927	London Midland & Scottish Rly [74]
The Lady Armaghdale	–	0–6–0T	1898	**Severn Valley Rly**
The Lady D	–	4wDM	1944	**Moseley Railway Museum [75]**
The Lady of the Lake	2690	D11/2	11/1924	London & North Eastern Rly
The Lancashire Fusilier	D52	Peak	6/1962	British Railways
The Lancer	6155	Royal Scot	7/1930	London Midland & Scottish Rly
The Lass o'Ballochmyle	37692	37/5	5/1963	British Railways
The Law Society	90013	90/0	11/1988	British Railways
The Leicestershire Regiment	5503	Patriot	7/1932	London Midland & Scottish Rly [76]
The Life Guardsman	6150	Royal Scot	5/1930	London Midland & Scottish Rly
The Liverpool Daily Post	86252	86/2	1965	British Railways
The Liverpool Phil	90014	90/0	10/1988	British Railways
The Lizard	3259	Duke	9/1895	Great Western Rly [77]
THE LOCOMOTIVE & CARRIAGE INSTITUTION	47584	47/4	1964	British Railways
The London Irish Rifleman	6138	Royal Scot	9/1927	London Midland & Scottish Rly [78]
THE LONDON STANDARD	47573	47/4	1964	British Railways
The Lord Provost	69	Duke	8/1874	Highland Rly [79]
The Lord Provost	510	I	6/1921	North British Rly
The Lord Provost	47709	47/7	1966	British Railways
The Lovat Scouts	6128	Royal Scot	8/1927	London Midland & Scottish Rly [80]
The Loyal Regiment	6158	Royal Scot	8/1930	London Midland & Scottish Rly
The Magistrates' Association	56086	56	1980	British Railways
The Major	1	I	12/1885	**Mersey Rly [81]**
The Major	7	4wDM	1937	**Amberley Chalk Pits Museum [82]**
The Manchester Guardian	86253	86/2	1965	British Railways
The Manchester Guardian	86044	86/0	12/1965	British Railways
The Manchester Regiment	6148	Royal Scot	11/1927	London Midland & Scottish Rly [83]
The Manchester Regiment	D49	Peak	10/1961	British Railways
The Meynell	352	D49/2	3/1929	London & North Eastern Rly [84]
The Middlesex Regiment	6149	Royal Scot	11/1927	London Midland & Scottish Rly [85]
The Middleton	283	D49/2	8/1933	London & North Eastern Rly
The Morpeth	365	D49/2	12/1934	London & North Eastern Rly [86]
The Morris Dancer	47206	47/0	1965	British Railways

Name	Number	Class	Date	Railway
The National Trust	43169	43	9/1981	British Railways
The Needles	2423	H2	9/1911	Southern Rly [87]
The Newspaper Society Founded 1836	43196	43	7/1982	British Railways
The Nile	1676	Newton	4/1868	London & North Western Rly
The Nile	1676	rPrecedent	5/1891	London & North Western Rly
The Nile	1352	Prince/W	1/1916	London & North Western Rly
The Northamptonshire Regiment	6147	Royal Scot	10/1927	London Midland & Scottish Rly [88]
The Northern Lights	37251	37/0	1965	British Railways
The North Staffordshire Regiment	6141	Royal Scot	10/1927	London Midland & Scottish Rly [89]
The Norwegian Monarch	4027	Star	9/1909	Great Western Rly [90]
The Oakley	366	D49/2	12/1934	London & North Eastern Rly
Theocritus	–	Bogie	12/1854	Great Western Rly (bg)
Theodore	360	bCrewe	3/1855	London & North Western Rly
The Old Contemptibles	6127	Royal Scot	8/1927	London Midland & Scottish Rly [91]
Theorem	183	aCrewe	11/1847	London & North Western Rly
Theorem	183	DX	c.1860	London & North Western Rly
Theorem	792	Samson	2/1864	London & North Western Rly
Theorem	792	Whitworth	6/1893	London & North Western Rly [92]
The Percy	288	D49/2	8/1933	London & North Eastern Rly
The Permanent Way Institution	47974	47/4	5/1964	British Railways
The Pioneer No 1	1	Sentinel	6/1923	Jersey Rly [93]
The Pioneer No 2	2	Sentinel	1/1924	Jersey Rly [94]
The Pirate	2971	Saint	12/1903	Great Western Rly [95]
The Pirate	409	Scott	4/1914	North British Rly
The Port of Felixstowe	47291	47/0	1966	British Railways
The Prince	2	0–4–0TT	1863	Festiniog Rly [96]
The Prince	2313	4P	1928	London Midland & Scottish Rly
The Princess	1	0–4–0TT	1863	Festiniog Rly [97]
The Princess Royal	6200	Princess	7/1933	London Midland & Scottish Rly
The Prince of Wales's Own Regiment of Yorkshire	55005	Deltic	5/1961	British Railways
The Prince of Wales's Volunteers (South Lancashire)	6137	Royal Scot	9/1927	London Midland & Scottish Rly [98]
The Puckeridge	368	D49/2	12/1934	London & North Eastern Rly
The Pytchley	298	D49/2	9/1933	London & North Eastern Rly
The Queen	57	2–2–2	1849	North British Rly
The Queen	1213	Newton	4/1872	London & North Western Rly
The Queen	1213	rPrecedent	4/1892	London & North Western Rly
The Queen	3041	3031	10/1894	Great Western Rly [99]
The Queen	3041	replica	1983	**Great Western Rly [100]**
The Queen Mother	47722	47/7		British Railways
The Queen's Own Hussars	43096	43	7/1978	British Railways

[73] Originally named *Phoenix*; renamed in May 1936.
[74] Originally named *Hector*; renamed in May 1936.
[75] 2ft gauge.
[76] Renamed *The Royal Leicestershire Regiment* in November 1948.
[77] Originally named *Lizard*. Renamed in January 1904.
[78] Originally named *Fury*; renamed in October 1929.
[79] Later renamed *Sir James*, and then *Aldourie*.
[80] Originally named *Meteor*; renamed in April 1936.
[81] Preserved at the Rail Transport Museum, Thirlmere, New South Wales, Australia.
[82] 2ft gauge.

[83] Originally named *Velocipede*; renamed in October 1935.
[84] Originally named *Leicestershire*; renamed in June 1932.
[85] Originally named *Lady of the Lake*; renamed in May 1936.
[86] Rebuilt in August 1942 by Thompson with inside cylinders, renumbered 2768 and reclassified D49/4.
[87] Built for the London, Brighton & South Coast Railway. Nameplates fitted by the Southern Railway in April 1927.
[88] Originally named *Courier*.
[89] Originally named *Caledonian*; renamed in June 1936.
[90] Originally named *King Henry* until July 1927. Renamed *The Norwegian Monarch* in July 1927, and *Norwegian Monarch* in

November 1927.
[91] Originally named *Novelty*; renamed in June 1936.
[92] Transferred to Engineer's Department as no. 5099 *Engineer* from May 1923 to July 1932.
[93] Sentinel-Cammell steam railcar. 3ft 6in gauge.
[94] Sentinel-Cammell steam railcar. 3ft 6in gauge. Later renamed *Portelet*.
[95] Previously named *Albion* until March 1907; reverted to *Albion* in July 1907.
[96] 1ft 11½in gauge.
[97] Name later changed to *Princess*. 1ft 11½in gauge.
[98] Originally named *Vesta*; renamed in May 1936.
[99] Originally named *Emlyn*. Renamed *The Queen* in 1897 and *James Mason* in June 1910.
[100] A non-working replica at Madame Tussaud's, Windsor.

Name	Number	Class	Date	Railway
The Queen's Own Mercian Yeomanry	47528	47/4	1967	British Railways
The Quorn	336	D49/2	6/1929	London & North Eastern Rly [101]
The Railway Mission	47725	47/7		British Railways
The Railway Observer	37890	37/7	10/1963	British Railways
The Ranger (12th London Regt.)	6165	Royal Scot	10/1930	London Midland & Scottish Rly
The Red Arrows	91004	91	6/1988	British Railways
The Red Cross	43147	43	5/1981	British Railways
The Red Dragon	47671	47/4	1/1966	British Railways [102]
The Red Knight	755	King Arthur	3/1923	Southern Rly [103]
The Red Knight	73110	5MT	10/1955	British Railways
The Rifle Brigade	6146	Royal Scot	10/1927	London Midland & Scottish Rly [104]
The Rock	–	0–4–0DM	1941	**Irchester Narrow Gauge Railway Museum** [105]
The Romney Hythe and Dymchurch Railway	73118	73/1	1966	British Railways
The Roumanian Monarch	4028	Star	9/1909	Great Western Rly [106]
The Round Tabler	86220	86/2	1966	British Railways
The Royal Air Force	6159	Royal Scot	8/1930	London Midland & Scottish Rly
The Royal Alex	73101	73/1	1965	British Railways
The Royal Army Ordnance Corps	5505	Patriot	7/1932	London Midland & Scottish Rly [107]
The Royal Army Ordnance Corps	**45112**	**45**	**1962**	**British Railways**
The Royal Army Ordnance Corps	47972	47/4	1/1965	British Railways
The Royal Artilleryman	6157	Royal Scot	8/1930	London Midland & Scottish Rly
The Royal Artilleryman	**45118**	**45**	**1962**	**British Railways**
The Royal Bank of Scotland	87012	87/0	1974	British Railways

Name	Number	Class	Date	Railway
The Royal British Legion	86244	86/2	1965	British Railways
The Royal Dragoon	6153	Royal Scot	7/1930	London Midland & Scottish Rly
The Royal Horse Guardsman	6151	Royal Scot	6/1930	London Midland & Scottish Rly
The Royal Leicestershire Regiment	45503	Patriot	7/1932	British Railways [108]
The Royal Logistics Corps	47033	47/0	1964	British Railways
The Royal Naval Reserve 1859 – 1959	D812	Warship	11/1959	British Railways
The Royal Northumberland Fusiliers	55011	Deltic	8/1961	British Railways
The Royal Pioneer Corps	45506	Patriot	8/1932	British Railways [109]
The Royal Pioneer Corps	D54	Peak	8/1962	British Railways
The Royal Regiment of Wales	43032	43	10/1976	British Railways
The Royal Warwickshire Fusilier	D59	Peak	2/1962	British Railways
The Royal Warwickshire Regiment	6131	Royal Scot	9/1927	London Midland & Scottish Rly [110]
The Rt.Hon. Viscount Cross, G.C.B., G.C.S.I.	258	8D	12/1905	Great Central Rly
The Rufford	370	D49/2	1/1935	London & North Eastern Rly
The Saltire Society	37406	37/4	1965	British Railways
The Sapper	47142	47/0	1964	British Railways
The Sapper	47306	47/3	1964	British Railways
THE SCOTSMAN	91003	91	4/1988	British Railways
The Scott	–	4wPM	5/1927	Ravenglass & Eskdale Rly [111]
The Scottish Horse	6129	Royal Scot	8/1927	London Midland & Scottish Rly [112]
The Scottish Hosteller	37420	37/4	1965	British Railways
Theseus	254	bCrewe	12/1849	London & North Western Rly
Theseus	1002	L/Bloomer	1851	London & North Western Rly
Theseus	–	Caesar	11/1862	Great Western Rly (bg)
The Silcock Express	47231	47/0	1965	British Railways
The Sinnington	374	D49/2	1/1935	London & North Eastern Rly
The Snapper, The East Yorkshire Regiment, The Duke of York's Own	4780	V2	8/1937	London & North Eastern Rly
The Somerset Light Infantry (Prince Albert's)	4016	Castle	10/1925	Great Western Rly [113]
The Sorter	08701	08	1960	British Railways
The South Durham	375	D49/2	1/1935	London & North Eastern Rly
The South Staffordshire Regiment	6143	Royal Scot	10/1927	London Midland & Scottish Rly [114]
The South Wales Borderer	6156	Royal Scot	7/1930	London Midland & Scottish Rly
The South Wales Borderers	4037	Castle	6/1926	Great Western Rly [115]
The Southwold	292	D49/2	8/1933	London & North Eastern Rly
The Spanish Monarch	4029	Star	10/1909	Great Western Rly [116]
The 1211 Squadron	–	0–6–0DM	1957	**Battlefield Steam Rly**
The Staintondale	376	D49/2	2/1935	London & North Eastern Rly
The Statesman	47785	47/7		British Railways

London Midland & Scottish Railway Royal Scot class 4–6–0 no. 6151 *The Royal Horse Guardsman*, passing Hatch End with a Holyhead–Euston express on 1 September 1934. (Photo: LCGB Ken Nunn Collection)

[101] Originally named *Buckinghamshire*. Renamed *The Quorn* in May 1932.

[102] Also named (on the other side) *Y Ddraig Goch*.

[103] Nameplates fitted in 1925.

[104] Originally named *Jenny Lind*; renamed in May 1936.

[105] Metre gauge.

[106] Originally named *King John*. Renamed *The Roumanian Monarch* in June or July 1927, and *Roumanian Monarch* in November 1927. The name was removed in November 1940 and the words STAR CLASS painted on the splashers.

[107] Originally named *Wemyss Bay*; renamed *The Royal Army Ordnance Corps* in August 1947.

[108] Built by London Midland & Scottish Railway and originally named *The Leicestershire Regiment*. Renamed in November 1948.

[109] Built by the London Midland & Scottish Railway; name applied by British Railways.

[110] Originally named *Planet*; renamed in May 1936.

[111] 15in gauge.

[112] Originally named *Comet*; renamed January 1936.

[113] *Knight of the Golden Fleece* until 1938. Rebuilt from Star class.

[114] Originally named *Mail*; renamed in July 1934.

[115] *Queen Philippa* until March 1937. Rebuilt from Star class.

[116] Originally named *King Stephen*. Renamed *The Spanish Monarch* in June or July 1927, and further renamed *Spanish Monarch* in November 1927. Nameplates were removed in November 1940, and the words STAR CLASS were painted on the splashers.

Name	Number	Class	Date	Railway
The Storeman	5162	J94	1944	War Department
The Suffolk Regiment	2845	B17/1	6/1935	London & North Eastern Rly
The Swedish Monarch	4030	Star	10/1909	Great Western Rly [117]
The Talisman	419	Scott	9/1914	North British Rly [118]
The Territorial Army 1908–1958	70048	Britannia	7/1954	British Railways
The Tetrarch	2559	A3	3/1925	London & North Eastern Rly
Thetis	–	1Sussex	4/1838	London & South Western Rly [119]
The Toleman Group	47016	47/0	1963	British Railways
"The Tyke"	08745	08	1960	British Railways
The Tynedale	377	D49/2	2/1935	London & North Eastern Rly
The Welch Regiment	6139	Royal Scot	10/1927	London Midland & Scottish Rly [120]
The Welshman	–	**0–6–0ST**	**1890**	**Chatterley Whitfield Mining Museum**
The Wemyss Coal Co. Ltd	20	**0–6–0T**	**1939**	**Bo'ness & Kinneil Rly**
The West Yorkshire Regiment	6130	Royal Scot	8/1927	London Midland & Scottish Rly [121]
The White Knight	2576	A3	10/1924	London & North Eastern Rly
The Wolf	3349	Bulldog	3/1900	Great Western Rly
The York and Ainsty	211	D49/2	5/1932	London & North Eastern Rly
The York & Lancaster Regiment	6142	Royal Scot	10/1927	London Midland & Scottish Rly [122]
The Zetland	220	D49/2	5/1932	London & North Eastern Rly
Thirlestaine Hall	6965	M/Hall	7/1944	Great Western Rly [123]
Thirlwall	41	0–6–0	1855	Newcastle & Carlisle Rly [124]
Thisbe	126	Acis	12/1862	London, Chatham & Dover Rly
Thisbe	6	Ilfracombe	2/1873	Shropshire & Montgomeryshire Rly [125]
Thisbe	–	0–6–2T	1911	Shropshire & Montgomeryshire Rly [126]
T.H. Ismay	1921	Jubilee	1900	London & North Western Rly
Thistle	77	Rose	7/1863	London, Chatham & Dover Rly
Thistle	–	Metro	9/1863	Great Western Rly (bg)
Thistle	–	0–4–0ST	1912	Chatham Dockyard [127]
Thomas	–	**0–6–0T**	**1947**	**Nene Valley Rly**
Thomas	4	**0–4–0ST**	**1950**	**Yorkshire Dales Rly**
Thomas	–	**J94**	**11/1952**	**Mid-Hants Rly** [128]
Thomas	08500	08	1958	British Railways
Thomas	–	**0–4–0VB**	**1979**	**Telford Horsehay Steam Trust** [129]
Thomas Adam	5	N	12/1887	Great North of Scotland Rly
Thomas Bach	2	**0–4–0ST**	**1904**	**Llanberis Lake Rly** [130]
Thomas Barnardo	60055	60	9/1991	British Railways
Thomas B. Macaulay	479	Prince/W	12/1913	London & North Western Rly
Thomas Burt MP 1837–1902	401	**0–6–0ST**	**1950**	**Stephenson Railway Museum & North Tyneside Steam Rly**
Thomas Campbell	2249	Prince/W	12/1913	London & North Western Rly
Thomas Carlyle	265	Precedent	1/1882	London & North Western Rly
Thomas Carlyle	265	rPrecedent	7/1894	London & North Western Rly
Thomas Cook	91008	91	7/1988	British Railways

Name	Number	Class	Date	Railway
Thomas Edmondson	6	**0–4–0T**	**1918**	**South Tynedale Rly** [131]
Thomas Gray	637	Prince/W	1/1914	London & North Western Rly
Thomas Hardy	70034	Britannia	12/1952	British Railways
Thomas Hardy	92012	92		British Railways
Thomas Houghton	2512	George V*	11/1910	London & North Western Rly
Thomas Lord	2	Bo-Bo	1921	Metropolitan Rly [132]
Thomas Moore	2205	Prince/W	11/1913	London & North Western Rly
Thomas Savery	1557	John Hick	1898	London & North Western Rly
Thomas Savery	1498	2Experiment	5/1909	London & North Western Rly
Thomas Telford	47825	47/4	8/1964	British Railways
Thompson	871	**0–6–0DH**	**1966**	**War Department** [133]
Thor	146	Craven	1/1876	East Lancashire Rly
Thor	47091	47/0	1965	British Railways
THOR	47846	47/4	5/1965	British Railways
Thoresby Colliery	58032	58	1985	British Railways
Thoresby Colliery	58046	58	10/1986	British Railways [134]
Thoresby Park	2830	B17/1	4/1931	London & North Eastern Rly [135]
Thorin Oakenshield	16	**4wDM**	**1939**	**Leighton Buzzard Rly** [136]
Thornaby	08817	08	1960	British Railways
Thornaby Demon	37512	37/5	7/1961	British Railways
Thornaby T.M.D.	37069	37/0	1962	British Railways
Thornaby TMD	56069	56	1979	British Railways
Thornbridge Hall	6964	M/Hall	5/1944	Great Western Rly [137]
Thornbury Castle	5063	Castle	6/1937	Great Western Rly [138]
Thornbury Castle	7027	**Castle**	**8/1949**	**British Railways (Western Region)**
Thornhill	3	2–4–0T	1880	Manx Northern Rly [139]
Thornton Heath	380	D3	7/1893	London, Brighton & South Coast Rly
Thornycroft Hall	7924	M/Hall	9/1950	British Railways (Western Region)
Thorpe Hall	2837	B17/1	3/1933	London & North Eastern Rly
Thorpe Marsh Power Station	56077	56	1980	British Railways
Three Bridges	383	D3	12/1893	London, Brighton & South Coast Rly
Three Bridges C.E.D.	09009	09	1959	British Railways
Throwley Hall	6963	M/Hall	4/1944	Great Western Rly [140]
Thruster	D853	Warship	8/1961	British Railways
"Thumper"	752	0–6–0ST	1879	South Eastern & Chatham Rly [141]
Thunderbolt	204	bCrewe	4/1848	London & North Western Rly
Thunderbolt	409	1Precursor	10/1874	London & North Western Rly
Thunderbolt	3079	3031	2/1899	Great Western Rly
Thunderbolt	1102	2Precursor	11/1904	London & North Western Rly
Thunderer	44	0–4–2	1836	Liverpool & Manchester Rly
Thunderer	–	0–4–0	3/1838	Great Western Rly (bg) [142]
Thunderer	41	Goliath	7/1849	East Lancashire Rly
Thunderer	–	Caesar	7/1851	Great Western Rly (bg)
Thunderer	37	0–6–0	8/1856	Birkenhead, Lancashire & Cheshire Junction Rly [143]
Thunderer	504	Dreadnought	1885	London & North Western Rly

[117] Originally named *King Harold*. Renamed *The Swedish Monarch* in July 1927, and *Swedish Monarch* in November 1927. Nameplates were removed in November 1940, and the words STAR CLASS were painted on the splashers.

[118] Ran as *Talisman* from December 1931 to February 1938, and again from May 1940 to March 1947. 9419 is the 1924 number. Became no. 2428 in November 1946, and British Railways no. 62428 in September 1949.

[119] Unsatisfactory in service, it was rebuilt by Fairbairns in 1842, returning as no. 26 *Gazelle*.

[120] Originally named *Ajax*; renamed in May 1936.

[121] Originally named *Liverpool*; renamed in June 1935.

[122] Originally named *Lion*; renamed in May 1936.

[123] Nameplates fitted in September 1947.

[124] Became North Eastern Railway no. 489 in 1862.

[125] Built for the London & South Western Railway as no. 283, later duplicated as no. 0283. This Ilfracombe Goods class engine was withdrawn in December 1913 and sold to the Shropshire & Montgomeryshire Railway in December 1914, becoming their no. 6 *Thisbe*. It was laid aside in September 1935 and finally scrapped in May 1937.

[126] Later became no. 9 of the Longmoor Military Railway.

[127] 18in gauge.

[128] This is the same engine, HE 3781/1952, as *Linda* on the Kent & East Sussex Railway.

[129] 2ft gauge.

[130] 1ft 11½in gauge. Also named *Wild Aster*.

[131] 2ft gauge.

[132] Officially a rebuild of an earlier, unnamed, locomotive built in 1905. Most of the 'rebuilds' were in fact new machines, but the first few might have incorporated some material from the earlier locomotives.

[133] Reported as being at Queenborough rolling mills in 1998.

[134] Originally named *Ashfordby Mine*.

[135] Renamed *Tottenham Hotspur* in January 1938.

[136] 2ft gauge.

[137] Nameplates fitted in June 1947.

[138] Renamed *Earl Baldwin* in July 1937.

[139] 3ft gauge. Became Isle of Man Railway no. 14 when the two railways amalgamated in 1905.

[140] Nameplates fitted in January 1947.

[141] This nickname came from the sound it made when in motion!

[142] Built under a patent of T.E. Harrison, the 0–4–0 chassis, with the cylinders, was separate from the boiler, which followed on a six-wheeled, unpowered, chassis, with the tender behind that. The 6ft driving wheels were geared up in the ratio of 27:10. The engine ceased 'work' at the end of 1839.

[143] Became Great Western Railway no. 101.

Name	Number	Class	Date	Railway
Thunderer	1120	2Precursor	1/1905	London & North Western Rly
Thunderer	5703	Jubilee	1936	London Midland & Scottish Rly
Thunderer	**50008**	**50**	**1968**	**British Railways**
Thundersley	**80**	**79**	**1909**	**London, Tilbury & Southend Rly**
Thurlow	73	Duke	1/1885	Highland Rly [144]
Thurso	13	Belladrum	7/1862	Highland Rly [145]

London, Tilbury & Southend Railway 4–4–2T no. 80 *Thundersley*, at Southend Central, as restored for preservation, on 2 March 1956. (*Photo: LCGB Ken Nunn Collection*)

Name	Number	Class	Date	Railway
Thurso Castle	27	Castle	1913	Highland Rly
Tidmarsh Grange	6847	Grange	10/1937	Great Western Rly
Tiger	–	1Sussex	5/1838	London & South Western Rly [146]
Tiger	8	2–2–0	9/1839	Midland Counties Rly
Tiger	–	Priam	4/1840	Great Western Rly (bg)
Tiger	103	Bison	8/1848	London & South Western Rly
Tiger	117	aCrewe	5/1850	London & North Western Rly [147]
Tiger	121	Peel	3/1857	Stockton & Darlington Rly
Tiger	2116	4–4–0ST	5/1860	Great Western Rly (bg) [148]
Tiger	117	Problem	c.1860	London & North Western Rly
Tiger	16	Tiger	12/1861	London, Chatham & Dover Rly
Tiger	103	Lion	6/1864	London & South Western Rly
Tiger	1439	2Precursor	11/1905	London & North Western Rly
Tiger	–	**0–4–0DH**	**1954**	**Bo'ness & Kinneil Rly**
Tiger	D854	Warship	9/1961	British Railways
Tiger	50028	50	1968	British Railways
Tiger Moth	37004	37/0	1960	British Railways
Tigress	104	Bison	9/1848	London & South Western Rly
Tilbury	3	Class 1	1880	London, Tilbury & Southend Rly
Tilbury Docks	9	Class 1	1880	London, Tilbury & Southend Rly
Tilbury Docks	51	51	1900	London, Tilbury & Southend Rly
Tillington	591	E5	4/1904	London, Brighton & South Coast Rly
Times	3	Times	3/1849	Stockton & Darlington Rly
Times	2198	cSentinel	1929	London & North Eastern Rly
Timour	–	Iron Duke	8/1849	Great Western Rly (bg)
Timour	–	Rover	7/1873	Great Western Rly (bg)

Name	Number	Class	Date	Railway
Timour	3056	3031	3/1895	Great Western Rly [149]
Tinsley TMD Silver Jubilee 41A, 1966–1990	47186	47/0	1964	British Railways
Tinsley Traction Depot Quality Approved	47375	47/3	1965	British Railways
Tintagel	3269	Duke	6/1896	Great Western Rly [150]
Tintagel	3269	Bulldog	5/1907	Great Western Rly
Tintagel	745	King Arthur	11/1919	Southern Rly [151]
Tintagel	73084	5MT	7/1955	British Railways
Tintagel Castle	5011	Castle	7/1927	Great Western Rly
Tintern Abbey	4067	Star	1/1923	Great Western Rly [152]
Tintern Abbey	5087	Castle	11/1940	Great Western Rly [153]
Tiny	–	0–4–0T	5/1862	London & North Western Rly [154]
Tiny	–	0–4–0ST	12/1862	Brecon & Merthyr Rly [155]
Tiny	**2180**	**0–4–0VB**	**1/1868**	**Great Western Rly (bg) [156]**
Tiny	–	**0–4–0ST**	**1949**	**Keighley & Worth Valley Rly**
Tipton	29	0–6–0	1858	South Staffordshire Rly
Titan	34	0–4–0	1834	Liverpool & Manchester Rly
Titan	45	1Hercules	2/1842	London & South Western Rly
Titan	2126	4–4–0ST	10/1866	Great Western Rly (bg) [157]
Titan	18	Clio	9/1867	East Lancashire Rly
Titan	508	Dreadnought	1884	London & North Western Rly

London, Brighton & South Coast Railway E5 class 0–6–2T no. 591 *Tillington*, at East Croydon on 22 June 1912. (*Photo: LCGB Ken Nunn Collection*)

Name	Number	Class	Date	Railway
Titan	3348	Bulldog	3/1900	Great Western Rly
Titan	7	2Precursor	6/1904	London & North Western Rly
Titan	47612	47/4	1965	British Railways
Titania	5	2–2–2WT	1851	Whitehaven & Furness Junction Rly
Tite	–	2–2–2	7/1844	London & South Western Rly [158]
Titley Court	2953	Saint	3/1913	Great Western Rly
Tityos	–	Fury	10/1842	Great Western Rly (bg)
Tiverton Castle	5041	Castle	7/1935	Great Western Rly
T.J. Hare	1195	George V*	10/1910	London & North Western Rly

[144] Renamed *Rosehaugh* in 1898.

[145] Originally named *Lovat*. Renamed *Thurso* in 1874.

[146] An unsatisfactory design, it was rebuilt by Fairbairns in 1842, returning as no. 24 *Elk*.

[147] Previously Liverpool & Manchester Railway 0–4–2 no. 58; became a London & North Western engine in 1846 and was renewed in 1850 as no. 264 *Clarendon*.

[148] Built for the South Devon Railway.

[149] Renamed *Wilkinson* in July 1901.

[150] Nameplates removed in August 1930, to avoid confusion with Castle class locomotives.

[151] Built for the London & South Western Railway to Robert Urie's design. Nameplates fitted by the Southern Railway in 1925.

[152] Rebuilt to Castle class in November 1940 as no. 5087.

[153] Rebuilt from Star class no. 4067.

[154] 18in gauge, Crewe Works Tramway.

[155] Built to the order of Thomas Savin, the contractor who worked both the Brecon & Merthyr Railway and the Cambrian Railways. When he went bankrupt in 1866 *Tiny* was located at Llynclys, on the Cambrian, and in October 1868 it was apparently being used on the line between Porthywaen and Savin's collieries at Coed-y-Go. The B&M valued it

at £500, and sold it to Savin for £450. So *Tiny*, although officially a B&M locomotive, never operated on its home system and never received a B&M number.

[156] Built for the South Devon Railway.

[157] Built for the South Devon Railway.

[158] Originally no. 8 *Cheltenham* of the broad gauge Bristol & Gloucester Railway. In August 1856 it was sold to Thomas Brassey for working the North Devon Railway, a broad gauge concern which later passed to the London & South Western Railway. There it is thought to have become the NDR's *Tite*.

Name	Number	Class	Date	Railway
Toad	–	0–4–0ST	1887	Caldon Low Quarry [159]
Tobago	5635	Jubilee	1934	London Midland & Scottish Rly
Tobruk	1232	Bo-BoDE	1941	Longmoor Military Rly [160]
Toby	–	**0–4–0VB**	**1890**	**Nene Valley Rly**
Tockenham Court	2954	Saint	3/1913	Great Western Rly
Toddington Grange	6848	Grange	10/1937	Great Western Rly
Todmorden	28	2–2–2	2/1841	Manchester & Leeds Rly
Toffo	**2**	**4wDM**	**1959**	**South Yorkshire Rly** [161]
Tom	–	**0–4–0DH**	**1954**	**Telford Steam Rly**
Tomatin	**1**	**4wDM**	**1963**	**Scottish Mining Museum – Prestongrange**
Tom Bombadil	**15**	**4wDM**	**1941**	**Leighton Buzzard Rly** [162]
Tomlinson	2587	0–4–0T	1894	London & North Western Rly

British Railways (ex-LNER) EM1 class Bo-Bo electric locomotive no. 26000 *Tommy*, at Gorton in November 1955. (*Photo: RAS Marketing*)

Name	Number	Class	Date	Railway
Tommy	26000	EM1	1941	London & North Eastern Rly
Tom Paine	**141R73**	**141R**	**1948**	**Société Nationale des Chemins de fer Français** [163]
Tom Parry	–	**0–4–0ST**	**1935**	**Buckinghamshire Railway Centre**
Tom Rolt	**7049**	**0–6–0DM**	**1944**	**Steamtown, Carnforth**
Tom Rolt	**7**	**0–4–2ST**	**1948**	**Talyllyn Rly** [164]
Tonbridge	905	Schools	5/1930	Southern Rly
Tonga	5632	Jubilee	1934	London Midland & Scottish Rly
Tonnidae	47125	47/0	1964	British Railways
Tooting	65	A1	8/1874	London, Brighton & South Coast Rly
Topham	**10**	**0–6–0ST**	**1922**	**North Downs Steam Rly**
Topi	1013	B1	12/1946	London & North Eastern Rly
Top of the Pops	43002	43	2/1976	British Railways
Topsy	–	0–4–0T	1/1867	London & North Western Rly [165]
Tor	31	0–6–0ST	1874	Brecon & Merthyr Rly
Tor Bay	3290	Duke	3/1897	Great Western Rly [166]
Torch	51	2–2–2	1838	Grand Junction Rly
Torch	51	aCrewe	2/1849	London & North Western Rly
Torch	895	L/Bloomer	1851	London & North Western Rly

Name	Number	Class	Date	Railway
Tornado	–	Iron Duke	3/1849	Great Western Rly (bg)
Tornado	2139	0–6–0ST	12/1854	Great Western Rly (bg) [167]
Tornado	803	Problem	c.1860	London & North Western Rly
Tornado	–	Rover	7/1888	Great Western Rly (bg)
Tornado	3026	3031	8/1891	Great Western Rly [168]
Tornado	1995	2Experiment	10/1906	London & North Western Rly
Tornado	70022	Britannia	8/1951	British Railways
Tornado	37073	37/0	1962	British Railways
Toronto	3459	Bulldog	2/1904	Great Western Rly
Torpedo	RL5	0–4–0ST	9/1887	Woolwich Arsenal [169]
Torquay	3372	Bulldog	12/1900	Great Western Rly
Torquay Manor	7800	Manor	1/1938	Great Western Rly
Torridge	3	2–4–2T	1896	Bideford, Westward Ho! & Appledore Light Rly
Torrington	21C131	rWC	6/1946	Southern Rly
Tortworth Court	2955	Saint	4/1913	Great Western Rly
Tory	15	Tory	11/1838	Stockton & Darlington Rly
Total Energy	47379	47/3	1965	British Railways
Totland	W23	O2	10/1890	Southern Rly [170]
Totnes Castle	5031	Castle	5/1934	Great Western Rly
Toton Traction Depot	58050	58	3/1987	British Railways
Tottenham	34	Class 1	1892	London, Tilbury & Southend Rly
Tottenham Hotspur	2830	B17/1	4/1931	London & North Eastern Rly [171]
Tottenham Hotspur	2870	B17/4	5/1937	London & North Eastern Rly [172]
Touchstone	114	2–2–2	1840	Great Western Rly [173]
Toulon	142	E1	3/1879	London, Brighton & South Coast Rly
Toulouse	140	E1	3/1879	London, Brighton & South Coast Rly
Touraine	116	E1	7/1877	London, Brighton & South Coast Rly
Tow Law	57	Shotley	3/1852	Stockton & Darlington Rly [174]
Towneley	20	2–2–2	1/1841	Manchester & Leeds Rly
Townsend Hook	**4**	**0–4–0T**	**1880**	**Amberley Chalk Pits Museum** [175]
Towy	–	?	?	Llanelly Rly
Towy	914	0–6–0	1868	Great Western Rly [176]
Towyn	46	S/Goods	8/1864	Cambrian Railways
Tracery	2558	A3	2/1925	London & North Eastern Rly
Track 29	47479	47/4	1964	British Railways
Trader	12	Tory	9/1842	Stockton & Darlington Rly [177]
Trafalgar	114	2–2–2	8/1844	South Eastern Rly [178]
Trafalgar	221	aCrewe	9/1848	London & North Western Rly
Trafalgar	–	Caesar	6/1853	Great Western Rly (bg)
Trafalgar	221	DX	c.1860	London & North Western Rly
Trafalgar	–	0–4–0ST	12/1871	Chatham Dockyard [179]
Trafalgar	3055	3031	3/1895	Great Western Rly [180]
Trafalgar	1940	Jubilee	1900	London & North Western Rly
Trafalgar	273	aSentinel	1928	London & North Eastern Rly
Trafalgar	5682	Jubilee	1936	London Midland & Scottish Rly
Trajan	128	Adrian	8/1866	London, Chatham & Dover Rly
Tramp	–	2–2–0	10/1836	London & South Western Rly
Tranmere	14	II	1/1888	Mersey Rly
Tranquil	2570	A3	9/1924	London & North Eastern Rly
Transit	3	1Sussex	6/1838	London & South Western Rly
Transit	3	Lion	6/1870	London & South Western Rly
Transit	43305	Clayton	1928	London & North Eastern Rly
Trans-Jordan	5633	Jubilee	1934	London Midland & Scottish Rly

[159] 3ft gauge. Caldon Low Quarry was owned by the London & North Western Railway.

[160] Built by the Whitcomb Locomotive Co. of Rochelle, Illinois, under the US Government's Lend–Lease programme.

[161] The modern, preserved South Yorkshire Railway.

[162] 2ft gauge.

[163] Preserved at Bressingham.

[164] Rebuilt from 3ft gauge locomotive built in 1948 for Bord na Mona (the Irish Turf Board). Regauged to 2ft 3ins and entered service with the Talyllyn Railway in 1991. It was originally intended to name the

locomotive *Irish Pete*, a clever pun on its origins.

[165] 18in gauge, for Crewe Works Tramway.

[166] Originally named *Torbay* (all one word) until December 1903.

[167] Built for the South Devon Railway.

[168] Built as a broad gauge convertible. Rebuilt to 4–2–2 in June 1894.

[169] 18in gauge. Nameless until about 1901.

[170] Originally London & South Western Railway no. 188.

[171] Originally *Thoresby Park*. Renamed *Tottenham Hotspur* in January 1938.

[172] Originally *Manchester City*. Renamed

Tottenham Hotspur (May 1937), and *City of London* and streamlined for working the East Anglian express (September 1937).

[173] Built for the Chester & Birkenhead Railway.

[174] Some sources show this engine as no. 56.

[175] 3ft 2¼in gauge. From Dorking Greystone Lime Co.'s quarry at Betchworth, Surrey.

[176] Built for the Llanelly Railway.

[177] Rebuilt from no. 12 *Briton*, originally built in June 1837.

[178] Built for the Gravesend & Rochester Railway.

[179] 18in gauge.

[180] Renamed *Lambert* in July 1901.

Name	Number	Class	Date	Railway
Transmark	47314	47/3	1965	British Railways
Travancore	5590	Jubilee	1934	London Midland & Scottish Rly
Traveller	2089	George V	8/1911	London & North Western Rly
Traveller	2144	cSentinel	1928	London & North Eastern Rly
Treago Castle	5019	Castle	7/1932	Great Western Rly
Trecatty	–	0–6–0DM	1959	*Gwili Rly*
Tredegar	–	0–6–0	?	Sirhowy Rly [181]
Treffrey	1392	0–6–0T	1873	Great Western Rly [182]
Treflach	55	Small Pass	12/1865	Cambrian Railways
Treforest	–	0–6–0	6/1851	Taff Vale Rly
Treforest	21	0–6–0	1862	Taff Vale Rly
Trefusis	3289	Duke	3/1897	Great Western Rly
Tregeagle	3371	Bulldog	12/1900	Great Western Rly
Tregenna	3291	Duke	3/1897	Great Western Rly [183]
Tregenna Castle	5006	Castle	6/1927	Great Western Rly
Tregothnan	3347	Bulldog	2/1900	Great Western Rly
Trelawney	3369	Bulldog	11/1900	Great Western Rly
Trellech Grange	6828	Grange	2/1937	Great Western Rly
Trematon Castle	5020	Castle	7/1932	Great Western Rly
Tremayne	3370	Bulldog	12/1900	Great Western Rly
Tremorfa Steelworks	37711	37/7	12/1962	British Railways
Tremorfa Steelworks	56073	56	1980	British Railways
Tren Nwyddau Amlwch	47330	47/3	1965	British Railways
Trent	–	2–2–2	9/1839	Birmingham & Derby Junction Rly
Trent	24	2–2–2	1/1841	Manchester & Leeds Rly
Trent	112	Rocklia	4/1849	London & South Western Rly
Trent	830	Samson	8/1864	London & North Western Rly
Trent	112	Lion	2/1869	London & South Western Rly
Trent	830	Whitworth	1/1900	London & North Western Rly
Trent	–	0–6–0ST	?	Aberford Rly [184]
Trent	18	4wDM	1949	*West Lancashire Light Rly* [185]
Trent 2	–	0–4–2	1839	St Helens Rly [186]
Trentham	92	aCrewe	10/1846	London & North Western Rly
Trentham	894	L/Bloomer	1851	London & North Western Rly
Trentham	305	1Experiment	1883	London & North Western Rly
Trentham	2120	2Precursor	5/1905	London & North Western Rly
Trentham Hall	5915	Hall	7/1931	Great Western Rly
Tre Pol and Pen	3271	Duke	7/1896	Great Western Rly
Tre Pol and Pen	37671	37/5	10/1964	British Railways
Tresco	3288	Duke	3/1897	Great Western Rly [187]
Tresco Abbey	4072	Star	2/1923	Great Western Rly [188]
Tresco Abbey	5092	Castle	4/1938	Great Western Rly [189]
Tretower Castle	5064	Castle	6/1937	Great Western Rly [190]
Tretower Castle	5094	Castle	6/1939	Great Western Rly
Trevithick	428	DX	c.1860	London & North Western Rly
Trevithick	–	Victoria	7/1863	Great Western Rly (bg) [191]
Trevithick	3270	Duke	6/1896	Great Western Rly
Trevithick	202	B2	4/1897	London, Brighton & South Coast Rly [192]
Trevithick	2327	Remembrance	4/1935	Southern Rly [193]
Trevone	34096	rWC	11/1949	British Railways (Southern Region)
Trevor Hall	5998	Hall	6/1940	Great Western Rly
Trevose Head	2425	H2	12/1911	Southern Rly [194]
Trewithen	–	0–6–0	1873	Pentewan Rly [195]
Trigo	2595	A3	2/1930	London & North Eastern Rly
Trimbush	60536	A2	5/1949	British Railways (Eastern Region)
Trinidad	3465	Bulldog	3/1904	Great Western Rly
Trinidad	5634	Jubilee	1934	London Midland & Scottish Rly
Trinity Hall	5916	Hall	7/1931	Great Western Rly
Trio	–	0–4–2	1/1838	London & South Western Rly
Triplex	1874	aCrewe	6/1846	London & North Western Rly [196]
Triton	40	0–4–2	8/1848	Manchester, Sheffield & Lincolnshire Rly
Triton	26056	EM1	7/1953	British Railways
Triumph	–	0–6–2T	1934	*Sittingbourne & Kemsley Light Rly* [197]
Triumph	D855	Warship	10/1961	British Railways
Triumph	50042	50	1968	*British Railways*
Trocadero	118	E1	8/1877	London, Brighton & South Coast Rly
Trojan	–	0–4–0ST	1897	*Alexandra (Newport & South Wales) Docks & Rly* [198]
Trojan	D856	Warship	11/1961	British Railways
"Trotter"	3	0–2–4	3/1834	Dundee & Newtyle Rly [199]
Trouville	114	E1	5/1877	London, Brighton & South Coast Rly
Trouville	89	B4	11/1892	London & South Western Rly
True Blue	225	aSentinel	1928	London & North Eastern Rly
True Briton	244	aSentinel	1928	London & North Eastern Rly
Trumpeter	–	0–4–0ST	3/1876	Woolwich Arsenal [200]
Truro	–	0–4–2	12/1853	West Cornwall Rly
Truscott	364	D3	6/1892	London, Brighton & South Coast Rly
Tryfan	D10	Peak	2/1960	British Railways
Tryfan	60094	60	2/1992	British Railways
TSW Today	43010	43	4/1976	British Railways
Tubal	312	bCrewe	5/1853	London & North Western Rly
Tubal	312	DX	c.1860	London & North Western Rly
Tubal	828	Samson	8/1864	London & North Western Rly
Tubal	828	Whitworth	7/1890	London & North Western Rly
Tubal	2017	2Precursor	3/1906	London & North Western Rly
Tubal Cain	8	0–6–0	1854	Whitehaven & Furness Junction Rly
Tubal Cain	26	S/Goods	2/1863	Cambrian Railways
Tudor Grange	6857	Grange	11/1937	Great Western Rly
Tudor Minstrel	E528	A2	2/1948	British Railways (Eastern Region)
Tufton	169	Panther	5/1863	Stockton & Darlington Rly
Tugwell	1	2–4–0	9/1844	Bristol & Gloucester Rly (bg)
Tulsehill	42	A1	6/1877	London, Brighton & South Coast Rly
Tulyar	55015	Deltic	10/1961	*British Railways*
Tunbridge Wells	279	D1	12/1879	London, Brighton & South Coast Rly
"Turbomotive"	6202	Princess	1935	London Midland & Scottish Rly [201]
Turin	302	Lyons	1/1878	London, Brighton & South Coast Rly
Turk	345	bCrewe	9/1854	London & North Western Rly
Turk	345	DX	c.1860	London & North Western Rly
Turk	829	Samson	8/1864	London & North Western Rly
Turk	829	Whitworth	1/1892	London & North Western Rly

[181] Built some time between 1832 and 1853.

[182] Built for the Cornwall Minerals Railway. The name may have been corrected later to *Treffry*.

[183] Nameplates removed in July 1930 to avoid confusion with new Castle class locomotive.

[184] This is probably the same *Trent* that worked on the Easingwold Railway in 1924–5.

[185] 2ft gauge.

[186] Originally no. 23 on the Manchester & Birmingham and London & North Western Railways. Sold in 1860 to the St Helens Railway. When this was absorbed by the LNWR in July 1864 *Trent* became no. 1368. It was sold in the same year to Isaac Boulton as his no. 9. Boulton altered it to 0–6–0ST and sold it in 1871 to the Cowbridge Railway, only to repurchase it and finally sell it in August 1873 to Chell Ironstone Mines.

[187] Renamed *Isle of Tresco* in February 1904.

[188] Rebuilt in April 1938 to Castle class as no. 5092.

[189] Rebuilt from Star class no. 4072.

[190] Renamed *Bishop's Castle* in September 1937.

[191] Shown as *Trevethick* in some official records.

[192] Rebuilt to class B2x in June 1910.

[193] Rebuilt from London, Brighton & South Coast Railway L class 4–6–4T no. 327 *Charles C. Macrae*.

[194] Built for the London, Brighton & South Coast Railway. Nameplates applied by the Southern Railway in August 1926.

[195] 2ft 6in gauge.

[196] Originally no. 54 *Medusa*. Altered to a two-cylinder compound in August 1878 by F.W. Webb. In August 1895 it was again rebuilt, this time as a triple-expansion locomotive, numbered 1874 and named, appropriately, *Triplex*. It was unable to haul a single inspection saloon, the only duty required of it, and was condemned in October 1903.

[197] 2ft 6in gauge.

[198] Became Great Western Railway no. 1340.

[199] 4ft 6in gauge.

[200] 18in gauge.

[201] Originally turbine driven and unnamed, although semi-officially nicknamed the "Turbomotive". Rebuilt by British Railways as a four-cylinder conventional locomotive in August 1952, and named *Princess Anne*. Destroyed in the Harrow and Wealdstone accident on 8 October 1952.

Name	Number	Class	Date	Railway	Name	Number	Class	Date	Railway
Tweed	–	Caesar	2/1857	Great Western Rly (bg)	*Tyne*	–	Caesar	5/1859	Great Western Rly (bg)
Tweed	146	Tweed	12/1858	London & South Western Rly	*Tyne*	11	0–6–0	1865	South Hetton Rly [211]
Tweed	19	0–6–0	1861	Stockton & Darlington Rly [202]	*Tyneside*	–	0–4–0	1835	Wylam Colliery [212]
Tweeddale	90	Strath	5/1892	Highland Rly [203]	*Tyneside*	54	2–2–2	4/1842	Stockton & Darlington Rly [213]
Tweeddale	880	I	8/1906	North British Rly	*Tyneside Venturer*	25	DE Railcar	1931	London & North Eastern Rly
Tweedside	34	cSentinel	1929	London & North Eastern Rly	**Tynwald**	**7**	**2–4–0T**	**1880**	**Isle of Man Rly [214]**
Twells	4	2–2–0	1834	London & Greenwich Rly	*Typhon*	71	2–2–2	5/1841	Grand Junction Rly
Twineham	510	E4	12/1900	London, Brighton & South Coast Rly	*Typhon*	97	2–4–0	3/1850	Manchester, Sheffield &
Twineham Court	2952	Saint	3/1913	Great Western Rly					Lincolnshire Rly
Twin Sisters	–	0–6–0	8/1828	Liverpool & Manchester Rly [204]	*Typhon*	71	bCrewe	5/1853	London & North Western Rly
Twizell	**3**	**0–6–0T**	**1891**	**Beamish Museum**	*Typhon*	–	Caesar	4/1855	Great Western Rly (bg)
T.W. Lewis	**39**	**4wDM**	**1954**	**Leighton Buzzard Rly [205]**	*Typhon*	444	Samson	9/1873	London & North Western Rly
Twll Coed	**8**	**4wDM**	**1956**	**Llanberis Lake Rly [206]**	*Typhon*	444	Whitworth	10/1890	London & North Western Rly
Tyler	12	0–6–0	6/1866	London & South Western Rly (ed) [207]	*Typhon*	1481	George V	4/1913	London & North Western Rly
Tylney Hall	6919	Hall	6/1941	Great Western Rly [208]	**Typhoon**	**7**	**4–6–2**	**1926**	**Romney, Hythe & Dymchurch**
Tyne	11	?	?	St Helens Canal & Rly					**Rly [215]**
Tyne	8	0–4–0	1836	Newcastle & Carlisle Rly [209]	*Typhoon*	37009	37/0	1961	British Railways
Tyne	8	0–6–0	c.1857	Newcastle & Carlisle Rly [210]	*Tyrwhitt*	5657	Jubilee	1934	London Midland & Scottish Rly

[202] Ex-West Hartlepool Harbour & Railway, absorbed by the North Eastern Railway in 1865.

[203] Renamed *Grandtully* in 1897.

[204] Built by Stephenson and used on the construction of the Liverpool & Manchester. Although taken into stock, it was never numbered. Much slower than the other engines, it was used for goods trains, and at night for maintenance duties. Later sold to the Bolton & Leigh Railway. The name, incidentally, probably derives from its having two vertical boilers.

[205] 2ft gauge.

[206] 1ft 11½in gauge.

[207] Originally no. 230 of Loco Dept.

[208] Nameplates fitted in August 1947.

[209] Withdrawn in 1857. Replacement had same name and number.

[210] Became North Eastern Railway no. 457 in 1862.

[211] Believed to be the same engine as *Chancellor*, no. 3 of the Wrexham, Mold & Connah's Quay Railway.

[212] Is this really an industrial locomotive, and so outside the scope of the present work? In his defence, the author submits that in those early years the distinction was not so cut and dried as it later became, and craves the reader's indulgence for including an interesting pioneer.

[213] Some sources give the building date as October 1842.

[214] 3ft gauge.

[215] 15in gauge.

U

Name	Number	Class	Date	Railway
Uckfield	27	D1	3/1876	London, Brighton & South Coast Rly
Udaipur	5591	Jubilee	1934	London Midland & Scottish Rly
Uddingston	107	165	7/1878	North British Rly [1]
Uddingston	109	72	9/1880	North British Rly
Uganda	5636	Jubilee	1934	London Midland & Scottish Rly
Ulleswater	81	2–2–2	1859	Lancaster & Carlisle Rly
Ulleswater	144	Peel	3/1860	Stockton & Darlington Rly
Ullswater	16	0–4–0ST	1875	Whitehaven, Cleator & Egremont Rly
Ulster	5739	Jubilee	1936	London Midland & Scottish Rly
Ulva	87	Scotchmen	8/1866	London, Chatham & Dover Rly
(Ulverstonian)	08678	08	1959	British Railways
Ulysses	28	2–2–2	12/1846	Manchester, Sheffield & Lincolnshire Rly
Ulysses	–	Caesar	7/1853	Great Western Rly (bg)
Ulysses	3058	3031	4/1895	Great Western Rly [2]
Ulysses	26057	EM1	8/1953	British Railways (Eastern Region)
Umberslade Hall	4975	Hall	1/1930	Great Western Rly
Umpire	1000	L/Bloomer	1851	London & North Western Rly
Umpire	36	bCrewe	3/1855	London & North Western Rly
Umpire	2151	cSentinel	1928	London & North Eastern Rly
Umseke	1028	B1	5/1947	London & North Eastern Rly
Una	998	L/Bloomer	1851	London & North Western Rly
Una	297	bCrewe	11/1852	London & North Western Rly
Una	2147	0–6–0ST	1862	Great Western Rly (bg) [3]
Undaunted	D857	Warship	12/1961	British Railways
Underley	83	2–4–0	1859	Lancaster & Carlisle Rly
Underley Hall	6928	Hall	11/1941	Great Western Rly [4]
Undine	163	Undine	12/1859	London & South Western Rly
Unicorn	47	2–2–0	8/1840	Stockton & Darlington Rly [5]
Unicorn	233	aCrewe	3/1849	London & North Western Rly
Unicorn	2157	Samson	11/1874	London & North Western Rly
Unicorn	2157	Whitworth	11/1896	London & North Western Rly
(Unicorn)	08060	08	1953	British Railways
Union	–	2–2–0	1830	Bolton & Leigh Rly
Union	186	Windsor	2/1865	Stockton & Darlington Rly
Union	–	0–4–0ST	?	Garstang & Knott End Rly [6]
Union	2101	Clayton	1928	London & North Eastern Rly
Union Castle	21C2	MN	6/1941	Southern Rly
Union of South Africa	4488	A4	6/1937	London & North Eastern Rly [7]
Unique	–	2–4–0Fs	1924	Sittingbourne & Kemsley Light Rly [8]
United Provinces	5578	Jubilee	1934	London Midland & Scottish Rly
United States Lines	21C12	MN	1/1945	Southern Rly
United Transport Europe	47218	47/0	1965	British Railways
University of Bradford	43056	43	7/1977	British Railways
University of Dundee	47550	47/4	1964	British Railways
University of East Anglia	86237	86/2	1965	British Railways
University of Edinburgh	47470	47/4	1964	British Railways
University of Exeter	43177	43	11/1981	British Railways
University of Kent at Canterbury	73112	73/1	1966	British Railways
University of Leicester	47535	47/4	1965	British Railways
University of London	86634	86/6	10/1965	British Railways
University of Nottingham	47444	47/4	1964	British Railways
University of Oxford	47705	47/7	1967	British Railways
University of Stirling	47677	47/6	5/1964	British Railways
University of Strathclyde	47640	47/4	1/1966	British Railways
University of Surrey	73117	73/1	1966	British Railways
Upminster	21	Class 1	1884	London, Tilbury & Southend Rly
Upnor Castle	–	0–4–0DM	1954	Festiniog Rly [9]
Upperton	361	D1	1/1887	London, Brighton & South Coast Rly
Uppingham	–	0–4–0ST	1912	Rutland Railway Museum
Uppingham	923	Schools	12/1933	Southern Rly [10]
Upton	29	4–2–0	7/1841	Birmingham & Gloucester Rly
Upton Castle	5065	Castle	7/1937	Great Western Rly [11]
Upton Castle	5093	Castle	6/1939	Great Western Rly
Upton Park	6	Class 1	1880	London, Tilbury & Southend Rly
Uranus	93	2–2–2	1847	Stockton & Darlington Rly [12]
Uranus	93	0–6–0	4/1867	Stockton & Darlington Rly
Urquhart Castle	35	Castle	1911	Highland Rly
Usk	–	0–4–0WT?	?	Alexandra (Newport & South Wales) Docks & Rly [13]
Usk	15	0–6–0ST	12/1862	Brecon & Merthyr Rly
Usk	9	2–4–0	4/1865	Brecon & Merthyr Rly [14]
Usk Castle	5032	Castle	5/1934	Great Western Rly
Uskmouth No 1	–	0–4–0ST	1952	Dean Forest Rly
Utilis	–	0–4–2	1832	Bolton & Leigh Rly [15]
Utrillas	35	0–4–0WT	1907	West Lancashire Light Rly [16]

[1] Later renamed *Leuchars*.
[2] Renamed *Grierson* in May 1895.
[3] Built for the South Devon Railway.
[4] Nameplates fitted in September 1947.
[5] Formerly no. 15 *Unicorn* of the Midland Counties Railway, purchased in 1844. Bury type.
[6] Purchased in 1875 from the Lancashire Union Railway.
[7] Temporarily renamed *Osprey* in the late 1980s.
[8] 2ft 6in gauge. Fireless locomotive.
[9] 1ft 11½in gauge.
[10] Before entering service, this engine was renamed *Bradfield* following objections from the headmaster at Uppingham School. He considered that displaying the school's name on a locomotive constituted advertising, which he did not deem proper.
[11] Renamed *Newport Castle* in September 1937.
[12] Purchased from the Edinburgh & Glasgow Railway in 1855.
[13] May just possibly have been Brecon & Merthyr Railway no. 15; no. 15 was sold to one C.D. Phillips in July 1881, and was working on a Newport dock contract in 1885.
[14] Renumbered 21 in 1888.
[15] Said to have been later rebuilt as a 2–4–2; if so, this must have been the only 2–4–2 tender engine ever to run in this country.
[16] 1ft 11½in gauge.

V

Name	Number	Class	Date	Railway
Vale of Pickering	59203	59/2		NationalPower
Vale of Rheidol	37426	37/4	1965	British Railways [1]
Vale of York	59201	59/2		NationalPower
Valiant	5707	Jubilee	1936	London Midland & Scottish Rly
Valiant	**50015**	**50**	**1968**	**British Railways**
Valliant	21	aSentinel	1927	London & North Eastern Rly
Valorous	D858	Warship	12/1961	British Railways
Valour	1165	9P	7/1920	Great Central Rly
Vampire	43	2–2–2	1838	Grand Junction Rly
Vampire	30	2–2–0	10/1840	Midland Counties Rly
Vampire	43	bCrewe	10/1848	London & North Western Rly
Vampire	885	Samson	10/1874	London & North Western Rly [2]
Vampire	885	Whitworth	1/1896	London & North Western Rly
Vampire	37013	37/0	1961	British Railways
Vancouver	3463	Bulldog	3/1904	Great Western Rly

Great Central Railway 9P class 4–6–0 no. 1165 *Valour*, at King's Cross on 3 May 1924, in early LNER days. (*Photo: LCGB Ken Nunn Collection*)

Name	Number	Class	Date	Railway
Vandal	59	2–2–2	1839	Grand Junction Rly
Vandal	36	2–2–0	4/1841	Midland Counties Rly
Vandal	59	aCrewe	7/1848	London & North Western Rly
Vandal	980	S/Bloomer	1854	London & North Western Rly
Vandal	138	Saxon	4/1857	London & South Western Rly
Vandal	2060	Dreadnought	1885	London & North Western Rly
Vandal	1117	2Precursor	11/1904	London & North Western Rly
Vanguard	2998	Saint	3/1903	Great Western Rly [3]
Vanguard	2220	George V	8/1911	London & North Western Rly
Vanguard	D801	Warship	11/1958	British Railways
Vanguard	50024	50		British Railways
Vanquisher	D859	Warship	1/1962	British Railways
Van Tromp	–	0–6–0	3/1845	Gravesend & Rochester Rly [4]
Varna	348	bCrewe	9/1854	London & North Western Rly

Name	Number	Class	Date	Railway
Vasidae	47278	47/0	1965	British Railways
Vauban	–	0–4–0ST	11/1877	Woolwich Arsenal [5]
Vaughan Williams	92041	92		British Railways
Vauxhall	27	0–6–0	1858	South Staffordshire Rly
Velindre	1	0–6–0ST	1905	Gwendraeth Valleys Rly [6]
Velinheli	**–**	**0–4–0ST**	**1886**	**Launceston Steam Rly [7]**
Velocipede	187	aCrewe	11/1847	London & North Western Rly
Velocipede	302	1Experiment	1883	London & North Western Rly
Velocipede	2584	2Precursor	11/1906	London & North Western Rly
Velocipede	6148	Royal Scot	11/1927	London Midland & Scottish Rly [8]
Velocity	60538	A2	6/1948	British Railways (Eastern Region)
Velocity	87023	87	1974	British Railways
Venice	307	Lyons	4/1878	London, Brighton & South Coast Rly
VENICE SIMPLON ORIENT EXPRESS	47791	47/7		British Railways
Ventnor	125	2–2–2	7/1857	London, Brighton & South Coast Rly [9]
Ventnor	–	2–4–0T	1868	Isle of Wight Rly [10]
Ventnor	W12	A1	9/1880	Southern Rly [11]
Ventnor	333	F	8/1881	London, Brighton & South Coast Rly
Ventnor	W16	O2	6/1892	Southern Rly [12]
Venum	37072	37/0	1962	British Railways
Venus	18	2–2–0	1831	Liverpool & Manchester Rly
Venus	7	Chaplin	6/1838	London & South Western Rly
Venus	–	Wolf	9/1838	Great Western Rly (bg)
Venus	8	2–2–2	7/1840	London & Brighton and South Eastern Railways Joint Committee [13]
Venus	25	?	1/1841	Newcastle & Carlisle Rly [14]
Venus	–	Priam	10/1841	Great Western Rly (bg)
Venus	–	2–4–0	9/1844	London & South Western Rly (bg) [15]
Venus	73	2–2–2WT	7/1850	Manchester, Sheffield & Lincolnshire Rly
Venus	41	2–4–0	1857	Taff Vale Rly
Venus	152	Panther	7/1860	Stockton & Darlington Rly
Venus	7	Lion	7/1870	London & South Western Rly
Venus	2	0–4–2WT	1885	Longmoor Military Rly [16]
Venus	HMF 13.906	0–6–0DH	1944	Longmoor Military Rly [17]
Venus	70023	Britannia	8/1951	British Railways
Verdun	615	C	7/1889	North British Rly
Vernon	251	bCrewe	1/1850	London & North Western Rly
Vernon	5661	Jubilee	1934	London Midland & Scottish Rly
Verona	121	E1	7/1878	London, Brighton & South Coast Rly
Versailles	112	E1	4/1877	London, Brighton & South Coast Rly
Vespasian	129	Adrian	8/1886	London, Chatham & Dover Rly
Vesper	–	Caesar	3/1854	Great Western Rly (bg)
Vesta	24	2–2–0	1831	Liverpool & Manchester Rly
Vesta	56	2–2–2	1837	Liverpool & Manchester Rly [18]
Vesta	8	Chaplin	8/1838	London & South Western Rly
Vesta	–	Priam	12/1841	Great Western Rly (bg)
Vesta	7	2–2–2	4/1842	Manchester, Sheffield & Lincolnshire Rly

1. Named on one side only. On the other side, the locomotive is named *Y Lein Fach*.
2. Transferred to Engineer's Department 1897–May 1923, and named *Engineer*.
3. Named *Vanguard* in March 1907, and renamed *Ernest Cunard* in December 1907.
4. Later became South Eastern Railway no. 116.
5. 18in gauge.
6. Shown bearing the name *Kidwelly* in the makers' photograph. Later Great Western Railway no. 26.
7. 2ft gauge.
8. Renamed *The Manchester Regiment* in October 1935.
9. Name applied by Stroudley in March 1871.
10. Later Southern Railway no. W15. Scrapped in 1925.
11. Originally London, Brighton & South Coast Railway no. 84 *Crowborough*. Sold to the Isle of Wight Central Railway in November 1903, becoming their no. 12, and nameless. Named *Ventnor* by the Southern Railway. Withdrawn in May 1936.
12. Previously London & South Western Railway (and Southern Railway) no. 217. Named *Ventnor* by the Southern Railway on transfer to the Isle of Wight.
13. Became South Eastern Railway no. 51.
14. Either 0–6–0 or 0–4–2. Became North Eastern Railway no. 473 in 1862.
15. Originally no. 2 *Industry* on the Bristol & Gloucester Railway, a broad gauge concern which was later taken over by the Midland Railway, who renumbered it 269. In 1856 the locomotive was sold to Thomas Brassey for working the North Devon Railway, a broad gauge line which later passed to the London & South Western Railway. It is thought to have become the NDR's *Venus*.
16. 18in gauge. Came in 1906 from the School of Military Engineering, Chatham, who in turn obtained it from the Royal Arsenal Railway at Woolwich.
17. 750mm gauge. Built by Gmeinder & Co. of Mosbach (works no. 4147), 1944. Originally used for hauling V2 rockets.
18. Replacement for above engine.

Name	Number	Class	Date	Railway
Vesta	365	aCrewe	5/1855	London & North Western Rly
Vesta	8	Lion	7/1870	London & South Western Rly
Vesta	–	0–6–0T	1916	**Penrhyn Castle Industrial Railway Museum** [19]
Vesta	6137	Royal Scot	9/1927	London Midland & Scottish Rly [20]
Vesuvius	43	2–2–2	1836	Liverpool & Manchester Rly [21]
Vesuvius	–	Fury	9/1846	Great Western Rly (bg)
Vesuvius	119	1Vesuvius	10/1851	London & South Western Rly
Vesuvius	111	0–6–0	11/1852	Manchester, Sheffield & Lincolnshire Rly
Vesuvius	119	2Vesuvius	12/1869	London & South Western Rly
Vesuvius	644	Dreadnought	1888	London & North Western Rly
Vesuvius	1137	2Precursor	1/1905	London & North Western Rly
Veteran	–	0–4–0	5/1831	Bolton & Leigh Rly [22]
Viceroy	320	bCrewe	5/1854	London & North Western Rly
Vich Ian Vohr	361	Scott	12/1911	North British Rly
Victim Support	47787	47/7		British Railways
Victor	–	0–6–0	1864	Llanelly Rly [23]
Victor	307	1Experiment	1883	London & North Western Rly
Victor	1430	2Precursor	5/1905	London & North Western Rly
Victor	2996	0–6–0ST	1951	**Strathspey Rly**
Victor	–	4wDM	1953	**Sittingbourne & Kemsley Light Rly** [24]
Victor	37298	37/0	1965	British Railways
Victor Emanuel	–	Victoria	10/1856	Great Western Rly (bg)
Victor Hugo	1134	Prince/W	10/1913	London & North Western Rly
Victor Hugo	92001	92		British Railways
Victoria	–	0–6–0	1832	Bolton & Leigh Rly [25]
Victoria	5	2–2–0WT	5/1836	London & Greenwich Rly
Victoria	14	0–4–0	1838	Newcastle & Carlisle Rly
Victoria	–	Rennie	11/1838	London & South Western Rly [26]
Victoria	–	0–6–0	1839	Llanelly Rly
Victoria	6	4–2–0	7/1839	Birmingham & Gloucester Rly
Victoria	–	2–2–2	1840	Lancaster & Preston Junction Rly
Victoria	9	2–2–2	11/1845	Chester & Birkenhead Rly
Victoria	7	2–2–2T	1850	London & Blackwall Rly
Victoria	83	Peel	7/1854	Stockton & Darlington Rly
Victoria	–	Victoria	8/1856	Great Western Rly (bg)
Victoria	3	0–6–0T	1857	Whitehaven, Cleator & Egremont Rly [27]
Victoria	899	0–4–2	1857	Great Western Rly [28]
Victoria	153	Canute	6/1859	London & South Western Rly
Victoria	827	Problem	c.1860	London & North Western Rly
Victoria	8	0–6–6–0F	1866	Burry Port & Gwendraeth Valley Rly [29]
Victoria	256	Victoria	12/1868	London, Brighton & South Coast Rly [30]
Victoria	1	S/Goods	6/1872	Cambrian Railways
Victoria	–	0–4–0ST	11/1873	Woolwich Arsenal [31]
Victoria	9	2–2–2	9/1884	Great Western Rly [32]
Victoria	614	0–4–4T	4/1886	Lancashire & Yorkshire Rly
Victoria	11	II	12/1887	Mersey Rly [33]
Victoria	365	D3	7/1892	London, Brighton & South Coast Rly
Victoria	–	2–4–0T	1895	Rye & Camber Tramway [34]
Victoria	723	721	1896	Caledonian Rly
Victoria	65	51	1903	London, Tilbury & Southend Rly
Victoria	2112	2Experiment	9/1907	London & North Western Rly
Victoria	5565	Jubilee	1934	London Midland & Scottish Rly
Victoria and Albert	21	2–2–2	7/1848	Shrewsbury & Chester Rly
Victoria and Albert	1944	Alfred	6/1901	London & North Western Rly
Victorious	1950	Alfred	6/1901	London & North Western Rly
Victorious	D860	Warship	1/1962	British Railways
Victorious	50036	50	1968	British Railways
Victor Wild	4474	A3	3/1923	London & North Eastern Rly [35]
Victory	8	0–6–0	1829	Stockton & Darlington Rly
Victory	22	2–2–0	1831	Liverpool & Manchester Rly
Victory	–	2–2–2	1838	Sheffield & Rotherham Rly
Victory	123	DX	c.1860	London & North Western Rly
Victory	234	0–4–0ST	1880	War Department
Victory	1	0–4–0ST	1919	Birmingham Museum of Science and Industry [36]
Victory	–	0–6–0T	3/1920	Llanelly & Mynydd Mawr Rly [37]
Victory	5712	Jubilee	1936	London Midland & Scottish Rly
Victory	–	0–4–0ST	1945	**Colne Valley Rly** [38]
Victory	–	0–4–0ST	1945	**Caerphilly Railway Society**
Victory	09025	09	1962	British Railways
Vienna	148	E1	10/1880	London, Brighton & South Coast Rly
Vigilant	37	Dawn	11/1862	London, Chatham & Dover Rly
Vigilant	–	0–4–0ST	1882	**Northamptonshire Ironstone Railway Trust**
Vigilant	D861	Warship	2/1962	British Railways
Viking	37057	37/0	1962	British Railways
Viking	D862	Warship	3/1962	British Railways
Village of Chantry	59102	59/1	10/1990	ARC Ltd
Village of Great Elm	59104	59/1	10/1990	ARC Ltd
Village of Mells	59103	59/1	10/1990	ARC Ltd
Village of Whatley	59101	59/1	10/1990	ARC Ltd
Vimiera	1675	Newton	4/1868	London & North Western Rly
Vimiera	1675	rPrecedent	5/1891	London & North Western Rly
Vindictive	13	Claughton	7/1920	London & North Western Rly [39]
Vindictive	5726	Jubilee	1936	London Midland & Scottish Rly
Violet	224	aCrewe	9/1848	London & North Western Rly
Violet	224	DX	c.1860	London & North Western Rly
Violet	38	Dawn	4/1863	London, Chatham & Dover Rly
Violet	763	Samson	5/1863	London & North Western Rly
Violet	–	Metro	7/1864	Great Western Rly (bg)
Violet	763	Whitworth	3/1893	London & North Western Rly
Viper	–	Wolf	8/1838	Great Western Rly (bg) [40]
Viper	16	0–6–0	12/1852	South Staffordshire Rly
Virago	375	bCrewe	10/1855	London & North Western Rly
Virgil	–	Bogie	9/1854	Great Western Rly (bg)
Virgo	–	Leo	12/1841	Great Western Rly (bg)
Viscount	105	bCrewe	5/1847	London & North Western Rly
Viscount	402	1Precursor	9/1874	London & North Western Rly

[19] 1ft 11½in gauge.

[20] Renamed *The Prince of Wales' Volunteers (South Lancashire)* in May 1936.

[21] Became London & North Western Railway no. 125 in 1846.

[22] Later rebuilt to 0–6–0.

[23] Later went to Cardigan & Carmarthen Railway.

[24] 2ft 6in gauge.

[25] Later rebuilt to 0–4–2T.

[26] An unsuccessful design, the entire class was sent to Fairbairns for rebuilding. *Victoria* returned as no. 20 *Princess*, November 1841.

[27] Became Furness Railway no. 113.

[28] Built for the Llanelly Railway.

[29] A Fairlie articulated locomotive with double boiler, originally built to 3ft 6in gauge for service in Queensland, Australia. It was rebuilt in May 1896, and seems to have been quite successful on the Burry Port & Gwendraeth Valley Railway. It was by far the most powerful locomotive on that line.

[30] Rebuilt by Stroudley and name applied in October 1871; renumbered 483 in October 1881.

[31] 18in gauge. Renamed *Boxer* in about 1901.

[32] This 2–2–2 passenger locomotive was reconstructed from an experimental 4–2–4 express passenger tank locomotive. Probably inspired by the very successful broad gauge 4–2–4Ts designed by James Pearson for the Bristol & Exeter Railway, this engine was a complete failure. It derailed itself while still in Swindon Works, and never entered service. Indeed, for many years the GWR denied all knowledge of the engine! The rebuild, which incorporated a few parts of the original, lasted until March 1905. Work on a second 4–2–4T was halted, and the parts were incorporated in a 2–2–2, no. 10 *Royal Albert*.

[33] Later Alexandra (Newport & South Wales) Docks and Railway no. 6.

[34] 3ft gauge.

[35] Converted from Class A1 in 1942.

[36] 2ft gauge. Later renamed *Leonard*.

[37] Became Great Western Railway no. 704.

[38] Built by Andrew Barclay, Kilmarnock, as works no. 2199. The following locomotive, now with the Caerphilly Railway Society, was also built by Andrew Barclay, as works no. 2201.

[39] Later renumbered 2430.

[40] Renamed *Teign* in 1846. Original name restored in 1851.

Name	Number	Class	Date	Railway
Viscount	1737	2Precursor	3/1905	London & North Western Rly
Viscount Churchill	2975	Saint	3/1905	Great Western Rly [41]
Viscount Churchill	2984	Saint	7/1905	Great Western Rly [42]
Viscount Churchill	111	Castle	9/1924	Great Western Rly [43]
Viscount Horne	5086	Castle	12/1937	Great Western Rly [44]
Viscount Portal	7000	Castle	5/1946	Great Western Rly
Viscount Ridley	1241	B1	10/1947	London & North Eastern Rly [45]
Viso	112	0–6–0	1852	Manchester, Sheffield & Lincolnshire Rly [46]
Vivid	35	Vivid	7/1839	London & South Western Rly
Vivid	35	2Hercules	8/1854	London & South Western Rly
Vivien	748	King Arthur	8/1922	Southern Rly [47]
Vivien	73117	5MT	11/1955	British Railways
Vixen	–	Caesar	6/1854	Great Western Rly (bg)
Vizier	23	2–2–2	1837	Grand Junction Rly
Vizier	38	Vivid	9/1839	London & South Western Rly
Vizier	35	2–2–0	4/1841	Midland Counties Rly
Vizier	23	2–2–2	11/1842	Grand Junction Rly
Vizier	1	0–6–0	12/1846	Lancaster & Carlisle Rly
Vizier	23	bCrewe	5/1854	London & North Western Rly
Vizier	38	Lion	6/1871	London & South Western Rly
Vizier	2148	1Precursor	8/1874	London & North Western Rly
Vizier	2202	2Precursor	10/1905	London & North Western Rly
Voice of the North	91026	91	11/1990	British Railways
Volante	32	2–4–0T	1/1856	Birkenhead, Lancashire & Cheshire Junction Rly [48]
Volcano	–	Caesar	6/1851	Great Western Rly (bg)
Volcano	117	1Vesuvius	8/1851	London & South Western Rly
Volcano	2140	0–6–0ST	11/1854	Great Western Rly (bg) [49]
Volcano	117	Volcano	8/1869	London & South Western Rly
Voltaire	92038	92		Société Nationale des Chemins de fer Français
Volunteer	9	0–4–2	12/1860	Cambrian Railways
(Volunteer)	13014	08	1952	British Railways
Vortigern	4	2–2–2	2/1842	South Eastern Rly
Vortigern	S4	0–4–0DM	1941	Admiralty
Voltigeur	33	2–4–0T	2/1856	Birkenhead, Lancashire & Cheshire Junction Rly [50]
Voltigeur	3059	3031	4/1895	Great Western Rly [51]
Vortimer	5	2–2–2	2/1842	South Eastern Rly
Vrachtverbinding	90128	90/0	3/1989	British Railways
Vulcan	19	2–2–0	1831	Liverpool & Manchester Rly
Vulcan	–	0–6–0	4/1835	Leicester & Swannington Rly
Vulcan	–	Wolf	11/1837	Great Western Rly (bg)

Name	Number	Class	Date	Railway
Vulcan	44	0–6–0	5/1846	Joint Board of Management [52]
Vulcan	33	2–4–0	6/1847	Manchester, Sheffield & Lincolnshire Rly
Vulcan	22	2–2–2	11/1849	Shrewsbury & Birmingham Rly
Vulcan	115	1Vesuvius	7/1851	London & South Western Rly
Vulcan	275	bCrewe	11/1851	London & North Western Rly
Vulcan	29	0–6–0	1853	Taff Vale Rly
Vulcan	14	0–6–0	8/1860	Whitehaven & Furness Junction Rly
Vulcan	73	Aeolus	3/1861	London, Chatham & Dover Rly
Vulcan	3	0–6–0	11/1862	Brecon & Merthyr Rly
Vulcan	115	Volcano	8/1869	London & South Western Rly
Vulcan	275	Newton	9/1870	London & North Western Rly
Vulcan	2169	0–6–0ST	3/1874	Great Western Rly (bg) [53]
Vulcan	118	0–4–0ST	8/1878	London & South Western Rly [54]
Vulcan	–	0–4–2T	1883	School of Military Engineering, Chatham [55]
Vulcan	275	rPrecedent	1/1888	London & North Western Rly
Vulcan	3330	Duke	7/1899	Great Western Rly
Vulcan	3330	Bulldog	12/1908	Great Western Rly
Vulcan	–	0–4–0ST	1918	**Peak Rail**
Vulcan	6133	Royal Scot	9/1927	London Midland & Scottish Rly [56]
Vulcan	75	0–6–0D	1936	War Department
Vulcan	9312	WD2–8–0	1945	War Department
Vulcan	70024	Britannia	10/1951	British Railways
Vulcan	37087	37/0	1962	British Railways
Vulcan	47623	47/4	1965	British Railways
Vulcan Enterprise	37905	37/9	4/1963	British Railways
Vulcan Heritage	86228	86/2	1965	British Railways
Vulture	47	2–2–2	1838	Grand Junction Rly
Vulture	9	2–2–2	9/1839	Midland Counties Rly
Vulture	7	2–2–2	5/1840	London & Brighton and South Eastern Railways Joint Committee [57]
Vulture	–	Priam	10/1840	Great Western Rly (bg)
Vulture	30	1Eagle	12/1844	London & South Western Rly
Vulture	47	aCrewe	5/1847	London & North Western Rly
Vulture	853	L/Bloomer	1851	London & North Western Rly
Vulture	4	Tiger	8/1861	London, Chatham & Dover Rly
Vulture	30	2Eagle	12/1862	London & South Western Rly
Vulture	–	0–6–0ST	11/1863	Swansea Vale Rly
Vulture	1165	1Precursor	11/1878	London & North Western Rly
Vulture	–	0–4–2T	1885	Woolwich Arsenal [58]
Vulture	2257	2Precursor	8/1905	London & North Western Rly

[41] Renamed *Sir Ernest Palmer* (February 1924) and *Lord Palmer* (October 1933).

[42] Originally named *Churchill*; renamed *Viscount Churchill* in 1906, and *Guy Mannering* in 1907.

[43] Rebuilt in 1924 from Churchward's 4–6–2 locomotive *The Great Bear*.

[44] Rebuilt from Star class engine no. 4066, previously named *Malvern Abbey* and *Sir Robert Horne*.

[45] Nameplates only fitted in December 1947.

[46] Became Oxford, Worcester & Wolverhampton Railway no. 33.

[47] Built for the London & South Western Railway. Nameplates applied by the Southern Railway in 1925.

[48] Later became Great Western Railway no. 97.

[49] Built for the South Devon Railway.

[50] Became Great Western Railway no. 98.

[51] Renamed *John W. Wilson* in March 1908.

[52] Birmingham & Gloucester and Bristol & Gloucester Railways, formed on 14 January 1845. Standard gauge. The locomotives passed to the Midland Railway on 3 August 1846, and were renumbered into Midland stock wef February 1847.

[53] Formerly the South Devon Railway, absorbed by the GWR in 1876.

[54] Built for the Southampton Docks Co.

[55] 18in gauge.

[56] Renamed *The Green Howards* in May 1936.

[57] Became London & Brighton Railway no. 15.

[58] 18in gauge.

W

Name	Number	Class	Date	Railway
Wadborough	35	0–4–2	1/1844	Birmingham & Gloucester Rly
Waddon	**54**	**A1**	**2/1876**	**London, Brighton & South Coast Rly [1]**
Wadebridge	**21C107**	**WC**	**8/1945**	**Southern Rly**
Waggoner	**192**	**J94**	**1953**	**Museum of Army Transport, Beverley**
Wagner	92019	92		British Railways
(Wainwright)	**70**	**USA**	**1943**	**Southern Rly [2]**
Wakefield	32	2–2–2	3/1841	Manchester & Leeds Rly
Wakering	71	69	1903	London, Tilbury & Southend Rly
Walberton	561	E4	11/1901	London, Brighton & South Coast Rly
Wales	–	0–6–0	1843	Llanelly Rly [3]
Waleswood	**–**	**0–4–0ST**	**1906**	**Battlefield Steam Rly**
Wallington	12	D1	7/1874	London, Brighton & South Coast Rly
Wallsworth Hall	5974	Hall	4/1937	Great Western Rly
Walrus	**3271**	**0–4–0DM**	**1949**	**Cholsey & Wallingford Rly**
Walrus	**2**	**4wDM**	**1952**	**Groudle Glen Rly [4]**
Walrus	33009	33/0	1961	British Railways
Walsall	2	2–2–2	3/1849	South Staffordshire Rly
Walsingham	2802	B17/1	11/1928	London & North Eastern Rly [5]
Walter	6	2–2–0WT	11/1836	London & Greenwich Rly [6]
Walter Burgh Gair	433	11E	10/1913	Great Central Rly
Walter K Whigham	4487	A4	4/1937	London & North Eastern Rly [7]
Walter Long	3426	Bulldog	5/1903	Great Western Rly
Walter Robinson	3057	3031	4/1895	Great Western Rly [8]
Waltham	–	0–4–0T	1916	Woolwich Arsenal [9]
Walthamstow	36	Class 1	1892	London, Tilbury & Southend Rly
Walton Grange	6849	Grange	10/1937	Great Western Rly
Walton Hall	5918	Hall	7/1931	Great Western Rly
Walton Park	4	0–6–0ST	1908	Weston, Clevedon & Portishead Rly [10]
Walworth	32	D1	5/1876	London, Brighton & South Coast Rly
Wanborough	402	E5	9/1904	London, Brighton & South Coast Rly
Wandering Willie	499	Scott	11/1920	North British Rly
Wandle	58	A1	11/1875	London, Brighton & South Coast Rly
Wandsworth	2	D1	12/1873	London, Brighton & South Coast Rly
Wanstead	33	Class 1	1892	London, Tilbury & Southend Rly
Wantage Hall	5962	Hall	7/1936	Great Western Rly
Wapping	71	A1	1/1872	London, Brighton & South Coast Rly [11]
Warbleton	221	D1	7/1885	London, Brighton & South Coast Rly
Wardley Hall	5950	Hall	4/1935	Great Western Rly
Wardley Opencast	56130	56	1984	British Railways
Wardour Castle	5066	Castle	7/1937	Great Western Rly [12]
Warfield Hall	4976	Hall	1/1930	Great Western Rly
Warhawk	–	Caesar	3/1861	Great Western Rly (bg)
Warlock	–	Iron Duke	8/1848	Great Western Rly (bg)
Warlock	–	Rover	11/1876	Great Western Rly (bg)
Warlock	3060	3031	4/1895	Great Western Rly [13]
Warnham	270	D1	5/1880	London, Brighton & South Coast Rly
Warningcamp	581	E4	9/1903	London, Brighton & South Coast Rly
Warrington	–	2–2–0	4/1831	Warrington & Newton Rly
Warrington	**150**	**J94**	**1944**	**Peak Rail**
Warrington Yard	47311	47/3	1965	British Railways
Warrior	349	bCrewe	9/1854	London & North Western Rly
Warrior	–	Caesar	3/1861	Great Western Rly (bg)
Warrior	426	1Precursor	10/1874	London & North Western Rly
Warrior	1925	Jubilee	1900	London & North Western Rly
Warrior	**–**	**J94**	**1954**	**Dean Forest Rly**
Warrior	D863	Warship	4/1962	British Railways
Warspite	5724	Jubilee	1936	London Midland & Scottish Rly
Warspite	50014	50	1968	British Railways
Warwick Castle	4081	Castle	3/1924	Great Western Rly
Warwickshire	1002	2Experiment	12/1909	London & North Western Rly
Warwickshire	**–**	**0–6–0ST**	**1926**	**Severn Valley Rly**
Warwickshire	320	D49/3	5/1928	London & North Eastern Rly [14]
Washington	12	4–2–0	8/1840	Birmingham & Gloucester Rly
Wasp	241	bCrewe	5/1849	London & North Western Rly
Wasp	979	S/Bloomer	1854	London & North Western Rly
Wasp	–	Metro	8/1862	Great Western Rly (bg)
Wasp	–	0–4–0ST	1891	Lancashire & Yorkshire Rly [15]
Wastwater	17	0–6–0ST	1898	Whitehaven, Cleator & Egremont Rly [16]
Watcombe Hall	4977	Hall	1/1930	Great Western Rly
Waterbuck	1011	B1	11/1946	London & North Eastern Rly
Waterfield	457	E3	12/1895	London, Brighton & South Coast Rly
Waterford	3310	Badminton	1/1899	Great Western Rly
Waterloo	4	2–2–2	8/1848	Liverpool, Crosby & Southport Rly [17]
Waterloo	220	aCrewe	8/1848	London & North Western Rly
Waterloo	220	DX	c.1860	London & North Western Rly
Waterloo	748	Samson	2/1864	London & North Western Rly
Waterloo	748	Whitworth	11/1889	London & North Western Rly
Waterloo	51909	cSentinel	1929	London & North Eastern Rly
Watersmeet	21C130	WC	5/1946	Southern Rly
Water Witch	220	aSentinel	1928	London & North Eastern Rly
Wath ETD 41F	08509	08	1958	British Railways
Watkin	123	2–2–2WT	5/1856	Manchester, Sheffield & Lincolnshire Rly
Watkin	**–**	**0–4–0VB**	**1893**	**Penrhyn Castle Industrial Railway Museum [18]**
Watling Street	521	A2/3	5/1947	London & North Eastern Rly
Watt	229	aCrewe	11/1848	London & North Western Rly
Watt	229	Problem	c.1860	London & North Western Rly
Watt	–	Victoria	2/1864	Great Western Rly (bg)
Watt	2585	2Precursor	1/1906	London & North Western Rly
Wavell	172	GWR2301	4/1896	War Department [19]
Waverley	–	Abbot	4/1855	Great Western Rly (bg)
Waverley	806	Problem	c.1860	London & North Western Rly
Waverley	487	Abbotsford	10/1878	North British Rly [20]
Waverley	2031	2Precursor	3/1905	London & North Western Rly
Waverley	2990	Saint	9/1905	Great Western Rly
Waverley	876	H	8/1906	North British Rly
Waverley	509	A2/1	11/1944	London & North Eastern Rly
Waverley	**–**	**4–4–2**	**1948**	**Mull Rail [21]**
Waverley	47708	47/7	1965	British Railways
W.C. Brocklehurst	2155	George V	11/1910	London & North Western Rly
Wear	30	Miner	6/1845	Stockton & Darlington Rly
Wear	–	Caesar	4/1859	Great Western Rly (bg)
Weasel	2173	0–4–0WT	3/1873	Great Western Rly (bg) [22]

---

[1] Sold to the South Eastern & Chatham Railway in 1904 as their no. 751; to service stock in 1932 as no. 680S, later DS680. Preserved at the Montreal Railway Historical Museum, Canada.

[2] Now no. 21 on the Kent & East Sussex Railway.

[3] Formerly *Prince of Wales*, until about 1856.

[4] 2ft gauge.

[5] Rebuilt by Edward Thompson to Class B2 and renumbered 1602.

[6] Previously named *William*.

[7] Originally named *Sea Eagle*; renamed in October 1947.

[8] Originally named *Tartar*; renamed in July 1901.

[9] 18in gauge.

[10] Later sold to the East Kent Railway, becoming their no. 4.

[11] Sold to the Kent & East Sussex Railway in January 1905 as their no. 5 *Rolvenden*.

[12] Renamed *Sir Felix Pole*, April 1956.

[13] Renamed *John G. Griffiths* in March 1909; name removed in March 1914.

[14] Originally built with Lentz Oscillating Cam poppet valves. In March 1938 rebuilt with piston valves and assimilated into Class D49/3.

[15] 18in gauge Horwich Works internal system.

[16] Became Furness Railway no. 112.

[17] Renamed *Antelope* or *Gazelle* by October 1850.

[18] 1ft 11½in gauge.

[19] Originally Great Western Railway no. 2478.

[20] Originally named *Montrose*. Renamed in 1880 on transfer to the Carlisle route following the fall of the first Tay Bridge.

[21] 10¼in gauge.

[22] Built for the South Devon Railway.

Name	Number	Class	Date	Railway
Weaver	26	2–4–0	1/1853	Birkenhead, Lancashire & Cheshire Junction Rly [23]
Wednesbury	3	2–2–2	4/1849	South Staffordshire Rly
W.E. Dorrington	260	Claughton	8/1914	London & North Western Rly
Wee Scotland	88	2–2–2WT	1850	North British Rly
W.E.Gladstone	10	Bo-Bo	1921	Metropolitan Rly [24]
Welbeck Abbey	2819	B17/1	11/1930	London & North Eastern Rly
Wellington	–	0–6–0	c.1835	South Hetton Coal Co. [25]
Wellington	–	0–4–2	1836	Bolton & Leigh Rly
Wellington	39	0–4–2	1836	Joint Board of Management [26]
Wellington	13	0–4–0	1838	Newcastle & Carlisle Rly
Wellington	218	aCrewe	8/1848	London & North Western Rly
Wellington	–	Caesar	11/1853	Great Western Rly (bg)
Wellington	218	Problem	c.1860	London & North Western Rly
Wellington	–	**0–4–0ST**	**1873**	**Tanfield Rly**
Wellington	–	0–6–2T	1886	Longmoor Military Rly [27]
Wellington	3028	3001	8/1891	Great Western Rly [28]
Wellington	1490	2Experiment	1/1909	London & North Western Rly
Wellington	289	Clayton	1928	London & North Eastern Rly
Wellington	902	Schools	4/1930	Southern Rly
Wellington	5075	Castle	8/1938	Great Western Rly [29]
Wellington Road	55	51	1900	London, Tilbury & Southend Rly [30]
Wells	34092	**WC**	**9/1949**	**British Railways (Southern Region) [31]**
Welsh Guardsman	6117	Royal Scot	10/1927	London Midland & Scottish Rly
Welsh Guardsman	71516	**J94**	**1944**	**Gwili Rly**
Welsh Pony	–	**0–4–0TT**	**1867**	**Festiniog Rly [32]**
Wembley 1924	15	Bo-Bo	1921	Metropolitan Rly [33]
Wemyss	5648	Jubilee	1935	London Midland & Scottish Rly
Wemyss Bay	5505	Patriot	7/1932	London Midland & Scottish Rly [34]
Wendy	1	**0–4–0ST**	**1919**	**Hampshire Narrow Gauge Railway Society [35]**
Wenhaston	4	0–6–2T	1916	Southwold Rly [36]
Wennington	70	2–2–2	1859	Lancaster & Carlisle Rly
Wennington	52	51	1900	London, Tilbury & Southend Rly
Wensleydale	20173	20	1966	British Railways
Werfa	49	0–6–0	1860	Taff Vale Rly
Westbourne	520	E4	6/1901	London, Brighton & South Coast Rly
West Brighton	158	E3	10/1891	London, Brighton & South Coast Rly
West Burton Power Station	56028	56	1977	British Railways
Westcliff	38	37	1897	London, Tilbury & Southend Rly
Westergate	575	E5	4/1903	London, Brighton & South Coast Rly
Western Advocate	D1055	Western	3/1963	British Railways
Western Ambassador	D1051	Western	1/1963	British Railways
Western Australia	5568	Jubilee	1934	London Midland & Scottish Rly
Western Buccaneer	D1018	Western	4/1963	British Railways
Western Bulwark	D1073	Western	12/1963	British Railways
Western Campaigner	D1010	**Western**	**10/1962**	**British Railways**
Western Cavalier	D1021	Western	6/1963	British Railways
Western Centurion	D1026	Western	12/1963	British Railways
Western Challenger	D1019	Western	5/1963	British Railways
Western Champion	D1015	**Western**	**1/1963**	**British Railways**
Western Chieftain	D1057	Western	4/1963	British Railways
Western Consort	D1065	Western	6/1963	British Railways
Western Courier	D1062	**Western**	**5/1963**	**British Railways**
Western Crusader	D1004	Western	5/1962	British Railways
Western Dominion	D1060	Western	4/1963	British Railways
Western Dragoon	D1034	Western	4/1964	British Railways
Western Druid	D1067	Western	7/1963	British Railways

Name	Number	Class	Date	Railway
Western Duchess	D1044	Western	11/1962	British Railways
Western Duke	D1043	Western	10/1962	British Railways
Western Emperor	D1036	Western	8/1962	British Railways
Western Empire	D1059	Western	4/1963	British Railways
Western Empress	D1037	Western	8/1962	British Railways
Western Enterprise	D1000	Western	12/1961	British Railways
Western Envoy	D1061	Western	4/1963	British Railways
Western Explorer	D1002	Western	3/1962	British Railways
Western Firebrand	D1012	Western	11/1962	British Railways
Western Fusilier	D1023	**Western**	**9/1963**	**British Railways**
Western Gauntlet	D1070	Western	10/1963	British Railways
Western Gladiator	D1016	Western	2/1963	British Railways
Western Glory	D1072	Western	11/1963	British Railways
Western Governor	D1054	Western	3/1963	British Railways
Western Guardsman	D1025	Western	11/1963	British Railways
Western Harrier	D1008	Western	9/1962	British Railways
Western Hero	D1020	Western	5/1963	British Railways
Western Huntsman	D1024	Western	10/1963	British Railways
Western Hussar	D1028	Western	2/1964	British Railways
Western Invader	D1009	Western	9/1962	British Railways
Western King	D1039	Western	9/1962	British Railways
Western Lady	D1048	**Western**	**12/1962**	**British Railways**
Western Lancer	D1027	Western	1/1964	British Railways
Western Legionnaire	D1029	Western	7/1964	British Railways
Western Leviathan	D1014	Western	12/1962	British Railways
Western Lord	D1047	Western	2/1963	British Railways
Western Mail	56038	56	1978	British Railways
Western Marksman	D1032	Western	12/1963	British Railways
Western Marquis	D1046	Western	12/1962	British Railways
Western Monarch	D1049	Western	12/1962	British Railways
Western Monitor	D1063	Western	5/1963	British Railways
Western Musketeer	D1030	Western	12/1963	British Railways
Western Nobleman	D1058	Western	3/1963	British Railways
Western Pathfinder	D1001	Western	2/1962	British Railways
Western Patriarch	D1053	Western	2/1963	British Railways
Western Pioneer	D1003	Western	4/1962	British Railways
Western Prefect	D1066	Western	6/1963	British Railways
Western Prince	D1041	**Western**	**10/1962**	**British Railways**
Western Princess	D1042	Western	10/1962	British Railways
Western Queen	D1040	Western	9/1962	British Railways
Western Ranger	D1013	**Western**	**12/1962**	**British Railways**
Western Regent	D1064	Western	5/1963	British Railways
Western Reliance	D1068	Western	7/1963	British Railways
Western Renown	D1071	Western	11/1963	British Railways
Western Rifleman	D1031	Western	12/1963	British Railways
Western Ruler	D1050	Western	1/1963	British Railways
Western Sentinel	D1022	Western	7/1963	British Railways
Western Sovereign	D1038	Western	9/1962	British Railways
Western Stalwart	D1006	Western	6/1962	British Railways
Western Star	–	Priam	11/1841	Great Western Rly (bg)
Western Star	4010	Star	5/1907	Great Western Rly
Western Star	70025	Britannia	9/1952	British Railways
Western Sultan	D1056	Western	3/1963	British Railways
Western Talisman	D1007	Western	8/1962	British Railways
Western Thunderer	D1011	Western	10/1962	British Railways
Western Trooper	D1033	Western	1/1964	British Railways
Western Vanguard	D1069	Western	10/1963	British Railways
Western Venturer	D1005	Western	6/1962	British Railways
Western Viceroy	D1052	Western	2/1963	British Railways

---

[23] Later went to the Great Western Railway.

[24] Carried this name from 1953. *William Ewart Gladstone* up to 1942.

[25] Hackworth double-tender design, *c.* 1835–7.

[26] Birmingham & Gloucester and Bristol & Gloucester Railways, formed on 14 January 1845. Standard gauge. The locomotives passed to the Midland Railway on 3 August 1846, and were renumbered into Midland stock wef February 1847. This locomotive is said to have come from the Bolton & Leigh Railway, retaining its name.

[27] Originally named *Kitchener*. Ex-Taff Vale Railway no. 168.

[28] Built as broad gauge convertible. Rebuilt to 4–2–2 in July 1894.

[29] *Devizes Castle* until October 1940.

[30] Later renamed *Bow Road*.

[31] Renamed *City of Wells*, March 1950.

[32] 1ft 11½in gauge.

[33] Officially a rebuild of no. 15, built in 1908, but incorporating little if any of the original. Name removed in 1942 and never restored.

[34] Renamed *The Royal Army Ordnance Corps* in August 1947.

[35] 2ft gauge.

[36] 3ft gauge.

Name	Number	Class	Date	Railway
Western Viscount	D1045	Western	12/1962	British Railways
(Western Waggoner)	**03144**	**03**	**1961**	**British Railways**
Western Warrior	D1017	Western	3/1963	British Railways
Western Yeoman	D1035	Western	7/1962	British Railways
Westfield	123	165	4/1877	North British Rly
Westhall	10	Seafield	9/1858	Highland Rly [37]
Westham	226	D1	5/1885	London, Brighton & South Coast Rly
West Ham	35	Class 1	1892	London, Tilbury & Southend Rly
West Ham United	2872	B17/4	7/1937	London & North Eastern Rly
Westminster	204	Belgravia	1/1872	London, Brighton & South Coast Rly
Westminster	73	B4	10/1901	London, Brighton & South Coast Rly [38]
Westminster	67	51	1903	London, Tilbury & Southend Rly
Westminster	1550	GeorgeV*	1910	London & North Western Rly
Westminster	17	0–6–0ST	1914	Longmoor Military Rly
Westminster	908	Schools	7/1930	Southern Rly
Westminster Abbey	4069	Star	1/1923	Great Western Rly [39]
Westminster Abbey	5089	Castle	10/1939	Great Western Rly [40]
Westminster Abbey	43027	43	9/1976	British Railways [41]
Westminster Hall	5917	Hall	7/1931	Great Western Rly
Westmorland	1534	2Experiment	12/1909	London & North Western Rly
Westmorland	2760	D49/1	6/1929	London & North Eastern Rly
Westol Hall	7925	M/Hall	10/1950	British Railways (Western Region)
Weston	–	2–2–2T	1866	Weston, Clevedon & Portishead Rly [42]
Weston	3	0–6–0ST	1881	Weston, Clevedon & Portishead Rly [43]
Weston-super-Mare	3729	Bulldog	9/1906	Great Western Rly
West Riding Union	47	0–4–0	11/1845	Manchester & Leeds Rly
West Thurrock	26	Class 1	1884	London, Tilbury & Southend Rly
Westward Ho	3030	3031	12/1891	Great Western Rly [44]
Westward Ho	21C136	rWC	7/1946	Southern Rly
Westwood Hall	4978	Hall	2/1930	Great Western Rly
West Yorkshire Enterprise	56075	56	1980	British Railways
West Yorkshire Metropolitan County	43121	43	9/1977	British Railways
Weymouth	3331	Duke	8/1899	Great Western Rly
Weymouth	3331	Bulldog	7/1907	Great Western Rly
Weymouth	34091	WC	9/1949	British Railways (Southern Region)
Whaddon Hall	6970	M/Hall	9/1944	Great Western Rly [45]
Wharncliffe	4	0–6–0	1849	South Yorkshire Rly
Whatley	56001	56	1977	British Railways
Wheatley	1	0–6–0ST	1861	Buckley Rly [46]
Wheatstone	262	Precedent	1/1882	London & North Western Rly
Wheatstone	262	rPrecedent	4/1897	London & North Western Rly
Wheldale	**S134**	**J94**	**5/1944**	**Yorkshire Dales Rly [47]**
Whernside	2	2–2–2WT	5/1850	North Western Rly
Whernside	D6	Peak	11/1959	British Railways
Whetham	–	Sir Watkin	9/1866	Great Western Rly (bg)
Whig	17	Tory	3/1839	Stockton & Darlington Rly
Whimple	21C125	rWC	3/1946	Southern Rly [48]
Whippingham	295	D1	10/1877	London, Brighton & South Coast Rly
Whiston	**3694**	**J94**	**1950**	**Foxfield Rly**
Whitbourne Hall	5940	Hall	8/1933	Great Western Rly
Whitby	198	Roseberry	12/1866	Stockton & Darlington Rly
White	3392	Atbara	9/1900	Great Western Rly [49]
Whitechapel	**50**	**A1**	**12/1876**	**London, Brighton & South Coast Rly [50]**
Whitechapel	27	Class 1	1884	London, Tilbury & Southend Rly
Whitehaven	2	0–4–2	8/1846	Whitehaven & Furness Junction Rly
Whitehead	**–**	**0–4–0ST**	**1908**	**Southport Railway Centre**
White Horse	3029	3031	11/1891	Great Western Rly [51]
White Horse of Kent	44	2–2–2	9/1844	Croydon and Dover Joint Committee [52]
Whiteinch	74	72	5/1882	North British Rly [53]
White Raven	21	2–4–2T	1863	St Helens Canal & Rly
Whitfield	–	0–6–0ST	1857	West Somerset Mineral Rly [54]
Whitgift	916	Schools	5/1933	Southern Rly
Whittington	56	Small Pass	12/1865	Cambrian Railways [55]
Whittington Castle	5021	Castle	8/1932	Great Western Rly
Whitwell	W26	O2	12/1891	Southern Rly [56]
Whitworth	447	DX	c.1860	London & North Western Rly
Whitworth	1045	Samson	1/1865	London & North Western Rly
Whitworth	1045	Whitworth	9/1889	London & North Western Rly
Whitworth	211	B2	12/1897	London, Brighton & South Coast Rly [57]
Whixall	13	0–6–0ST	1/1862	Cambrian Railways [58]
Whorlton Hall	6929	Hall	11/1941	Great Western Rly [59]
Wick Hall	5995	Hall	1/1940	Great Western Rly
Wickham	300	2–4–0	11/1861	Lancashire & Yorkshire Rly
Wickwar	7	2–2–2	7/1844	Bristol & Gloucester Rly (bg)
Widgeon	1777	George V	10/1911	London & North Western Rly
Wightwick Hall	**6989**	**M/Hall**	**3/1948**	**British Railways (Western Region)**
Wigmore	261	D1	4/1882	London, Brighton & South Coast Rly
Wigmore Castle	3021	3001	4/1891	Great Western Rly [60]
Wigmore Castle	5022	Castle	8/1932	Great Western Rly
Wilberforce	23	Director	1832	Stockton & Darlington Rly [61]
Wilbert	**–**	**J94**	**12/1953**	**Dean Forest Rly**
Wild Aster	**2**	**0–4–0ST**	**1904**	**Llanberis Lake Rly [62]**
Wild Duck	1595	George V	9/1911	London & North Western Rly
Wildebeeste	1010	B1	11/1946	London & North Eastern Rly
Wildfire	3	0–2–2	1830	Liverpool & Manchester Rly [63]
Wild Fire	–	Priam	4/1840	Great Western Rly (bg)
Wildfire	8	bCrewe	10/1844	London & North Western Rly
Wildfire	77	Fireball	5/1847	London & South Western Rly [64]
Wildfire	77	Falcon	3/1865	London & South Western Rly

[37] Renamed *Duncraig* and altered from 2–4–0 to 4–4–0, June 1873.

[38] Name removed in about 1906; rebuilt to class B4x in November 1923.

[39] Rebuilt to Castle class no. 5089, October 1939.

[40] Rebuilt from Star class no. 4069 *Westminster Abbey*, and previously *Margam Abbey* until May 1923.

[41] Originally named *Glorious Devon*.

[42] Formerly Furness Railway no. 35, purchased by WC&PR in 1899.

[43] Originally built for industrial use. Became *Cwm Mawr* on the Burry Port & Gwendraeth Valley Railway in 1894, and was sold to Avonside Engine Co. in 1904. Date of purchase by WC&PR not known.

[44] Rebuilt to 4–2–2 in October 1894.

[45] Nameplates fitted May 1947.

[46] Became no. 1 of the Wrexham, Mold & Connah's Quay Railway, and later no. 1B of the Great Central Railway.

[47] Originally War Department no. 5118 *King Feisal*.

[48] Originally named *Rough Tor*. Renamed *Whimple* from 3 May 1948.

[49] Temporarily renamed *Powerful* for a City Imperial Volunteers' Special, 29 October 1900.

[50] Rebuilt to class A1x in 1920. Transferred to the Isle of Wight in May 1930 as no. W9 *Fishbourne*; returned to the mainland in 1936 as no. 515S in service stock; returned to running stock in 1953 as no. 32650. Preserved by the London Borough of Sutton and on long-term loan to the Kent & East Sussex Railway as their no. 10 *Sutton*.

[51] Rebuilt to 4–2–2 in July 1894.

[52] Became South Eastern Railway no. 44.

[53] Originally named *Coatbridge*. Renamed *Whiteinch* for a while before reverting to *Coatbridge*.

[54] This engine is thought to have started life as London & North Western Railway 0–6–0 no. 1837, built by Sharp Stewart (works no. 1011) in 1857. It was altered to 0–6–0ST by the LNWR in 1870 before being sold into industrial service. *Whitfield* seems to have worked on the West Somerset Mineral Railway (then leased to the Ebbw Vale Company) for a few months in 1895. It ended its days at South Hetton Colliery in 1947.

[55] Later altered to 2–4–0T.

[56] Previously London & South Western Railway (and Southern Railway) no. 210.

[57] Rebuilt to class B2x in June 1910.

[58] Later renamed *Green Dragon*.

[59] Nameplates fitted in December 1946.

[60] Built as broad gauge convertible. Rebuilt to 4–2–2 in March 1894.

[61] May have been built in 1833.

[62] 1ft 11½in gauge. Also named *Thomas Bach*.

[63] Renamed *Meteor* before entering service.

[64] Originally named *Hecla*; renamed in June 1852.

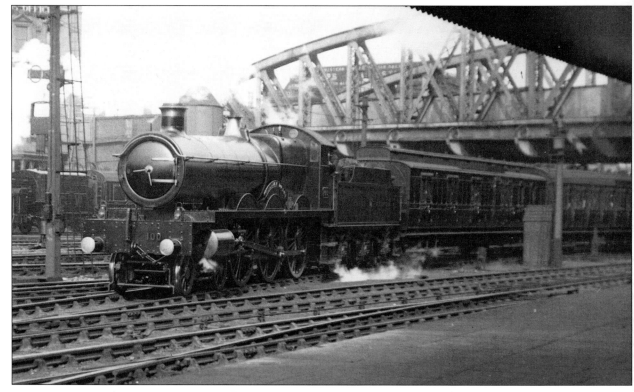

Great Western Railway. The pioneer Churchward 4–6–0 no. 100 *William Dean*, here seen leaving Paddington. (*Photo: RAS Marketing*)

Name	Number	Class	Date	Railway
Wildfire	468	Samson	10/1874	London & North Western Rly
Wildfire	468	Whitworth	11/1890	London & North Western Rly [65]
Wildlife	8	2–2–2	1837	Grand Junction Rly
Wild Swan	4467	A4	2/1938	London & North Eastern Rly
Wild Swan	47003	47/0	1963	British Railways
Wilkington	–	0–4–2	1841	Birmingham & Derby Junction Rly
Wilkinson	3056	3031	3/1895	Great Western Rly [66]
Willbrook	60150	A1	6/1949	British Railways (Eastern Region)
Willesden Intercity Depot	87016	87/0	1974	British Railways
Willesden Yard	47317	47/3	1965	British Railways
Willesley Hall	6967	M/Hall	8/1944	Great Western Rly [67]
Willey Hall	7926	M/Hall	10/1950	British Railways (Western Region)
William	6	2–2–0WT	11/1836	London & Greenwich Rly [68]
William	–	**0–4–0T**	**1956**	**Peak Rail**
William	–	**0–4–0DM**	**1957**	**Severn Valley Rly**
William Beveridge	60056	60	9/1991	British Railways
William Booth	60032	60	12/1990	British Railways
William Cawkwell	767	G.Britain	1894	London & North Western Rly
William Cawkwell	2269	2Experiment	12/1906	London & North Western Rly
William Cookworthy	37207	37	11/1963	British Railways
William Cowper	1321	Prince/W	2/1914	London & North Western Rly
William Cubitt	323	B2	12/1896	London, Brighton & South Coast Rly [69]

Name	Number	Class	Date	Railway
William Dean	2900	Saint	2/1902	Great Western Rly [70]
William Ewart Gladstone	10	Bo-Bo	1922	Metropolitan Rly [71]
William Francis	6841	**Garratt**	**1937**	**Bressingham Museum [72]**
William Froude	1534	John Hick	1898	London & North Western Rly
William Froude	1138	George V	2/1913	London & North Western Rly
William Gwynne	21	4–2–0	12/1840	Birmingham & Gloucester Rly
William H. Austen	24	**0–6–0ST**	**1953**	**Kent & East Sussex Rly**
William IV	–	0–4–0	9/1830	Liverpool & Manchester Rly [73]
William IVth	14	Majestic	1831	Stockton & Darlington Rly [74]
William Pearson	09026	09	1962	British Railways
William Penn	6	Bo-Bo	1921	Metropolitan Rly [75]
William Shakespeare	70004	Britannia	3/1951	British Railways
William Shakespeare	87034	87/0	1974	British Railways
William Siemens	1559	John Hick	1898	London & North Western Rly
William Siemens	2154	George V	2/1913	London & North Western Rly
William Webb Ellis	86254	86/2	1966	British Railways
William Whitelaw	2563	A3	7/1924	London & North Eastern Rly [76]
William Whitelaw	4462	A4	11/1937	London & North Eastern Rly [77]
William Wordsworth	70030	Britannia	11/1952	British Railways
Willingdon	255	D1	2/1882	London, Brighton & South Coast Rly
Willington	–	0–4–2	?	Birmingham & Derby Junction Rly
Willington Hall	7927	**M/Hall**	**10/1950**	**British Railways (Western Region)**

[65] Transferred to Engineer's Department 1923–November 1927, and renamed *Engineer Northampton*.

[66] Originally named *Timour*, renamed in July 1901.

[67] Nameplates fitted January 1946.

[68] Later renamed *Walter*.

[69] Rebuilt to class B2x in September 1908.

[70] Previously no. 100. Named *Dean* in June 1902, and *William Dean* in November 1902.

[71] Name removed in 1942. Restored in 1953 as *W.E. Gladstone*.

[72] 0–4–0 + 0–4–0 Beyer-Garratt locomotive.

[73] Built by Braithwaite & Ericsson. Sometimes referred to as *King William IV*. Its trials were unsatisfactory and the Liverpool & Manchester Railway declined to purchase it, hence the absence of a number.

[74] The spelling is variable. As well as the above, *William IV* and *William the IVth* have been noted.

[75] Name removed between 1942 and 1947.

[76] Renamed *Tagalie* in 1941. Converted from Class A1 in 1942.

[77] Originally named *Great Snipe*. Renamed in July 1941.

London, Brighton & South Coast Railway D1 class 0–4–2T no. 255 *Willingdon*. Although an indifferent photograph, it does show the standard of cleanliness which was normal in Stroudley's time for an inner suburban locomotive. (*Photo: Lens of Sutton*)

Name	Number	Class	Date	Railway
Will Scarlet	1356	0–6–0T	11/1873	Great Western Rly [78]
Will Shakspere	51	2–2–2	1856	Oxford, Worcester & Wolverhampton Rly
Wilmington	343	F	1/1882	London, Brighton & South Coast Rly
Wilson	291	2–4–0	6/1861	Lancashire & Yorkshire Rly
Wilson Worsdell	60127	A1	5/1949	British Railways (Eastern Region)
Wilton	21C141	WC	10/1946	Southern Rly
Wilton-Coalpower	56117	56	1983	British Railways
Wilton Endeavour	47361	47/3	1965	British Railways
Wimblebury	**7**	**J94**	**1/1956**	**Foxfield Rly**
Wimbledon	6	D1	1/1874	London, Brighton & South Coast Rly
Wimpole Hall	5963	Hall	7/1936	Great Western Rly
Wincanton	34108	rWC	4/1950	British Railways (Southern Region)
Winchburgh	218	211	1856	North British Rly [79]
Winchelsea	400	E5	7/1904	London, Brighton & South Coast Rly
Winchester	901	Schools	3/1930	Southern Rly
Winchester Castle	5042	Castle	7/1935	Great Western Rly
Windermere	–	0–4–0	11/1838	Manchester & Bolton Rly
Windermere	–	?	?1846	Preston & Wyre Railway, Harbour & Dock Co.
Windermere	83	2–4–0	4/1846	Grand Junction Rly
Windermere	–	0–4–0T	1850	Kendal & Windermere Rly
Windermere	259	aCrewe	4/1855	London & North Western Rly
Windermere	259	aCrewe	10/1857	London & North Western Rly [80]
Windermere	143	Peel	11/1859	Stockton & Darlington Rly
Windermere	789	George V	6/1916	London & North Western Rly
Windle	**–**	**0–4–0WT**	**1909**	**Middleton Rly**
Windsor	40	2Hercules	7/1852	London & South Western Rly
Windsor	176	Windsor	4/1865	Stockton & Darlington Rly
Windsor	–	Swindon	1/1866	Great Western Rly (bg)
Windsor	40	2Vesuvius	2/1874	London & South Western Rly
Windsor	64	B4	8/1901	London, Brighton & South Coast Rly [81]
Windsor Castle	3080	3031	3/1899	Great Western Rly
Windsor Castle	4082	Castle	4/1924	Great Western Rly [82]
Windsor Castle	**3080**	**3031**	**?**	**Great Western Rly [83]**
Windsor Lad	2500	A3	6/1934	London & North Eastern Rly
Windward Islands	5637	Jubilee	1934	London Midland & Scottish Rly

Name	Number	Class	Date	Railway
Wineham	563	E4	12/1901	London, Brighton & South Coast Rly
Winfield	**–**	**4wDM**	**1948**	**East Lancashire Rly**
Winnipeg	3462	Bulldog	2/1904	Great Western Rly
Winslow Hall	5975	Hall	5/1937	Great Western Rly
Winston Churchill	**9**	**4–6–2**	**1931**	**Romney, Hythe & Dymchurch Rly [84]**
Winston Churchill	**21C151**	**BB**	**12/1946**	**Southern Rly**
Winter	192	Panther	7/1866	Stockton & Darlington Rly
Winterstoke	2976	Saint	4/1905	Great Western Rly
Winterstoke	2985	Saint	7/1905	Great Western Rly [85]
Wirral	1	2–2–2	9/1840	Chester & Birkenhead Rly
Wissington	**–**	**0–6–0ST**	**1938**	**North Norfolk Rly**
Witch	14	2–2–2	1837	Grand Junction Rly
Witch	14	aCrewe	1846	London & North Western Rly
Witch	–	Priam	12/1846	Great Western Rly (bg)
Witch	2004	Newton	4/1871	London & North Western Rly
Witch	2004	rPrecedent	5/1891	London & North Western Rly
Witch	1379	Prince/W	1/1916	London & North Western Rly
Witchingham Hall	6966	M/Hall	5/1944	Great Western Rly [86]
Withdean	245	D1	12/1881	London, Brighton & South Coast Rly
Witherslack Hall	**6990**	**M/Hall**	**4/1948**	**British Railways (Western Region)**
Withyham	281	D1	11/1879	London, Brighton & South Coast Rly
Witton Castle	27	Tory	5/1840	Stockton & Darlington Rly
Wivelsfield	463	E4	12/1897	London, Brighton & South Coast Rly
Wivern	29	2–2–0	9/1840	Midland Counties Rly
Wizard	21	2–2–2	1837	Grand Junction Rly
Wizard	5	2–2–0	5/1839	Midland Counties Rly
Wizard	39	Vivid	10/1839	London & South Western Rly
Wizard	21	bCrewe	2/1845	London & North Western Rly [87]
Wizard	–	Iron Duke	9/1848	Great Western Rly (bg)
Wizard	39	Minerva	7/1856	London & South Western Rly
Wizard	39	2Vesuvius	2/1874	London & South Western Rly
Wizard	872	Precedent	6/1877	London & North Western Rly
Wizard	872	rPrecedent	8/1895	London & North Western Rly
Wizard of the Moor	6391	Director	10/1924	London & North Eastern Rly
W.M. Thackeray	979	Prince/W	1/1914	London & North Western Rly
Woking Homes 1885–1985	73134	73/1	1966	British Railways
Woldingham	401	E5	7/1904	London, Brighton & South Coast Rly [88]
Wolf	39	2–2–2	8/1840	Midland Counties Rly
Wolf	–	Wolf	7/1841	Great Western Rly (bg)
Wolf	2115	4–4–0ST	8/1859	Great Western Rly (bg) [89]
Wolfe	1524	Newton	11/1866	London & North Western Rly
Wolfe	1524	rPrecedent	3/1890	London & North Western Rly
Wolfe	421	8F	1941	Longmoor Military Rly
Wolfe Barry	209	B2	9/1897	London, Brighton & South Coast Rly
Wolferton	51	B4	7/1901	London, Brighton & South Coast Rly [90]
Wolf Hall	7928	M/Hall	10/1950	British Railways (Western Region)
Wolfhound	1489	George V	4/1911	London & North Western Rly
Wolf of Badenoch	2006	P2	9/1936	London & North Eastern Rly
Wolf of Badenoch	506	A2/2	5/1944	London & North Eastern Rly [91]
Wolf of Badenoch	87027	87/0	1974	British Railways
Wollaton Hall	5999	Hall	6/1940	Great Western Rly
Wolseley	3391	Atbara	9/1900	Great Western Rly
Wolseley Hall	5964	Hall	7/1936	Great Western Rly
Wolsingham	55	0–4–2	5/1847	Stockton & Darlington Rly
Wolstanton No 3	**–**	**0–6–0DM**	**1960**	**Foxfield Steam Rly**
Wolverhampton	9	0–6–0	7/1849	South Staffordshire Rly
Wolverhampton	–	Swindon	2/1866	Great Western Rly (bg)
Wolverhampton	3452	Bulldog	10/1903	Great Western Rly

[78] Built for the Severn & Wye & Severn Bridge Railway.

[79] Ex-Edinburgh & Glasgow Railway, absorbed by NBR in 1865.[79] Replacement of above engine, which was sold to the Lancaster & Carlisle Railway.

[80] Replacement of above engine, which was sold to the Lancaster & Carlisle Railway.

[81] Renamed *Norfolk* in December 1908.

[82] This engine exchanged identities with 7013 *Bristol Castle* in February 1952, so that an engine named *Windsor Castle* could haul HM King George VI's funeral train from Paddington to Windsor. The exchange of names and numbers was permanent.

[83] Non-working replica built for Madame Tussaud's, Windsor.

[84] 15in gauge scale model, Canadian prototype.

Originally named *Doctor Syn*.

[85] Named *Winterstoke* in February 1906, and *Peveril of the Peak* in April 1907.

[86] Nameplates fitted May 1946.

[87] Previously no. 381 *Sardinian*.

[88] Rebuilt to class E5x in May 1911.

[89] Built for the South Devon Railway.

[90] Name removed in about 1906.

[91] Rebuild of previous engine.

Name	Number	Class	Date	Railway
Wolverine	2021	Prince/W	12/1911	London & North Western Rly
Wolverton	08629	08	1959	British Railways
Wolverton	**1009**	**2–2–2**	**1991**	**London & North Western Rly** [92]
Women's Royal Voluntary Service	47854	47/4		British Railways
Wonder	296	Clayton	1928	London & North Eastern Rly
Wonersh	77	A1	7/1880	London, Brighton & South Coast Rly [93]
Wood	–	Hawthorn	1/1866	Great Western Rly (bg)
Woodbastwick Hall	2813	B17/1	10/1930	London & North Eastern Rly
Woodbine	**–**	**0–4–0DM**	**1936**	**Swindon & Cricklade Rly**
Woodcock	336	bCrewe	5/1854	London & North Western Rly
Woodcock	1799	George V	10/1911	London & North Western Rly
Woodcock	4489	A4	5/1937	London & North Eastern Rly [94]
Woodcock	4493	A4	7/1937	London & North Eastern Rly
Woodcock Hall	6968	M/Hall	9/1944	Great Western Rly [95]
Woodendean	499	E4	6/1900	London, Brighton & South Coast Rly
Woodgate	494	E4	11/1899	London, Brighton & South Coast Rly
Woodgrange	37	37	1897	London, Tilbury & Southend Rly
Woodlands	58	Woodlands	8/1848	Stockton & Darlington Rly
Woodlark	89	2–2–2	1844	Liverpool & Manchester Rly [96]
Woodlark	147	aCrewe	11/1851	London & North Western Rly
Woodlark	147	DX	c.1860	London & North Western Rly
Woodlark	794	Samson	3/1864	London & North Western Rly
Woodlark	794	Whitworth	1/1895	London & North Western Rly
Woodman	82	0–4–0	10/1843	Brighton, Croydon & Dover Joint Committee [97]
Woodmancote	464	E4	12/1897	London, Brighton & South Coast Rly
Woodpecker	2147	cSentinel	1928	London & North Eastern Rly
Woodside	393	D3	4/1896	London, Brighton & South Coast Rly
Woolacombe	21C144	rWC	10/1946	Southern Rly
Woollas Hall	5965	Hall	8/1936	Great Western Rly
Woolmer	**010–70074**	**0–6–0ST**	**1910**	**War Department**
Woolston Grange	6858	Grange	12/1937	Great Western Rly
Woolton	–	0–4–0	3/1839	Manchester & Bolton Rly
Woolwich	**–**	**0–4–0T**	**1916**	**Woolwich Arsenal** [98]
Woolwinder	2554	A3	12/1924	London & North Eastern Rly [99]
Wootton Hall	**4979**	**Hall**	**2/1930**	**Great Western Rly**
Worcester	3	2–2–2	5/1839	Birmingham & Gloucester Rly
Worcester	158	Cobham	9/1879	Great Western Rly
Worcester	3027	3031	11/1894	Great Western Rly [100]
Worcestershire	1471	2Experiment	1/1910	London & North Western Rly
Wordsworth	82	bCrewe	4/1846	Grand Junction Rly
Wordsworth	1020	Newton	8/1873	London & North Western Rly
Wordsworth	1020	rPrecedent	5/1891	London & North Western Rly
Wordsworth	1661	2Experiment	5/1909	London & North Western Rly
Worksop Depot	58011	58	1983	British Railways
Worplesdon	407	E6	12/1904	London, Brighton & South Coast Rly
Worsley Hall	5919	Hall	7/1931	Great Western Rly
Worsley-Taylor	438	11E	12/1913	Great Central Rly
Worthing	147	2–2–2	7/1861	London, Brighton & South Coast Rly [101]
Worthing	355	D1	5/1886	London, Brighton & South Coast Rly
Wotton Tramway	**–**	**0–4–0TG**	**1872**	**Metropolitan Rly**
Wotton No 2	–	0–6–0ST	2/1899	Metropolitan Rly
W.P. Allen	60114	A1	8/1948	British Railways (Eastern Region)
W.P. Awdry	**4**	**J94**	**12/1953**	**Dean Forest Rly** [102]
Wraysbury Hall	6969	M/Hall	9/1944	Great Western Rly [103]
Wrekin	56	2–2–2	c.1849	Great Western Rly [104]
Wrekin	33	0–4–2	12/1852	Shrewsbury & Chester Rly
Wren	**–**	**0–4–0ST**	**1887**	**Lancashire & Yorkshire Rly** [105]
Wren	47316	47/3	1965	British Railways
Wrottesley Hall	4980	Hall	2/1930	Great Western Rly
Wroxall	–	2–4–0T	1872	Isle of Wight Rly [106]
Wroxall	W4	E1	11/1878	Southern Rly [107]
Wroxham Broad	**1**	**2–6–4T**	**1992**	**Bure Valley Rly** [108]
W.S. Moorsom	11	4–2–0	6/1840	Birmingham & Gloucester Rly [109]
Wulfruna	86633	86/6	1/1966	British Railways
Wycliffe	142	Peel	7/1859	Stockton & Darlington Rly
Wycliffe Hall	5920	Hall	8/1931	Great Western Rly
Wye	–	Caesar	5/1859	Great Western Rly (bg)
Wye	10	2–4–0	4/1865	Brecon & Merthyr Rly
Wye	1359	0–4–0T	1876	Great Western Rly [110]
Wye	76	River	11/1895	Great Western Rly [111]
Wyke Hall	7929	M/Hall	11/1950	British Railways (Western Region)
Wyn	223	0–4–0ST	1883	War Department
Wyncliffe	–	0–4–0ST	1901	Fishguard & Rosslare Railways & Harbours
Wynnstay	4	0–4–2	10/1859	Cambrian Railways [112]
Wynnstay	3311	Badminton	1/1899	Great Western Rly
Wynyard Park	2818	B17/1	11/1930	London & North Eastern Rly
Wyre	–	2–2–2	?	Preston & Wyre Railway, Harbour & Dock Co.
Wyre	269	bCrewe	6/1851	London & North Western Rly
Wyre	614	S/Bloomer	1854	London & North Western Rly
Wyre	1166	Samson	6/1879	London & North Western Rly [113]
Wyre	1166	Whitworth	1/1896	London & North Western Rly

[92] Replica locomotive displayed at Milton Keynes Central station.

[93] Rebuilt to class A1x in 1911. Transferred to the Isle of Wight in 1927 as no. W3, later W13 *Carisbrooke*; returned to the mainland in 1949 as no. 32677.

[94] Renamed *Dominion of Canada* in June 1937.

[95] Nameplates fitted March 1947.

[96] Sold to St Helens Railway. Became London & North Western Railway no. 147 in 1846.

[97] Became South Eastern Railway no. 82.

[98] 18in gauge. Now preserved on the Bicton Woodland Railway as their no. 1.

[99] Converted from Class A1 in 1942.

[100] Built as broad gauge convertible, and originally named *Thames*. Renamed in December 1895.

[101] Rebuilt by Stroudley and name affixed in August 1871.

[102] Named *G B Keeling* when first preserved.

[103] Nameplates fitted June 1947.

[104] Built for the Shrewsbury & Birmingham Railway.

[105] 18in gauge Horwich Works internal system.

[106] Later Southern Railway no. W16. Withdrawn in 1933.

[107] Formerly London, Brighton & South Coast Railway no. 131 *Gournay*. Transferred to the Isle of Wight in June 1933 by the Southern Railway.

[108] 15in gauge.

[109] Later sold to the Taff Vale Railway, one of three sold to that company. The others were *Columbia* and *Gloucester*.

[110] Built for the Severn & Wye & Severn Bridge Railway.

[111] Rebuilt from 2–2–2 no. 76 of 1856.

[112] Later went to the Brecon & Merthyr Railway as their no. 12.

[113] Transferred to Engineer's Department 1902–1925, and renamed *Engineer Bangor*.

X

Name	Number	Class	Date	Railway		Name	Number	Class	Date	Railway
Xancidae	47010	47/0	8/1963	British Railways		Xanthus	26	Tiger	8/1862	London, Chatham & Dover Rly
Xancidae	47054	47/0	12/1964	British Railways		Xerxes	–	Caesar	1/1863	Great Western Rly (bg)

Y

Name	Number	Class	Date	Railway
Yard No DY326	**–**	**4wDM**	**1955**	**Caledonian Railway (Brechin)**
Yarm	92	Peel	3/1855	Stockton & Darlington Rly
Yarmouth	W2	E1	10/1880	Southern Rly [1]
Yarmouth	337	F	10/1881	London, Brighton & South Coast Rly
Yataghan	–	Wolf	8/1841	Great Western Rly (bg)
Y Ddraig Goch	47671	47/4	1/1966	British Railways [2]
Yeo	–	2–2–2	12/1857	London & South Western Rly (bg) [3]
Yeo	–	2–6–2T	12/1897	Lynton & Barnstaple Rly [4]
Yeo	**–**	**2–6–2T**	**1978**	**Fairbourne & Barmouth Steam Rly [5]**
Yeoman Challenger	59004	59/0	1/1986	Foster-Yeoman
Yeoman Endeavour	59001	59/0	1/1986	Foster-Yeoman
Yeoman Enterprise	59002	59/0	1/1986	Foster-Yeoman
Yeoman Highlander	59003	59/0	1/1986	Foster-Yeoman
Yeovil	21C104	rWC	7/1945	Southern Rly
Yes Tor	21C126	rWC	3/1946	Southern Rly
Yes Tor	60043	60	6/1991	British Railways
Yeti	**10**	**0–4–0DH**	**1986**	**Snowdon Mountain Rly [6]**
Yiewsley Grange	6859	Grange	12/1937	Great Western Rly
Yimkin	**26**	**4wDM**	**1942**	**Leighton Buzzard Rly [7]**

Name	Number	Class	Date	Railway
Y Lein Fach	37426	37/4	1965	British Railways [8]
Yoker	485	165	1/1878	North British Rly [9]
Yolland	11	2–4–0	6/1866	London & South Western Rly (ed) [10]
York	42	0–4–2	1836	Liverpool & Manchester Rly
York	6	0–4–2	7/1839	Manchester & Leeds Rly
York	159	Panther	2/1862	Stockton & Darlington Rly
York Festival '88	43093	43	6/1978	British Railways
Yorkshire	1561	2Experiment	1/1910	London & North Western Rly
Yorkshire	234	D49/1	10/1927	London & North Eastern Rly
Yorkshire Cricket Academy	43115	43	3/1979	British Railways
Yorkshire Evening Post	43157	43	4/1981	British Railways
Yorkshire Evening Press	43109	43	1/1979	British Railways
Yorkshire Hussar	238	aSentinel	1928	London & North Eastern Rly
Yorkshire Post	43193	43	6/1982	British Railways [11]
Ypres	612	C	8/1892	North British Rly
Ypres	505	11F	12/1922	Great Central Rly
Yr Wyddfa	**3**	**0–4–2T**	**1895**	**Snowdon Mountain Rly [12]**
Yvonne	**2945**	**0–4–0VB**	**1920**	**Northampton & Lamport Rly**

[1] Formerly London, Brighton & South Coast Railway no. 152 *Hungary*. Transferred to the Isle of Wight as no. W2 by the Southern Railway in June 1932.

[2] Also named (on the other side) *The Red Dragon*.

[3] Built by Thomas Brassey at Birkenhead for the Grand Junction Railway of Canada. When this fell through, the locomotive (with *Dart*) was diverted to the broad gauge North Devon Railway, which was taken over by the London & South Western on 1 January 1863.

[4] 1ft 11½in gauge. Became Southern Railway no. 759 in 1923.

[5] 12¼in gauge.

[6] 800mm gauge. Rack and pinion locomotive.

[7] 2ft gauge.

[8] Also named (on the other side) *Vale of Rheidol*.

[9] Later renamed *Blairadam*. It is, however, not certain that the name *Yoker* was in fact carried.

[10] Formerly no. 229 of the Loco Dept.

[11] Originally named *Plymouth SPIRIT OF DISCOVERY*.

[12] 800mm gauge. Rack and pinion locomotive.

Z

Name	Number	Class	Date	Railway	Name	Number	Class	Date	Railway
Zambesi	D864	Warship	5/1962	British Railways	Zest	D869	Warship	7/1961	British Railways
Zamiel	11	2–2–2	1837	Grand Junction Rly	Zetes	–	Caesar	2/1855	Great Western Rly (bg)
Zamiel	11	bCrewe	3/1845	London & North Western Rly	Zetland	86	0–6–0	?1847	Stockton & Darlington Rly [3]
Zamiel	635	Samson	9/1873	London & North Western Rly	Zillah	2	2–2–2	9/1840	Chester & Birkenhead Rly
Zamiel	635	Whitworth	1890	London & North Western Rly	Zillah	4	0–4–2?	9/1840	Birkenhead Rly [4]
Zamiel	401	Prince/W	12/1915	London & North Western Rly	Zillah	5	2–4–0	6/1857	Birkenhead, Lancashire & Cheshire Junction Rly [5]
Zanzibar	5638	Jubilee	1934	London Midland & Scottish Rly					
Zealous	D865	Warship	6/1962	British Railways	Zillah	419	Samson	2/1865	London & North Western Rly
Zebra	–	Wolf	8/1841	Great Western Rly (bg)	Zillah	419	Samson	1866	London & North Western Rly
Zebra	148	Panther	3/1860	Stockton & Darlington Rly	Zillah	419	Whitworth	1890	London & North Western Rly
Zebra	2127	4–4–0ST	10/1866	Great Western Rly (bg) [1]	Zillah	1947	Alfred	6/1901	London & North Western Rly [6]
Zebra	D866	Warship	3/1961	British Railways	Zina	–	Caesar	12/1853	Great Western Rly (bg)
Zeebrugge	502	11F	10/1922	Great Central Rly	Zopyrus	2	2–4–0T	2/1857	Birkenhead, Lancashire & Cheshire Junction Rly [7]
Zenith	D867	Warship	4/1961	British Railways					
Zeno	1	2–4–0T	2/1857	Birkenhead, Lancashire & Cheshire Junction Rly [2]	Zopyrus	404	Samson	1/1865	London & North Western Rly
					Zopyrus	404	Whitworth	3/1894	London & North Western Rly
Zeno	401	Samson	1/1865	London & North Western Rly	Zulu	D870	Warship	10/1961	British Railways
Zeno	401	Whitworth	1894	London & North Western Rly	Zygia	4	0–4–2?	4/1857	Birkenhead, Lancashire & Cheshire Junction Rly [8]
Zephyr	172	Undine	6/1860	London & South Western Rly					
Zephyr	49	Reindeer	7/1865	London, Chatham & Dover Rly	Zygia	418	Samson	1/1865	London & North Western Rly
Zephyr	D868	Warship	5/1961	British Railways	Zygia	418	Whitworth	3/1893	London & North Western Rly

[1] Built for the South Devon Railway.

[2] Became London & North Western Railway no. 401.

[3] Purchased from the Lancashire & Yorkshire Railway in 1854; formerly their no. 219, and no. 4 of the Blackburn, Darwen & Bolton Railway.

[4] According to the makers, this locomotive was an 0–6–0.

[5] Later passed to the London & North Western Railway.

[6] Previously named *Australia*. Renamed in June 1911.

[7] Became London & North Western Railway no. 404.

[8] Later passed to the London & North Western Railway.

APPENDIX I

CLASS NOTES

A class, Metropolitan Railway.   First introduced in 1864, these were 4–4–0 tank locomotives, designed and built by Beyer, Peacock & Co. of Manchester. They were very effective, and forty-nine were built for the Metropolitan. Only the first eighteen were named. Further very similar locomotives were built for the Metropolitan District Railway, and for other railways. The last survivor, Metropolitan no. 23, has been preserved.

A1 class, London, Brighton & South Coast Railway.   These were the famous 'Terrier' class, a nickname first applied by the drivers and which gained universal currency. Introduced in 1872, fifty of these small 0–6–0 tanks were built. Originally intended for London suburban work and the South London line in particular, they worked all over the system. Several minor railways bought examples, and so did the London & South Western Railway and the South Eastern & Chatham Railway. Most received new boilers with extended smokeboxes, thus becoming Class A1x. Although withdrawals started as long ago as 1901, the last survivors are still at work on preserved lines today.

A1 class, London & North Eastern Railway.   See class A3.

A2 class, Furness Railway.   These 0–4–0 tender locomotives worked mineral trains, hauling iron ore to Barrow-in-Furness. They were introduced in 1846, and were of Edward Bury design, with bar frames and domed-top firebox. Only one survives, the well-known *"Coppernob"*, preserved in the National Railway Museum. There were five classes of these 0–4–0s, all very similar, and they were highly successful in this case, long outliving similar Bury types on other railways. One, which had been converted to 0–4–0ST for industrial use and which had survived, has recently been restored to its former condition.

A2 class, London & North Eastern Railway.   See 2400 class.

A2 class, London & North Eastern Railway.   This, the second A2 class, started off with Edward Thompson's appointment as chief mechanical engineer on Sir Nigel Gresley's death in 1941. Thompson had been responsible for maintaining Gresley's engines, and he was well aware of their shortcomings – in particular the conjugated valve motion for the inside cylinder of the three-cylinder designs. Some V2 class 2–6–2s under construction at Doncaster were finished as 4–6–2s and became class A2/1. The Gresley P2 class 2–8–2s were rebuilt as 4–6–2s, keeping their original names, and became class A2/2. Class A2/3 was a development of class A2/2 for new construction. Thompson was very keen that both inside and outside connecting rods should be the same length, so the result was a large gap between the bogie wheels and the driving wheels. The engines looked ungainly and did not run smoothly. Thompson's tenure of office was short, and he was succeeded by the much-loved and respected Arthur Peppercorn who, as chief draughtsman, had been planning his own revised version of the design during the closing months of the Thompson regime. Thompson took the Gresley A4 and, without the streamlining, brought it thoroughly up to date. This was the second class A2. Most of the names were of racehorses.

A3 class, London & North Eastern Railway.   These famous engines were Nigel Gresley's first 4–6–2 design, and the first two, *Great Northern* and *Sir Frederick Banbury*, appeared just in time to receive Great Northern Railway livery and numbers, 1470 and 1471 respectively. They were classed A1. The next one, no. 1472, entered service in February 1923 with its new owner's initials on the tender. Between December 1923 and March 1924 it underwent a general repair at Doncaster, when it was renumbered 4472 and named *Flying Scotsman*. *Flying Scotsman* was exhibited at the 1924 Wembley Exhibition, just opposite the Great Western Castle class locomotive. The GWR placed a large notice by their engine, proclaiming *Caerphilly Castle* as Britain's most powerful passenger locomotive. A trial was arranged, and on both the LNER main line and on its own ground the GWR engine had the better of it. Gresley modified the valves and increased the boiler pressure on one of his 4–6–2s, with remarkable results. The modified engine was classed A3, and most of the remainder were dealt with over time. The remaining unmodified engines were classified A10 after 1945, leaving the A1 designation clear for the locomotives designed by Edward Thompson and Arthur Peppercorn. Most of the names were of racehorses.

A4 class, London & North Eastern Railway.   There were thirty-five of these most famous engines, and there was a good deal of renaming. They were originally numbered 2509–12, 4482–98, 4462–9, 4499–500, and 4900–3, which is why the preserved *Mallard* bears her original number, 4468. In 1946 Edward Thompson embarked on a renumbering scheme in which the A4s would have had three-digit numbers, but later in the same year there was a second renumbering, in which they were renumbered from 1 upwards, in no particular order. The only one not to be taken over by British Railways was the first *Sir Ralph Wedgwood*, no. 4469. This engine was destroyed by a direct hit in a bombing raid on York in the Second World War; a plaque marks the spot in the Great Hall of the National Railway Museum, near the sectioned *Ellerman Lines*. The first four A4s – *Silver Link*, *Quicksilver*, *Silver King* and *Silver Fox* – were originally painted in two-tone grey for working the 'Silver Jubilee' express between London and Newcastle. Those named after Dominions and the Empire of India were painted blue for working the 'Coronation' express between London and Edinburgh, as were *Golden Fleece*, *Golden Plover* and *Golden Shuttle* for the 'West Riding' express between London and Leeds and Bradford. The next batch of A4s were painted green, like *Flying Scotsman* or *Green Arrow*, for general service. It was more practical to use whatever A4 was available for whatever train, so it was decided to repaint the whole class in blue, simply because it looked best! But in the Second World War they all soon became plain black and very dirty, and with the initials on the tenders abbreviated to NE. After 1945 the 'garter blue' was restored, and after nationalization, and experiments with, *inter alia*, a vivid purple, some of the class were painted a shade of light blue. This did not wear well, so 'Brunswick green', very much akin to the old Great Western colour, was adopted for the rest of the engines' lives. Details of the renumbering schemes are as follows:

Original LNER No.	First 1946 No.	Second 1946 No.	BR No.
2509	–	14	60014
2510	–	15	60015
2511	–	16	60016
2512	–	17	60017
4482	–	23	60023
4483	585	24	60024
4484	–	25	60025
4485	587	26	60026
4486	588	27	60027
4487	–	28	60028
4488	–	9	60009
4489	–	10	60010
4490	–	11	60011
4491	–	12	60012
4492	–	13	60013
4493	–	29	60029
4494	–	3	60003
4495	–	30	60030
4496	–	8	60008
4497	–	31	60031
4498	–	7	60007
4462	–	4	60004
4463	–	18	60018
4464	–	19	60019
4465	–	20	60020
4466	605	6	60006
4467	–	21	60021
4468	–	22	60022
4469	–	–	–
4499	–	2	60002
4500	–	1	60001
4900	–	32	60032
4901	–	5	60005
4902	–	33	60033
4903	–	34	60034

A10 class, London & North Eastern Railway.   See A3 class.
Abbot class, Great Western Railway (broad gauge).   Designed by Daniel Gooch, these were 4–4–0 tender

locomotives. The leading wheels were mounted in the main frames, not in a bogie. The first appeared in February 1855, and the last were withdrawn in November 1876.

Abbotsford class, North British Railway. An express passenger 4–4–0 design by Dugald Drummond, first introduced in 1876 and built by Neilson & Co. of Glasgow for the inauguration of through expresses from London via the Midland Railway's Settle and Carlisle line, opened the previous year. There were twelve of these engines, and they were the prototypes of many more, with progressive enlargement, built for several railways. The last survivor was withdrawn by the London & North Eastern Railway in 1924.

Acis class, London, Chatham & Dover Railway. Fourteen 0–6–0 goods engines, designed by W. Martley and entering service in 1861. Quite successful, they lasted until 1908.

Adrian class, London, Chatham & Dover Railway. Six 0–6–0 goods engines designed by William Martley, very similar to the Acis class noted above. They entered service in 1866 and gave good service. Kirtley modernized them in 1885–90, giving them numbers and removing the names, and the last was withdrawn in 1910.

Aeolus class, London, Chatham & Dover Railway. Four 4–4–0s were built in 1860–1 by Robert Stephenson & Co. for the Smyrna & Aidin Railway in Turkey, but were left on the builders' hands. Always on the look-out for bargains, the LCDR snapped them up at a bargain price and found them reasonably reliable. They were rebuilt with saddle tanks in 1873 and transferred to suburban work. *Aeolus* and *Comus* were withdrawn in 1905 and the last, *Bacchus*, in 1909.

Alecto class, London & South Western Railway. Ten 2–2–2 passenger engines built from 1847 by Fairbairn & Co. Basically similar to the Mazeppa class, they were never as successful and were given light work. Withdrawals commenced in 1863 and by 1872 they were all gone.

Alfred the Great class, London & North Western Railway. A class of 4–4–0 four-cylinder compound express locomotives designed by F. W. Webb, and first introduced in May 1901. A development of the earlier Jubilee class, with a larger boiler, they proved to be little better than the Jubilees, and frequently needed to be piloted.

Atbara class, Great Western Railway. These double-framed 4–4–0s were similar to the contemporary Bulldog class, except for having 6ft 8½in driving wheels compared with the Bulldogs' 5ft 8in. They were first introduced in 1900, and many of their names commemorated places and personalities connected with the South African War. In December 1912 they were renumbered; the original numbers are those quoted in this list. For ease of reference, the following table is appended:

Old No.	New No.	Old No.	New No.	Old No.	New No.	Old No.	New No.
3373	4120	3383	4129	3393	4139	3403	3703
3374	4121	3384	4130	3394	4140	3404	3704
3375	4122	3385	4131	3395	4141	3405	3705
3376	4123	3386	4132	3396	4142	3406	3706
3377	4124	3387	4133	3397	4143	3407	3707
3378	4125	3388	4134	3398	4144	3408	3708
3379	4126	3389	4135	3399	4145	3409	3709
3380	4127	3390	4136	3400	3700	3410	4146
3381	4128	3391	4137	3401	3701	3411	4147
3382	–	3392	4138	3402	3702	3412	4148

No. 3382 was scrapped after its involvement in the Henley-in-Arden accident of 1911. The class was not very long-lived, the last examples being withdrawn in 1931.

The very similar Flower class continued the numbers above.

Aurora class, East Lancashire Railway. Five 2–2–2s, very similar to the same Railway's Bacchus class. Nos 15 *Aeolus*, 21 *Prometheus* and 38 *Phantom* were later rebuilt as 2–4–0s. All were withdrawn by 1880.

B class, London, Brighton & South Coast Railway. Stroudley's no. 151 *Grosvenor*, a 2–2–2 express passenger locomotive which was completed on 24 December 1874, and later assimilated into the G class.

B1 class, London & North Eastern Railway. This was Thompson's answer to the LMS 'Black Five': a go-anywhere, do-anything mixed traffic 4–6–0. The plan was to name the class after antelopes and such-like African game, and the management tried to popularize them as the Antelope class. But the men referred to them as 'B1s' – until 1005 *Bongo* appeared! Whether the name, constantly repeated, sounded like loose valve gear at slow speeds 'Bongos' they became! Of course, the supply of big game names soon ran out, so, after commemorating one or two directors, most of the engines were left nameless.

B2 class, London, Brighton & South Coast Railway. The LB&SCR's first 4–4–0 tender engines, they were introduced in 1895 to R.J. Billinton's design. Twenty-five were built, and it was soon clear that their boilers were far too small. They were all fitted with bigger boilers, becoming **Class B2x**.

B2 class, London & North Eastern Railway.   After the withdrawal of the last of the 'Sir Sam Fay' class 4–6–0s, which the Great Central had classified Class 1 and the London & North Eastern Railway had dubbed Class B2, the designation B2 was available for Edward Thompson to use for his rebuild of Sandringham class engines. The main difference was the removal of the inside cylinder and the installation of a B1 class boiler.

B3 class, London, Brighton & South Coast Railway.   Class B2 engines were under-boilered, so R.J. Billinton completed no. 213 *Bessemer* with a larger boiler, thus creating the sole example of Class B3. A further reboilering made it uniform with class B2x.

B4 class, London, Brighton & South Coast Railway.   By the end of the nineteenth century the express passenger services were both leisurely timed and frequently late: it was evident that more powerful locomotives were needed. The B2 class were quite under-boilered, so Robert Billinton designed a revised version with a much bigger boiler. Thirty-three eventually entered traffic, between December 1899 and October 1901. Although a vast improvement on their predecessors, there was nevertheless scope for improvement. In particular, the frames were on the thin side, and suffered from fractures over the driving axles. Twelve were rebuilt (virtually new engines) to class B4x, but none had names. The last of these were withdrawn by the end of 1951.

B4 class, London & South Western Railway.   These were 0–4–0Ts, first designed by William Adams in 1891 for service in the docks at Devonport and as station pilots. Ten were built initially, then a further ten for work in Southampton Docks, acquired in 1891. The practice then began of naming the locomotives after places across the Channel. A further five were built by Dugald Drummond in 1908, to a slightly smaller design originally known as class K14, but soon integrated into class B4. They were useful machines, and moved about the L&SWR and Southern as required. Withdrawal commenced in 1948 and was complete by October 1963. Some were sold for industrial service.

B17 class, London & North Eastern Railway.   The Sandringham class (the name being taken from the first one) was designed by the North British Locomotive Co. of Glasgow to Sir Nigel Gresley's requirements. They were for the Great Eastern section, which had short turntables and so the engines had short tenders. This was the basic B17 design. Once they had proved their worth, more were ordered for elsewhere on the LNER, the later engines being fitted with LNER 4,200-gallon tenders. They were classified **B17/4**, the basic design becoming **B17/1**. Later, a pair of B17/4s, *East Anglian* and *City of London*, were fitted with streamlining for the 'East Anglian' express from Liverpool Street to Norwich. This made them look like miniature A4s, but the train itself was not streamlined, neither were the timings very exciting. Some class members were fitted with Thompson B1 boilers, and Thompson rebuilt some more drastically to class B2, so that they looked very like B1 class engines. One of these was *Royal Sovereign*, which was the royal engine for journeys between London and Wolferton, the station for Sandringham.

Bacchus class, East Lancashire Railway.   Four 2–2–2 passenger engines, introduced in 1846. The last was withdrawn in 1877.

Badminton class, Great Western Railway.   Twenty double-framed 4–4–0s, first introduced in December 1897 and used on expresses between Paddington and Bristol, Exeter, Shrewsbury and South Wales. The first GWR class to be built with Belpaire fireboxes. No. 3297 *Earl Cawdor* was rebuilt in 1903 with a very large boiler with round-topped firebox, and a double-window cab of almost North Eastern Railway appearance. Nothing like it had been seen on the Great Western before – or since. The experiment, for such it was, was not over-successful, and the engine reverted to type in 1906. Like so many GWR locomotives, the Badminton engines were renumbered in December 1912:

Old No.	New No.	Old No.	New No.	Old No.	New No.	Old No.	New No.
3292	4100	3297	4105	3302	4110	3307	4115
3293	4101	3298	4106	3303	4111	3308	4116
3294	4102	3299	4107	3304	4112	3309	4117
3295	4103	3300	4108	3305	4113	3310	4118
3296	4104	3301	4109	3306	4114	3311	4119

The old numbers are used in this list.   The last Badminton was withdrawn in 1931.

Banking class, Great Western Railway (broad gauge).   Four 0–6–0 saddle tanks, introduced in October 1852. Apart from *Juno*, they were all withdrawn by December 1883. *Juno* was sold to the South Devon Railway, who, already having a *Juno* in their fleet, renamed the newcomer *Stromboli*. In 1876, when the SDR became part of the Great Western, the name was retained, together with the GWR number 2138. The engine had received various improvements meanwhile, such as cast-iron brake blocks and a cab, and lasted until June 1889.

BB class, Southern Railway.   The **West Country** and **Battle of Britain** classes were designed by Mr O.V.S. Bulleid, the Southern Railway's chief mechanical engineer. They were in fact mechanically identical. The WC class came first, and was named after towns, villages, beauty spots, etc., of the West Country. When more engines were required, this time for service in Kent, it was felt that West Country names were inappropriate, so names connected with the Battle of Britain, largely fought over Kent, were chosen. There was some renaming: *Wells* became *City of Wells*, *Blandford* became *Blandford Forum*, while *Rough Tor* lasted only a few days. No. 34071 started life as *615 Squadron*. Of the BB class, locomotives named after squadrons are listed under S, and then in numerical order: *257 Squadron* comes before *601 Squadron*. The locomotives of both classes were a smaller and lighter edition of the **Merchant Navy class**, and the only way an observer could distinguish the three classes was by the shape of the nameplates.

The Southern Railway numbered these engines from 21C101 upwards, with both BB and WC names scattered more or less at random. The number was intended to show the engine's wheel arrangement, and was one of Mr Bulleid's ideas. British Railways renumbered them into a series beginning at 34001, with 34071 onwards built new with BR numbers.

Many of these engines were rebuilt without the 'air-smoothed' casing, but the original nameplates were reused. Rebuilds are shown with a small r in the classification column, i.e. rBB or rWC. The following is a list of those engines which were rebuilt, the dates being their re-entry into traffic in their altered condition:

Number	Date	Number	Date	Number	Date	Number	Date
21C101	11/1957	21C124	2/1961	21C145	10/1958	34085	6/1960
21C103	9/1957	21C125	11/1957	21C146	2/1959	34087	12/1960
21C104	2/1958	21C126	2/1958	21C147	10/1958	34088	4/1960
21C105	6/1957	21C127	9/1957	21C148	3/1959	34089	11/1960
21C108	7/1960	21C128	8/1958	21C150	8/1958	34090	8/1960
21C109	1/1961	21C129	12/1958	21C152	9/1958	34093	5/1960
21C110	2/1959	21C131	12/1958	21C153	11/1958	34095	1/1961
21C112	1/1958	21C132	10/1960	21C156	12/1960	34096	4/1961
21C113	10/1957	21C134	8/1960	21C158	11/1960	34097	3/1961
21C114	3/1958	21C136	9/1960	21C159	3/1960	34098	2/1961
21C116	4/1958	21C137	3/1958	21C160	11/1960	34100	9/1960
21C117	11/1957	21C139	1/1959	21C162	4/1959	43101	9/1960
21C118	10/1958	21C140	10/1960	34071	5/1960	34104	5/1961
21C121	1/1959	21C142	1/1959	34077	7/1960	34108	5/1961
21C122	12/1957	21C144	5/1960	34082	4/1960	34109	3/1961

Belgravia class, London, Brighton & South Coast Railway. Six 2–4–0 passenger engines designed by William Stroudley and introduced in 1872. *Goodwood*, the last of the class, was withdrawn in 1902.

Belladrum class, Highland Railway. This class took its name from the first engine in the series, a small 2–2–2 by William Barclay. There were only two engines, and the first was rebuilt as a 2–2–2T.

Birkbeck class, Stockton & Darlington Railway. Two 0–6–0 mineral engines, 63 *Birkbeck* and 64 *Larchfield*, both completed in February 1849. They represented a break from the long boiler outside cylinder arrangement, having their fireboxes between the second and third axles, and inside cylinders. *Larchfield* was withdrawn in 1873, and *Birkbeck* in 1857.

Bison class, London & South Western Railway. Ten 0–6–0 goods engines, designed by J.V. Gooch and built at the L&SWR's Nine Elms Works, London, entered traffic in 1845–8. By the early 1860s they had become outclassed, and the last two were withdrawn in 1887.

Bluebell class, London, Chatham & Dover Railway. Six more Dawn class 2–4–0 express engines were ordered from Sharp, Stewart & Co., but with sufficient modifications for them to be considered a separate class. All were successful in service, attaining well over a million miles. The last was withdrawn in 1908.

Bo-Bo electric locomotives, Metropolitan Railway. These locomotives were built in 1922. Officially a 'rebuild' of earlier, unnamed, locomotives dating from 1906. Only two locomotives were actually rebuilt; so much work went into the operation that it was deemed more economical to scrap the earlier locomotives and build new. They were used on through passenger trains between Baker Street and Aylesbury, which changed over to steam traction at Harrow (later at Rickmansworth). In the rush hour these trains were extended to Liverpool Street and possibly to Aldgate. The class numbered twenty. They were replaced by new multiple-unit trains in 1960 when the electrification was extended to Amersham and Chesham, and the through service to Aylesbury ended.

Bogie class, Great Western Railway (broad gauge). Sir Daniel Gooch's 4–4–0 saddle tank design, which, in enlarged form, was copied by the South Devon Railway, Bristol & Exeter Railway, and Vale of Neath Railway.

Britannia class, British Railways. The first 'standard' class for use on the unified national system appeared in 1951, and was supposed to be based on the best designs of the four main line companies. In practice, the design team was almost entirely ex-London Midland & Scottish. This was the first two-cylinder 4–6–2 to run in this country (the only other one was the Clan class, British Railways) and did in fact work on all Regions. Ultimately fifty-four were built, and all except no. 70047 were named. The first fourteen went to the Eastern Region lines out of London (Liverpool Street) to Norwich and Ipswich, although no. 70004 *William Shakespeare* received a special finish and was exhibited at the Festival of Britain in London. It afterwards went to the Southern Region for working the prestige 'Golden Arrow' Pullman car train. Those allocated to the Western Region received the names of old broad gauge locomotives. Most went to the London Midland Region, but the final five, allocated to Scotland, received suitably Scottish names. Ultimately, they all ended their days on the London Midland Region, and withdrawals began in June 1965 with the arrival of the diesels. No. 70000 *Britannia* and no. 70013 *Oliver Cromwell* have been preserved.

Brougham class, Stockton & Darlington Railway. Two 4–4–0s, 160 *Brougham* and 161 *Lowther*, designed by William Bouch to cope with the exposed conditions on the route to Tebay over Stainmore Summit, for which they were fitted with large enclosed cabs. *Brougham* entered service in August 1860, and *Lowther* in October of that year. They were withdrawn in 1888. They were very similar, apart from the cabs, to the Saltburn class which immediately followed them.

Bulldog class, Great Western Railway.   A large class (156) of inside-cylinder 4–4–0s with double frames, and with detail variations between batches. Earlier engines were virtually an enlarged version of the Duke class. They originally worked in Cornwall, but spread over most of the system in later years. Withdrawals started in 1930, but the last few were scrapped by British Railways in 1951.

The locomotives were renumbered into one consecutive series in December 1912, but the original numbers only are given in this list. To aid the enquirer, old and new numbers for each locomotive are given:

Old No.	New No.	Old No.	New No.	Old No.	New No.	Old No.	New No.	Old No.	New No.	Old No.	New No.
3253	3300	3339	3327	3366	3354	3443	3381	3470	3408	3725	3435★
3262	3301	3340	3328	3367	3355	3444	3382	3471	3409	3726	3436★
3263	3302	3341	3329	3368	3356	3445	3383	3472	3410	3727	3437★
3264	3303	3342	3330	3369	3357	3446	3384	3701	3411	3728	3438★
3268	3304	3343	3331	3370	3358	3447	3385	3702	3412	3729	3439
3269	3305	3344	3332	3371	3359	3448	3386	3703	3413	3730	3440★
3273	3306	3345	3333	3372	3360	3449	3387	3704	3414	3731	3441
3279	3307	3346	3334	3413	3361	3450	3388	3705	3415	3732	3442
3280	3308	3347	3335	3414	3362	3451	3389	3706	3416	3733	3443
3282	3309	3348	3336	3415	3363	3452	3390	3707	3417	3734	3444
3286	3310	3349	3337	3416	3364	3453	3391	3708	3418	3735	3445
3312	3311	3350	3338	3417	3365	3454	3392	3708	3419★	3736	3446
3316	3312	3351	3339	3418	3366	3455	3393	3710	3420★	3737	3447
3318	3313	3352	3340	3419	3367	3456	3394	3711	3421★	3738	3448
3322	3314	3353	3341	3420	3368	3457	3395	3712	3422	3739	3449
3324	3315	3354	3342	3421	3369	3458	3396	3713	3423★	3740	3450
3325	3316	3355	3343	3422	3370	3459	3397	3714	3424★	3741	3451
3327	3317	3356	3344	3423	3371	3460	3398	3715	3425★	3742	3452
3330	3318	3357	3345	3424	3372	3461	3399	3716	3426★	3743	3453
3331	3319	3358	3346	3425	3373	3462	3400	3717	3427★	3744	3455
3332	3320	3359	3347	3426	3374	3463	3401	3718	3428★		
3333	3321	3360	3348	3427	3375	3464	3402	3719	3429★		
3334	3322	3361	3349	3428	3376	3465	3403	3720	3430		
3335	3323	3362	3350	3429	3377	3466	3404	3721	3431★		
3336	3324	3363	3351	3430	3378	3467	3405	3722	3432★		
3337	3325	3364	3352	3431	3379	3468	3406	3723	3433★		
3338	3326	3365	3353	3432	3380	3469	3407	3724	3434		

★ These locomotives were unnamed.

C class, North British Railway.   Designed by Matthew Holmes as an updated version of Dugald Drummond's 18in 0–6–0 goods, the class was introduced in 1888 and ultimately totalled 168. All passed to the LNER in 1923, and withdrawal did not commence until 1931 (apart from no. 676 *Reims*, destroyed in an accident in 1926). Twenty-five engines went to France in 1917; on their return in 1919 they received appropriate names. The North British Railway was the only company to give names to those of its locomotives which went overseas in the war. *Maude* has survived into preservation; otherwise the class became extinct in 1966.

C2 class, Great Northern Railway.   The Great Northern named but few of its locomotives, and the appearance of no. 990 *Henry Oakley* (named after the General Manager) in 1898 created a sensation. It was the first British 4–4–2 locomotive, a wheel arrangement hitherto considered American. The class was soon followed by no. 251, which had a much bigger boiler (class C1), and which formed the front-line Great Northern motive power until the coming of the Gresley 4–6–2s. Both nos 990 and 251 have been preserved.

C11 class, London & North Eastern Railway.   See H class, North British Railway.

Caesar class, Great Western Railway (broad gauge).   These were 0–6–0 tender engines, incorporating Pyracmon, Caesar, Ariadne and Caliph classes. They were a mixed bunch of early goods engines.

Canute class, London & South Western Railway.   Twelve express passenger 2–2–2 locomotives, designed by J.H. Beattie and built in 1856–9 at the railway's Nine Elms Works. They suffered badly from lack of adhesion, and were not as good as the earlier engines by J.V. Gooch. No. 134 *Ironsides* was rebuilt as a 2–4–0 in 1856, but this engine seemed always prone to hot trailing axleboxes, a fault that was never really cured. They spent most of their time at country depots, and the last one was withdrawn in 1885.

Carbrook class, Caledonian Railway.   Twenty-nine express passenger 4–4–0 locomotives, designed by Dugald Drummond, and introduced in 1884 and 1894. Only two were named. They were very similar to the same designer's Abbotsford class for the North British Railway, and Drummond built further very similar engines after moving to the London & South Western Railway. The Carbrook engines were much rebuilt by Drummond's successors, and lasted until 1930.

Cardean class, Caledonian Railway.   Also known as the 903 class. Five of these imposing and very famous 4–6–0 express locomotives were built in 1906 for the heavy 'West Coast' expresses between Glasgow and Carlisle. Generally similar to the 49 or Sir James Thompson class, the cylinder diameter was reduced and the diameter of the boiler increased. Only no. 903 *Cardean* was named, after the estate of Mr Edward Cox, the deputy chairman of directors at the time, but lost its name when that gentleman severed his connection with the railway. No. 907 was destroyed in the Quintinshill accident of 1915. All (except no. 907) were withdrawn by the London Midland & Scottish Railway.

Castle class, Great Western Railway and British Railways.   These engines were first introduced in 1923 and were still being built as late as August 1950, when Swindon Works was withdrawing the earliest examples. The design was a development of the Star class, and several Stars were rebuilt as Castles, an operation involving little more than extending the frames at the rear and fitting a new boiler and cab. Such engines usually kept their names, such as *Tresco Abbey*. While most were named after castles, some were renamed after topical events, for example aircraft in the Battle of Britain (*Defiant*, *Fairey Battle*, etc.) and an Elgar Festival (*Sir Edward Elgar*). The names displaced by such renaming were recycled on later engines, with the result that some names, such as *Denbigh Castle*, were carried by as many as four engines at different times! Several Castles have been preserved.

Castle class, Highland Railway.   David Jones of the Highland Railway had introduced the first British 4–6–0 with his 'Jones Goods' design, the first of which is preserved. He then designed a passenger version, but he was forced to retire following an accident before the engines were built. His successor, Peter Drummond, looked over the drawings, and made one or two alterations – principally the design of chimney and cab – and the Highland Railway's Castle class appeared! They were very successful. First introduced in 1900, the last were withdrawn by the London Midland & Scottish Railway in April 1947. A measure of their success can be gauged from the fact that a further fifty were built by the North British Locomotive Co. during the First World War for the Etat Railway of France; these examples, virtually identical apart from their air brakes, lasted until 1933–7.

Chancellor class, Great Western Railway.   Eight 2–4–0 locomotives built in 1862 at Wolverhampton. No. 154 was the only one to receive a name, *Chancellor*. While it was being built, Sir William Harcourt, then Chancellor of the Exchequer, visited the works. The last one was withdrawn in May 1920.

Chaplin class, London & South Western Railway.   Three 2–2–2WT locomotives, generally similar to the second Sussex class. They were completed in 1856, and were worn out by 1877.

Charon class, East Lancashire Railway.   Two 0–6–0 goods engines, introduced in 1857–9, and lasting until 1881. After amalgamation with the Lancashire & Yorkshire Railway in 1859, a further twenty-eight engines of the same design were built, but none had names.

Chichester class, London, Brighton & South Coast Railway.   The Chichester class comprised two 2–2–2 singles, built by J.C. Craven at Brighton Works in 1864. They were nos 172 *Chichester* and 173, which never received a name. Chichester received its name in 1870, when Stroudley had succeeded Craven, and was withdrawn in 1886.

City class, Great Western Railway.   A very celebrated class of double-framed express passenger 4–4–0s, which combined the double frames of William Dean with the 6ft 8½in driving wheels and the Standard No. 4 taper boiler of G.J. Churchward. Cylinders were 18in diameter × 25in stroke.

The class's main claim to fame is the exploit of *City of Truro*, which was timed by C. Rous-Marten at 102.3mph down Wellington Bank with an 'Ocean Mails' special in 1904. This speed was subsequently examined and rejected by C.J. Allen, who considered that Rous-Marten's stop-watch was capable of a significant error over a quarter-mile; but there is no doubt that *City of Truro* was very fast, and the legend is secure!

The first City was introduced in April 1907 (if one excepts no. 3405 *Mauritius*, which was a rebuilt 'Atbara' of September 1902). The class worked on West of England, Birmingham, and South Wales expresses until superseded by 4–4–2s and 4–6–0s in each case. The last one went to the scrapheap in 1931.

Like so many GWR locomotives, the Cities were renumbered in December 1912:

Old No.	New No.	Old No.	New No.	Old No.	New No.	Old No.	New No.
3400	3700	3405	3705	3433	3710	3438	3715
3401	3701	3406	3706	3434	3711	3439	3716
3402	3702	3407	3707	3435	3712	3440	3717
3403	3703	3408	3708	3436	3713	3441	3718
3404	3704	3409	3709	3437	3714	3442	3719

Clan class, British Railways.   These 4–6–2 general purpose locomotives were introduced in 1952. Only ten were built and, as the name suggests, they were mainly employed in Scotland. They consisted of a Britannia class chassis with a smaller boiler, and in appearance they strongly resembled their larger sisters. None has been preserved.

Clan class, Highland Railway.   Designed by C. Cumming and introduced in 1919; eight were built. They were the last express locomotives built by the Highland Railway, the last four being delivered in 1921. The last survivor was withdrawn by British Railways in the late 1940s.

Claud Hamilton class, Great Eastern Railway.   Designed by James Holden (or, more accurately, by his chief draughtsman, Fred V. Russell), this class of express passenger 4–4–0 locomotives made its appearance in 1900. The first one, numbered 1900 and named *Claud Hamilton* after the chairman of the company, Lord Claud Hamilton, was exhibited at Paris where it gained a gold medal, and became the precursor of a very successful line of express locomotives for the GER. It was the only one to carry a name. After 1923 the London & North Eastern Railway classified these locomotives as class D16.

Claughton class, London & North Western Railway.   Mr C.J. Bowen Cooke's masterpiece, a four-cylinder 4–6–0 which was introduced in January 1913 and handled front-line express passenger trains in the L&NWR's final years. After some fiddling with the numbers, it was arranged that the company's official war memorial was a Claughton, no. 1914 *Patriot*. Later on, some of the Claughtons were fitted with a larger boiler. (Bowen Cooke had wanted to do this from the outset but had been prevented by weight considerations.) The Claughtons were supposed to be rebuilt into the Patriot class, but apart from the wheel centres on the first one or two, the latter engines were entirely new.

Clayton steam railcars, London & North Eastern Railway.   In the mid-1920s the LNER experimented with geared steam railcars. The basic idea was a small, high-pressure boiler and a high-speed engine, with the drive to the wheels via a gearbox. Horsepower was nominally 100. The carriage part was built as light as possible, to reduce the demands on the power unit, which meant (a) that there was little reserve to haul a trailer if the railcar generated more passenger traffic than it could accommodate; (b) there was little reserve strength in the event of an accident; and (c) the vehicle wore out more quickly than ordinary stock. In addition, a fault in either the power unit or the passenger half of the vehicle meant that the whole car was out of commission, and the passenger part was difficult to keep clean while the power unit was being repaired or refuelled. Two manufacturers' products were tried: Claytons, and Sentinel-Cammell. The names were of old-time stage-coaches. All the Clayton cars were out of service by 1937.

Cleveland class, Stockton & Darlington Railway.   Three 0–6–0 long-boiler mineral engines: 60 *Cleveland*, 61 *Star*, and 62 *Southend*. Built by Gilkes, Wilson & Co., they entered service in 1848–9. The cylinders were inside the frames. The first two lasted until 1870, but *Southend* was only withdrawn in 1876.

Clio class, East Lancashire Railway.   Three 2–4–0T engines introduced in 1867 and rebuilt to 2–4–0 tender engines in 1869. They were then included in the Craven class, and lasted until 1882.

Clyde class, London & South Western Railway.   Probably the best known of Joseph Beattie's express engines were the thirteen 2–4–0s built with 7ft driving wheels. No. 157 *Clyde* was the first to enter service, in January 1859, and the last was no. 100 *Python* in October 1868. They were sent to work the London to Southampton and Salisbury expresses, where they won much prestige but they were in fact little better than the already capable 6ft 6in 2–4–0s of the Undine and Falcon classes. As more modern engines arrived, they were cascaded to local and cross-country work, and the last was withdrawn in February 1899.

Clyde Bogie class, Highland Railway.   Eight 4–4–0s by David Jones, with 'Crewe-type' framing, they were introduced in 1886, and the last was withdrawn by the LMS in 1930.

Cobham class, Great Western Railway.   Ten express passenger 2–2–2 engines, first introduced in 1878. Only three had names. The last one was withdrawn in December 1914.

Commerce class, Stockton & Darlington Railway.   These were three long-boiler 0–6–0 mineral engines, designed by William Bouch. They entered service in 1847 and the last two were withdrawn in 1876. The most striking feature of the design was the coupling rods. In order to keep the outside cylinders as close together as possible, the connecting rods were next to the wheels, with the coupling rods outside them. In order to clear the crankpins on the leading pair of wheels, the connecting rods had a large forged eye. The design was unsatisfactory on several counts, most notably the very uneven weight distribution and oscillation at speed owing to the short wheelbase. However, given the slow speeds of the mineral trains, this last may not have been too serious a handicap.

County Class, Great Western Railway.   There were two County Classes, which had very little in common apart from their names.

       1County: 4–4–0 passenger locomotives designed by G.J. Churchward and introduced in 1904. Principally used on the lightly loaded passenger trains between Shrewsbury and Craven Arms, they had a reputation for rough riding and they were all gone before 1939. There is some speculation in enthusiast circles as to just why Churchward built these locomotives at all.

       2County: 4–6–0 passenger locomotives designed by F.W. Hawksworth and introduced in 1945. They were non-standard in several ways, principally with their very high boiler pressure of 280lb/sq. in, a figure only equalled by the Bulleid Merchant Navy and West Country classes on the Southern. It is sometimes alleged that they were the precursors of a still-born design for a 4–6–2 (Hawksworth, as chief draughtsman, had done much of the design work for Churchward's *Great Bear*), but Hawksworth himself always denied this. More likely they made use of the flanging blocks for producing London Midland & Scottish 8F class 2–8–0s, which the Great Western had built in quantity during the war. The second County class worked mainly in Cornwall, and were quietly successful.

Craven class, East Lancashire Railway.   Twelve 2–4–0 passenger engines, first introduced in 1862. The class also incorporates no. 113 *Juno*, an odd engine assembled from spare parts, and the Clio class after they had been rebuilt from 2–4–0Ts to 2–4–0 tender engines. The last one was withdrawn in 1901.

Crewe-type, London & North Western Railway.   This particular family of designs originated with William B. Buddicom (1816–87). Early Grand Junction and L&NWR 2–2–2s showed a marked tendency to break their crank axles, so Buddicom rebuilt some with a plain axle and outside cylinders. To obviate the tendency for cylinders to work loose, Buddicom arranged inside frames and bearings for the driving axle, with outside frames for the leading and trailing axles, and with the outside cylinder securely bolted between the two. There were three main varieties: (a) 2–2–2 passenger engines, shown as 'aCrewe'; (b) 2–4–0 goods engines, shown as 'bCrewe'; and (c) 2–4–0T tank engines, shown as 'cCrewe'. Many of the names were reused, both on other 'Crewe-type' locomotives, and on subsequent L&NWR classes.

D1 class, London, Brighton & South Coast Railway.   In total, 125 of these useful 0–4–2 passenger tank locomotives were built to William Stroudley's designs, the first entering service in 1873. Originally intended for London suburban work, they gravitated to country branches. The last were withdrawn by British Railways in 1951.

D2 class, London, Brighton & South Coast Railway.   See Lyons class.

D3 class, London, Brighton & South Coast Railway.   Designed by Robert Billinton and introduced in 1892, these 0–4–4T engines were intended to replace Stroudley's D1 class on London suburban work. Thirty-six were built, and they ended their days on country branches. The author well remembers them on the Guildford to Horsham line in the late 1940s and early 1950s. The last ones were withdrawn in 1953.

D11/2 class, London & North Eastern Railway.   The Great Central Railway's Director class 4–4–0s (see classes 11E and 11F, Great Central Railway) was so successful that, immediately after the formation of the London & North Eastern Railway in 1923, the new chief mechanical engineer, Mr (later Sir) Nigel Gresley, ordered a further twenty-four for use in Scotland, on the routes of the former North British Railway. They differed from the GCR machines only in having the chimneys and domes made a little lower to clear the Scottish loading gauge. They were given appropriate Scottish names, drawn from the 'Waverley' novels of Sir Walter Scott. Unlike their GCR predecessors, which had cast nameplates, the Scottish Directors had their names painted on the splashers in the North British Railway style.

D16 class, London & North Eastern Railway.   See Claud Hamilton class, Great Eastern Railway.

D49 class, London & North Eastern Railway.   Designed at Darlington to Sir Nigel Gresley's requirements, this class of three-cylinder 4–4–0s first appeared in October 1927. The inside cylinder's valve was driven by Gresley's conjugated motion, thereby obviating the need for a third set of Walschaerts' valve gear.

    There were three varieties: (a) D49/1: piston valve engines; (b) D49/2: fitted with rotary cam-operated Lentz poppet valves; and (c) D49/3: fitted with oscillating cam-operated Lentz poppet valves. The oscillating cam valve gear proved unsatisfactory, and in 1938 all D49/3 engines were converted to ordinary piston valve cylinders, thereby being assimilated into class D49/1. The engines were mostly used in the north-east and in Scotland. They were successful, though with a reputation for rough riding at speed. (The Great Western Railway's first County class, also outside-cylinder 4–4–0s, had the same characteristic.) *Morayshire*, the last in service, was withdrawn in July 1961 and has been preserved.

Dawn class, London, Chatham & Dover Railway.   Five express passenger 2–4–0s designed by William Martley and introduced in 1862. All were successful in service, attaining well over a million miles. The last was withdrawn in 1907.

'Dean Goods', Great Western Railway.   See GWR 2301 class.

Deltic class, British Railways.   A very successful class of Co-Co diesel-electric locomotives, which at the time of their introduction were the most powerful single-unit diesel locomotives in the world at 3,300hp. A direct development of the pioneer 'Deltic', the name came from the triangular arrangement of the cylinders in the two diesel engines each locomotive carried. The first ones entered service in April 1959, and the last was withdrawn only with the onset of the High Speed Trains (HSTs) in 1979 which effectively made them redundant. Originally numbered from D9000, they were renumbered as Class 55:

Old No.	New No.	Old No.	New No.	Old No.	New No.
D9000	55022	D9008	55008	D9016	55016
D9001	55001	D9009	55009	D9017	55017
D9002	55002	D9010	55010	D9018	55018
D9003	55003	D9011	55011	D9019	55019
D9004	55004	D9012	55012	D9020	55020
D9005	55005	D9013	55013	D9021	55021
D9006	55006	D9014	55014		
D9007	55007	D9015	55015		

DFG class, London & South Western Railway.   The 'Double-Framed Goods' engines were built by Beyer Peacock & Co. of Manchester when it became clear that the railway's requirements for new motive power were outstripping the Nine Elms Works' capacity of about eight to ten locomotives per annum. Twenty-four were built, the first entering service in March 1866. Only the first six were named. They were very successful and long-lasting, the last four being withdrawn by the Southern Railway in December 1924.

Director class, Great Central Railway.   See 11E and 11F classes, Great Central Railway.

Director class, Stockton & Darlington Railway.   Sometimes known as the Wilberforce class. First introduced in 1832, the five locomotives of this class were Hackworth-type 0–6–0 mineral engines. They were arranged with vertical cylinders driving on to a plain axle, from which coupling rods transmitted the drive to the wheels. The firebox was directly below the smokebox and chimney, to which it was linked by a return-tube system. Thus the driver stood at one end and the fireman at the other, each on a separate tender carrying water and coal respectively. Very successful engines, they lasted until around 1850, and several were sold for further use.

Dreadnought class, London & North Western Railway.   The Dreadnought class three-cylinder compounds were designed by Mr F.W. Webb and first introduced in 1884. With a 2–2–2–0 wheel arrangement, they were similar to the first Experiment class but slightly larger. They were not very successful.

Duchess class, London Midland & Scottish Railway.   The official designation was 'Princess Coronation' class, but in spite of the fact that only ten of the thirty-eight engines were named after duchesses, the nickname 'Duchess' seems to have stuck! On paper, they were less powerful than the 'Princess Royal' class (with a tractive effort of 40,000lb, compared with 40,285lb for the earlier engines) but when it came to hauling seventeen-coach trains over Shap and Beattock Summits, there was no comparison! The first locomotives were streamlined, for working the 'Coronation Scot' express, but later examples were built without the streamlined casing. After the Second World War all were destreamlined. Details are as follows:

No.	S or N/S	Date Removed	No.	S or N/S	Date Removed	No.	S or N/S	Date Removed
6220	S	9/1946	6233	N/S	–	6246	S	9/1946
6221	S	5/1946	6234	N/S	–	6247	S	5/1947
6222	S	5/1946	6235	S	4/1946	6248	S	12/1946
6223	S	8/1946	6236	S	12/1947	6249	N/S	–
6224	S	5/1946	6237	S	1/1947	6250	N/S	–
6225	S	2/1947	6238	S	11/1946	6251	N/S	–
6226	S	6/1947	6239	S	6/1947	6252	N/S	–
6227	S	2/1947	6240	S	6/1947	6253	N/S	–
6228	S	7/1947	6241	S	1/1947	6254	N/S	–
6229	S	11/1947	6242	S	3/1947	6255	N/S	–
6230	N/S	–	6243	S	5/1949	6256	N/S	–
6231	N/S	–	6244	S	8/1947	46257	N/S	–
6232	N/S	–	6245	S	8/1947			

Duke class, Great Western Railway. Designed for the steep gradients of Devon and Cornwall, this class of double-framed 4–4–0s first appeared in 1895. Sixty were built and all were named. Numbers ran from 3252 to 3331 (not continuously), and like so many GWR locomotives, the Dukes were renumbered in December 1912. Details are:

Old No.	New No.	Old No.	New No.
3252	3252 *Duke of Cornwall*	3257	3256 *Guinevere*
3253	3300 *Pendennis Castle*	3258	3257 *King Arthur*
3254	3253 *Boscawen*	3259	3258 *The Lizard*★
3255	3254 *Cornubia*	3260	3259 *Merlin*
3256	3255 *Excalibur*	3261	3260 *Mount Edgcumbe*
3262	3301 *Powderham*	3287	3276 *St. Agnes*
3263	3302 *Sir Lancelot*	3288	3277 *Isle of Tresco*★
3264	3303 *St. Anthony*	3289	3278 *Trefusis*
3265	3261 *St. Germans*	3290	3279 *Tor Bay*★
3266	3262 *St. Ives*	3291	3280 *Tregenna*
3267	3263 *St. Michael*	3312	3311 *Bulldog*
3268	3304 *River Tamar*★	3313	3281 *Cotswold*
3269	3305 *Tintagel*	3314	3282 *Chepstow Castle*
3270	3264 *Trevithick*	3315	3283 *Comet*
3271	3265 *Tre Pol and Pen*	3316	3312 *Isle of Guernsey*★
3272	3266 *Amyas*	3317	3284 *Isle of Jersey*★
3273	3306 *Armorel*	3318	3313 *Jupiter*
3274	3267 *Cornishman*	3319	3285 *Katerfelto*
3275	3268 *Chough*	3320	3286 *Meteor*
3276	3269 *Dartmoor*	3321	3287 *Mercury*
3277	3270 *Earl of Devon*	3322	3314 *Mersey*
3278	3271 *Eddystone*	3323	3288 *Mendip*
3279	3307 *Exmoor*	3324	3315 *Quantock*
3280	3308 *Falmouth*	3325	3316 *St. Columb*
3281	3272 *Fowey*	3326	3289 *St. Austell*
3282	3309 *Maristow*★	3327	3317 *Somerset*
3283	3273 *Mounts Bay*	3328	3290 *Severn*
3284	3274 *Newquay*	3329	3291 *Thames*
3285	3275 *St. Erth*	3330	3318 *Vulcan*
3286	3310 *St. Just*	3331	3319 *Weymouth*

★ These names were altered during the lives of the locomotives; see main list for details.

In later years, Duke class boilers were mounted on Bulldog class frames, to produce the 3200 (later 9000) class, which went by the happy soubriquet 'Dukedogs'.

Duke class, Highland Railway. Seventeen 4–4–0s designed by David Jones and retaining the 'Crewe-type' framing.

Dunalastair class, Caledonian Railway. The CR's locomotive engineer, J.F. MacIntosh, was contemplating the 4–4–0 express engines designed by his predecessor Dugald Drummond. His works manager, Robert Urie, is said to have remarked: 'Why not build the same engine, but with a much bigger boiler?' MacIntosh did so, and the result was the 721 or Dunalastair class. The design was enlarged further to produce the 766 or Dunalastair II class, and the first engines of each series were named *Dunalastair* and *Dunalastair II* respectively. Of the Dunalastair class, fifteen were built but only three were named: no. 721 *Dunalastair*, after the estate near Pitlochry of Mr J.C. Bunten, the then chairman of the Caledonian Railway, no. 723 *Victoria* and no. 724 *Jubilee*. These last two commemorated Queen Victoria's Diamond Jubilee of 1897. There were also Dunalastair III and Dunalastair IV classes, but none of these engines was named. All were highly successful.

Dunalastair II class, Caledonian Railway. Also known as the 766 class. Very similar to the 721 or Dunalastair class, but with boiler pressure raised from 160 to 175lb/sq. in and the cylinder diameter increased from 18¼in to 19in. Fifteen of these fine 4–4–0s were built, but only two were named: no. 766 *Dunalastair II* and no. 779 *Breadalbane*. The Marquis of Breadalbane was a director of the Caledonian Railway.

DX class, London & North Western Railway. This 0–6–0 goods engine by John Ramsbottom was the first example of a 'mass-produced' design. The first one, no. 355 *Hardman*, appeared in September 1858, and Crewe built nearly eight hundred of them! Only the first fifty-four were named.

E1 class, London, Brighton & South Coast Railway. Seventy-eight of these 0–6–0 goods tank engines were built to William Stroudley's designs, the first entering service in 1883. Intended for short-distance freight, they were found to be quite effective on passenger work and a number were painted in passenger livery. All were named, mostly after European destinations which, it was hoped, might be considered within the LBSCR's sphere of influence! The last were withdrawn by British Railways in 1960, and one is preserved.

E Special class, London, Brighton & South Coast Railway. One locomotive, no. 157 *Barcelona*, built in 1884 by William Stroudley for the Tunbridge Wells–Eastbourne line, where freight loadings were more than the standard E1 class could manage. *Barcelona* had a standard E1 chassis fitted with larger cylinders and boiler. The arrival of E3 and E4 class 0–6–2Ts spelled the end of *Barcelona*'s reign, and it was withdrawn in June 1922.

E3 class, London, Brighton & South Coast Railway. Sometimes called 'Small Radials', these 0–6–2T locomotives were designed by Robert Billinton and first entered traffic in November 1894 on suburban passenger work. They were moderately successful, though somewhat underpowered, and when the more powerful E4 class entered traffic, the E3s were relegated to medium-distance goods work and yard shunting before being packed off to country branch lines. Nevertheless, they had a good innings, the last not being withdrawn until November 1959.

E4 class, London, Brighton & South Coast Railway. Sometimes called 'Large Radials', these 0–6–2T locomotives were extremely useful, both on London suburban traffic and more generally throughout the system. First introduced in December 1897, a total of seventy-five were built, the last being withdrawn in June 1963. Four were rebuilt with larger boilers to class E4x.

E5 class, London, Brighton & South Coast Railway. When further locomotives of the E4 class were required, the opportunity was taken to redesign the cylinders and provide a larger firebox. The result was a very successful class of thirty 0–6–2T locomotives which were first introduced in November 1902 and lasted until January 1956. Intended for London suburban passenger work, they had a fine turn of speed and could help out on the main line in an emergency. Later, they retreated to the country branches in the face of electrification. Four were rebuilt with larger boilers as class E5x.

E6 class, London, Brighton & South Coast Railway. When more goods tank engines were required to augment class E3, advantage was taken to produce a design based on class E5. The result was a class of twelve attractive, efficient locomotives. The first one entered service in December 1904 and they lasted until December 1962. Some were rebuilt with bigger boilers, becoming class E6x.

Eagle class, London & South Western Railway. There were two Eagle classes, the first lasting from 1843 to 1862, and the second from 1862 to 1865. The two classes had nothing in common.

1Eagle: four 2–2–2s assembled at the L&SWR's Nine Elms Works, London. *Eagle*, *Hawk*, *Falcon* and *Vulture* entered service in 1843–4 and lasted until 1862–3. They spent most of their time on London suburban services.

2Eagle: three 2–4–0 engines, also built at Nine Elms. *Eagle*, *Hawk* and *Vulture* reused the names of the above class. They spent most of their time in the West Country, and were all gone by 1886.

Earl class, Great Western Railway. Also known as the 3200 class, these 4–4–0 passenger locomotives were constructed using the frames of withdrawn Bulldog class locomotives and boilers from withdrawn Duke class engines. They appeared in 1936–9 and, with their outside frames, presented a most archaic appearance. Someone coined the soubriquet 'Dukedogs' for the class, and it stuck – in enthusiast circles anyway! The Earls after whom they were named were, in some cases, directors of the GWR, and it is said that they considered themselves affronted that their names should be carried by such small locomotives. At any rate, the names were removed and transferred to new Castle class locomotives – which were much more impresive! The 3200 class was closely associated with the Cambrian main line from Shrewsbury through Welshpool to Aberystwyth and Pwllheli. In 1946 the whole class was renumbered in the 9000 series. One has been preserved, and has had its name restored.

Echo class, London, Chatham & Dover Railway. Five 4–2–0 express engines, designed by T.R. Crampton with his patent arrangement of the driving axle behind the firebox, and the cylinders driving a 'dummy' intermediate shaft coupled to the driving wheels by coupling rods. It was not unlike an inside-cylinder 4–4–0 with the front pair of driving wheels removed, leaving the axle in situ. They entered service in 1862, but could only manage very limited loads. From 1863 onwards, Mr Martley rebuilt them as 4–4–0s, replacing the jackshaft with an orthodox pair of driving wheels. In this condition they ran until 1906.

Edward Pease class, Stockton & Darlington Railway. These were two inside-cylinder, long-boilered 2–4–0s, with the firebox behind the rear axle. No. 114 *Edward Pease* and no. 115 *Meynell* both entered service in 1856. Originally the only protection for the enginemen was a weatherboard, but a cab of William Bouch's characteristic 'biscuit-tin' shape was added later. After at least one rebuilding, both were withdrawn in 1877.

Egmont class, London, Brighton & South Coast Railway.   Two 2–2–2 tank locomotives, nos 222 and 223, appeared in May 1866 to the designs of J.C. Craven. Intended for suburban passenger work in the Crystal Palace and Croydon–Wimbledon area, they were transferred to country branch work soon after Stroudley succeeded Craven. No. 222 received a substantial rebuild in 1874 and received the name *Egmont*, after the seventh Earl of Egmont who resided at Cowdray Park. No. 223 was withdrawn in January 1882, but *Egmont* lasted two years longer.

ELBloomer class, London & North Western Railway.   See L/Bloomer class.

EM1 class, London & North Eastern Railway and British Railways.   'Tommy' was built by the LNER in 1941 for the proposed Manchester–Sheffield–Wath electrification. The wheel arrangement was Bo-Bo. After the Second World War it was loaned to the Netherlands Railways, where it acquired the nickname '*Tommy*'. The name was made official on its return to the UK. Fifty-seven more of the class were built by BR in 1950 for freight work on the newly electrified Manchester–Sheffield–Wath line, and some later received names. They were originally numbered in the 26XXX series, but were renumbered in 1967 into the 76XXX series. Most lasted until the closure of the Woodhead route in 1981.

EM2 class, British Railways.   The passenger version of class EM1, with a Co-Co wheel arrangement. Seven were built between 1953 and 1954 and all were given classical names. They were numbered in the 27XXX series, and in 1967 it was planned to renumber them to 77XXX. However, they were withdrawn in 1968 and sold to the Netherlands Railways before they could be renumbered. *Electra* has recently been repatriated for preservation.

England class, Great Western Railway.   Eight 2–4–0 passenger locomotives were built for the standard gauge by George England & Co., Hatcham Ironworks, in 1862. They were to the standard Great Western pattern, with outside sandwich frames. The whole class was renewed at Stafford Road Works, Wolverhampton, between 1878 and 1883, with little or nothing left of the originals. While no. 154 was under construction in November 1878, the Works were visited by Sir William Harcourt, the Chancellor of the Exchequer, and it was named *Chancellor* in his honour. It was the only one of the class to receive a name. The last one was withdrawn in May 1920.

Enigma class, London, Chatham & Dover Railway.   Three passenger 2–4–0s built at Longhedge Works, London, to W. Martley's design. Work started in 1865, but owing to shortage of cash the first was not completed until 1869. Mr Martley remarked that it was an enigma to him how completion was ever achieved, so at the chairman's suggestion *Enigma* she became! The class was relegated to country work when more modern power displaced them from the main line expresses, but they did good work until withdrawal in 1906.

Enterprise class, Stockton & Darlington Railway.   Four Hackworth-type 0–6–0 mineral engines, the first of which entered service in 1835. The fire grate was at one end of a U-shaped flue, which ran the length of the boiler and returned to exhaust into the chimney, which was alongside the firegrate. The cylinders were at the other end, mounted vertically and driving downwards to the rear pair of wheels. The controls were at the cylinder end, and thus the driver stood on a tender carrying water at one end, and the fireman stood on a tender carrying coal at the other. The direct drive on to the rear axle meant that it could not be sprung, and so the locomotives tended to damage the track. *Enterprise* was rebuilt by W. & A. Kitching, a firm that still survives as Whessoe. They were withdrawn in 1841, and all four were rebuilt by Timothy Hackworth in 1842. *Enterprise* emerged as no. 8 *Leader*, *Briton* as no. 12 *Trader*, and no. 11 *Beehive* as no. 11 *Bee*. *Tees*, rebuilt in 1848, seems to have kept its name and number unaltered.

Eskdale class, Stockton & Darlington Railway.   There were fifteen engines in this class, only two of which had names. These were no. 200 *Eskdale*, and no. 201 *Carlton*, both entering service in 1867. Built by Hopkins, Gilkes & Co., they were inside-cylinder, long-boilered 0–6–0 mineral engines of more or less conventional design. The last of the class was withdrawn in 1909.

Europa class, London, Chatham & Dover Railway.   Mr Martley's last and best 2–4–0 express engines, entering service in 1873. The last two of the six were completed after Martley's death and were never named. They were relegated to local trains and main line piloting, and lasted until 1909.

Experiment class, London & North Western Railway.   The L&NWR had two Experiment classes, which had nothing in common.

1Experiment: no. 66 *Experiment* was the first of a class of forty three-cylinder compound 2–2–2–0s introduced by Mr Webb in 1884. In appearance they were rather like the preserved *Hardwicke*, but with tiny outside cylinders, and no coupling rods. They were not very successful, but Webb persevered with compounding, ultimately to his railway's great disservice.

2Experiment: it was ironic that Mr Whale, in the 'clean sweep' of compounds that followed Mr Webb's retirement, should have chosen both the number and name, no. 66 *Experiment*, of Webb's first and worst compound locomotive class, for his own simple and straightforward 4–6–0 express engines – which were as successful as their predecessors were not. They remained in front-line service for the rest of the company's existence.

F Class, Great North of Scotland Railway.   The GNSR preferred to use 4–4–0 tender engines for all purposes, and the F class, designed by the GNSR's last locomotive engineer, Thomas Heywood, were really mixed traffic locomotives. Introduced in 1920, they had 6ft 1in driving wheels and 18in × 26in cylinders. The first was withdrawn in 1947, and the last, *Gordon Highlander*, went in 1958 and is preserved.

F class, London, Brighton & South Coast Railway.   William Stroudley's first 2–2–2 design, later incorporated in G class.

F class, South Eastern Railway.   The Folkestone continental expresses were increasing in weight and the Mail class 2–2–2s could no longer cope, so James Stirling introduced his F class 4–4–0s to replace them. Eighty-eight of these 4–4–0 express passenger locomotives were eventually built, the first one appearing in December 1883. They worked passenger trains all over the system. Most were eventually reboilered to become class F1, and the last ones were withdrawn by British Railways. Only one was named: no. 240 *Onward*, for the Paris Exhibition of 1889. On 16 March 1890 it re-entered normal work, with its name removed.

Fairbairn class, London & South Western Railway.   This is not the correct designation. These locomotives were rebuilt by Fairbairns from less-than-successful machines optimistically purchased by the railway. *Southampton* retained its name, but all the others were renamed:

New Name	Number (1846)	Old Name	Original Maker
Southampton	16	*Southampton*	Summer, Groves & Day
Queen	17	*Garnet*	G. & J. Rennie
Albert	18	*London*	G. & J. Rennie
Briton	19	*Deer*	G. & J. Rennie
Princess	20	*Victoria*	G. & J. Rennie
Prince	21	*Reed*	G. & J. Rennie
Giraffe	22	*Renown*	C. Tayleur & Co.
Antelope	23	*Sam Slick*	C. Tayleur & Co.
Elk	24	*Tiger*	C. Tayleur & Co.
Reindeer	25	*Pegasus*	C. Tayleur & Co.
Gazelle	26	*Thetis*	C. Tayleur & Co.

Falcon class, London & South Western Railway.   Seventeen 2–4–0 express passenger engines, very similar to the Undine class. The first entered service in June 1863. Not all were exactly alike, and most were sent to London (Nine Elms) for the Southampton and Salisbury traffic, but four were initially stationed at Exeter. Latterly many were employed on local trains and branch lines in Dorset and Hampshire. Withdrawal took place between 1882 and 1898.

Fenton class, London & South Western Railway.   This is not the correct designation. These four miscellaneous 2–2–2s were built by Fenton, Murray & Jackson of Leeds in 1839–40, and lasted until 1856.

Fireball class, London & South Western Railway.   Twenty-eight 2–2–2 locomotives by Rothwell & Co. of Bolton. Delivered in 1846–8, they were quite successful. No. 80 *Hornet* worked the first train into Waterloo station. This was the Up night mail from Southampton, which arrived at 4.30 a.m. on 13 July 1848. The last survivor was withdrawn in December 1872.

Flower class, Great Western Railway.   Twenty double-framed 4–4–0s, very similar to the Atbara class, but with a slightly different frame design. They all appeared in May–July 1908, and had relatively short lives, the last disappearing in April 1931. Like so many GWR locomotives, the Flowers were renumbered in December 1912:

Old No.	New No.	Old No.	New No.	Old No.	New No.	Old No.	New no.
4101	4149	4106	4154	4111	4159	4116	4164
4102	4150	4107	4155	4112	4160	4117	4165
4103	4151	4108	4156	4113	4161	4118	4166
4104	4152	4109	4157	4114	4162	4119	4167
4105	4153	4110	4158	4115	4163	4120	4168

Fury class, Great Western Railway (broad gauge).   A mixed bunch of early goods engines, this class comprised 0–6–0 tender engines, incorporating Hercules and Premier classes, together with *Bacchus*.

G class, London, Brighton & South Coast Railway.   William Stroudley's larger 2–2–2 passenger locomotive design, first introduced in December 1880. The class eventually numbered twenty-four. They worked expresses between London and Brighton and Portsmouth. The last one was withdrawn in 1914.

G class, Metropolitan Railway.   Four 0–6–4T locomotives were designed by Charles Jones for passenger and freight work at the country end of the Metropolitan Railway, the first one entering service in December 1915. They were reasonably satisfactory, and were sold to the London & North Eastern Railway in 1935, losing their names at that time. They became LNER class M2, and the last ones were withdrawn in October 1948.

G. Britain class, London & North Western Railway.   The Greater Britain class of 2–2–2–2s first appeared in 1891 and were three-cylinder compounds designed by Mr F.W. Webb. They had two small high-pressure cylinders mounted outside the frames, and one large low-pressure cylinder mounted between the frames. They thus resembled 2–4–2s but without coupling rods. They could top 80mph under favourable circumstances, but seemed to have little power in reserve for dealing with heavy loads. Thus they were only moderately successful.

Gem class, London & South Western Railway.   Six 2–4–0 goods engines, entering traffic in 1862–3. Most went to the West Country, and were withdrawn in 1884–5.

George V class, London & North Western Railway.   The George V class was a superheated version of the second Precursor class. It was a 4–4–0, designed by C.J. Bowen Cooke and introduced in July 1910. But Mr Bowen Cooke was not quite sure about superheating, and at the same time he introduced a saturated version, the Queen Mary class. Since these were all eventually rebuilt with superheated boilers, they are shown here with an asterisk, e.g. George V★.

Giraffe class, East Lancashire Railway.   Two engines built in 1857 substantially to London & South Western Railway design (possibly the Undine class). It is thought that they might have been part of a cancelled L&SWR order, since they were from a batch of five engines, one of which went to the Glasgow & South Western Railway and the other two to Egypt. They were withdrawn in 1878–9.

Gladstone class, London, Brighton & South Coast Railway.   William Stroudley's final express engines, these 0–4–2s were first introduced in 1882. Thirty-six were built, and they remained on main line work virtually until electrification. D.E. Marsh is said to have considered rebuilding them as inside-cylinder 4–4–2s, but contented himself with reboilering them. The last one was withdrawn in 1933.

Glen class, North British Railway.   A small-wheeled version of the Scott class, the Glens were a very successful 4–4–0 design and were used all over the North British system. The first ones appeared in 1913. They gave good service and were finally withdrawn by British Railways.

Glenbarry class, Highland Railway.   Eighteen 2–2–2s, most of which were altered to 2–4–0. They were of the 'Crewe-type' appearance favoured by the Highland.

Goliath class, East Lancashire Railway.   Five goods locomotives, built 1848–9. It is not certain but research seems to indicate that they were 0–4–0 tender locomotives of Edward Bury pattern: bar frames, domed firebox and generally a very light and spindly construction. (They would have been not unlike the preserved locomotive *"Coppernob"*, at the National Railway Museum at York.) The last was withdrawn in May 1876.

Grange class, Great Western Railway.   Small-wheeled 4–6–0 passenger locomotives, they were very similar to the Manor class, but had a bigger boiler; the two classes were thus very hard to tell apart. Some were rebuilt from withdrawn 43XX class 2–6–0s.

GWR2301 class, War Department.   In both world wars the War Department requisitioned numbers of the Great Western Railway's 2301 class 0–6–0 goods locomotives, colloquially known as 'Dean Goods' after their designer. Light but powerful, they were ideal for working over temporary or damaged track. At least one was captured by the Germans, and in the early 1950s a number were still working as the property of French National Railways, as Class 030W. The GWR's Swindon Works prepared the locomotives for service overseas, fitting them with Westinghouse brakes and some with condensing apparatus as well. Even in the 1950s there were still examples to be found with the War Department, though by now in a somewhat run-down condition.

H class, North British Railway.   A celebrated class of 4–4–2 express passenger locomotives designed by W.P. Reid specifically for the Waverley Route between Edinburgh and Carlisle. They were introduced in 1906 and were successful up to a point. Said to be heavy on coal, they were in fact little more voracious than many other British locomotives. More were built in 1910, and their sphere of activity widened. When superheated they were known as **class I**. Under the London & North Eastern Railway they became **class C11**. They were withdrawn between May 1933 and December 1937, but no. 875 was reinstated and ran until the summer of 1939.

H1 class, London, Brighton & South Coast Railway and Southern Railway.   D.E. Marsh's first 4–4–2 design for the LB&SCR, soon after he arrived from the Great Northern Railway where he had been chief draughtsman under H.A. Ivatt. The locomotives were built by Kitson & Co. of Leeds, to Great Northern drawings amended in red ink, so it was no wonder that they closely resembled the (unnamed) Great Northern Railway large-boilered 4–4–2s. Five engines, they were numbered 37 to 41, and the first one appeared in December 1905. No. 39 was named *La France* in June 1913 to haul M. Raymond Poincaré, the President of the French Republic, from London to Portsmouth, and retained this name until renamed *Hartland Point* by the Southern Railway. Otherwise the engines were unnamed until Southern Railway days, when the following names were applied:

No.	SR No.	BR No.	Name	Withdrawn
37	2037	32037	*Selsey Bill*	July 1951
38	2038	32038	*Portland Bill*	July 1951
39	2039	32039	*Hartland Point*	February 1951
40	2040	–	*St. Catherine's Point*	January 1944
41	2041	–	*Peverill Point*	March 1944

H2 class, Southern Railway.   The London, Brighton & South Coast Railway built these six 4–4–2 express passenger locomotives at Brighton Works, the first one appearing in June 1911. Very similar to Class H1, these locomotives were superheated. (Class H1 used saturated steam in LB&SCR days, but superheated boilers were later fitted by the Southern Railway.) None was named by the Brighton company, but after the formation of the Southern Railway the following names were applied:

No.	SR No.	BR No.	Names	Withdrawn
421	2421	32421	*South Foreland*	August 1956
422	2422	32422	*North Foreland*	September 1956
423	2423	32423	*The Needles*	May 1949
424	2424	32424	*Beachy Head*	April 1958
425	2425	32425	*Trevose Head*	September 1956
426	2426	32426	*St. Alban's Head*	August 1956

Beachy Head was the last 4–4–2 tender locomotive to work in this country. The two classes could easily be distinguished at sight: on class H1 the footplate swept up over the cylinders and down again before the driving wheel splashers, whereas on class H2 the footplate went over the cylinders and then remained level until just before the firebox.

Hall class, Great Western Railway.   A very successful mixed traffic locomotive, which was the Great Western's equivalent to the London Midland & Scottish Railway's class 5 and the London & North Eastern Railway's class B1. All were named after Halls, except the first one, *Saint Martin*. This engine was a Saint class 4–6–0 which was rebuilt with 6ft diameter driving wheels instead of the previous 6ft 8½in. *Saint Martin* was very successful, but the rest were built new; no further Saints were modified.

Hawthorn class, Great Western Railway (broad gauge).   Twenty 2–4–0 tender engines, designed by Joseph Armstrong, Daniel Gooch's successor as locomotive superintendent. First introduced in April 1865, many of them lasted to the end of the broad gauge in 1892. When built, *Avonside* was unimaginatively named *Slaughter*. This had nothing to do with the engine's accident-proneness or otherwise, and everything to do with Mr Slaughter of Slaughter, Gruning & Co. of Bristol, the contractors who built the engines! Nevertheless, the name was changed shortly afterwards.

Helensburgh class, North British Railway.   In 1879 Dugald Drummond built three express passenger 4–4–0 tank locomotives for the fast business trains between Glasgow and the outer suburban towns of Helensburgh, Craigendoran and Dumbarton. All three were named, and renamed, and the last one was withdrawn by the London & North Eastern Railway in March 1926.

Hercules class, London & South Western Railway.   There were two classes with this name, with nothing in common between the two designs.

   1 Hercules: seven 0–4–2 goods locomotives. *Hercules*, *Ajax* and *Atlas* were built by Jones, Turner & Evans; and the remainder by Sharp, Roberts. No. 48 *Hercules* was the first to appear, in August 1840, and nos 42 *Atlas* and 44 *Pluto* were the last to remain in service, being withdrawn in March 1864.

   2 Hercules: fifteen 2–4–0 goods locomotives, designed by J.V. Gooch and completed by his successor J.H. Beattie. They entered traffic in 1851–4, and were used on mixed traffic duties. The last one was withdrawn in 1884.

I class, North British Railway.   See H class, North British Railway.

I2 class, London, Brighton & South Coast Railway.   These were 4–4–2T locomotives, designed by D.E. Marsh for suburban services. Ten engines appeared between December 1907 and August 1908; none was named. Since they were very much less than successful, the opportunity was taken to sell two of them, by now Southern Railway nos 2013 and 2019, to the War Department in March 1942. They spent the remainder of the war on the Longmoor Military Railway, and were renumbered 72400 and 72401. No. 72400 was named *Earl Roberts*. After the war they were moved to a siding at Guildford, where the author, then a schoolboy, remembers being mystified by them. They were scrapped in 1951.

Ilfracombe Goods class, London & South Western Railway.   For the opening of the steeply graded railway from Barnstaple to Ilfracombe, W.G. Beattie asked Beyer, Peacock & Co. of Manchester to design a light 0–6–0 tender locomotive. The first was delivered in February 1873. They were similar to several that Beyer, Peacock had built for export. Withdrawal commenced in 1905 as they eventually became superseded, and their light weight of 24t 7½cwt made them very attractive to Col. H.F. Stephens, a gentleman who in the early years of the twentieth century made a business of buying up light railways and licking them into shape. None of these engines was named by the L&SWR, but Stephens named and allocated his purchases as follows:

L&SWR No.	Light Railway	No. and Name	Laid Aside	Broken Up
0349	Kent & East Sussex	7 *Rother*	12/1932	10/1938
0283	Shropshire & Montgomery	6 *Thisbe*	9/1935	5/1937
0284	Kent & East Sussex	9 *Juno*	3/1935	10/1939
0300	Shropshire & Montgomery	5 *Pyramus*	10/1930	3/1932
0324	Shropshire & Montgomery	3 *Hesperus*	5/1939	11/1941
0394	East Kent	3 (unnamed)	8/1933	3/1935

'Immingham' class. See 8F class, Great Central Railway.

Iron Duke class, East Lancashire Railway. Two long-boilered 0–6–0 goods engines, broadly similar in design. No. 43 *Phoenix* was built in 1847, and no. 46 *Iron Duke* in 1850. Both were withdrawn in 1880.

Iron Duke class, Great Western Railway (broad gauge). These celebrated 4–2–2 locomotives originated with Daniel Gooch's 2–2–2 *Great Western*, the first locomotive to be built at Swindon, in 1846. The load on the leading axle proved too great and it broke near Shrivenham after only a few months' service; the engine was subsequently rebuilt as a 4–2–2. All the wheels were mounted rigidly in the main frames. More were built later. These were the famous 'Gooch 8ft singles', which lasted to between 1871 and 1887. They were then 'renewed' as the Rover class: that is to say, they were withdrawn and scrapped, and replaced by very similar engines which inherited most – but not all – of the names of their predecessors.

J1 and J2 classes, London, Brighton & South Coast Railway. J1 class consisted of one locomotive, a 4–6–2T named *Abergavenny*, which had inside Stephensons valve gear. A close sister was no. 326 *Bessborough*, which had outside Walschaerts valve motion and was classed J2. Both were used on the best expresses between London and Brighton. Both lost their names (officially, that is! They were both referred to by their names by railwaymen, enthusiasts and passengers alike for the rest of their lives!) at the Grouping in 1923, and both lasted into the 1950s.

J36 class, London & North Eastern Railway. This was the LNER classification of the North British Railway's C class.

J94 class. This was the London & North Eastern Railway classification for the ex-War Department 0–6–0STs designed by the Hunslet Engine Co. of Leeds and built in quantity by most manufacturers for the military during the Second World War. Many went into industry, and the type became a standard with the National Coal Board. As noted above, the LNER purchased seventy-five after the war and designated them Class J94. Many have survived into the preservation era, and many preserved lines were operated in their early days by a Hunslet Austerity and a couple of ex-BR Mark 1 coaches. The designation has been used here to identify all those of the design listed, whether ex-LNER or not, for purposes of identification only.

John Bull class, East Lancashire Railway. Four 2–4–0s, introduced in 1849. Nos 44 *John Bull* and 45 *Caliban* were rebuilt as 2–4–0Ts. All were withdrawn by 1880.

John Hick class, London & North Western Railway. These engines, introduced in 1894, were a smaller-wheeled version of the Greater Britain class (see G. Britain class). With 6ft driving wheels, they had all the faults of the larger engines but none of the virtues. Contemporary writers had scarcely a good word to say for them, though O.S. Nock, in his *The Premier Line* (Ian Allan, 1952) tries to be kind.

Jones Tanks, Highland Railway. Three 2–4–0Ts with 'Crewe-type' framing, which were converted to 4–4–0T, still with the 'Crewe-type' framing which was much favoured by the Highland Railway. They were introduced by David Jones, locomotive superintendent.

Jubilee class, London Midland & Scottish Railway. Sir William Stanier's first three-cylinder 4–6–0, these engines suffered quite prolonged teething troubles. In short, they would not steam. Once this had been sorted out, they were very successful and worked all over the LMS. In the L&NWR tradition, the names were a mixture of colonies, admirals, classical allusions, battles, ships' names and pioneer locomotives, many of which last had previously been carried by Royal Scot class locomotives. Introduced in 1934–6, they lasted until the end of steam and some have been preserved.

Jubilee class, London & North Western Railway. A class of 4–4–0 four-cylinder compound express locomotives designed by F.W. Webb, and first introduced in March 1899. They were not very successful, though they were capable of occasional good work. Some of the names were perpetuated in the LMS Jubilee class, mentioned above.

K1 class, London & North Eastern Railway. See K4 class.

K2 class, London & North Eastern Railway.   A mixed traffic 2–6–0 design by Mr (later Sir) Nigel Gresley for the Great Northern Railway, and first introduced in 1914. There were variations: class K2/2 was the basic 1914 design; class K2/1 was a 1931 rebuild of class K1 (which dated from 1912 on the Great Northern); and class K2/2, which was fitted with a side-window cab for use in Scotland. Of these, some of class K2/2 were named after Scottish lochs.

K4 class, London & North Eastern Railway.   These 2–6–0 locomotives were designed by Sir Nigel Gresley for the West Highland Line, the first appearing in 1937. Only six were built, and all were given suitable Scottish names:

Name	Original No.	BR No.
Loch Long	3441	61993
The Great Marquess	**3442**	**61994**
Cameron of Lochiel	3443	61995
Lord of the Isles	3444	61996
MacCailin Mor	3445	61997
MacLeod of MacLeod	3446	61998

No. 3442 was originally named *MacCailein Mor*, but the spelling mistake was quickly noticed and the engine was renamed within a fortnight. No. 3445 *MacCailin Mor* (spelt correctly this time!) was rebuilt by Edward Thompson with two cylinders and renumbered 1997; it formed the prototype of his class K1, of which 70 were built by British Railways. This engine, however, was the only one to carry a name.

King class, Great Western Railway.   A development of the Castles, themselves a development of the Stars. These engines were planned as the Cathedrals class and were to be named after English cathedrals, but this was changed with the permission of the reigning monarch and they became the King class. The first *King William III* was written off after the Shrivenham accident in March 1936, and replaced by a new locomotive with the same name and number. *King George VI* was originally named *King Henry II*, and *King Edward VIII* was originally named *King Stephen*.

King Arthur class, Southern Railway.   The earliest ones were built for the London & South Western Railway by Robert Urie, and the rest by R.E.L. Maunsell for the Southern. Sir John Elliott, then PR officer for the Southern, had the idea of naming the engines after the Arthurian legends, and consulted Sir Herbert Walker, the General Manager, and Maunsell. Maunsell is said to have replied: 'Tell Sir Herbert I have no objection, but I warn you it will not affect the performance of the engines!' In the event they were highly successful, and were the mainstay of Southern express passenger services until the arrival of the Merchant Navy and West Country classes.

L class, London, Brighton & South Coast Railway.   The two J class 4–6–2 tank locomotives were only just able to cope with the longest and heaviest runs on the system, so Mr L. Billinton prepared an enlarged version of the design, with a four-wheeled trailing bogie making a 4–6–4T wheel arrangement. The first one, no. 327 *Charles C. Macrae*, entered service in March 1914. Seven were built, of which only the first one and nos 329 *Stephenson* and 333 *Remembrance* had names. No. 333 was the official war memorial locomotive, and carried a plaque inscribed:

IN GRATEFUL REMEMBRANCE
OF THE 532 MEN OF THE
L.B.&S.C.RLY WHO GAVE THEIR
LIVES FOR THEIR COUNTRY
1914–1919

In service the first 4–6–4Ts were originally prone to water surging in the tanks, and later examples were built with well tanks under the boiler and back tanks under the coal bunker. The earlier ones were altered to conform. They gave good service, but the electrification of most of the former LB&SCR made them redundant. To improve their radius of action, R.E.L. Maunsell converted them to 4–6–0 tender engines between 1934 and 1936, gave them all names, and restyled them as class N15x, or the Remembrance class, as shown in the following table.

No.	Name	Date	Rebuilt	Name	Withdrawn
327	*Charles C. Macrae*	4/1914	4/1935	*Trevithick*	1/1956
328	–	9/1914	2/1936	*Hackworth*	1/1955
329	*Stephenson*	10/1921	12/1934	*Stephenson*	7/1956
330	–	12/1921	9/1935	*Cudworth*	8/1955
331	–	12/1921	4/1936	*Beattie*	7/1957
332	–	3/1922	11/1935	*Stroudley*	1/1956
333	*Remembrance*	4/1922	6/1935	*Remembrance*	4/1956

The Southern Railway renumbered the locomotives 2327–33, and British Railways further renumbered them 32327–33. See Remembrance class.

L class, Southern Railway.   In 1914 the South Eastern & Chatham Railway introduced a new class of express passenger 4–4–0 locomotives. All were unnamed, and all became Southern Railway locomotives in 1923, receiving an A prefix to their numbers to distinguish them from the other two constituents of the Southern. During the General Strike of 1926, no. A763 was unofficially named *Betty Baldwin*, the name being neatly applied with gold leaf on the leading splasher. It remained until the locomotive was next repainted, in May 1927. This was the only L class 4–4–0 to carry a name.

Lancing class, London, Brighton & South Coast Railway.   Three large 2–2–2s were designed by J.C. Craven, and appeared in 1858 and 1861. Initially used on London–Brighton expresses, they later worked on most main lines of the system and were withdrawn by 1886.

Large Ben class, Highland Railway.   A larger-boilered version of the Small Ben class (officially Class U), the Large Bens first appeared in 1908, only two years after the last of the earlier class entered service. Six were built, again named after Scottish mountains. Not so long-lasting as their smaller sisters, the last one in service was no. 14422 *Ben a'Chaoruinn* (Highland Railway no. 62), withdrawn by the London Midland & Scottish Railway in March 1937.

L/Bloomer class, London & North Western Railway.   The Large Bloomers (a nickname which gained at least semi-official currency) were a class of 2–2–2 express passenger locomotives designed by John Ramsbottom and first introduced in 1851. They had 7ft diameter driving wheels, which distinguished them from the Small Bloomers of 1854 (6ft 6in driving wheels) and the three Extra-Large Bloomers of 1861 (7ft 6in driving wheels). The locomotives appeared at a time when Mrs Amelia Bloomer was trying to introduce certain reforms in ladies' dress. Without the decent skirting of an outside frame, and with most of their wheels uncovered, quite clearly they were 'Bloomers'! Very effective locomotives, they lasted until the early 1880s on front-line duties.

Leader class, British Railways (Southern Region).   Though never named, the Leader class locomotive was so celebrated (or infamous) that it seems a pity to omit it. No. 36001 was always referred to as the Leader. The concept of a double-ended tank locomotive to replace the M7 class 0–4–4 tank engines was well advanced by nationalization, and British Railways allowed the experiment to proceed. Only one locomotive, no. 36001, was completed and subjected to trials. It usually had to be towed back to base by an older, more orthodox, and infinitely more reliable locomotive. The engine never hauled a revenue-earning train. It was ordered to be scrapped, together with the incomplete nos 36002 and 36003, in 1951.

Leo class, Great Western Railway (broad gauge).   Eighteen 2–4–0 tender engines for goods work, first introduced in January 1841. To increase the adhesive weight, they were all altered to 2–4–0 tank engines. The last was withdrawn by June 1874.

Lion class, London & South Western Railway.   A class of inside-framed 0–6–0 goods engines by Joseph Beattie. Thirty-eight were built, no. 101 *Lion* entering service in December 1863. Although used primarily on main line freight work, no. 16 *Salisbury* was regularly employed on passenger trains, and its prominent nameplate misled unwary passengers into mistaking it for the train's destination! So, after complaints, the engine was renamed *Stonehenge*. The last of the class was withdrawn in June 1906. The combined name, date and number plate from no. 92 *Charon* survives in the National Railway Museum, York.

Loch class, Highland Railway.   Eighteen 4–4–0s by David Jones, in which he at last abandoned the 'Crewe-type' framing around the outside cylinders. They were his last design for the Highland, with 6ft 3½in driving wheels. Introduced in 1896, the last survivor was withdrawn by British Railways in 1950.

Lochgorm Tanks, Highland Railway.   Three small 0–6–0T shunters, designed by William Stroudley and celebrated as the forerunners of the LB&SCR's Terrier class.

Locomotion class, Stockton & Darlington Railway.   These were no. 1 *Locomotion* and her sisters, 0–4–0 locomotives designed by George Stephenson. *Locomotion* is credited with hauling the inaugural train on the S&DR on 27 September 1825. No. 2 *Hope* may have been originally named *Bedlington*; if so, it can only have been for a very short while. With their two vertical cylinders, the engines were very similar to Stephenson's Killingworth Colliery locomotives. In motion, the vertical pistons caused a 'bouncing' motion, which caused the unsprung locomotives to be unstable at any speed much over 8 or 10mph. These pioneers lasted into the 1840s, albeit much rebuilt, and no. 1 *Locomotion* survives to this day.

Lord Nelson class, Southern Railway.   At the time of their introduction in 1926, they were the most powerful passenger locomotives in the UK (on a tractive effort basis, that is. Tractive effort, which is measured in lb,★ is a theoretical

---

★ The Phillipson formula for calculating a locomotive's tractive effort is:

$$\text{Tractive effort} = \frac{0.85 \, d^2 \, s \, n \, p}{2 \, w}$$

where d = cylinder diameter (in inches); s = piston stroke (in inches); n = number of cylinders; p = boiler pressure in lb/sq. in; and w = driving wheel diameter (in inches).

calculation and has largely fallen into disuse as a means of rating a locomotive's performance. Horsepower is much more meaningful. But when the Lord Nelsons appeared, tractive effort was the yardstick!). Designed by R.E.L. Maunsell, there were sixteen of these most impressive 4–6–0s. But they were disappointing, and were much improved by O.V.S. Bulleid, who fitted new cylinders and made other improvements. Initially designed for the Dover boat trains, they ended their service on the 'Ocean Liner' expresses between Waterloo and Southampton Docks and lasted to the end of Southern steam.

L/Scotchmen/Large Scotchmen class, London, Chatham & Dover Railway.   Six 0–4–2 well tank engines, designed by William Martley. They were an enlargement of the Scotchmen class. The first entered service in 1873 and they were very successful. They lasted until 1914.

Lyons class, London, Brighton & South Coast Railway.   These were a tender version of the very successful D1 class 0–4–2Ts. First introduced in 1876, there were fourteen engines, almost all named after European resorts. The last were withdrawn in 1907. They are sometimes known as class D2.

Mails class, South Eastern Railway.   For working the Folkestone tidal expresses, J.I. Cudworth designed two large and powerful 2–2–2 locomotives in 1861. Six more, slightly smaller, appeared in 1865–6. Known as the 'Mail Singles', they handled the continental expresses for many years. They were unnamed, but for a short time no. 72 was named *Excalibur* and no. 81 *Flying Dutchman*, and both appeared in a royal blue livery instead of the usual holly green. They had a good innings, the last ones being withdrawn in February 1890.

Majestic class, Stockton & Darlington Railway.   First appearing in 1831, the six members of this class were Hackworth-type 0–6–0 mineral engines. The vertical cylinders were mounted ahead of the smokebox on a kind of outrigger, and drove downwards on to a plain axle. Coupling rods transmitted the drive to the wheels. The driver stood on a tender carrying water at the cylinders end, and the fireman stood on a tender carrying coal at the firebox end. The engines were unsteady in service, and one authority mentions a stabilizing weight mounted under the firebox. They seem to have been prone to derailments and were clearly not as successful as hoped. *Northumbrian* and *Lord Brougham* were dismantled in 1838, and the last one went in 1841 after a life of just ten years.

Manor class, Great Western Railway.   A small-boilered class of 4–6–0 locomotives, intended for use on lines subject to axle-loading restrictions. After initial problems with draughting had been satisfactorily solved after 1945, they were very successful on the lines of the former Cambrian Railways, and lasted to the end of Western Region steam.

Mazeppa class, London & South Western Railway.   Ten 2–2–2 express engines were built at the L&SWR's Nine Elms Works, entering traffic in 1847. They were fast runners and trouble-free, and the railway was well pleased with them. The last was withdrawn in 1870.

Medium Goods, Highland Railway.   Ten 'Crewe-type' 2–4–0s with 5ft 1½in driving wheels.

Medusa class, East Lancashire Railway.   Four engines built in 1846 as 2–2–2s. Later no. 1 *Medusa* was rebuilt as a 2–4–0T, but it is not clear if the others were similarly altered. No. 10 *Diomed* was exchanged for a Lancashire & Yorkshire Railway 2–2–2 (their no. 90), which took the same name and number on the ELR. All were withdrawn by 1869.

Merchant Navy class, Southern Railway.   See MN class.

Metro./Metropolitan class, Great Western Railway (broad gauge).   Sir Daniel Gooch designed these 2–4–0 well tanks to operate the Metropolitan Railway, which opened from Paddington to Farringdon. They were the first engines to have condensing gear (whereby the exhaust steam was diverted into the water tank, condensed, and reused, in an attempt to alleviate the smoke nuisance in the tunnels). They were also the only broad gauge engines built for the Great Western with outside cylinders. Not very successful, they were soon moved to country areas, and some were converted into 2–4–0 tender engines.

M/Hall class, Great Western Railway.   The Hall class proved very successful, and the design of the frames was altered at the front end to facilitate production. This produced the Modified Hall class, and the two are distinguishable by looking at the framing. On the Modified Hall the frames are visible above the curved footplating below the smokebox door; on the original Hall class the frames are not visible. There were over three hundred Halls and Modified Halls. While some of the names are well-known, many are obscure. Also, one wonders if there was any difference between *Broughton Hall*, *Broughton Grange* and *Broughton Castle*!

Miner class, Stockton & Darlington Railway.   These locomotives were very similar to the Tory class, with return-flue boilers which had the smokebox immediately above the firebox. The cylinders were mounted at the other end, at a fairly steep angle, and drove the wheels nearest the firebox. Thus all axles could be sprung. The arrangement did, however, mean that the driver stood on a tender carrying water at the cylinders end, and the fireman stood on a tender carrying coal at the firebox end. There were six locomotives, and they were quite successful. No. 29 *Miner* entered service in June 1845. The last to be withdrawn, no. 33 *Shildon*, went in 1877.

Minerva class, London & South Western Railway.   The first of four classes of 2–4–0 well tanks for the London suburban services and for country branch line work. There were three engines, built in 1856 and withdrawn by 1883.

MN class, Southern Railway. The Merchant Navy class engines, designed by O.V.S. Bulleid, were originally numbered from 21C1 to 21C20. The remainder of the class were built new by BR, and numbered 35021–30, the earlier engines being renumbered 35001–20 to suit. No. 21C13 *Blue Funnel* later had the shipping company's motto *Certum Pete Finem* added to the nameplate in smaller letters. (A rough translation is 'Make a Good Job of It'!) All of these engines were rebuilt without the 'air-smoothed' casing, chain-driven valve gear, oil baths and other Bulleid idiosyncrasies, but the original nameplates were reused.

N class, Great North of Scotland Railway. Two 4–4–0s designed by James Manson and introduced in 1887. Both were named, but the names were removed in the 1890s by William Pickersgill. Driving wheels were of 5ft 7in diameter, and cylinders were 17½in × 26in. They were used on both passenger and freight work, and were withdrawn by 1936.

N class, Southern Railway. The South Eastern & Chatham Railway introduced the first N class locomotive, a 2–6–0 mixed traffic engine, in 1917 when the first example appeared. Eleven more were completed before the SE&CR became merged in the Southern in 1923, and further construction brought the final total to sixty-nine. They worked all over the Southern Railway, and lasted to the end of steam in the 1960s. A very successful design indeed, they were capable of working almost anything. One or two examples have been preserved, and have since been named.

N7 class, London & North Eastern Railway. A class of 0–6–2T locomotives introduced by A.J. Hill on the Great Eastern Railway in January 1915 for London suburban duties, and subsequently multiplied by the London & North Eastern Railway. One has been named in preservation.

N15 class, Southern Railway. See King Arthur class.

N15x class, Southern Railway. See Remembrance class.

Nelson class, London & South Western Railway. J.H. Beattie's second class of 2–4–0WTs, again for the London suburban services and country branches. There were three engines, built in 1858 and withdrawn by 1885.

Newton class, London & North Western Railway. These 2–4–0s were first designed by John Ramsbottom in 1866. Seventy-six were built initially, with more built by F.W. Webb after Ramsbottom's retirement. They had 6ft 7½in driving wheels, and shared main line duties with the Problem class 2–2–2s until they were renewed as improved Precedent class engines, a process started in 1887. See rPrecedent class.

Nile class, London & South Western Railway. J.H. Beattie's third class of 2–4–0WTs, again for the London suburban services and country branches. There were three engines, built in 1859 and withdrawn in 1882.

O2 class, London & South Western Railway and Southern Railway. Designed by William Adams for lighter suburban services and branch line work, the first of these 0–4–4T locomotives entered service on 12 December 1889. Seventy were built and, in accordance with L&SWR policy at the time, none had names – apart from no. 185 *Alexandra*. This was specially named for the opening of the Brookwood–Bisley branch on 12 July 1890, and the first shoot of the National Rifle Association at the Bisley Ranges, an event attended by HRH the Princess of Wales, afterwards Queen Alexandra. No. 185 hauled the special train and, as well as the name, received a representation of the Prince of Wales's feathers and a monogram of the company's initials. It became nameless again in November 1896, the date of the next repaint. It was the only member of its class to bear a name until Southern Railway days, when engines transferred to the Isle of Wight were named after places on the island. Isle of Wight locomotives differed from their mainland sisters: they had Westinghouse brakes, with the pump prominent on the smokebox side and an air tank on top of a side tank. A deep-toned hooter replaced the usual whistle, and the bunkers were later enlarged to carry 3 tons of coal instead of the original 1½ tons.

P class, South Eastern & Chatham Railway. Mr H.S. Wainwright was impressed by the A1 or Terrier class 0–6–0T locomotives on the neighbouring London, Brighton & South Coast Railway, and also by the very small tank locomotives on the London & South Western Railway specifically designed for push-and-pull trains. As a means of economical working for branch lines, the idea of a control system whereby the train could run in reverse, with the locomotive pushing at the back while the driver controlled it from a cab at the leading end of the first coach, had much to commend it, and most of the main line companies adopted it. Usually, superannuated tank locomotives were used; the SE&CR was one of the few to design a class specifically for the job (the Great Western was another, with its 14XX class). Class P consisted of eight small 0–6–0T engines, the first two of which appeared in 1909 and the rest in 1910. As push-and-pull passenger locomotives they were something of a failure, being underpowered, but they did well at shunting and harbour work. All lasted to be withdrawn by British Railways, and two were sold to the preserved Bluebell Railway. There they were named: no. 323 became *Bluebell*, and no. 327 *Primrose*.

P2 class, London & North Eastern Railway. In 1934 Sir Nigel Gresley introduced the first (and last) 2–8–2 passenger design to run in the United Kingdom. The engines were for the Edinburgh–Aberdeen main line, which abounds in sharp curves and heavy gradients. The first one, no. 2001 *Cock o'the North*, had poppet valves, and was subjected to testing at the Vitry testing plant in France. No. 2002 *Earl Marischal* had Walschaerts valve gear. Both had a curious semi-streamlined form at the front end, which wind-tunnel experiments indicated would eliminate the problem of drifting smoke interfering with the driver's forward vision. This was reasonably satisfactory on *Cock o'the North*, with the sharper exhaust from the poppet valves, but was not so successful on *Earl Marischal*. The latter received an extra set of smoke deflectors, but the decision was taken to alter *Cock o'the North* to Walschaerts valve gear, and at the same time to give both engines (and the rest of the class) an A4-type wedge-shaped front, but without the faring over the boiler or the valances over the wheels. The engines were not entirely satisfactory in service. There was talk of the long-coupled wheelbase not riding well on the sharp curves, and the coal consumption was high. On the credit side, they were absolute masters of any load the traffic people cared to give them. Edward Thompson rebuilt them as 4–6–2s in 1943–4, retaining their names. Thompson placed the bogie in advance of the outside cylinders, thus producing a locomotive which looked 'wrong', and was no improvement on the original 2–8–2 design as far as riding was concerned, and was definitely detrimental to the load-hauling capacity.

Panther class, Stockton & Darlington Railway.   Twenty-five long-boilered 0–6–0 mineral engines, introduced in 1860. The first six were built by R. & W. Hawthorn, another fifteen by Gilkes, Wilson & Co., and the last four at Shildon Works in 1863–4. Quite successful, they lasted into the early 1900s.

Patriot class, London Midland & Scottish Railway.   These engines were originally supposed to be rebuilds of the L&NWR Claughton class, but, although wheel centres may have been reused on the first one or two examples, they were in fact entirely new. They consisted of a Royal Scot class 4–6–0 three-cylinder chassis with a smaller boiler. (The Claughtons had had four cylinders.) Sir William Stanier rebuilt most (if not all) with larger taper boilers after the Second World War. The names were a mixture, in the L&NWR tradition. *Patriot* was the official war memorial locomotive, and for many years carried a wreath on Armistice Day. *Private E. Sykes V.C.* and *Private W. Wood, V.C.* were both named in honour of LMS engine drivers, who were duly photographed with 'their' engines for publicity purposes. For some unexplained reason (probably sheer carelessness), Wood had a comma after his name and Sykes hadn't!

Peak class, British Railways.   In all, 193 of these 1Co-Co1 diesel-electric locomotives were built, the first taking to the rails in 1959. The first ten, which were named after mountains, had Sulzer twelve-cylinder 12LDA28–A twin-bank pressure-charged engines of 2,300bhp at 750rpm, and the remainder, which were named after regiments, had Sulzer 12LDA28–B engines, with inter-cooling, of 2,500bhp at 750rpm. In later years the first group became class 44 and the second group class 45.

Peel class, Stockton & Darlington Railway.   Nine inside-cylinder, long-boilered 0–6–0s, first introduced in 1852. There is a possibility that these locomotives were not originally built as long-boiler engines, but were altered to this form later. Successful engines, the last one was withdrawn in 1911.

Pegasus class, East Lancashire Railway.   Two 0–4–2 goods engines, taken into stock in 1847. In 1863 they were 'rebuilt' as 2–4–0s, with very little, if any, of the original engines incorporated. *Pegasus* was the last to go, in 1885.

Phaeton class, East Lancashire Railway.   Six 2–4–0s for passenger work, first introduced in 1848. A successful design, they lasted until 1882.

Pierremont class, Stockton & Darlington Railway.   Two engines, no. 98 *Pierremont* and no. 101 *Marske*. They were long-boilered 2–4–0 passenger locomotives, with inside cylinders. Entering service in 1855, they were successful and lasted until 1876 and 1882 respectively. Another two of broadly the same design, no. 99 *Ayton* and no. 100 *Stobart*, were built by the Shildon Works Co. in 1855 but were less successful than the earlier pair, and both were gone by 1882.

Planet class, Stockton & Darlington Railway.   Two locomotives, no. 10 *Planet* and no. 11 *North Star*. They were 2–2–0 passenger locomotives, very similar to the Liverpool & Manchester Railway engine of the same name. *Planet* entered service in November 1830, and *North Star* in March 1831. Both seem to have been very successful on light passenger work, and lasted until they wore out in 1839 and 1842 respectively.

Pluto class, East Lancashire Railway.   Two 0–4–2 goods engines, introduced in 1850 and withdrawn by 1876.

Precedent class, London & North Western Railway.   These 2–4–0s were designed by F.W. Webb and first appeared in 1874. Driving wheels were 6ft 6in diameter.

rPrecedent class, London & North Western Railway.   These engines were officially rebuilds of the original Precedent class. They had thicker frames and higher boiler pressure. They carried for the most part the same names and numbers as the Newtons they replaced, and even the same nameplates with the original building date unaltered. But in fact they were completely new locomotives, and should therefore be considered as renewals. They include Hardwicke, the sole survivor, which has been restored to its original L&NWR number of 790.

Precursor class, London & North Western Railway.   There were two Precursor classes, which had nothing in common.

1Precursor: the first Precursor class comprised 2–4–0s designed by F.W. Webb; they first appeared in 1874. Driving wheels were 5ft 6in diameter.

2Precursor: after Webb's retirement, his successor, George Whale, placed in service in 1904 a simple and straightforward 4–4–0 named *Precursor*. The L&NWR tradition of reusing names meant that there were now two Precursor classes, one a 2–4–0 and one a 4–4–0. The prefixes 1 and 2 have been added here to minimize confusion.

Priam class, Great Western Railway (broad gauge).   These were 2–2–2 tender engines, incorporating the Prince class, and all Fire Fly class engines not rebuilt as tank engines.

Priam class, Stockton & Darlington Railway.   Gilkes, Wilson & Co. built twelve 2–4–0 long boiler locomotives with outside cylinders in 1847 for the Newmarket & Great Chesterford Railway, who found that they could only afford to pay for six of them. The WS&DR took the rest. There is a suggestion in one source that no. 65 *Stephenson* may originally have been named *Newmarket*. Although designed as passenger engines, they worked mainly on mineral traffic, on which they were quite successful. All lasted into the 1870s.

Prince/W class, London & North Western Railway.   The Prince of Wales class were inside-cylinder express passenger 4–6–0s introduced in 1911 by C.J. Bowen Cooke. They were a superheated version of the Experiment class (the second Experiment class, that is). They were reasonably successful, and the last was withdrawn in May 1949.

Princess of Wales class, Midland Railway.   S.W. Johnson produced four series of 4–2–2 express passenger locomotives for the Midland Railway. The first, in June 1887, had 7ft 4in driving wheels. The 1893 and 1896 batch were similar but had piston valves instead of slide valves. The third lot, which appeared in 1896, had 7ft 9in driving wheels. In 1899 came no. 2601 *Princess of Wales*, the only one to receive a name. This one and her nine sisters were again very similar, differing only by an inch or two here and there. But they were equipped with huge eight-wheeled tenders which, when full, weighed more than the locomotives themselves!

Princess Royal class, London Midland & Scottish Railway.   These were Sir William Stanier's first express passenger design. Named after members of the royal family, they present a trap for the unwary: *Duchess of Kent* is NOT a Duchess class locomotive! *Princess Elizabeth* set up a record for a non-stop run from London to Glasgow and back. These 4–6–2s lasted until the end of steam on the London Midland Region of British Rail.

Problem class, London & North Western Railway.   Sometimes called the Lady of the Lake class, these were 2–2–2 express engines by John Ramsbottom. The first appeared in 1859, and sixty were built. They were renewed over the years, receiving Webb boilers, chimneys and cabs. Their final years were spent as main line pilots.

Queen class, Great Western Railway.   There were twenty-one of these 2–2–2s, of which ten had names. First introduced in 1873, the last survivor was withdrawn in April 1914.

Raigmore class, Highland Railway.   The Highland Railway had two Raigmore classes. The first was a class of four very small 2–2–2 engines, designed by William Barclay and rebuilt by William Stroudley as 2–4–0s. When they were all gone, the name was reused for a pair of 2–4–0s designed by David Jones for local passenger work.

Reindeer class, London, Chatham & Dover Railway.   William Martley designed this class of six 2–4–0 passenger locomotives, all entering traffic in July 1865. They had 6ft 6in driving wheels. At first, they worked the London Victoria–Dover services, but were supplanted by the larger Europa class in 1873. As was customary on the LC&DR in Martley's time, the engines were named but not numbered, but after his successor William Kirtley took office the numbers 44 to 49 were allotted and the names were gradually removed. The last one to go was *Talisman*, by now no. 48, in 1908.

Remembrance class, Southern Railway.   Officially designated class N15x, they were 4–6–0 tender engines rebuilt from the London, Brighton & South Coast Railway L class 4–6–4 tank engines. *Remembrance* and *Stephenson* retained their names; the rest were either named or renamed after bygone locomotive engineers. *Remembrance* was the official war memorial locomotive, and carried a plate under the nameplate commemorating the LB&SCR men killed in the First World War. The practice of adding an x to a class designation when the engines were improved came from the LB&SCR; in this instance it was illogical because the engines should have been class Lx, as they had nothing in common with the King Arthur or N15 class. Indeed, the locomotive department thought at first that they were getting a 'hotted-up' King Arthur, and the rebuilds had a brief fling on the two-hour Bournemouth expresses. But they soon settled down to all-stations locals, which was much more their scene! They lasted until the 1950s.

Rennie class, London & South Western Railway.   Not the correct designation. These five 2–2–2s were built by George and John Rennie, a London firm, in 1838. Not very successful, they were all sent to Fairbairns in 1841 for extensive rebuilding.

Richmond class, London, Brighton & South Coast Railway.   The first one, *Richmond*, was an enlarged Lyons class 0–4–2, intended for express passenger work, and entered service in 1878. A total of six were built, and the last one was withdrawn in 1904.

River class, Great Western Railway.   A class built as 2–2–2s in 1855–6 and altered to 2–4–0 in 1895. They lasted until December 1918.

River class, Highland Railway.   None of these engines bore names in service, and so they do not figure in the preceding pages, but they are a fascinating 'might-have-been'. The Highland Railway's locomotive superintendent, F.G. Smith, designed six large 4–6–0s in 1915. However, as he did not get on with the civil engineer, Alexander Newlands, he did not consult him over the new design and the first Newlands knew about them was when the first one arrived from the builders. It was intended to name them after Highland rivers, and the first one was named *River Ness*. Newlands forbade the engines' use on the grounds that they were too heavy for the underline bridges, and they were sold (at a profit!) to the Caledonian Railway. The Caledonian never named them. As for Mr Smith, he was called before the directors and invited to resign. But after the 1923 Grouping, it was agreed that the locomotives would be less harmful to the track than Newlands had feared, and they returned to work on the Highland main line after all!

River class, Southern Railway.   The Southern's first chief mechanical engineer was R.E.L. Maunsell, who came from the South Eastern & Chatham Railway, and already had a prototype 2–6–4 express passenger tank locomotive in service. Maunsell multiplied the class to twenty examples, one of which, no. 890 *River Frome*, had three cylinders. (The rest had two.) Concern was expressed about the engines' tendency to roll at speed, and matters came to a head with the Sevenoaks accident in 1927, in which thirteen passengers were killed. The engines were then converted to 2–6–0 tender engines, losing their names in the process. (The popular press dubbed them the 'Rolling Rivers'.) They became class U, and the three-cylinder example became the prototype of class U1. In preservation, a converted River class locomotive has had its name restored.

Roach class, East Lancashire Railway.   Four long-boilered 2–2–2s, with all wheels ahead of the firebox, built in 1846. In 1848 they were rebuilt as 2–4–0s, with lengthened wheelbase and shortened boilers, and in 1858 they were rebuilt again, this time as 0–6–0s. All were gone by 1878.

Rocklia class, London & South Western Railway.   Six 2–2–2 locomotives built by Christie, Adams & Hill of the Thames Bank Ironworks, Rotherhithe. They entered traffic in 1848–9 and were reasonably successful. No. 114 *Frome* worked a special train carrying the Prince of Wales (afterwards King Edward VII) from London to Gosport on 14 December 1861, the day the Prince Consort died. Withdrawals started in 1868 and the last went in 1870.

Rokeby class, Stockton & Darlington Railway.   These were two long-boilered 2–4–0 passenger engines, no. 38 *Rokeby* and no. 39 *Ruby*, entering service in 1847. The outside cylinders were kept as close together as possible, with the coupling rods mounted outside the connecting rods. To clear the crankpins on the first pair of driving wheels, the crossheads were made exceptionally wide and provided with a vertical slot, into which the crankpins fitted. The locomotives had bar frames. The short wheelbase and overhang at each end must have made them unsteady at speed, and they were soon relegated to mineral and shunting duties. They were rebuilt in 1860, losing the slotted crossheads in favour of a more orthodox design, and gaining cabs. They were also fitted with William Bouch's feed water heater, which consisted of piping the boiler feed water round the chimney. *Ruby* was scrapped in 1871, and *Rokeby* followed in 1875.

Rose class, London, Chatham & Dover Railway.   Six 2–4–0 tank engines for suburban work, designed by W. Martley and entering service in 1863. They moved to country branches when they were displaced by more modern power in the London area, and lasted until 1883.

Roseberry class, Stockton & Darlington Railway.   William Bouch designed four 0–6–0ST locomotives in 1866 for banking duties on the Skinningrove Mine branch. The cumbersome-looking rectangular water tanks just met on the top of the boiler, justifying the saddle tank description, but the flat top made the engines look more like pannier tanks. They had inside cylinders, and were of long boiler type. With a total weight in excess of 46 tons, they were inclined to damage the track, and were later rebuilt as 0–6–0 tender engines. As such they were quite satisfactory, no. 199 *Escomb* lasting until 1911.

Rossendale class, East Lancashire Railway.   These were four long-boilered 0–6–0 goods locomotives dating from 1852, and lasting until 1882.

Rover class, Great Western Railway (broad gauge).   These were replacements of the Iron Duke class, and, while the first two or three may have incorporated parts from their predecessors, the rest were entirely new engines. Visually, they can easily be distinguished by having cabs; the Iron Dukes were without cabs. They were not quite the same mechanically – an inch or two here and there – but the main dimensions, with the 8ft driving wheels, were the same. Even the Gooch-style safety valve casing was reproduced. They lasted until the end of the broad gauge in 1892.

Royal Scot class, London Midland & Scottish Railway.   These famous engines were born of a motive power crisis. By 1926 the LMS had no suitable locomotives for hauling the increasingly heavy expresses between London and Glasgow, so they borrowed a GWR Castle. This showed that it could comfortably do the job, so the GWR were asked for the loan of a set of Castle drawings; the LMS wanted fifty Castles in service as soon as possible! The GWR refused, but Mr Maunsell of the Southern was more co-operative. He loaned a set of Lord Nelson drawings, on the strict understanding that they were for looking at, not copying. The drawings were dispatched to the North British

Locomotive Co. in Glasgow, with instructions to design a three-cylinder 4–6–0 and to build the engines straight off the drawing-board. They did so with good effect: North British had two factories in Glasgow, and the first engine from each was photographed with *Royal Scot* nameplates! The engines were originally named after famous pioneer locomotives, but there was a change of policy and they were renamed after regiments. Sir Henry Fowler, the LMS chief mechanical engineer, who had had no hand in the design but who was involved with the Boy Scouts, was solemnly photographed in Scout uniform beside *The Boy Scout*. *Fury* was an experimental ultra-high-pressure compound locomotive, which never hauled a revenue-earning train and which killed a man when a boiler tube burst on trial. She was rebuilt by Stanier with a taper boiler, and was most successful. The original Royal Scot boilers were not too good: the smokeboxes were difficult to keep airtight and mileage decreased between shoppings as the engines got older. Stanier and his successors then converted the entire class to taper boiler form, though it is doubtful how much of the original engines was reused. They were always referred to as 'Converted Royal Scots' – the term 'rebuilt' seemed to be frowned upon! The engines were rebuilt (or converted!) at the following dates:

Number	Date Rebuilt	Number	Date Rebuilt	Number	Date Rebuilt	Number	Date Rebuilt	Number	Date Rebuilt
46100	6/1950	6114	6/1946	6128	6/1946	46142	2/1951	46156	5/1954
6101	11/1945	6115	8/1947	6129	12/1944	46143	6/1949	6157	1/1946
46102	10/1949	6116	5/1944	46130	12/1949	6144	6/1945	46158	9/1952
6103	6/1943	6117	12/1943	6131	10/1944	6145	1/1944	6159	10/1945
6104	3/1946	6118	12/1946	6132	11/1943	6146	10/1943	6160	2/1945
46105	5/1948	6119	9/1944	6133	7/1944	6147	9/1946	6161	10/1946
46106	9/1949	6120	11/1944	46134	12/1953	46148	7/1954	46162	1/1948
46107	2/1950	6121	8/1946	6135	1/1947	6149	4/1945	46163	10/1953
6108	8/1943	6122	9/1945	46136	3/1950	6150	12/1945	46164	6/1951
6109	7/1943	46123	5/1949	46137	3/1955	46151	4/1953	46165	6/1952
46110	1/1953	6124	12/1943	6138	6/1944	6152	8/1945	6166	1/1945
6111	10/1947	6125	8/1943	6139	11/1946	46153	8/1949	46167	12/1948
6112	9/1943	6126	6/1945	46140	5/1952	46154	3/1948	6168	4/1946
46113	12/1950	6127	8/1944	46141	10/1950	46155	8/1950	6169	5/1945
								6170	11/1935

Nos 6100–24 were built by the North British Locomotive Co. Ltd at their Queen's Park Works, Glasgow, and nos 6125–49 were built by the same company's Hyde Park Works, Glasgow. Nos 6150–69 were built by the LMS at Derby Works. No. 6399 *Fury* (no. 6170 on rebuilding) was built by the North British at Hyde Park Works.

An engine numbered 6100 went to America in 1933 with an eight-coach train for exhibition at the Chicago World Fair, after which it toured North America. There is some doubt as to whether it was the real 6100; it is said to have been no. 6152, but there is doubt about that also.

The first two Royal Scots were withdrawn on 13 October 1962 and the last on 1 January 1966.

Ruby class, London, Chatham & Dover Railway.   Always on the look-out for bargains, the LC&DR's General Manager discovered six 2–4–0s lying unused on the Dutch Rhenish Railway and snapped them up at £2,500 each! They entered service in 1861 and did well on the Victoria–Dover expresses. In 1864–5 they were rebuilt as 2–4–0Ts, and the last, no. 70 *Pearl*, was withdrawn in 1891.

S15 class, Southern Railway.   These small-wheeled 4–6–0 locomotives first appeared on the London & South Western Railway in 1920, and were intended for main line express freight work. After the formation of the Southern Railway, more were built in 1927 to an improved design. None was named, but one or two names have appeared in preservation.

S160 class, United States Army Transportation Corps.   Over two thousand of these 2–8–0 locomotives were built by American builders during the Second World War prior to the D-Day invasion. They were designed by a certain Major Marsh, to the British loading gauge. Thus they were very small engines by American standards, and scarcely giants to British eyes. Many were stored in the UK prior to D-Day, and a large number were put to work to help the hard-pressed British railway companies. Their American characteristics included a water gauge quite different to those on British engines; when handled by British crews there were one or two cases of the gauge being seriously misunderstood, resulting in boiler explosions. After the invasion, all were sent to Europe, and later passed into the hands of several railway administrations. Examples have been brought back to the UK from Poland (K&WVR) and Hungary. The Mid-Hants Railway's example, *Franklin D. Roosevelt* (Alco, works no. 71533 of 1944), came from Greece, having previously seen service in Italy! All have had their USATC numbers restored.

Saint class, Great Western Railway.   G.J. Churchward's two-cylinder 4–6–0 express passenger design. The class had a fairly complex history, being directly derived from no. 100, named *Dean* and then *William Dean*, which appeared in 1902 before Churchward's predecessor had retired. There is, however, no doubt that the design was 100 per cent Churchward! Some were built as 4–4–2s, to compare with the French locomotives nos 102, 103 and 104, before being converted to 4–6–0. While most were named after saints, there were further series named after courts, ladies, knights and kings. The kings were renamed to make way for the King class. The Saint class locomotives were very successful indeed.

Saltburn class, Stockton & Darlington Railway.   Four 4–4–0 passenger locomotives designed by William Bouch entered service in 1862. With outside cylinders, they were very similar to the Brougham class which immediately preceded them – except that the enclosed cabs of the latter were replaced by the scantiest of weatherboards. The bogie, while pivoted, had no side play and so did little to help the locomotives round curves. The driving wheels were 7ft ½in in diameter, which suggests fast passenger work. After various rebuildings and reboilerings, the last, *Morecambe*, was withdrawn in 1888.

Samson class, East Lancashire Railway.   Five goods engines, introduced in 1846. A long-boilered 0–6–0 design, but also including no. 23 *Elk*, believed to have been a 2–2–2. All were withdrawn by 1878.

Samson class, London & North Western Railway.   These small 2–4–0s were first introduced in 1863 to the designs of John Ramsbottom. With 6ft 1½in driving wheels, they were soon outclassed on main line work, but continued on less important duties until renewed as Whitworth class engines.

Sandringham class, London & North Eastern Railway.   See Class B17.

Saxon class, London & South Western Railway.   Twelve 2–4–0 goods engines with 5ft coupled wheels were turned out from Nine Elms Works in 1855–7. All were named after ancient tribes. No. 139 *Lombard* exploded its boiler in 1857, after the driver tampered with the safety valves. Distributed throughout the system, they were used on light goods work and the last were withdrawn in 1885.

S/Bloomer class, London & North Western Railway.   See L/Bloomer class.

Schools class, Southern Railway.   One of the most successful 4–4–0 designs in the world. First introduced in March 1930, forty were built, all named after famous public schools. First intended for the demanding Hastings line via Tonbridge, the class also showed its mettle on the pre-war two-hour Bournemouth expresses, and on the Direct Portsmouth line prior to electrification. They were finally displaced from the Hastings line by the diesel-electric multiple-unit trains of 1957–8. The last survivors were withdrawn in December 1962.

Scotchmen class, London, Chatham & Dover Railway.   These fourteen 0–4–2 well tank locomotives were designed by Neilson & Co. of Glasgow, in consultation with William Martley, the LCDR's locomotive superintendent. They were generally similar to engines being supplied to the Great Northern Railway. They were delivered in 1866, named after Scottish rivers and islands. The drivers dubbed them 'Scotchmen', though William Kirtley, who succeeded Martley on the latter's death, referred to them much more prosaically as the E class! They were very successful, lasting until 1908. See also L/Scotch class.

Scott class, North British Railway.   A celebrated class of 4–4–0 express passenger locomotives, designed by W.P. Reid and first introduced in 1909. The first six were chiefly employed on the Edinburgh–Perth expresses. A further ten were built in 1911. Very successful, they were later modernized and the last one was withdrawn by British Railways in 1952. A smaller-wheeled version was also introduced, known as the Glen class.

Seafield class, Highland Railway.   Seven 2–4–0s of the 'Crewe type', with 5ft driving wheels. Two, *Fife*(I), later *Dingwall*(II), and *Westhall*, later *Duncraig*, were rebuilt as 4–4–0s.

Sentinel Steam Railcars, Jersey Eastern Railway.   These were similar in conception and design to the much more numerous Sentinel cars constructed for the London & North Eastern Railway. The Jersey Eastern Railway started off as standard gauge, but converted to 3ft 6in gauge. The railcars were to this gauge.

Sentinel Steam Railcars, London & North Eastern Railway.   In the mid-1920s the LNER experimented with geared steam railcars. The basic idea was a small, high-pressure boiler and a high-speed engine, with the drive to the wheels via a gearbox. Horsepower was nominally 100. The carriage part was built as light as possible, to reduce the demands on the power unit, which meant (a) that there was little reserve to haul a trailer if the railcar generated more passenger traffic than it could accommodate; (b) there was little reserve strength in the event of an accident; and (c) the vehicle wore out more quickly than ordinary stock. In addition, a fault in either the power unit or the passenger half of the vehicle meant that the whole car was out of commission, and the passenger part was difficult to keep clean while the power unit was being repaired or refuelled. Two manufacturers' products were tried: Claytons, and Sentinel-Cammell. The Sentinel railcars were in four distinct varieties, distinguished in the main list as follows: aSentinel: 100hp, two cylinders; bSentinel: 200hp, twin engine; cSentinel: 100hp, six cylinders; and dSentinel: Twin articulated railcar.

The first three varieties consisted of a power unit with four coupled wheels, and a passenger coach articulated to it. A four-wheeled bogie supported the other end of the coach. Thus the configuration was rather like an articulated lorry. The twin articulated railcar *Phenomena* had its power unit in the middle and a coach articulated to each end.

The names were of old-time stage-coaches. Again, this was a good idea, although *Bang Up* has rather an ominous sound!

In service, the cars were moderately successful. A number of lightweight four-wheeled trailer coaches were built for them, specifically for dealing with an excess of passengers. The last of the Sentinels was withdrawn by British Railways in the late 1940s.

SFG class, London & South Western Railway.   The Single Framed Goods engines were built by Beyer Peacock & Co. of Manchester to W.G. Beattie's requirements. Thirty-six were eventually built, the first entering service in July 1874. Less successful than the elder Beattie's Double Framed Goods engines, they were nevertheless long-lasting and the last three were withdrawn by the Southern Railway in December 1925.

Shotley class, Stockton & Darlington Railway.   These were two 0–6–0 mineral engines, designed by William Bouch, which entered service in 1852. They had inside cylinders. They gave good service, but were replaced in 1866. Their actual fate is unknown.

Sir Daniel class, Great Western Railway.   These were the first standard gauge locomotives to be built at Swindon, first appearing in 1866. There were thirty of these 2–2–2s, of which only four carried names. Of the named engines, only *Sir Daniel* completed its life as a 2–2–2; the remainder were reconstructed as 0–6–0 goods engines: no. 380 *North Star* in February 1902, no. 381 *Morning Star* in July 1902, and no. 471 *Sir Watkin* in January 1901. Final withdrawal dates were: *Sir Daniel* in May 1898; of the 0–6–0 conversions no. 380 went in September 1911; no. 381 in December 1919, and no. 471 in November 1912. The last example of all, no. 474, lasted until February 1920. *Sir Daniel* was named after Sir Daniel Gooch, the company's first locomotive engineer and later chairman. Sir Watkin Wynne was a director.

Sir James King class, Caledonian Railway.   Also known as the 908 class. Ten of these imposing 4–6–0 express passenger locomotives were built to J.F. McIntosh's design in 1906. They were very similar to the 903 or Cardean class, but with 5ft 9in driving wheels instead of the 6ft 6in of the earlier class. Only two were named: no. 908 *Sir James King*, after the late chairman of directors, and no. 911 *Barochan*, after the residence of the then chairman, Sir Charles Renshaw. All were withdrawn by the London Midland & Scottish Railway.

Sir James Thompson class, Caledonian Railway.   Also known as the 49 class. These two 4–6–0 express locomotives were built in 1903 for the Carlisle–Glasgow expresses. Only no. 49 *Sir James Thompson* was named, after a former general manager and chairman of the company. When more locomotives were needed, J.F. McIntosh produced the 903 or Cardean class.

Sir Watkin class, Great Western Railway (broad gauge).   These six 0–6–0 tank engines were the only side-tank engines built for the Great Western broad gauge. Initially they worked goods trains on the Metropolitan Railway, for which they had condensing apparatus (whereby the exhaust steam was diverted into the water tank, condensed and reused, in an attempt to alleviate the smoke nuisance in the tunnels). After 1869, when the broad gauge vanished from the Metropolitan, they were converted to saddle tanks and lost the condensing gear. *Bulkeley*, *Fowler* and *Saunders* were sold to the South Devon Railway in 1872. In 1876 the SDR was absorbed by the GWR, and these three were numbered 2157–9. Incidentally, Sir Watkin Wynne was a director of the company.

Skye Bogie class, Highland Railway.   David Jones's 4–4–0 design for the Kyle of Lochalsh line. The 'Crewe-type' framing was used.

Small Ben class, Highland Railway.   Officially Class C, the Small Bens were designed by Peter Drummond and first introduced in 1898. They were 4–4–0 passenger locomotives, with 6ft driving wheels. As the class name implies, all were named after Scottish mountains. The first one was to have been named *Ben Nevis* until it was pointed out that Ben Nevis was in North British Railway territory, so the name was hurriedly changed to *Ben-y-Gloe*. Twenty were built, and the last one, no. 54398 *Ben Alder* (Highland Railway no. 2) was withdrawn in February 1953 by British Railways.

Small Goods class, Cambrian Railways.   The Small Goods class of 0–6–0 engines was introduced in 1861, and all were named. They had 4ft 6in wheels and 16in × 24in inside cylinders. Names were removed between 1886 and 1891. Long-lasting, the last of these engines were withdrawn in 1947.

Small Goods class, Highland Railway.   A batch of ten 'Crewe-type' 2–4–0s. Another long-lasting design, the first appeared in 1863 and the last was withdrawn in 1923.

Small Pass class, Cambrian Railways.   The Small Passenger class consisted of twelve 2–4–0 locomotives designed and built by Sharp, Stewart & Co. The last of them were withdrawn in 1922.

Snaigow class, Highland Railway.   In 1916 Christopher Cumming designed a modern and powerful 4–4–0 for the Highland Mails. Two locomotives were built, no. 73 *Snaigow* and no. 74 *Durn*. They were the first 4–4–0s to be fitted with outside Walschaerts valve gear. They were quite successful, but wartime conditions prevented more being built. As non-standard engines, they were soon withdrawn by the London Midland & Scottish Railway.

Sondes class, London, Chatham & Dover Railway.   A class of six 4–4–0ST engines, designed by Thomas Russell Crampton for main line duties. Crampton was nominally the civil engineer, but he was 'a bit of a genius', with a fairly successful patent locomotive design to his credit. In the Sondes class, the cylinders were mounted about halfway along the boiler and drove the rear pair of driving wheels, thus anticipating later French locomotives. They were built in 1857 and proved most unsatisfactory, being over-powered and prone to derailment. William Martley, the locomotive superintendent, rebuilt them in 1865 as orthodox outside-framed 2–4–0 tank engines for London suburban use. They were withdrawn in 1909. Lord Sondes was a director of the company.

Special Tank class, Highland Railway.   The Duke of Sutherland had largely financed the construction of the Highland main line north of Inverness. He made a practice of maintaining his own locomotive and saloon coaches. In 1895 he invested in a new locomotive, named *Dunrobin*, and sold its predecessor to the unsuspecting Highland. They renamed it *Gordon Castle* (it had previously also borne the name *Dunrobin*), and found that His Grace had had far the better part of the bargain! It was rebuilt from a 2–4–0T to a 4–4–0 T in 1896.

Special Tank class, London & North Western Railway.   A class of 0–6–0ST locomotives for shunting and departmental work, designed by John Ramsbottom and first appearing in 1870. A total of 260 were built. A handful were named for special work at Liverpool Riverside station, Wolverton works, etc.

Standard class, London & South Western Railway.   This was Joseph Beattie's fourth attempt at a 2–4–0WT for London suburban services and country branches, and this time he got it right! No fewer than eighty-five were built, but only the first five were named. The first entered service in 1863. Nos 33 *Phoenix*, 36 *Comet* and 76 *Firefly* were built by the L&SWR at Nine Elms Works, London, and the rest by Beyer Peacock & Co. of Manchester. Construction continued up to 1875, although Mr Beattie had died in 1871 and had been succeeded by his son W.G. Beattie. It was the younger Beattie who ordered the last examples, which included nos 298, 314 and 329. While the rest of the class had gone to the scrapheap by 1899, these three were retained to work the Wenfordbridge branch in Cornwall, and were only withdrawn in December 1962. No. 298 survives as BR 30587 and is part of the National Collection; no. 314 also survives, as BR 30585.

Star class, Great Western Railway.   These 4–6–0s were the production version of G.J. Churchward's experimental four-cylinder engines. As more were built, Swindon soon ran out of Star names; there were Knights, Queens, Kings and Abbeys, many of which were later rebuilt as Castles.

Stella class, Great Western Railway.   Twenty-five 2–4–0s entered traffic in 1884–5, only one of which received a name. The GWR sold the brand-new no. 3201 to the Pembroke & Tenby Railway, who named it *Stella* and numbered it 8. In 1896 the GWR took over the P&TR and *Stella* became no. 3201 again. But it retained its name for several years. *Stella* was the last one of the class to be withdrawn, lasting until October 1933.

Strath class, Highland Railway.   Twelve 4–4–0s by David Jones, with the usual 'Crewe-type' framing. First introduced in 1892, the last survivors were withdrawn by the LMS in 1931.

Summers class, London & South Western Railway.   This is not the correct designation. These two locomotives were built by Summers, Groves & Day. No. 40 *Fly* was a 2–2–0 Planet-type engine, delivered in 1839 and soon rebuilt as a 2–2–2. It was withdrawn in 1849. *Southampton*, also supplied in 1839, equally proved a doubtful asset, and was rebuilt by Fairbairns in 1841.

Sussex class, London & South Western Railway.   There were two Sussex classes on the L&SWR, and they had nothing in common.

1Sussex: twelve 2–2–2 tender locomotives were ordered from Charles Tayleur & Co. of the Vulcan Foundry, Newton-le-Willows. No. 1 *Sussex* was the first to be delivered, in April 1838, and no. 4 *Locke* was the first to be withdrawn, in March 1852. The last to go was no. 3 *Transit*; rebuilt as a 2–2–2T, it lasted until 1871.

2Sussex: a class of eight 2–2–2WT engines for London suburban and branch line work, first introduced by J.H. Beattie in 1852. The last was withdrawn in 1877.

Swindon class, Great Western Railway (broad gauge).   Fourteen 0–6–0 tender engines, for goods traffic. First introduced in November 1865, they lasted in some cases up to the end of the broad gauge in May 1892.

T19 class, Great Eastern Railway.   First introduced in 1886, there were 110 of these 2–4–0 express passenger locomotives to James Holden's design. Only one of them, no. 760 *Petrolea*, ever bore a name; it was one of ten locomotives equipped to burn oil. Oil-gas lighting for carriages was introduced on the GER in 1878, and complaints over the discharge of waste from the gas plant at Stratford led to its use as a locomotive fuel. When electric lighting for coaches arrived, GER locomotives reverted to burning coal. The T19 class provided front-line express power for many years, and after the introduction of the Claud Hamilton class in 1900 a number were rebuilt, first with a larger boiler, and then with a leading bogie in place of the single carrying axle, thus producing an effective 4–4–0 for secondary work.

Tartar class, London & South Western Railway.   Six 2–2–2WT locomotives, built to J.H. Beattie's designs, for branch line work. They entered service in 1852, and the last was withdrawn in 1874.

Teutonic class, London & North Western Railway.   These were easily the best of the Webb compounds. The wheel arrangement was 2–2–2–0; they looked rather like a normal 2–4–0, but the driving wheels were uncoupled. They first appeared in 1889, and were the first of Mr Webb's compounds to feature a slip eccentric for the valve of the inside low-pressure cylinder. When the engine backed down to couple up to a train, the slip eccentric was in reverse gear. Then, when the engine started in forward gear, the slip eccentric sometimes failed to slip, with the engaging result that the rear driving wheels slipped violently in forward gear while the front pair rotated in reverse! The locomotive would, of course, be stationary during this performance, and it was not unusual for another engine to be summoned to get the train under way! But, nevertheless, it was a Teutonic, no. 1309 *Adriatic*, which averaged 56.6mph from Euston to Crewe on the last night of the 1895 Race to Aberdeen, while *Jeanie Deans* regularly worked the 2 p.m. 'Corridor' express from January 1891 to August 1899.

The Duke class, Stockton & Darlington Railway.   Two 0–6–0 locomotives intended for banking duties, and designed by William Bouch. No. 80 *The Duke* appeared in May 1854, and no. 135 *Eden* in November 1858. So *The Duke* must have been adjudged a success. As in the Commerce class, the outside cylinders were kept as close together as possible, with the coupling rods mounted outside the connecting rods. To clear the crankpins on the first pair of driving wheels, the coupling rods had a large eye forged in them, into which the crankpins fitted. The whole complication could have been obviated by adopting inside cylinders! Both engines were withdrawn in 1882.

Tiger class, London, Chatham & Dover Railway.   Designed by that brilliant but eccentric engineer Thomas Russell Crampton, these were twenty-four 4–4–0 tender engines generally similar to the Sondes class, and suffering the same faults. They entered service in 1861 and were rebuilt as 2–4–0s from 1862; the last was withdrawn in 1907.

Times class, Stockton & Darlington Railway.   There were two locomotives, no. 3 *Times* and no. 2 *Graham*, which entered service in 1849. They were built by Alfred Kitching, of the Hope Town Foundry, Darlington (a firm still in existence, though now known as Whessoe), and very little is known about them. They seem to have been 0–6–0 mineral locomotives, with inside cylinders and long boilers, and both vanished from the railway in 1865.

Tory class, Stockton & Darlington Railway.   Sixteen 0–6–0 mineral locomotives to Timothy Hackworth's design, first entering service in 1838. The individual engines showed differences between one other, but in general the cylinders were inclined, driving directly on to the wheels. This arrangement avoided the jackshaft drive of the Majestic class, and at the same time allowed all the axles to be sprung. The engines were very similar to the Miner class, and had the driver's controls at one end and the firebox at the other. Hence a tender was needed at each end. The driver stood on a tender carrying water, while the fireman stood on another carrying coal. Several were rebuilt, *Bee* starting life as *Beehive*, and *Leader* was rebuilt from *Enterprise*, both of the Enterprise class. *Derwent*, built in 1845, has survived.

Tweed class, London & South Western Railway.   Six 2–4–0 passenger engines, all named after rivers, entered traffic in 1858–9. Built to J.H. Beattie's design, they worked from London, and latterly from Salisbury, and lasted until 1877–9.

U class, Southern Railway.   See River class, Southern Railway.

Ulysses class, East Lancashire Railway.   Five 0–6–0s built in 1856, probably the last to have the 'haycock'-type domed firebox as exemplified by the preserved Furness Railway locomotive *"Coppernob"*. The last went for scrap in 1882.

Undine class, London & South Western Railway.   Twelve 2–4–0 express passenger locomotives, with 6ft 6in driving wheels, were built to Joseph Beattie's design, entering service in 1859–60. Most of them worked from London on the Salisbury and Southampton expresses, and the last ones were withdrawn in December 1886.

USA class, Southern Railway.   Concurrently with the S160 class, the United States Army Transportation Corps identified a need for a small 0–6–0T for shunting duties when the American armies reached Europe in 1944. Accordingly, construction was put in hand with several American locomotive building firms. After 1945 the Southern Railway required a replacement for the B4 class 0–4–0Ts in Southampton Docks and, as the American locomotives were being sold off as 'war surplus', a very advantageous deal was concluded. After some small modifications to suit British conditions, the class took up their duties in Southampton Docks, and lasted to the end of steam. In later years some entered departmental service and received the names of bygone locomotive engineers.

V2 class, London & North Eastern Railway.   Sir Nigel Gresley's mixed traffic 2–6–2 design. In all, 184 were built from 1936 onwards, and six were named. *Green Arrow* is the sole survivor.

V4 class, London & North Eastern Railway.   A lightweight 2–6–2 designed by Gresley in 1941 just before his death; only two were built and only the first carried a name, *Bantam Cock*. The other was known unofficially as *"Bantam Hen"*!

Ventnor class, London, Brighton & South Coast Railway.   Two 2–2–2 passenger locomotives were completed at Brighton Works in 1856. Although intended for main line work, they spent most of their time on London–Brighton semi-fasts. Both were modified and named by Stroudley. They were laid aside in 1880 and scrapped in 1882.

Venus class, East Lancashire Railway.   Ten 2–2–2s, first introduced in 1848. They were the ELR's standard passenger class. Nos 25 *Venus*, 31 *Orion* and 50 *Banshee* remained as 2–2–2s; the rest were rebuilt as 2–4–0s. All were withdrawn by 1882.

Venus class, London & South Western Railway.   Nine 2–2–2 locomotives were ordered from Sharp, Roberts in 1838, and all were delivered in that year. The first withdrawals were in 1852, but no. 8 *Vesta*, albeit much rebuilt, survived until 1872.

Vesuvius class, London & South Western Railway.   There were two Vesuvius classes, with nothing in common.

1 Vesuvius: nine large 2–2–2 express engines, designed by J.V. Gooch and built at Nine Elms Works, were built in 1849–53. Gooch resigned during their construction, having secured an appointment with the Eastern Counties Railway, and it was left to his successor J.H. Beattie to see the engines into traffic. Reasonably successful, they lasted until 1880.

2 Vesuvius: thirty-two large 2–4–0 express engines designed by Joseph Beattie in 1869. They had 6ft 6in driving wheels. Not all were named, those that were taking the names and numbers of older locomotives which were placed on the duplicate list – a device for replacing a locomotive but still keeping it in service. The exception was no. 280 *Persia*, which was used to convey the Shah on his state visit to Windsor in 1873. This was the occasion when that monarch demanded that the driver be instantly beheaded for going too fast! The second Vesuvius class were good engines, and several were rebuilt and modernized in the 1880s. The last were withdrawn in 1899.

Victoria class, Great Western Railway (broad gauge).   These were 2–4–0 passenger engines with four-wheeled tenders. Introduced in August 1856, they numbered eighteen engines, and construction ended in May 1864. Moderately useful, they had all gone by June 1881. It seems that a train to Weymouth, hauled by *Victoria*, ran away down Upwey bank. The train ran through the station and across the road, ending up just short of the Somerset Hotel. This gave rise to a song with the refrain 'Victoria in the gin shop'!

Victoria class, London, Brighton & South Coast Railway.   Two 2–2–2 express engines, built in 1868 at Brighton works by J.C. Craven. No. 255 was named *Hastings* and no. 256 *Victoria* in 1871 by W. Stroudley. *Hastings* was withdrawn in 1888 and *Victoria* in 1891.

Vivid class, London & South Western Railway.   Five 2–2–2 locomotives by Rothwell & Co., in service between 1839 and 1870.

Volcano class, London & South Western Railway.   Eighteen 2–4–0s with 6ft driving wheels, designed by J.H. Beattie and built at Nine Elms Works, entered service between 1866 and 1872. The final six, nos 25 *Reindeer*, 26 *Gazelle*, 118 *Etna*, 5 *Ganymede*, 11 *Minerva* and 31 *Leeds*, were built by W.G. Beattie, Joseph Beattie's son and successor. They were mostly named after volcanoes, perhaps appropriately since the L&SWR was known to Great Western enginemen at Basingstoke as 'Blaze an' Smoke'! They were modernized by William Adams in turn, and the last were withdrawn in 1897.

Warship class, British Railways.   There were seventy-six of these diesel-hydraulic locomotives, built under the British Transport Commission's pilot modernization scheme. While other Regions preferred diesel-electric locomotives, the Western Region opted for diesel-hydraulics. They were much influenced by the successful V200 class on the German Federal Railways, and would have liked to obtain one for evaluation tests. Unfortunately, this was not possible owing to loading gauge limitations. The first five locomotives, nos D600–D604, were of 2,000hp and of the A1A–A1A type, built by the North British Locomotive Co. of Glasgow, who were the UK licensees of the MAN (German) diesel engines and transmission. Then came three 2,000hp units (nos D800–D802) from Swindon Works, with Maybach engines and of the Bo-Bo wheel arrangement, and lastly six 1,000hp Bo-Bo units with MAN engines (nos D6300–D6305) from North British. It was decided to multiply the D800–D802 batch, and a further sixty were built with detail variations. D803–D832 came from Swindon with Bristol Siddeley–Maybach MD650 engines and Mekydro transmissions. A further thirty-three, nos D833–D865, came from North British with MAN L12V18/21BS engines and Voith transmissions. The engines and transmissions were built by NBL under licence. (An acquaintance of the writer's, who was serving his apprenticeship at Swindon at the time, reported that the Maybach engines and Mekydro transmissions arrived with German-language instructional literature, which caused severe headscratching in certain quarters!)

In 1959 a new engine by Paxman was tested in no. D830 *Majestic*. The experiment was fairly successful, but this locomotive was the first of the class to be withdrawn. The D800–D870 series were built to resemble a scaled-down German V200; the five North British A1A–A1As were quite different in appearance. All are now withdrawn, apart from preserved examples.

WC class, Southern Railway.   See BB class.

WD 2–8–0 class/WD 2–10–0 class, War Department.   During the Second World War, with the invasion of Europe being planned, a need was perceived for a heavy freight locomotive to operate the railway system in the wake of the Allied armies. (The Germans could hardly be counted on to leave serviceable locomotives behind!) So Mr R.A. Riddles designed first a 2–8–0 based on the London Midland & Scottish Railway 8F class 2–8–0, and then a ten-coupled version.

Unlike the equivalent German 52 class 2–10–0, the British locomotives were built in quantity, straight off the drawing-board, with no detail variations whatsoever. (All sorts of Nazi organizations had had a hand in the German 52 class, with the result that some had Brotan boilers, some had condensing tenders and so on. Many different ideas were tried out.) The 2–8–0 first appeared in early 1943 and the 2–10–0 in June 1944. Most were shipped straight to Europe, but many were loaned to the British railway companies prior to shipment. After the war the London & North Eastern Railway bought a number of the 2–8–0s, which they classified O7, and British Railways, after nationalization, bought many more, and also a number of the 2–10–0s. In the preservation era it was discovered that almost all the British examples had been scrapped, so a 2–8–0 was repatriated from Sweden and a number of 2–10–0s from Greece and Eastern Europe. Some of these have since received names.

Western class, British Railways. These are the Co-Co diesel-hydraulic locomotives for the Western Region, sometimes known as the 52 class. Seventy-four were built, the first entering service in December 1961. They had two Maybach MD655 engines of 1,380bhp at 1,500rpm. The design was not trouble-free, and while they did good work it was decided that diesel-hydraulic traction was non-standard and would be phased out. By June 1979 they had all gone, apart from seven which have been preserved. Originally numbered D1000–D1073, they were classified 52 but were not renumbered into the 52xxx series.

Whitworth class, London & North Western Railway. The renewals of the Samson class 2–4–0 passenger locomotives, with 6ft 6in driving wheels.

Wilberforce class, Stockton & Darlington Railway. See Director class, Stockton & Darlington Railway.

Windsor class, Stockton & Darlington Railway. Twelve inside-cylinder, long-boilered 0–6–0 mineral locomotives to William Bouch's design, first entering service in 1865. All were rebuilt at least once, and gave good service. The last were withdrawn in 1910.

Wolf class, Great Western Railway (broad gauge). Single driving tank engines, incorporating six unclassified engines; six Stars, three Firefly class, and the whole of the Sun class. A mystery surrounds that most famous of Great Western pioneer locomotives, *North Star*. While six of the Star class were altered to 2–2–2 tanks, or 4–2–2 tanks, there is no record of *North Star* having been altered. Moreover, the engine as preserved at Swindon up to 1906 (when it was scrapped; what is preserved at Swindon today is a replica incorporating some of the original parts) showed no sign of having been altered. Yet Swindon records consistently included it in the Wolf class!

Woodlands class, Stockton & Darlington Railway. A passenger 2–4–0 design, first introduced in 1848. They had inside cylinders and were of the long-boiler type, with the firebox behind the wheels and the cylinders and smokebox ahead of them. Six were built, with detail variations, and they lasted, albeit with various rebuildings, until 1881.

Yankee class, Highland Railway. Five 4–4–0T engines which, improbably, were built by Dubs & Co. of Glasgow for the Uruguay Eastern Railway in 1891. The Uruguayans being unable to pay for them, they were snapped up by the Highland at the bargain price of £1,500 each. They looked very British, and once the headlamps and cowcatchers were removed one would never have guessed that they had been built for South America. They gave good service, and the last survivors were withdrawn by the LMS in 1934.

03 class, British Railways. These were 204hp 0–6–0 diesel-mechanical shunters. In all, 230 were built between 1957 and 1962. None was named while in BR service.

04 class, British Railways. A class of 0–6–0 diesel-mechanical shunting locomotives, of 204hp. In all, 140 were built between 1952 and 1962. All are now withdrawn. None was named while in BR service.

05 class, British Railways. A 204hp diesel-mechanical 0–6–0 shunter, of which sixty-nine were built. They were limited to a maximum speed of 18mph. None was named in BR service, but a few have been preserved and some have received names.

08 class, British Railways. First introduced in 1953, this is the standard British Railways 350bhp 0–6–0 diesel-electric shunting locomotive, limited to a maximum speed of 15mph. In all, 472 have been built. Tractive effort is 35,000lb. They are a development of a pre-war English Electric design for the London Midland & Scottish Railway. Many more have been built for the War Department and industrial use, and redundant ex-BR examples find a ready market in industry and the preserved railways. They were very successful indeed.

09 class, British Railways. These were exactly the same as the class 08 engines, except that their maximum speed is 27mph, and the tractive effort is 25,000lb.

1 class, Great Central Railway. Six 4–6–0 express engines, built by J.G. Robinson in 1912–13 and known as the Sir Sam Fay class. Handsome engines with inside cylinders and 6ft 9in driving wheels, they were nevertheless outclassed by the Director class 4–4–0s, and ended their days on local passenger work. The last was scrapped in 1947.

1 class, London, Tilbury & Southend Railway. Having previously been worked by the Great Eastern Railway, the LTSR commenced working its own system in 1880 with thirty express tank locomotives of the 4–4–2 wheel arrangement. Built by Sharp Stewart & Co. and numbered 1–30, the design was officially anonymous. However, it is generally believed to be the work of William Adams, who had left the Great Eastern two years previously. The railway extended from Fenchurch Street to Shoeburyness, and in the rush hours worked an intensive passenger service. In 1892 a further six engines were built to essentially the same design. All were named after places on the system.

I class, Mersey Railway.   These were nine 0–6–4T engines built by Beyer Peacock in 1885–6 for the railway's opening. At the time of their construction they were the most powerful locomotives in the country. They lasted until the electrification of the Mersey Railway in 1903, and were all subsequently sold into industrial use, one or two even finishing up in Australia. The exceptions were three which went to the Alexandra Docks Railway in South Wales.

1A class, Great Central Railway.   Eleven 4–6–0s generally known as the Glenalmond class. Introduced in 1913–14, they were virtually identical to Class 1 except in having 5ft 7in driving wheels. Four were named. They were intended for fast freight traffic, and the last was withdrawn in 1949.

II class, Mersey Railway.   These were six 2–6–2T engines, built by Beyer Peacock in 1887–8 for an extension of the Mersey Railway. Less powerful than Class I, they were nevertheless preferred by the enginemen. After electrification in 1903, all were bought by the Alexandra Docks Railway in 1903 and 1904.

III class, Mersey Railway.   Three 2–6–2T engines built by Kitsons of Leeds, broadly similar to the Beyer Peacock locomotives of Class II. All went to the Alexandra Docks Railway in 1905.

4 class, Great Central Railway.   This was a broad grouping for several 0–4–0ST and 0–6–0ST engines acquired from miscellaneous sources. *Bismarck* and *Moltke* were typical contractors' 0–6–0STs built by Manning Wardle, cabless and with inside cylinders. They were bought in 1880. *Bismarck* was scrapped in 1905, and *Moltke* in 1922. *Ajax*, also by Manning Wardle, was bought in 1876, and *Humber* was by Hudswell Clark and acquired in 1911. All were employed shunting at Grimsby.

4MT class, British Railways.   These were 2–6–0 mixed traffic locomotives, based on a postwar London Midland & Scottish Railway design. Well over a hundred were built, but none was named by British Railways. One or two have been preserved, and have received names in preservation.

4P class, London Midland & Scottish Railway.   The term '4P class' related to the power of a locomotive, irrespective of design. In theory, a train of sufficient weight to call for a 4P class locomotive could be hauled by any within that bracket, whether it was an elderly Midland 4–4–0 or one of the latest 2–6–4 tank locomotives. Just about the only 4P class locomotive to receive a name was no. 2313, a parallel-boiler 2–6–4T of Fowler's design, which was under construction at Derby Works in 1928 during a visit by HRH the Prince of Wales (afterwards King Edward VIII) and was named *The Prince* in his honour. The name was painted on the side tanks and was carried for a number of years.

5 class, Great Central Railway.   Twelve 0–6–0ST engines introduced by Harry Pollitt on the Manchester, Sheffield & Lincolnshire Railway in 1897. No. 889 rejoiced in the nickname '*Little Dick*'. The MS&LR restyled itself the Great Central Railway with effect from 1 August 1897. (This class should not be confused with the very much larger and better-known Class 5 of the London Midland & Scottish Railway.)

5 class ('Black Fives'), London Midland & Scottish Railway.   Sir William Stanier's general purpose 4–6–0 design, first introduced in 1934 and subsequently multiplied to no fewer than 842 examples. Some locomotive designers held that, for maximum economy, one should prepare a special design for each and every line, but the 'Black Fives' could be seen everywhere between Bournemouth and Thurso, Holyhead and Shoeburyness, handling everything from a main line express (in extremis!) to a pick-up freight. The last ones in service with British Railways worked until the very end of steam traction in 1968, and several have been preserved.

5MT class, British Railways.   First introduced in 1951, this was R.A. Riddles's version of Sir William Stanier's class 5 for the London Midland & Scottish Railway. A very successful mixed traffic 4–6–0, initially none was named. Later, those allocated to the Southern Region took the names of withdrawn members of the King Arthur class, and took over their workings on the Bournemouth expresses. One or two have been preserved.

7 (Armstrong) class, Great Western Railway.   These four extremely handsome double-framed 4–4–0s were not unlike a coupled version of the 3021 class of bogie singles. They were renumbered in December 1912, as follows: no. 7 became 4171; no. 8 became 4172; no. 14 became 4170 and no. 16 became 4169. The last one, 4169 *Charles Saunders*, was withdrawn in 1930.

7F class, London Midland & Scottish Railway.   These celebrated 2–8–0 freight locomotives were built by the Midland Railway for the Somerset & Dorset Joint Railway, which the Midland owned jointly with the London & South Western Railway. The arrangement was that the Midland looked after the locomotives and rolling stock, while the L&SWR saw to the track, civil engineering and signalling. After 1923 the arrangement was continued by the London Midland & Scottish Railway and the Southern Railway. The 7F 2–8–0s were first introduced in February 1914, and lasted until the end of the S&DJR. None carried names prior to withdrawal. Two have been preserved, and one is occasionally named.

8D class, Great Central Railway. Two 4–4–2 express engines to J.G. Robinson's design. No. 258 *The Rt. Hon. Viscount Cross, G.C.B., G.C.S.I.* and no. 259 *King Edward VII* were introduced in 1905 and 1906 respectively. They were four-cylinder compounds, and lasted until 1947.

8E class, Great Central Railway. Two 4–4–2 express engines built in 1906 by J.G. Robinson, nos 364 *Lady Henderson* and 365 *Sir William Pollitt*. Lady Henderson became Lady Farringdon on her husband's accession to that title in 1917. The class lasted until 1947.

8F class, Great Central Railway. Ten 4–6–0s designed by J.G. Robinson and first introduced in 1906. They were intended for the Immingham express fish traffic. Often called the 'Immingham' class, only no. 1097 *Immingham* was named. The last was withdrawn in 1950.

8F class, London Midland & Scottish Railway. Sir William Stanier's 2–8–0 heavy freight design, first introduced in 1935. In all, 624 were built for the LMS, plus further examples for the War Department. These saw service in the Middle East during the Second World War, and examples were to be found in Iraq, Egypt and Turkey. The WD named several of its engines, but the LMS never did. Nevertheless one or two preserved ex-LMS locomotives have been named in preservation.

9F class, British Railways. These 2–10–0 heavy freight locomotives first appeared in September 1957 although preliminary plans had been for a 2–8–2. Although the driving wheels were no more than 5ft in diameter, the locomotives showed that they had a fine turn of speed when required; one has been timed at 90mph. The last one to be built was also the last steam locomotive for British Railways; as such, no. 92220 was named *Evening Star*. Built at Swindon, it was further embellished with a Great Western-style copper cap to the chimney and was painted in express passenger colours. It was the only one to be named by British Railways, but others have been named in preservation. In all, 251 were built, but they were a short-lived class: in the race to dieselize, the first ones were withdrawn in May 1964 and by June 1968 they were all gone. Quite a number have been preserved, including, of course, no. 92220 *Evening Star*.

9P class, Great Central Railway. Six 4–6–0 express engines, with outside cylinders. The first was introduced in 1917 and the rest in 1920. No. 1165 was named *Valour* in commemoration of the Great Central employees who were killed in the First World War. The last one was withdrawn in 1947.

10 class, British Railways. In all, 146 of these 350hp 0–6–0 diesel-electric locomotives were built between 1955 and 1962. They were intended for shunting and transfer freight working, and had a maximum speed of 20mph. None was named in BR service, but a few have been preserved and some have received names.

11B class, Great Central Railway. Forty 4–4–0 passenger engines, first introduced in 1901. Only nos 1014 *Sir Alexander* and 1021 *Queen Mary* were named. The last went in 1950.

11C class, Great Central Railway. Two 4–4–0s, rebuilt in 1907 from class 11B. They were a development of class 11B.

11E class, Great Central Railway. The celebrated Director class, there were fifteen of these 4–4–0 express engines. Introduced by J.G. Robinson in 1913, they were among the most successful of his engines.

11F class, Great Central Railway. A development of the Director class, there were six of these 4–4–0 express engines, built in 1922, the last year of the Great Central's independent existence. A further twenty-four were built by Sir Nigel Gresley for the London & North Eastern Railway for service in Scotland, and were given Scottish names (see class D11/2, London & North Eastern Railway). No. 506 *Butler-Henderson* is preserved.

14 class, Highland Railway. Two 'Crewe-type' 2–4–0s, which started and ended their careers nameless.

14XX class, Great Western Railway. These 0–4–2T locomotives were introduced in 1932 to C.B. Collett's design, primarily to replace the 517 class 0–4–2Ts, of which they were a modernized version. They were intended for branch line work. Ninety-five were built, the majority fitted for auto-train working. (Auto-train is another name for push/pull working, an explanation of which is given in the notes on the P class, South Eastern & Chatham Railway.) None was named by the Great Western Railway or British Railways, but four have been preserved and some have received names.

19 class, North British Railway. Twenty-four of these small 4–4–0T locomotives were built by Dugald Drummond, the first ones appearing in 1880. All were named. They were used on branch lines and for local traffic all over the system. In 1884 six more were built, but these were never named. The last ones were withdrawn by the London & North Eastern Railway in 1933.

20 class, British Railways. A total of 228 of these 1,000hp Bo-Bo diesel-electric locomotives were built between 1957 and 1968. They were used principally in pairs on freight work. None was named while in BR service.

24 class, British Railways. In all, 151 examples were built of these general purpose Bo-Bo diesel-electric locomotives between 1958 and 1961. They were powered by a Sulzer 6LDA28A diesel engine of 1,160hp. None was named in BR service, but names have appeared in preservation.

25 class, British Railways. In all, 327 of these 1,160hp general purpose Bo-Bo diesel-electric locomotives were built between 1961 and 1967. The class was sub-divided as follows: class 25/1 was dual-braked (except no. D5217) and fitted with steam-heating; class 25/2 was also dual-braked, nos D7585–94 had steam-heating and D7523/35/41 had none; and class 25/3 was dual-braked and without steam-heating. In all cases the maximum speed was 90mph. None was named in BR service, but the class has been found useful on preserved railways and many have been given a further lease of life and some have been named.

26 class, British Railways. Forty-seven of these general purpose Bo-Bo diesel-electric locomotives were built by the Birmingham Railway Carriage & Wagon Co. between 1958 and 1959. They were powered by a Sulzer 6LDA28 engine of 1,160hp. Maximum speed was 75mph.

31 class, British Railways. In all, 263 of these very successful A1A-A1A diesel-electric locomotives were built between 1957 and 1962. Originally they had Mirrlees JSV12T diesel engines of 1,250hp, but in 1964–9 they were re-engined with English Electric 12SVT engines of 1,470hp. There have been varieties within the class: class 31/0 has electromagnetic control, while class 31/1 also has dual brakes. Several have been preserved, and some have since received names.

33 class, British Railways. Sometimes called 'Cromptons'. Ninety-eight of these Bo-Bo diesel-electric locomotives were built in 1961–2 by the Birmingham Railway Carriage & Wagon Co. Ltd. The Sulzer 8LDA28A diesel engine gave 1,550hp at 750rpm. Class 33/0 was the standard locomotive; class 33/1 comprised nineteen push/pull-fitted locomotives for working between Bournemouth and Weymouth with TC (Trailer Control) coach sets; and class 33/2 consisted of twelve locomotives built with specially slim bodies (2.64m as against 2.81m, or 8ft 8in as against 9ft 3in in old money!) for use on the Hastings line, with its narrow tunnels.

37 class, British Railways. A very successful class of 1,750hp Co-Co diesel-electric locomotives, introduced between 1960 and 1965. There are several sub-divisions of this numerous class, e.g. 37/7. They were used on both passenger and freight work.

37 class, London, Tilbury & Southend Railway. Twelve 4–4–2 tank locomotives, introduced in 1897–8 by Thomas Whitelegg, the Tilbury's locomotive superintendent. Numbered 37–48, they were, like their predecessors, named after places on the system. An enlargement of the successful class 1, the engines were only just capable of keeping up with the increasing loads. All were rebuilt in 1905–11, which enhanced their capacity.

40 class, British Railways. A series of 1-Co-Co-1 diesel-electric locomotives introduced in 1958 for general service on BR. Those named after mountains were known as the Peak class. Most are now withdrawn, and the survivors will not last much longer. Some examples have been preserved.

42XX class, Great Western Railway. The first of these unique (for Great Britain) 2–8–0T locomotives was no. 4201, introduced in 1910 by G.J. Churchward for South Wales mineral traffic over short distances. Many were built subsequently, fifty-four of which were converted to the 2–8–2T wheel arrangement. None was named prior to the preservation era.

43 class, British Railways. These are the power cars of the High Speed Trains (HSTs), which at first were regarded as coaching stock and numbered accordingly, but have more recently been regarded as locomotive power in their own right and numbered in the 43XXX series; most have received names. The first HSTs entered service in 1976, and were designed for a top speed of 125mph – hence the 'InterCity 125' logo. The power cars incorporate a guard/luggage compartment, but the guards much prefer to ride in a passenger coach, away from the noise of the Paxman 'Valenta' 12RP200L diesel engine. The wheel arrangement is Bo-Bo. A missed opportunity is the absence of controls at the rear, non-streamlined, end; this makes shunting a power car in the confines of a depot not the easiest of tasks. In service, these engines have been in the forefront of passenger services on non-electrified lines in most parts of the country, and only now (1999) are being cascaded down to cross-country work.

44 and 45 classes, British Railways. See Peak class.

47 class, British Railways. First introduced in 1962, these 2,750bhp diesel-electric locomotives are one of the largest and most successful classes of diesel-electric locomotive introduced in the earlier stages of the dieselization programme. They are equally at home on a 90mph passenger train or a 1,000-ton freight. Over 500 were built, and there are several sub-classes, e.g. 47/7. Now coming to the end of their lives, they are being withdrawn, but there are moves to preserve at least one example.

49 class, Caledonian Railway. Also known as the Sir James Thompson class. These were two 4–6–0 express locomotives built in 1903 for the Carlisle–Glasgow expresses. Only no. 49 *Sir James Thompson* was named, after a former general manager and chairman of the company. When more locomotives were needed, J.F. McIntosh produced the 903 or Cardean class.

50 class, British Railways. Based on the prototype locomotive no. DP2 and first numbered D400 to D449, these 2,750hp Co-Co diesel-electric locomotives first entered service in 1967. They were designated mixed traffic, and although they first worked on express passenger trains on the then non-electrified sections of the West Coast main line, they were also fitted with a slow-speed control for hauling merry-go-round coal trains at 3mph while the trains were either being loaded at the pitheads or discharging at the power stations. Very successful in service, they worked on the Western Region after complete electrification displaced them from the West Coast main line.

51 class, London, Tilbury & Southend Railway. Eighteen 4–4–2 tank engines, numbered 51–68 and named after places on or near the system. A progressive enlargement of the 37 class, they entered service in 1900–3.

52 class, British Railways. See Western class.

56 class, British Railways. In all, 135 of these 2,400hp Co-Co diesel-electric locomotives were built for British Railways between 1977 and 1984. The first thirty were built in Romania, and the rest by British Rail Engineering Ltd.

58 class, British Railways. These 3,300hp Co-Co diesel-electric locomotives, first introduced in 1983, are intended for heavy freight. Fifty have been built. Power comes from a Ruston Paxman RK3ACT diesel engine of 2,460kW at 1,000rpm. All are equipped with slow speed control for merry-go-round coal trains.

60 class, British Railways. A Co-Co diesel-electric locomotive for heavy freight, with 3,100bhp and intended to work 4,000-tonne loads. First introduced in 1990.

69 class, London, Tilbury & Southend Railway. Apart from a couple of 0–6–0 tender engines, these ten 0–6–2 tank engines were the only goods locomotives the 'Tilbury' ever owned. Introduced in 1903, they were the work of Thomas Whitelegg and handled the railway's goods traffic very successfully up to the company's absorption by the Midland Railway in 1912.

72 class, North British Railway. Twenty-four 4–4–0T engines of a very neat and somewhat diminutive design, introduced by Dugald Drummond in 1880 for suburban and branch line work. A further six, without names, were added by Matthew Holmes in 1884. The last was withdrawn in 1933.

73 class, British Railways. Designed for the Southern Region, these Bo-Bo locomotives are termed 'electro-diesel'. That is to say, they are straightforward diesel-electric locomotives with a 600hp diesel engine, but are also able to take 675 volts DC from the third rail in the Southern area. They then develop 1,600hp. Thus they can operate throughout the system. Forty-nine were built.

79 class, London, Tilbury & Southend Railway. Four 4–4–2 tank engines, numbered 79–82 and named after places on or near the system. A progressive enlargement of the 51 class, they entered service in 1909. More engines of the same basic design were built by the London Midland & Scottish Railway after 1923, a splendid endorsement of the design (or perhaps an indictment of the LMS's then inability to do better!)

86 class, British Railways. A large class of Bo-Bo electric locomotives for the West Coast 25kV electrification from London Euston to Crewe, Carlisle and Glasgow. First introduced in 1965, they are rated at 3,600hp continuous rating and can reach 100mph. There are several sub-divisions of the class, denoting variations in the electrical equipment fitted.

87 class, British Railways. First introduced in 1973, these Bo-Bo electric locomotives for the West Coast main line are rated at 5,000hp and can reach 110mph. Sub-class 87/1 has thyristor control.

89 class, British Railways. So far, there is only one of these 5,800hp Co-Co electric locomotives. The prototype, no. 89001 *Avocet*, entered service in October 1986; capable of 125mph, it is clearly intended for express passenger work. It weighs 105 tonnes and is almost 65ft long.

90 class, British Railways. Built in 1987–90 at Crewe Works, these Bo-Bo electric locomotives develop 5,000hp. Class 90/1 has the electric train heating equipment isolated and the drop-head buckeye couplers removed.

91 class, British Railways. A class of 6,090hp Bo-Bo electric locomotives built between 1988 and 1991. They are fitted with thyristor control, and have a design maximum speed of 140mph. Drop-head buckeye couplers are fitted. This class is owned by Eversholt Train Leasing Co. (owner code SAB).

92 class, British Railways. Built between 1993 and 1995, these Co-Co freight locomotives are designed for working through the Channel Tunnel. They are electric locomotives, designed to take power either at 25,000 volts AC from overhead equipment in France, or at 750 volts DC from the third rail on the Southern Region of British Railways. They develop 6,700hp on the 25,000 volt AC, or 5,360hp on the 750 volt DC. Examples of the class are owned by SNCF (French Railways) as well as British owners.

107 class, London & South Western Railway. Six 2–2–2 locomotives were built for the Italian–Austrian Railway in 1847 by Stothert & Slaughter of Bristol. The L&SWR locomotive engineer, J.V. Gooch, had designed them as a side commission (with the approval of the L&SWR Board), and then arranged for all six to undertake their proving trials on the L&SWR. The Italians, for reasons of their own, decided only to accept four, and offered *Ombrone* and *Bizenzia* to the L&SWR at £2,000 each. They thus became nos 107 *Gem* and 108 *Ruby* respectively. *Gem* was withdrawn in 1862, and ·*Ruby* lasted until 1868.

141R class, French National Railways. With the end of the Second World War in sight, a French delegation placed orders with American and Canadian locomotive builders for a large number of general purpose 2–8–2 locomotives.

These were classified 141R by the Société Nationale des Chemins de fer Français (SNCF) and were most successful. Some were equipped to burn oil. They worked all over France, and were only made redundant by electrification. One has been preserved in this country.

157 class, North British Railway.   Six 0–4–2 tanks introduced by Dugald Drummond in 1877. The weight on the rear carrying axle proved excessive, and within five years they were altered to 0–4–4Ts. They became LNER class G8, and the last survivors were withdrawn in 1925.

165 class, North British Railway.   A class of light 0–6–0 tank engines introduced by Dugald Drummond in 1875 for branch line work. Twenty-five were built, all named after places on the system. Engines tended to be stationed in the area of their name, and on reallocation were occasionally renamed. Thus some had two names, and one example had three. They became LNER class J82, and the last was withdrawn in 1926.

211 class, North British Railway.   A class of 2–2–2 express locomotives built for the Edinburgh & Glasgow Railway, which the NBR absorbed in 1865. They were rebuilt at least once, and Dugald Drummond built two more in 1876.

233 class, North British Railway.   A class of seven ex-Edinburgh & Glasgow Railway 2–4–0 passenger locomotives, which received names during Dugald Drummond's time as locomotive superintendent.

317 class, North British Railway.   A class of 0–4–2 locomotives, built for the Edinburgh & Glasgow Railway, which the NBR had absorbed in 1865. Intended for main line goods work, they ended their days on branch passenger work and on the Edinburgh suburban trains. They received names during Dugald Drummond's superintendency.

317 class, North British Railway.   Following the withdrawal of the veterans that made up the first 317 class, the numbers were available for new developments. These were twelve 4–4–0 express locomotives for the Aberdeen road, first appearing in 1903. They were Matthew Holmes's last design, and but for his death the class might have been bigger. Numbers were 317–28. The class was never rebuilt, and the last was withdrawn by the London & North Eastern Railway in July 1926.

418 class, North British Railway.   A class of 2–4–0 passenger locomotives designed by T. Wheatley and first introduced in 1873. Five of them received names during Dugald Drummond's time as locomotive superintendent.

627 class, Lancashire & Yorkshire Railway.   These were 4–4–0 passenger locomotives, with 6ft driving wheels, designed by W. Barton Wright and first introduced in 1880. Of the 110 built, only a handful had names.

721 class, Caledonian Railway.   See Dunalastair class.

757 class, Southern Railway.   These two 0–6–2T locomotives were built in December 1907 for the Plymouth, Devonport & South Western Junction Railway. In spite of its grandiose title, the line extended only from Bere Alston to Callington, serving various tin and copper mines. In spite of being completely non-standard, they remained in the Plymouth area until they were withdrawn by British Railways.

766 class, Caledonian Railway.   See Dunalastair II class.

863 class, Lancashire & Yorkshire Railway.   Very similar to the 627 class of 4–4–0 passenger locomotives, first appearing in June 1885.

903 class, Caledonian Railway.   Also known as the Cardean class. Five of these imposing 4–6–0 express locomotives were built in 1906 for the heavy West Coast expresses between Glasgow and Carlisle. Generally similar to the 49 or Sir James Thompson class, but the cylinder diameter was reduced and the diameter of the boiler increased. Only no. 903 *Cardean* was named, after the estate of Mr Edward Cox, the deputy chairman of directors at the time, but lost its name when that gentleman severed his connection with the railway. No. 907 was destroyed in the Quintinshill accident of 1915. All (except no. 907) were withdrawn by the London Midland & Scottish Railway.

908 class, Caledonian Railway.   Also known as the Sir James King class. Ten of these imposing 4–6–0 express passenger locomotives were built to J.F. McIntosh's design in 1906. They were very similar to the 903 or Cardean class, but with 5ft 9in driving wheels instead of the 6ft 6in wheels of the earlier class. Only two were named: no. 908 *Sir James King*, after the late chairman of directors, and no. 911 *Barochan*, after the residence of the then chairman, Sir Charles Renshaw. All were withdrawn by the London Midland & Scottish Railway.

1076 class, Great Western Railway.   Sometimes called the Buffalo class, from the only member of the class to receive a name, there were 266 of these 0–6–0 tank engines. The first examples were side tanks, followed by saddle tanks. First introduced in 1870, all were rebuilt with saddle tanks, and then all but thirteen with pannier tanks. The last was not withdrawn until 1946.

1738 class, Midland Railway.   Designed by S.W. Johnson, the class first appeared in 1882 with locomotive no. 1562. In all, 265 locomotives were eventually built, although there were some differences between batches. Only one example of this series of 4–4–0 passenger locomotives was named, no. 1757 *Beatrice*.

1813 class, Great Western Railway.   Forty 0–6–0 tank engines, introduced in 1882. The first one was sold to the Pembroke & Tenby Railway, becoming their no. 7 *Holmwood*. In 1896 the GWR absorbed the P&TR and no. 1813 returned to the fold; however, it kept its name until withdrawal. All but two were rebuilt with saddle tanks, and all but one were further altered to pannier tanks. All but ten were superheated. The last was withdrawn in 1949.

2301 ('Dean Goods') class, Great Western Railway.   See GWR2301 class.

2400 class, North Eastern Railway.   This was Sir Vincent Raven's Pacific, or 4–6–2, design. Basically an enlarged and elongated Z class 4–4–2, it appeared in 1922, at the very end of the North Eastern Railway's independent existence. Comparative trials suggested that there was very little to choose between no. 2400 and the first Gresley 4–6–2s, with 180lb boiler pressure and short-travel valves. But Sir Nigel chose to develop his own design, and the Raven 4–6–2s were not perpetuated. The names were added by the LNER.

3001 class, Great Western Railway.   These were similar to the 3021 class, but were built for the standard gauge at the outset. Photographs show that some of these engines were not named at first. They were all converted to 4–2–2 at the same time as their ex-broad gauge sisters.

3031 class, Great Western Railway.   With the end of broad gauge in sight, William Dean produced a class of 2–2–2s that were designed to be easily convertible to standard gauge. The broad gauge wheels were temporarily outside both sets of double frames. While running on the broad gauge, the engines were unnamed, and received names when they were converted to standard gauge. After an accident involving no. 3021 *Wigmore Castle*, when she broke her leading axle in Box Tunnel, concern was expressed about the weight on the leading pair of wheels. They were then rebuilt a second time, with a leading bogie. Further locomotives of the new 3031 class were then built new to the 4–2–2 design. In their 4–2–2 state, these are considered by many to be the most beautiful locomotives ever to run in this country.

3200 class, Great Western Railway.   See Earl class, Great Western Railway.

APPENDIX II

COMPANY NOTES

In the earliest days, almost all locomotives were named. The concept of a class of identical engines took some time to become established; there were enough problems in making something that would work! Some engineers, notably J.C. Craven of the London, Brighton & South Coast Railway, firmly believed in horses for courses, and produced a fresh design for virtually every job on the railway. Later, quite a few railways reacted, and made a clean sweep of virtually all names. Apart from a few oddities and/or special occasions, the London & South Western Railway, the South Eastern & Chatham Railway, the Midland Railway, the North Eastern Railway, the Great Northern Railway, the Great Eastern Railway, the North Stafford Railway and the Furness Railway, to name quite a handful, in their later years at any rate did not make a practice of naming their locomotives. At the other extreme, in William Martley's time on the London, Chatham & Dover Railway all locomotives were named but not numbered, and in William Stroudley's time the LB&SCR named everything except 0–6–0 goods engines! The following notes are intended to amplify the policies pursued by those railways that did name their motive power.

British Railways. At first, BR began with a series of heroic names, drawn from the pages of history, for the Britannia class 7 4–6–2 locomotives. The class 6 4–6–2s were named after Scottish clans, and so became known as the Clan class. The solitary class 8P 4–6–2 was named *Duke of Gloucester*. Otherwise, names were exceptional. A few class 5MT 4–6–0s allocated to the Southern Region took the names of withdrawn King Arthur class locomotives, and the last steam locomotive of all, a class 9F 2–10–0, was named *Evening Star*. With its diesel and electric locomotives, there seem to be three policies operating concurrently. Some of the best steam era names have been perpetuated. Names that will generate a spot of (preferably free) publicity have resulted in locomotives being named after, among other things, provincial newspapers. And there have been some homely touches; as noted above, *Cookie* was named after the depot cat. (N.B. British Railways restyled itself British Rail in 1965.)

Caledonian Railway. Extending from Carlisle to Edinburgh and Glasgow, to Oban in the west and Aberdeen in the north, the Caledonian named locomotives only occasionally. Usually directors or their estates were commemorated. The Caledonian Railway became part of the London Midland & Scottish Railway in 1923.

Festiniog Railway. This railway, on the narrow gauge of 1ft 11½in, extends from Portmadoc to Blaenau Ffestiniog, in North Wales. One of the earliest narrow gauge railways to introduce steam power, the line really became famous for its adoption of the Fairlie articulated type, examples of which continue working there to this day.

Furness Railway. This line had its headquarters at Barrow-in-Furness, and only named its locomotives in the early days. Names were a mixed bag. The Furness Railway became part of the London Midland & Scottish Railway in 1923.

Great Central Railway. See Manchester, Sheffield & Lincolnshire Railway.

Great Eastern Railway. Only three locomotives were named. The first, *Mogul*, gave its name to the 2–6–0 wheel arrangement. The second, *Petrolea*, commemorated its oil-burning apparatus. The third, *Claud Hamilton*, commemorated the chairman, and was specially named for the Paris Exhibition of 1900. By a neat bit of fiddling, the locomotive was also given the number 1900. The GER became part of the London & North Eastern Railway in 1923.

Great Northern Railway. Only three locomotives were named. The first was no. 990 *Henry Oakley*, named after the general manager; happily this engine survives in the National Collection. The other two were the first two of Nigel Gresley's 4–6–2 locomotives, *Great Northern* and *Sir Frederick Banbury*. The third, which appeared after the formation of the London & North Eastern Railway, was the immortal *Flying Scotsman*. The GNR became part of the London & North Eastern Railway in 1923.

Great North of Scotland Railway. This was quite a small company, with lines radiating from Inverness. It was notable for using 4–4–0 locomotives for most services, including freight, and for not owning any 0–6–0 locomotives. Names were sparingly applied, and were something of a mixed bag. The Ballater branch provided rail access to Balmoral, and saw a great deal of royal traffic. The GNSR became part of the London & North Eastern Railway in 1923.

Great Western Railway. In the early broad gauge days, all engines were named but not numbered. This ended as a general rule when the GWR got involved with standard gauge operations, but the Rover class 4–2–2s and their renewals remained identified by name only up to the end of the broad gauge in 1892. Thereafter the GWR, ever publicity-conscious, named its passenger engines with themes: Stars, Saints, Ladies, Knights, Courts, Castles, Kings, Counties (two series), Halls, Granges, Manors and so on. There was one incident when certain directors objected to their names being applied to what later became known as the 'Dukedog' class,★ and insisted that their names be borne by Castles. The engines ran nameless thereafter, but in preservation the surviving 'Dukedog' has had its original name, *Earl of Berkeley*, restored. In 1948 the Great Western Railway was nationalized to form the Western Region of British Railways.

Highland Railway. The main line extended from Perth to Inverness, taking the tracks over Druimuachdar Summit, at 1,484ft the highest point reached by a British main line. A long branch extended from Dingwall to Kyle of Lochalsh. North of Inverness the line extended to Wick and Thurso, the latter being the most northerly place in Scotland reached by a main line. Locomotives were named from the earliest days, usually after places on the lines to which they were allocated, and a locomotive's transfer to another part of the system usually meant a renaming. Locomotives were also named after personalities connected with the railway, such as the Duke of Sutherland. The Highland Railway became part of the London Midland & Scottish Railway in 1923.

Jersey Railway. The line opened in 1870, running from St Helier to St Aubin, a distance of 3¾ miles, and to standard gauge. The extension to La Moye, and then to Corbière, was opened on 31 August 1884, to the 3ft 6in gauge. The original section was then converted to the 3ft 6in gauge, with through running over the 7½ miles from St Helier to Corbière commencing on 5 August 1885. After several years of running at a loss, the destruction by fire of the St Helier terminus and a sizeable proportion of the carriage stock in October 1936 seemed a good opportunity to close the railway permanently. Locomotives were named after localities and other Jersey features.

Liverpool & Manchester Railway. This pioneer railway, after starting with a mixed bag of names, settled down to animal names for goods locomotives and bird names for passenger engines. Thus *Lion*, which has been preserved, is an 0–4–2 goods locomotive. The line ultimately became part of the London & North Western Railway.

London, Brighton & South Coast Railway. This company was formed in 1846 from the amalgamation of the London & Croydon and the London & Brighton Railways. Initially, almost all engines were named, and some were not numbered. With the advent of J.C. Craven as locomotive superintendent in 1847 names were dropped, only to be reintroduced when William Stroudley succeeded Craven on the latter's retirement in 1869. Stroudley named virtually everything apart from the 0–6–0 goods engines, choosing for the most part towns and villages served by the LB&SCR, and European towns that might be regarded as coming within the LB&SCR's sphere of influence. This policy was continued by his successor R.J. Billinton. When D.E. Marsh took over in 1905, the locomotive livery was changed from the bright gamboge to be seen on the preserved *Gladstone* and *Boxhill* locomotives to burnt umber, and almost all names were removed. Henceforth, names were applied only to some of the railway's largest and most prestigious locomotives. The LB&SCR became part of the Southern Railway in 1923.

London, Chatham & Dover Railway. At first, in William Martley's time as locomotive superintendent, all locomotives were named and none was numbered. Names were somewhat fanciful, such as *Frolic* and *Flirt*. After Martley's death, his successor William Kirtley introduced numbers and removed all names. The LC&DR formed a working union with the South Eastern Railway in 1900, styled the South Eastern & Chatham Railway, although the LC&DR Company retained its independent existence until 1923. It then became part of the Southern Railway.

London Midland & Scottish Railway. Torn between the 'name everything' policy of the former London & North Western and the 'name nothing' policy of the Midland, the LMS named only its six-coupled passenger locomotives. The Royal Scot class was initially named after pioneer locomotives, with a bas-relief representation of its early namesake included below each nameplate; subsequently the locomotives were renamed after regiments of the British Army. In order not to offend regiments that were not so favoured, some of the Class 5 4–6–0 mixed traffic locomotives were also named. The Patriot and Jubilee classes retained the L&NWR tradition of a happy-go-lucky mixture. The Princess class 4–6–2s were named after members of the royal family, and the Princess Coronation or Duchess class engines were mostly

---

★These engines were produced by marrying the boiler of a Duke class engine with the frames of a Bulldog class. The name 'Dukedog' was coined by an enthusiast, and never had official standing; officially the engines were 9000 or 90XX class.

named after more royals, duchesses and cities. The London Midland & Scottish Railway became part of British Railways in 1948.

London & North Eastern Railway. This company was formed in 1923 by amalgamating the Great Northern, Great Central, Great Eastern, North Eastern, North British, and Great North of Scotland Railways. There were several naming policies. Sir Nigel Gresley named his first 4–6–2s after racehorses, and the streamlined A4 class after birds. Edward Thompson and Arthur Peppercorn in their turn continued the racehorse theme (and so did the Eastern Region of British Railways for their Deltic class diesels). Gresley, meanwhile, revived the heroic Scottish names of the North British H and I classes for his P2 class 2–8–2s, and continued the 'Waverley' novels theme for his Scottish Director class built soon after the Grouping. He later turned to names of counties and, more imaginatively, names of hunts for his 4–4–0 designs. The B17 class was named after a mixture of stately homes and football teams. Interestingly, Gresley's most spectacular passenger design, the four-cylinder compound 4–6–4 no. 10000, never had a name. The LNER became part of British Railways in 1948.

London & North Western Railway. With very few exceptions, the names for each class were a very mixed bag. Classical allusions, historical figures, railway directors, colonies, ships from the Royal Navy, flora and fauna were just some of the sources tapped. This meant that it was virtually impossible to tell a locomotive's class from its name alone; a further complication was the railway's habit of recycling many of the names from one generation of locomotives to the next. Some of the names were quite beautiful, like *Luck of Edenhall*. O.S. Nock explains that the name is 'that of a family heirloom of the Musgraves, of Eden Hall, near Penrith. The legend is told in a ballad by Uhland, which Longfellow translates:

> This flashing glass of crystal tall,
> Gave to my Sires the Fountain Sprite;
> She wrote in it 'If this glass doth fall,
> Farewell, then, O Luck of Edenhall.'

The London & North Western Railway became part of the London Midland & Scottish Railway in 1923.

London & South Western Railway. At its fullest extent, the L&SWR stretched from London (Waterloo) to Portsmouth, Salisbury, Exeter, Plymouth, Bude, Ilfracombe and Padstow. Locomotives were named up to W.G. Beattie's term of office, and there was a disconcerting habit of reusing names and numbers of locomotives that had been withdrawn. Thus there were two Hercules classes, two Eagle classes, and so on. These have been distinguished by a prefix 1 or 2 as appropriate.

William George Beattie was the son of Joseph Hamilton Beattie, his predecessor. Unfortunately, he was less successful as an engineer, and after the fiasco of his 348 class of (unnamed) 4–4–0s, he retired on grounds of ill-health. Thereafter locomotives were for the most part unnamed. The Southampton Docks Co. named its shunters, and when the L&SWR took over the docks, William Adams and his successors continued this tradition. Thus only the smallest locomotives were named. The L&SWR became part of the Southern Railway in 1923.

London & South Western Railway (Engineering Department). In its earliest days, when track maintenance was put out to contract, the L&SWR's civil engineer maintained his own fleet of locomotives for ballasting work, etc., quite independently of the railway's main fleet for running the trains. Engineering Department locomotives were named but not, initially, numbered. This unusual practice ended in 1888.

Longmoor Military Railway. This line ran from Bordon to Liss in Hampshire via Longmoor Down, and was built and operated as a training exercise for the Railway Operating Division of the Royal Engineers. It started life as the Woolmer Instructional Military Railway, and changed its name to the Longmoor Military Railway (because, so it is said, the initials WIMR were said to stand for the 'Will It Move Railway?') The locomotive names were a mixture of generals, battles, garrisons and similar names appropriate to the military mind.

Manchester & Milford Railway. The first proposal to connect Manchester with the port of Milford Haven surfaced in 1845, but the company really became established with the start of construction in 1860. The company was perpetually short of cash, so the only stretch that was built was the 40-mile line from Aberystwyth to Pencader, with running powers over the Great Western Railway thence to Carmarthen. Its locomotives were named after places on the system and after local worthies. In 1906 the line was leased to the Great Western, who later absorbed it outright, and its locomotives were renumbered into that company's stock.

Manchester, Sheffield & Lincolnshire Railway. The title gives a good description of the line's whereabouts. All locomotives were named in the early days, usually with names derived from classical mythology. In 1859 the Locomotive & Stores Committee decided to cease naming locomotives, and existing names were removed as the engines came in for repair. On 1 August 1897 the MS&L changed its name to Great Central Railway. With J.G. Robinson as its locomotive superintendent, a cautious return was made to the policy of naming some of the best express locomotives. The Great Central Railway became part of the London & North Eastern Railway in 1923.

Martin Mill Military Railway. This little-known concern ran between Dover and Deal. Its main purpose was to accommodate some very large rail-mounted guns which were used during the Second World War to shell Calais. In order not to give away the exact position of the guns, diesel locomotives were used, and these were supplied by the London Midland & Scottish Railway, that company having by 1939 quite a sizeable fleet of 0–6–0 diesel-electric locomotives. Accordingly, a suitable number were transferred to the military, and when they required repair or overhaul they were returned to the LMS – who promptly replaced them with others from its stock, and returned the repaired machines to service on its own system. Thus, there was a rotating fleet of diesel-electrics in military service. The War Department nevertheless saw fit to renumber and name those locomotives in its charge at any one time, which makes things rather confusing for the locomotive historian! Names were of a military nature, similar to those of the Longmoor Military Railway.

North British Railway. This railway extended from Berwick to Edinburgh, Glasgow and Aberdeen. Beyond Glasgow the NBR operated the West Highland Railway from Glasgow to Fort William and Mallaig. Locomotives were named from the earliest days, usually after places on the lines to which they were allocated, and a locomotive's transfer to another part of the system sometimes meant a renaming. The NBR became part of the London & North Eastern Railway in 1923.

A War Department Dean Goods 0–6–0 being rerailed on the Longmoor Military Railway. This was an Open Day, as the crowds testify, and, playing to the gallery, the railway's steam crane was being used. Normally, a simple derailment would be dealt with by jacks and packing. (*Photo: Author*)

South Devon Railway. This line continued the Great Western and Bristol & Exeter main line to the west from Exeter to Plymouth. The line followed the South Devon coast, with formidable gradients which are a bugbear to this day. Originally, it was intended to operate the line by the atmospheric principle, whereby the trains were attached to a piston in a tube. As the air was pumped out of the tube ahead of the piston, the atmospheric pressure behind it forced it forward. In practice, this was a failure. Steam locomotives on the 7ft ¼in gauge were designed by Daniel Gooch of the Great Western, and were 4–4–0ST for passenger trains and 0–6–0ST for goods. All received classical names. In 1876 the line, together with the Bristol & Exeter and the Cornwall Railway, amalgamated with the Great Western, giving that company a through route from Paddington to Penzance.

South Eastern Railway. This railway extended from London to Dover and Folkestone. In the very earliest days locomotives were named, usually with classical or Kentish connotations. From Cudworth's time as locomotive superintendent the engines were nameless, apart from no. 240 of James Stirling's F class. This was named *Onward* (the company motto) for the Paris Exhibition of 1889. After comparative trials on the Paris, Lyon & Mediterranean Railway, *Onward* was landed at Dover on 30 January 1890. It re-entered traffic on 16 March, nameless. The SER formed a working union with the London, Chatham & Dover Railway in 1900, styled the South Eastern & Chatham Railway, although the SER Company retained its independent existence until 1923. It then became part of the Southern Railway.

Southern Railway. Locomotives were first named as a deliberate public relations policy. First was the N15 class, which became the King Arthurs. Then came the Lord Nelson class, named after famous admirals of former times. The Remembrance class, rebuilt from redundant express passenger tank locomotives, remembered bygone locomotive engineers, as well as the war dead of the London, Brighton & South Coast Railway, and the Schools class engines were named after famous public schools. The Merchant Navy class commemorated the shipping companies using Southampton Docks, and the smaller West Country and Battle of Britain classes marked places in the West Country, and famous personalities, places and squadrons connected with the Battle of Britain respectively. The former London,

Brighton & South Coast Railway 4–4–2 locomotives of classes H1 and H2 were named after headlands on the south coast. But the River class names were removed when those locomotives were converted from 2–6–4T to 2–6–0 tender engines – again for public relations reasons: since the Sevenoaks accident the 'Rolling Rivers' had received a very bad press. The Southern Railway became part of British Railways in 1948.

Stockton & Darlington Railway.   This pioneer line, opened in 1825, started off by naming every locomotive regardless. The first four, *Locomotion*, *Hope*, *Black Diamond* and *Diligence*, were very similar though not quite identical. No. 5 *Royal George* was the first of a long line of 0–6–0 mineral engines by Timothy Hackworth, all of which were broadly similar in that they had a tender at each end. The first, which was pushed ahead of the engine, carried the fireman and the coal, while the second, pulled behind the engine, carried the driver and the water supply. The preserved engine *Derwent* gives a good idea of the type. Then came the celebrated long-boilered type of mineral locomotive, which had a long boiler relative to its diameter and a quite small firebox. This was ideal for a locomotive which spent long periods in refuge sidings, waiting for faster passenger trains to pass, before making a tremendous effort to haul its train to the next refuge siding. The boiler became in effect a reservoir for steam, and the small firebox ensured economical coal consumption. Such locomotives lasted for many years, the last only being withdrawn by the London & North Eastern Railway after 1923. The S&DR itself was absorbed by the North Eastern Railway in 1875. The NER removed almost all engine names.

Talyllyn Railway.   Opened in 1865 on the narrow gauge of 2ft 3in, the Talyllyn was still using its original locomotives, coaches and track in 1951. In that year it was taken over by the world's first railway preservation society, which operates it to this day. Locomotive names are a mixture of local geographical features and worthies connected with the railway.

West Somerset Mineral Railway.   This most interesting railway was standard gauge, though there was no regular connection with the rest of the railway network. It ran inland from Watchet in Somerset to Combe Row. There a tremendous cable-worked incline ran up Brendon Hill, and the line continued along the top of the Brendons to Gupworthy, now a remote hamlet. But when the line opened in 1859 iron ore was being mined in the area, and the line hoped for revenue from this traffic. But cheaper ores from abroad killed the business, though the railway lingered on until 1909. From 1864 the railway was leased by the Ebbw Vale Company and its successors. The locomotives were mainly 0–6–0STs, though one or two 0–4–0STs worked on the top section above the incline. Names were a mixed bunch. It is worth noting that, in spite of persistent allegations to the contrary, *Brendon* and *Atlas* never worked on the WSMR. *Brendon* is said to have been shipped to South Wales by mistake; Roger Sellick, in his definitive history of the line, says that it is 'practically certain' that it never ran on the WSMR. *Atlas* was one of Sharp, Stewart's Order E492 (1657 of 1865) which became Brecon & Merthyr Railway no. 18.

LOCOMOTIVE DESIGNERS

First of all, how were engines designed? Locomotive designs didn't just happen: they were carefully worked out by a drawing-office team, headed by a chief draughtsman. In charge was the locomotive superintendent, a title later changed to chief mechanical engineer. He laid down policy, and took a greater or lesser involvement in the evolution of each new design. The remit from the Traffic Department might read: 'A locomotive to haul passenger trains of x tons from a to b at an average of y miles per hour', and the Drawing Office would come up with a number of suggestions. Constraints included considerations of weight (owing to the capacity of underline bridges), length (to fit existing turntables), width (to avoid hitting platform edges), and height (to avoid hitting tunnels). The chief mechanical engineer might (or might not) lay down ideas such as wheel arrangement, number of cylinders, and so on. G.J. Churchward of the Great Western supervised the drawing office in detail, sitting down with individual draughtsmen to discuss problems. At the other extreme, H.S. Wainwright of the South Eastern & Chatham, who was really a carriage designer, left everything to Robert Surtees, the chief draughtsman, and contented himself with simply devising the painting scheme. History remembers Churchward as one of the greatest locomotive engineers this country has ever produced. The South Eastern & Chatham directors asked Mr Wainwright to resign.

The design was attributed to the CME, whether or not he actually 'designed' it himself. He received the credit if the locomotive were a success but he also received the blame if it were not. With this caveat, the following tables are offered in an attempt to be helpful.

Locomotives were built either at the railways' own workshops or by private firms, some of which have been mentioned in this book. The locations of the various companies' works are indicated below.

British Railways
British Railways inherited all the locomotive, carriage and wagon building plants of all the railways.
> Robert A. Riddles (1948–54)

In 1965 British Railways restyled itself British Rail.

Caledonian Railway
The works were at St Rollox, Glasgow.
> Robert Sinclair (1847–56)
> Benjamin Connor (1856–76)
> George Brittain (1876–82)
> Dugald Drumond (1882–90)
> Hugh Smellie (1890)
> John Lambie (1890–5)
> John Farquharson McIntosh (1895–1914)
> William Pickersgill (1914–22)

Cambrian Railways
The works were at Oswestry. Locomotives were supplied by private manufacturers, e.g. Sharp, Stewart & Co. of Manchester.
> Alexander Walker (–1879)
> William Aston (1879–98)
> H.E. Jones (1898–1922)

Furness Railway

The works were at Barrow-in-Furness. Locomotives were supplied by private manufacturers, e.g. Sharp, Stewart & Co. of Manchester.

    R. Mason★ (1890–7)
    William Frank Pettigrew (1897–1918)
    D.J. Rutherford# (1918–22)

★   Prior to 1890, Furness Railway locomotives were designed, as well as built, by the builders, usually Sharp, Stewart & Co. of Manchester.

Rutherford was the railway's 'engineer', and was primarily a civil engineer. He delegated locomotive matters to the chief draughtsman, Ernest Sharples.

Glasgow & South Western Railway

The works were at Kilmarnock.

    Patrick Stirling (1853–66)
    James Stirling★ (1866–77)
    Hugh Smellie (1877–90)
    James Manson (1890–1912)
    Peter Drummond# (1912–18)
    Robert Harben Whitelegg (1918–22)

★   Younger brother of Patrick Stirling.
Younger brother of Dugald Drummond.

Great Central Railway (see also Manchester, Sheffield & Lincolnshire Railway)

Locomotive works were at Gorton, Manchester. Coaches and waggons were built at Dukinfield.

    Harry Pollitt (1897–1900)
    John George Robinson (1900–22)

Great Eastern Railway

The works were at Stratford, East London.

    Robert Sinclair (1862–5)
    William Kitson (1865–6)
    Samuel Waite Johnson (1866–73)
    William Adams (1873–8)
    Massey Bromley (1878–81)
    Thomas William Worsdell (1881–5)
    James Holden# (1885–1907)
    Stephen Dewar Holden★ (1908–12)
    A.J. Hill (1912–22)

James Holden came from the Great Western, where he had been a very successful carriage designer. He delegated most of his locomotive work to his chief draughtsman, Fred V. Russell.

★   Son of James Holden.

Great Northern Railway

The works were at Doncaster.

    Benjamin Cubitt (1846–8)
    Archibald Sturrock (1850–66)
    Patrick Stirling (1866–95)
    Henry Alfred Ivatt (1896–1911)
    Herbert Nigel Gresley (1911–22)

Great North of Scotland Railway

The works were originally at Kittybrewster, Aberdeen, but in 1902 they were moved to Inverurie.

Daniel Kinnear Clark (1853–5)
J.F. Ruthven (1855–7)
William Cowan (1857–83)
James Manson (1883–90)
James Johnson★ (1890–4)
William Pickersgill (1894–1914)
Thomas E. Heywood (1914–22)

★   Son of S.W. Johnson of the Great Eastern and Midland Railways.

Great Western Railway
The works were at Swindon.
Daniel Gooch★ (1837–64)
Joseph Armstrong (1864–77)
William Dean (1877–1902)
George Jackson Churchward (1902–21)
Charles Benjamin Collett (1921–41)
Frederick William Hawksworth (1941–7)

★   He became Sir Daniel Gooch Bt in 1866.

Highland Railway
The works were at Lochgorm, just outside Inverness.
William Barclay (1855–65)
William Stroudley (1865–70)
David Jones (1870–96)
Peter Drummond (1896–1912)
Frederick George Smith (1912–15)
Christopher Cumming (1915–22)
David C. Urie★ (1922)

★   Son of R.W. Urie of the London & South Western Railway.

Hull & Barnsley Railway
Locomotives were supplied by private manufacturers.
Matthew Stirling★ (1885–1922)

★   Matthew Stirling was the son of Patrick Stirling and the nephew of James Stirling.
In 1922 the Hull & Barnsley Railway was absorbed by the North Eastern Railway, which became part of the London & North Eastern Railway the following year.

Lancashire, Derbyshire & East Coast Railway
Locomotives were supplied by private manufacturers.
Robert Absolom Thom (1902–7)
In 1907 the Lancashire, Derbyshire & East Coast Railway was absorbed by the Great Central Railway.

Lancashire & Yorkshire Railway
The works were at Horwich.
William Jenkins (1854–67)
William Hurst (1868–76)
W. Barton Wright (1876–86)
John Audley Frederick Aspinall★ (1886–99)
Henry Albert Hoy (1899–1904)
George Hughes (1904–22)

★   He became Sir John Aspinall in 1917.

In 1922 the Lancashire & Yorkshire Railway merged with the London & North Western Railway, and in 1923 became part of the London Midland & Scottish Railway.

London, Brighton & South Coast Railway
The locomotive works were at Brighton. Carriages and waggons were built at Lancing.

John Gray (1845–7)
Thomas Kirtley★ (1847)
John Chester Craven (1847–69)
William Stroudley (1870–89)
Robert John Billinton (1890–1904)
Douglas Earle Marsh (1905–11)
Lawson Boskovsky Billinton# (1911–22)

★ Brother of Matthew Kirtley of the Midland Railway.
Son of R.J. Billinton.

London, Chatham & Dover Railway
The works were at Longhedge, Battersea.

Benjamin Cubitt (–1860)
William Martley (1860–74)
William Kirtley (1874–98)

In 1899 the London, Chatham & Dover Railway formed a working union with the South Eastern Railway known as the South Eastern & Chatham Railway. In 1923 the SE&CR became part of the Southern Railway.

London Midland & Scottish Railway
The LMS inherited works at Crewe, Derby, Horwich, Stoke, St Rollox, Kilmarnock and Inverness.

George Hughes (1923–5)
Sir Henry Fowler★ (1925–31)
Ernest John Hutchings Lemon★★ (1931–2)
William Arthur Stanier# (1932–44)
Charles Edward Fairburn (1944–5)
Henry George Ivatt## (1945–7)

★ He became Sir Henry Fowler in 1918.
★★ He later became Sir Ernest Lemon.
He became Sir William Stanier in 1943.
Son of H.A. Ivatt of the Great Northern Railway.

In 1948 the London Midland & Scottish Railway was nationalized to form the London Midland Region and part of the Scottish Region of British Railways.

London & North Eastern Railway
The LNER inherited works at Doncaster, Darlington, Gateshead, Stratford, Gorton, Cowlairs, Inverurie, Dukinfield, Shildon and York.

Herbert Nigel Gresley★ (1923–41)
Edward Thompson (1941–6)
Arthur Henry Peppercorn (1947)

★ He became Sir Nigel Gresley in 1936.

In 1948 the London & North Eastern Railway was nationalized to form the Eastern and North Eastern Regions, and part of the Scottish Region of British Railways.

London & North Western Railway

Francis Trevithick, son of the great Cornish pioneer Richard Trevithick, oversaw the Northern Division and James Edward McConnell the Southern Division, with headquarters at Crewe and Wolverton respectively, until 1857, when the divisions were amalgamated and Crewe assumed supremacy. McConnell resigned in 1882.

    John Ramsbottom (1857–71)
    Francis William Webb (1871–1903)
    George Whale (1903–9)
    Charles John Bowen Cooke (1909–20)
    Capt Hewitt Pearson Montague Beames (1920–1)
    George Hughes (1922)

In 1922 the London & North Western Railway merged with the Lancashire & Yorkshire Railway, and in 1923 became part of the London Midland & Scottish Railway.

London & South Western Railway

The works were originally at Nine Elms, London, and then moved to Eastleigh.

    Joseph Woods (1835–41)
    John Viret Gooch★ (1841–50)
    Joseph Hamilton Beattie (1850–71)
    William George Beattie# (1871–8)
    William Adams (1878–95)
    Dugald Drummond (1895–1912)
    Robert Wallace Urie (1912–22)

★   Elder brother of Sir Daniel Gooch of the Great Western.
Son of J.H. Beattie.

London, Tilbury & Southend Railway

The repair works were at Plaistow. Locomotives were supplied by private manufacturers.

    Thomas Whitelegg (1880–1910)
    Robert Harben Whitelegg★ (1910–12)

★   Son of T. Whitelegg.

In 1912 the London, Tilbury & Southend Railway was absorbed by the Midland Railway, which in turn became part of the London Midland & Scottish Railway in 1923.

Manchester, Sheffield & Lincolnshire Railway

Locomotive works were at Gorton, Manchester. Coaches and waggons were built at Dukinfield.

    Richard Peacock (–1854)
    William Grindley Craig (1854–9)
    Charles Reboul Sacre (1859–86)
    Thomas Parker (1886–1903)
    Harry Pollitt (1893–7)
    John George Robinson (1897–1922)

In 1897 the Manchester, Sheffield & Lincolnshire Railway changed its name to Great Central Railway.

Maryport & Carlisle Railway

Locomotives were supplied by private manufacturers.

    Hugh Smellie (1870–8)
    James Campbell (1878–?)
    William Coulthard (?–1904)
    J.B. Adamson (1904–22)

In 1923 the Maryport & Carlisle Railway became part of the London Midland & Scottish Railway.

Metropolitan Railway

The works were at Neasden. Locomotives were supplied by private manufacturers.

> Robert H. Burnett (1864–72)
> Joseph Tomlinson (1872–85)
> J.J. Hanbury (1885–93)
> T.S. Raney ('temporarily in charge of the locomotive running department') (1893–5)
> T.F. Clark (1896–1905)
> Charles Jones (1906–23)
> George Hally (1923–33)

In 1933 the Metropolitan Railway became part of the London Passenger Transport Board.

Midland Railway

The works were at Derby.

> Matthew Kirtley (1844–73)
> Samuel Waite Johnson (1873–1903)
> Richard Mountford Deeley (1903–9)
> Henry Fowler★ (1909–22)

★   He became Sir Henry Fowler in 1918.

In 1923 the Midland Railway became part of the London Midland & Scottish Railway.

North British Railway

The works were at Cowlairs, Glasgow.

> William Hurst (1855–67)
> Thomas Wheatley (1867–74)
> Dugald Drummond (1875–82)
> Matthew Holmes (1882–1903)
> William Paton Reid (1903–19)
> Walter Chalmers (1919–22)

In 1923 the North British Railway became part of the London & North Eastern Railway.

North Eastern Railway

The works were at Gateshead and Darlington. Coaches and waggons were built at York. There were also works at Shildon, inherited from the Stockton & Darlington Railway. William Bouch of the Stockton & Darlington Railway continued designing locomotives for that line until he retired in 1875, several years after the North Eastern had absorbed it in 1863.

> Edward Fletcher (1854–83)
> Alexander McDonnell (1883–4)
> (Interregnum) 1884–1885
> Thomas William Worsdell (1885–90)
> Wilson Worsdell★ (1890–1910)
> Vincent Litchfield Raven# (1910–22)

★   Younger brother of T.W. Worsdell.
He became Sir Vincent Raven in 1917.

In 1923 the North Eastern Railway became part of the London & North Eastern Railway.

North London Railway

The works were at Bow.

> William Adams (1853–73)
> John Carter Park (1873–93)
> Henry J. Pryce (1893–1908)

After 1908 the North London Railway was worked by the London & North Western Railway, and in 1923 became part of the London Midland & Scottish Railway.

North Staffordshire Railway

The works were at Stoke.

L. Clare (1876–82)

Luke Longbottom (1882–1902)

John Henry Adams (1902–15)

John Albert Hookham (1915–22)

In 1923 the North Staffordshire Railway became part of the London Midland & Scottish Railway.

Rhymney Railway

Locomotives were supplied by private manufacturers.

Cornelius Lundie (1861–1905)

In 1923 the Rhymney Railway became part of the Great Western Railway.

South Eastern Railway

The works were at Ashford.

James I'Anson Cudworth (1845–76)

Alfred M. Watkin# (1876)

Richard Mansell (1877–8)

James Stirling★ (1878–98)

\# Son of Sir Edward Watkin, the company chairman.

★ Brother of Patrick Stirling of the Great Northern.

In 1899 the South Eastern Railway formed a working union with the London, Chatham & Dover Railway known as the South Eastern & Chatham Railway. In 1923 the SE&CR became part of the Southern Railway.

South Eastern & Chatham Railway

The works were at Ashford. The Longhedge, Battersea, Works of the London, Chatham & Dover Railway were closed.

Harry Smith Wainwright (1899–1913)

Richard Edward Lloyd Maunsell (1913–22)

In 1923 the South Eastern & Chatham Railway became part of the Southern Railway.

Southern Railway

The SR inherited works at Eastleigh, Brighton and Ashford.

Richard Edward Lloyd Maunsell★ (1923–37)

Oliver Vaughan Snell Bulleid★ (1937–47)

★ These two names are often mispronounced. Maunsell rhymes with 'cancel' (i.e. the u is silent); 'Bulleid' rhymes with 'succeed'.

In 1948 the Southern Railway was nationalized to form the Southern Region of British Railways.

Taff Vale Railway

Locomotives were supplied by private manufacturers.

Joseph Tomlinson (1858–69)

B.S. Fisher (1869–73)

Tom Hurry Riches (1873–1911)

John Cameron (1911–22)

In 1923 the Taff Vale Railway became part of the Great Western Railway.

Wirral Railway

Locomotives were supplied by private manufacturers.

Eric G. Barker (1892–1902)

T.B. Hunter (1903–22)

In 1923 the Wirral Railway became part of the London Midland & Scottish Railway.

APPENDIX IV
ACKNOWLEDGEMENTS AND SOURCES

This book could not have been compiled without referring to the work of many railway historians and writers, some of whom alas have passed on to the Happy Shunting Grounds. In particular, the staff of the Library of the National Railway Museum have been most helpful, especially Philip Atkins and Mrs Lynne Thurston. My sons Alexander Warburton and Richard Pike were indispensable in sorting out all the problems that the word processor could throw at them. Richard also generously allowed me to use several of his photographs; these have been credited in the usual manner. All other photographs are from my own collection, some of them taken when I was very young indeed. The staff at Sutton Publishing, Rupert Harding, Sarah Cook, Joyce Percival, Glad Stockdale and Mary Critchley, have performed the miracle of bringing this book to life. Many other people have given help and/or encouragement, and most of all I would like to thank my wife Patricia, who suggested this work, lived to regret it, and then put up with my pounding the word processor for what seemed like an eternity.

The following works have been consulted, and are recommended to the reader seeking further information on a particular locomotive.

ABC of British Railways Locomotives (Ian Allan, various editions)

Allen, Cecil J. *British Pacific Locomotives* (Ian Allan, 1975)

Barton, D.B. *The Redruth and Chasewater Railway* (D. Bradford Barton Ltd, 1966)

Baxter, Bertram and Baxter, David, *British Locomotive Catalogue 1825–1923*, vol. 5B (Moorland Publishing Co., 1988)

Boyd, J.I.C. *Narrow Gauge Rails to Portmadoc* (Oakwood Press, 1949)

——, *Narrow Gauge Rails in Mid-Wales* (Oakwood Press, 1952)

Bradley, D.L. *Locomotives of the L&SWR Parts 1 and 2* (Railway Correspondence & Travel Society, 1965)

——, *The Locomotive History of the South Eastern Railway* (Railway Correspondence & Travel Society, 1985)

——, *The Locomotive History of the London, Chatham & Dover Railway* (Railway Correspondence & Travel Society, 1979)

——, *The Locomotive History of the South Eastern & Chatham Railway* (Railway Correspondence & Travel Society, 1980)

——, *Locomotives of the LB&SCR, Parts 1, 2 and 3* (Railway Correspondence & Travel Society, 1969)

——, *Locomotives of the Southern Railway, Parts 1 and 2* (Railway Correspondence & Travel Society, 1975)

Brown, G.A., Prideaux, J.D.C.A. and Radcliffe, H.G. *The Lynton and Barnstaple Railway* (Atlantic Transport Publishers, 1996)

Butcher, Alan C. (ed.) *Railways Restored* (Ian Allan, 1993, and later editions)

Clinker, C.R. *et al.*, *The Midland Counties Railway* (Railway & Canal Historical Society, 1989)

Cormack, J.R.H. and Stevenson, J.L. *Highland Railway Locomotives, Book 1* (Railway Correspondence & Travel Society, 1988)

Davies, W.J.K. *The Ravenglass & Eskdale Railway* (David & Charles, 1981)

Dow, George, *Great Central*, vol. 3 (Ian Allan, 1971)

Dunn, J.M. *The Stratford-upon-Avon & Midland Junction Railway* (Oakwood Press, 1952)

Ellis, C. Hamilton, *The Midland Railway* (Ian Allan, 1953)

——, *The North British Railway* (Ian Allan, 1955)

Fox, Peter and Hall, Peter (eds), *Preserved Locomotives of British Railways* (Platform 5 Publishing, 1995, 9th edn)

Fox, Peter and Bolsover, Richard, *British Railways Pocket Book No. 1: Locomotives* (Platform 5 Publishing, 1996)

Goodman, John, *LMS Locomotive Names* (Railway Correspondence & Travel Society, 1994)

Griffiths, Denis, *Heavy Freight Locomotives of Britain* (Patrick Stephens Ltd, 1993)

Hambleton, F.C. *Locomotives Worth Modelling* (Percival Marshall, no date)

Haresnape, Brian, *Gresley Locomotives* (Ian Allan, 1993)

——, *Stanier Locomotives* (Ian Allan, 1981)

——, *Loco Profile no.12: BR Britannias* (Profile Publications, 1973)

—— and Peter Rowledge, *Drummond Locomotives* (Ian Allan, 1982)

Household, Humphrey, *Narrow Gauge Railways* (Alan Sutton Publishing, 1989)

Kidner, R.W. *English Narrow Gauge Railways* (Oakwood Press, 1947)

——, *The Narrow Gauge Railways of Wales* (Oakwood Press, 1947)

——, *Mineral Railways* (Oakwood Press, 1954)

Lambert, Anthony J. *Nineteenth Century Railway History Through The Illustrated London News* (David & Charles, 1984)

Locomotives Illustrated, various issues

MacLeod, A.B. *The McIntosh Locomotives of the Caledonian Railway* (Ian Allan, 1948)

Macmillan, Nigel S.C. *The Campbeltown & Machrihanish Light Railway* (David & Charles, 1970)

Marshall, John, *A Biographical Dictionary of Railway Engineers* (David & Charles, 1978)

Mason, Eric, *The Lancashire & Yorkshire Railway in the Twentieth Century* (Ian Allan, 1954)

Moffat, Hugh, *East Anglia's First Railways* (Terence Dalton Ltd, 1987)

Morgan, John Scott, *The Colonel Stevens Railways* (David & Charles, 1990)

Nock, O.S. *The Premier Line* (Ian Allan, 1952)

——, *Locomotives of the North Eastern Railway* (Ian Allan, 1954)

——, *British Locomotives of the 20th Century* (Patrick Stephens Ltd, 1985)

Paar, H.W. *The Severn & Wye Railway* (David & Charles, 1963)

Pearce, T.R. *The Locomotives of the Stockton & Darlington Railway* (Historical Model Railway Society, 1996)

Redman, Ronald Nelson, *The Railway Foundry Leeds* (Goose & Son, 1972)

Reed, Brian, *Loco Profile no. 3: Great Western 4-cylinder 4–6–0s* (Profile Publications, no date)

___, *Loco Profile no. 10: The Met Tanks* (Profile Publications, 1971)

___, *Loco Profile no. 22: Merchant Navy Pacifics* (Profile Publications, 1972)

——, *Loco Profile no. 32: The Brighton Gladstones* (Profile Publications, 1973)

Railway Correspondence & Travel Society, *The Locomotives of the Great Western Railway* (published in several parts from 1952 onwards)

Railway Correspondence & Travel Society, *Locomotives of the LNER* (published in several parts from 1963 onwards)

Robbins, Michael, *The Isle of Wight Railways* (Oakwood Press, 1953)

Rogers, Col. H.C.B. *Thompson & Peppercorn, Locomotive Engineers* (Ian Allan, 1979)

Rowledge, J.W.P. *Loco Profile no. 37: LMS Pacifics* (Profile Publications, 1974)

Rush, R.W. *The East Lancashire Railway* (Oakwood Press, 1983)

Sellick, Roger, *The West Somerset Mineral Railway* (David & Charles, 1970)

Smith, Martin, *Britain's Light Railways* (Ian Allan, 1994)

Stuart, D.H. and Reed, Brian, *Loco Profile no. 15: The Crewe Type* (Profile Publications, 1971)

Tayler, A.T.H., Thorley, W.G.F. and Hill, T.J. *Class 47 Diesels* (Ian Allan Ltd, 1979)

Thomas, R.H.G. *The Liverpool & Manchester Railway* (B.T. Batsford Ltd, 1980)

Tourret, R. *War Department Locomotives* (Tourret Publishing, 1976)

Webb, Brian, *AC Electric Locomotives of British Rail* (David & Charles, 1979)

___, *The Deltic Locomotives of British Rail* (David & Charles, 1983)

Whittle, G. *The Newcastle & Carlisle Railway* (David & Charles, 1979)

Wilkinson, Reg, *The Wantage Tramway* (Oakwood Press, 1995)

Yeadon, Willie B. *A Compendium of L&NWR Locomotives 1912–1949, Part One: Passenger Tender Engines* (Challenger Publications, 1995)

Young, Robert, *Timothy Hackworth and the Locomotive* (Locomotive Publishing Co., 1923)